The JEWS IN RUSSIA

The JEWS IN RUSSIA

THE STRUGGLE FOR EMANCIPATION

LOUIS GREENBERG

Two volumes in one

With a new foreword by Alfred Levin

SCHOCKEN BOOKS • NEW YORK

To the memory of the brothers

HARRIS BOTWINIK

1872–1929

HYMAN BOTWINIK

1889–1940

The cause of Russian Jewry lay close to their hearts.

First published by SCHOCKEN BOOKS 1976

Published by arrangement with Yale University Press

Clothbound edition available from AMS Press, Inc.

Library of Congress Cataloging in Publication Data

Greenberg, Louis, 1894-1946.
The Jews in Russia.

Reprint of the ed. published by Yale University Press, New Haven, which was issued as Miscellany 45 and 54 of Yale historical publications.
Originally presented as the author 's thesis, Yale, 1941.
Bibliography: v. 1, p.
CONTENTS: v. 1. 1772-1880.—v. 2. 1881-1917.
Includes index.
1. Jews in Russia—History. 2. Jews—Emancipation. I. Title. II. Series: Yale historical publications: Miscellany; 45, [etc.].

DS135.R9G68 1976 947'.004'924 75-36489

Manufactured in the United States of America

FOREWORD

BY ALFRED LEVIN

THE Jewish problem in the Russian Empire was not properly Russian. It was inherited by the Russians with their piecemeal absorption of the Polish-Lithuanian state from the mid-seventeenth century on. A significant influx of Jews into Poland in the Middle Ages stemmed from circumstances favorable both to the Polish government, which was eager to stimulate commercial life, and to the Jews, who were granted a remarkable degree of cultural autonomy and economic opportunity. But in the circumstances of medieval Polish life the expansion of the Jewish population brought complex problems. For the Jews entered Poland as a city people in an agrarian society organized feudally with a proud aristocracy at one end of the social structure and a vast, enserfed peasantry at the other. They were non-Christian with special religio-judicial autonomy in a society officially, culturally, and emotionally Roman Catholic. The Poles competed culturally and politically on a frontier of the Roman Catholic world with the Orthodox Russians for the land and soul of the East European plain. National consciousness and faith were identified more intensely as the political danger from Russia loomed larger and in the aftermath of the Counter-Reformation. And the Jews were further insulated from Polish culture by the regular use of their jargon—basically a German dialect with Polish accretions and Hebrew remnants. The cultural reactions, positive and negative, which arose from these intricately juxtaposed circumstances were further complicated by the attitudes of the dominant Russian element. The ingrained prejudices of an Orthodox, essentially agrarian society were supplemented by the implications of the official nationalism of Russia's ruling spheres in the nineteenth and early twentieth centuries: an official policy reminiscent of the efforts at cultural standardization of the sixteenth and seventeenth centuries.

The Jewish question in Russia must be viewed in the perspective of the pattern of Russian civilization as a whole and particularly as a significant ingredient of one of its major elements, the national minorities which the Russians absorbed in their relentless expansion over Eurasia. Like all other segments and strata of Russian society, these numerous, non-Russian peoples were subjected to the statist concept whereby duty to the society, as embodied in the state, was the prime prerequisite, the *raison d'être*, for their existence. They suffered from the same negative aspects of this concept (e.g., arbitrary disposition of populations and property, efforts at imposition of ideological and cultural uniformity) as did the Great Russians, but with the added disabilities imposed on them by the Russian state. Thus the problems of the Jews, like those of other minorities in Russian society, impinged on many major elements of the Russian cultural pattern—its autocracy, Orthodoxy, nationalism, and agrarianism. The complexities of the solutions are self-evident.

But there were important differences between the Jews and other minorities in European Russia which were likely to make their position more difficult. They were a minority within a minority, without definite territorial designation, unlike minorities that had at one time controlled the territory they occupied. They could be identified (aside from their physical characteristics when these were in evidence) by dialect, faith, and usually occupation though, as elsewhere in Europe, some of their intellectual and economic elite rejected these cultural indices. They were identified in the popular psychology as strangers within the gates: as a craft-commercial stratum whose virtues were largely ignored and whose vices were exaggerated. They were unusually exotic as non-Christians, and their faith was equated with hostility toward Christianity and Christians.

From the perspective offered, we can perhaps gain some insight into the workings of the official Russian mind in consistently pursuing the contradictory policies of Russification by enticement or force and territorial, cultural, and economic isolation. The official solution of the Jewish problem was relatively simple. Let the Jew assimilate as completely as possible. His Christianization would automatically eliminate the millenial religious prejudice, and the expansion of his cultural horizon would lead him from his reputedly "parasitic" economic interests to more "useful" agricultural and industrial pursuits. If he resisted this kind of assimilation the administration had perforce to keep him locked up and restricted in the Pale of Settlement to protect the "basic Russian" population from exploitation.

Within the Jewish fold, the intellectual, religious, and economic leadership reacted to official policy variously according to their horizons and interests. They considered whether assimilation was at all possible in Russian society and whether old patterns and prejudices could be easily renounced by either Russian or Jew. As a group, they naturally rejected the official religious solution. Most of them saw their salvation in the elimination of civil and economic discrimination. Basic disagreement focused on the necessity for and the degree of assimilation. While the protagonists of the enlightenment saw at least a modicum of assimilation as necessary and perhaps inevitable, the conservative and orthodox elements were fearful that assimilation would alienate a significant part of the Jewish intellectual leadership from its cultural heritage. These questions were never resolved under the old regime and, except for the army of emigrants and the resourceful or fortunate few, the mass of Russian Jewry which remained led a culturally restricted, economically depressed existence.

Life under the Soviet regime has not resolved these problems. Traditional Russian attitudes at the official and unofficial levels seem to have changed little. But, to a degree, we are able to ascertain the direction of Jewish life with the elimination of the Pale and the urbanization and industrialization of Russian society. Cultural restriction and, apparently, educational limitations still weigh heavily on the Jewish community. The Jews seem to have benefited somewhat from the need of the regime, committed to technological advancement, to husband its reserves of expertise. But in the broad perspective urbanization, with its cosmopolitan aftereffects, was bound to broaden the horizon of the Jews and beget competition with their purely parochial interests. The elimination of the Jewish middle class seems to have produced no marked change in non-Jewish attitudes toward them, and the tradition of literacy, learning, and competition offered advantages that could also stimulate old hostilities. Some have assimilated to the new official ideology of Russification, Communism, and atheism from motives varying from conviction to self-interest. With greater urbanization there appears to be a broad stratum of religious indifference. There remains also a stolid conservatism in matters of faith and culture. But much of the Jewish population evinces a vital interest in matters Jewish as evidenced by the lively attraction of anything connected with Israel—from diplomats to athletic performers—and of scattered Jewish cultural events such as folksong concerts. While suffering from pressures and restrictions proceeding from the official ideology, Jewish life is far from a state of collapse.

The significance of Dr. Louis Greenberg's study lies not only in his recognition of the basic ingredients of the Jewish question in Russia but in his provision of a careful historical presentation and analysis of the realities as he understood them. If we are to derive a valid image of Jewish society on the eve of the Revolution of 1917—

the background for life under the Soviets—this perspective is indispensable. Dr. Greenberg has established an original analysis of the relationship between the chilling realities of "not belonging" and the rise of all aspects of intellectual activity in the effort to escape from a nearly hopeless situation. In this connection he has offered a most objective account of the Haskalah movement in Russia and its far-reaching intellectual and economic aftermath. For he indicates how it opened the way to a study of the actualities of Jewish life in Russia, which led in turn to a quest for salvation through various channels: assimilation, emigration, Zionism, and even revolution. Insofar as it brought the Jews into currents of *belles lettres* and political literature it drew some into the revolutionary and oppositional movements as "activists," theorists, or both. And the Jews, like most major minorities, provided a significant part of the leadership for a wide range of liberal oppositionist and revolutionary elements (Gessen, Vinaver, Professor Pergament, Gershuni, Akselrod, Trotsky). Orthodox and conservative circles regarded them as misfits in their effort to help non-Jews solve their revolutionary and political problems. Yet this was the challenge they were bound to accept—and it proved fatal for some.

For the historian, Dr. Greenberg has thoroughly documented the doleful circumstances, sometimes extreme, that generated Jewish intellectual ferment in Russia. He has utilized the official statistical data available to account for the harsh meaning of restrictive economic and social policies in terms of food, clothing, and shelter. The herring-a-day meal certainly provided no grounds for support of bureaucratic Russia. From the evidence adduced it appears to be self-evident that whatever Jewish policies the tsarist regime decided to pursue, at the least the elimination of restrictive residence and occupational legislation had to precede intellectual emancipation for the mass of the Jewish population and was necessary even for the economic health of the Empire. The unbearable economic burden imposed by that largest of ghettoes, the Pale of Settlement, precluded the possibility of advancement in any area of endeavor except for the hardiest few with strong will and temperament.

Again, for the historian, the author has delineated rather sharply the discouraging record of the remarkably parochial, almost obscurantist, attitudes of Russia's modern rulers toward their Jewish subjects. To the contemporary world these men appeared as cosmopolitan sophisticates. Yet details concerning the sentiments of Alexander II, for example, offer significant material for an estimate of the true nature of his liberalism even in the earlier years of his reign.

A singular characteristic of the present study is the abundance of material it provides to indicate the tenacity of some basic Russian attitudes in the nineteenth and twentieth centuries. It brings into relief the surprising ease with which the intelligentsia accepted the stereotype of the Jew as a dangerous economic and social pariah. At the turn of the century some of the leading literary figures, including Gorky (as the author notes) and Kuprin, tended to join in protest against Jewish disabilities or analyze the roots of racial violence. In this connection it is perhaps of more than passing interest to note that Jews among the Populists rejected the concept of Jewish nationality on much the same grounds as official Soviet ideology: absence of a true language, territory, and political organization. And they vigorously opposed the argument that faith served as a unifying bond. Again, some of the prerevolutionary limitations have a familiar ring, for example difficulties experienced in the establishment of a truly Jewish press and the limitation of the number of synagogues in major centers like Moscow and Odessa. And the author throws some illuminating beams of statistical light on charges of Jewish exploitation of the peasantry, the negative influence of the Jews on their economic status, and the reputed disdain of the Jews for farming.

Dr. Greenberg focuses considerable attention on the varying degrees of suspicion of the government's motives entertained by the Jewish population. Jewish intellectual leaders sensed the dangers inherent in blind resistance to official proposals. But most of the Jewish fold saw the matter in the light of physical suffering and deprivation and of unfulfilled hopes. The element of compromise was conspicuous by its absence in the political pattern of the Russian Empire. At best the matter lies in one of those areas of cultural clash which required (and requires) a long period of mutual accommodation.

The posthumous second volume of this study, dealing with the last forty years of the old regime, is regarded by some specialists as more parochial than the first (written originally as a doctoral dissertation under the careful guidance of Professor George Vernadsky). There is no reason to doubt that, given his scholarly equipment and perspective, the author would have accepted some qualitative changes arising from more intensive study of the period during the last two decades. This would apply especially to the Stolypin-Kokovtsov period. Peter Stolypin emerges as something more than another mediocre reactionary from the bureaucratic milieu. Few indeed are the statesmen of the nineteenth and twentieth centuries who took significant action to adapt their societies to kaleidoscopic social, economic, and intellectual change. Stolypin was not the greatest of these but he occupied an unusually difficult position. The society in which he acted had just departed timidly (if violently) from a long autocratic tradition. And he manipulated an enormous bureaucracy which adapted itself with only the greatest difficulty to the circumstances of even a diluted constitutionalism. The intellectuals had, as noted, almost no tradition of compromise and a large segment was suspicious of, if not hostile toward, constitutional government. In these circumstances Stolypin had perforce to compromise with his society and his authorities to realize what he might of his program. And he was bound to retain much of the cultural pattern of the aristocracy close to the court. Reared largely in the Baltic region, he was a Great Russian nationalist. And he was not averse to resorting to the more negative techniques of the bureaucracy. He might utilize the rabidly antisemitic Union of the Russian People but, if only out of prudence, he did try to restrain their penchant for riot. And he chose to employ them, with all of the risk implied, primarily as a counterweight to the revolutionary left—as fanatical supporters of the throne who might influence the peasant and worker-peasant.

Yet Stolypin's Jewish policy was empirical. It arose from an understanding of the plight of the Jews in the Lithuanian area in which he was reared and where he had served as an appointed marshal of the nobility and governor. If he was unsuccessful in his effort to remove Jewish disabilities (an effort he initiated) it was because he understood the limitations of bureaucratic powers. If he would not allow the Jews to participate in local self-government or limited their representation, he was certainly governed as much by his Great Russian nationalism as by any ingrained prejudices. The Poles and Finns, too, suffered from these attitudes. At the very least, despite serious violations of the spirit and letter of the new constitutionalism (as in the Law of June 3, 1907), he kept the vital minority question alive. Until the archives of the Council of Ministers are opened, no definitive judgments concerning Stolypin are possible.

Nor, from a long perspective, was the Duma which Stolypin encountered and to an extent dominated entirely ineffective. From more recent studies of the Duma period we know that while parliament was not yet strong enough to bend the determined will of the autocrat and bureaucrat in any sphere of policy, opposition to the regime was clearly articulated by representatives of almost every segment of Russian public opinion and was widely heard. The government prevailed in the debates on the new zemstvos in the non-Russian western provinces, with their disproportionate representation for the Russian peasantry, and in the assault on Finnish autonomy. But it is not at all certain that because of these victories Stolypin's position or that of the regime were rendered more secure. In a multinational society non-Russian interests would demand a hearing.

Dr. Louis Greenberg saw all of these events through the eyes of a scholar and an American Jew professionally dedicated to the propagation and preservation of his faith. Some of his judgments may emerge as too harsh for the tastes of the practiced historian. But the realities of Jewish life in the last century of the old regime were themselves harsh.

VOLUME I

1772-1880

CONTENTS

PREFACE

THE struggle for Jewish emancipation is a recurrent theme in modern Jewish history. During the last hundred and fifty years, since the French Constitutional Assembly conferred the rights of citizenship upon Jews, the civic status of European Jewry has had a chequered history. The rise and fall of its civic fortunes has run parallel to the progress or retrogression of the democratic idea.

This book deals with the rise and development of the movement for civic rights carried on by Russian Jewry during the second half of the nineteenth century. In Russia, as in Western Europe, the cause of Jewish freedom was borne forward and backward by alternating tides of progress and reaction. Russian Jews began their quest for civic rights about a century later than their Western brethren because democratic thought had made no perceptible inroads into the land of the tsars up to the middle of the nineteenth century. During the first half of that century, a few feeble and timid voices were raised on behalf of Jewish equality by Jewish intellectuals who had come into contact with Western enlightenment. The aspirations for a new status began to assume the proportions of a movement during the reign of Alexander II, when a new era, known as the period of the Great Reforms, was inaugurated. This régime saw the abolition of serfdom and the introduction of many democratic reforms.

Encouraged by the new spirit of liberalism and by the friendliness of government and press, Jews for the first time in the history of Russia ventured to assert their claim to civic equality. Some of the rights to which they aspired were the removal of the Pale (the area circumscribing their residence), the right to own land, and eligibility for government service. In brief, their goal was to achieve abolition of discriminatory legislation which deprived them of civic rights enjoyed by corresponding classes of non-Jews in Russia. When the government abolished some of the humiliating and oppressive laws and granted a number of minor concessions, Jewish hopes for imminent emancipation soared high. Because of this new confidence in the government, the movement for secular education known by the Hebrew name of *Haskalah*, hitherto unpopular with the masses, made rapid strides. Out of *Haskalah* came the trends towards Russification, assimilation, and religious reforms.

During the second part of Alexander's reign a spirit of reaction set in. The high hopes for the expected redemption were dashed to earth and the movement for civic equality received a shattering blow. Other channels for freedom were sought. It was during this period that the revolutionary movement began to attract considerable numbers from Jewish ranks. Then, too, the first voices were heard urging the Jew to seek his own national emancipation through the revival of his Hebrew culture and the redemption of Palestine, historic Jewish homeland.

This volume, which is devoted primarily to the Alexandrian period, also presents introductory material leading up to that era. The first five chapters give the historic background both of the movement for emancipation and of the forces involved in the struggle for Jewish rights. The book ends with the death of Alexander II in 1881, a date which marks the return of complete absolutism and militant reaction. A forthcoming volume will continue the story of the Russian-Jewish struggle for freedom and of its achievement.

For unstinted assistance in the preparation of this work, the author is deeply indebted to Professor George Vernadsky of Yale University, under whose guidance this study was originally written as a doctoral dissertation and later revised and enlarged for publication. The writer wishes also to acknowledge the valuable literary and technical aid in the preparation of this manuscript for print rendered by Professor Leonard Woods Labaree, editor of the Yale Historical Series. The author is happy to record his grateful appreciation to Doctor Louis Finkelstein, president of The Jewish Theological Seminary of America, to Professors Louis Ginzberg and Alexander Marx of that institution and to Professor Harry Rudin of Yale University for having given of their valuable time to a critical reading of this manuscript in whole or in part. Many warm thanks are due to Professor Erwin R. Goodenough for helpful suggestions regarding this work and for his sincere encouragement and friendly guidance in the capacity of Director of Graduate Studies of the History Department during the years of the writer's residence work at Yale University. To two kind and generous friends, Dr. Maurice L. Zigmond, director of the Hillel chapter at the University of Connecticut, and Mr. Samuel H. Freedman, editor of the New York *Call*, who spent many wearisome hours seeking out errors in punctuation and rhetorical gaucheries, this author is deeply indebted. An expression of appreciation should not be omitted for the never failing courteous assistance rendered by the library staffs of Yale University and The Jewish Theological Seminary of America as well as for the material made available at The New York Public

Library. A word of thanks is also due to Mr. Isaac Rivkind, cataloguer at the Jewish Theological Seminary Library for his helpful suggestions in bibliography. It should also be recorded that Congregation Bnai Jacob, of New Haven, which the writer has served since 1928, has made it possible for him to pursue his studies and research at Yale. The author also wishes to register his grateful appreciation for the devoted services of the subscription committee, which was organized and directed by Mr. J. P. Botwick, Mr. Louis Linderman, Mr. Joseph I. Sachs, and a recently deceased friend, Mr. William Lesnow. The final word of appreciation the writer reserves for his wife, Batyah, for her assistance in the translations from the Hebrew and Yiddish sources, for helping to smooth out many a rough spot in the manuscript, and for her steadfastness in performing so many of the laborious chores that go with the preparation of a manuscript for print.

L. G.

New Haven, Connecticut,
February 2, 1944

EXPLANATIONS

IN transliterating from the Russian, Hebrew, and Yiddish, the author followed with slight modifications the method employed by the Yale University Library.

P. P. S. Z.—Polnoe Sobranie Zakonov Rossiskoi Imperii. Sobranie Pervoe.
V. P. S. Z.—Polnoe Sobranie Zakonov Rossiskoi Imperii. Sobranie Vtoroe.
Z. M. N. P.—Zhurnal Ministerstva Narodnago Prosveshcheniia.

All Russian dates in this book are according to the Julian calendar.

I

HOW THE RUSSIAN-JEWISH PROBLEM BEGAN

IN ancient times, some believe as far back as twenty-six hundred years, Jewish communities already existed upon Russian soil. There is a theory that the first Jewish settlers consisted of stragglers from the ten tribes of Israel who found their way to the shores of the Black Sea after their exile from the Northern Kingdom of Palestine in the year 719 B.C.E.[1] Of this we have no proof, but records left by historians of Armenia and Georgia tell us that Jewish settlements appeared in the Caucasus and in Transcaucasia soon after the destruction of Jerusalem in 586 B.C.E., and that by the end of the fourth century B.C.E. cities in Armenia had large Jewish populations.[2] From the ruins of tombstones, synagogue inscriptions, and Greek sources, we learn that in the Crimea more than two thousand years ago there were well-organized Jewish communities whose origin undoubtedly dates back many centuries more.[3] To these communities in the fifth and sixth centuries C.E. flocked large numbers of Eastern Jews seeking refuge from the persecutions of the church in Byzantium, so that by the eighth century Jews comprised the largest single group among the peoples of the Crimea, or Tauris, as it was then called.

From the early centuries of the Common Era, these Greek-Taurian colonies were the center of Christian missionary activity conducted by the Byzantine church with the object of converting Jews and pagans. The Jews not only stubbornly resisted and contested these efforts, they even vied with the church in seeking converts for their own faith among the pagan peoples in whose midst they lived. This contest centered particularly among the Khazars, a heterogeneous people of Finnish-Turkish origin who held dominion over the region from the Sea of Azov to the Volga between the seventh and tenth centuries C.E. All three religions—Mohammedan, Christian, and Jewish—were eager to win over this powerful

1. A. Harkavy, *Ha-Yehudim U-Sefat Ha-Slavim,* pp. 108–110.
2. *Regesty i Nadpisi,* I, 37–42.
3. On the early history of the Jews of Russia see A. Firkovich, *Abne Zikkaron;* I. Berlin, *Istorich. Sudby Evreiskago Nar. na Ter. Russ. Gos.,* pp. 52–80; I. L. Levinsohn, *Teudah Be-Yisrael,* pp. 33–34; S. M. Dubnow, *History of the Jews in Russia and Poland,* I, 13–18; Max L. Margolis and Alexander Marx, *A History of the Jewish People,* pp. 525–527.

conquering people, but only a part of them went over to Christianity and Islam, while the most important elements, such as the king and the nobility—and with them a great many of the rank and file—embraced Judaism.

The story of this conversion, which occurred some time between the seventh and eighth centuries, is related in the accounts of medieval Arab travelers. A somewhat similar version is found in the exchange of letters between Joseph, King of the Khazars, and the Spanish-Jewish statesman, Hasdai Ibn Shaprut. Learning of the existence of a Jewish kingdom and hopeful that this might prove to be the kingdom of the long-lost ten tribes, Hasdai Ibn Shaprut sent a letter to the kagan (king) of the Khazars, part of which reads as follows:

Then I humbled myself, adoring the God of heaven, and I sought around me a faithful messenger to send him to your country that I might learn the whole truth regarding the happy condition of the king my master as well as his subjects, our brothers. . . . He that proves the hearts of man knows that I have not done this in order to be honored, but solely to know the truth, to discover whether the exiled Israelites have somewhere a state or kingdom free from all foreign domination and tribute; for, if it be so, I, renouncing all my honors and dignities, and leaving my family, will cross mountains and hills, and will go over earth and ocean, till I come to the place where lives the king my master, that I may see his greatness and his splendour, the glory of his ministers, the peace and prosperity of the remnant of Israel; when I see this my eyes will be illumined, my loins will rejoice and my lips will praise God, Whose infinite goodness is not withdrawn from the afflicted. I therefore ask Your Majesty to bethink him of the eager desires of his servant, and notwithstanding the great distance to command his private scribes to send an affirmative answer to his servant, that I might know all concerning their condition, and that I might learn how Judaism was brought into your country. . . .

Joseph, King of the Khazars, replied (about the year 960):

We are of the posterity of Japhet and descendants of his son Togarma. We read in the genealogical books of our forefathers that Togarma had ten sons; we are the issue of Khozar, the seventh. It is set down in our chronicles that from his days onward our ancestors had to fight against peoples more numerous and more powerful than they. . . . Some centuries later there came a descendant of Khozar, King Bulan, a wise man and God-fearing, who drove away the soothsayers and purified the country of idolatry. . . . The king of Edom (Christians) and of Ishmael (Mohammedans) sent their ambassadors to him with great treasures, and also sent their learned men to convert them to their religion. But the king in his wisdom also sent for a learned Israelite, well versed in all matters; and he then had them as it were complete, so that each one expounded with fire the principles of his own religion and sought to refute the arguments of his antagonists. . . . Then the king said to the monk: "Of the two religions, that of the Israelite and that of the Ishmaelite, which is to be preferred?" The priest replied: "That of the Israelite." Then he asked the Cadi: "Between the faith of the Israelite and the faith of the Edomite, which is to be preferred?" The Cadi replied: "The religion of the Israelite is much to be preferred to the religion of the Nazarenes." To this the prince answered: "You both acknowledge that the faith of the Israelite is the wiser and the better; I therefore choose that religion, the religion of Abraham." From that time on God always helped him and strengthened him, and he and his people were all circumcised. He then sent for the wise men of Israel, who expounded before him the law and the precepts. From that time on we have followed his religion: God be praised for it eternally. . . .[4]

During the reign of the Jewish kagans, the Khazar kingdom rose to great power and prosperity. The rulers exhibited a remarkable spirit of tolerance toward other faiths. In their supreme court, for example, there were judges representing all the religions in Khazar territory; two for the Mohammedans, two for Jews and Christians, and one heathen judge for the Slavonian Russians and other pagan peoples under Khazar rule. When, in 921, a Khazar king ordered the partial destruction of a mosque and the execution of a muezzin, it was not because of religious intolerance, but in retaliation for the destruction of a Jewish synagogue by the Mohammedans in a land called Babunj, for the Khazars sought to protect Jewish rights wherever they could. Especially did the Jews of the Byzantine lands look to the Khazars for protection. Fleeing the persecution of the church, many sought asylum in the Khazarian Jewish kingdom.

During Khazar rule and for a time after that, Jews were held in high esteem by the inhabitants. Russians thought of the Jew as a clever merchant and a carrier of culture, and indeed regarded him as a "veritable symbol of perfection." Much of this admiration was undoubtedly merited, but the idealization was to a large extent due to reflected glory. The Jews, identified with this powerful ruling people, shared their reputation. Even the qualities of physical

4. Translation by Maurice Samuel of E. Fleg, *The Jewish Anthology,* pp. 151–154.

prowess and heroism for which the Khazars were famed were indiscriminately ascribed to the Jewish people as a whole.

Khazar rule witnessed the flowering of Jewish life in their domains and the emergence of Jewish communities in the principality of Kiev, "mother of Russian cities." Due to the ties between the Khazars and the Jews living in the vicinity of Kiev, Khazar-Jewish communities were established in the region during the tenth and eleventh centuries. In 1016, after fifty years of conquest by the Russians, the Khazar kingdom was completely vanquished, and a large portion of the Jewish-Khazarian population of Tauris (Crimea) was removed to the principality of Kiev.

Christianity had become the state religion of Russia. The spirit of tolerance, which had existed in ancient Russia for centuries, began to give way to intolerance and enmity as hatred for the Jew and Judaism was sown by the Greek-Orthodox clergy. By the twelfth century the significance attached to the word *Zhid* indicated the changed attitude toward the Jew. Previously, the word had connoted what it literally stood for—a member of the Jewish people—but now it became a term of opprobrium, synonymous with enmity toward Christ and the Russian people.[5] This antagonism represented more than the intolerance bred of differing theological beliefs; it was rooted in ancient rivalries which began before the conversion of the Khazars and persisted after their downfall, when the Russian people and their ruler became the objects of conversional competition. Before Vladimir, Prince of Kiev, adopted Christianity and made it the official religion of the whole Russian people about the end of the tenth century, he, too, like Bulan of the Khazars conducted a test of faiths in which Khazarian Jews participated. This time Christianity was the victor. Though the Greek-Orthodox church became powerfully entrenched in Russia, it did not cease to look upon the Jew as a dangerous rival whom it both hated and feared.

In spite of growing intolerance, the position of the Jews in Russia until about the sixteenth century was much better than that of their West-European brothers, whose legal status was that of *servi camerae* (property of the king). The Jews of Russia were free men. They were members of the city merchant class and enjoyed liberty of worship even after the Russian state was converted to Christianity. During the Middle Ages, when there were Jewish ghettos in other parts of Europe, there was no segregation of Jews in Russia. The fact that most of the Jews lived in cities in medieval days gave rise to the theory that there were restrictions circumscribing their

5. I. Berlin, *Ist. Sud. Ev. Nar.*, pp. 166–169.

area of residence. This conjecture is unsupported by any recorded evidence and is rejected by reputable historians, who maintain that the idea of segregating Jews was completely foreign to both ancient and medieval Russia.[6]

Nor were the Jews subjected to maltreatment at the hands of the non-Jewish population. A Russian scholar cites the fact that throughout the Middle Ages, with the single exception of the attack upon the Jews in 1113, there were no antisemitic manifestations. These riots, though motivated to some extent, perhaps, by anti-Jewish feeling, were for the most part expressions of class revolt during a period of political and economic unrest, when excesses were perpetrated against non-Jews as well as upon Jews.[7] A comparison of the effects of the Crusades upon Russian and West-European Jewry also leads one to the conclusion that Russian Jewry fared relatively well. In Western Europe these religious expeditions were accompanied by wholesale massacres of Jews and annihilation of entire communities. The period witnessed the most harrowing experiences of Jewish martyrdom and the most brutal expressions of religious hatred. Though the Russian natives were not completely unaffected by the fanatical fervor engendered by the Crusades, there were no anti-Jewish outbreaks during these periods of religious ferment. Moreover, Jews fleeing persecution in Western Europe often found refuge in Russia. Comparative toleration of Jews there at a time when virulent antisemitism was rampant in Western Europe may be ascribed to the fact that the church was established in Russia several centuries later than in other parts of Europe, and its anti-Jewish agitation had not yet sufficiently taken root.

The latter part of the fifteenth century, however, saw the rise of a movement which had serious consequences for the Jews of Russia. Called the "Judaizing heresy" because it resulted in many apostasies from the Christian church, this proselyting movement added fuel to growing anti-Jewish animosity. Its initiator was said to be the learned Jew Zechariah of Kiev, who was in the employ of Prince Michael Olelkovich. In the city of Novgorod, whither he journeyed when the prince was invited to assume the rulership of the principality, Zechariah converted to Judaism some prominent Russian ecclesiastics. After his departure, missionary activities were carried on by the converts.

In 1478, when Novgorod was annexed to Moscow, Ivan III,

6. N. D. Gradovsky, *Otnosheniia k Evr. v Drev. i Sovremen. Rusi,* p. 11; I Berlin, *Ist. Sud.,* pp. 150–151.
7. Gradovsky, *Otnosh. k Evr.,* p. 244.

Grand Duke of Moscow, brought with him to the capital a number of priests, including the two who had been converted to Judaism by Zechariah. As a result of their efforts, a number of government officials and high-ranking clergy joined the secret sect, among them the daughter-in-law of the grand duke, and the metropolitan of Moscow. For a time, practically the entire government consisted of Judaizers or sympathizers.[8] Their influence in both church and government circles was so strong that Judaizing activities were not checked by the religious authorities.

The first to demand strong measures against the heretics was Gennadi, Archbishop of Novgorod. Learning in 1487 of the existence of the heresy from a convert who re-embraced the Christian faith, he dispatched an epistle to Moscow demanding ruthless suppression of the movement. A great admirer of the Catholic inquisition and its methods, this ecclesiastic urged that the apostates be burnt at the stake. Two special Church Assemblies were convened in the capital for the purpose of dealing with the heretics, but because of the Judaizers' influence in the court, not much headway was made by church authorities. At the beginning of the sixteenth century, when high-placed members of the sect lost their influence in the court, the church finally succeeded in suppressing the Judaizing heresy. Some converts were burnt at the stake and others imprisoned for life.

For an explanation of the rise and spread of this apostasy, one must look beyond the Jewish influences associated with it. The successful appeal of the Judaic doctrines must to a large extent be ascribed to disaffection within the church which set in not alone in Russia but in other parts of Eastern and Western Europe in the centuries preceding the Reformation. Numerous dissenting groups, repudiating church doctrines and rites which, they believed, obscured the soul of Christianity, broke away from the established church and organized dissident sects. Among these was a Judaizing sect which arose in Bulgaria in the fourteenth century, and was suppressed by a Church Assembly in 1360. Coincident with the Judaizing heresy in Novgorod arose a dissenting sect known as the *Strigolniki*. Many of its adherents were drawn to Judaism because they saw in it the spirit of that primitive Christianity they were seeking to revive.[9]

8. Z. Casdai, *Ha-Mityahadim,* p. 16.

9. On Judaizing heresy see *Jewish Encyc.,* VII, 369–370; G. Vernadsky in *Speculum,* October 1933, pp. 436–454; S. M. Dubnow, *Hist. J. Rus. Pol.* I, 36–37; E. Golubinsky, *Istoria Russkoi Tserkvi,* II, part I, 560–607; S. Dolgov, *Eresi Zhidovstvuiushchikh,* pp. 113–125.

Obviously, fear of Jewish influence since earliest times, culminating in the Judaizing heresy, lay at the root of the anti-Jewish policies of tsarist Russia. From the sixteenth century, when the Muscovy Tsardom set about consolidating independent principalities into a unified empire, it became fixed Russian policy not to admit Jews into its territories even for temporary purposes. In 1555 the Polish king Sigismund Augustus demanded that Ivan the Terrible, first tsar of the Russians, admit Lithuanian Jews for business purposes. The tsar categorically refused. In a communication reflecting the prevailing hostile and superstitious attitude toward the Jews, Ivan spoke of them as importers of poisonous medicines and as misleaders from the Christian faith.[10] N. Varadinov, official historian of the Ministry of the Interior, refers to this fear of Jewish influence in the following observation:

> The history pertaining to Jewish affairs since 1649 bears the stamp of distrust toward the followers of the Mosaic faith. One of the reasons for this attitude is the fact that Jews, through their false teachings, have lured to their religion adherents of other faiths, even those of the Christian persuasion. Because of this, their civic rights were constantly limited and their immigration from other countries forbidden. On several occasions they were completely driven out from Russia.[11]

Determined to keep Jews out and to get rid of those already in Russia as a result of illegal penetration or territorial acquisition,[12] the government persistently legislated against them. In 1727 a decree was issued that "all Jews found to be residing in the Ukraine and in other Russian towns shall be forthwith expelled beyond the frontier and not permitted under any circumstances to re-enter Russia." Before leaving the country Jews were to exchange all their gold and silver specie for copper money.[13] In 1742 another edict reaffirmed the decree of banishment and non-admission, an exception being made for those who would embrace the Greek-Orthodox faith.[14]

Concerned over the economic losses resulting from this *ukaz*, the Senate recommended to Empress Elizabeth "that for the furtherance of the interests of the state and for the development of trade," Jews be allowed to visit Little Russia and Riga for business purposes. Economic considerations could not modify her attitude. "I

10. Dubnow, *Hist. J. Russ. Pol.,* I, 243.
11. N. Varadinov, *Istoria Ministerstva Vnutrennikh Del,* II, 129.
12. In 1654, the Ukraine with its large Jewish population was annexed to Moscow.
13. *P. P. S. Z.,* VII, no. 5063.
14. *Ibid.,* XI, no. 8673.

seek no gain at the hands of the enemies of Christ," [15] the empress wrote on the document submitted by the Senate. A letter written by a friend to Elizabeth shows the antipathy which prevailed in the upper circles. Describing a visit in 1738 to the city of Nezhin in the Ukraine, the writer states: "The Jews there are very numerous. I saw them, the dogs." [16]

Catherine II ascended the throne of Russia in 1762 and continued the policy of her predecessors. She issued a manifesto in the first year of her reign permitting the immigration of all foreigners except Jews.[17] That this policy reflected not her own views but political considerations may be gathered from the following incident. Soon after Catherine became empress, the question of admitting Jews was raised in the Senate. The empress feared she might antagonize the clergy and offend the religious sensibilities of the Russian people. She refused to commit herself on the subject, requesting that the matter be postponed. In relating the incident later, she observed: "How often it proves insufficient to be enlightened, to have the best of intentions and even the power to carry them out." [18]

Such was the policy of the Russian government in respect to the Jews until the year 1772, when, as a result of the first partition of Poland, Russia inherited a Jewish population of two hundred thousand souls.[19] Through the subsequent partitions of 1793 and 1795, which added other Polish-Lithuanian provinces, the number of Jews grew to nine hundred thousand.[20] Since it was no longer possible to resort to banishment as a means of solving its Jewish problem, the government set about to limit Jewish rights within its realms through special legislation.

The first manifesto issued by Catherine II to the new provinces under her dominion was indicative of the discriminatory policy to be pursued under tsarist rule. Dated August 16, 1772,[21] the proclamation made a distinction between the Jewish and non-Jewish subjects. The latter were promised that they could exercise the rights they had enjoyed under their former government throughout the Russian Empire. The locale in which Jews could exercise their former rights was specifically limited to the territory in which they were living at the time of the partition.

15. *Ibid.*, XI, no. 8840.
16. *Arkhiv Kniazia Vorontsova,* I, 84.
17. *P. P. S. Z.,* XVI, no. 11, 720.
18. *Russky Arkhiv,* 1865, p. 494.
19. Dubnow, *Hist. J. Russ. Pol.,* I, 307.
20. *Sbornik Materialov ob Economicheskom Polozhenii Evreev v Rossii,* Preface, p. xviii.
21. *P. P. S. Z.,* XIX, no. 13,850.

Because of this specific limitation of area for the exercise of Jewish rights, the year 1772 may be regarded as the official establishment of the Jewish Pale in Russia. Some Jewish historians, however, consider the year 1791 the official date, because a decree that year specifically barred Jews from definite areas. The *ukaz* declared that they were to be allowed to enjoy the privileges of citizens and burghers in White Russia only, but that they did not possess the right of registering as merchants in the towns and sea-ports of the rest of the empire.[22] Even within the Pale, Jews were singled out from among the Christian populace for discriminatory legislation through the imposition of a double tax upon Jewish merchants and burghers.[23]

The first earnest attempt to solve the Jewish problem was made in the early years of the reign of Alexander I. The winds of liberalism then blowing in Western Europe made themselves felt in Russia, too, and gave promise of bringing relief to the Jews. In November, 1802, the tsar ordered the creation of a "Committee for the Amelioration of the Jews." The inclusion in the committee of Count Kochubei and Adam Chartoryzki, close friends of Alexander I and known for their liberal views, augured well for a favorable solution of the Jewish problem. That the committee approached its task in a humane and rational spirit may be seen from an observation recorded in its journal of September, 1803. "Since reforms effected by the authority of the state," the journal pointed out, "are generally lacking in stability, particularly when traditions of centuries have to be overcome, it is more desirable and safer to lead the Jews to self-improvement by opening to them the roads that will lead them to happiness." Instead of the use of force through government agencies, the committee advised the encouragement of voluntary activities without interference. "A minimum of restrictions, a maximum of liberties," it stated, "these are the ingredients of a good social order." [24] The committee also decided on a novel and unprecedented step—to invite deputies from the Jewish communities of the provincial capitals as advisers on the needs of their people. "The population was stirred," writes Gessen, a historian of Russian Jewry. "It was the first time that the Russian government wanted to listen to the Jews themselves." [25]

22. *Ibid.*, XXIII, no. 17,006. The Russian scholar A. D. Gradovsky (*Sobranie Sochineni*, VII, 366) dates the beginning of the Pale as the year 1769, when foreign Jews were permitted to immigrate into Russia on the condition that they settle only in the New Russian province. (*P. P. S. Z.*, XVIII, no. 13,383.)

23. *Ibid.*, XXIII, no. 17,224.

24. *Russky Arkhiv*, 1903, I, 254–255.

25. J. Gessen, *Evrei v Rossii*, p. 77.

The work of the committee resulted in the "Statute Concerning the Organization of the Jews," issued with the sanction of the tsar on December 9, 1804.[26] Prefacing the new charter, which Dubnow, the famous Russian-Jewish historian, characterizes as a "mixture of liberties and disabilities,"[27] was a preamble stating that it was prompted by a "solicitude for the welfare of the Jews as well as for the native population of those provinces in which these people are allowed to live." The illiberal aspect of the statute is evident in the last part of the sentence, which officially confirmed the existing Pale of Settlement. The liberal features of the charter included permission granted to Jews to send their children to all schools of the empire, and inducements held out by the government to those who would engage in agriculture. Paragraph twenty-nine states that "when the Jews shall evince diligence and application in agriculture, manufacture, industry, and commerce, the government will adopt the necessary measures for equalizing the taxes imposed on them with those levied on the other subjects of the empire."

Because the general reaction in Europe after the Congress of Vienna, the liberal tendencies of the first half of Alexander I's reign suffered a setback during the latter part of his rule. After the war of 1812, Jews had hoped that their patriotism and loyalty to Russia during the trying years of the Napoleonic invasion would be rewarded by improvement of their legal status.[28] In the face of the political reaction which gripped Russia, their hopes were doomed to disappointment.

The position of the Jews was made even more difficult during the reign of Nicholas I. For the first time in Russia, Jews were conscripted into the much dreaded military service, in connection with which additional discriminatory disabilities were imposed. The "Statute of Conscription and Military Service" promulgated August 26, 1827,[29] provided that in addition to supplying recruits for the army to serve a term of twenty-five years, Jews also had to produce cantonists[30] from the ages of twelve to twenty-five. The Jewish communities were charged with the duty of filling the required quota of recruits. In case of failure the community elders were liable to severe punishment and even to military service.

In April, 1835, a new code of regulations was issued which con-

26. *P. P. S. Z.*, XXVIII, no. 21,547.
27. Dubnow, *Hist. J. Russ. Pol.*, I, 342.
28. For tributes paid by military authorities to Jewish patriotism and valor see S. M. Ginsburg, *Otechestvennaia Voina 1812 goda i Russkie Evrei.*
29. *V. P. S. Z.*, II, nos. 1329, 1330.
30. Juvenile conscripts. Among the Jews this word applied to any child drafted for military service, although the term specifically designated children of soldiers subject to conscription.

firmed the anti-Jewish legislation of the law of 1804 and appended the restrictive by-laws promulgated since that time.[31] The Pale of Settlement was now clearly defined. It consisted of Lithuania (provinces of Kovno, Vilno, Grodno, and Minsk); the southwestern provinces (Vohlyn and Podol without any territorial restrictions); White Russia (Vitebsk and Mogilev minus the villages); Little Russia (Chernigov and Poltava minus the crown hamlets); New Russia (Kherson, Ekaterinoslav, Taurida, and Bessarabia minus Nikolaev and Sevastopol); the province of Kiev minus the capital; and the Baltic provinces (for old settlers only). Rural settlements in the 50-verst [32] zones along the western frontier were to be closed to newcomers.

With the accession of Alexander II, new hope entered the Jewish ghetto. The disastrous results of the Crimean War had convinced the ruling class that if Russia were to regain her prestige as a great power, new and vital changes in her system of government would have to be made. This realization was responsible for the period of "Great Reforms" which resulted in the abolition of serfdom, the granting of local self-government, and the institution of court and military-service reforms. The Jews, too, benefited from the new policies. The cantonist system, which had subjected the Jewish youth to virtual martyrdom, was abolished on August 26, 1856—the day Alexander II was crowned.[33] During the reign of the Tsar Liberator, laws favoring special classes of Jewry were enacted. Some groups were accorded the right of unrestricted residence and the opportunity for government service.

These reforms, inaugurated by the new ruler whom Jews hailed as the "Emperor of Mercy," encouraged them to believe that emancipation was no longer a vain dream. In an atmosphere of new hope and intensified civic aspirations, the movement for secular education known by the Hebrew name of *Haskalah* (enlightenment) gained fresh impetus. The program by which its exponents hoped to obtain civic emancipation for the Jews, first made its appearance in Russia during the twenties of the nineteenth century, when it failed to make headway because of the oppressive policies of the government. Recharged with new energies in the liberal era of Alexander II, *Haskalah* continued throughout his reign to play a dominating role in the campaign for Jewish emancipation.

31. *V. P. S. Z.*, X, no. 8054.

32. One verst is equal to 0.6629 mile. Residence along the border was barred to Jews on the ground that they might engage in smuggling.

33. *V. P. S. Z.*, XXXI, no. 30,888.

II

THE WEST-EUROPEAN BACKGROUND OF *HASKALAH*

SINCE the *Haskalah* movement was destined to play an important part in the Jewish struggle for civic equality, it is necessary to devote some space to its origin and history. The source of *Haskalah* may be traced to French rationalism of the eighteenth century. The ideas of French Enlightenment profoundly influenced the thinking and aspirations of a considerable portion of Prussian Jews, whose social and commercial contacts exposed them to the intellectual currents of their day. Hence, it was in Prussia that the *Haskalah* movement first assumed significant proportions.

To appreciate why French Enlightenment made such a strong appeal to the rightless Jews of Prussia, one need but recall the outstanding principles preached by the leaders of the movement. The articles of faith of the Religion of Enlightenment, as summarized by Carl L. Becker, were as follows:

1. Man is not natively depraved.
2. The end of life is life itself, the good life on earth, instead of the beatific life after death.
3. Man is capable, guided solely by the life of reason and experience, of perfecting the good life on earth.
4. The first and essential condition of the good life on earth is the freeing of men's minds from the bonds of ignorance and of their bodies from the arbitrary oppression of the constituted social authorities.[1]

These ideas made a particular appeal to the Jewish intellectuals, since their people was the special object of oppression and was regarded as eternally accursed. The Jews no doubt also found solace in the French philosophers' critical attitude toward history. "The history of great events in the world," said Voltaire, apostle of the rationalists, "is scarcely more than a history of crimes." In order to be happy, asserted Chastellux, there is far greater need of forgetting than of remembering, since the great object of enlightened

1. Carl L. Becker, *The Heavenly City of the Eighteenth Century Philosophers,* pp. 102–103.

men should be "to raise the edifice of Reason on the ruins of opinion." [2] A philosophy promising the inauguration of a new era for the Jew found many adherents among Jewish intellectuals. In the triumph of the spirit of enlightenment, they visioned their own deliverance not only from the judgments of the past, but also from the intolerable conditions of the present.

Christian Wilhelm Dohm (1751–1820), writer, diplomat, and personal friend of Frederick the Great, gives us an account of the legal position of the Jews in Europe in the second half of the eighteenth century. "In almost all parts of Europe," he states, "the laws of the state aim to prevent as much as possible the influx of these unfortunate Asiatic refugees—the Jews. . . . Everywhere the Jew is denied the privilege of service to the state. He is not allowed to engage in agriculture, nor is he permitted to acquire property. The only branch of economic activity left for him in which to eke out a livelihood is petty trade. When a Jew has several sons, he has the privilege of having with him only one, since the oldest alone is allowed to marry and raise a family. The others he must send away. His daughters remain with him only if they are lucky enough to marry Jews of his own city who have the right to stay there." "Very rarely," observes this Christian historian, "is a Jewish father fortunate enough to live among his children and grandchildren, and to establish the welfare of his family on a permanent foundation." [3]

Examination of the special Jewish codes of Prussia and Austria in the second half of the eighteenth century confirms the assertions made by Dohm. From the official code regulating the status of the Jews of Prussia, issued by Frederick the Great, April 17, 1750,[4] we learn that the number of Jews in his provinces was definitely limited. Those allowed residence in Prussia were divided into Jews with regular protection, and those without regular protection (*ordentliche und ausserordentliche Schutzjuden*). Jews of the first category could transmit their privileges to the eldest son, while those of the second category could not. There was also a third class whose privilege of residence depended on the official position they held in the Jewish community—as, for example, rabbis, cantors, religious teachers, and other community functionaries—or on the services they rendered to the aforementioned privileged classes of Jews. To insure full and prompt payment for protection privileges, the entire

2. *Ibid.*, pp. 93–94.
3. *Über die bürgerliche Verbesserungen der Juden*, pp. 8–10.
4. *Novum Corpus Constitutionum Pruss-Brand.*, ed. by Christian Otto Mylius, Vol. 1751–1760, pp. 118–146.

Jewish community—*in solidum*—was held responsible for each individual Jew. Jews were denied the privilege of pursuing a trade and of melting silver or gold. They were forbidden to acquire real estate, and it was stipulated that the Jews of Berlin were not to add any new houses to the forty they already owned there.

A legal code issued later in the century, dealing with the status of the Jews in Austria, breathed a more tolerant spirit, but still essentially denied them basic rights. This document, the *Toleranzpatent* (Edict of Toleration) of Joseph II, promulgated January 2, 1782,[5] allowed Jews, in order to make them more useful to the state, to send their children to all the secondary and higher institutions of learning maintained by the government. The code also permitted them to engage in handicrafts, subject to certain reservations and restrictions. These concessions constituted the tolerant features of the edict, while the remainder of the code confirmed most of their former disabilities. The *Toleranzpatent* explicitly stated that it was not the intention of the king to increase the number of Jews in his lands or to change the conditions which regulated their toleration there. Places which had never admitted Jews would continue to bar them, while the privilege of residence in Vienna was to be obtained by the payment of a special tax (*Schutzgeld*) determined by the government. Jews were to continue to pay double court and chancery taxes.

Such was the status of European Jewry at the time when the Encyclopaedists were preaching their doctrines of tolerance and reason. The first to react to the ideas of the French rationalists and to initiate the struggle for Jewish emancipation were the Jews of Prussia. Their legal position was not better than that of any other portion of Jewry in Europe, but among them were wealthy and cultured Jews who had the opportunity to become aware of the ideas of French Enlightenment.

The rise of this class was due to the economic and financial policies of Frederick William I and Frederick the Great. In their desire to build up the silk and satin industry in Prussia, both monarchs encouraged rich and enterprising Jews to establish factories in their kingdom. They granted them government subsidies, in some cases even monopolies; accorded them special privileges in the conduct of their business, and through special decrees even supplied their factories with child labor from Christian orphanages.[6] Official

5. A. F. Pribram, *Urkunden und Akten zur Geschichte der Juden in Wien*, I, 495–500.

6. *Acta Borussica, Die Preussische Seidenindustrie in 18. Jahrhundert und ihre*

records of the 1760s reveal the leading rôle Jews played in the silk industry of Prussia. Figures relating to October, 1766, show that more than half of the working looms and 60 per cent of all the manufactured silk in the warehouses belonged to Jews.[7]

That Frederick was disturbed by Jewish domination of the silk industry may be seen from a royal order addressed to the military counselor, Moss. The king complains that though he has been urging Moss for a long time to attract Christian merchants to the silk industry, there have been no results. He admonishes his counselor not to give up the attempt, but to offer further inducements to Christian merchants. Frederick assures Moss that if Christians capable and willing to engage in the industry are found, there will be no Jews left in it within a period of one year.[8]

"In spite of his aversion for Jews," states a German-Jewish historian, "Frederick the Great always turned to them for help whenever he needed money." Jews, for example financed the Seven Years' War, and some acquired large fortunes.[9] Due to the governmental policy of favoring industrialists and bankers and of admitting only the richest Jews into its provinces, the number of wealthy Jews continued to increase in Berlin, where the bulk of German-Jewish wealth was concentrated.[10] In the 1780s only ten of the 120 members of the Jewish community in Berlin had a capital of less than one thousand thalers, and many owned tens of thousands.[11]

These rich Prussian Jews associated with the French residents of Berlin, who formed the dominant element of the industrial and progressive circles of the Prussian capital. It was through these Frenchmen that wealthy Jewish youth became familiar with the teachings of the French Encyclopaedists. Henriette Herz relates in her memoirs how that contact was brought about. "First to learn the French language were the daughters of the wealthy Jews. The parents did not object because of practical reasons, since French was the key to European civilization. At first the young Jewesses used their French to conduct elegant conversations with army officers and court cavaliers who came to borrow money from their

Begründung durch Friedrich den Grossen, Vol. I, no. 30, p. 28; no. 65, p. 67; no. 99, p. 102; no. 146, p. 140; no. 180, p. 172.

7. *Ibid.,* no. 523, pp. 529–530; no. 531, pp. 534–535.

8. *Acta Borussica, Die Handels, Zoll- und Akzisepolitik Preussens,* 1740–1786, III, Part I, 387.

9. Ludwig Geiger, *Geschichte der Juden in Berlin,* p. 65.

10. This rich class represented but a fraction of the number of Jews who lived in poverty in the Germanic states.

11. Geiger, *Ibid.,* p. 43.

fathers. Later, however, they utilized their knowledge of French for the more important purposes of familiarizing themselves with French classics and modern writers." [12]

One may reasonably assume that French literature appealed to Prussian Jewish youth not only because it was fashionable and a mark of culture, but also because it held out to them the cherished hope of legal equality. For as the historian Graetz puts it: "Between the social position of the cultured Jews and their legal standing there was a deep chasm. In the burgher classes the Jews of Berlin were the first to be millionaires—no indifferent matter, considering the important place held by money at that time—yet, according to the law, they were treated like peddlers." [13] The attacks of the philosophers on feudal institutions, whose chief characteristics were class privilege and religious intolerance, encouraged the Jew to believe that his redemption was not far off. "The world is changing," observed an eighteenth-century Jew. "Once a man's worth was determined by rank and birth, now it is determined by money." [14]

The popularity of the French rationalists with the Jews of Germany may also be explained by the hope that the ideas of enlightenment which came from across the Rhine might remove the barrier that separated the Jew from his Gentile neighbor, a barrier made especially intolerable by his improved social position. The Encyclopaedists' merciless attacks on the superstitions of religion, their vitriolic denunciations of church authority, and their insistence that reason should be the guiding principle in the institutions which regulate the affairs of men, struck a responsive chord in the hearts of intellectual Jews. In their pathetic eagerness to acquire political and social emancipation, they turned against those traditions and practices of their own faith which, to their mind, could not stand the test of reason, and which, they believed, were the only barriers to the acquisition of civic rights and social equality. "Voltaire's famous phrase, '*Ecrasez l' Infâme*'—abolish superstition," writes a Jewish scholar, "found a strong echo in the circles of Jewish intellectuals." [15] "Voltaire," to quote another Jewish authority,

12. Henriette Herz, *Ihr Leben und ihre Erinnerungen,* Hrsg. von J. Fürst, pp. 119–120.

13. H. Graetz, *History of the Jews,* V, 414.

14. Kingsley Martin, *French Liberal Thought in the Eighteenth Century,* p. 69. On the attitudes to Judaism and the Jew on the part of Voltaire and other representatives of French Enlightenment see S. W. Baron, *A Social and Religious History of the Jews,* II, 201–204.

15. I. Zinberg, *Die Geschichte fun der Literatur bei Yiden,* VII, book I, 117.

"had more admirers in the tents of Jacob than in German homes." [16]

The center and cradle of Jewish enlightenment was Berlin, the residence of Moses Mendelssohn (1729–1786), regarded as the father and originator of the *Haskalah.* Author of a number of noted philosophical treatises—one of which earned for him a prize from the Prussian Academy of Sciences—Mendelssohn also gained fame as a writer and interpreter of Judaism. The many notable and influential Christian friendships he enjoyed, among which was that of the famous philosopher and dramatist, Lessing, contributed much to his prestige and influence in Jewry. Though regarded as the father of the reform movement in Judaism, this theologian and scholar did not seek to make any changes in the Jewish religion. As a matter of fact, he strictly adhered all his life to orthodox observances and ritual.

The aim of this German-Jewish philosopher was not the reformation of the Jewish faith, but the modernization and improvement of Jewish education, through which he sought to raise the cultural level of his people. As a young man of twenty-one he published the first Hebrew weekly, *Kohelet Musar* (A Miscellany of Ethics), for the purpose of cultivating a taste for pure Hebrew, which he hoped would replace the jargonized Hebrew of the ghetto. Through his initiative there was established in Berlin in 1778 the first Jewish school where, in addition to the Pentateuch and Talmud—the traditional subjects of the ghetto *heder*[17]—the curriculum also included German, French, and general subjects.

Mendelssohn reached the high watermark of his Jewish activities when he translated the Pentateuch and a few books of Hagiographa into German. With the aid of a group of Jewish scholars he wrote a Hebrew commentary on the Pentateuch. The German translation was written in Hebrew characters for the benefit of those who could not read German. In a letter to a Christian friend, Adolf Hennings, Mendelssohn spoke of this effort as "the first stage on the road to enlightenment, from which my nation unfortunately is still so far away that one sometimes begins to doubt the future of the Jewish people." [18] The translation of the Bible which, under the name of *Paths of Peace*, appeared in the years 1780–1783, was enthusiastically received by the progressive circles of Jewry. His

16. Graetz, *History of the Jews,* V, 411.

17. Heder—Literally a room. A term applied to the elementary school of the ghetto.

18. M. Kayserling, *Moses Mendelssohn, sein Leben und seine Werke,* p. 522.

masterful German rendition, which faithfully preserved the beauty of the original Hebrew text, was extolled in prose and verse. "This edition," writes Israel Zinberg, "was destined to form a milestone in the cultural history not only of German Jewry, but of East-European Jewry as well." [19] For a special edition of Mendelssohn's Bible was made in 1836–38 for Polish-Russian Jewry, and a later one appeared in Vilno in 1843–53.

Next in importance to Mendelssohn as a leader of the enlightenment was Naphtali Herz Wessely (1725–1805), one of his collaborators on the commentary to the Pentateuch. Wessely was a prolific writer whose literary activities embraced exegesis, poetry, and essays on problems of Jewish life. Soon after the promulgation of Joseph II's Edict of Toleration, he published a pamphlet in Hebrew, *Dibre Shalom Ve-Emet* (Words of Peace and Truth). This brochure is regarded as the opening manifesto of the *Haskalah* and beginning of modern Hebrew literature.

Wessely hailed the *Toleranzpatent* with joy because, he believed, it gave the Jews an opportunity to realize the most cherished doctrines of the *Haskalah*. The opening of the general schools for Jews and the permission to establish normal schools of their own filled his heart with deep gratitude to "his Majesty, the Great Emperor, Joseph II, who loves humanity and brings joy to people." [20] Directing his message to the Jewish communities in the lands of the emperor, Wessely proposed a program of education for Jewish children, consisting of two parts—one dealing with secular subjects, or, as he called it, "studies of man," and the other a study of religion.[21] Of all peoples, he complained, the Jews, especially those of Germany and Poland, are the only ones who have neglected secular education. He deplored the fact that so many Jews who are men of reason, great understanding, and piety, should from childhood be exclusively concerned with religious study.[22] But, he hopefully declared, now things can change, due to the humanitarianism of Joseph II, who had not forgotten the long forgotten children of Israel.[23] The author of *Dibre Shalom Ve-Emet* shared Mendelssohn's contempt for the Judeo-German dialect, describing it as German speech that has become distorted in the mouths of Jews so that those living in German-speaking lands have become "a people of

19. *Ges. Lit. Yid.*, VII, Book 1, 63. On Mendelssohn see also Meyer Waxman, *A History of Jewish Literature,* III, 63–77; Shalom Spiegel, *Hebrew Reborn,* pp. 47–72.
20. From the title page.
21. *Dibre Shalom Ve-Emet,* p. 1.
22. *Ibid.*, p. 9.
23. *Ibid.*, p. 14.

stammerers." [24] He suggested that after the children in the normal schools received their first training in the elementary secular subjects, they should take up a study of the Scriptures translated by Mendelssohn so that they might learn a pure German and a pure Hebrew.[25]

The program advocated by Mendelssohn and Wessely gained many enthusiastic followers among progressive German and Polish Jews, who regarded the modernization of Jewish education as one of the means of helping Jewry emerge from the medieval ghetto and merge with the civilization of Europe. In line with this objective, in 1783, a group of young *maskilim* (followers of the *Haskalah*) formed a Society for the Promotion of the Hebrew Language for the purpose of publishing in Königsberg a Hebrew monthly modelled after the then popular *Berliner Monatsschrift*. In the prospectus setting forth the aims of this periodical, which was to have a German supplement, the founders appealed to Jewish youth not to remain indifferent to the demands of the times, "times of education and enlightenment." "See," they exclaimed, "how all the nations strive after knowledge, concern themselves with the education of their children and their youth. . . . How can we sit by with folded arms? Arise, brethren, close your ranks! With sure steps set out in search of those treasures which are more precious than the greatest fortunes; and faithful guides, men of truth and knowledge, will illumine our paths." [26]

The literary quality of this first organ of the Enlightenment, called *Ha-Measef* (The Collector), was rather poor. Its style was didactic and its material tendentious. In the course of its existence it did not produce a single outstanding literary figure.

The chief emphasis of *Ha-Measef* was laid upon the need for secular education. To give secular knowledge religious and historic sanction in the eyes of its readers, the monthly presented in its biographical section the lives of famous Jews who, in addition to Jewish scholarship, had also possessed secular culture, such as Maimonides, Abravanel, and Manasseh ben Israel.

The writers of this *Haskalah* periodical also stressed the importance of Gentile approval. Discussing the need of a systematic study of the Hebrew language, the author of one article, Mordecai Schnaber, urged his point with the following argument: "What will

24. *Ibid.*, pp. 24–25.
25. *Ibid.*, p. 23.
26. *Ha-Measef*, 1784, p. 13.

our neighbors, the Gentiles, say when they find that they know more Hebrew than we do?" [27]

Patriotism, too, was a dominant note in *Ha-Measef*. The task of the school, it maintained, was to train useful and patriotic subjects. Through a proper education, the leaders of the *Haskalah* pointed out, the Jews could train such citizens, and thus prove themselves deserving of the favorable attention of the government. "In our own days," runs an article on children's education, "the sun of justice and healing has begun to shine on the downtrodden and unfortunate people, for God has caused His spirit to move the hearts of rulers and councilors to be benevolent and gracious unto us. It is, therefore, the primary duty of parents to guide and lead their children in the righteous way, to implant in them good manners and civility, so that they may be worthy of the loving-kindness of the rulers." [28]

The pages of *Ha-Measef* are replete with eulogies extolling the virtues of enlightened despotism, including extravagant tributes to Ludwig XVI, Catherine II, Joseph II, and Frederick the Great.[29] The faith that the writers of the *Haskalah* had in benevolent monarchy was undoubtedly inspired by the views of the French rationalists on enlightened despotism. "It was the Enlightenment," states a modern scholar "that Voltaire cared about, and not the form of government. Enlightened despotism seemed more likely to preserve civil liberty than a popular or an aristocratic government." [30] According to Voltaire, a monarchy, in any case, was preferable to a democracy. He preferred to obey a fine lion, much stronger than himself, than two hundred rats of his own species.[31] Wessely seems to echo Voltaire's sentiments when in a poem dedicated to Joseph II extolling the *Toleranzpatent*, he declares, "One man of great reason can set the erring on the right path. . . . When the ruler is a man of great wisdom, the people cease to be uncivilized." [32]

Thus the two chief instruments by means of which the early *maskilim* hoped to achieve Jewish emancipation were a benevolent monarchy and secular education. They were confident that as soon as the Jew qualified for citizenship, the "gracious king" would bestow upon him the gift of civic equality. Therefore they kept harp-

27. *Ibid.,* 1784, p. 185.
28. *Ibid.,* 1784, p. 134.
29. *Ibid.,* pp. 65–69; 1785, pp. 17–20.
30. Martin, *French Liberal Thought.,* p. 141.
31. *Ibid.,* p. 140.
32. *Ha-Measef,* 1784, p. 164, p. 171.

ing upon the need of secular education as the necessary requisite for the attainment of that end.

These ideas were prevalent among the cultured and wealthy Jews of Prussia and had a nucleus of adherents in Russia. But it was not until the latter part of the reign of Nicholas I that they found expression in an organized movement.

III

THE FIRST ATTEMPT AT EMANCIPATION

IT is generally agreed that the Russian *Haskalah* was strongly affected by the writings of Mendelssohn and his school. There is reason to believe, however, that even without the stimulus from the West, the Jews of Russia would have attempted to emerge from the ghetto by reforming their system of education and mode of life. "This kinship" (between east and west), observes a Jewish historian, "really existed, and was recognized both by the people and the intellectuals. But unfortunately the legend about the ancestor from Berlin grew to such disproportionate dimensions that it pushed into the background all the other ancestors of the progressive Jews of the western Russian borderlands." [1] Another authority goes even further in refuting the importance of Prussian influence. He maintains that the creators of the Polish-Lithuanian Enlightenment were not the disciples of the *Measfim* (Writers for the magazine *Ha-Measef*) but were the products of the same current of thought that gave birth to the Prussian *Haskalah*.[2]

A study of the views on secular education held by Rabbi Elijah of Vilno (1720–1797), outstanding rabbinic authority of Lithuanian Jewry of the eighteenth century, seems to substantiate the opinion that Russian Jewry produced its own sponsors of enlightenment independent of Prussian influence. This great rabbi and scholar, better known as the Gaon,[3] strongly favored the acquisition of secular knowledge. Baruch Shick, or Baruch of Shklov, informs us that when he visited the Gaon he "heard from his saintly lips that if one is ignorant of the secular sciences, one is a hundredfold more ignorant of the wisdom of the *Torah*, for the two are inseparable." [4] Another rabbi cites as the Gaon's opinion that "all sciences are essential for an understanding of the Holy *Torah*." [5]

The Gaon himself wrote on Hebrew grammar, mathematics, and geography. To facilitate the study of the Bible and make it more intelligible to the lay student he prepared a geography with a map

1. P. Marek, *Ocherki po Istorii Prosveshcheniia Evreev v Rossii*, p. 2.
2. I. Zinberg, *Evreiskaia Starina,* 1928, p. 17.
3. The title *Gaon,* a Hebrew term which is the equivalent of "His Excellency," was originally conferred upon the heads of the Talmudical academies in Babylonia. Later this term was applied to outstanding Jewish scholars.
4. Introduction to the Hebrew translation of *Euclid.*
5. Rabbi Israel of Shklov, Introduction to *Peat Ha-Shulhan.*

of Palestine.[6] Rabbi Elijah also revolutionized the study of the Talmud by his rejection of the scholastic-dialectic method known as *Pilpul* (casuistry) and his insistence that reason and the rules of logic should be employed in Talmudic interpretation.

That the Gaon shared the *maskilim's* dissatisfaction with the prevailing method of Jewish education is evidenced by his attempt to change and improve it. But his interest in secular studies was hardly prompted by the considerations that motivated the activities of the *maskilim.* It is inconceivable that this saint and mystic, who lived in an isolated world, literally poring day and night over sacred tomes, ever dreamed of emerging from the ghetto. Nor could his insistence on the rigid and unquestioning fulfillment of all the precepts of the Talmudic authorities be harmonized with the religious views of even the earlier leaders of the Enlightenment. His sanction of secular studies must, nonetheless, have given a strong impetus to the advancement of those studies among Russian Jewry. As a modern writer puts it: "There is no doubt that unwittingly, and certainly unintentionally, the Gaon was the harbinger of the *Haskalah* in Lithuania." [7]

The views of the Gaon certainly must have encouraged the cultural activities of a remarkable group of rabbis and scholars of the White Russian city of Shklov, who grouped themselves around the wealthy Jew, scholar, and patron of learning, Joshua Zeitlin. In the latter part of the eighteenth and at the beginning of the nineteenth century, Shklov was an important Jewish commercial and intellectual center. Of its widespread renown in the Jewish world we learn from correspondence between this community and Jews of Bukhara.

In 1802, the Jews of Kizil Gar addressed a letter to their coreligionists in Shklov, inquiring whether there was any truth in the report that there were Jews in Russia and whether Bukhara Jews would be allowed to go there for business purposes.[8] In their reply, dated the first day of Hanukkah,[9] 1803, the Jews of Shklov informed their Bukharian brethren that Shklov "was a city and mother in Israel, a city full of wise men and writers, a city whose Jewish inhabitants are among the rich and famous in the land." Thus at the time the *Haskalah* was launched in Prussia, a community already existed in Russia possessing a similar group of cultured and rich Jews engaged in the pursuit of enlightenment.

6. Map reprinted in second volume of *Perezhitoe.*
7. J. Klausner, *Historyah shel Ha-Safrut Ha-Ibrit Ha-Hadashah,* III, 11.
8. Letter published in *Perez.,* II, 274–280.
9. Hanukkah—Feast of Lights held in commemoration of the Maccabean victory, 165 B.C.E.

The outstanding Jew of Shklov was Zeitlin, a friend of Prince Potemkin and manager of his estates. Upon the death of the prince, Zeitlin retired to his own large estate at Ustie, where he gave refuge and hospitality to Jewish scholars. He built a synagogue and established a library and laboratories for scientific experiments.[10]

Another prominent resident of Shklov was Leb Nevakhovich (1776–1831), author of *Vopl Dcheri Iudeiskoi* (Lament of the Daughter of Judea), the first defense of the Jews written in the Russian language. In the latter part of Catherine II's reign, Nevakhovich, together with Abraham Perets, Zeitlin's son-in-law, removed to St. Petersburg. A man of great wealth and extensive commercial activities, which included shipbuilding for the government, Perets was an important figure in the capital. Among his close friends were the noted government officials, Speransky and Kankrin.[11]

Perets, Nevakhovich, and the Polish court councilor and financier, Nota Notkin, were among the first members and founders of the Jewish community in St. Petersburg.[12] Catherine II might have referred to them when she wrote to a foreign correspondent: "There have been three or four Jews in Petersburg for a long time. One of my priests gave them lodging. They are tolerated against the law: we pretend we don't notice them." [13]

Nevakhovich wrote his *Vopl Dcheri Iudeiskoi*—evidently with a view to helping the Jewish cause—after Alexander I named a special committee in 1802 to find a solution for the Jewish problem. A Jewish historian believes the book was effective in correcting erroneous impressions about the Jews among Russian readers, and in influencing the Jewish code of 1804.[14] The *Vopl*, published in 1803 in the "privileged Breitkopofov printing house," was dedicated to Victor Kochubei, a member of the Jewish Committee,[15] who later became minister of the interior. A Hebrew translation of the book[16] which the author made a year later was dedicated to Nota Notkin,

10. A vivid account of Shklov as a center of learning is given by Zeitlin's son-in-law, Rabbi Bernard Nathanson. See S. I. Fuenn, *Kiryah Neemanah,* pp. 277–278.

11. On the relations between Perets and Speransky see G. R. Derzhavin, *Zapiski,* p. 476, and M. Korff, *Zhizn Grafa Speranskago,* I, 102n.

12. On the founding of the Jewish community in St. Petersburg see L. Gordon, *Voskhod,* 1881, I and II. About the first Jews in that city see Prince N. Golitsyn, *Istoria Russkago Zakonod. o Evreiakh,* pp. 174–175.

13. I. G. Orshansky, *Russk. Zakonod. o Evreiakh,* p. 251.

14. J. Gessen, *Budushchnost,* 1902, supplement to weekly, III, 114–117.

15. A special committee of government officials appointed for the task of dealing with the Jewish problem.

16. A Russian reprint of the book, made by Gessen from a copy found in the Imperial Public Library, appears in *Budushchnost,* 1902, III. The Hebrew copy is reprinted in the second volume of *Ha-Abar,* 1918. All quotations here are from the Hebrew text.

a deputy on the same committee, where he evidently played an important part.

In the introduction the author states that he was moved to this literary effort by "his love for the Emperor and the Fatherland; his exultation over the present enlightened period, his pride that he can call the Russians his compatriots, and the deep compassion he feels for his coreligionists." He pleads with the followers of the New Testament, who boast of their compassion and loving-kindness, to take pity on the Jews, not to believe the false charges made against them, and not to despise them. Instead of looking for the Jew in the man, he urges Christians to look for the man in the Jew. Overwhelmed by the many favors Russia has showered upon persecuted Israel, the writer exclaims: "All these favors are engraved upon the tablets of my heart, and I shall not cease to speak of the glory of the sons of Russia all the days of my life." [17] The book ends with an expression of faith in Alexander, to whom Nevakhovich refers as "our King, our Helper," and with an appeal to the Jews to shake off the "dust of ignorance" and acquire secular knowledge.[18]

Nevakhovich's work reflects the marked influence of German-Jewish enlightenment and French rationalism. He, too, speaks of wisdom as "the means of man's salvation" and expresses that faith in enlightened absolutism and secular knowledge which characterized the German-Jewish *maskilim*. While there is reason to believe that the Russian *Haskalah* came into being independently of and simultaneously with that of Prussian-Jewish enlightenment, there is no doubt of the significant influence the latter exerted upon the former. This influence was exercised not alone through the writings of the Prussian *maskilim*, but also through commercial and cultural intercourse. Many East-European Jewish scholars traveled abroad in quest of secular knowledge. Berlin, the residence of Mendelssohn, represented the Mecca of enlightenment to men in pursuit of *Haskalah*, the "Daughter of Heaven."

One such "wandering" scholar, Mendel Levin (1741–1819), is regarded by a Jewish historian as the connecting link between the Galician and the Lithuanian pioneers of the *Haskalah* movement.[19] Born in Satanov, province of Podol, Levin spent some time in Shklov, Berlin, and Galicia.

As stated above, commercial intercourse was instrumental in

17. *Kol Shavat Bat Yehudah,* p. 34.
18. A few years after the publication of this book, Nevakhovich embraced the Greek-Orthodox faith. The famous scientist Elias Mechnikov is his grandson.
19. I. Zinberg, *Ges. Lit. Yid.,* V, 332.

bringing about intellectual contact between Prussian, Galician, and Russian Jewries. A. B. Gottlober of Vohlyn, writer and active champion of the enlightenment, describes how Galicia, which received its *Haskalah* from Prussia, influenced the southwestern center of Russia. "The Jews of the big Galician cities were the first who were illumined by the light of wisdom that shone forth from Mendelssohn and his disciples. And whenever they would come for business purposes to Russian cities, they would bring with them some spices of their enlightenment and culture. The youth would taste it and their eyes would light up. In this respect Brody particularly distinguished itself, for it was a city full of wise and learned men, and its commercial activities were mostly with Russia. Wherever a merchant of Brody would come, he would captivate the youth with his beautiful speech. Their eyes would open, and, realizing that they were barren of any knowledge, they would begin to study. The merchant of Brody was their guide and teacher." [20]

Further proof of the influence of Galician intellectuals on Russian Jewry of the southwest is furnished by the fact that the new type of schools established in 1822, in Uman, and in 1826, in Odessa, were headed by educators from Galicia. Another such school was founded in Vilno in 1830 by a Galician pedagogue.[21]

Galicia was also responsible for shaping the views and activities of the outstanding writer and reformer, Isaac Baer Levinsohn (1788–1860), sometimes called the Russian Mendelssohn. Unlike most children of his time, Levinsohn, who was born in the small town of Kremenits, Podol, received instruction in the Russian language in addition to the usual education of his day. As a young man he became ill from mental exertion and went to Brody for medical care. He came into contact with the leading scholars of Galician Jewry and soon became a prominent figure among them. During his stay in Galicia he compiled a grammar of the Russian language in Hebrew, and for a time taught Hebrew in one of the modern schools there.

In 1820 Levinsohn returned to his native town, where he commenced the writing of his most important work, *Teudah Be-Yisrael* (A Testimony in Israel), published in Vilno in 1828. In this work the author undertook to convince his coreligionists that the program of *Haskalah,* which advocated the study of the Hebrew language and grammar, the acquisition of secular sciences and the pur-

20. A. Fridkin, *Abram Baer Gottlober un zein Epohe,* p. 84.

21. S. M. Ginsburg, Introduction to *Kazennyia Evreiskiia Uchilishcha,* I, 37. Interesting information about the Uman school is given by S. M. Stanislavsky in *Voskhod,* 1884, Book 4, pp. 132–133.

suit of handicrafts and agriculture, was not in conflict with the Jewish faith. Citing numerous passages from the Talmud and medieval authorities, he sought to prove that such a program was in harmony with the best traditions and historic experiences of the Jews. In support of his proposal for the economic readjustment of Jewish life, he quoted Jewish as well as non-Jewish sources pointing to the Jews as a historically agricultural people to whom trade was a foreign acquisition.[22] He noted with satisfaction that the unfortunate circumstances which forced the Jews of the Middle Ages to turn to trade and commerce, the only means of livelihood then open to them, were now happily things of the past. "Now that the dark night of bigotry has given way to the sun of science and enlightenment; now that in Russia civic rights, permission to work the land, to attend schools, build factories, and practice arts and crafts are given to the Jews, it is up to them to take advantage of the benevolence extended to them and not to neglect the opportunities agriculture offers them." [23]

The profound impression that Levinsohn's book made on the Jewish youth, especially on Talmudic students, is described by Gottlober, who relates that, in defiance of the "fanatics," countless young men started to study the Hebrew and Russian languages. Clubs were formed in each city with the assistance of the few *maskilim* found here and there.[24]

In 1839 Levinsohn published his *Bet Yehudah* (The House of Judah), which is a critical study of the Jewish religion. At the end of the second part he outlined a five-point program of reform for Russian Jewry, which became the official program of the leaders of the *Haskalah*. The author suggested:

1. That modern schools be established for children of both sexes, and theological seminaries set up in the cities of Warsaw, Vilno, Odessa, and Berdichev. In addition to Jewish studies, students should receive instruction in secular subjects.
2. That a chief rabbi and council be appointed to have charge of the spiritual life of Russian Jewry.
3. That competent preachers be obtained to instruct the people.
4. That at least a third of the people be encouraged to engage in agriculture.
5. That Jews be discouraged from ostentatious display and luxurious living.[25]

22. *Tehudah Be-Yisrael,* pp. 173–174.
23. *Ibid.,* p. 177.
24. A. Fridkin, *Abram Baer Gottlober un zein Epohe,* p. 211.
25. *Bet Yehudah,* Part 2, pp. 130–134.

The writings of Levinsohn and the activities of the progressive groups in the various towns failed to gain any appreciable following among the masses of Russian Jewry. There were a number of reasons why the people were unresponsive to the call of *Haskalah*. To begin with, there was the usual resistance to innovation. For several centuries before they came under the rule of Russia, the Jews of Poland had been accustomed to living in a secluded world of their own apart from any social or cultural contact with their non-Jewish environment. The training which Jewish children received in the *heder* or *yeshibah* (Talmudical school) consisted of a study of the Pentateuch, Talmud, and religious codes translated into the Yiddish vernacular. The study of Hebrew as a language was practically unknown. The language of the native country and other secular subjects found no place in the curriculum, since pupils were not being prepared for any contact with the world outside the ghetto. Consequently all non-religious studies came to be regarded as taboo.

The program of the *maskilim* sought to effect a radical change in the traditional system of education and thus appeared to the orthodox masses of Jewry as an attempt to undermine the very foundation of the Jewish faith. "It is because of this suspicion," relates a contemporary, "that the *Hassidim*[26] could not tolerate the Jews of Brody, and the *Hassidic* Rabbi of Opt used to curse them, charging that they brought atheism into Russia." [27] A Jewish writer recalls that when he was a child he used to hear the *Hassidim* speak with anger about the "Teudke,[28] may his name be blotted out forever." [29] These sentiments were shared by all orthodox Jewry, *hassidic* or otherwise.

Another factor which contributed toward the distrust of *Haskalah* was the large number of conversions among Prussian Jewry in the last decade of the eighteenth and the first of the nineteenth centuries. There were, to be sure, influences other than *Haskalah* responsible for these mass desertions, but orthodox Jewry attributed them solely to the movement for enlightenment.

The chief deterrents to the progress of *Haskalah*, however, were the policies of Alexander I and Nicholas I. A study of these policies will make clear why the movement could not take root during their reign and why governmental attempts at "reforming" the Jew were destined to fail.

26. *Hassidim*—members of a religious sect who were the disciples of the wonder-rabbis, and who regarded piety as preferable to learning. For more on *Hassidism* see Chapter V in this book.

27. A. Fridkin, *Abram Baer Gottlober.*, p. 84.

28. *Teudke*—a derogatory diminutive for the writer of *Teudah Be-Yisrael.*

29. Zinberg, *Ges. Lit. Yid.*, VIII, Book 2, 55.

IV

THE JEWISH POLICIES OF ALEXANDER I AND NICHOLAS I

WHILE the avowed intention of both Alexander I and Nicholas I was to break down the isolation of the Jews and to improve their political and economic status, their legislation served only to perpetuate and even to aggravate those very conditions. Alexander's law of 1804, with its clauses for educational and agricultural opportunities, was written in a more liberal spirit than any Jewish legislation heretofore, yet it left the Jew politically rightless and economically in a worse position than before. Article 34 of the statute ordered that Jews should within three and in some cases four years be deprived of the right to lease and manage taverns and inns in villages and thoroughfares, or even to reside there. This section brought ruin upon sixty thousand Jewish families—about half a million souls.[1]

The edict, though purporting to be a preparatory step in the economic readjustment of the Jews, proved disastrous because the government had made no provisions for the absorption of the evicted population into other occupations. A Russian writer thus describes the manner in which the expulsion from the villages was effected:

> Jews pleaded for extension of time, they cried and groaned, but to no avail. They were mercilessly driven under a guard of peasants and, in some cases, of soldiers! They drove them like cattle into the towns and hamlets, and there on open lots under the sky, they were left to contemplate the vicissitudes of fate.[2]

An official historian, friendly to the reign of Alexander I, thus notes the tragic results of those evictions:

> In the dead of winter half-naked Jews, driven from their domiciles into the towns, were crowded together in quarters that gave them no breathing space, while others, ill-sheltered, were left exposed to the bitter cold. . . . There developed among them disease and death.[3]

The ruthless and planless dislocation of such large numbers of

1. *Russky Arkhiv,* 1903, I, 258; S. M. Dubnow, *Hist. J. Russ. Pol.,* I, 346.
2. V. N. Nikitin, *Evrei Zemledeltsy,* p. 16.
3. N. Golitsyn, *Istoria Russkago Zakon. o Evreiakh,* pp. 686–687.

Jews created a serious problem for non-Jews as well. From a report of the Jewish Committee submitted to the emperor, we learn that many local authorities complained to the central government about their inability to take care of the refugees who swarmed their towns. They expressed fear "that these people, because of poverty, might cause riots or take to looting or murder." [4] There were also protests from landowners, whose source of income was depleted through these evictions.[5]

Complete removal from the villages was temporarily postponed because of unexpected circumstances. In 1807, Napoleon, for the purpose of settling certain Jewish questions, convened representatives of French Jewry in an assembly which he dignified by the name of The Sanhedrin.[6] The relations between Russia and France being strained at that time, this move was regarded by the Holy Synod as an attempt to unite world Jewry under the banner of France.[7] This suspicion prompted the Russian government to suspend the expulsions so as not further to antagonize its Jewish population. After the conclusion of the war between Russia and France, however, the evictions were renewed and completed.

Nor was the legislation enacted during the second half of Alexander's reign—a period more reactionary than the first—consistent with the avowed policies of the government to improve the Jewish position. A few illustrations will suffice. In 1821 Jews were forbidden to come to the interior Russian provinces even for business purposes.[8] In 1825, the provinces of Astrakhan and the Caucasus, which had been open to Jews since 1804, were declared closed to them.[9] In the same year the existing prohibition of residence in the province of Vohlyn within a radius of fifty versts from the border was extended to all border states.[10] Even Prince Golitsyn, a historian who lauded the Jewish policies of Alexander I, testifies to the misery experienced by the Jews during that emperor's reign. "One cannot deny," he states, "that during the period Jews were destined to suffer and Jewish tears flowed freely." [11]

Restrictive measures multiplied rapidly in the reign of Nicholas I, pointing to a desire on the part of the government to cut the Jews

4. *Russky Arkhiv,* 1903, I, 258.
5. S. M. Dubnow, *Hist. J. Russ. Pol.,* I, 346.
6. *Sanhedrin*—The legislative and judicial body in Palestine during the Second Commonwealth.
7. *P. P. S. Z.,* XXIX, no. 22,394.
8. *Ibid.,* XXXVII, no. 28,537.
9. *Ibid.,* XL, no. 30,404.
10. *Ibid.,* XL, no. 30,402.
11. Golitsyn, *Istoria Russ. Zak. Evr.,* p. 903.

off from Russian life, rather than to make them a part of it. A Russian-Jewish historian thus characterizes the policies of Nicholas I:

> In this legislation which sought to regulate Jewish life, one may perceive a cry of despair that, with all its power, the government is unable to uproot the Jew from the bosom of Russian life, or to destroy completely that material and spiritual connection between Jews and Christians which life itself had created.[12]

Painfully aware of the hostile attitude of the government which officially branded them as a people "more harmful than useful to the state," [13] the Jews sought comfort in the traditions and practices of their religion, to which they now clung with even greater tenacity. The missionary policies inaugurated in the second half of Alexander I's régime and continued through that of Nicholas I made them more than ever distrustful of the government and fearful for their faith.

Inducements offered to converts[14] in the way of exemptions from military service and taxes indicated that these régimes were seeking to lure Jews from their ancestral faith. The fact that a special committee was established [15] to care for Jews converted to Christianity is further evidence that the suspicion of the Jews was not groundless. An episode related by a Russian teacher reveals the missionary tendencies of the period. A Jew from the city of Chernigov sought to engage this teacher as an instructor for his children. At first the teacher refused but later he consented when the authorities pointed out to him that the Jew's children might be persuaded to embrace Christianity as a result of his instruction.[16]

Education as a means of strengthening the Christian faith and the authority of the state had become the basis of the school system during the reactionary period of Alexander I. The official historian of the Ministry for Public Education states that the new leaders of the ministry in the second half of Alexander's régime saw a source of political and religious upheaval[17] in the liberal policies of their predecessors of the first half of the reign. In a letter written to the emperor in 1816, Count N. Speransky expressed the prevalent

12. J. Gessen, *Istoria Evr. Naroda v Rosii,* II, 19.

13. *V. P. S. Z.,* III, no. 2558.

14. For the various privileges offered Jewish converts in the reigns of Alexander I and Nicholas I, see the imperial orders of August 13, 1820, *P. P. S. Z.,* XXXVII, no. 28,377; November 30, 1823, *ibid.,* XXXVIII, no. 29,662; September 25, 1830, *V. P. S. Z.,* V. no. 3951; January 23, 1851, *ibid.,* XXVI, no. 24,873.

15. *P. P. S. Z.,* XXXIV, no. 26,752.

16. *Kievskaia Starina,* 1894, April, p. 84.

17. S. V. Rozhdestvensky, *Istorichesky Obzor Deiatelnosti Minis. Nar. Prosv.,* p. 110.

view on the function of education. He stated that "Christian teaching should be at the basis not only of the social order but even more so of education." [18] In line with this policy, the Ministry for Public Education was merged with that of Public Worship, so that "Christian piety might always be the foundation of true education." [19] That the government also intended education to serve as a means of strengthening its own authority is indicated by the directions given in 1818 to the educational committee. The committee was instructed to use only textbooks which would best help to bring about "an enduring and blessed harmony between faith, knowledge, and authority." [20]

It is not surprising, then, in view of the Christian character of education, added to the general hostility directed against the Jews, that they remained unresponsive to the educational opportunities offered them. Out of 1,906 university students in Russia in 1835, only eleven were Jews.[21] Of the 2,866 students who attended the higher institutions of learning in 1840, fifteen were Jews, and of the total number of 80,017 pupils in the primary and secondary schools, forty-eight were of the Jewish faith.[22]

The failure to attract Jewish children to the general schools gave rise to a new plan, that of establishing special Jewish schools. With this thought in mind, Count Sergius Uvarov, minister of Public Education, during a visit in Germany in the latter thirties, discussed with German-Jewish leaders methods for educating their Russian coreligionists.[23] When on December 19, 1840, a committee was formed for the purpose of devising means for the radical reorganization of the Jews of Russia, it was understood that plans for education would play an important part in the program.

The lines along which the Nicholas government expected to work in "reforming" and re-educating Russian Jewry may be gathered from the anonymous memorandum which the members of the committee received from their chairman, P. D. Kiselev, minister for State Domains.[24] Asserting that, in spite of a series of coercive measures and restrictions imposed on them by the government,

18. E. K. Shmid, *Istoria Srednikh Uchebnykh Zavedeni v Ross.*, p. 135.
19. *P. P. S. Z.*, XXXIV, no. 27,106.
20. E. K. Shmid, *Ist. Sred. Ucheb. Zav.*, p. 136.
21. *Z. M. N. P.*, XII, 330.
22. *Ibid.*, XXXII, Division 3, 32–45.
23. He reported to Nicholas on those conversations in an official memorandum of March 17, 1841, *Dopolnenie K Sborniku Postanovleni po Ministerstvu Narod. Prosv.*, pp. 700–711.
24. The memorandum, which Jewish historians believe was written by Kiselev himself, was published by Dubnow, in *Voskhod*, 1901, books 4 and 5, pp. 29–40 and 3–9 respectively.

"the Jews are still in a state of vagrancy and harmful to the well-being of the country," the document invited the special attention of the members of the committee to the religious teachings of the Jews. These teachings, the memorandum averred, are responsible for the peculiar characteristics which distinguish the Jews from peoples of other faiths, and which are harmful not alone to the Jews themselves but also to the Russian subjects among whom they live. The anonymous author stated that, according to the admission of some Jews, "all the misfortunes of their coreligionists are caused by the superstition and fanaticism instilled by the Talmud." The memorandum then proposed that the committee direct its attention mainly to a consideration of the following two items: (1) The ethical and religious education of the Jew; (2) The abolition of those Jewish administrative and financial institutions which hamper the civic reorganization of the Jews.[25]

To achieve these ends, the note offered a plan for the reorganization of the spiritual and economic life of the Jews, which included the establishment of special schools for them under the supervision of the government. In line with this program, a law promulgated on November 13, 1844, stipulated that, without being barred from the general school system Jews could also open their own schools to be supported by funds from special taxes imposed on them. The law also provided for the teaching of the Jewish religion by instructors of the Jewish faith. Secular subjects might be taught by Jews as well as Christians. In addition to primary schools, two theological seminaries were also to be opened for training teachers and rabbis, the curriculum to correspond to that of a gymnasium.[26] Teachers and graduates of these schools were to enjoy the privileges offered by the corresponding government institutions.[27]

A secret supplement to this law containing the principles which the Ministry for Public Education was to follow[28] reveals the real purpose of the government's Jewish educational policies. "The purpose of educating the Jews," reads paragraph one, "is to bring about their gradual merging with the Christian nationalities, and to uproot those superstitions and harmful prejudices which are instilled by the teachings of the Talmud." The law specified that

25. This refers to the institution of the *Kahal* (Hebrew term for community), the Jewish community organization whose functions were religious, fiscal, and, in some cases, judicial. These *Kahals,* a carry-over from Poland, where they exercised considerable authority over Jewish life had been continually limited in power since Catherine II, and were completely abolished in 1844. See *V. P. S. Z.,* XIX, No. 18,546.

26. Gymnasium—A secondary educational institution.

27. *V. P. S. Z.,* XIX, no., 18,420.

28. *Sbornik Post. po Minis. N. P.,* II, no. 279, pp. 521–528.

principals of the primary schools and directors of the theological seminaries were to be only Christians.

Uvarov, the moving spirit of this educational project, knew that it would be no easy task to win the confidence of the Jews. To overcome anticipated resistance and secure coöperation for the newly created schools, he enlisted the services of a young German Jew, Dr. Max Lilienthal, the director of the modern Jewish school in Riga. This educator was held in high esteem by the Russian government and had been presented with a diamond ring by the emperor in recognition of his extraordinary success in developing the Riga school.[29]

Soon after this distinction was conferred upon him, Lilienthal was called to St. Petersburg in connection with the new task he was to undertake. When he informed the minister of the Jews' distrust regarding the government's proposed measure, in which they saw only a proselytizing scheme, Uvarov asked, "Well, what can the government do to remove their doubts?" "Grant them emancipation at once," the Jewish educator replied. He conceded that even a partial removal of their disabilities would gain the confidence of his coreligionists. The Russian official, however, evaded the issue by a vague reassurance that the intentions of the tsar were good.[30]

In his memoirs, written years later in America, Lilienthal reveals that he shared the suspicions of the Russian Jews. Reminiscing about his conversation with Uvarov, he states that after he had left the minister of education, he pondered upon the suspicious inconsistency of the government. Lilienthal could not understand why it made such a special effort to educate the Jews, when as a matter of fact, they already stood on a higher cultural level than the Russian masses.[31]

Considering the distrustful attitude of the Nicholas government toward education in general, which it regarded as more harmful than good for the masses,[32] its effort to educate the Jews could hardly have inspired confidence. A famous Russian writer observes that when Nicholas I ascended the throne, education ceased to be a virtue and came to be regarded as a crime.[33] Uvarov's sentiments concerning education and progress are revealed in a conversation

29. D. Philipson, *Max Lilienthal,* p. 19. On Lilienthal's accomplishments in the Riga school see the official testimony in *Dopol. K Sborn. Post. po Minis. N. P.,* p. 707.

30. Philipson, *Max Lilienthal,* pp. 246–247.

31. *Allgemeine Zeitung des Judentums,* 1855, p. 275.

32. On the restrictive measures designed to discourage the acquisition of both elementary and secondary education by the lower classes of the Russian people, see *Sbornik Rasp. p. Min. N. P.,* no. 509, p. 985; *Sbornik Post. po Minis. N. P.,* II, no. 41, pp. 71–72.

33. S. M. Solovev, *Zapiski,* p. 120.

with a Russian scholar, to whom the minister of education said: "I know what these liberals, journalists and their accomplices want. They will not succeed in planting their seeds in the field over which I stand guard. . . . If I could succeed in turning Russia back fifty years, I would feel that I had fulfilled my duty and could die in peace." [34] The régime's paradoxical concern with the education of the Jews caused a Russian educator to comment: "In the matter of education, Jews, who were regarded as a harmful element of the population, were put in an unusually privileged position as compared with the tens of millions of the Russian population who were not regarded as harmful." [35]

Toward the end of 1841, Lilienthal, at the request of Uvarov, undertook a tour of the important cities of the Pale to obtain the coöperation of the Jewish communities. In Vilno, the first city he visited for this purpose, the Jewish representatives confronted him with this challenging question:

> Doctor, are you fully acquainted with the leading principles of our government? . . . The course pursued against all denominations but the Greek-Orthodox proves clearly that the government intends to have but one church in the whole empire; that it has in view only its own future strength and greatness, and not our prosperity. We are sorry to state that we put no trust in the new measures proposed by the ministerial council, and we look with gloomy foreboding into the future.

Lilienthal then pointed out that their refusal to coöperate would not deter the government from proceeding with its plans. On the other hand, if they would support the project, their suggestions would be taken into consideration in shaping the policies of the Jewish school system. At this point their resistance weakened, but they still demanded a guarantee that their religion would not be encroached upon. Lilienthal assured them that as soon as he discovered that any measures against "our holy religion" were being undertaken, he would resign from his office. This solemn promise overcame their objections and they pledged their support.[36]

From Vilno Lilienthal proceeded to Minsk, where he encountered stubborn opposition. Orthodox Jews countered his arguments with this statement:

> As long as we are not granted civic rights, education will be only a misfortune for us. In his present cultural state the Jew does not disdain

34. A. V. Nikitenko, *Russkaia Starina,* LXIII, 532–533.
35. A. Beletsky, *Vopros ob Obraz. Russ. Ev. v. Tsarst. Imp. Nicol. Per.,* p. 40.
36. Philipson, *Max Lilienthal,* pp. 264–266.

the humiliating livelihood of a broker or usurer, and finds comfort in his religion. But when the Jew will receive a modern education, he will become sensitive to his legal disabilities, and then, dissatisfied with his bitter lot, he will be prompted to desert his faith. An honest Jewish father will never agree to train his child for conversion.[37]

Lilienthal was more successful in the southwest. In the cities of Berdichev and Odessa, where his arrival was anxiously awaited, he was given a royal welcome. Because of the activities of the "Friends of the New Enlightenment," the Jews of south Russia were more favorably disposed to the ideas of *Haskalah*. Lilienthal outlined the plans of the government at a meeting of representative Jews, and the assembly solemnly promised "to do and obey."[38]

The *maskilim* were the only ones who hailed the establishment of the Jewish government schools. Just as Wessely and his followers had acclaimed the *Toleranzpatent* in verse and prose, so now the Russian-Jewish champions of *Haskalah* eulogized Nicholas and Uvarov. The special prayer of thanksgiving, written by the historian Samuel Joseph Fuenn (1819–1891) of Vilno, is typical of the expressions of extravagant praise and naïve enthusiasm which the new government undertaking evoked from the *maskilim*. Fuenn thanked God "who caused us to find favor and grace in the eyes of the mighty rulers of Russia . . . whose heart is full of pure love for us," and expressed his implicit faith "in our emperor, whose throne is founded on justice and righteousness."[39]

The *maskilim* from abroad, too, added their voices to the chorus of praise. Abraham Goldberg of Rava, Galicia, wrote a Hebrew poem with the grandiloquent title *Masa Zafon* (A Prophecy from the North), in which he took his brethren to task for their failure to appreciate the blessings of education and agriculture. Describing the low state to which Israel had fallen because of ignorance, the author represents Nicholas, moved by pity, saying to himself, "I shall be like dew unto Israel, I shall be a source of living waters unto him."[40]

But the *maskilim* of Russia and of Western Europe had no effect upon the attitude of the bulk of Russian Jewry. The reaction of the masses to the special Jewish schools is aptly described by the novelist, Lev Levanda, in a short story called *Shkoloboiazn* (School

37. M. Lilienthal, *Allgemeine Zeitung des Judentums,* 1842, p. 605.

38. M. Morgulis, *Evreiskaia Biblioteka,* I, 173–174. On Lilienthal's activities in Russia see also Pauline Wengeroff, *Memoiren einer Grossmutter,* I, 118–137; J. S. Raisin, *The Haskalah Movement in Russia,* pp. 171–189.

39. *Pirhe Zafon,* II, 70–72.

40. *Masa Zafon,* p. 21.

Fear).[41] It is evident from the tale that school reform was regarded as an evil decree similar to military service.

Another cause for distrust of the government was the *ukaz* of 1843 ordering the eviction of all Jews from the towns and villages in the frontier zones bordering on Austria and Prussia.[42] This brought disaster to thousands of Jewish families. It was in the hope of obtaining the revocation of this edict and the amelioration of Jewish disabilities that the famous Anglo-Jewish philanthropist, Sir Moses Montefiore (1784–1885), came to Russia in 1846.

Sir Moses had received several previous invitations to visit Russia. In 1842, a Jewish deputation from Riga came to him with a request that he intercede on behalf of the Jews of the frontier zones, who were threatened with deportation. Lilienthal, too, at the suggestion of Uvarov, had asked him to come as a consultant in connection with the work of the Jewish Committee. But it was not until 1846 that Montefiore came to the land of his East-European brethren.[43]

In a conversation with the English visitor, Uvarov made it clear that before opportunities for gaining a livelihood would be granted to the Jews, they must first be educated along the new lines proposed by the government. He pointed to the orthodoxy of the Russian Jews and their adherence to the Talmud as the cause of their backwardness and inferior civic status. The minister assured the philanthropist that the government had no intention of converting his coreligionists through the special schools, but sought only to qualify Russian Jewry for more liberal treatment.

The Jewish emissary countered Uvarov's charges against the Talmud by reminding him that it was a work held in high esteem by many pious and learned Christians. In support of his contention that the Talmud was not a source of false teachings, as Uvarov averred, Montefiore quoted among other statements from eminent Christian scholars what the famous Christian Hebraist, Buxtorf, said in the preface to his Chaldaic and Talmudical Lexicon:

> The Talmud is a learned work or a large corpus of erudition; it contains manifold learning in all sciences; it teaches the most explicit and most complete, civil and canonical law of the Jews, so that the whole nation, as well as their Synagogue, might live thereby in a state of happiness—in the most desirable way.

41. *Ev. Bib.*, V, 65–88.
42. *V. P. S. Z.*, XVIII, no. 16,767.
43. P. Goodman, *Moses Montefiore*, pp. 78–79; *Diaries of Sir Moses Montefiore and Lady Montefiore*, edited by Dr. L. Loewe, I, 311; J. Gessen, *Perez.*, IV, 150. See especially S. M. Ginsburg, *Historische Werk,* II, 163–203.

It is the most luminous commentary of the Scriptural law as well as its supplement and support.
It contains most excellent teaching on jurisprudence, medicine, natural philosophy, ethics, politics, astronomy, and other branches of science, which make one think highly of the history of that nation and of the time in which the work was written.

Montefiore also refuted the minister's assertion concerning the ignorance of the Russian Jews by citing numerous works in Hebrew literature produced by them.[44]

Interviews with other government dignitaries were equally discouraging. Nor did Montefiore get any encouragement from Nicholas, to whom he made a most fervent plea "for the general alterations of all laws and edicts that pressed heavily on the Jews under his Majesty's sway." This appeal, voiced in an audience with the emperor on April 4, 1846, was productive only of the vague assurance "that he [the tsar], as well as his ministers, was most desirous for the improvement of the situation in every way possible."[45]

Returning to England after a few months' stay in Russia, Montefiore, at the request of the tsar, sent him a memorandum on the impressions he had gathered and his recommendations for the improvement of the Jewish position. His findings were based on a study of several representative Jewish communities he had visited, and on data dealing with the economic structure of Russian Jewry submitted to him by authoritative Jewish leaders. Montefiore defended his coreligionists against a number of charges commonly leveled against them. He refuted the charge about the disinclination of Jews to perform productive labor by pointing to the many Jewish artisans and craftsmen and to those engaged in stone-breaking, digging, load-bearing, etc. He answered the complaints often voiced about the large number of Jewish idlers by pointing to their restriction of residence, which deprived them of the opportunity enjoyed by the non-Jew of seeking work elsewhere when it was scarce in their own area. The writer, assuring the emperor that his Jewish subjects were most eager to engage in agriculture, cited numerous instances in which their willingness was frustrated by impediments put in their path by local officials. Countering the charge that most Jews were engaged in petty trade, Montefiore stated that only one fourth of the Jewish population sought a livelihood in this occupation. As to the oft-repeated accusation that Jews resorted to dishonest business practices, he suggested that the guilty

44. *Diaries,* I, 331–332.
45. *Ibid.,* 333–334.

be punished but that punishing a whole people for the wrongdoing of a few was unjust. In connection with the charge of Jewish smuggling, on the basis of which Jews were barred from living in frontier zones, the report called attention to the existence of such criminal activity in Moscow and St. Petersburg, where Jews did not reside. Montefiore concluded his report with a fervent plea for the abolition of laws restricting Jewish residence and activity within the Pale.[46] He asked that they be given real opportunities to engage in agricultural pursuits and urged the removal of such special taxes and restrictions "as at present they are made to bear in a greater number and to a greater extent than other classes of his Majesty's subjects." [47]

The emperor's observations on this report, noted by Kiselev on the margins of the document, came to light when the archives were opened after the Russian revolution. These notations record the tsar's favorable impression of the tenor of the report and his admission that there were certain inconsistencies in the laws concerning the Jews which should be rectified. Concerning the plea of the petitioner that Jews be given equal rights with Christians within the Pale, however, the emperor observed: "When Montefiore speaks of equalizing the rights of Jews with that of Christians—that cannot be permitted *and as long as I live I shall not permit it*. . . . The king must not forget that it is his duty to protect the rights of sixty million people. . . . The limitations created by law cannot be removed all at once. . . . If the present attempt to turn the Jews toward productive labor succeeds, time will of itself bring about the gradual abolition of those restrictions which are at present still necessary." [48]

Montefiore's visit upon which Russian and English Jewries placed so much hope,[49] proved fruitless either in improving the position of the Russian Jews or in effecting any change in their attitude toward the governmental schools. Lilienthal's sudden departure in 1845 for the United States only strengthened the suspicion that the whole educational scheme was actuated by proselytizing motives. The rumor spread that he had left Russia because the government had suggested his embracing the Greek-Orthodox faith. An article in the *Allgemeine Zeitung des Judentums* in 1848 confirmed the

46. Even within those provinces where Jews were permitted to reside, there were specified areas barred to them for residence or trade.

47. Memorandum published in *Diaries,* I, 360–373.

48. S. M. Ginsburg, *Hist. Werk,* II, 198–199.

49. A special prayer for the success of Montefiore's mission was offered up in all the synagogues of England. The text of the prayer is published in S. M. Ginsburg, *Hist. Werk,* II, 292.

suspicions of his Russian coreligionists. "Only when the Jew will bow to the Greek cross," Lilienthal wrote, "will the tsar be satisfied, irrespective of whether the converts be good or bad people." [50]

Vilno and Zhitomir were the first cities to open Jewish government schools, which began to function in 1847. Their budget was to be met by a special tax levied on Sabbath candles.[51] Out of fear of antagonizing the authorities, some Jews sent their children there, but the new schools never became popular. Nor did these educational institutions succeed in discouraging private instruction by *melamdim*,[52] who were regarded by the authorities as the disseminators of superstitious beliefs. According to the director of the schools of Vitebsk, the greater part of the pupils of the Jewish schools attended the classes for general subjects only, while they continued to receive their Jewish education from the *melamdim*.[53]

The incompetence and unpopularity of the Jewish teachers, who were chosen for their anti-orthodox behavior rather than for their knowledge, contributed greatly to the failure of the schools to gain the confidence of the Jewish population. Nor were the Christian principals, generally selected from the dregs of the country schools, capable of inspiring confidence, particularly since they knew neither the language nor the ways of the people with whom they dealt.[54]

In addition to their duties as principals of the Jewish government schools, these officials were charged with the supervision of the private Hebrew schools conducted by the *melamdim*. It was their duty to enforce the law which required that the *melamdim* pass an examination in the Russian language. The bribes which they accepted from the Jewish communities not to disqualify these traditional teachers soon made the post of principal a very lucrative one.[55] "In such a manner," writes a Jewish historian, "the people who were placed at the helm of Jewish education simultaneously occupied two remunerative posts: one, in the employ of the Ministry of Public Education as the official disseminators of culture, and the other in the employ of the local Jewish communities as most trusted and effective fighters of the educational policies of the same ministry." [56]

The corruption of the principals and the incompetence of the teachers, not to speak of the lack of confidence on the part of the Jewish population, were responsible for the negligible enrollment.

50. 1848, p. 233.
51. *V. P. S. Z.,* XIX, no. 18,545.
52. *Melamdim*—literally teachers. A term applied to the teachers of the *heder*.
53. *Z. M. N. P.,* CXII, Div. 6, 113.
54. L. Bramson, *Sbornik v polzu Nachalnykh Shkol,* p. 318.
55. P. Kulisher, *Voskhod,* 1892, June, p. 13.
56. P. Marek, *Och. po Ist. Pros. Evr.,* p. 62.

In 1852 the city of Shklov, with a Jewish population of over ten thousand, had a registration of twenty-seven pupils in its school. Vitebsk, which had a substantial Jewish population, enrolled thirteen in 1849, and nineteen in 1851. Starodub had eighteen in 1856.[57] In 1857, ten years after the government schools were established, the total number of pupils was 3,293.[58]

Embarrassed by the poor registration and attendance, officials sought to attribute them to the children's ill health and lack of clothing and necessary school materials. A Russian educator advanced a more likely reason for the failure of the schools when, in 1862, he wrote: "Moral education has to be imparted not in the spirit of the Christian religion, to which the Jews will never subscribe, but rather in the spirit of general human education, which is acceptable to each and everyone." [59]

But the work of the government schools was not altogether fruitless. Thousands of Jewish children received an introduction to secular education, and in the theological schools Jewish boys pursued a course of study which corresponded to that of a gymnasium. Summarizing the harsh régime of Nicholas I, a Jewish historian writes: "Yet the efforts of the Nicholas administration in the field of Jewish education were not in vain. The seeds were scattered by the wind, and the fertile ones sank deep into the ground. As soon as the political conditions changed and warm winds began to blow, these seeds began to sprout, yielding a rich harvest." [60]

Alexander I and Nicholas I sought to solve the Jewish problem in still another way. They tried to encourage Jews to engage in agriculture. In this connection they pursued a program much along the lines laid down by the Austrian monarch, Joseph II, who, to induce his Jewish subjects to settle on the land and engage in husbandry, deprived the Jews of Galicia of the right to sell liquors or lease landed property. Driven from their domiciles and deprived of centuries-old sources of livelihood, these Jews were left without any means of sustenance, for most of the available land had been allocated to German colonists who had responded to the emperor's call to colonize his "vacant and deserted land." [61] Though Joseph was well meaning, his failure to take into consideration existing condi-

57. *Ibid.*, p. 81. Figures taken from archives of the respective schools.

58. L. Bramson, *Sbornik v Polzu Nac. Shk.*, p. 312.

59. N. Barsov, *Shkoly na Vohlyni i Podoli*, p. 67. Quoted in I. M. Cherikover, *Istoria Obshchestva dlia Rasprostraneniia Prosveshcheniia mezhdu Evreiami v Rossii*, p. 14.

60. S. Posner, *Evrei v Obshchei Shkole*, p. 23.

61. S. K. Padover, *The Revolutionary Emperor, Joseph II*, pp. 302–303.

tions brought economic ruin to a third of Galician Jewry.[62] The governments of Alexander I and Nicholas I repeated these disastrous mistakes.

The first Russian official to suggest the economic readjustment of the Jews through agriculture was the liberal Lithuanian governor, I. S. Frisel. In the first government document dealing with farming by Jews, dated December 31, 1799, he recommended that they be given crown land, and that Jewish farmers be permitted to enjoy the same rights as other freeholders. Frisel also advocated that civic emancipation be granted to all Jews.[63]

Agricultural pursuits for Jews were also advocated by the poet, G. R. Derzhavin (1743–1816), who later became minister of justice. His recommendations were incorporated in a report submitted in 1800 to Emperor Paul, who had commissioned him to investigate the conditions of the Jews in White Russia in connection with the famine among the peasantry there. The title of the report, "An Opinion on How to Avert the Scarcity of Food through the Curbing of Jewish Usury, Their Reformation, etc.," indicates that the author was not an objective observer or investigator. Indeed, the first pages of chapter two of his "Opinion" reveal that Derzhavin, who heretofore had never come in contact with Jews, received his information about them from anti-Jewish sources.[64] Describing the Jews as a people whose usefulness as citizens is questionable and who somehow always manage "to lord it over the nations among whom they live," he ventured the following opinion:

> Since Providence, for the realization of some unknown purpose, has left this dangerous people on the face of the earth and did not destroy it, the governments under whose rule it lives ought to tolerate it. It is also the duty of these governments to take care of them in such a manner that the Jews may be useful to themselves and to the society in whose midst they live.[65]

In order to reform the Jews so as to make them more useful, he suggested that they be divided into four classes—merchants, town burghers, rural burghers, and a fourth class made up of peasants and other laborers. He further proposed that the steppes of Astra-

62. See A. Bravir's series of articles, "Yosef Ha-Sheni Ve-Yehude Galizyah," *Ha-Shiloah,* XXIII.

63. Frisel's report was published by S. A. Bershadsky in *Voskhod,* 1895, March, pp. 74–77.

64. "Opinion" is published in *Sochineniia Derzhavina,* VII, 229–305.

65. *Ibid.,* p. 246.

khan and New Russia[66] be opened for Jewish settlers. Like Frisel, Derzhavin stipulated that the Jewish peasants should remain free. He differed, however, with the Lithuanian governor in that he was satisfied to retain the prevailing disabilities for merchants and town burghers. It was Derzhavin who recommended the reorganization of Jewish life by expelling all Jews from villages and depriving them of the right of inn-keeping.[67]

From the self-righteous and solemn words with which the poet concluded his "Opinion," it is evident that he regarded his proposal as highly magnanimous. "In such a manner," he writes, "the Jews, who, as fanatic and stiff-necked enemies of the Christians are destined by fate to remain eternally scattered, will even in their sad state be well-established. And Emperor Paul Petrovich will be lauded by future generations as the first Russian monarch to have fulfilled the great commandment, 'Love thine enemy, do good unto those who hate you.' "[68]

Derzhavin, who was the first Russian government official to suggest the settlement of Jews on the uninhabited lands of New Russia, utilized the plan offered him by the wealthy Jew Notkin. Upon learning of the commission Derzhavin had received from Emperor Paul, Notkin wrote him explaining his project for the reorganization of the economic life of the Russian Jews. In addition to proposing the establishment of factories and various manufacturing industries to be subsidized by the government and private capital, the plan included the settlement of Jews in New Russia and the development of various branches of rural economy. It is interesting to note that this influential Jew did not suggest complete civic emancipation for his coreligionists. He ventured to ask for no more than that Jews be equalized with non-Jews in payment of taxes.[69]

Derzhavin's "Opinion," incorporating Notkin's plan, served as a basis for the Statute of 1804. To encourage agriculture among Jews, the government promised exemption from taxation for five years to those who would form free farming settlements on lands rented from landowners.[70] Poor Jews were allowed to settle on government land in White Russia and New Russia, where, in some provinces, thirty thousand desiatins[71] were allotted to them.[72] Jews

66. Territory around the Black Sea ceded to Russia by Turkey in 1774, following the Peace of Kuchuk Kainardji.

67. See first pages of this chapter.

68. *Ibid.*, p. 305.

69. Notkin's letter is published in J. Gessen's *Evrei v Rossii*, pp. 443–444. His project in *Ibid.*, pp. 444–446.

70. Par. 16.

71. One desiatin equals 2.7 acres.

72. Par. 17.

who would voluntarily remove to new lands were promised exemption from taxation for ten years plus the usual government loan granted to foreign colonists.[73] At the expiration of the privileged years, Jewish peasants, whether on government or private lands, were to pay the same taxes as non-Jewish peasants. This exemption from double taxes was also granted to those who would engage in husbandry within the Pale of Settlement.[74]

These concessions, however, were of little consequence in a plan which was doomed to failure for several reasons. The first obstacle was the psychological factor. The Jews, divorced from the soil for centuries and forced to make a living from trade and commerce, had come to regard work connected with the cultivation of the soil as a calling unfit for a Jew. The second obstacle was a natural reluctance to leave an accustomed habitat to start life anew in strange and uninhabitated places. Moreover, when in 1806 a group of enterprising Jews consisting of thirty-six families applied for land in New Russia, the unexpected difficulties they encountered revealed the total incapacity of the government to manage the colonization problem. In the hour of crisis, the government of Alexander I, like that of Joseph II, found that it had neither enough available or suitable land for all whom its decree made homeless, nor proper administrative machinery to handle the resettlement of the refugees.

During the régimes of Alexander I and Nicholas I, three attempts were made by the government to settle Jews on land. The first venture was made in the early years of the nineteenth century. According to the colonial office, approximately 645 families—3,618 souls—were settled in the newly established Jewish colonies of New Russia. In 1810, however, at the request of the authorities there, the immigration of new colonists was stopped by the central government,[75] lack of funds and inadaptability of the Jewish colonists to husbandry being given as the reasons. The official historian of the Ministry of the Interior advances the same reasons for the failure of the first colonization attempt.[76]

The documentary evidence which the Russian scholar V. N. Nikitin collected in his study of the new Jewish settlements in south Russia led him, however, to reject as unfounded the charge of the Jews' lack of industry or unfitness for agricultural work.[77] Two years later, the government admitted its own mistakes in handling the first attempt at Jewish colonization. A report of the Jewish

73. Par. 18.
74. Par. 19.
75. *P. P. S. Z.*, XXXI, no. 24,185.
76. Varadinov, *Ist. Min. Vn. Del.*, II, 84–85.
77. *Ev. Zem.*, Preface.

Committee ascribed the failure of the venture not merely to Jewish unfitness, but also to lack of available land and government funds.[78]

A second attempt at Jewish colonization was made in the early twenties, the initiative this time coming from the Jews themselves. The writers Borovoi and Nikitin attribute this move to the extreme poverty among the Jews of the western provinces, which was aggravated by the years of famine and the evictions from the villages.[79] This second attempt at Jewish farming was again curtailed because of the government's inability to handle and finance uncontrolled streams of destitute Jews. Nevertheless, 435 families, comprising 2,294 souls, managed to settle on the soil.[80]

Still another effort was made in the reign of Nicholas I to solve the Jewish problem through agriculture. Soon after the promulgation of the law of 1835, which offered attractive inducements to Jewish land settlers, the minister of finance, Kankrin, proposed that the waste lands of Siberia, too, be opened for Jewish colonization. Now, in addition to the thousands of applicants for land under the law of 1835, thousands more clamored for inclusion in the new Siberian venture. "There was not a town in the Western region," writes Nikitin, "where Jews did not plead for land in Siberia. Nay, more than that—they suddenly conceived such a strong attachment for Siberia that they were ready to fly there on wings." [81]

The Siberian project came to an abrupt halt when on January 5, 1837, the emperor personally ordered that further immigration of Jews to Siberia be terminated.[82] According to Nikitin, this imperial decree was issued at the suggestion of the chief of the gendarmes, General Benkendorf, and the minister of the interior, Bludov, both of whom contended that Jews would exercise a bad influence on the Siberian population.[83] The warning that Jews might set a bad example to the local population by their alleged aversion for productive labor and by their "unethical" trade practices led Nicholas to issue another restrictive decree limiting the rights of residence even of those Jews who had lived there before the Siberian project. By a law issued on May 15 of the same year, the settlement of Jews in Siberia was "decidedly and forever stopped." [84] "Thus," observes Borovoi, "ended the short-lived project of saving the Jews

78. *Russky Arkhiv,* 1903, I, 263–265.

79. S. J. Borovoi, *Evr. Zemledelcheskaia Colonizatsia v Staroi Rossii,* pp. 79–82; Nikitin, *Ev. Zem.,* p. 128.

80. Nikitin, *Ev. Zem.,* p. 122.

81. *Ibid.,* pp. 206, 217.

82. *V. P. S. Z.,* XII, no. 9,843.

83. Nikitin, *Ev. Zem.,* pp. 208–209.

84. *V. P. S. Z.,* XII, no. 10,242.

through settling them in Siberia. A plan which was intended to save the Jews was turned into one of saving the native population from the Jews." [85]

Nor was the procedure of settling colonists in the south better organized this time than in the previous two periods. Of the tens of thousands of families from White Russia and the Baltic provinces pleading for land, only 2,386 households were settled in the region of Kherson during the years 1837–1841. According to the official census, there were in 1844, 11,344 Jewish settlers in New Russia.[86]

In the middle of the forties, another spontaneous movement arose among Russian Jews to settle on the land. The immediate cause of this fourth and final attempt at colonization was the *Razbor*, a projected classification of Jews as useful and useless subjects. This survey was to serve as a pretext for further restrictions and disabilities to be imposed upon the Jewish masses, since, according to its specifications, most Jews would have been branded as useless subjects.[87] Because agricultural workers were to be considered among the useful subjects, Jews, eager to be classified in that category, applied for land. The fact that out of 10,830 families which made applications only 205 succeeded in obtaining land in the years 1844–51, is further proof of the lack of governmental coöperation.[88]

Jewish historians ascribe the failure of the economic readjustment of the Jews through the organization of farming colonies to the inconsistency of the Russian government and to bureaucratic inefficiency. S. J. Borovoi, whose study was made from colonial records, asserts that the hardships and sufferings of the new Jewish peasants were due to the incompetence and corruption of local officials who saw in the colonies mainly a source of personal enrichment. The writer quotes a government investigator who reported in an official record that "in none of the colonies did he find public funds. Everywhere he heard complaints that the overseers took everything for themselves and did not permit the Jews to inquire about the public monies." [89] In his report to Nicholas, Montefiore, too, complained of the gross inefficiency and negligence in the administration of these colonies. He informed the tsar that "the rye seed which the Israelites ought to have received in the month of August was not given to them before the month of October. The seed

85. Borovoi, *Ev. Zem. Col. Star. Ros.*, p. 138.

86. Nikitin, *Ev. Zem.*, p. 292.

87. The idea of the *Razbor*, projected in 1840, was under consideration for eighteen years, and was finally abandoned because of the opposition of high-ranking government officials.

88. *Ibid.*, p. 411.

89. Borovoi, *Ev. Zem. Col. Star. Ros.*, p. 56.

for the summer crops, which ought to have been given them in the month of March, they did not receive before the month of May. Thus they were obliged to put the seed into the ground very late in the season, and heavy rains which followed again caused the crop to fail." [90]

The writer Benjamin Mandelstam, one of the extreme *maskilim* who had implicit faith in the sincerity of the government's intention toward the Jews and who propagandized its educational projects among his coreligionists, gave the following account to Montefiore in 1846 about these agricultural experiments:

When the Jews learned about the land that was allotted to them in the region of Kherson, they wept with joy. They hastened to leave their native places and property, acquired horses and cows, each according to his means. They placed their wives and young children in the wagons, and with faith in the mercy of God and the grace of the tsar, they requested the administration to give them the subsidy which the government appropriated for their transportation. But the officials would not listen to the pleas of the unfortunate Jews, from whom they were accustomed only to take. . . . Despairing and hungry they started on their journey. Thus many of them perished from hunger and thirst, both men and cattle, with no one even to bury them. But the officials who feared that they would be held responsible, declared in their reports that the emigrants were in fine condition. And the kind tsar was happy, thinking that these unfortunates were blessing him. But they were not any longer among the living. Their memory was preserved only in the records of the officials so that the latter might continue to receive the allowance intended for these people and use it for their own benefit. Only a remnant of the emigrants reached the colonies and settled there. Then the same corruption followed. Fearing that they might be asked to render an account of income and expenses, the officials continued to cause all sorts of harm to the Jewish settlers. They denounced them to the higher authorities as poor and indolent workers, maintaining that because of their laziness the land allotted to them was being wasted.[91]

Jacob Lestchinsky, a modern economist and statistician, believes that Jewish leadership as well as the government was responsible for the collapse of the agricultural experiments, both in Austria and in Russia. "With a few honorable exceptions," he writes, "the Jewish masses, together with their rabbis and *hassidic* leaders, were buried in such obscurantism that the plans of the government, in es-

90. *Diaries,* I, 366.
91. *Hazon La-Moed,* II, 58–59.

sence progressive, and, as regards the prevailing conditions of Jewish life, revolutionary, were remote from their understanding and psychology." He emphasizes, however, that the seeds of failure were inherent in the government's approach to the problem, for a program which aimed at converting Jews into useful citizens without granting them the rights of citizenship could hardly have been expected to succeed. He also blames administrative corruption and incompetence which, as he put it, could kill the best of enterprises. Citing a number of instances of inefficiency on the part of both the Russian and Austrian governments, he concludes: "Both sides, the government administration and the Jews, were unprepared for such a difficult and complicated task as the creation of a Jewish agricultural class. But the seeds that were sown did ultimately produce results. Today,[92] both in New Russia and Galicia, there are thousands of Jewish families which derive their sustenance from rural economy." [93]

No account of Jewish life in Russia under Nicholas I would be complete if it failed to describe the cantonist system which imposed a military martyrdom on Jewish youth and terrorized the Jewish populace. According to the law of August 26, 1827, Jewish youths from the ages of twelve to eighteen were to be conscripted for military service. During these years they received preparatory training in the cantonist battalions. Later they were assigned to the regular army to serve an additional twenty-five years, the regular term of military service. Because the Jewish community was held responsible for the supply of the assigned quotas, children younger than twelve were often drafted to make up the deficiency. A Hebrew writer relates in his memoirs that in the city of Grodno, a child of five was recruited.[94]

To escape the severe punishment for failure to produce the required number of child recruits, Jewish communities were forced to appoint special agents whose duty it was to round up these children and deliver them to the military authorities. These *happers* (kidnappers), as they were called, kept the Jewish population in a state of dread and terror. A contemporary writer describes an incident he witnessed in his youth, which is typical of the terrifying activities of the *happers*. As he was walking in the streets of Minsk, he saw a coach stop near a Jewish home. Six strong men entered the house and soon emerged dragging a child whom they had gagged to silence his screams. An agonized woman, screaming, wrestled with them,

92. Written in the twenties of the present century.
93. J. Lestchinsky, *Schriften far Ekonomic un Statistic,* I, 30–32.
94. *Sefer Ha-Shanah,* ed. N. Sokolow, III, 86.

seeking vainly to free her child from their grasp. They threw her to the ground and dashed away with their prey, while the mother, bloody and bruised, beat her head against the pavement, wailing "My son, my fledgling!" [95]

Describing the horrors of the cantonist system, a Russian writer[96] says that in all the Jewish cities and towns was enacted the lamentation in Rama (Jeremiah, chapter 31): "Mother Rachel weeping for her children and refusing to be comforted." Even the official government records make mention of the tragic consequences of juvenile conscription. They state that the draft spread despair among Jewish mothers, who would rush to the graves of their parents to plead for divine intervention. Some died of grief and heartbreak.[97]

The conscripts' destination was usually as far away from the Pale as possible and the trip was an ordeal which initiated the children into a long career of physical suffering and spiritual torment. The military guards, in order that they might pocket the money allotted for transportation, forced these unfortunate children to make their journey, often lasting from six months to a year, on foot. The famous Russian writer, Alexander Gertsen (1812–1870), gives a graphic portrayal of such a march, which he encountered on a journey in the vicinity of Perm in the year 1835. The cantonists were falling into line ready to resume their march after a rest. "This was one of the most terrible scenes I have ever witnessed," writes Gertsen. "Poor, unfortunate children! The boys of twelve or thirteen managed somehow to stand up, but the little ones of eight and nine. . . . No artist's brush could paint the horror. Pale, emaciated, frightened faces looked out of the ludicrously clumsy soldiers' uniforms, casting about helpless, pitiful glances at the soldiers. From their blue lips and the blue veins under their eyes, it was obvious that they were suffering from fever and exposure. A sharp wind was blowing, and these sick children, loveless and helpless, were marching straight to their graves. I grasped the officer's hand, and crying 'Take good care of them!' flung myself into the carriage choking with tears." [98]

Much has been written both by Jewish and non-Jewish authors of the harrowing experiences of these juvenile soldiers during their years of training in the cantonist battalions. Many of these writings, which may be considered a part of the literature of Jewish

95. *Sefer Ha-Yobel Li-Kabod Nahum Sokolow,* p. 359.
96. N. S. Leskov, *Polnoe Sobranie Sochineni,* XXII, 57.
97. *Zhur Minist. Vnut. Del,* 1846, no. 14, p. 47 quoted in S. M. Ginsburg, *Hist. Werk,* III, 16.
98. A. Gertsen, *Byloe i Dumy,* I, 314–315.

martyrology, give firsthand accounts of the tortures designed to induce conversion among the youths. Not only were these hapless children forbidden to practice religious observances, speak the Yiddish language, visit Jewish homes or fraternize with each other, but they were forced to attend church services in the hope of securing their voluntary conversion. The recalcitrant were subjected to physical tortures and humiliations.

"The captain of our company was a veritable wild beast," a former cantonist relates in his memoirs. "Immediately upon our arrival they began to flog us, sometimes with ordinary rods, sometimes with rods soaked in salt water and at other times with bare twigs. And all these tortures were inflicted upon us so as to compel us to accept baptism. 'Get yourselves baptized, scoundrels, or else I will flog you to death!' the commander roared at us." [99]

Another cantonist's memoirs describe the method of coercion employed by the commander of his battalion, who vowed that as long as he lived no one under his command would remain a Jew. At his instructions, one of his subordinates compelled the Jewish boys to kneel at his bedside throughout the night, and on the following day deprived them of food. This process would be repeated until the boys yielded. In the course of a year all but one embraced Christianity.[100]

In this soul-saving campaign, some of the priests of the battalions, who were the official religious leaders of the children, would resort to torture. In the battalion of Nizhni Novgorod, for example, flogging was not sufficient. The priest would in addition pour icy water upon the obdurate ones—in the winter, out of doors.[101]

Missionary activity among the cantonists was under the direct supervision and personal guidance of the emperor, who applied himself to this task with the utmost severity and determination. In his zeal for gaining converts, he secretly abrogated the law requiring priests to obtain permission from the higher church authorities for every juvenile conversion. He directed the Holy Synod to issue special instructions and to detail a larger number of particularly dependable instructors in order to accelerate the progress of the undertaking. The tsar's personal interest is evident from the painstaking attention he gave to the reports submitted to him and from the notations of approval and disapproval through which he spurred the religious and military functionaries to greater efforts.[102]

99. P. I. Levensohn, *Voskhod,* 1884, VII, 25.

100. I. Itskovich, *Ev. Star.,* 1912, I, 59–60.

101. Quoted from official sources in S. M. Ginsburg, *Hist. Werk,* III, 99.

102. Quoted from official records in *Ibid.,* pp. 62, 64, 68, 69. Complete text of instructions for priests of cantonist institutions issued by Synod in 1843 published in *ibid.,* pp. 357–369.

In addition to the sadism engendered by the military system, officials were led by their anxiety to please the monarch to employ the cruel means mentioned above to gain converts. The results, to be sure, were gratifying, for most of their victims did capitulate and permit themselves to be "saved." Records of the number of conversions are incomplete, but from those available we learn that the percentage of converts was very high, in many instances reaching 100 per cent. In the battalions of Saratov in the year 1845, all the Jewish cantonists were baptized, including 130 who arrived in May and were converted within two weeks. In the same year those in charge of the Perm battalions joyfully reported similar successes to the Holy Synod. These achievements were due to the special pressure brought to bear upon the military and religious officials through the intensified program instituted by the emperor in 1843. Previously, results had not been quite so gratifying. In the half battalion of Verkhne-Uralsk, for example, only one third of the Jewish children were won over to baptism between the years 1836–42, and the battalion of Saratov, which in 1845 reported such perfect results, produced only 687 converts out of its 1304 Jewish recruits during the years 1828–1842.[103]

Considering the methods employed, it is remarkable that any had the courage and endurance to hold firm to their faith. Many youthful martyrs, who could not endure the ceaseless torture and would not abandon their faith, chose death in preference to baptism. "Suicide was not a rare phenomenon," reports the historian Ginsburg, on the basis of years of study of official sources. To this statement a former cantonist bears testimony when he relates that in 1845 there remained but two Jews in his group. Of the others who refused to be converted, three committed suicide by the knife, two by hanging, and several others by drowning.[104]

The heroism of the cantonist martyrs has provided subject matter for many a tale in which some actual incident has been embroidered by popular fancy. One of these relates that when Nicholas was reviewing his troops in Kazan, an official of one regiment arranged to have a group of Jewish cantonists baptized in his presence. The children were brought to the banks of the river Volga. But they had made a pact among themselves to commit suicide rather than submit to baptism. At the emperor's command to enter the water, they submerged never to rise again.[105]

Many cantonists who were not made of martyr stuff but who

103. S. M. Ginsburg, *ibid.*, pp. 63, 102.
104. *Ev. Star.*, 1909, III, 119.
105. *Ibid.*, II, 118.

were deeply attached to Judaism managed throughout their years of service to practice their religion secretly. Some sought to renounce their new faith when they reached the age of eighteen and became a part of the regular army. For this rebelliousness they were committed to prisons and monasteries and subjected to "corrective" torments, which many of them endured for years without recanting their original faith.[106]

The cantonist system was not the only source of terror for the Jews. In the days of Nicholas I, the Jewish populace was kept in constant dread and torment by their fear of the officials set over them. A Russian-Jewish writer describes the panic created by the visit of an official to a Jewish town. " 'Is he bringing with him any paper from the *gubernia* [provincial capital]?' the terror-stricken inhabitants would speculate. 'Is he coming for military recruits? What business brought him here?' When he would blow into town, the town would begin to shiver as though in a fever. . . . Close the stores! . . . Light the black candles! . . . Put old and young under oath. . . . About what? For what? God knows! The outcome, of course, is always the same. Again there would be a deputation waiting on the official, again there would be a protestation of reverential loyalty accompanied by the customary bribe." [107]

In the memoirs of a Russian contemporary, reference is made to the manner in which the government officials exploited the helplessness and rightlessness of the Jews for their self-aggrandizement. He relates how the *gorodnichi* (town bailiff) of Vinnitsy lived a merry life at the expense of the Jews. The Jewish community had to appoint a special group of men to provide for his maintenance. One supplied his kitchen with beef, another with bread, and a third with vodka and wine. One was even charged with the responsibility of refunding to the bailiff the losses he incurred at cards.[108]

The insecurity and other hardships suffered by Jews during the reigns of Alexander I and Nicholas I help explain why the *Haskalah* movement failed to take root during their rule. In face of mounting disabilities, it is small wonder the Jews did not subscribe to that faith in benevolent monarchy which was one of the tenets of the Enlightenment. Since their suspicions that educational reforms were merely a stepping stone to conversion were well-founded, the Jewish masses could view only with distrust any movement which

106. *Hist. Schriften,* I, 789–792. In addition to the sources cited on the cantonists see also A. Lewin, *Cantonisten;* Dr. N. Samter, *Judentaufen in 19 Jahrhundert,* pp. 38–44.

107. O. Rabinovich, *Sobranie Sochineni,* I, 27.

108. M. K. Chalago, *Kievskaia Starina,* 1894, Dec., p. 343.

gave these educational innovations unquestioning support. Nor did the sad experiences of the Jews with the agricultural experiments help give them confidence in the *Haskalah*, which advocated economic reconstruction through settlement on the land.

The underlying reasons for the attitude of the two monarchs toward the Jews may be summarized as follows. In the first place, ruler and people had the traditional prejudice and fear in regard to the Jew and his religion. This hostility—a carry-over from the Muscovy period—was intensified by the spirit of reaction that swept Europe after the Napoleonic wars. An added factor in the reign of Nicholas I was the emperor's personality, which militated against liberal treatment of any minority. A noted Russian writer thus characterizes him: "A despot by nature, with an instinctive aversion for every movement for and every expression of individual freedom and independence, Nicholas loved only the soulless mass movement of soldiers under command." [109] One can imagine that the Jews of the ghetto, with their outlandish and peculiar ways, must have seemed to him a sore on the body of the Russian people.

Unfriendly policies toward the Jews were also due in no small measure to the fact that the Jew as a human being was practically an unknown entity to the Russian people. Whatever notion did exist about him was usually distortion and caricature. Even in classic Russian literature the Jew appears either as an unreal being or as a ludicrous creature.

Among the factors responsible for the failure of contemporary Russian literature to give an adequate representation of the Jew, class prejudice played no small part. It should be borne in mind that the authors of that period were landed proprietors, members of the nobility, who had a general aversion for hucksters and merchants—occupations they associated with the Jew. The most important reason, however, for the failure of the authors of Great Russia to give a fair picture of the Jew was their total unfamiliarity with his way of life. To writers who up to the sixties rarely came into contact with the Jews, the dwellers of the ghetto with their medieval garb and peculiar mannerisms appeared grotesque and repellent. Even authors in the Ukraine and Polish regions, who did have opportunity to observe the Jew at closer range, knew virtually nothing of his inner life. A modern student of Russian literature observes that while their portrayal of Jews was more realistic in externals, the real and ideal life of the Jewish people, as expressed in their institutions and traditions, literature and folk-song, re-

109. S. M. Solovev, *Zapiski,* p. 116.

mained altogether unknown to Russian authors, regardless of the literary genre they employed.[110]

Writing in the early eighties, the famous Russian writer, M. E. Saltykov, deplored the unfair and unsympathetic attitude toward the Jew of both men of letters and the public. This attitude he ascribed to traditional prejudice and to total lack of knowledge concerning the Jew. "There is nothing more inhuman and irrational," he declared, "than this myth, which has its origin in the dark caverns of the remote past, and which, with a cruelty approaching idiotic self-satisfaction, perpetuates the mark of shame, estrangement, and hatred."

Deploring the lack of understanding, Saltykov asks: "What do we really know about the Jew except some scandals about Jewish concessionnaires, or questionable deals of lease-holders and innkeepers? Have we the least understanding of that numerous mass of Jewish artisans and petty traders which swarms in the squalor of the Jewish towns and multiplies at a furious rate, in spite of the curse stamped upon it and the ever-present threat of starvation." Only of late, he observed, have some rays of light begun to penetrate into our literature to illumine this agonizing world. "The first and foremost requirement," the writer concludes, "is knowledge, and knowledge will, undoubtedly, bring with it a feeling of humaneness." [111]

Unfortunately, during the régime of Nicholas I the government was sadly lacking in this "first and foremost requirement." The following extract from the writings of the famous Orientalist, Professor Daniel Khvolson, reveals the confusion in the minds of government leaders about Jews and their religious teachings: "When posterity will search in our official records, they will find there two interesting documents. One is a report of the minister of the interior submitted to Emperor Nicholas I in the year 1844, in which it is stated that in a secret Jewish book called *Rambam*,[112] it is ordained that Jews must steal Christian children, murder them and drink their blood. In the other report, submitted to the same monarch in 1850 by the minister for public education, this same book is recommended as a textbook in morality for Jewish youth." [113]

When the government did seek information about the Jews, it unfortunately went to the wrong sources. Information about the

110. J. Kunitz, *Russian Literature and the Jew,* p. 19.

111. M. E. Saltykov, *Sochineniia,* VII, 562, 565, 566.

112. Rambam—A contraction of the name of Rabbi Moses Maimonides (1135–1204), medieval codifier and philosopher. There is no book called *Rambam.*

113. *O Nekotorykh Sredne-Vekovykh Obvineniiakh protiv Evreev,* pp. 133–134.

Talmud was received from Johann Andreas Eisenmenger's (1654–1704) *Entdecktes Judentum* (Judaism Exposed), a volume described by reputable Christian scholars as a malicious distortion. The *Allgemeine deutsche Biographie*, published by the German Imperial Academy of Sciences in 1876, characterizes the book thus: "As a whole it is a collection of scandals. In part it is misinterpretation, other parts are distortion, and still others are but malicious inferences read into Judaism." [114]

Professor Khvolson describes the author of the *Entdecktes Judentum* as a shady character who was ignorant of the Talmud but who had Jewish renegades supply him with the type of information he sought. The charlatanism of the man is evident; he published the book only after the Jews refused to pay him thirty thousand florins for which he offered to suppress it.[115]

Nicholas I manifested his preference for this type of information when he ordered that *Derek Selulah* (The Trodden Path), a pamphlet by a Jewish convert, Temkin, defaming the Talmud, be published in Hebrew and Russian at the expense of the government.[116] The erudite Levinsohn, on the other hand, who refuted the charges made in *Derek Selulah* by pointing out the ignorance of the author and his distortions of the Talmudic text, made no impression on the leaders of the government. On the contrary, his championship of the Talmud only helped to weaken his influence in upper government circles.[117] Discussing the character of the sources from which the authorities drew their knowledge about Jews, a Christian historian observes: "For its own purpose of penetrating into the secret depths of the Jews, our government more than once turned for information to the literary assistance of certain people, for which it paid liberally. Unfortunately, however, the money was completely wasted." [118]

What the government could have learned about the inner life of its Jewish subjects had it gone to the proper sources or evinced a sincere desire to form an unbiased judgment is the subject of the next chapter.

114. V, 773.
115. D. Khvolson, *O Nekot. Sredne-Vek.*, pp. 135–137.
116. Varadinov, *Ist. Min. Vnut. Del*, IV, Book 1, 555–556. On the efforts of Nicholas to discredit the Talmud see also J. S. Raisin, *The Haskalah Movement in Russia*, pp. 144–147.
117. Zinberg, *Ges. Lit. Yid.*, VIII, Book 2, 96–97.
118. S. A. Bershadsky, *Litovskie Evrei*, p. 64.

V

THE CULTURAL AND MORAL STATUS OF RUSSIAN JEWRY

THE cultural life of the Russian Jew during the period dealt with in the last chapter was primarily of a religious nature. Secular education was still in its infancy and, for reasons already stated, unpopular with the masses. The number of intellectuals interested in secular studies was insignificant, but among them were a few who exercised an important influence and made significant literary contributions. In addition to Isaac Levinsohn (who was discussed in previous pages) Mordecai Aaron Günzburg (1795–1846) and Abraham Dob Lebensohn (1794-1878) also figured prominently as writers and leaders of *Haskalah* in the second quarter of the nineteenth century.

Günzburg, regarded as the creator of modern Hebrew prose, wrote on a variety of subjects in Hebrew, which was the literary medium of early *Haskalah*. His contributions included a "History of Russia" and a translation from the German of a work entitled "The History of Man." Günzburg cultivated in his readers a taste for modern culture and stimulated their interest in the world about them.

While Günzburg developed literary taste through his prose, Lebensohn awakened the aesthetic sense of his generation through the medium of poetry, a form of literary expression which had been dormant among the Jewish people for several centuries. A historian of modern Hebrew literature[1] believes that this poet's potentialities never came to full flowering because of his exclusively parochial education; that his emotional expressiveness was hampered by a mind accustomed to Talmudical dialectics. At the same time, Lebensohn's mastery of Biblical Hebrew contributed much toward the richness and lucidity of his style.

The Jewish masses were unacquainted with contemporary Hebrew literature not because they were illiterate, but because secular education was regarded as heretical. In fact, there was practically no illiteracy among Russian Jewry, for almost every male—and in many cases females, too—could read the prayer book and the Bible.

1. J. Klausner, *A History of Modern Heb. Lit.*, p. 29. On Günzburg and Lebensohn see also Meyer Waxman, *A History of Jewish Literature,* III, 212–214, 217–226; Zinberg, *Ges. Lit. Yid.*, VIII, book 2, chapter IV.

Learning was a universal pursuit in the Russian ghetto, where there was neither time nor age limit to the study of *Torah*.[2]

At a very tender age, sometimes as young as four, the male child began his school career. The commencement of his study was marked by a ceremony which sought to impress the mind of the initiate with the solemn significance of the occasion. Pauline Wengeroff, whose *Memoiren einer Grossmutter* (Memoirs of a Grandmother) contain valuable material on Russian-Jewish life of the nineteenth century, recounts Lilienthal's impressions of a ceremony he witnessed in the city of Brest. While visiting a local *heder*, he felt a stir of excited anticipation in the room.

Soon a poorly clad couple entered, the man carrying in his arms a young boy of about six, wrapped in a *talit* [prayer shawl]. Both father and mother were weeping with joy, grateful to God who had preserved them that they might witness this beautiful and meaningful moment. Having extended a cordial welcome to the newcomers, the *melamed* took the hero of the celebration into his arms and stood him upon a table. Afterwards the boy was seated on a bench and was the first to receive cake, nuts, raisins and dainties of which the happy mother had brought along an apron-full. The teacher then sat down near the youngster, placed a card with a printed alphabet before him and, taking a long pointer, began the first lesson by blessing his newly-initiated pupil that he may be raised for the study of *Torah*, marriage and good deeds.[3]

This occasion made a profound impression upon Lilienthal. The German-Jewish educator was averse to the kind of schooling the *heder* represented and he found the uncouthness of the *melamdim* repellent. Yet at the same time he was deeply moved by the devotion of even the most poverty-stricken parents to the education of their young.

Two types of schools provided elementary education: one instructed beginners in the prayers and the Pentateuch, and the other taught more advanced students the Talmud and its commentaries. While there was neither a supervised nor a prescribed course of study in these educational institutions—the choice of a particular tractate being left entirely to the discretion of each individual

2. Literally *Torah* means teaching. In Jewish tradition this term applies to the Pentateuch, the entire Bible, or to Rabbinic literature. *Torah* may also denote the spiritual heritage of the Jewish people. On concept of *Torah* see S. Schechter, *Some Aspects of Rabbinic Theology*, pp. 116–126; M. M. Kaplan, *Judaism as a Civilization*, pp. 409–416; R. T. Herford, *The Pharisees*, pp. 53–58; M. Kadushin, *Organic Thinking*, pp. 16–30.

3. Pauline Wengeroff, *Memoiren einer Grossmutter*, I, 122–123.

teacher—the curriculum on the whole was uniform throughout the Pale. No definite age limit or formal graduation marked the end of a pupil's school career. Its duration depended either on the financial circumstances of the parents or on the child's mental aptitude. In most cases the *heder* education ended at the age of twelve or thirteen. Those desiring to pursue the more advanced studies of the Talmud would do so through self-study in the local synagogue or by entering some *yeshibah*. In the first half of the nineteenth century a number of such Talmudic colleges existed, the most famous being the *Yeshibah* of Volozhin, in the province of Vilno, and the *Yeshibah* of Mir in the province of Minsk. Tuition in the *yeshibot* was free.

L. I. Mandelstam, noted educator and Bible scholar, gives a realistic account of student life in a *yeshibah*. In 1840, on his way to Moscow University where he was to be the first Jewish student, he spent a few days in Mir. There he had occasion to observe the routine of a Talmudic school.

This school which has become famous among Jews, is located in a rather large though old and dilapidated building not far from the synagogue. The building includes a large hall and a room where the students congregate for the entire day, from five in the morning until ten in the evening. Altogether there are about one hundred students, almost all of them striplings. Almost all are very poor and are maintained by contributions collected for this purpose in numerous Jewish settlements. . . . Of these funds each registered student receives seventy-five kopeks a week. With this allowance he has to maintain himself the entire week with the exception of Saturday, since on Sabbaths and holidays students are invited out for meals by the local residents.

Their daily routine is as follows: At five o'clock in the morning the students are already at work preparing for the lecture, after which they hold their morning service and have their breakfast consisting of bread and water. At eleven o'clock begins the instructor's discourse, which lasts around two hours. Then follows lunch, consisting of the so called *krupnik*—grits cooked in water. At three o'clock there is a review of the discourse. At six—*minha* (the afternoon service) followed by a study of *Yoreh Deah*[4] (Teacher of Knowledge). Although the *maarib* service (evening prayer) at eight or nine o'clock officially concludes the day's work, the students usually remain over their books till ten and twelve o'clock. The greater part of the student body sleeps in the school.[5]

4. A religious code compiled by the famed Talmudist, Rabbi Jacob ben Asher (1280–1340).

5. L. I. Mendelstam, *Perez.*, I, 24–25.

The Talmud was the province of the more scholarly minds, but every male member of the community engaged in some form of study according to his intellectual level. As Doctor Ginzberg put it: "Every Jew was either a teacher or a pupil, or both at the same time. The *lamdan* (learned man) did not belong to a distinct class; he was the representative *par excellence* of the people as a whole." [6]

In his autobiography, the Hebrew-Russian writer and champion of *Haskalah*, Abraham Paperna, gives us a glimpse into the cultural life of his native town. It is a description typical of Jewish life in Russia, particularly that of Lithuania in the days of Nicholas I.

Educational institutions in the modern sense of the word were conspicuous by their absence in our town. There was no government or public school of a secular character in Kopyl. The Christian population was without exception illiterate. The Jewish population, on the other hand, had an overabundance of schools, though of a special type. First, there were the *hadarim*—about twenty of them. Kopyl had a population of about three thousand souls, Jews, White Russians and Tartars. Jews constituted the majority. All Jewish male children from the ages of four to thirteen were taught in *heder*. Although education was not compulsory for girls, they, too, in most cases could read the prayers and the Pentateuch in the Yiddish translation. A Jew of Kopyl spared nothing for the education of his children. It was not rare for a poor man to sell his last candlestick or his only pillow to pay the *melamed*. . . . With the single exception of Meerke the idiot, who was both stoker in the bath house and water-carrier, there were no ignoramuses in Kopyl. And even this moronic water-carrier somehow knew the prayers and could quite satisfactorily recite the blessing over the *Torah*.[7]

Nor did study end at any particular time in the life of the Jew. Not only professional scholars but laymen with an average knowledge of the Talmud or of the more popular sacred literature would set apart some time of the day for study. For the more or less learned Jews of his town, relates Paperna, the synagogue was not only a house of worship but also a reading room and school for adults. Each day, after the morning and evening services, they would spend some time there in study.[8]

The famous Hebrew-Yiddish novelist S. J. Abramovich, known by the pen name of Mendele Moker Sefarim (Mendele the Bookseller), describes a typical synagogue scene in the period herein con-

6. L. Ginzberg, *Students, Schol. Saints,* p. 4.
7. A. I. Paperna, *Perez.,* II, 31–32.
8. *Ibid.,* p. 9.

sidered: "Every evening between *minha* and *maarib*, working men and other folk would gather around different tables to listen to the words of a lay teacher. At one, they would study *Midrash*, at another *Ein Yaakob* or *Hobot Ha-Lebabot* [9] (Duties of the Heart). At other tables would be heard lessons from the Bible or from moralistic and philosophic works."[10] Pauline Wengeroff, too, refers to the habit of adult study which prevailed among Jews of all classes. Her own father, a wealthy contractor, would rise at four each morning to spend a few hours over the Talmud before going to the synagogue for services.[11]

Since knowledge of *Torah* was the highest attainment, books, particularly sacred tomes, were the most cherished possessions. "Each well-to-do and self-respecting Jew," reports Paperna, "owned all the books he could acquire which were to his taste. A well-filled bookcase, containing a complete set of the Talmud with red leather binding, was the finest ornament for a Jewish householder. Books, like jewels, lent the home dignity and an air of aristocracy. Moreover, in case of need, this frozen capital could be converted into cash. One could pawn or sell these valuables, since books, like diamonds, had current value and therefore would find ready customers. In a pinch, one could give them as dowry to a daughter. The women had their own collection of volumes corresponding to their mental development and spiritual needs. Since they did not know Hebrew, their books, for the most part of a religious nature, were in Yiddish." [12]

Although the culture of Russian Jewry in the period under consideration was parochial, it cannot be said that secular sciences were completely foreign to them. The Talmud itself, product of the religious and literary activity of the Jewish people for about five hundred years—the first five centuries of the Common Era—contains an abundance of material on secular subjects. A Jewish scholar notes that since "the religious law of the Jews dealt with all the circumstances of life, the Talmud discusses the most varied branches of human knowledge—astronomy and medicine, mathe-

9. *Midrash*—A branch of Rabbinic literature containing homiletic interpretations of the Scriptures.

Ein Yaakob—A collection of popular stories and allegories from the Talmud compiled by Jacob ben Solomon ibn Habib (1460–1516) of Spain.

Hobot Ha-Lebabot—An ethico-philosophic work: its author was Bahya ben Joseph ibn Pakuda, a Spanish-Jewish philosopher and religious teacher, who lived in the first half of the eleventh century.

10. *Shlome Reb Hayem's,* Book I, 14, in vol. XVIII of Collected Works.

11. *Mem. Gross.,* I, 5, 9.

12. Paperna, *Perez.,* II, 17.

matics and law, anatomy and botany—thus furnishing valuable data for the history of science also." [13]

In an essay which attracted world-wide attention, the noted Orientalist, Emanuel Deutch, thus summarizes the versatile character of the Talmud: "It is a microcosm embracing, even as does the Bible, heaven and earth. It is as if all the prose and poetry, the science, the faith and speculation of the old world were, though only in a faint reflection, bound in it *in nuce*." [14]

Many of the rabbis of the Palestinian and Babylonian academies whose teachings and discussions are recorded in the Talmud were versed in the arts and sciences of their day. Certain tractates in this monumental work testify to a knowledge of natural history on the part of these scholars, while others indicate their familiarity with astronomy and mathematics. It was this knowledge that enabled the Talmudic sages to calculate the Jewish calendar, regarded as a truly brilliant achievement by Joseph Scaliger (1540–1609), an eminent authority on the history of the calendar and the greatest scholar of his day.[15]

A modern historian asserts that the successful transition from religious to secular education on the part of Jewish youth in modern days was due to their Talmudic training. "When the emancipation came," he declares, "the Jewish intellect, exercised for centuries in this dialectical training school, readily mastered the difficulties in various branches of learning in the universities." [16]

There is no doubt that the subtle, often hair-splitting disputations in the Talmud which developed and sharpened the mental powers of the Jew were in a great measure responsible for this special attainment in other fields of intellectual endeavor. But it was more than keenness of mind with which the Talmud equipped its students. The scientific knowledge contained in that encyciopaedic work was in itself of practical value to the student who entered a secular institution of learning. Though much of the Talmudic information was anachronistic and unsystematically presented, it nevertheless served as a helpful preparation for academic pursuits.

The primary purpose of the study of *Torah*, however, was pragmatic rather than intellectual. Study was to serve as a guide for living, and knowledge of the law was essential for the sake of the observance of the law. The standard guide for the Jews of Russia

13. *Jew. Enc.*, XII, 24.
14. *London Quarterly Review*, Oct., 1867, p. 224.
15. *Opus de Emendatione Temporum*, pp. 99–105.
16. D. Philipson, *Old European Jewries*, p. 258.

was the *Shulhan Aruk* (The Table Prepared).[17] This code, the universal guide for all Jewry of pre-emancipation days, regulated to the minutest detail every act of the Jew. From the moment he opened his eyes in the morning till he closed them at night, from the cradle to the grave, in the market place or in the synagogue, on week-days or holidays, on sad or happy occasions, the Jew was bound by the rules of the *Shulhan Aruk*. These rules prescribed his ritualistic observances and regulated his social, business, and filial relationships. Even his dress, diet, and personal hygiene were the subjects of precise regulation. Broadly speaking, this code covered the Jew's duties toward his Maker, toward his fellow men, and toward his own person.

The scrupulous adherence to ritual typical of the Russian Jew and the dominant rôle which religious observance played in his life is described in Wengeroff's *Memoiren*. She relates that "upon rising in the morning he (her father) strictly observed the rule not to walk four cubits (about six feet) without first washing his hands. Before taking the first bite, he leisurely recited the introductory morning prayers, following which he would repair to his study." Time in her father's house was measured by reference to the three daily prayers. It was either before or after the services, before or after *minha*, or between *minha* and *maarib*. Similarly, the time of the year was referred to in relation to the festivals. It was either before or after Hanukkah, before or after Purim, etc.[18]

The religious law which dominated the life of the Jew was reflected in his moral standards. Crimes of violence to persons or property were virtually unknown in the ghetto. More common were offenses related to the economic life, such as tax evasion, smuggling, and similar forms of lawlessness. These transgressions were due largely to the restrictions and disabilities which deprived the Jew of many legal sources of livelihood. They certainly were not the fruits of Talmudic teaching, as the government of Nicholas I averred.

Infidelity and drunkenness were practically non-existent in the life of the ghetto Jew. In his sociological study *The Jews*, Dr. Maurice Fishberg states: "The traditional purity of the Jewish home and family life which was one of the characteristics of the ghetto Jew of the past was responsible for the smaller number

17. A religious code based on the Talmud and its numerous commentaries, compiled by Rabbi Joseph Karo of the sixteenth century.

18. *Mem. Gross.*, I, 5–6. Purim commemorates the deliverance of the Jews of Persia from extermination at the hands of Haman. The story is recounted in the Biblical book of Esther.

affected with venereal diseases among them."[19] The same author attributes the rarity of alcoholism among Jews to social conditions fashioned by their religious life. He disputes the theory that it is a racial characteristic, pointing out that as soon as the Jew left the ghetto, his so-called racial immunity to alcoholism vanished. "It was the Jew of the ghetto," he observes, "isolated from his non-Jewish neighbor, who abhorred drunkenness as a sin, a disgrace only fit for a 'goi' (Gentile) but not for one of the chosen people."[20]

Talmudic law, which controlled the physical and moral conduct of the Jew, also guided him in the exercise of his social responsibilities. Among the manifold social duties dealt with in Rabbinic literature, the following branches of benevolent activity are prescribed for the Jewish communities: "Feeding the hungry, clothing the naked, visiting the sick, burying the dead and comforting the mourners, redeeming the captives, educating the orphans, sheltering the homeless and providing poor brides with dowries."[21]

A noted student of Jewish life describes the place of philanthropy among Jews as follows: "The practice of charity is a basic principle of Jewish life, and forms a prominent feature of every communal organization. Ordained in the Pentateuch as a commandment and emphasized throughout the Bible as a social duty, the relief of the poor has from earliest times always received the ready aid of the individual and the zealous care of the community. In all the centuries of gloom and oppression that have lain so heavily upon the people of Israel, the cry of the needy has never failed to be heard."[22]

The numerous philanthropic organizations which existed in the Russian Pale not only indicated the great need which existed, but also expressed the tradition of charity in Israel. The first official census, in 1897, when economic conditions were similar to those which prevailed in the reigns of Nicholas I and Alexander II, reported two thousand charitable agencies in the western provinces alone. These organizations included public kitchens, poor houses, free dispensaries, free loan associations, sheltering homes for strangers, funds for assisting poor brides and providing for Passover needs, and similar agencies. Not a single sizable town—not to mention the larger cities—was without some, if not all of these organizations.

The population was divided into givers and receivers, with the

19. Maurice Fishberg, *The Jews: A Study of Race and Environment,* p. 530.
20. *Ibid.,* p. 275.
21. *Moed Katan,* p. 27b.
22. Israel Cohen, *Jewish Life in Modern Times,* p. 75.

latter comprising about one fifth of the total number. The burden of social responsibility carried by the Jewish community was indeed a heavy one, since the contributing four fifths of the population were themselves, with but few exceptions, on the border line of poverty.[23]

The cultural and moral status of a people may be gauged not only from its way of life but also from its standards. Abramowich (Mendele Moker Sefarim), a most realistic and severe critic of Russian-Jewish life, thus characterizes the attitudes and aspirations of his generation:

To be considered a nice and respectable householder in the city of K., one needed but to own a house, a cow, and, in addition, to earn some sort of a livelihood. But to enjoy prestige, to be respected and popular, more than wealth was required. At one time in Lithuania—perhaps not so much to-day—*Torah* was held in higher esteen than money. A boor, no matter how rich, was nothing more than a boor. As the popular saying had it: 'Out of a pig's tail one cannot make a fur hat.' Such a one may push himself to the fore and have a say in things, and it was often necessary to look on and be silent. But never would such as he be voluntarily accorded a place of honor or listened to open-mouthed. Oh, no! To be worthy of that, one had to be learned, good, pious and come of a good family. Prestige depended not on the money bags but upon the mind and the heart.[24]

Some attention must also be given to the representative spiritual personalities, for they, too, serve as an index to the cultural and moral standards of their contemporaries and reflect the milieu which produced them. Men like the Gaon of Vilno, Israel Salanter, and Isaac Elhanan, after whom many institutions of Jewish learning have been named, became household words because of their supreme scholarship and piety, and even more so because of their saintliness of character and acts of public service.

Elijah Gaon, renowned for his matchless scholarship, was also known as Elijah the Saint because of the deep humaneness which characterized his life. This saintly man lived in dire poverty but would often give away his last piece of bread or pawn his meager belongings in order to assist the needy. The forbearance he exercised toward those who wronged him is exemplified in the following incident. A petty official for years withheld from the Gaon a stipend

23. *Sbornik Mat. Econ. Pol. Ev. Ros.,* II, 239–243, 282. On the philanthropy of Russian Jews see the study made by S. I. Ianowsky, *Evreiskaia Blagotvoritelnost.*
24. *Shlome Reb Hayem's,* Book I, 14, Vol. XVIII in Collected Works.

which had been bequeathed him in a will. Although Elijah had to endure extreme penury because of this deprivation, he refused to prosecute the guilty man. In explanation, the rabbi quoted a Talmudic opinion that humiliating a man in public is tantamount to the shedding of human blood.

So greatly revered was this scholar and saint that his opinion was sufficient to override a decision of the most influential lay leaders. When the Board of Jewish Charities in Vilno decided to centralize the collection and distribution of charity funds, the resolution was not put into effect because of the Gaon's objection that it would subject all applicants for charity to the humiliation of appearing before a public body. The Gaon insisted that the deserving poor should not have to undergo that indignity.[25] This tender regard for people's feelings did not apply to those in whom this zealot saw a threat to Judaism. An arch enemy of *Hassidism,* which he regarded as a menace to the faith and people of Israel, Rabbi Elijah was most severe and uncompromising in his fight against the *Hassidim* whom he placed under the ban of excommunication. As a result, the sect made but few inroads among the Jews of Lithuania, where the Gaon lived and exercised his greatest influence.

In the latter forties of the nineteenth century, a movement known as the *Musar* (Moral) School arose in Lithuania. The originator of this movement, which aimed at thorough preparation and training for the good life, was Rabbi Israel Lipkin (1810–1883), known as Rabbi Salanter after his place of residence, Salant, province of Kovno. This rabbi held that man could through meditation, self-criticism, and intensive study of moralistic works so retrain his mind and emotions that in time he would automatically follow the good and shun the evil. To illustrate how a religious act could become second nature through man's constant exercise of the will power, Rabbi Salanter pointed to the dietary laws, which were upheld by all Jews as a matter of course though observance entailed much sacrifice. Moreover, because of long training and continuous discipline in controlling food habits, forbidden foods not only did not require the constant conquest of temptation but even became abhorrent to the Jew. Similarly, a person could through a process of training and self-discipline so habituate himself to the perfect ethical life that anything contrary to this way of living would in time become repugnant to him.

For the purpose of such training, Rabbi Salanter established *Musar Stublach* (Moral Conventicles) where his disciples would

25. On Elijah of Vilno see L. Ginzberg, *Students, Scholars and Saints,* pp. 125–144; S. Schechter, *Studies in Judaism,* I, 73–98.

assemble to recite edifying passages from the Bible and from writings of Jewish moralists. In deepest earnest mounting to tearful melancholy, they would meditate upon sin and punishment, upon man's latter end and his destined accounting before the Heavenly Judge.

While the religious training prescribed by Rabbi Salanter may be regarded in a sense as ascetic, it never assumed extreme forms of self-denial or self-mortification. When the rabbi observed a tendency toward those extremes among his disciples, he sought to discourage it. It is pertinent to observe that ascetic cults among Jewry never engaged in the extreme practices which manifested themselves in other religions. Asceticism runs counter to the spirit of Judaism. As Professor Ginzberg puts it: "A religion that sanctifies even the so-called animal appetites and desires of man, elevating them into worship and religious exaltation, and instead of despairing of the flesh, highly recommends the satisfaction and joy of the body—such a religion could never produce excesses of asceticism found in other religions to whom the body and the material world are the seat of evil." [26]

Rabbi Salanter's mode of life, like that of all saints, did possess certain elements of asceticism, for he practiced self-discipline and self-denial. Guarding against the impurities which mar idle talk, he would often impose upon himself periods of complete silence. For the good of his soul he would deny himself the opportunity of attaining ordinary comforts, refusing many a remunerative office which offered an easier living. But the exercise of self-denial and self-discipline was directed not so much toward the salvation of his own soul as toward the service of his fellow men. At one period in his life Rabbi Salanter permitted himself the luxury of accepting four rubles a week for his services as head of a *yeshibah*, but he saw to it that these earnings were spent in feeding the poor in his home, which became a veritable guest house. When after the death of his wife he discovered that she had left some money, which through frugality she had managed to save, he forthwith distributed it among the needy.

The rabbi's deep and personal feeling of responsibility for these unfortunates is illustrated in the following incident. In order to expedite the repair of the *hekdesh* (poor house) which was in a most sorry state, he spent the night there sleeping on the floor. This tacit rebuke was most effective, for the officials of the community soon hastened to make the necessary repairs.[27]

26. Ginzberg, *Stud. Schol. Saints.*, pp. 188–189. See also Achad Ha-Am, *Al Poroshat Derakim,* III, 222–232. 2d edit. Berlin, 1921.

27. On Salanter see Ginzberg, *Stud. Schol. Saints,* pp. 145–195. Jacob Mark, *Gedolim fun Unser Zeit,* pp. 67–105; S. Rosenfeld, *Perez.,* I, 66–104.

Nobility of character, which characterized so many of the Talmudic authorities, was also exemplified in the personality of Rabbi Isaac Elhanan (1817–1896) of Kovno, regarded as the foremost rabbinic authority of his day. Although an uncompromising opponent of *Haskalah,* he chided those of his followers who harassed and embittered the lives of the *maskilim.* Instead of taunting and reviling these modernists, Rabbi Elhanan sought to win them over by kind and tolerant treatment. In matters of ritual, the sage of Kovno may be regarded as a fundamentalist since he insisted on the strictest observance of the letter of the law. In practice, however, he is known to have deviated from this course when the interests of the poor were at stake. In the famine year of 1869, disregarding the protests of some rabbis, he permitted the use of beans and peas on Passover when such foods are ordinarily forbidden. To Rabbi Salanter he wrote: "My family as well as the most prominent Jews of Kovno will eat peas on Passover, and I implore you, Rabbi Israel, to do likewise, so that the poor whose mainstay this food is will not suffer the embarrassment of regarding themselves as transgressors."

Although by inclination Rabbi Elhanan was meant for the cloistered life of the scholar, his sense of duty and love for his people led him to become the outstanding public servant of his generation. In spite of his inability to speak Russian, he managed through sheer force of personality to obtain favors from the government for Jewish communities and individuals who appealed to him to intercede on their behalf.[28]

Owing to their isolated existence, the social responsibilities of most of the scholars and saints of that period were limited to the service of their own people. Those, however, who had the rare experience of contact with the outside world, found the horizon of their idealism widening to include general social problems. Such a man was Manasseh ben Porat (1776–1818), better known as Manasseh Illier, after the town of his residence, Illya, province of Vilno. In the rich library of a relative, this brilliant Talmudist discovered the writings of the rationalists and humanitarians of the eighteenth century. They awoke in him an absorbing interest in universal problems, so that the betterment of the world order became the consuming ideal of his life, to the exclusion of his personal concerns. In one of his works he stated: "I am ashamed to worry about my needs and those of my family when I see how deep is the need and misery of the world. . . . I cannot rest, but must needs delve into the order of this world, point out its miseries, its sufferings, its

28. Jacob Mark, *Gedolim fun Unser Zeit,* pp. 105–125.

needs, and pray to God that He may light my eyes and point the way to the improvement of the world."[29] That improvement, he believed, could be achieved through the application of intelligence and reason, the formula upon which the rationalists and early *maskilim* pinned their hope.

In 1807, Manasseh Illier sought in his *Pesher Dabar* (Solution to the Problem) to bring unity into the ranks of Jewry by reconciling all the factions of the conflicting schools of thought through the harmonization of reason and faith. This book, of which but one copy is extant—in the British Museum—was assailed as heretical by orthodox leaders, who took great pains to suppress its circulation. Although a rationalist, and in the eyes of his orthodox contemporaries a heretic, this dreamer of the ghetto was throughout his life a deeply pious and scrupulously observant Jew.

That the products of Talmudic Judaism presented fertile ground for the sowing of advanced social ideas is also demonstrated by the comparatively large number of rabbinical students who fifty years later became deeply involved in the revolutionary movement. It is significant that the first Jewish revolutionary circle in Russia was established in the rabbinical seminary of Vilno. While this may rightly be ascribed to the fact that these students belonged to an educated class exposed to modern thought, one may also assume that indoctrination of humanitarian ideals through Talmudic training predisposed them to the idealistic aspects of the revolutionary movement.

This short survey of the cultural and moral status of Russian Jewry would be incomplete if it did not include some account of *Hassidism,* the movement which challenged the cultural and religious standards of Rabbinic Judaism and created a schism in the established order of Jewish life. This religious cult arose in the middle of the eighteenth century in the region of Podol, then belonging to Poland, primarily because of unbearable political disabilities and economic privations of Jews in that country. The deterioration of the central government made the position of the Jew most precarious, since his life and property depended entirely upon the whim of the *pan* (landowner). To provide entertainment for his guests, the *pan* would often compel a Jew to don the skin of a bear. Armed with clubs and whips, the company would then enjoy the sport of a mock bear hunt with the Jew as the quarry. It was also a common pastime of the Polish nobility to make their Jews chant portions from Hebrew liturgy for the amusement of the drunken revelers.

29. Introduction to *Tikun Kelali,* quoted in Isaac Spalter, *Alfe Manasseh,* II, 5–6.

Into this miserable existence, beset with constant fears and humiliations, came *Hassidism* to preach its gospel of joy, optimism, and self-worth through religious experience. Israel Baal Shem Tob,[30] creator of the movement, taught that prayer was acceptable to God only if it flowed from a joyous heart.[31] Weeping at prayer was an evil thing, only when tears were an expression of an overwhelming religious experience could it be regarded as good.[32] Singing, dancing, and swaying of the body both at prayer and at *hassidic* gatherings were employed to induce that state of spiritual exaltation called *hitlahabut*.

Hassidism also sought to raise the self-esteem of the unlearned, who were looked down upon in the Jewish community where scholarship was the criterion of a man's worth. Sincerity and ardor in praying were far more important than learning, proclaimed this new movement. In the matter of study, too, special stress was laid upon sincerity and devotion. According to the Besht (contraction for Baal Shem Tob), these qualities made the study of even one who did not understand its significance acceptable to the Lord. In a charming simile he tells us that just as a father delights in the unintelligible prattle of a baby, so does our Heavenly Father respond lovingly to the study of the simple.[33]

The importance which *Hassidism* attached to the emotional aspects of Judaism as opposed to the intellectual was an expression of the revolt of the masses against the aristocracy and autocracy of the learned class. By proclaiming the humble and unlettered to be the equals of the learned in the eyes of God, *Hassidism* invested the life of its devotees with a new-found dignity. In the *hassidic* courts where the rich and poor, learned and unlearned, mingled freely and were joined in common fellowship, the humble and ignorant felt themselves to be the equals of those whom they had been accustomed to regard as their betters.

At the head of each *hassidic* group stood the *Zadik*[34] upon whom the movement hinged. The *Hassidim* believed these leaders to be endowed with supernatural powers by means of which they could perform miracles both in the heavenly spheres and in the nether regions. They also believed that the *Zadik* served as an intermediary between his disciples and the Almighty, for one of the fundamental

30. Master of the Good Name; thus called because of his purported power to perform miraculous cures and feats by invoking the name of God.

31. *Sefer Zavaat Ha-Ribash,* p. 21; *Keser Shem Tob,* p. 23.

32. *Likute Yekarim,* p. 1.

33. *Ibid.,* p. 1.

34. *Zadik*—literally "righteous" or "saint." Also referred to as *Rebbe,* meaning "Master."

doctrines of the cult held that the Deity was most accessible through the intercession of the saint.

It was this saint worship or *Zadikism* which the religious authorities found most objectionable in *Hassidism*. S. A. Horodetzky, a student of mystic movements in Judaism, points out that the rabbis opposed the *hassidic* sects essentially for the same reason that the Pharisees objected to Jesus. It was not the teachings of the Nazarene, in essence the same as those of the prophets and sages, that the Pharisees found objectionable, but rather the significance attached to his personality. The Pharisees, whose cardinal doctrine was that the *Torah* must be the sole source of religious authority, were alarmed at the phenomenon of a man who constituted himself as an authority. Thus the religious leaders fought *Hassidism* not for its teachings, which were in no sense a departure from traditional Judaism, but for its investing the *Zadik* with undue authority and supernatural power and for its making his person rather than the *Torah* the focal point of Judaism.[35]

The virtual deification of the *Zadik* gave rise to other undesirable features which later led to the degeneration of *Hassidism*. Many of the *Zadikim* abused the faith of their followers in order to acquire wealth and power. They maintained luxurious courts to whose upkeep the very poorest contributed and they concerned themselves little with the spiritual or material welfare of their adherents. Another factor responsible for the deterioration of *hassidic* leadership was its dynastic system, whereby the mantle of the saint automatically passed on to his son regardless of his qualifications. As a result, charlatanism and ignorance were not uncommon characteristics of *hassidic* dynasties.

From its very inception *Hassidism* divided East-European Jewry into two hostile camps—*Hassidim* and *Mitnagdim* (Opponents). The latter were the followers of the established rabbinic authorities, many of whom waged a bitter fight against the new movement. The appeal of this cult, however, was so strong that soon after its birth the adherents of *Hassidism* outnumbered their opponents in numerous communities of Poland and Russia. While the strength of the movement was not the same in each area, it is safe to assert that at the beginning of the nineteenth century, when *Hassidism* was at its height, it counted among its adherents the majority of East-European Jewry.[36] The rabbis also denounced this rapidly rising sect because of the disregard for learning bred by its doctrines. The *maskilim*, who looked with disfavor upon both camps, were particu-

35. S. Horodetzky, Introd. to *Shibhe Baal Shem Tob,* p. 15.
36. S. Dubnow, *Toldot Ha-Hassidut,* pp. 2–3.

larly vituperative in their condemnation of *Hassidism*. Assailing its obscurantism and superstition, they contended that it presented the greatest obstacle to progress and emancipation.

But *Hassidism* also possessed many positive qualities and virtues. The disciples' visits to the *hassidic* courts, where they feasted, danced, sang, and listened with rapturous attention to the mystical words of the *rebbe* or to his wondrous tales, were experiences which brought joyous relief to an otherwise sordid and cheerless existence. These circles also fostered a spirit of mutual helpfulness and comradeship, upon which *Hassidism* laid special stress, so that many a petitioner who came to find miraculous aid from his *rebbe* would find material assistance from one of the *rebbe's* disciples. Through *Hassidism* not only was faith in divine Providence strengthened, but faith in the worth of the devotee himself. Even the humblest and most ignorant of Jews came to regard himself as of some consequence because of the democratic practices of the *Hassidim* and the democratic principles of *Hassidism*.

The most beautiful characteristics of the movement were exemplified in some of its nobler representatives. Outstanding among these was its founder, Israel Baal Shem Tob (1700–1760). From early childhood, this religious mystic, whose conception of God so closely resembled Pantheism, evinced an unusual love for nature. Often he would absent himself from *heder* and spend long hours on some hilltop or in the fields absorbed in meditation. God to him was an ever-manifest reality Who revealed Himself in the animate and inanimate, through the physical as well as through the spiritual qualities of man. The Besht sought to make joyousness a religious principle and the worship of God a joyous experience. Unlike the gloomy and stern preachers of his day, whom he often rebuked for their descriptions of the terrifying prospects of hell, he would fill the hearts of his listeners with an optimistic faith in the benevolence and forgiveness of the Almighty. The founder of *Hassidism* was, as Dr. Solomon Schechter put it, "a religious revivalist in the best sense; full of burning faith in his God and his cause; convinced utterly of the value of his work and the truth of his teaching." [37]

The life of this mystic has been embellished with innumerable tales of his wondrous deeds and miraculous cures. The content of these tales and many incidents in his life closely resemble those connected with the life of Jesus. The Besht, too, consorted with sinners and outcasts, whom he won over through service, friendship, and love. Indeed, the whole life of this remarkable man was filled to overflowing with a passionate love and devotion to God and man.

37. S. Schechter, *Studies in Judaism,* I, 19.

Another personality who enshrined himself in the hearts of the Jewish people was Levi Yizhak of Berdichev (1740–1809), known as "The Advocate of his People." This defense he conducted not in the courts of law but before the Judgment Seat of the Almighty, whom he addressed both as Judge and Defendant. In impassioned speech and heartrending tone, Levi Yizhak would storm the heavens demanding an explanation from the Lord for his affliction of Israel. Many of the utterances of this revered rabbi have become incorporated into Jewish folk-song, and Jewish folk-lore contains many a story of his defense of the Jew in whom he saw only good. It is related, for example, that when he chanced upon his coachman saying his prayers while greasing his wagon wheels, instead of chiding the driver for irreverence, Levi Yizhak addressed the Almighty as follows: "Observe, oh Lord, how truly holy are Thy people, who even when performing menial tasks do not forget to pray unto Thee." In him was represented at its best the democratic character of *Hassidism,* in which solicitude for the humble played so great a part. On one occasion, it is told, this *Zadik* deferred the blowing of the ram's horn on Rosh Hashanah so as to permit a humble villager to finish the preceding prayers through which he was laboriously plodding.[38]

Despite the unfavorable features that marred *Hassidism,* this movement produced so many saintly personalities, brought joy to so many, and left the Jew so rich a spiritual and cultural heritage, that it must be regarded as a decided contribution to Judaism. However *Hassidism* may have been corrupted by disreputable leaders who abused the confidence of the people, the ethical and moral standards of its devotees remained unimpaired. As far as their morals were concerned, the masses of Jewry, whether of the *hassidic* or *mitnagdic* (oppositional) alignment, certainly compared favorably with the non-Jewish population, with whom they were denied equality on charges of ignorance and immorality.

These charges were the result of prejudice and lack of knowledge of the inner life of the Jewish people. With the collapse of the Nicholas régime in the Crimean War and with the inauguration of the new emperor, a more sympathetic effort to understand the Jew began to replace centuries-old hostility. The reign of Alexander II made the first breach in the ghetto walls and gave promise of better days to come.

38. On Levi Yizhak see Jacob S. Minkin, *The Romance of Hassidism,* pp. 152–177.

VI

THE NEW ERA OF ALEXANDER II

THE inauguration of the reign of Alexander II ushered in one of the most hopeful and promising periods in Russian history. The mood of apathy and despair that engulfed the Russian people in the days of Nicholas I gave way to a spirit of exultant expectancy. To appreciate this change in mood, one must have some realization of the spirit of submission and resignation which prevailed under the Nicholas régime. "In practical life," writes a Russian publicist, "government came to mean 'officialdom.' 'Officialdom' permeated every phase of life. In that word were embodied law, truth, grace and punishment. The merchant engaged in trade by grace of the officials. The petty official drank vodka, got married, begat children and accepted bribes by grace of the higher officials. People breathed the air because the officials, indulging our weakness, released into the atmosphere the necessary amount of oxygen. The fish swam in the water, the birds sang in the forest, because it was permitted by 'officialdom.' "[1]

The régime of Alexander II promised to do away with the bureaucratic evils paralyzing the will of the people. The famous words uttered by the new emperor on his ascension to the throne pledging "education, equal justice, tolerance, and humaneness toward all," infused new life and energy into the atrophied veins of the Russian masses. Contemporary writers speak of the heightened mood that characterized the period. "There are periods in history," said the famous Russian publicist Michael Katkov in 1857, "when everyone unmistakably feels that he has a calling in life, when to the depths of the innermost soul one clearly hears the answers which bring peace and blessedness to the heart, restore reason, truth and balance to life. There are periods when the powers of man instantly renew themselves and ripen; when people with a quickening of the heart merge in the common cause and feeling. Happy are the generations which are destined to live in such a period! Thank God!—we are privileged to live in such an epoch!"[2]

In the same vein of glowing enthusiasm, contemporaries in later

1. Liubimov, *M. N. Katkov i Ego Istoricheskaia Zasluga,* pp. 182–184; quoted in S. M. Ginsburg, "Zabytaia Epokha," *Voskhod,* 1896, Jan., pp. 90–91.
2. *Russky Vestnik,* 1857, Dec., p. 204.

years reminisced about the period of the Great Reforms. In a lecture which marked the inauguration of his twenty-sixth year of teaching, Professor Nicholas Tagantsev, a noted legal scholar, spoke nostalgically of the "magic spell of those times, of the resurgence of youthful enthusiasm that animated the society of the day when I first began my teaching career. I might perhaps compare the spirit of that period to the exultation of mood experienced by one fortunate enough to witness the first sign of our southern spring, somewhere in Ialta, or on the seashore in the Caucasus, when every atom in creation is filled with creative powers, when throughout budding nature happily and resoundingly there is a quickening of the pulse of life." [3]

At a dinner celebrating his thirty-five years of literary activity, A. M. Skabichevsky referred to the first years of the Alexandrian era as a "great and wonderful time," when "people exultingly rejoiced in the feverish expectation of great events." "Before every one's eyes," he said, "there opened wide and distant horizons radiating all the rainbow colors. All of Russian life presented one brilliant dawn! It seemed as though the darkness of ignorance and stagnation had disappeared, and that each and all aimed at one goal: progress in religious tolerance, cessation of racial and religious strife, equal rights for men and women, equalization of all before the law, the raising of the standards of living for the working masses, etc. In one friendly and unanimous voice, all Russian literature preached these great principles. And it was a literature which measured up to the height of its calling!" [4]

Great as was the cause for rejoicing among the Russian people at the inauguration of the new reign, even greater was that of the Russian Jews. They saw in the new rule a promise of redemption not alone from the oppression which they shared in common with the Russian masses, but also from the additional disabilities and terrors they suffered as Jews.

The first important *ukaz* regarding the Jews was issued by the new emperor on the day of his coronation and sent a thrill of relief and joy through the Jewish ghetto. It was the decree abolishing juvenile conscription and the grievous injustices connected with it.[5] A Jewish poet, who in his childhood was among a group of newly recruited cantonists awaiting transportation to their destination, describes the joy he experienced when the order for their release came:

3. N. Tagantsev, *Vestnik Evropy,* December, 1892, pp. 820–821.
4. Quoted in S. M. Ginsburg, "Zab. Ep.," *Voskhod,* 1896, March, p. 87.
5. *V. P. S. Z.,* XXXI, no. 30,888.

At about one o'clock in the morning, while we were all asleep in the barracks, we were awakened by a great commotion in the street. The noise came nearer and nearer, and soon we heard vigorous knocks at the iron doors and shutters: "Get up children! A deliverance! You are free!" someone shouted. "An *ukaz* from the tsar to release you!", shouted another. "Praise God, children! Say *Hallel!*" [A special prayer of praise in the Jewish liturgy] several voices called out together. The news was to us as the sound of the great *Shofar* which will awaken the dead on the day of Resurrection. With a cry of joy we sprang from our wretched straw heaps, washed and fell to saying *Hallel.* I was the chazzan [cantor] and my choir accompanied me. After *Hallel* we all joined hands and danced a Jewish "Karehod" [folk dance]. It was a gruesome scene, making one laugh and weep in turn. After the dance I wrote my song, "The Deliverance" [Die Yeshuah] and arranged a beautiful melody for it.[6]

The abolition of juvenile conscription—a major reform—was followed during the years 1859 to 1865 by a series of minor reforms which strengthened the confidence of the Jews in the government. On December 2, 1857, the fifty-verst zones from the Polish border which hitherto had been closed to Jewish inhabitants, were opened.[7] On October 27, 1858, Jews were allowed to reside in the frontier zones of the border provinces in the West, as well as in that of Bessarabia.[8] In 1859, Jewish merchants of the first guild,[9] together with foreign Jews, were granted, subject to certain conditions, the right to reside and trade all over Russia.[10] In the following year Jewish soldiers who completed their term of service in the Guard regiments were permitted to remain permanently in the capital.[11] In 1861, Jewish graduates of higher institutions of learning, possessing academic degrees, were made eligible for government service throughout Russia. The holders of such degrees were also allowed to engage in trade and commerce outside the Pale.[12] On December 11 of the same year, merchants of the first and second guilds were granted the right of permanent residence in the city of Kiev, while all other Jews were permitted temporary residence there for business, medical, and various other purposes.[13]

6. *A Jewish Bard, Being the Biography of Eliakum Zunser,* p. 20.
7. *V. P. S. Z.,* XXXII, no. 32,513.
8. *Ibid.,* XXXIII, no. 33,659.
9. Merchants who paid an annual tax of about a thousand rubles.
10. *V. P. S. Z.,* XXXIV, no. 34,248.
11. *Ibid.,* XXXV, no. 36,339.
12. *Ibid.,* XXXVI, no. 37,684.
13. *Ibid.,* XXXVI, no. 37,738.

The impression this concession made on the Jews is reflected in the enthusiastic comments of the contemporary Jewish press. "Who could have foretold," a correspondent exclaims, "that Kiev, the mother of Russian cities, where not so long ago the appearance of a Jew was forbidden, would now become the friendly refuge of the Jews?" [14] Another correspondent records his joy at having heard Jewish speech on the streets of Kiev.[15]

In the sixties, the government removed the restrictions against Jewish residence in certain sections of a number of cities within the Pale. And in 1865, all Russia was opened for one of the largest classes of Jewry when on June 28, the government abolished the Pale for all artisans and their families.[16]

During the reign of Alexander II, the legal position of the Jews in the Kingdom of Poland was also greatly improved. The Jews of Poland who constituted one-eighth of the general population, had been living under severe legal disabilities. Of the 453 Polish cities only 246 were open to them. In thirty-one of these there were zone restrictions for all Jews excepting the wealthy and the cultured. In ninety cities Jewish residence was either altogether forbidden or limited to certain sections. In the more than one hundred border towns, no new Jewish settlers were permitted.

Through the efforts of Marquis Wielopolski, a prominent Polish statesman who was highly influential with the Russian government, Alexander II, in 1862, issued an *ukaz* abolishing the oppressive disabilities of the Polish Jews. This imperial order permitted them to acquire land and purchase real estate in all cities, and removed all residence restrictions in the Kingdom of Poland. The law made Jews eligible for witnessing all legal documents, and declared the testimony of a Jew in criminal cases to have the same validity as that of a non-Jew.[17]

Indicative of the greater confidence the government now placed in the Jews are the following laws dealing with military service and education. In 1859, humiliating phrases in the oath taken by Jewish recruits were eliminated.[18] Two years later Jewish privates became eligible for advancement to the rank of non-commissioned officer and office clerk.[19] The following year, the office of supervisor of

14. *Ha-Carmel,* 1862, no. 15.
15. *Ibid.,* 1863, no. 34.
16. *V. P. S. Z.,* XL, no. 42,264.
17. J. Gessen, *Istoria Evr. Naroda v. Ros.,* II, 185–197. See also I. P. Kelberin, *Cherta Osedlosti,* pp. 54–55.
18. *V. P. S. Z.,* XXXIV, no. 34,975.
19. *Ibid.,* XXXVI, no. 37,624.

the Jewish government schools, which in the days of Nicholas I could be filled by Christians only, was opened to Jews.[20]

The official memoranda dealing with the Jewish problem reflect the change in the attitude of the upper administrative circles. The Jewish Committee, which in preceding régimes kept piling one disability after another upon the Jew, now took a different stand. In 1856 it reported to Alexander II that "the aim of the government, as stated in 1840, to bring about the union of the Jewish with the general population, is hampered by the temporarily established restrictions which contradict the general legislation and create confusion." [21]

And when, in 1856, the minister of the interior, Count Lanskoi, communicated with the provincial authorities regarding the advisability of removing certain restrictive measures against the Jews, he received answers which were both sympathetic and favorable. Count Stroganov, governor-general of New Russia and Bessarabia, urged complete emancipation of the Jews on the ground that "the existence at the present time of any legal limitations for Jews is out of harmony both with the spirit and tendencies of the times, as well as with the aim of the government to merge them with the native population of the empire." [22]

In the same spirit, the provincial government attorney, I. N. Kozakovsky, submitted to the minister a "Project for the Organization of Jewry," in which he strongly urged the granting of complete civic equality to the Russian Jews. He contended that both the Jewish and non-Jewish populations would profit from such a step. The following closing lines of this scholarly and humane document typify the practical idealism of the reformers of those days:

> And so, science, experience, the interests of the government, the interests of the residents of Great Russia, as well as of the Western region, and the interest of the Jews themselves, all speak loudly in favor of my suggested measure. They all urge: remove the disabilities imposed on the Jews; organize commercial and trade schools for them; and that same people which at present is regarded as the scourge of the population of the Western provinces, will be transformed into arteries, carrying life-giving sap into all parts of the empire.[23]

20. *Ibid.,* XXXVII, no. 38,641.
21. *Ibid.,* XL, no. 42,264.
22. *Ibid.,* par. 5.
23. Project published in *Voskhod,* 1881, Book 5.

The equalization of the legal status of the Jews with that of the rest of the population was also advocated by Prince N. A. Orlov in a note which he submitted to the emperor in 1858. This document, which deals chiefly with the question of religious dissent, contains some interesting observations on the Jewish problem. "I know and expect," he says, "that my thoughts [on the Jews] will be strongly censured. Prejudice against the Jews is still strong in Russia, and perhaps for a long time they will not get their due. We can only comfort ourselves with the hope that sooner or later prejudice will disappear through education, and in the meantime repeat the words of Guizot: 'La verité est une; ceux qui la cherchent consciencieusement finissent toujours par s'accorder.' "[24] (There is but one truth; those who seek it conscientiously always find it in the end.)

The Russian press, too, reflected the favorable change in attitude toward the Jews. An article in the ***Russky Invalid*** (Russian Veteran), a publication of the Ministry of War, indicates the new spirit of friendship and tolerance preached by the organs of public opinion. Appearing in 1858, it reads in part as follows:

Let us be worthy of our age; let us give up the childish habit of presenting the Jews in our literary works as ludicrous and ignominious creatures. On the contrary, remembering the causes which brought them to such a state, let us not forget the innate ability of the Jews for the arts and sciences; and by offering them a place among us, let us utilize their energy, readiness of wit, and skill as a new means for satisfying the ever-growing needs of our people.[25]

The influential *Russky Vestnik* (Russian Messenger), too, pleaded the cause of the Jews. Referring to the oft-repeated charges as to their unethical practices, the writer Pavlov asks:

Has society a right to blame others for disregarding the ethical precepts when it itself fails to act accordingly? Should not society first trouble itself to fulfill those obligations which truth and Christian love impose upon it, and only then, if anyone so pleases, let him speak about the dirtiness and the swindling of the Jews. . . . The time for making attacks on the Jews has passed, and passed forever. Rather let us defend ourselves against their justified attacks, and through our actions nullify the truth of Shylock's famous words: 'The villainy you teach me, I will execute.'[26]

24. "Zametka Kniazia Orlova," *Russkaia Starina,* 1881, XXXI, 94.
25. 1858, no. 39. Quoted in *Voskhod,* 1896, p. 141.
26. 1858, XVIII, November, Book 1, 126.

This remarkable change of attitude on the part of the leaders of Russian thought was hailed with enthusiasm by Jewish writers. One of the latter noted with satisfaction the "spirit of conciliation, tolerance, and education worthy of our time" manifested by the Russian press and literature.[27] The writer Levanda declared that the Russian writings of the first decade of the Alexandrian period formed a glorious page in the history of the Russian Jews. He asserted that the Russian champions of Jewish rights could be compared with such men as Macaulay and Disraeli.[28]

The broad liberal spirit of this era was evidenced in the new aims and policies of the Ministry of Education, marking a complete departure from those of the Nicholas government. Both the curriculum and the administration of the Russian schools underwent a thorough revision. It was evident from the very beginning of the new reign, that the former police-bureaucratic method of administering the school system was at an end.[29] Whereas education in the former régime was designed to strengthen and perpetuate class privilege, it was now organized along more democratic and humanitarian lines. The preamble of the new law for education prepared in 1862, stated that the "aim of the gymnasiums is to give students a comprehensive general education that would prepare them for rational human living rather than train them for successful activity in a particular class." [30]

The administration of the schools also became more democratic. Bureaucratic school management by a single head was replaced by faculty meetings which shared responsibility for the conduct of the schools. In a communication sent by the curator of the Vilno school region to his subordinates in 1859 instructing them to hold such staff meetings, he requested that there be no formalities at these sessions. "I would like to see," he wrote, "more freedom, more progress, more new and enlightened ideas, and a complete break with the old routine." [31]

The liberal tendencies manifested in its general educational policies were reflected in the attitude of the government to the problem of Jewish education. A new policy was instituted in educating Jewry—a policy which quickly gained the confidence of the masses. The missionary efforts of the former régimes were discontinued. E. P. Kovalevsky, minister of education, stated in 1859 that "there

27. I. Tarnopol, *Opyt Sovremennoi i Osmotritelnoi Reformy v Oblasti Iudaisma v. Rossii,* p. 32.
28. L. Levanda, *K Voprosu o Evreiakh v Zapadnom Krae,* pp. 12–13.
29. *Evr. v Obsh. Shk.,* p. 24.
30. *Ibid.,* p. 24.
31. P. Marek, *Och. Ist. Pros. Evr.,* p. 144.

would be as little interference as possible in the instruction of religion, and that this subject would be left rather to the supervision of the parents with no pressure exercised by the government."[32] The new regulations dealing with Jewish education, issued in 1859, attested to the sincerity of the minister's statement. Jewish religious instruction in the schools was made optional with the alternative of engaging private instructors for that purpose, if the parents so desired.[33] The discontinuance of proselytizing through education was part of the new policy concerning Jewish conversions. A decree issued December 1861, forbade the baptizing of Jewish children under fourteen without consent of their parents.[34] In 1864, the government stopped the gifts of money made to Jewish privates upon embracing the Greek-Orthodox faith.[35] And in March of 1866, the government abolished the practice of lessening the punishment for non-Christian offenders who during trial would embrace Christianity.[36]

As a result of this friendlier attitude toward the Jew, the *Haskalah* propaganda for secular education reached its high watermark in the first half of Alexander's reign. The response was widespread, wholehearted, and enthusiastic. "If you should ask," writes one of the heroines of a contemporary novel to a friend, "what kind of society is that of the city of G., I can positively state that the population there is not educated, but self-educating. I do not know who introduced the idea of education here, but I do know that it has struck deep roots. Everybody is studying here, both young and old, especially women. . . . All thirst for knowledge. Though frugal in every other way, the residents of the city of G. spare nothing where education is concerned."[37]

Interest in general culture found adherents even in the *yeshibot* which were the bulwark of the old type of education. Jewish literature dealing with that period is replete with descriptions of secret excursions of Talmudical students into the realm of forbidden knowledge. In the dead of night, these lads would stealthily enter the screened and deserted portion of the women's synagogue; there, safe from intrusion, by the light of a candle or of the moon, they would devour forbidden fruits of knowledge, such as a Hebrew periodical, a Russian textbook, or a German grammar.

32. Quoted in Posner, *Evr. Obsh. Shk.*, p. 25.
33. *V. P. S. Z.*, no. 34,461.
34. *Ibid.*, XXXVI, no. 37, 709.
35. *Ibid.*, XXXIX, no. 40,703.
36. *Ibid.*, XLI, no. 43,138.
37. L. O. Levanda, "Goriachee Vremia," *Ev. Bib.*, I, 41.

The call to education was the keynote of the Hebrew and Russian-Jewish periodicals which came into existence in the early sixties. Invariably the theme of the correspondents' reports in these weeklies was of the status of education in their respective communities. As for the acute economic problems of Russian Jewry, they were hardly discussed in the pages of the Jewish publications; the all-absorbing subjects that engaged the attention of the Jewish writers were education and emancipation, the former even overshadowing the latter. In his zeal to accelerate the program of enlightenment, a writer in *Razsvet* (Dawn) went so far as to propose compulsory education for the Jews of Russia. He argued that, though other Western European countries had not instituted compulsory education, it was important that Russia should do so because of the greater need for it.[38]

As in Western Europe, so in Russia the program of enlightenment fostered an intense feeling of patriotism and a strong attachment to the language and the culture of the fatherland. "Our fatherland," declared *Razsvet*, "is Russia. And just as her air is ours, so too, must her language be ours." [39] In order to absorb the Russian spirit and accustom the Jewish child from its infancy to the sound of the Russian tongue, Zeiberling, the Jewish censor and social worker, advised his coreligionists to engage Russian nurses for their children.[40] *Razsvet* advocated the replacement of German, hitherto the language of instruction in Jewish government schools, by Russian. German, the paper argued, may be the object of study for anyone who so desires, but it certainly should not take the place of "the beautiful and rich Russian language, which is the inheritance of everyone who calls Russia his fatherland." [41]

In their zeal for the dissemination of the Russian language and culture as a means of bringing Jewish youth closer to Russian life, Jewish supervisors and teachers of the special Jewish schools even went to the extent of using police coercion upon resisting parents.[42] It was through these instructors that Jewish subjects, which formerly comprised the bulk of the curriculum, were gradually cut down to give more time to the study of the Russian language. In some school regions, the German language and Jewish subjects were eliminated. As a result of the patriotic zeal of Jewish school officials who believed it was their mission to Russify their coreligionists, the

38. 1860, no. 29, p. 462.
39. 1860, no. 13, p. 201.
40. J. Zeiberling, *Z. M. N. P.*, 1862, CXV, 66.
41. 1861, April 21, p. 764.
42. Marek, *Och. Ist. Pros. Evr.*, p. 192.

Jewish government schools, as a Jewish historian put it, became Russian schools for Jews.[43]

By this time, however, pupils of the special Jewish schools were eager to be transferred to the general government schools, and the most cherished ambition of students of rabbinic seminaries was to be admitted to a university. In 1864, the Hebrew poet L. O. Gordon commented in a letter to a friend on the change that had come over the Jewish community in its attitude to secular education:

> I remember that in your city there was one Jewish student in the gymnasium. The youth would walk to school stealthily. He never appeared in the street in his student uniform, but would always leave it with the janitor of the gymnasium. He would come to school attired in his orthodox garb. Once there, however, he would change into his uniform, hide his earlocks behind his ears, and become a completely different person. This was his usual routine. Today, however, there is not a town where Jewish children do not drink the refreshing waters from strange fountains. And they do it openly, without embarrassment.[44]

Russian schools which had been open for Jews since 1804 and had attracted but a negligible number now became the object of their enthusiastic quest. Jewish youth flocked to the secondary and higher institutions of learning. Jews were so eager to have their children registered in the gymnasiums that parents would often falsify their birth certificates if they were past the age of admission.[45] In their thirst for knowledge many Jews not qualified for matriculation in a university as regular students were satisfied to be accepted as auditors.[46]

A Jewish student of the sixties gives us a description of his feelings upon being matriculated at the University of Moscow. "After a few days," he relates, "I was registered and received my university card. When together with Shlossberg I walked out of the old building of the university, we crossed over to the opposite street, took off our hats, bowed our heads in reverence to the sanctuary which had taken us unto itself, and embraced each other. Proudly we walked home, eager to shout to every one we met: 'Do you know, we are university students!' It was as though our feeling of estrangement toward the Christians about us had fallen away from us. We felt

43. *Ibid.,* p. 219.
44. *Igrot Gordon,* I, 90.
45. Posner, *Evr. Obsh. Shk.,* p. 36.
46. *Ibid.,* p. 36.

as though we belonged to a new society, wherein there were neither Judeans nor Hellenes." [47]

The rapid growth of the number of Jewish students in the Russian school system may be seen from the following figures. In 1853, there were 159 Jewish students in all the gymnasiums and pre-gymnasiums of Russia, comprising 1.25 per cent of the total student body. Ten years later this number had increased to 552, constituting 3.2 per cent of the total number.[48] In 1873, the number of Jewish students in all secondary schools for men rose to 2,362, or 13.2 per cent of the general number.[49]

Previous to this period, Jews who lived in the seclusion of the ghetto remained aloof from the people about them. Now that they were emerging spiritually and, in some cases physically, from their isolation, events about them took on a new and personal significance. In the memoirs of his childhood, a Jewish writer recalls the enthusiasm with which his parents and teachers hailed the emancipation of the serfs in 1861. "Their faces glowed with joy," he relates, "just as though they themselves had been liberated." [50] Panegyrics extolling the Tsar-Liberator and the new era he had inaugurated filled the pages of Hebrew periodicals. One of these magazines greeted the end of Russian serfdom with the verse from Solomon's Song of Songs: "The time of the (birds') singing is come, and the voice of the turtle-dove is heard in our land." [51] Another eulogizes the emperor in the words: "Happy is the land whose ruler seeks your good and teaches you to be useful." [52]

The emergence of the Russian Jew from his isolation also resulted in a profound change in his attitude to Gentile opinion. Accustomed to a life of humiliation and degradation, the Jew in the ghetto had hitherto remained practically indifferent to Gentile opinion about him. In intense devotion to his faith and its traditions he had found compensation for the contempt in which the world held him. In fact, believing as he did in the spiritual superiority of his way of life, he often disdained rather than envied the Gentile world. Now that he was beginning to make contact with the outside world, he became painfully sensitive to non-Jewish opinion. The contemporary press offers numerous examples of this psychological change. "There was a time," observed a correspondent from Warsaw, "when

47. V. O. Garkavy, *Perez.*, IV, 281.
48. Posner, *Evr. Obsh. Shk.*, p. 38.
49. *Z. M. N. P.*, CLXVI, 44; for more statistics see *Evr. Entsik.*, XIII, 61–62.
50. *Keneset Yisrael,* I, 855.
51. *Ha-Meliz,* 1861, no. 26.
52. *Ha-Carmel,* 1861, no. 38.

Jews submitted to the ridicule of the Polish *pany*. Now they have become sensitive and conscious of their dignity."[53] Another correspondent complained of the social aloofness between Jew and non-Jew which even commercial relations failed to break. "It seems to me," he regretfully concluded, "that for a long time to come the Gentile will differentiate strictly between his business and social relationship with the Jew."[54]

On the other hand, a friendly gesture on the part of a non-Jew evoked enthusiastic comment in the Jewish press. In the sixties, government representatives often appeared at celebrations in Jewish schools, farewell dinners, examinations, etc. Their manifestation of interest was joyously welcomed by the *maskilim*, who were eager to convince the world that the "light of education also shone upon the Jew." The admission of a Jew to a Gentile club, a rare occurrence in those days, elicited jubilant expressions of triumph and gratification. A Jew in Kovno, who was elected to the nobility club, delivers himself thus: "What happened! What miracles! . . . They elected me not in spite of my being a Jew, but because of it, so that I might serve as an instrument for the expression of their highest ideal."[55]

In their pathetic eagerness to bridge the gulf which separated them from their Christian neighbors, Jews interpreted a friendly gesture on the part of non-Jews as evidence of a complete change of heart. Every minor concession granted by the government was hailed as an assurance of coming civic emancipation. The mere phraseology of a government order pertaining to them, notes a Jewish journalist, in which the invariable "It is forbidden" of the pre-Alexandrian period was replaced by "It is permitted," was a source of greatest encouragement to the Jewish people, regardless of the insignificance of the new concession.[56]

Confident of the government's good intentions, leaders of the *Haskalah* felt that the Jew must now prove his fitness for civic equality. Like their predecessors of the forties, these *maskilim* constantly emphasized secular education, usefulness to the state and patriotism as prerequisites for civic rights. They held that the Jew must earn "the gift of emancipation."[57]

Other voices, however, insisted that emancipation should not depend on Russification but should be granted the Jew as of right. *Razsvet* gave expression to this view in an editorial disagreeing with

53. *Ha-Meliz,* 1863, no. 15.
54. *Razsvet,* 1860, no. 5, p. 72.
55. *Ha-Carmel,* 1861, no. 49, Russian Supplement.
56. *Ev. Star.,* VI, 341.
57. *Ha-Meliz,* 1861, no. 36, pp. 568–9.

those who made Russification and moral improvement a condition for Jewish equality. "History has proved," asserted Osip Rabinowich, author of the editorial, "that our legal equality never depended on the status of our education, but rather on the degree of the political development of the nations among whom we lived. . . . We should seek to improve ourselves not for the sake of achieving our civic equality—that we have a right to expect by virtue of our belonging to the human family and in spite of all our faults and weaknesses. We should strive after perfection out of pure love for the highest ideal of Perfection." [58] The view that the civic status of the Jew generally depends on the degree of civilization attained by his Gentile neighbors, rather than on his own spiritual and mental development, was shared by the writer Ioakhim Tarnopol.[59] He also pointed out how the rightlessness of the Jew tended to discourage Jewish youth and cool their ardor for secular education, since such education, unaccompanied by civic rights, only accentuated the Jews' feeling of inferiority.[60]

Because the south of Russia responded to the *Haskalah* even before the reign of Alexander II, a considerable group of Jewish intellectuals in the fifties and early sixties were already becoming increasingly depressed by the legal and social discriminations they suffered as Jews. The Jewish jurist and journalist, A. Dumashevsky, pictured the pathetic situation of intellectuals who no longer fitted into their old environment and yet were not admitted into Gentile society. He represented the Gentiles as saying to these Jewish misfits: "Education, even that of a university, gives you the civic rights of honorary citizenship, but not those of ordinary citizenship. Go to your 'Moshkes' and 'Berkes,' [61] for with them and among them is your place." Depressed and humiliated, the Jewish intellectual goes back to his former environment, only to be rebuffed with: "Among us live the Berkes and the Moshkes. Go to your own kind." Only emancipation, the writer asserted, could save the Jew from the horns of this dilemma. As for their qualification for citizenship, he, too, believed that civic freedom would create civic virtues.[62]

The fact that education did not improve the economic position of the Jews was another argument for the futility of enlightenment unaccompanied by civic rights. In an editorial in which the editor of

58. 1860, no. 6, p. 85.
59. *Opyt. Sov.*, pp. 262–3.
60. *Ibid.*, pp. 44–45.
61. A derogatory use of Jewish names.
62. Quoted by I. Sosis in *Ev. Star.*, VI, 29–30.

Razsvet discussed the limited opportunities for Jews in the free professions, he summarized his conclusions thus: "From what was said above, one can easily convince himself that so far education has given the Jew nothing." [63]

Despite expressions of impatience and disillusionment heard here and there, the mood of Russian Jewry in the liberal era of the reign of Alexander II was on the whole one of hope and confidence. This spirit of high hope and joyous expectancy is epitomized in the rousing call which the novelist, Levanda, issued to his brethren:

> The morning has arrived! Hear, ye brothers! Awaken ye who are slumbering! The night guards are gradually descending from their posts. Do you hear? The morning hour has struck! Soon the sound of the morning bell will be heard, and on the street people will appear. Soon, soon, perhaps the door of our little hut, too, will open and we will rush forth to the great celebration of our good mother. Long may she live and joy may she bring to her children and grandchildren! [64]

63. 1860, no. 18, p. 284.
64. L. Levanda, *Sion,* 1861, no. 2, p. 26.

VII

THE JEWISH POLICIES OF ALEXANDER II

THE high hopes of the Jews that they would obtain civic equality in the reign of Alexander II did not materialize. A number of reasons militated against the fulfillment of their expectations, not the least important being the political views and attitude of the emperor himself. Modern historians agree that the liberalism of the Tsar-Liberator was greatly exaggerated by his contemporaries. According to Professor George Vernadsky, "Alexander II had, in fact, the same ideals of enlightened absolutism as Nicholas I; but Alexander was of a much gentler and more tolerant disposition than Nicholas." [1] The reforms effected in the reign of Alexander II, certainly did not reflect his political convictions. These reforms represented a concession on his part to the growing demands for social and political change, for the tsar feared that complete resistance to the currents of the time might bring about the disruption of his empire.[2]

Research in government archives opened to scholars after the revolution of 1917 substantiates the opinion of these writers.

In 1858, the minister of finance, Brock, suggested to the Jewish Committee that a number of discriminatory laws which limited Jewish commercial activities in certain branches of Russian industry be abolished. He urged the lifting of such restrictions because he believed that they had an adverse effect upon manufacture and commerce and retarded the progress of social development of the country. When the committee submitted to the emperor the minutes of the session in which Brock's project appeared verbatim, Alexander underlined the word *progress* and made the following marginal notation in his own handwriting: "What kind of a word is *progress?* Please do not mention this word in official documents." [3]

That the tsar's personal attitude toward Jews was not much different from that of his father, we may learn from an incident related by Rabbi Jacob Maze. When Maze was a student in the Alexandrian Gymnasium in Kerch, he relates in his memoirs, the emperor came

1. G. Vernadsky, *A History of Russia,* p. 151. On character of Alexander see Peter Kropotkin, *Memoirs of a Revolutionist,* pp. 147–153.

2. A. Kornilov, *Modern Russian History,* II, 5.

3. A photographic copy of the emperor's notation made from *Arkhiv Gosud. Soveta. Dokumenty Ev. Komit.,* no. 2, appears in S. M. Ginsburg, *Hist. Werk,* II, 250.

to visit the city in 1876. The students of the school were to go out in a special boat to meet His Majesty. Young Maze was thrilled at the prospect of meeting the kindly and gracious monarch face to face. During a sleepless night of excited anticipation he had even made up his mind to recite the benediction prescribed by Jewish ritual for the occasion of meeting a great personality. Finally, the great moment arrived, and the emperor was passing by, reviewing class after class. "As he was nearing my group and my lips began to move preparatory to uttering the benediction," the writer relates, "I was struck speechless by the following conversation between the tsar and commandant of the fort. 'Who built these redoubts [military forts], the Greek-Orthodox people or the Jews?' the tsar asked. When the commandant replied that both had had a share in their construction, Alexander observed, 'The inferior redoubts must have been built by the Jews.' "[4]

Even in the liberal era of his reign, observes a modern Jewish historian, Alexander II could not conceive of the idea of granting the Jews civic equality. The thought that, as human beings and citizens, they were entitled to civic rights without first earning them through some special meritorious deeds was completely foreign to him.[5]

In the matter of minor legal changes or reforms regarding his Jewish subjects, the emperor had no consistent policy but permitted himself to be guided by the advice of his ministers or local authorities. When the governor-general of Kiev, Dondukov-Korsakov, urged that the leasing of land be forthwith prohibited to Jews without waiting for the disposition of the entire Jewish problem, Alexander noted his agreement with the official. On the other hand, he later concurred with the contrary opinion of the minister of the interior that the measure could be decided only in conjunction with the consideration of the general Jewish problem. The tsar showed the same inconsistency in a number of other instances.[6]

The historian Gessen believes that the reforms of the first ten years of his reign were effected because of Alexander's vacillation in minor matters of Jewish policy. Government leaders had felt the need of these legal changes in the previous régime but could do nothing about them because of the determined opposition of Nicholas[7] to any reform whatsoever. But even in the minor concessions

4. J. Maze, *Zikronot,* I, 73–4.
5. S. M. Ginsburg, *Hist. Werk.,* II, 125–126.
6. *Ev. Entsik.,* I, 810.
7. *Ibid.,* I, 810.

which Alexander did grant because of either pressure or practical necessity, he made sure to specify limitations.

When, for example, during the Crimean War the minister of the interior, with the approval of the finance and war ministers, recommended that Jewish sutlers be allowed to sell their wares in localities outside the Pale, the emperor, in confirming the recommendation, added in his own handwriting: "Through the duration of the war leave these sutlers where they are, but do not admit any more." [8] In November of the same year, the tsar permitted the war minister to employ Jewish tailors and cutters in military units and military educational institutions situated in the interior of Russia, stipulating, however, that no more than one tailor or cutter be allowed for a regiment or an academy.[9]

When asked to grant privileges not dictated by practical or immediate necessity, Alexander was unyielding. Thus, in 1858, he rejected the suggestion of the ministers for both education and the interior that the right of residence throughout Russia be granted to Jewish ex-soldiers. "I absolutely do not agree," [10] he wrote on the report. Neither practical nor humanitarian considerations could move the emperor from his decision not to grant the Jews complete emancipation. In minor matters his policy was flexible and subject to the influence of his advisers, but he was adamant in his refusal to abolish the Pale, despite the recommendations of his most important officials.

In 1858, Lanskoi, minister of the interior, acting on a report he had received from the governor-general of New Russia, submitted to the Jewish Committee a memorandum warmly supporting the liberal views of the southern administrator, who had urged on humanitarian as well as utilitarian grounds that the initial step in the emancipation of Russian Jewry be taken by abolishing the Pale of Settlement. Endorsing these views, Lanskoi pointed out that the merging of the Jewish with the non-Jewish population of Russia which the government sought to effect, would be expedited through legal equalization of the Jew with the rest of the inhabitants. He also expressed the opinion that the miserable condition of the Jews was due to their lack of civic rights.

The Jewish Committee rejected Lanskoi's recommendation, stating that the emancipation of the Russian Jews would be accomplished gradually in proportion to the increase of education among

8. *V. P. S. Z.,* XXX, no. 29,378.
9. *Ibid.,* XXX, no. 29,850.
10. *Ev. Entsik.,* I, 811.

them and to their absorption into useful occupations. Alexander sanctioned the opinion of the committee by noting: "Entirely correct." [11]

Nor was Alexander influenced by the opinions of high local and central administrative officials who urged the removal of residence restrictions and other oppressive disabilities against the Jews. In 1861, both the minister of the interior and the minister of education submitted a memorandum to the Jewish Committee suggesting remedial legislation for the Jews of the Northwest. These recommendations were prompted by a report describing the unhappy state of the population of that region sent by Nazimov, governor-general of Vilno. In their memorandum the ministers explained the reasons for the unfortunate conditions prevailing there. The poverty of the population, they pointed out, was due to the disproportionately large number of Jews engaged in trade and commerce. Because of the abnormal competition among the Jews it was almost impossible for them to make an honest living. The ministers attributed the "ignorance and low moral level" of the Jewish population to the legal disabilities which restricted Jews in their choice of occupation and residence. Only by lifting these restrictions could a change in the cultural and moral status of the Jew be effected. The policy of the government—making the gradual moral improvement of the Jew the condition of Jewish emancipation—only meant the perpetuation of their present miserable status, as well as that of the non-Jewish population. The authors of the memorandum wholeheartedly supported Nazimov's suggestion that the right of residence throughout Russia be granted to merchants of all guilds and to graduates of secondary and higher institutions of learning.

Finance Minister Reitern also recommended a more liberal policy toward the Jews. In a memorandum submitted to the Jewish Committee advocating the removal of the Pale, he advanced much the same reasons. The opening of the interior provinces of Russia to the Jews, he asserted, would not only benefit them but would also improve the economic condition of the non-Jewish population of the Pale. It would, moreover, be a boon to those living in the interior of Russia where there was a dearth of commercial energy and enterprise. Reitern shared the views of the ministers of the interior and education that an improvement in the legal and economic status of the Jews would raise their cultural and moral level.[12]

In 1861, Prince Vasilchikov, governor-general of Kiev, Podol, and Vohlyn, urged the central government to remove the residence

11. *Ibid.*, I, 814–815. See also J. Gessen, *Perez.*, I, 144–163.
12. J. Gessen, *Ist. Evr. Nar. Ros.*, II, 148–149.

restrictions for Jewish artisans and graduates of the special Jewish schools. Such a reform, the prince stated, would raise the prestige of education among the Jews, give their youth a wider field for activity, and encourage civic loyalty and patriotism among them.[13]

A majority of the local administrators favored opening the interior of Russia to such large portions of Jewry as would virtually have abolished the Pale. These recommendations were made by the officials in answer to an inquiry sent in 1856 by Minister of the Interior Lanskoi, who requested them to offer suggestions for merging the Jewish with the non-Jewish population, and for directing the Jews into more useful activity.[14]

Alexander remained steadfast in his decision not to grant Jews civic equality. Like his father, he had no confidence in their moral qualities. He, too, maintained that only through their "moral" improvement—which, in his opinion, could be achieved only through Russification and productive activities—would the Jews earn their civic rights. In the matter of reform, the tsar adhered to the policy he had set forth in an *ukaz* to the Jewish Committee in the second year of his reign, when he had set a limit to the extent of Jewish emancipation. That *ukaz*, issued in March, 1856, ordered officials "to revise all existing legislation regarding the Jews, so as to bring them into harmony with the general policy of merging this people with the native population, so far as the moral status of the Jews will allow it." [15] In view of Alexander's opinion of Jewish morality, this conditional clause held out little hope for the complete emancipation of his Jewish subjects.

Evidently aware of Alexander's attitude, a group of influential Jews attempted to gain at least partial civic privileges for select groups of Russian Jewry. In 1856, a group of first guild merchants headed by the prominent financier Evzel Günzburg submitted to the tsar a memorandum in which they pleaded for partial civic rights for the most useful elements of the Russian Jews. Among these they listed the rich merchants "who for many years developed the life, activities and rich resources of the country," the younger generation "trained in the spirit and under the supervision of the government," and the conscientious and qualified artisans[16] who earned their bread by the sweat of their brow. In their eagerness to obtain the desired rights for these groups, the petitioners prac-

13. *Ibid.*, II, 150.
14. History of the inquiry and the substance of the replies appear in *V. P. S. Z.*, XL, no. 42,264.
15. *Ibid.*
16. About residence privileges granted merchants and artisans, see chapter VI.

tically sanctioned the government's policy of dividing Jews into "useful" and "useless" citizens. They asked that the groups for which they pleaded be "differentiated from the other classes of Jewry who have not as yet given any evidence of their good intentions, usefulness and industry." They implored "the gracious monarch to distinguish the wheat from the chaff and, as an encouragement to good and praiseworthy activity, to bestow a number of modest privileges upon the deserving and educated among us." [17]

Count Kiselev, chairman of the Jewish Committee, was also petitioned by a Jewish group for special civic rights. Thirty-four medical students submitted to him a memorandum in which they prayed that the secret decree of Nicholas I barring Jews from government service in general, and from service in the medical department of the army in particular, be removed.[18] They were grateful for the educational opportunities the government offered them, "but," stated the petitioners, "our people judges education by its practical benefits." Through civic enfranchisement the authors of the petition hoped to bridge the chasm that separated them from their Gentile neighbors. "Having discarded the errors of our coreligionists and finding the company of our Christian colleagues and learned teachers so congenial, we find it painful to be reminded at the very outset of our career of our unfortunate origin." [19]

Russian public opinion and influential government officials, as has been pointed out, favored Jewish rights in the first period of Alexander's reign, and it was largely the emperor's determined opposition that prevented legal equality with the rest of the population. Toward the middle of the sixties, however, these elements became less friendly and the movement for Jewish emancipation consequently suffered a serious setback.

Largely responsible for this unfavorable change on the part of the press and the government was the Polish uprising in 1863, which affected adversely all national minorities in Russia. This rebellion intensified the patriotism of the Russian people and alienated those previously sympathetic to the Jewish cause. Influential Russian papers like *Kievlianin* (The Kievite), *Golos* (The Voice), and *Vilensky Vestnik* (The Vilno Messenger), which first favored civic rights for Jews, reversed their stand after the uprising.

General M. N. Muravev, who was charged with the task of crushing the Polish insurrection, was suspicious and hostile toward the Jews. In a letter to the minister of education, written in 1864,

17. J. Gessen, *Perez.*, I, 155–6. See also I. Cherikover, *Ist. Obsh. Rasp. Pros.*, p. 15.
18. Concerning privileges granted special classes see chapter VI.
19. I. Cherikover, *Ist. Obsh. Rasp. Pros.*, pp. 15–16.

Kornilov, curator of the Vilno school region, informed his superior that General Muravev found "that he could rely on one people only, on the Greek-Orthodox clergy and on the Russian administration." [20] Kornilov's own attitude to the Jews is made evident by his references to them in his correspondence. Regarding a director of a Vilno gymnasium whose dismissal he urged in a communication to the assistant minister of education, he observed: "He is undoubtedly of the Greek-Orthodox faith, he is a Russian, but for some reason he favors the Jews." [21] And in a letter to Bishop Nil, Kornilov pictures the Poles and the Jews as a greater evil for Russia than the Mongols were.[22]

This hostility seriously hampered the work of Russification, for the officials of the Northwest exhibited an antagonism which defeated the very purpose of the government program. "It is well known," observed a distinguished Russian publicist, "how vociferous our Russificators of the Northwest were about the importance of Russian education and Russian schools for Jews, and yet there are people in that region who openly boast that they flunk Jewish students on the examinations and make all sorts of difficulties for their admission into the schools." [23]

The Polish uprising also affected the policies of the Kiev and Odessa school authorities, who became hostile to all non-Russian groups.[24] The most reactionary administration was in the Vilno school region. It sponsored the Jewish convert Jacob Brafman (1825–1879) whose book, *Kniga Kagala* (The Book of the *Kahal*), was a factor contributing to anti-Jewish feeling. Brafman, who previous to his conversion had unsuccessfully tried many professions, was after baptism appointed professor of Hebrew at the Greek-Orthodox Seminary in Minsk. That his cultural attainments were rather limited is indicated by Kornilov's decision not to entrust Brafman with the teaching of general subjects. Since, however, the curator regarded the former Jew as indispensable and "irreplaceable" for the purpose of clarifying "the complex and dark Jewish question," he strongly urged Governor-General Kaufman to appoint him censor of Jewish books, or to render him financial assistance that he might proceed with his research.[25]

How Brafman's cultural deficiencies made him the butt of ridicule is told by a Jewish writer. He relates that the convert once asked

20. I. Kornilov, *Russkoe Delo v Severo-Zapadnom Krae,* p. 49.
21. *Ibid.,* p. 81.
22. *Ibid.,* p. 36.
23. B. F. Korsh, quoted in Voltke, *Sborn. Pol. Nach. Shk.,* p. 512.
24. See M. Morgulis, *Sborn. Pol. Nach. Shk.,* p. 384.
25. *Russ. Delo.,* pp. 128–129.

the famous Orientalist A. Harkavy, librarian of the Imperial Library of St. Petersburg, for some information about a "book" called *Ibid* or *Ibidem*, which "authors quote so often." Whereupon Harkavy, seizing upon this opportunity to expose the man's ignorance, asked him to sign his name on a public library slip applying for a book of that title.[26]

In 1867, Brafman published a series of articles in the *Vilensky Vestnik* entitled "Evreiskiia Bratstva v Gorodakh Zapadnoi Rossii" (Confraternities in the Cities of Western Russia). His thesis was that in every town of western Russia there existed a Jewish confraternity which sought to exploit the non-Jewish population. In 1869, the articles appeared in Vilno in book form. In the latter year he also published his *Kniga Kagala* which received wide attention in the Russian press and aroused outraged protests on the part of the Jews. The author charged that the Jews formed a state within a state, and that the Jewish state was governed by the laws of the Talmud which sought to exploit and enslave the non-Jewish populations in whose midst they lived. Brafman asserted that he based his charges on a study of a series of documents of the *Kahal* of Minsk of the years 1795–1803 which he translated from Hebrew into Russian. Students of the rabbinic seminary of Vilno who, unaware of his intentions, had assisted the author of *Kniga Kagala* in his research, published statements in Russian newspapers accusing Brafman of deliberately distorting and falsifying the text of the Hebrew records.[27] A number of Jewish publicists refuted the charges made by the Jewish renegade, pointing out that the documents were forgeries. The Jewish writer Shereshevsky called attention to the fact that a third of the transactions quoted in *Kniga Kagala* were dated on Saturdays or feastdays, when writing, according to Jewish law, is forbidden.[28]

The anti-Jewish press and the reactionary elements in the government exploited Brafman's writings. They used his "discoveries" as proof that the Jews themselves were to blame for the disabilities the government imposed upon them. "The Russificators," observes a Jewish publicist, "were quick to seize upon this 'brilliant' idea of the Jew who 'saw the light,' and acclaimed him a great patriot and journalist."[29] The interest which the government showed in *Kniga Kagala* may be seen from the fact that the second edition, issued in 1871, was published at the expense of the state.[30]

26. M. Kagan, *Perez.*, III, 140.
27. P. Marek, *Och. Ist. Pros. Evr.*, p. 205.
28. *Jew. Encyc.*, III, 346.
29. I. Orshansky, *Ev. v Ross.*, p. 192.
30. *Ev. Entsik.*, IV, 917–922, article by J. Gessen and M. Morgulis based on ma-

It is difficult to establish whether Brafman's writings in themselves were responsible for the anti-Jewish policies in the second half of Alexander's reign, or whether they but served as a pretext. The fact is that toward the end of the sixties and throughout the seventies, policies toward the Jews were fashioned by the determination to break the separatism against which Brafman warned. A visit which the tsar paid in 1870 to the Kingdom of Poland, now known as the By-Vistula region, contributed toward this determination. Repelled at the sight of the medieval attire of the Polish Jews, he ordered the administration there to revive Nicholas' prohibition against the Jewish form of dress decreed in 1850.[31]

In connection with this prohibition, the State Council soon took up the entire Jewish question, since it realized that the change in dress alone would not destroy that Jewish separatism which, according to Brafman, constituted a menace to the state. That objective, the council believed, could be achieved through weakening the social ties that held Jews together, and through attracting Jewish youth into general government schools. The members of the council were now of the opinion that the special Jewish schools had merely a temporary and transitional value for the Russification of the Jews. They believed that in the general educational institutions, where from childhood on Jews came into close contact with Christians and were subjected to the influence of Christian teachers, a thorough eradication of deep-rooted Jewish prejudices could be effected.[32]

As a result of these deliberations, a special Jewish committee for the reorganization of Jewish life was established at the Ministry of the Interior in 1871. As the first step toward the attainment of its program, the committee suggested curtailment of Jewish government schools. Since the new generation, they pointed out, was willing to attend general educational institutions, there was no need to maintain special schools. Accordingly, all Jewish government schools were closed in 1873 excepting in localities where there were no general schools.[33] The two rabbinic institutions were also closed, because it was contended that they were permeated with a spirit of Jewish "exclusiveness" [34] and were nurseries of Talmudic orthodoxy.[35] Incidentally, these seminaries had never satisfied the bulk of Jewry either, since the Jewish masses had regarded the graduates of these

terial from archives of Ministry for Public Education. On the personality of Brafman, see also A. Paperna, *Perez.*, II, 49–53.

31. Dubnow, *Hist. J. Russ. Pol.*, II, 190.
32. Gessen, *Ist. Ev. Nar. Ros.*, II, 201–203.
33. *V. P. S. Z.*, XLVIII, no. 52,020.
34. Kornilov, *Russ. Delo*, p. 168.
35. Voltke, *Sborn. Pol. Nach. Shk.*, p. 510.

schools as government functionaries charged with the mission of breaking down the stubbornness of their coreligionists.[36] These rabbinic seminaries were now transformed into normal schools for the training of Jewish teachers.[37]

A further step in attracting Jewish youth to the general schools, suggests Gessen, should have been to offer Jewish graduates opportunities in government service and the right of unrestricted residence. Such, in fact, were the recommendations which a number of high government officials made to the Jewish Committee when the projected school reform of 1873 was discussed. The ministers of finance and education urged the abolition of the Pale for the graduates of secondary schools, while two members of the committee proposed removal of all residence restrictions even for graduates of elementary schools, and the governor-general of the Southwest suggested the opening of the interior of Russia for all Jews.[38]

But the anti-Jewish sentiments which dominated upper government spheres in the seventies militated against such proposals. The view of another member of the Jewish Committee, V. Grigorev, whose opinion Gessen believes was "without a doubt" influenced by the *Kniga Kagala*, reflected the predominant sentiments of the government. Grigorev stated that "as long as the Jews remain what they are, the government cannot treat them on a footing of equality with other nationalities of the Empire. . . . The government cannot grant them unconditional residence all over Russia. Such permission should be granted to them only when the measures adopted by the government to transform them into productive and useful citizens in their present places of residence will prove successful."[39]

This spirit of reaction was also responsible for the restrictions on Jews in the municipal reforms promulgated in 1870. The change in attitude on the part of the government in the second half of Alexander's régime can clearly be seen by contrasting the *Zemstvo* (rural self-government) and judicial reforms of 1864 with the law of town government of 1870. While the two former statutes stipulated no exceptions for the Jews, so that at least juridically they were on an equal footing with the rest of the population, the latter law decreed that only a third of the town representatives could be non-Christian, and that no Jew was eligible for the post of mayor.[40]

In the matter of military service, too, discriminatory stipulations

36. M. Morgulis, *Voprosy Evr. Zhizni,* p. 170.
37. *V. P. S. Z.,* XLVIII, no. 52,020.
38. J. Gessen, *Ist. Ev. Nar. Ros.,* II, 204–205.
39. *Ibid.,* II, 205.
40. *V. P. S. Z.,* XLV, no. 48,498, paragraphs 35 and 88.

were made for Jews. On December 28, 1876, a law granted recruiting committees the authority to require police evidence to corroborate, whenever doubtful, the claim of Jewish recruits to exemption from military service for family reasons. The decree specifically stated that such corroborative testimony could be required only of Jews.[41] And on May 9, 1878, another law was issued placing the obligation of military service in the case of Jews upon the entire group. Thus, in the event of failure to fill the assigned quota of recruits, Jews who for family reasons were entitled to exemptions would be drafted to make up the deficiency.[42] In respect to jury service, too, there was discriminatory legislation. In 1877 the number of Jews eligible for such service was limited in nine western provinces containing large Jewish populations.[43]

During the last years of Alexander's reign a radical change was discernible in the attitude of the government toward Jewish education. The anti-Jewish press and some circles in the Department of Education became concerned over the large number of Jews in Russian educational institutions. In 1880, the *Novoe Vremia* (Modern Times), which had only recently changed from a liberal to a reactionary organ, published an alarming article entitled "Zhid Idet" (The Jew is Advancing). The anti-Jewish press in the provincial cities quickly followed suit in echoing this alarm.

The first to suggest a *numerus clausus* for Jewish students in Russian schools was the curator of the Odessa school region. Angered by participation of Jews in the political demonstrations of the students of the gymnasiums, he made his proposal to the emperor in person. Commenting on this suggestion the tsar observed: "And not so long ago we intended to break down the separatism of the Jews by attracting them to the Russian schools! Circumstances have changed. Now, according to your report, the number of Jews in the gymnasiums of Odessa is growing larger than that of the Christians." [44]

The unfriendly spirit toward the Jew which prevailed in upper government circles in the seventies found expression at the Congress of Berlin in 1878. At the eighth session of that international gathering held on June 28th, a memorandum submitted by the *Alliance Israelite Universelle* (a French-Jewish organization founded in 1860 for the defense of Jewish rights) was discussed. The leaders of the alliance petitioned the Congress to guarantee religious free-

41. *Ibid.,* LI, no. 56,780.
42. *Ibid.,* LIII, no. 58,490.
43. *Ibid.,* LIII, no. 57,589.
44. Posner, *Evr. Obsh. Shk.,* p. 47.

dom and civic and political equality to the Jews of Serbia, Bulgaria, Roumania, and Turkey. The representatives of all the great powers, with the exception of Russia, agreed to equalize the Jews in their civic rights with the rest of the population of the Balkan countries. In explaining his objection to the proposal, Prince Gorchakov, the Russian delegate, asked the Congress not to compare the Jews of Berlin, Paris, London, or Vienna with their coreligionists of Serbia and Roumania, or those who lived in some provinces of Russia. The former, he declared, certainly were deserving of civic and political equality, while the latter were the scourge of the native populations.[45]

Indicative of the trend of the period was the ritual murder charge brought in the obscure locality of Sacheri, in the Caucasus, against several Jews who were tried in the district court of Cutais, in 1879. This was the first case of such a nature to be tried in the new reformed courts. Because the Christian girl who was found dead showed no marks of a ritual murder—it was not even established that she was murdered—the indictment made no reference to the cause of the child's death. To cast suspicion on the defendants and give the case the character of a ritual murder, the indictment constantly emphasized that the crime occurred on the eve of the Jewish Passover, the customary time, according to the medieval legend, for ritual murders. The defendants were freed for lack of evidence, but the trial created the impression among the Russian people that the Jews were officially accused of using Christian blood for religious purposes.[46]

Russian public opinion since the Polish rebellion was not averse to believing the worst of the Jew, as had been strikingly evidenced by its reaction to the pogrom in Odessa eight years before the ritual murder case. In 1871, when for three days Jews were beaten, their homes and shops looted, and their synagogues desecrated, not the hooligans but their victims were the objects of censure. Two gymnasium teachers openly justified the actions of the mob in their classroom lectures, and prominent jurists expressed sympathy with the rioters.[47] A contemporary Jewish publicist charges that in discussing the events in Odessa, the leading Russian papers assumed such a hostile and provocative tone toward the Jews that a general crusade against them might have resulted.[48]

45. *British and Foreign State Papers,* LXIX, 946–964. Gorchakov's observation on p. 960.

46. A complete stenographic report of the court proceedings of this trial is published in *Ev. Bib.,* VII, 1–188.

47. I. Orshansky, *Ev. v Ros.,* pp. 156–158.

48. *Ev. Bib.,* III, 419.

The anti-Jewish reaction set in motion by the Polish insurrection and further inflamed by the writings of Brafman became even more intensified in the seventies. Some Jewish writers attribute the increased antisemitic sentiment of the Russian masses in those years to the growth of the Pan-Slavic sympathies which engendered a spirit of chauvinism in the years preceding the Russo-Turkish War.[49] All Jewish historians agree that the participation of Jews in the revolutionary movement in the seventies strengthened the anti-Jewish feeling of the government and the press.

Nevertheless, the policy of granting special privileges to selected groups of Jews was not abandoned even in the reactionary period of Alexander's reign. On January 30, 1867, even Jewish physicians who did not possess the academic doctoral degree were made eligible for government service in the Department of the Ministry of the Interior throughout Russia, except in the capital provinces.[50] In the same year, soldiers who completed their term of service were allowed to reside in all parts of the Empire.[51] In 1868, the government abolished the law forbidding Jews to move from the Kingdom of Poland to the Russian Pale or vice versa.[52] And in 1879, the government lifted residence restrictions for all graduates of higher institutions of learning, a privilege hitherto enjoyed only by those who received higher academic degrees.[53]

As a result of these laws, government service was opened to Jews. A number of Jewish physicians received posts in the army and many served in the Russo-Turkish War. "The military orders of that time," states an historian, "abound in such names as Grossman, Sher, Shapiro, Rabinowich, etc." [54] Between twenty and thirty Jewish jurists were engaged in the Department of Justice, occupying positions as court officials, chief secretaries, and judges.[55]

Despite the reactionary spirit of the era, until the very end of Alexander's reign, some high government officials still advocated removal of the Pale and granting of complete emancipation to the Jews. In 1880, N. A. Nekliudov, an official at the Ministry for Justice, and V. D. Karpov, an official at the Ministry of the Interior, submitted to the Jewish Committee a memorandum refuting the charge that Jews engaged in unproductive activity and exploited

49. Posner, *Evr. Obsh. Shk.*, p. 46. See also A. E. Kaufman, *Ev. Star.*, 1913, pp. 210–211.

50. *V. P. S. Z.*, XLII, no. 44,195.

51. *Ibid.*, XLII, no. 44,745.

52. *Ibid.*, XLIII, no. 46,038.

53. *Ibid.*, LIV, no. 59,236.

54. M. L. Usov, *Evrei v Armii*, p. 65.

55. G. Litovsky, *Perez.*, III, 163.

the population. They based their defense of the Jews upon reports of local administrators whose testimony they cited. It was not for the sake of the Jews alone, they stated, that they were advocating removal of the Pale, but also for the sake of the non-Jewish population therein, as well as for the development of trade and commerce in the interior of Russia.

"The unrestricted choice of a place of residence," these two officials argued, "is the natural right of every citizen, a principle recognized by every civilized country in Europe. Only the criminal is denied the exercise of that right, and that for a specified term only. Reason does not justify placing a population of several million in the same category as criminals, nay, even in a worse position than criminals, for that population is forever condemned to one and the same place." [56] A majority of the committee supported the report, but the proposals were doomed to failure because of the gathering strength of the reactionary forces and intense anti-Jewish feeling.

The Jews, however, did not give up the hope which the era of the Great Reforms had kindled. Despite Alexander's failure to grant them emancipation, they continued throughout his reign to regard him as their friend and benefactor. Nor did the reactionary relapse extinguish their hopes for the eventual triumph of their cause, in which they continued to believe as an inevitable outcome of Russian progress. Illustrative of this spirit of confidence is the following extract from an article in the Russo-Jewish weekly, *Den* (Day):

> One cannot with impunity do violence to the natural progress of events in a land where there exist railways, freedom of the press, equality before the law, and where serfdom was abolished in principle. The oppression of particular groups in such a country cannot endure—it is bound to crash. This is the order of the time against which all the barking must prove unavailing.[57]

56. Memorandum quoted in J. Gessen, *Ist. Ev. Nar. Ros.*, II, 209. Memorandum also published by Gessen under name *O Ravnopravii Evreev, Zapiska N. A. Nekliudova i V. Karpova* (About Jewish Equality, a Memorandum by N. A. Nekliudov and V. Karpov.), St. Petersburg, 1907.

57. 1869, no. 21, p. 323.

VIII

THE JEWS AND RUSSIAN PUBLIC OPINION IN THE NEW ERA

IN the reign of Alexander II the struggle for Jewish emancipation assumed new form and direction. A new Jewish intelligentsia, whose training and outlook were decidedly different from those of their predecessors of the forties, appeared on the Russian scene.

Up to the fifties of the nineteenth century, Jewish intellectuals had practically no knowledge of the Russian language or culture. The cultural language of the *Haskalah* in Russia, as in Prussia, was German. The other languages beside Yiddish which Russian Jews spoke were those of the racial groups in whose midst they lived. In Lithuania and White Russia the languages spoken were Polish, Lithuanian, and White Russian. In Courland, German was the predominant tongue, and in the Southwest, Polish and Ukrainian. In the fifties, the new type of *maskil* produced by the rabbinic seminaries and Russian universities was educated in the literature and language of Russia. Through the medium of this newly acquired tongue, the intellectuals were made aware of the spirit of liberalism that was manifesting itself in Russia and of the sympathetic attitude which the Russian press began to evince toward the Jew. "We first awakened," relates a representative of the new group of *maskilim*, "when we heard around us human voices, the voice of the Russian people speaking through the Russian press." [1] The champions of Jewish emancipation were no longer compelled to rely only upon the government for sympathy and aid; now they could state their grievances and appeal for justice to the Russian people. "The Russian Jewish intellectuals," writes a Jewish historian, "for the first time sensed a new force, the force of public opinion." [2]

It was for the purpose of influencing Russian public opinion through acquainting it with the plight and problems of the Jew that a group of Jewish leaders undertook to found a weekly in the Russian language. Odessa, chosen for the headquarters of this publication, was particularly suited to this purpose. Because of its commercial contacts with foreign countries, this southern seaport metropolis

1. L. Levanda, *Voskhod,* 1881, VI, 134.
2. Zinberg, *Ist. Ev. Pech.*, p. 38.

developed a large group of Europeanized Jews who spoke Russian. Writing in 1858, Ioakhim Tarnopol of Odessa informs us that the Jews of his city constituted a unique class in Jewry, being the first to adopt the ideas and manners of the modern Europeans who came to their shores. These Jews exercised quite an influence over their coreligionists in the surrounding provinces.[3]

In December 1856, Tarnopol, together with the novelist and journalist Osip Rabinowich, submitted an application to the curator of the Odessa school region, Nicholas Pirogov, for permission to issue a Russian-Jewish weekly to be called *Razsvet* (Dawn). The seven-point program of their policy included interpretation of government decrees, preaching of patriotism, genuine piety and morality, and dissemination of useful knowledge. The applicants expressed the hope that their organ would be of great service to the Russian Jew and that it would "assist our government in its constant and sincere efforts to improve the conditions of our people and raise its moral and cultural level." [4]

The historian Gessen doubts whether the seven points which the future editors outlined in their application completely covered the entire program they intended to follow. He believes it was due to political expediency that they omitted mention of the question of Jewish rights. He suggests that the applicants probably had hoped to escape suppression by discussing the problem of Jewish equality in a circuitous manner. From a work by Tarnopol we learn that one of the aims of the contemplated Russo-Jewish newspaper was to champion the cause of Jewish civic rights. Discussing the task of a Jewish journal, he says: "The aim of such a magazine ought to be to facilitate the self-improvement of the Jew, but at the same time to point out that such a program can succeed only with the improvement of the civic status of the Jews." [5] In his memoirs, Levanda, one of the important collaborators on *Razsvet*, asserts that the organizers of this first Russo-Jewish periodical proposed to go beyond the program for inner reforms which the old *maskilim* pursued. "We decided," he writes, "to wage a defensive and offensive fight. The defensive was to be directed against attacks from the outside, when our human or religious rights were assailed, and the offensive was to be waged against our inner enemy: bigotry, stagnation, institutional inefficiency, and corruption, as well as against our national vices, weaknesses, etc." [6]

3. Tarnopol, *Opyt. Sov.*, p. 85.
4. J. Gessen, *Perez.*, III, 40–41.
5. *Opyt. Sov.*, p. 83.
6. *Voskhod,* 1881, VI, 142.

Although Pirogov and the governor-general of the Odessa region, Count Stroganov, in notes to the central government, urged that the application be acted upon favorably, permission for the issuance of *Razsvet* was not granted for almost four years. Eradication of Jewish "fanaticism and separatism" was the purported aim of the government, yet it hesitated to allow the establishment of a Russian-Jewish organ which aimed at that very goal. The inconsistency of the government in this matter was especially evident when the Jewish Committee decided to reject the application for publication of the magazine in Russian, suggesting that it be printed either in Hebrew or in Yiddish instead. Through the persistent efforts of Pirogov, however, permission to publish *Razsvet* was finally granted, and it made its first appearance on May 27, 1860.[7]

The first articles on the Jewish question appearing in the periodical indicated its sponsorship of the struggle for Jewish civic rights. Because of rigid government censorship, this phase of the program met with disheartening obstacles and frustrations. The Jewish journalist I. Chatskin, who planned to publish a series of articles on the civic status of the Jews, informed his readers in the issue in which his second article was to have appeared, that "certain conditions" made it impossible for him to continue the subject.[8] "Certain conditions" probably referred to the local censor who, on instructions from the central government, ruled out the treatment of Jewish civic equality without special permission.[9] Number 20 of the magazine appeared without the usual editorial, the censor having suppressed it because of its reference to the Pale.[10]

Still, the aim of the paper was not completely nullified. The subject of Jewish rights was skillfully brought in through the "Survey of the Foreign Jewish Press," a feature conducted by Professor Alexander Georgievsky, a non Jewish collaborator.[11] His articles stressed the fact that in all civilized countries the Jews were marching rapidly on the road to civic equality. In his first survey, Georgievsky recorded that in Sardinia the Jews had been granted civic freedom, that in Austria many Jewish disabilities had been abolished, and that in Prussia the outlook was promising. The author

7. On the history of this first Russian-Jewish weekly, see J. Gessen, *Perez.*, III, 37–59; L. Levanda, *Voskhod,* 1881, VI; Zinberg, *Ist. Ev. Pech.*, ch. 5; S. Borovoi, *Historische Schriften,* I, 595–608.

8. No. 2, p. 23.

9. Zinberg, *Ist. Ev. Pech.*, p. 47.

10. Letter of Rabinowich to Rosenthal, *Ev. Star.*, 1911, pp. 85–87.

11. Professor Georgievsky (1830–1911), who held important posts in the Ministry of Education, was appointed to the Senate in 1898. He was an active advocate of Jewish emancipation. See *Ev. Entsik.*, VI, 338; also *Novy Entsik. Slovar,* XIII, 103–104.

admitted that occasionally a "medieval voice quavering with age" was still heard, but such a voice was powerless to disturb the general harmony. Discussing those states which had not yet conferred civic equality upon their Jewish citizens, Georgievsky attributed the failure not to Jewish unworthiness nor to popular Christian disapproval, but to "bad" governments.[12]

Razsvet was the first Jewish paper in Russia to dissociate the question of Jewish civic equality from that of self-improvement. While it preached Russification and was the first to advocate the replacement of German by Russian in the special Jewish schools, it nevertheless refused to adhere to the accepted doctrine of the *maskilim* of the forties—that Russification and Europeanization be made the condition of emancipation. This old *Haskalah* platform was also opposed by the Russian contributor Georgievsky. He asserted that, with the exception of Peter the Great who, anxious to accelerate the education of his upper classes, refused to permit them to marry until they acquired an elementary education, he knew of no instance where civic rights were contingent on the acquisition of education.[13]

In its crusade against the "inner enemy"—ghetto ways and practices—the magazine often followed the beaten path of *Haskalah*. *Razsvet*, too, spoke of the "beneficient rays of education which enlightened the minds of men," and called upon modern rabbis to impress upon their parishioners that obedience to the laws of the state was as sacred a duty as obedience to the laws of God.[14] This appeal was made in connection with an effort to enforce the Nicholas law of 1850, which had attempted to compel the Jews to replace their ghetto garb with modern dress.[15] Like the *maskilim* of former days, *Razsvet* regarded Yiddish as a distorted speech. Its writers argued that only upon replacing that jargon with Russian could the Jews of Russia, like their coreligionists of Western Europe, become a civilized people.[16]

The response of the Jewish reading public to the first Russian-Jewish paper was not encouraging. After six months of publication it had only 640 subscribers.[17] At one time the editor expressed doubt as to the possibility of carrying on much longer. However, the weekly came to a quick end because of censorship, not financial difficulties. In a letter to Levanda, Rabinowich explained that, due

12. No. 4, p. 56.
13. No. 2, p. 26.
14. No. 12, p. 184.
15. *V. P. S. Z.,* XXV, 24,127.
16. No. 13, pp. 200–201.
17. Zinberg, *Ist. Ev. Pech.,* p. 58.

to unceasing conflict with the censor, he had decided to suspend publication.[18] In the last number of *Razsvet*, issued May 19, 1861, an announcement by E. Soloveichik and Lev Pinsker stated that, because of Rabinowich's determination to give up his weekly, they would take the paper over and issue it under the name of *Sion* (Zion). In his parting words the editor of *Razsvet* charged his successors: "All for the truth, nothing for expediency. Walk, but do not falter. It is better to keep silent altogether than speak in a dual tongue."[19]

The first number of *Sion* appeared July 7, 1861, with the same motto as *Razsvet*—"Let there be light!" It was marked "second year," thereby stressing the fact that it was a continuation of the previous publication. To avoid conflicts with the censor, the new Russian-Jewish paper limited its journalistic activity and devoted more attention to works of historic and scientific content. In an editorial explaining the change of policy, the editors expressed the view that in dealing with the problem of civic equality for Jews "the straight line is not always the shortest." It was their opinion that no arguments or complaints, no matter how justified, could cause a sudden change in attitude toward the Jews. All they hoped to accomplish was to modify that attitude somewhat through acquainting the Russian public with the literature, history, and conditions of Jewish life.[20] Though it curtailed its journalistic activity, *Sion* promised nevertheless to defend the Jews from unjust attacks and accusations.

But the academic nature of the magazine did not save it from the grip of the censor. Its refutation of charges made against the Jews by unfriendly papers soon involved it in difficulties. In the forty-third number of *Sion*, the editors announced that because they were constantly impeded in their attempt to disprove groundless accusations against the Jewish religion and thus were prevented from presenting Judaism in its true light, they regarded it as their duty to terminate publication until they could obtain permission to issue a paper with a wider program. Such permission, however, was not forthcoming, so that for seven years there was no Russian-Jewish press in Russia.

Yet even during this period Russian Jewry did not remain without an organ for public expression. For the early sixties, when *Razsvet* and *Sion* had appeared, also saw the birth of the Hebrew and Yiddish press in Russia. One of these periodicals was the Hebrew

18. Letter published by Gessen in *Perez.*, III, 56–58.
19. No. 52, p. 827.
20. No. 1, p. 3.

weekly *Ha-Meliz* which came into existence in 1860 in Odessa under the editorship of Alexander Zederbaum (1816–1893) and Dr. Aaron Goldenblum (1827–1913). The latter, born and educated in Prussia, was in charge of the German supplement which the paper issued.

From the point of view of content and style, *Ha-Meliz* was typical of the old *Haskalah* school. Education and patriotism were the dominant topics of editorial discussions and correspondents' contributions. The very name of the weekly and the subtitle it carried, "The Mediator between the Jewish People and the Government, between Religion and Education," aptly described its character. In his first article, "Der Zeitgeist und das Judentum," Dr. Goldenblum pleaded with his readers to manifest loyalty to the state because of the friendlier attitude the world was now manifesting toward the Jews. In a like vein, the Hebrew editor constantly urged his coreligionists to demonstrate their usefulness to the state.[21]

The literary quality of the publication during its first years was rather low, as was also the standard of its scientific discourses. This weekly reflected the undeveloped style and immaturity of the Hebrew literature of the period. So limited was its appeal that in its fourth year it had less than a thousand subscribers.[22]

Another Hebrew weekly, *Ha-Carmel*, which appeared in Vilno in 1860, was typically *Haskalah* both in style and program. Edited by the historian and *maskil* S. I. Fuenn, it had both a German and a Russian supplement. From the point of view of current interest and political maturity, it was even inferior to *Ha-Meliz*. The fact that this new Hebrew paper was not much superior to the *Pirhe Zafon* of 1844, which had been edited and prepared by practically the same group of writers, indicates that these had made no advance in the ensuing fourteen or fifteen years. Levanda aptly characterized the intellectuals who comprised the personnel of the Hebrew publications in the early sixties: "Trained in the traditions of the Mendelssohn school of the end of the eighteenth century, these intellectuals were a vague, international, neither Jewish nor German group, notable for superficial dilettantism and academic rationalism. Clinging to a philosophy and to points of view which the West had long abandoned, they constituted an anachronism which made them entirely unfit for the life of their times." [23]

The two short-lived Russian-Jewish weeklies, on the other hand, were edited by the new type of Russian-Jewish intellectual, a prod-

21. Editorials in nos. 2, 3, 9, 15, etc., 1860.
22. L. Rosenthal, *Toldot Hebrat Marbe Haskalah Be-Yisrael.*, I, 11.
23. *Voskhod,* 1881, VI, 136–137.

uct of the culture of nineteenth-century Russia. This modern Jewish intellectual regarded himself not only as a subject of the Russian government, but also as a member of the Russian people. Typical of the new Jewish intelligentsia was the editor of *Razsvet,* Osip Rabinowich (1817–1869). Born in the province of Poltava, Rabinowich received a secular education in addition to the customary religious training. His first literary contribution appeared in the Russian *Odessky Vestnik* (Odessa Messenger). In that article he criticized certain religious practices which he believed required modification. He also contributed to a Russian magazine, *Literaturnye Vechera* (Literary Evenings), published in Odessa from time to time by a group of Russian writers. His popularity increased and his reputation as a writer was established when, in 1859, the prominent Russian magazine *Russky Vestnik* published his *Shtrafnoi* (The Penalized), a short novel dealing with Jewish life under the Nicholas régime. The story made a profound impression not only on Jewish but on non-Jewish readers as well. Popular legend had it that Rabinowich's story was a contributing factor in the abolition of the cantonist system. So much importance was attached to the book that in the homes of some educated Jews, the *Hagadah*[24] was replaced by the *Shtrafnoi* on Passover nights. "In Rabinowich," says his biographer, "the Russian Jews had their best representative. He was the first to employ the Russian language in championing the rights of his people. Through his journalistic writings he exercised a beneficent influence upon his coreligionists, awakening in them their spiritual strength." [25]

The author of *Shtrafnoi* used his literary gifts in fighting not only the external enemies of the Jew but also his people's own failings. In answer to criticism leveled against an article in the first number of *Razsvet* in which Levanda had pointed out some undesirable aspects of Jewish life, the editor stated: "If we are to succeed in rendering a public service, we must expose all sick areas, no matter how painful the removal of the bandages may be. . . . Our motto is —light. Our goal is—progress. Our reward—the consciousness of duty well done." [26] Rabinowich disagreed with those who maintained that it was not advisable to discuss publicly Jewish faults which were the result of conditions over which the Jews had no control. "We have no more to fear from the exposure of our weaknesses than any other people," he asserted. "Through self-knowledge alone will we earn the respect of others." [27]

24. The story of Israel's slavery and redemption from Egypt.
25. J. Gessen, *Gallereia Evreiskikh Deiatelei,* pp. 39, 70–71.
26. *Razsvet,* no. 3, pp. 36–7.
27. No. 6, pp. 84–85.

Another outstanding writer, representative of the new type of Jewish intellectual, was the novelist and publicist Lev Levanda (1835–1888) whose name has frequently been mentioned here. Born in Minsk, Levanda studied in the rabbinical school of Vilno and upon graduation was appointed instructor in the government school of his native town. He also held the office of the "Learned Jew" (expert on Jewish affairs) at the office of the governor-general of Vilno. He wrote for many Russian and Russo-Jewish newspapers and periodicals and was at one time editor of *Vilenskiia Gubernskiia Vedomosti* (Vilno Province News). Most of Levanda's writings are of Jewish content. His best known novels are *Goriachee Vremia* (Feverish Age) and *Ocherki Proshlago* (Sketches from the Past).

During the entire reign of Alexander II, this novelist preached Russification as the best solution to the Jewish problem.[28] For the purpose of making this message effective among the masses of Russian Jewry, he favored the plan of founding a Russo-Jewish organ. During the existence of *Razsvet* he was Rabinowich's closest collaborator, charged with the special task of conducting the campaign for Jewish self-improvement. In line with this program, he wrote articles and sketches of Jewish life in which he exposed Jewish faults and weaknesses.

It was on the question of whether the weekly should deal publicly with Jewish failings that the founders of the paper clashed. Because of his opposition to this policy, Tarnopol resigned from the editorship of *Razsvet*.[29]

Ioakhim Tarnopol (1810–1900), whose birthplace was Odessa, was a cultured Jew who even in the forties did not share the prevalent view that acquisition of secular knowledge would solve the Jewish problem. In a memorandum submitted to the assistant minister of education, he stated that while the Jews took to heart the demands of the "enlightened times," they could not remain silent about their needs and just demands.[30] Tarnopol wrote a series of articles and essays dealing with the Jewish question, some of which appeared in the *Russky Invalid*. In 1855 he published a book in French advocating reforms in the Jewish religion, and urging emancipation of the Jews on humanitarian as well as utilitarian grounds. Later he translated part of the volume into Russian under the title *Opyt Sovremennoi i Osmotritelnoi Refromy v Oblasti Iudaisma* (An Essay on the Contemporary Reform of Judaism).

28. After the pogroms of 1881, Levanda lost his faith in assimilation and was converted to the ideal of Zionism.
29. Beginning with no. 20 Rabinowich was the only editor of *Razsvet*.
30. *Ev. Entsik.*, XIV, 762.

Tarnopol, a wealthy merchant who engaged in writing as an avocation, was representative of a new element which, beginning with the later fifties, assumed a leading rôle in the struggle for Jewish rights. This new group consisted of rich and cultured Jewish capitalists who had acquired their wealth as railway builders, contractors, and financiers during the initial stages of the industrialization of Russia. Many of them, taking advantage of the law which granted first-guild merchants unrestricted residence rights, made the capital their temporary or permanent headquarters. Thus Petersburg became the center of a Jewish financial class which in the reign of Alexander II played an important rôle in the history of Russian Jewry.

To accelerate the diffusion of culture among Russian Jews and thus facilitate acquisition of civic rights, a group of these wealthy Jews decided to organize a society for that purpose. In his history of the "Society for the Promotion of Culture among Jews," Leon Rosenthal (1817–1887), its first treasurer, gives us the chief reason for the founding of the organization. "Whenever Jewish leaders broached the question of civic rights to government representatives," he writes, "the latter countered by charging them with the task of educating the masses of Jewry." [31]

The society which had its central office in St. Petersburg, started to function on December 18, 1863. The organization was under the supervision of the Ministry of Education, and admitted to membership persons of both sexes without distinction of faith. The charter members were representatives of the upper Jewish bourgeoisie, most of whom lived in the capital. Evzel Günzburg, prominent financier and Jewish leader, was chosen president. Among outstanding representatives of the liberal Russian press who accepted honorary membership were A. Kraevsky, editor of *Golos* (The Voice) and *Otechestvennyia Zapiski* (Fatherland Notes), P. Usov, editor of *Severnaia Pochta* (The Northern Post), and I. V. Vernadsky, editor of *Economist.*[32] In accepting membership in the society, most of these leaders of Russian thought stated that they regarded the work of the new organization as a preparation for Jewish emancipation.[33]

The Society for the Promotion of Culture among Jews adopted a three-point program of activity: to promote knowledge of the Russian language among the Jews, to subsidize poor Jewish students in the general schools, and to publish books on useful knowledge. The

31. L. Rosenthal, *Toldot Heb. Mar.*, Preface, p. VII.
32. Cherikover, *Ist. Obsh. Ras. Pros.*, pp. 45–46.
33. *Ibid.*, p. 53.

society undertook to encourage Jewish writers by paying them honorariums and by publishing their works.

As its first activity the organization decided to issue a literary-scientific journal in Russian containing studies by Jewish scholars on various aspects of Judaism. Outstanding Russian-Jewish scholars and writers, Professor Daniel Khvolson and Albert Harkavy among them, prepared articles for the publication. Because of censorship difficulties, however, the volume, completed in 1864, did not appear until 1868. Unable to cope with censorship, the society abandoned the idea of issuing annual publications.

It was also because of censorship impediments that plans for translation of the Bible into Russian did not materialize in the first years of the society's existence. The suggestion made by Professor Khvolson as early as 1864 to publish such a translation received the enthusiastic approval of Jewish writers and leaders.[34] The Jewish intelligentsia believed that just as Mendelssohn's rendition of the Pentateuch into German had promoted the knowledge of the German language among the Jews of Prussia, so would a translation of the Scriptures into Russian accelerate the diffusion of that language among Russian Jewry. It was this point that the society stressed in its application for permission to issue a Hebrew edition of the Bible accompanied by a Russian translation. "It is not sufficient," the applicants wrote, "to teach the Russian language in the special Jewish schools. We have to open a path for that speech into the Jewish home. Because Jews read the Scriptures each Sabbath and on festivals, they would through such a translation quickly acquire the Russian tongue." The application was denied.[35]

The reason for the denial is probably to be found in the fact that up to 1869 no official translation of the Old Testament existed in the Russian language. A rendition into the Church Slavonic language was the only one permitted in Russia. After the official Church translation of the Bible into Russian was completed and its use sanctioned by the Holy Synod, the society was granted the permission it sought. In 1871, it was given the right to use the translation of the Pentateuch which L. I. Mandelstam had published in Berlin in 1862 for the benefit of Russian Jews. Before Mandelstam's translation was adopted, a heated controversy raged over a suggestion made by Professor Khvolson. This converted Jewish scholar had participated in the preparation of the Church Bible, and he recommended that the same translation be used for the society's

34. *Ibid.*, p. 95.
35. *Ibid.*, p. 96.

purposes. His proposal was rejected in favor of Mandelstam's translation especially made for Jews.

In 1875, the society issued another translation of the five books of Moses, prepared by the Hebrew poet L. O. Gordon in collaboration with I. S. Gerstein, who occupied the post of "Learned Jew" at the office of the governor-general of Vilno. Four thousand copies of this edition were sold in Russia.[36]

In the early sixties, leading Jewish intellectuals proposed the translation of the Hebrew prayers into Russian, but here again government impediments delayed action for almost ten years. When permission was finally granted, a series of translations of the Jewish liturgy into Russian appeared, and the government—most likely in keeping with the new policy of Russification—encouraged their distribution. Thus the governor-general of Vilno instructed local authorities to assist in spreading the prayer book which the Rabbi of Grodno, O. Gurwich, had rendered into Russian.[37] In the early seventies there were also published Russian translations of the Passover *Hagadah*, of the prayer book for the High Holy Days, and of the Psalms, all subsidized by the society.[38]

One of the most important publications of the society was *Mirovozreniia Talmudistov* (The Philosophy of the Talmudists), of which the first volume appeared in 1874 and the second and third two years later. This work, undertaken at the suggestion of Professor Khvolson, was first written in Hebrew and later rendered into Russian by L. Levanda and L. O. Gordon. It contained the substance of the ethical and religious teachings of the Jewish authorities of Talmudic and post-Talmudic periods.

These books were published with a view to refuting the charges made against the Talmud in the anti-Jewish press and in *Kniga Kagala* of Brafman. "The purpose of this work," wrote the society to a Talmudic scholar whose services it solicited, "is to acquaint Russia with the lofty ethical teachings hidden in our thirty centuries old literature." [39] Brafman greeted the appearance of the Talmudic publication with an attack in the Russian *Golos* on the publishers and their work. The poet Gordon's reply in the same paper called forth an even more denunciatory article from the author of *Kniga Kagala* and a sharp editorial by the newspaper itself which bristled with insinuations against the society.[40]

36. *Ibid.*, pp. 100–101.
37. *Ibid.*, p. 102.
38. *Ibid.*, p. 102.
39. *Toldot Heb. Mar.*, II, 48.
40. I. Cherikover, *Ist. Obsh. Ras. Pros.*, p. 94.

The activities of the society were not limited to the publication of books of Jewish content in the Russian language. In its attempt to cultivate the taste of the masses, a good part of which was able to read Hebrew literature, it subsidized Hebrew writers and their works. In spite of its dislike for Yiddish, the society made a financial grant to the first Yiddish newspaper *Kol Mebasser* (The Herald), which appeared in October, 1862, as a supplement to *Ha-Meliz.* In offering the subsidy, however, it stipulated that the paper "should seek through a gradual refinement of the vulgar jargon to evolve a simple German as its medium of expression." Probably out of fear of losing his readers, who did not understand German, Editor Zederbaum did not change the style of his paper and the subsidy was withdrawn the following year.[41]

There were elements among the intelligentsia of the sixties and seventies who considered Hebrew as well as Yiddish objectionable. Representative of this viewpoint was the Russian Hebrew weekly *Den* which thus voiced its impatience with the literary policies of Zederbaum. "At a time when all the organs of the Russian Jews have been striving to replace the repulsive jargon which is the current speech of the Jews by a correct Russian, Mr. Zederbaum continues to express himself in his publication not only in Hebrew, but in a monstrous jargon which even Jews cannot understand." [42]

Den had come into existence in Odessa in 1869. Sponsored by the local branch of the Society for the Promotion of Culture among Jews, organized two years before, it preached complete Russification and fusion with the Russian people. Its writers reflected the ideology of the leaders of the Odessa branch of the society, who regarded as their main task "the acquisition of Russian for the Jew as a national language." [43]

In its Russification program *Den* went much further than its predecessors, *Razsvet* and *Sion.* While these two supported the special Jewish schools, *Den* insisted that Jews must get their education with the rest of the population in general schools.[44] All special institutions which made for the perpetuation of Jewish separatism were frowned upon. Only religion, *Den* asserted, distinguished the Jew from the Russian people. Complete fusion with the native and dominant population was the one and only Messiah to whose arrival the "best and most enlightened portion of Russian Jewry" was looking forward with feverish anticipation. The only

41. *Ibid.,* p. 121.
42. 1870, editorial of no. 47.
43. Cherikover, *Ist. Obsh. Ras. Pros.,* p. 239.
44. *Den,* 1869, p. 133.

impediment to the coming of the "Messiah," as *Den* saw it, lay in the legal disabilities which set the Jew apart from the Russian people.[45]

In their campaign for civic equality, the writers pointed to the practical advantages that Russia would gain from the Jew's civic emancipation. They contended that the changed economy brought about by the liberation of the serfs and the inauguration of the new industrial era required fresh energy and commercial enterprise. The Jewish merchants, they maintained, could be just as useful to Russia as the Jewish artisans, and should, therefore, be given the same right of residence all over Russia.[46]

Den also saw in the Jew the most effective medium for the Russification of the various racial groups inhabiting the border regions of Russia. This idea was advanced by I. G. Orshansky, the ablest publicist of the paper and one of the most brilliant Jewish scholars and writers of the period. In a series of articles on the "Question of the Russification of the Jews," he emphasized the importance for Russia of the Russification of all its foreign nationalities and their complete absorption by the dominant population. The achievement of this end, however, Orshansky contended, could not be brought about by "a system of legal disabilities, discriminatory exceptions and privileges," but rather "through a fair and equal treatment of all." The writer pointed out that as a result of the liberal policies of the government, even before it embarked upon the Russification policies, the Jews were the first to regard themselves as Russians both in nationality and in citizenship.[47]

Writers for *Den* were confident that civic equalization of the Jews was at hand. They even spoke of a date when that long-awaited ideal was to be realized.[48] But instead of the expected emancipation, there occurred in Odessa the pogrom of 1871, as a result of which this Russo-Jewish weekly came to an abrupt end. For not only was Orshansky's indignant editorial on the riots suppressed, but even a description of the events was forbidden to the paper.[49] Hampered in its attempt to refute arguments of the anti-Jewish press as to the cause of the Odessa pogrom, *Den* suspended its publication on June 8, 1871.

Short-lived though these Russian-Jewish publications were, they served during the brief span of their existence to bring to the fore personalities who made a permanent impress on Jewish, and, in some cases, also on Russian life. One such personality was the aforemen-

45. *Ibid.,* 1869, no. 10, p. 151.
46. *Ibid.,* 1870, no. 50, p. 817.
47. *Ibid.,* 1870, no. 13, p. 219.
48. 1870, no. 52, p. 851.
49. 1871, no. 16, p. 234.

tioned I. G. Orshansky (1846–1875), chief collaborator on *Den*. A native of Ekaterinoslav, Orshansky studied law in the universities of Kharkov and Odessa. The latter university offered him a post on its faculty on the condition that he embrace Christianity but he declined the offer. The first literary efforts of Orshansky, who was also a student of the Talmud and Jewish philosophy, appeared in the volume of essays issued in 1866 by the Society for the Promotion of Culture among Jews. During his student years in the University of New Russia, in Odessa, he was a contributor to the Russian press there and to the Hebrew *Ha-Meliz*. After the suppression of *Den*, he went to St. Petersburg, where he wrote for *Novoe Vremia*.

In his two volumes on the Russian Jews, Orshansky deals with the social, economic, and legal aspects of the Jewish problem. His *Evrei v Rossii* (The Jews in Russia) is rich in factual material and gives a comprehensive account of Jewish conditions. His *Russkoe Zakonodatelstvo o Evreiakh* (Russian Legislation about Jews) presents a keen analysis of the legal status of Russian Jewry with an interpretation of the causes responsible for Jewish legislation. This work, described by Gessen as "excellent in every respect," was regarded as a notable contribution both in Russia and abroad. The famous French scholar, Leroy-Beaulieu, who read the book in manuscript, refers to it in his works.[50]

Besides books and articles on Jewish problems, Orshansky also wrote on various aspects of Russian law. He contributed to *Sudebny Vestnik* (Court Messenger), to *Zhurnal Grazhdanskago i Ugolovnago Prava* (Journal of Civil and Criminal Law), and wrote a number of legal theses which earned for him the reputation of a learned jurist. The Russian legal scholar, S. A. Muromtsev, considers Orshansky's *Izsledovaniia po Russkomu Pravu Semeinomu i Nasledstvennomu* (Studies of the Russian Law of Family and Heredity) one of the best contributions to the legal literature of Russia.[51]

In tribute to the memory of a man who was regarded by Russian Jewry as one of its outstanding champions, a memorial, modeled by the famous Russian-Jewish sculptor Antokolsky, was erected on Orshansky's grave in Ekaterinoslav fifteen years after his untimely death.

Another important publication subsidized by the Society for the Promotion of Culture among Jews was *Evreiskaia Biblioteka* (The Jewish Library). This annual, first issued in St. Petersburg in 1871 by the journalist Adolph Landau (1841–1902), was practically the

50. Gessen, *Gal. Ev. Deiat.*, p. 109.
51. *Ibid.*, pp. 149–150.

only Russo-Jewish organ functioning throughout the seventies. Its purpose, as stated by the editor, was "to acquaint the Russian public with the nature of the Jewish past, its present, and with what the Jews could become under more favorable conditions." [52] As an annual the *Evreiskaia Biblioteka,* whose scholarly articles on Jewish history and Judaism were of high quality, could not give much space to current problems. It recorded only the most important events of Jewish interest and contested anti-Jewish attacks that had appeared in the Russian press. This publication met with an encouraging response, the first volume attaining a sale of 2,600.[53]

Among the prominent writers and scholars who contributed to *Evreiskaia Biblioteka* were Orshansky, Levanda, and Michael Morgulis (1837–1913). The last named was a recognized legal authority on Jewish affairs as well as author of numerous essays on the Jews of Russia. His outstanding contribution to Landau's periodical was a series of articles dealing with the history of secular education of Russian Jewry. It was in this publication, too, that Levanda's novel *Goriachee Vremia* first saw the light of day.

A number of important Gentile Russian writers and scholars, sympathetic to the Jewish cause, also wrote for the magazine. One of these, the noted art critic, V. Stasov, was an ardent defender both of Jewish rights and of Jewish talent. He rejected the assertion that Jews lacked artistic creativity, stating that only fools and ignorant people could repeat such nonsense.[54] In his defense of Jewish rights he went further than most Jewish leaders of his day. Whereas the latter in their aspirations for civic equality for the Jew urged the submergence of his national identity, Stasov insisted that Jews were entitled to both civic rights and the right of Jewish national self-expression as well. He contended that the Jew could best express his talent through the medium of his own national heritage, and he scored those Jewish artists who, as he put it, were "jumping from their skins" in an effort to run away from themselves as Jews.[55]

In the last two years of Alexander's reign two more Russo-Jewish weeklies, *Razsvet* [56] and *Russky Evrei* (The Russian Jew) were issued in St. Petersburg. *Razsvet,* which first appeared September 13, 1879, under the editorship of M. Kulisher, adopted a program similar to that of *Den* of Odessa. In an article outlining his editorial policy, Kulisher stated that it was the duty of the Jewish Intelligentsia to work for the redemption of Russian Jewry not alone

52. Preface to Volume II.
53. Zinberg, *Ist. Ev. Pech.,* p. 187.
54. *Ev. Bib.,* II, 463.
55. *Ibid.,* VII, 273–278.
56. Not to be confused with the Odessa *Razsvet* of 1860.

for the sake of the Jews, but for the sake of Russia as well. By devoting their time to the needs of the Jews of Russia, the Jewish intellectuals, far from separating themselves from Russian citizenry, the editorial maintained, were performing their duty as Russian citizens.[57]

The contention that Jews were seeking to solve the Jewish problem as Russian citizens and not as Jews was also put forth by Isaac Orshansky (a brother of I. G. Orshansky). In an article entitled "Is There a Jewish Question?",[58] the author expressed disagreement with Russian publicists who suggested that the only function of *Razsvet* should be defending the special interests of Jews. In support of his argument that no special Jewish aspirations were involved in the Jewish struggle for human rights, he compared the demands of the Finns and natives of the Baltic provinces with those of the Jews. The former were aspiring after the status of a distinctively civic, political, and cultural entity; the Jews, on the other hand, were seeking only to put an end to their own distinctiveness. He summed up the fundamental difference between the Jewish and any other national problem in Russia as follows: while the aim of every other nationality constituting a problem in Russia was to perpetuate itself as a distinctive entity, the Jewish problem was to destroy the causes which made for perpetuation of the Jews as a separate group.[59] Even in the midst of the gathering storm of reaction which clouded the last years of Alexander's reign, *Razsvet* still held on to its faith in assimilation, declaring that "redemption of the Jews lies in their assimilation with the peoples among whom they live."[60]

The outstanding figure of *Razsvet* was its acting editor, the ethnologist, jurist, and historian, M. Kulisher (1847–1919). Born in Vohlyn, he received his early training in the rabbinic school of Zhitomir. Soon after his graduation from the University of St. Petersburg, he was appointed assistant district attorney in that city. Before long he gave up his legal practice and devoted himself to writing. A prolific writer, he contributed to numerous Russian and German newspapers and magazines, and in the course of his literary career served as editor of *Pravda* (Truth) in Odessa and *Zaria* (Dawn) in Kiev. *Zaria* was established for the purpose of defending Poles, Ukrainians, and Jews against the attacks of the newspaper *Kievlianin*.

57. No. 1, p. 4.
58. *Razsvet,* 1879, nos. 2 and 3.
59. *Razsvet,* 1879, no. 3, p. 107.
60. 1880, p. 403.

As an historian, Kulisher was primarily interested in tracing the relations of the world to the Jew. His thesis was that economic interests shaped the policies which governments adopted toward them. His ethnological studies led him to the conclusion that the ill treatment of the Jew was also attributable to the remnant of barbarism left from jungle days.[61]

The group of able writers who collaborated in *Razsvet* made it a live and interesting paper. Its contemporary, *Russky Evrei*, on the other hand, was a rather colorless product. "*While Razsvet*," observes Zinberg, "held its readers by its pathos and youthful energy, *Russky Evrei* completely lacked temperament and passion." [62] Of the latter's two editors, one was devoid of literary ability and the other of sufficient knowledge of Russian. The literary character of the paper was somewhat improved when Dr. Judah Leb Kantor (1849–1915) assumed its editorship toward the end of 1879. Dr. Kantor, at that time a teacher in a Petersburg gymnasium and subsequently government rabbi of Libau, was a gifted journalist both in Russian and Hebrew. But even he failed to give this weekly more vitality or color. *Russky Evrei* engaged a great deal in apologetics, refuting the charge that the Jews contributed disproportionately large numbers to the ranks of the Russian revolutionaries. In its philosophy of Russification and Jewish nationalism, however, it was rather vague and not entirely consistent.

In summary, the literary quality and the scientific standards of the Russo-Jewish press in the régime of Alexander II were on the whole high, reflecting the remarkable cultural progress which had been effected in a short span of time. Although it achieved little in the struggle for civic rights, this press did succeed in bringing the Jewish problem to the notice of Russian public opinion, and in serving as a medium for the expression of Russian sentiments sympathetic to the Jewish cause.

These publications also were undoubtedly a contributing factor to the significant growth of education during the period. For while they differed on the philosophy of Russification, some advocating partial and others complete assimilation, they were unanimous in their propaganda for secular education. How effective this propaganda was may be inferred from a comparison of the percentages of Jewish students in the Russian schools between the years 1865 and 1881. In 1865 Jewish students in all Russian universities comprised 3.2 per cent of the total number; in 1881 this figure rose to

61. *Ev. Entsik.*, IX, 903–904. Kulisher's studies were noted by the anthropologist Edward B. Tylor and are quoted by American and European scholars.

62. Zinberg, *Ist. Ev. Pech.*, pp. 246–247.

8.8 per cent. In the school region of Vilno, which in the days of Nicholas I offered greatest resistance to secular education, the percentage of Jews in all the gymnasiums and pre-gymnasiums increased from 6.9 in 1865 to 26.7 in 1881.[63]

It should, of course, be borne in mind that this phenomenal progress in Jewish responsiveness to propaganda for education was primarily due to the confidence the reforms of Alexander II inspired. It was this encouragement from the government, combined with the exhortations of the Jewish press, that produced a new generation of Jews who regarded themselves no longer merely as subjects of the Russian government but as part and parcel of Russian culture and the Russian people.

63. S. Posner, *Evr. Obsh. Shk.,* Supplements 54, 58. For figures of Jewish students in Russian educational institutions in reign of Alexander II see also *Ev. Entsik.,* XIII, 61–62.

IX

TRENDS TOWARD ASSIMILATION

THE contact with the outside world which caused a revolution in the mental and spiritual outlook of the Russian Jew affected his attitude not only to Jewish education but also to the Jewish religion. In Prussia, the struggle to emerge from the ghetto resulted in the formation of a religious reform movement which reinterpreted religious doctrine and modernized the divine service to make it more adaptable to the conditions of the time and environment. One of the innovations in the reform service was the introduction of the sermon in the German language. Another consisted in the adoption of a revised and abridged prayer book in which the omission of prayers for the restoration of Zion constituted the most radical change. The hope of returning to Palestine, cherished by Israel for centuries, was relinquished as evidence that the Jews had no other aspirations save that of being citizens of their respective countries.[1]

Emulating the example of their coreligionists, the *maskilim* in Russia, too, began to sponsor religious reforms. Back in the forties, a few feeble voices had been raised advocating changes in the practice of the Jewish religion. Because of their small number and the insignificant influence they exercised on the Jewish masses, intellectuals of those days did not dare to preach vital changes. All that M. A. Günzburg, outstanding writer of the period, ventured to suggest was that the traditional gabardine be discarded in favor of modern German garb. It was his opinion that the difference in dress was responsible for the barrier that existed between the Jewish and Christian populations.[2]

In the fifties, Tarnopol, writing in Odessa, where orthodoxy was never strongly entrenched, advocated religious changes modeled on the Western European style.[3] He suggested that religious customs and rites not in harmony with an emancipated people be eliminated.[4] He also advised his Russian brethren to follow the example of their coreligionists in Western Europe, where a Jew could be recognized

1. On the reform movement see *Jew. Fncyc.,* X, 347–351; D. Philipson, *The Reform Movement in Judaism.*
2. *Leket Amarim,* pp. 89–91.
3. *Opyt. Sov.,* pp. 34–35.
4. *Ibid.,* Preface, pp. x, xxvii.

as such only in the synagogue, while outside of it he was "of one heart and one spirit with his Christian brother." [5]

In the sixties and the seventies, as a result of the movement for Russification, the demand for religious reforms became more vocal and insistent. The *maskilim* contended that traditional Judaism, which regulated every act of the Jew's daily existence—including dress and diet—fostered a social as well as a spiritual separatism which stood in the way of Russification. In order to bridge the gulf which separated the Jews from the Russian people, the *maskilim* considered it of utmost importance to make such changes in Judaism as would eliminate its peculiarly distinctive features. The advice of the poet Gordon, "Be a Jew in your tent, and a man in the street," became the slogan of the *Haskalah*.

Outstanding champion of religious reforms in the sixties was Moses Leb Lilienblum (1843–1910). A native of Kaidan, near Kovno, he received the customary education of his day in Bible and Talmud. In his early youth he became acquainted with medieval Jewish philosophy and *Haskalah* literature. These writings had a profound effect on his religious outlook. He made his first demand for religious reforms in a series of articles called "Orhot Ha-Talmud" (The Ways of the Talmud), published in *Ha-Meliz*.[6] His thesis was that the Talmudic authorities did not view Judaism as a static religion incapable of change or reinterpretation. He maintained that the Talmud was permeated with the spirit of reform and that in their religious legislation the Talmudic rabbis sought to suit their new enactments to the spirit and needs of the times. The author of "Orhot Ha-Talmud" appealed to religious leaders of his day to exercise their authority as interpreters of the law, and ease the rigorous practices which encumbered modern Jewish life. "I plead with you, leaders of the people, accept the voice of one who loves his people and his faith." [7]

Because the rabbis failed to respond to his appeal, Lilienblum published an additional series of four articles[8] entitled "Nosofot" (Supplements) in which he assumed a more belligerent tone, challenging the spiritual leaders to refute his arguments. This time the representatives of orthodox Jewry responded with a severe attack on the religious reformer, branding him as an atheist. As was to be expected, the rabbis were not induced to reverse religious policies of generations by the arguments of some unknown young author.

5. *Ibid.*, p. XIII.
6. 1868, nos. 13–29.
7. 1868, no. 29, p. 217.
8. *Ha-Meliz,* 1869, nos. 8–12.

But in spite of Lilienblum's failure to effect a change in the attitude of the religious authorities of his day, his "Orhot Ha-Talmud" may be regarded as a significant contribution to modern Judaism. "It is valuable," says a modern Jewish writer, "because it enunciates, probably for the first time in Hebrew literature, the view of Judaism as a historical growth, in contradistinction to the view that Judaism is a petrified system, serenely indifferent to all possible changes in the conditions of life and ways of thinking of the outside world." [9]

The attacks of the champions of orthodoxy did not dampen the reformer's spirit; they only spurred him on to a more aggressive stand. Having removed to Odessa, he felt freer to advocate his cause in a more outspoken manner. To his support came the Hebrew poet Leon Gordon (1831–1892), who in a number of satirical poems ridiculed the rabbis for clinging to obsolete interpretations of Jewish law and for failure to take cognizance of the changed circumstances and needs of the masses. His poem "Barburim Abusim" (Fatted Fowl) is typical of the biting sarcasm with which this battler for religious reforms attacked the rabbis for their backwardness and pedantry. A poor woman comes to a rabbi to inquire whether the fowl she slaughtered for Passover are *kosher*. The rabbi declares both birds *tref* (ritually unfit to eat) because of some doubtful ritualistic imperfection. The poet concludes the poem with these satiric words: "You must not despair, poor woman! Jews are charitable! You can support yourself by begging!" [10]

"Kozo Shel Yud" (The Dot on the I) is another poem in which he criticizes religious leaders for dogmatic and rigorous interpretation of Jewish laws. In this case a woman is condemned to eternal loneliness because in the divorce which she obtained from her first husband his name was spelled without the necessary *Yud* (a letter of the Hebrew alphabet corresponding to the English *i* or *j*). The poet pours out his venom on the rabbi, branding him a heartless creature—"Rabbi Wofsi's was a Tartar soul indeed"—and summarizes the tragedy of the woman in the line "A letter's dot has proven my ruin." [11]

For all his denunciations of the spiritual leaders, Gordon protested that he was not an iconoclast bent on annihilating the faith of the Jews. In a letter to a friend he stated: "I do not believe in destroying all memories of the past with which the life of our people is bound up. . . . I seek the golden mean to unite pure faith with reason and the needs of the time." [12]

9. Leon Simon, *Moses Leb Lilienblum,* p. 9.
10. *Kol Shire Yehudah Leb Gordon,* IV, 157, 160.
11. *Ibid.,* pp. 5–43.
12. *Igrot,* I, 148.

The religious institution which the champions of Russification were especially anxious to modernize was the synagogue, since they regarded that institution as an effective medium for Russification of the Jews. It will be recalled that it was primarily for the purpose of Russification that the translation of the Bible and the prayer book was undertaken by the Society for the Promotion of Culture among Jews. It was with this object in view that in 1866 a "Russian-Jewish Society" was organized in Zhitomir for the purpose of establishing a synagogue that would facilitate Russification of the Jews and assist them in "their merging in the civic sense with the native Russian population." *Ha-Carmel*, which reported on the founding of this Zhitomir society, quoted approvingly a statement from *Volynskiia Gubernskiia Vedomosti* to the effect that "the synagogue can have the most decisive influence on the education of the masses of Russian Jewry. . . . We see that in Western Europe the Jews started to speak the language of their respective countries only when that language began to be heard in the synagogue sermon." [13]

The sponsors of Russification through the synagogue had the most ardent supporters and collaborators in the modern rabbis who were trained in the seminaries of Vilno and Zhitomir. These ministers, referred to as government rabbis, introduced the custom of preaching in Russian and advocated Russification and patriotism on every occasion. Typical of these rabbinic expressions of patriotism is the declaration of Rabbi Mark Pomerants, in an address delivered on a solemn occasion, that for the Jews Alexander II was Moses the Redeemer.[14] Another illustration of the patriotic exhortations frequently sounded from the pulpit is furnished by a sermon of Rabbi Minor, who, on the occasion of the birthday of the empress, July 22, 1871, charged the women of his congregation as follows: "Arise, ye daughters in Israel! Awaken from your deep slumber, and look around. All strive toward that high destiny on which it is written: Be a Russian of the Mosaic faith!" [15]

That the rabbinic schools of Vilno and Zhitomir were largely responsible for the spirit of patriotism which animated these rabbis is indicated in the accounts of their former students. One of them, L. Binshtok, relates that in these institutions the Russian language and the Russian spirit reigned supreme, and that each student "was proud of the might of Russia." [16]

The rabbis who were favored by the government and the *maskilim*

13. Zinberg, *Ist. Ev. Pech.*, pp. 127–128.
14. *Ibid.*, p. 127.
15. Z. Minor, *Rechi*, p. 251.
16. *Russky Vestnik*, 1865, no. 11, p. 233.

failed, however, to gain adherents among the masses of Russian Jewry, who had no confidence in the spiritual leadership of ministers lacking both Talmudic erudition and the piety of the traditional rabbis. Since they were unpopular with the masses and there was little demand for spiritual leadership among the Russified Jews, the seminary-trained rabbis found it difficult to obtain posts. Their position was not secure or pleasant even when they did procure a rabbinic post.

Some progressive Jewish leaders urged that Jewish communities be compelled to accept as spiritual leaders only those designated by the government. Influential local government administrators also took this stand. In his report on Jewish schools, Postels, an official in the Ministry of Education, discussed the insecure position of modern rabbis and recommended that both their appointment and their service be controlled by the government.[17] The central government, however, rejected these suggestions, leaving the choice of rabbis to the Jewish communities.[18]

In summing up the movement for religious reform, it may be said that neither the masses nor the progressive elements in Jewry were particularly affected. Because of the failure of government rabbis to strike root within Russian Jewry, the plan for utilizing the synagogue as a means of Russification did not materialize. The attempt to reform Judaism for the purpose of making it more rational and more adaptable to the needs of the times also failed, for neither old nor young were interested in such changes. The old persisted in clinging to their ways of life, while the young tended to grow altogether indifferent to religion in any form. The well-known Hebrew-Yiddish writer and critic, David Frishman, aptly characterized these two attitudes. "My grandfather would rather submit to martyrdom seven times a day than yield one letter of the law, while as for myself, if there remain but one letter for me to observe, I shall completely disregard it if it will in any way prove burdensome." [19]

The young Jewish intelligentsia was averse not only to religion; it also set its face against the program and the character of both the old and the new *Haskalah*. This revolt was influenced by contemporary Russian literature, particularly by the works of two famous Russian writers, Chernyshevsky and Pisarev.

N. G. Chernyshevsky (1828–1889) was a Utopian socialist whose writings dealt chiefly with economic and political problems. He

17. *Otchot Postelsa po Obozreniiu Ev. Uchilishch,* pp. 23–24.
18. *Ev. Entsik.,* XIII, 227–230. *V. P. S. Z.,* XXXVI, no. 37,189.
19. David Frishman, *Kol Kitbe,* VIII, 32.

preached the organization of society on a communistic basis along the lines advocated by Fourier, Blanc, and Owen. In his attitude to religion, he was a materialist strongly under the influence of the German anti-theistic philosopher, Ludwig Andreas Feuerbach. His famous novel *Chto Delat?* (What Is To Be Done?), in which he expounded his philosophy, had a profound effect on the youth of Russia.[20]

The Russian critic, D. I. Pisarev (1841–1868), was greatly affected by the teachings of Chernyshevsky, and in turn exercised a tremendous influence on Russian thought. Pisarev was also a disciple of the French philosopher August Comte (1798–1857), founder of the philosophic system known as positivism. According to this philosophy, utility is the test of every institution and impulse. For the purpose of governing human society on a reasonable or scientific basis, Comte advocated study and application of the exact methods of the natural sciences in the affairs of the state.

Pisarev became the Russian apostle of positivism. He valued only useful and positive knowledge and deprecated aesthetics as useless and superfluous. "The more indifferent society becomes to the great and vital problems of life," he averred, "the more passionate its adherence to beautiful forms. . . . Periods of political stagnation in Europe were always golden periods of pure art." [21] The Russian exponent of positivism believed that aesthetics and realism were irreconcilables. "Realism, therefore," he urged, "should seek to annihilate aesthetics, which at the present time poisons and paralyzes all branches of our activity, beginning with the upper spheres of scientific endeavor and ending with the most ordinary relationships between man and woman." [22]

Chernyshevsky and Pisarev found eager adherents among Russian and Jewish youth. The first writer to reflect the views of Pisarev in Hebrew literature was Abraham Uri Kovner (1842–1909), whose two Hebrew booklets *Heker Dabar* (A Critique) and *Zeror Perahim* (A Bouquet of Flowers), published respectively in 1865 and 1868, evoked a veritable storm in the Jewish literary world.

In his first book, the author denied the existence of Jewish literature in the European sense of the word. The writings of the *mas-*

20. Speaking of the influence of this novel, Peter Kropotkin says: "It became the watchword of Young Russia, and the influence of the ideas it propagated has never ceased to be apparent since." *Russian Literature,* p. 305.

21. D. Pisarev, *Sochineniia,* II, 273.

22. *Ibid.,* IV, 58–59. A Brief exposition of the theories of Chernyshevsky and Pisarev in English in addition to Kropotkin's work is to be found in *The Spirit of Russia* by T. Masaryk, Vol. II; A. Brückner, *A Literary Hist. of Russia,* Ch. XI. See also the study of Pisarev by V. Kirpatin, *Radicalny Raznochinets D. I. Pisarev.*

kilim, he insisted, did not mirror either the spirit, the real needs, or the character of the Jewish people. "Because," he wrote, "Jewish writers do not know or understand the spirit of the time, or the needs of the people, we cannot expect them to write useful books for the masses . . . Why do they boast of spreading light in Israel when they themselves are immersed in darkness? Why do they so proudly proclaim their wisdom and knowledge when in reality they are ignoramuses?" [23]

In spite of the low esteem in which Yiddish was held by Jewish intellectuals, Kovner maintained that it was their duty to translate books on natural sciences into that language since it alone was spoken and understood by the masses. By rendering such works into "artificial" Hebrew, then in vogue, no useful purpose was served, he declared.[24] Realist that he was, he had no sentiment for either language, but judged them only according to their usefulness. Both Hebrew and Yiddish, he believed, would in time be replaced by the living Russian tongue.[25]

Kovner denounced the writers of the *Haskalah* for their idealization of the Hebrew language. "The Hebrew tongue," he declared, "like any other is made up of dead letters containing nothing sacred in themselves. Only the thoughts and ideas expressed through the medium of the language may assume holiness. Our writers, however, have turned the language itself, the dead letters, into a sacred entity in whose honor they constantly sing songs of praise." [26]

A consistent disciple of Pisarev, he appraised the value of a writer according to his contribution to the natural sciences. Just as his Russian master had sought to uncrown the poet laureate Pushkin because he did not measure up to the realists' standards of utility, so Kovner attempted to remove from his pedestal the famous Hebrew philologist, poet, and Bible exegete, S. D. Luzatto (1800–1865). Luzatto, who was professor of semitics at the rabbinic college of Padua and author of many Hebrew and Italian volumes on Biblical exegesis, archaeology, and kindred subjects, was one of the most gifted and original personalities of his time. Of him Kovner said: "Luzatto boasts of his mastery of the Hebrew language. We won't attempt to deny that. But to what purpose did he utilize his knowledge? Did he popularize in that language the phenomena of nature and natural sciences in order to enlighten Jews and cure them of superstitions?" [27]

23. A. Kovner, *Heker Dabar,* pp. 44–45.
24. *Ibid.,* pp. 54–55.
25. *Ibid.,* p. 56.
26. Kovner, *Zeror Perahim,* pp. 95–96.
27. *Ibid.,* pp. 112–114.

In his review of two volumes of poetry, Kovner took occasion to inveigh against Jewish poets of his day. His complaint was that these poets still regarded art as an end in itself, when, according to him, all other peoples had already come to the conclusion that the arts were only a means for serving useful and practical needs.[28]

Kovner's vitriolic attacks on the writers of the *Haskalah* brought forth a storm of abuse from the offended literati who branded him with such names as "nihilist" and "extinguisher of light." The young publicist M. G. Morgulis came to his defense.[29] Characterizing the controversy as a struggle between the old and the new generations, Morgulis warned the *Haskalah* writers of the futility of ranting and raving against a young crusader who, to his mind, represented the ideas and spirit of the younger generation.[30] In commenting on this battle of ideas, a modern historian refers to it as a counterpart of the struggle between the old generation and the new in the Russia of that period described in Turgenev's novel *Fathers and Sons*.[31]

Lilienblum, the "son" who first rebelled against the traditional religion of the fathers, now, under the influence of Chernyshevsky and Pisarev, joined the rebels against the old generation of *maskilim*. He lost interest in the question of religious reform and abandoned the idea of harmonizing religion with life. In his last article dealing with this problem—"Tikun Medini Ve-Tikun Safruti" (State and Literary Reforms) [32]—he attacked the backwardness not only of the rabbis but of the writers of the *Haskalah*. "At a time," he exclaims, "when all thinking elements in Russia are aroused by the new ideas of Chernyshevsky and Pisarev, which offer a solution to the great problem of universal happiness, our honored men of letters make a big noise about some comment on a Biblical text, and pore over ancient tomes whose ideas are as dried up as their withered leaves." He concludes the article with the impassioned appeal: "Provide bread! Fresh air! Concern yourselves with the peace and happiness of our suffering brethren and sisters! Save our youth from extinction! Show them the road to life so that they may not exhaust themselves blundering in the dark!" [33]

28. *Ha-Meliz,* 1866, nos. 39–42. Kovner's career as a Hebrew writer ended with the publication of *Zeror Perahim.* He became involved in a theft scandal as a result of which he was exiled to Siberia; he was baptized there, left the Jewish field of writing, and made a name for himself as a Russian writer. His youthful years are described in his autobiography published in the *Istorichesky Vestnik,* 1903, bks. 3–4.

29. *Ha-Meliz,* 1866, nos. 12–18.

30. *Ibid.,* 1866, pp. 280–281.

31. Zinberg, *Ist. Ev. Pech.,* p. 149.

32. *Ha-Shahar,* II, 366–375.

33. *Ibid.,* II, 373.

Pisarev's influence is especially evident in Lilienblum's glorification of the natural sciences as a means to the material enhancement of life. "The more we discover about the laws of nature, the greater will be her usefulness to us," he affirmed.[34] Chiding the Jews for living in what he called an "unsubstantial world," he urged Jewish writers to develop a more realistic attitude to life and make the Jews forget the imaginary world to which they were clinging. "The purpose of life," he reminded them, "is life itself." [35]

These critical blasts by young rebels at the *Haskalah* ideology and at its most revered and cherished instrument—the Hebrew language—were expressions of the growing tendency among the Jewish intelligentsia toward assimilation. Leon Rosenthal, a *maskil* of the old school, describes the temper of the revolt in his history of the Society for the Promotion of Culture among Jews. "The belief then prevailed," he writes, "that Israel was like unto all the other peoples, hence it had no need of a special Jewish culture. . . . They [the new intellectuals] declared war upon our sacred tongue." [36]

Not only did the new Jewish intellectuals deprecate the idealization of the Hebrew tongue and deride the current artificial imitation of the Biblical style, they also questioned the adequacy of Hebrew for the expression of modern thought and predicted its imminent disappearance. In a series of articles published in *Den*[37] entitled "A National and Practical View on the Hebrew Language," Morgulis pointed to the "inexorable" fact that in Western Europe Hebrew had been replaced by the language of the land. "This fact," he asserted, "should convince everyone that with the progress of scientific development the Biblical tongue was bound to disappear from literature, and that in the course of time Hebrew would give way in Russia to the living language of the land."

Belief in the impending disappearance of Hebrew as a cultural medium of Jewish expression was also shared by the Hebrew poet Gordon, who, though an exponent of Russification, lamented this prospect in the elegiac lines.

> Alas! Am I to be the last of the singers of Zion?
> and you the last of the readers? [38]

On the part of the anti-*Haskalah* intellectuals, however, these prognostications of doom were doubtless fathered by the proverbial wish.

34. *Ibid.,* IV, 508.
35. *Ibid.,* IV, 705.
36. *Toldot. Heb. Mar.,* Intro., p. XIII.
37. 1869, nos. 3 and 5.
38. *Ha-Shahar,* II, 354.

For to them Hebrew was but an impediment on the road to complete identification with the Russian people.

In their eagerness to assimilate with the Russians, these Jewish Russificators even sought to prove the existence of a spiritual affinity between the two peoples. Tarnopol spoke of the "striking and distinct" similarity between the Slavs and the Jews in manners and customs as well as in forms of speech and religious expressions.[39] I. Warshavsky, publicist and philologist, asserted in *Den* that his linguistic studies had convinced him that the spirit of the Russian language was uniquely similar to that of the Hebrew tongue. He found that Russian idioms which expressed the psychological traits of the Russian people showed a marked resemblance to Hebrew idioms. This similarity, the author contended, made the Russian language most suitable for conveying the meaning of a Hebrew text, and afforded an easy transition into the Russian language to the Jew permeated with the spirit of the Hebrew language and its literature.[40] The same idea was expressed by M. Shapiro in an article on the significance of Hebrew for Russian philology.[41]

Attempts were also made to prove by scientific analysis the error of considering the Jews a nationality. This approach is to be found in an anonymous article "The Jewish Problem and the Welfare of Russia,"[42] the sentiments of which Israel Zinberg characterizes as representative of Jewish academic youth of the seventies.[43] "We maintain," asserts the writer, "that the Jews, thrown by historic circumstances on the soil of European civilization, have always lacked, as they still do today, the most essential elements that make for a live, independent, and real nationality." Pointing out that the Jews have none of the attributes that make for nationhood, such as a common language, a land, and a political organization to assure their independence, he asks: "And so, where is the instrument by means of which one can hope to maintain or create that which would have the slightest semblance of a living nationality?"

The author ridiculed exponents of Jewish nationalism who saw in the Jewish faith a bond that united them into a nation. Regarding such a concept of nationalism as a scientific myth, he insisted that Judaism united the Jews only into a religious fraternity. "As a nation," he declared, "the Jews have no place in the economy of European civilization. As a religious fraternity their rôle may not

39. *Opyt. Sov.*, p. 253.
40. *Den,* 1871, no. 2, p. 28.
41. *Ibid.,* 1871, nos. 3–4.
42. *Ev. Bib.,* V, 1–47.
43. *Ist. Ev. Pech.,* pp. 189–190. See also S. M. Dubnow, *Pisma o Starom i Novom Evreistve,* pp. 217–219.

be ended as yet."[44] The transformation of Russian Jews into Russians of the Mosaic faith, according to the writer, offered the key to the solution of the Jewish problem.[45]

There is no doubt that these polemics were prompted by more than a quest for scientific truth; they were to a considerable degree actuated by a yearning for a new status for the Jew. To Jewish Russificators, the concept of Jewish nationalism represented a barrier to their cherished objective—national and cultural fusion of the Jew with the Russian people. Thereby they hoped not only to solve the political aspects of the Jewish problem but also to find fulfillment for that inner need of a sense of "belonging." In the pathetic outcry of one of the characters of Levanda's *Goriachee Vremia*, the author gives voice to this desperate longing which oppressed the hearts of Jewish youth of the period. "I experience," laments Sarin, the hero of the novel, "the torments of hell when I realize how like a dog without a master I am, wandering aimlessly in the street like a lonely canine, with no one to be faithful to, with no one to love or be loved by."[46]

The indignity of belonging nowhere and the great need of belonging somewhere experienced by the intelligentsia of the time were in great part responsible for the awakening of the Jewish national movement. Against the voices of the Russificators urging the renunciation of all Jewish national conceptions and aspirations were now raised the voices of Smolenskin and Ben-Yehuda calling upon the Jews to rouse their dormant national energies and to direct them toward their own spiritual regeneration and the rebuilding of their historic homeland.

44. *Ev. Bib.,* V, 41–42.
45. *Ibid.,* V, 45.
46. *Ibid.,* I, 54.

X

NATIONALISTIC TRENDS

THE nineteenth century, which is known as the century of nationalism and democracy, saw the unification of Germany and Italy and the emancipation of several small and oppressed minorities. Minorities which failed to achieve independence pressed their demands for national self-determination.

The doctrine of the right of national self-expression for each people was first enunciated in the eighteenth century, along with the demand for natural rights for the individual. "It was in the intellectual milieu of the eighteenth century," writes a modern historian, "that the first systematic doctrines of nationalism were expounded." [1] The nationalism advocated then was a sort of humanitarian nationalism because it was devoid of jingoism and intolerance, and was motivated by a regard for the best interests of all peoples. Its chief exponent was Johann Gottfried von Herder (1744–1803), who is said to have been the first to employ the term nationalism.[2]

Herder believed that nature itself, with its varying climatic and topographic conditions, divided humanity into distinct national units. The physical environment of each region fashioned the customs, manners, language, and culture of the peoples inhabiting it. These national traits, transmitted from generation to generation, became an integral part of the character of the people.[3] Herder regarded the particular language of each nationality as its most significant and precious possession. "Language," he asserted, "is the index to the mind and character of a people." [4] To him national self-expression was as important as enlightenment, these being "the two poles around which all the moral culture of mankind revolves." [5]

In France, Herder's views on nationalism were shared by Rousseau (1712–1778). In his *Considèration sur le gouvernment de Pologne*, Rousseau declared that "it is national institutions which form the genius, the character, the tastes and the customs of a peo-

1. C. J. H. Hayes, *The Historical Evolution of Modern Nationalism,* 1931 edition, p. 16.
2. *Am. Hist. Review,* XXXII, 722.
3. *Sämmtliche Werke,* XIV, 84.
4. *Ibid.,* XIII, 363.
5. *Ibid.,* XIV, 121.

ple; which make one people and not another; which inspire the ardent love of country founded on habits impossible to trace back to their source."[6] The nationalistic doctrines enunciated by these eighteenth-century philosophers received a powerful stimulus from the French Revolution, which proclaimed the right of national self-determination.

Nationalistic sentiment was further stimulated by the philosophy and literature of the first decades of the nineteenth century—the Age of Romanticism. In reaction against the rationalism of the eighteenth century, romanticism extolled emotion in preference to reason, idealized the common man, and glorified the past. This romantic attitude toward the past fostered a reverence for history and awakened the national loyalties of the European peoples, resulting in an intensified study of their respective spiritual and cultural heritage. Scholars were busily engaged studying the language, folk-ways, music, and history of their particular nationalities.

The romanticists believed that only through the cultivation of that culture which is a product of its own national genius and deeply rooted in its historic traditions can a people find self-realization. "The best culture of a people," declared Herder, "is not hastily acquired; it does not permit itself to be forced through a foreign language. That culture flourishes most beautifully upon its native soil, or I might say thrives only through the dialect which a people inherits and passes on to posterity. . . . Truly as God tolerates all languages in the world, so should also a ruler not alone tolerate but honor the various languages of the peoples he rules."[7] And the Slovak poet Jan Kollar stated in 1824: "It is a mistake to call the country in which we dwell by the holy name of fatherland; the true undying homeland, against which might and deceit cannot prevail, is custom, speech and concord."[8]

The ideas of the romantic movement left their impress upon the literature of European Jewry. In the opinion of a historian of Hebrew literature, the second period of modern Hebrew literature (1820–1860) was completely dominated by the influence of the romantics.[9] Even the "Science of Judaism"[10] may be said to have had its basis in romanticism. These scientific studies of Israel's history, religion, and culture were undoubtedly stimulated by the attention which the romantics centered upon their own respective cultures.

6. Quoted in Hayes, *Hist. Evol. of Mod. Nat.*, 1931 edition, p. 25.

7. *Briefe zu Beförderung der Humanität*, I, 147.

8. Hayes, *Hist. Evol. of Mod. Nat.*, 1926 edition, p. 54.

9. J. Klausner, *Historyah shel Ha-Safrut Ha-Ibrit Ha-Hadashah*, II, 1.

10. A critical and scientific study of Judaism and the history of the Jews. In Hebrew it is known as *Hakmat Yisrael* and in German as *Wissenschaft des Judentums*.

Also in its purpose this "science" had an element of romanticism since one of its aims was to revive interest in the Jewish cultural heritage, which it was feared was rapidly disintegrating and would soon be forgotten.

This concern about the imminent disappearance of Jewish culture was voiced by Leopold Zunz (1794–1886), founder of *Wissenschaft des Judenthums.* He declared that since Jews were leaning toward the ideals of other peoples, acquiring foreign tongues, bringing into their midst strange cultures and digging a grave for Rabbinic literature, it was therefore "the duty of science to rouse itself and demand an account of all that was created in that literature whose end apparently has come." [11]

The Hebrew scholar Klausner believes that the "Science of Judaism" was born in Prussia because there assimilation and the flight from Judaism assumed most alarming proportions. It could not be expected, he states, "that a people with an ancient culture would surrender without a struggle all the cultural values which gave it life and spiritual strength." [12] The Galician historian Solomon Judah Rapoport (1790–1867), one of the founding fathers of *Hakmat Yisrael,* regarded the study of Israel's past and the cultivation of the Hebrew language as a dike against the tides of assimilation and as a means of preserving the Jewish people.[13]

The most cherished ambition of the Jewish scientists, however, was to win the world's respect for Judaism and through their scholarly endeavors create for their people "that place of honor in the world which it deserves to occupy." [14] Thus they hoped to achieve their prime and ultimate objective—emancipation. Zunz's declaration that "the emancipation of the Jew would follow as a result of the emancipation of Judaism" (when the world will accord Judaism its rightful place), was the credo of most of those engaged in that branch of Jewish learning.[15]

The use of Jewish Science as a means toward that end instead of as an end in itself was severely scored by Samuel David Luzatto, contemporary Biblical exegete, poet, philologist, and scion of a distinguished line of Italian-Jewish poets and scholars. He spoke contemptuously of the ulterior motives which actuated the Jewish savants, charging that they "extolled the virtues of our ancients" not out of love or reverence for the Jewish past but in order to court the admiration of the world, so that it might grant the Jew emanci-

11. L. Zunz, *Gesammelte Schriften,* I, 4.
12. Klausner, *Hist. Saf. Ib. Had.,* II, 2.
13. *Bikkure Ha-Itim,* 1827, p. 12.
14. *Monatsschrift für Gesch. u Wissen. des Jud.,* 1922, p. 90.
15. *Zur Geschichte und Liter.,* p. 21.

pation.[16] Luzatto deprecated the motive of his colleagues because he had little faith in the worthwhileness of their prized objective. For this gifted scholar did not believe in emancipation as the panacea for Israel's ills. It was his conviction that Jewry's welfare was dependent upon its national solidarity, which he saw weakening in quest of the mirage of emancipation. He warned those whom he believed willing to buy emancipation at the cost of Judaism not to allow "our *Nationalstolz* to be extinguished and the language of our fathers to be forgotten by our seed." [17]

The chief purpose of the study of Judaism, Luzatto held, should be to acquaint Jews with their cultural heritage, so as to raise its prestige among them and thereby strengthen national Jewish consciousness. He believed that the most indispensable instrument for attaining that end and for fostering love of Judaism was the Hebrew language and literature, which should be perpetuated at all costs. Because of this objective and because, as he put it, "Love for the Hebrew language burns within me," [18] Luzatto spent many years in the study of Hebrew philology, in which field he had few peers in the nineteenth century. Contrary to the practice of most of his colleagues, who in trying to make Jewish culture known to the world employed European languages, Luzatto wrote many of his works in Hebrew. At one time this versatile linguist and author of many works in Italian and French resolved: "I will write only in Hebrew and through that language give expression to the age-old national emotions which live within me in their full vigor." [19]

To revive an interest in the medieval poets, Luzatto devoted himself to the task of collecting and editing their literary creations. Particularly dear to him were the works of the Spanish-Jewish poet Judah Ha-Levi, whose religious and national ardor was so expressive of Luzatto's own feelings and in whose concept of the Jew and Judaism he found support and inspiration.

In his youth a disciple of the rationalistic school, Luzatto soon broke away to become its most determined opponent and he may be regarded as the Jewish representative *par excellence* of romanticism. Like the romantics, he gave precedence to emotion over reason. "I have a heart and it is worth more than you, my dear brain," [20] he argued in a debate with himself. To him Judaism was primarily a religion of the heart, a religion of goodness and righteousness. After a study of the wisdom and lives of the great Greek and Roman phi-

16. *Igrot Shadal,* p. 1367.
17. *Ibid.,* p. 660.
18. *Ibid.,* p. 1246.
19. *Pardes,* III, 121.
20. *Ibid.,* III, 115.

losophers, said Luzatto, he came to appreciate more than ever the naïve wisdom and the simple virtues of the Talmudic sages whose ethical teachings represented the philosophy of the heart. A romantic nationalist, zealous for the recognition and perpetuation of the national and cultural character of the Jewish people, he strenuously opposed the religious reformers who rejected this principle. In a letter to Abraham Geiger, leader of the Reform movement in Germany, he appealed: "Let your portion be among those who lead the multitude to righteousness, and let your strength and power and learning serve as holy instruments to save the errant from sin, to revive the love of Hebrew literature among the people of your generation and to kindle in their hearts a Jewish pride. And may this year see an end to the servility and spiritual degradation of those who say: 'We are Germans, we are just like you, your culture is our culture, your morality our morality!' It is not so! It is not so!" [21]

Samuel David Luzatto is acknowledged to be a forerunner of modern Jewish nationalism. Thirty years after his death, Moses Leb Lilienblum—in his earlier years, under the influence of positivism scornful of this romantic's ideas, but now a convert to Zionism—hailed Luzatto as one of the foremost creators of the Jewish national idea.[22]

The first Russian-Jewish disciple of the Romantic school was the Hebrew poet Micah Joseph Lebensohn (1828–1852) of Vilno. From his correspondence with the Russo-French Jewish scholar, Senior Sachs (1816–1892), it is apparent that during his stay in Berlin Lebensohn became thoroughly familiar with literary currents of Europe in general and of Germany in particular. German literature of that period was strongly under the influence of *Jung Deutschland,* a movement which preached political freedom, social equality, and national self-determination. Young Germany had a political and spiritual affinity with movements known as Young Austria, Young Italy, and Young Poland, all of which doubtlessly contributed to Lebensohn's ideology.[23] That he was greatly influenced by Hebrew literature and the literary personalities of Western Europe is clear from the declaration in his introduction to the *Shire Bat Zion* (Songs of the Daughter of Zion). "I am grateful to Leopold Zunz and Samuel D. Luzatto, who advised me to cease to sing alien songs and, instead, to sing songs of Zion." He refers remorsefully

21. Quoted in Klausner, *Hist. Saf. Ib. Had.,* II, 106.
22. *Kol Kitbe M. L. Lilienblum,* III, 96–99.
23. Klausner, *Hist. Saf. Ib. Had.,* III, 258–261. See also his *Yozrim U-Bonim,* I, 127.

to his translation of the *Harisot Troyah* (The Destruction of Troy), exclaiming: "What have you and I, dear reader, in common with the city of Troy? . . . Come with me, dear reader, and let me carry you on the wings of song to our own Holy Land—the Land of Zion." [24]

Both the title and subject matter of his poems *Shire Bat Zion* and *Kinor Bat Zion* (The Lyre of the Daughter of Zion) reflect his nationalistic sentiments. His poems not only are a romantic glorification of Israel's ancient past, but also show the beginnings of Zionist aspirations in modern Hebrew literature. In his poem *A Driven Twig* he ascribes the suffering of the Jew to his homelessness. Asked why it is being tossed about on the raging sea, the driven twig replies that because it was broken off from its own tree,

"Therefore am I tossed,
Therefore am I lost upon the raging sea." [25]

The trend toward nationalism found even clearer expression in the first modern Hebrew novelist, Abraham Mapu of Kovno (1808–1868). Mapu regarded *belles lettres* as the most effective instrument for stemming the tide of assimilation among the Jewish youth of Russia. He ascribed the rapid growth of assimilation among the Jews of Germany and France to their lack of such a literature. "Through our literature," he declared, "we must turn the hearts of our youth to a love of the Hebrew language, lest they forsake that language as a worthless thing." [26] He believed fiction to be of greater importance for the national regeneration of the Jews than the scientific studies of Judaism then in vogue, and he deliberately chose, according to his own testimony, to dedicate his efforts to fiction rather than to scientific study of Judaism.[27]

Mapu's best known novels are *Ahabat Zion* (The Love of Zion), *Ashmat Shomron* (The Guilt of Samaria), and *Ait Zabua* (The Painted Hawk). As suggested by their titles, the subject matter and characters of the first two novels are drawn from Biblical times. Through glowing descriptions of Israel's ancient glory, its kings, princes, and prophets, he sought to awaken the national pride of the Jew and to inspire hope in the renewal of a national life upon the ancestral soil. In *The Painted Hawk*, the author makes the hero the exponent of Zionist ideals, which were quite new in his time. Un-

24. *Kol Shire Adam U-Mikal,* IV, xi-xii.
25. *Ibid.,* IV, 71–72.
26. Preface to part III of *Ait Zabua.*
27. See letter to Gurland, *Ha-Boker Or,* 1879, July, pp. 839–40.

like the popular ambition of the Jewish youth of his day, who aspired to professional and scientific careers, Azriel, hero of the novel, dreams of becoming a farmer in Palestine and of dedicating his life to the propagation of the ideal of agricultural pursuit on the soil of Israel's ancient homeland.

Mapu was also the first writer to present the *maskil* type, universally idealized in the literature of the period, in a critical light. Elisheba, heroine of *The Painted Hawk*, repulses the *maskil* Emil, upbraiding him for exchanging his Hebrew name Abner for the fashionable one of Emil.[28] She expresses her contempt for him because "in the wickedness of his heart" he denies himself to his people.[29]

"Mapu planted within us a national pride and the right Hebrew spirit" Klausner declares in summarizing the profound effect of Mapu's writings on his generation, ". . . With bonds of love he tied us to that land in which our highest hopes repose." [30]

The slumbering sentiments of nationalism, which Lebensohn and Mapu stirred through their poems and novels, found an echo in the Jewish press of the sixties. Although *Razsvet* and *Sion* advocated Russification, they at the same time insisted that there was no reason for Jews to give up their national identity. Observing that the Jews were beginning to come into closer contact with non-Jewish peoples, the former noted that "happily Jews do not cease being Jews but preserve their distinctive national characteristics." "While sharing in the common life of all nations through participation in their education and in their achievements," stated *Razsvet*, "Jews should at the same time preserve, develop, and perfect their own national heritage." The writer defined national heritage as follows:

> A common religion, a common holy language, a great common past, distinctive traits of physiognomy and character, common customs and mutual sympathy—these bind the Jews scattered all over the world into a distinct nationality, destined by Providence to fulfill its mission in a way different from all other peoples.[31]

In this weekly the journalist I. Galberstat also scored intellectual Jewish youth for their indifference to and ignorance of their own culture. "It is a shame to admit, though it is the sad truth," the author complained, "that we learn about ourselves through foreign sources; lightmindedly we accept as truth all stereotyped errors

28. *Ait Zabua,* Part I, 56.
29. *Ibid.,* Part I, 120.
30. *Yozrim U-Bonim,* I, 191.
31. *Razsvet,* no. 52, p. 835.

about the Jews, deny our identity and thus become not participants in European civilization but its slaves."[32] Galberstat rebuked the reform Jews of Germany who for the sake of convenience showed a "lamentable heroism" in throwing off the religious customs of their fathers. "These religious customs," he asserted, "are creations of the spirit and thought of our people; they have become an integral part of the life of our nation; they have grown into our habits and manners. . . . If we give up these historically developed practices which unite all Jews, what will take their place?"[33]

Sion, too, rejected assimilation as the solution to the Jewish problem. Reviewing an article in the Russian press in which a Jewish journalist advocated complete Russification of the Jews, J. Goldendach, a noted collaborator of *Sion*, declared: "All highminded Jews would welcome a closer friendship between the Jewish and the Russian people, but complete fusion predicated on the surrender of the Jewish identity would appeal to no one. . . . At a time when so much blood is being shed for national emancipation, Jewish assimilationists advise the Jews to commit national suicide!"[34] Goldendach rejected the argument of the writer that, lacking in territory, Jews cannot be regarded as a nation. This was only clever sophistry without regard to reality, he declared; for just as a plant transplanted to another soil does not lose its original nature, neither has the Jew deprived of his homeland lost his national character.

Further evidence of *Sion's* stand on the question of Jewish nationalism is furnished by the controversy between this periodical and the Ukrainian *Osnova* (Foundation). In answer to the charge that the Jews of south Russia never made a serious effort to break down their clannish exclusiveness in the relations with non-Jewish neighbors, *Sion* pointed out that the welfare of a country with a heterogeneous population did not require that each racial or religious group give up its national identity. *Osnova*, in its insistence that small nationalities voluntarily allow themselves to be swallowed up by the "fate and spirit of the one dominant nation," had adopted the point of view of the medieval inquisition, *Sion* declared, and failed to see that variety means life while uniformity spells death.[35]

While the *Evreiskaia Biblioteka* was not, as its editor put it, a "fanatical champion" of Jewish nationalism, it nevertheless saw no reason why secular education and acquisition of civic rights by the Jews should be contingent upon their national extinction. That

32. *Ibid.*, no. 9, p. 141.
33. *Ibid.*, no. 10, p. 161.
34. *Sion*, No. 6, p. 95.
35. *Ibid.*, no. 10, p. 160.

national existence does not depend on the possession of territory has been proved by the survival of the Jews themselves for a period of more than fifteen hundred years. Nationality was determined rather by a people's physiological and cultural characteristics, the author argued, and he failed to see why the Jew alone, whose national character was certainly developed to a high degree, should be made an exception and asked to give up his national existence.[36]

On the question of nationalism and assimilation there were, as has been pointed out, sharp and divided opinions. It should be noted, however, that in Russia assimilation never assumed the extreme form or proportions that it did in Germany. With the exception of the student youth and two organs of public opinion, Jewish secular thought in Russia opposed the obliteration of national Jewish identity and aspirations advocated by the majority of German-Jewish intellectuals.

There were a number of factors responsible for this difference in assimilationist tendencies and ideologies. The most important was undoubtedly the superior numerical and religious strength of Russo-Polish Jewry, which for centuries constituted the largest Jewish center in Europe. With traditional Judaism so widely and deeply entrenched, it is self-evident that assimilation would make but feeble inroads. Furthermore, German Jewry had established contact with the non-Jewish world at least a century before Russian Jewry began to emerge from the ghetto. Besides these religious and social factors, another important aspect to be considered is the different political circumstances under which the two Jewries struggled for emancipation.

Because the fight of the German Jew for civic equality coincided with the struggle of the Germanic states for national unity and political liberty, the Jews in these states were eager to prove that they did not constitute a nation within a nation. The wars of liberation against Napoleon and the subsequent struggle for national unity intensified the nationalistic sentiments of German intellectuals, arousing a patriotism that was accompanied by intolerance toward all non-Germanic minorities.

In Russia, political and national conditions were altogether different. The people were united under a strong central government and therefore did not consider minority groups a menace to their national strength. Especially was the period of the Great Reforms, when the Jew launched his campaign for civic rights, free from chauvinism. The leaders of Russian thought who championed the cause of humanitarianism and freedom were not troubled by the

36. Preface to vol. II, p. vi.

controversial question of dual Jewish nationalism. The attitude of Russian liberals to the question may be epitomized in the statement made by a contemporary Russian writer. "It is enough for me to know that the Jew, who is created in the image of God, is hounded and persecuted, in order for us to proclaim him worthy of human rights and wish him a better lot." [37] It was undoubtedly due in large measure to this liberal attitude, in addition to the other factors mentioned, that the philosophy of the Jewish Russificators did not assume the self-effacing character of Western-Jewish assimilationism.

Russo-Jewish thought, however, did little to check the tide of assimilation that engulfed the Jewish student youth of Russia in the sixties and seventies. Instead of battling this tide, the Russian-Jewish press devoted most of its energies to fighting the opponents of secular education and Russification. As to the futility of attempts made by religious reformers to check the abandonment of Judaism, a modern writer has the following to say:

> Lilienblum and Gordon had demanded that certain religious customs should be abolished in conformity with the changed outlook of the younger generation; but actually the younger generation had entirely cast away religion and was given over to frivolity and self-indulgence. Judaism, and with it the Hebrew language and literature, had fallen on evil days; and if this state of things had continued unchanged, the Hebrew literature of the period of *Haskalah* controversy was bound to become extinct.[38]

The man who undertook to stem the rising tide of assimilation among the Jewish youth of the seventies by championing the cause of Jewish nationalism was the novelist and publicist, Peter Smolenskin (1842–1885). Born in Monastryshchina, province of Mogilev, Smolenskin started his literary career in 1867, in the Hebrew *Ha-Meliz*. His earliest works, written during his residence in Odessa, had given indication of his nationalistic tendencies. In *Ha-Gemul* (The Reward), a story dealing with the Polish uprising which he translated and adapted from the German, he sought to show that the Jews can expect no reward for sacrifices made on behalf of other peoples' causes; on the contrary, what they reap from such sacrifices is the contempt of the contending sides. And in his first original novel, *Simhat Hanef* (The Joy of the Flatterer), the hero stressed love of and loyalty to Israel as of greater moment for a Jew than secular education. While other Jewish intellectuals of the period

37. Quoted in Zinberg, *Ist. Ev. Pech.*, p. 53.
38. J. Klausner, *A Hist. of Modern Heb. Lit.*, tr. by Herbert Danby, p. 85.

urged their people to better themselves by emulating the ways of other nations, Simon, the chief character of the story, seeks to strengthen his people's self-respect by pointing out that there are many things other nations can learn from the Jews.

Smolenskin's chief ambition was to publish a Hebrew periodical in which he could be free to preach his ideas without hindrance of government or editorial censorship. Realizing that he had no chance of receiving permission for such a publication in Russia, he left his native land determined to found a magazine abroad and traveled through Western Europe and England. The Jewish communities he visited and studied made a painful impression on him.

The new brand of Judaism of the Western Jews who styled themselves members of the Mosaic faith he found hollow, meaningless, and fruitless. Their reform temples, which banned the Hebrew language and traditional prayers, appeared to him artificial and lifeless, totally lacking in Jewish spirit and religious fervor. This type of religion, which cut itself away from its traditional forms and national hopes, offered no promise of a vital or glorious future for Israel. Far from sharing the admiration of Russian-Jewish intellectuals for the manner in which their enlightened brethren in the West were solving their Jewish problem, he could feel only contempt for them. To Smolenskin the "emancipated" Jews appeared spiritual slaves who had sold their birthright for a mess of pottage.

To fight the movement toward assimilation, he founded the Hebrew monthly *Ha-Shahar* (Dawn) in Vienna in 1869. The introductory article outlining the program of his periodical promised that the magazine would be dedicated to the renaissance of the Hebrew language, which the editor considered an indispensable instrument for the spiritual revitalization of the Jewish people and of its national hopes. Referring to the slogan of the assimilationists, "Let us be like the nations," he exhorted his readers: "Yes, indeed, let us be like the nations! Let us pursue knowledge and justice, let us be loyal citizens in the lands of our exile, but let us like them be unashamed of the rock from which we were hewn. And like them let us treasure and honor the language of our people! Just as other subjugated nations are not ashamed to hope for their national redemption, neither is it a disgrace for us to hope for an end of our exile." [39]

It may well be that Smolenskin's residence in Vienna, then the capital of Austria-Hungary and the classical arena wherein oppressed nationalities struggled for national freedom, influenced his

39. *Ha-Shahar,* I, preface, p. vi.

Jewish aspirations in a similar direction. It is suggested that another factor which gave added impetus to Smolenskin's national ideology was the unification of Italy.[40]

But while the editor of *Ha-Shahar* drew inspiration from the struggle and victories of other oppressed nationalities of his times, he found greatest support for his nationalistic ideology in Judaism itself. In a series of articles entitled "Am Olam" (An Eternal People) he refuted the basic tenet of the reformists that the Jews are only a religious group. The *Torah*,[41] he maintained, was not only the religious guide of the Jews but also their national mainstay. For it is the *Torah* that unites the spirit and the heart of Israel, even as land and government unite a people. The reason the Jews were not lost among the nations, he asserted, was that in the *Torah* they found everything that other peoples derive from land and government.[42] In Judaism, Smolenskin declared, religion and nationalism go hand in hand, and the Hebrew language is the basic essential for both.[43] He considered the Jews who sought to discard that language from worship and study as traitors to their religion and their people. "For without a Hebrew language there can be no *Torah*, and without a *Torah* there can be no nation." [44] So vital to the preservation of the Jews and Judaism did he regard the Hebrew language, that he insisted that even Jewish scientific works should be written in Hebrew. This language, he maintained, would make such works the common property of all Jewry, even as the *Torah* is the heritage of all Israel.[45]

Smolenskin scored the reformists for eliminating from the service the prayers for the restoration of Zion. Regardless of whether the hope for the return to Palestine would ever be realized, the maintenance of that hope, he insisted, was essential for the preservation of the Jews. He did not share the optimism of assimilationists who believed that the civic emancipation of the Jew was at hand. He was not even sure of the permanence of the rights Jews had already obtained in some countries of Western Europe. Smolenskin believed that, essentially, the nations really wanted the Jews to remain Jews; hence no attempt at self-effacement on their part would procure for them the coveted equality among the nations.[46]

Nor could this prophet of Jewish nationalism see any contradic-

40. Klausner, *Yozrim U-Bonim,* I, 206.
41. For a definition of term *Torah,* see page 57.
42. *Ha-Shahar,* III, 660.
43. *Ibid.,* IV, 131.
44. *Ibid.,* IV, 66.
45. *Ibid.,* IV, 66.
46. *Ibid.,* III, 672–3.

tion between the Jew's loyalty to his adopted land and his devotion to the hope for Zion's restoration. "Though a Jew may cling to his hope of Redemption," he declared, "he will not on that account lose his affection for the land of his adoption if she but consider him her son, just as a man does not give up the goods and delights of this world for the sake of his hope in the world to come." [47]

Of all his criticisms of reformists and assimilationists, the most notable was directed at Moses Mendelssohn. In an article entitled "Et Lataat" (Time to Plant), Smolenskin bitterly assailed the German-Jewish philosopher as the originator of anti-nationalistic and reform ideology. Castigating him for his translation of the Bible into German, he contrasted Mendelssohn's effort with that of Martin Luther. He pointed out that while the German reformer rendered the Scriptures into the vernacular so that his people might understand them, Mendelssohn translated the Bible from the Hebrew, which was accessible to most Jews, into a tongue foreign and unknown to them.[48]

The editor of *Ha-Shahar* charged that Mendelssohn's ideas and those of his disciples constituted a menace to Judaism and the Jewish people. But he reminded them defiantly that neither alien enemies nor internal foes could destroy the Jews. Concerning this idol of the *maskilim*, who stood unchallenged on his pedestal, he dared predict that "there would come a day when the eyes of the blind will be opened, and they will be ashamed of their teachers who had neither understanding nor judgment." [49]

Two outstanding Hebrew critics of our day summarize the place assigned to Smolenskin in modern Hebrew literature and in modern Jewish history. Reuben Brainin speaks of him as "the greatest national philosopher of our latest period, one of the foremost creators of the national literature of our day and the solitary champion of nationalism, who declared war on the assimilationists, gathering under his banner men of courage." [50] Although Smolenskin did not preach or envisage a program of practical Zionism, Klausner acclaims him as the standard-bearer of the Zionist ideal. "For if," as he puts it, "literary creations have it in their power to produce social and national movements, though other contributing factors may also be responsible for their birth, then we have a right to regard both our present day national ideal and the Zionist ideol-

47. *Ibid.,* IV, 8.
48. *Ibid.,* VI, 296.
49. *Ibid.,* VI, 307.
50. R. Brainin, *Smolenskin Ve-Toldotov,* pp. 5–6, 8.

ogy based upon it as largely the creation of Peter Smolenskin." [51]

The call sounded by Smolenskin found ready response among a large portion of Russian-Jewish youth. Disappointed at the failure of the government to grant the Jews civic equality and disheartened by the intensified anti-Jewish campaign which the nationalistic Russian press conducted after the Russo-Turkish War, young people lent a more attentive ear to the doctrines of Jewish nationalism preached by the editor of *Ha-Shahar*. Even Levanda, who in the sixties joyfully heralded the imminent emancipation of Russian Jews, began to despair of its realization. Sadly he observed in 1879 that "the Jewish problem in Russia would for a long time yet be the object of legislative debates." [52]

Another factor which helped gain adherents for Smolenskin's cause among Russian Jews was the strong antisemitism which swept Germany as a result of the Franco-Prussian War. Jewish national sentiment was also in no small measure stimulated by the heightened spirit of nationalism that gripped Europe after the Balkan Wars.

Evidence of awakened interest in the plight of their own people was furnished by Jewish youth during the acute economic crisis following the bad harvests from which Russian Jewry suffered in the late seventies. "Never before," observes a noted contemporary, "had been manifested such a readiness among the Jewish intelligentsia to serve the common weal of their people, to come nearer to the masses from which they had kept aloof, oblivious to their needs and problems." [53]

The change of heart on the part of Jewish youth is reflected in the novel *Nakip Veka* (The Scum of the Age), written by the Russian-Jewish writer Grigori Bogrov (1825–1885), and published in the *Razsvet* in 1879 and 1880. The hero, in severing connections with his cosmopolitan circle, bitterly denounces his former colleagues for disloyalty to their own people. In relation to the nations in whose midst they live, he reminds them, they are only like guests at a party, subject to dismissal at any time.[54]

The outstanding figure in this period of national resurgence was Eliezer Perlman, known as Ben Yehuda (1858–1922), the self-styled disciple of Smolenskin. Ben Yehuda, who was born in the town of Lushki, province of Vilno, showed an interest in *Haskalah* literature in his early youth. As a student in the *Realschule* of

51. *Yozrim U-Bonim,* I, 221.
52. *Russky Evrei,* 1879, p. 3.
53. *Ibid.,* 1880, p. 913.
54. *Razsvet,* 1880, no. 7, p. 273.

Dwinsk, he came under the influence of socialism and lost interest in the Hebrew language, in which he had shown great promise. The Russo-Turkish War, however, caused a decided change in him. In an autobiographical sketch[55] he relates how deeply stirred he was by the sentiments of racial solidarity expressed by the Russian press in regard to the Balkan Slavs for whose national freedom Russia was fighting. One night, as he was reading one such article, he began to think of his own people. He asked himself, "Why should we be any less worthy than any other people? What about our nation? Our language? Our land?"

This thought gave him no peace until he decided to work for the resettlement of Palestine. To realize his ideal he determined to go to Paris to study medicine and then, as a physician, to settle in the Holy Land. In the French capital he became acquainted with a Russian writer to whom he confided his cherished dream, and who encouraged him and urged him to express his ideas in print.

Following this advice, Ben Yehuda wrote an article "Sheelah Nikbadah" (An Important Problem), which appeared in *Ha-Shahar*.[56] Rejecting the thesis that Jews were not a nation, he pointed out that they possessed all the attributes of nationality, such as a common history, common memories, a feeling of common solidarity, and a common language, Hebrew.[57] The two factors which had saved the Jews from national extinction, he asserted, were their unique religion and the antagonism of other nations. These factors could no longer serve to save the Jews from national death. What we need today, he declared, is a national center to serve as the heart feeding the blood arteries of the nation.[58] He appealed to Jewish writers to work in this cause and to organize a society for the promotion of colonization in the Holy Land. "If we only do this," he proclaimed, "we shall be able to stand up and the redemption of Israel will come speedily."

Ben Yehuda took Smolenskin to task for suggesting "half-measures." An open letter to the editor of *Ha-Shahar*[59] criticized him for his failure to preach a return to Zion. The cultivation of the Hebrew language and literature alone, Ben Yehuda contended, was not enough. "If I did not believe in the possibility of Israel's redemption I would discard the Hebrew language as a worthless thing." [60] His contention was that Hebrew could be revived only in

55. *Sefer Zikkaron,* ed. N. Sokolow, pp. 188–192.
56. *Ha-Shahar,* IX, 360–366.
57. *Ibid.,* IX, 363.
58. *Ibid.,* IX, 364–365.
59. *Ha-Shahar,* X, 241–245.
60. *Ibid.,* X, 242.

a land where Jews constituted a majority. "Let us therefore," he appealed, "increase the number of Jews in our desolate land. Let us revive the nation, and the language, too, will be revived." [61] Ben Yehuda had no doubts about the ability of the Jewish religion to survive. "The Jewish faith," he asserted, "can live on in the Diaspora. It will assume new form according to time and environment, and will share the lot of all other religions. But as for the Jewish nation, it can exist only on its own soil. Only upon the soil can it find rejuvenation and bloom forth in splendor as in the days of yore!" [62]

Thus, two years before the pogroms of 1881, which were responsible for the *Hibat Zion* (Love of Zion) movement aiming at colonization of Jews in Palestine, and nineteen years before the first Zionist Congress launched Zionism as a political movement, Ben Yehuda had already formulated the Zionist program.[63]

So it was that as the hope of achieving the status of equality was fading for the Jews in Russia, new hope was kindled in many hearts by the ideas of Smolenskin and Ben Yehuda. The first bolstered up their morale by awakening an interest in their own national culture; the second held out the hope of an independent life on the soil of their ancestors.

61. *Ibid.*, X, 244.
62. *Ibid.*, X, 245.
63. In 1882 Ben Yehuda settled in Palestine. He is regarded as the creator of modern Hebrew as a living tongue. In 1912 he organized the first Hebrew daily in Jerusalem, *Doar Ha-Yom* (Daily Post). He is the author of *Milon Ha-Lashon Ha-Ibrit*—Thesaurus Totius Hebraitatis—a complete dictionary of ancient and modern Hebrew with French and German translations.

XI

JEWS IN THE REVOLUTIONARY MOVEMENT

THUS far we have discussed Jewish movements which were motivated exclusively by the desire to solve the problem of the Jew. Now we must deal with Jewish participation in the Russian revolutionary movement, which, though directed toward other ends, had an important bearing on the Jewish problem.

The secret anti-government activity which began in the reign of Alexander II was brought about by the refusal of the tsar to grant a constitutional régime and by his failure adequately to solve the land needs of the peasantry.[1] The spirit of rebellion spread to the non-Russian racial minorities of the empire, resulting in the Polish uprising of 1863 and in signs of unrest in the Ukraine and the Caucasus. The rebelliousness of the heterogeneous groups was motivated by both political dissatisfaction and national aspirations.

Of all these elements, the Jews were the most loyal to the government of Alexander II. The minor reforms granted by the emperor did little to alleviate their economic condition and improved their legal status only to an inconsiderable extent; yet his abolition of some of the cruel laws of Nicholas I elicited their grateful allegiance. Lev Deich, an important Jewish revolutionist, testifies to this absence of the spirit of revolt among the Jewish masses, ascribing it in part to their devotion to Alexander II. He believes furthermore that their isolation and their cowed spirits, crushed by centuries of oppression, militated against rebelliousness.[2]

Neither was there any spirit of unrest manifest among the educated and wealthy of Jewry. The special privileges they enjoyed secured for the government the good-will of the very classes which by virtue of contact with Russian thought were most exposed to revolutionary ideas.

Of the negligible number of Jewish revolutionists in the sixties, the most important was the converted Jew, Nicholas Utin, sometimes referred to as the first Russian Marxist. He attracted atten-

1. On the provisions of the peasant reform of 1861 see G. Vernadsky, *A History of Russia,* pp. 152–155; A. Kornilov, *Modern Russ. Hist.,* II, 45–54. On the attitude of the liberal as well as the radical elements in Russia toward the manner in which the government disposed of the land problem of the peasantry, see A. A. Kornilov, *Obshchestvennoe Dvizhenie pri Aleksandre Vtorom,* Ch. XI.

2. L. Deich, *Rol Evr. v Russk. Revol. Dvizhenii,* pp. 28–29.

tion in 1861 during the anti-government student demonstrations, in which he played a conspicuous rôle. He was also one of the leaders of the party *Zemlia i Volia* (Land and Freedom).[3] When the famous revolutionary of the sixties, Serno Solovevich, was arrested, Utin succeeded him on the party's central committee.

In Geneva, whither he fled to avoid arrest, Utin took over the editorship of the periodical *Narodnoe Delo* (The Case of the People), founded by the Russian anarchist, Michael Bakunin (1814–1876). In the famous struggle between Marx and Bakunin in the First (Socialist) International, Utin supported Marx, thus adding fuel to the anti-Jewish sentiments of their opponent.[4] Utin played an important rôle in the Socialist International. In 1870, he and a group of his followers created the Russian section of that body and at their invitation Karl Marx agreed to represent them on the central committee of the International.[5]

In the early seventies, with the growth of a Jewish student body which came into closer contact with the Russian intelligentsia, the number of Jewish revolutionaries increased considerably. But it was as Russians concerned with the plight of the Russian people, particularly the peasantry, and not as Jews engaged in the battle for Jewish rights, that these students joined the revolutionary movement. In his memoirs, a Jewish revolutionary of the period thus describes his attitude to the Russian peasants: "We are *Narodniki*,[6] the mujiks are our natural brothers." [7]

Upon their own people most of the early Jewish revolutionists looked with contempt, stigmatizing them as bourgeois and orthodox. Neither did they have any sympathy for the Jewish workers, most of whom were artisans. "For us," records Lev Deich, "there existed

3. This secret revolutionary group, which consisted of students and some writers, was organized in 1862 and existed only two years. It should not be confused with the more important revolutionary organization of the same name formed in 1877. About the earlier *Zemlia i Volia* see A. A. Kornilov, *Obsh. Dvizh. pri Aleks. Vto.*, pp. 146–147. L. F. Panteleev, *Iz Vospominani Proshlago*, I, 249–339; II, 1–148. Panteleev was one of active participants in the earlier *Zemlia i Volia.*

4. On Bakunin's unfriendly attitude to Jews, whom he regarded as enemies of Russia and the Slavic races, see V. Bogucharsky, *Aktivnoe Narod. Semides. Godov*, pp. 76–77.

5. V. Bogucharsky, *Akt. Narod. Semides. God.*, pp. 48, 90–91. For more details on Utin see *Historische Schriften*, III, 82–91; L. F. Panteleev, *Iz Vosp. Prosh.*, I, Ch. XXIV; A. Kornilov, *Obsh. Dvizh. pri Aleks. Vto.*, p. 147. Utin did not stay long in the revolutionary movement. In a letter to the tsar written in 1877, he pleaded to be forgiven for the sins of his youth. He died in the early nineties. Bogucharsky, *Akt. Narod. Semides God.*, p. 48; *Hist. Schr.*, III, 89–90.

6. The Russian socialists of the seventies called themselves *Narodniki* (Populists), because their program called for revolutionary propaganda among the masses of the people, chiefly the peasants.

7. Morris Winchevsky, *Zukunft*, 1906, XI, 38.

but one unhappy, dispossessed people, consisting mainly of tillers of the soil and partly of factory workers whose speech was the dominant Russian language. The artisans we regarded as exploiters." Since most of the working elements among the Jews, he adds, consisted of craftsmen who did not hesitate to engage in petty trade, the Jewish revolutionaries looked upon them as *geschäftmacher* (tradesmen).[8]

To these Jewish champions of the Russian masses, all specifically Jewish matters—religious, cultural, or national—were anathema. "For us," reminisces Aaron Zundelevich, a prominent revolutionary leader of the seventies, "Jewry as a national organism did not present a phenomenon worthy of support. Jewish nationalism, it seemed to us, had no *raison d'être*. As for religion, that cement which combines the Jews into one unit, it represented to us complete retrogression. . . . For a Jewish *Narodnik* the motto—'Go to the people'—meant go to the Russian people."[9]

The Jewish revolutionaries maintained that emancipation of the Jews depended on emancipation of the Russian people, with whom, they believed, the Jews should completely assimilate.[10] Discussing his reasons for devoting himself to the Russian revolutionary movement in preference to the struggle for Jewish emancipation, Paul Akselrod, an eminent revolutionary, explains that to him the Jewish problem shrank and paled into insignificance in face of the expected era of equality and fraternity which the pending "enthronement of the poorest and most downtrodden" promised to inaugurate. He was confident that the Jewish problem would be solved with the liberation of the masses. It was because of this belief, he asserts, that he dedicated himself to the redemption of the poor and humble in Russia.[11] Similar views were expressed in the memoirs of Vladimir Iokhelson, another outstanding revolutionist.[12]

Yet, though most of the revolutionaries did not admit it, and were perhaps not fully conscious of it themselves, there is good reason to believe that the disabilities from which their own people suffered did contribute toward their interest in the revolutionary movement. This became more apparent in the late seventies and the eighties, when the government's attitude toward the Jews became more hostile. A Jewish *Narodnik*, H. Magat, in a letter written in 1879, points to Jewish suffering as a motivating force in his revolutionary activity. "I see," he cries out, "two and a half million

8. L. Deich, *Rol Evr. Rus. Rev. Dviz.*, p. 56.
9. S. L. Zitron, *Drei Literarische Dorot*, II, 109.
10. *Ibid.*, II, 124.
11. P. B. Akselrod, *Perezhitoe i Peredumannoe*, Bk. I, 73.
12. V. Yokhelson, *Byloe*, 1918, July, p. 56.

people in bondage, and I say: 'One must stand up on behalf of this humiliated and defenseless people, and fight for its freedom.' "[13]

The extent of Jewish influence upon the early revolutionary movement in Russia is a controversial subject. Deich maintains that Jewish influence was negligible both in number and in importance.[14] The Jewish historian, Cherikover, on the other hand, through a study of later and more elaborate sources, assigns a place of far greater importance to Jewish revolutionaries. He states that, while the Jews had no share in the creation of the movement and did not produce even one outstanding philosopher, theoretician, or pamphleteer among the *Narodniki*, they did play an important rôle as organizers and "technicians" of the revolution.[15] This complete absence of Jews from among the original leaders and theoreticians of the movement he ascribes to their isolation in the ghetto, from which they were just beginning to emerge during the early stages of the revolution.

An article in *Katorga i Ssylka* (Hard Labor and Exile), based on official data culled from tsarist archives, furnishes statistics on the relative representation in the revolutionary movement of various classes and racial groups of Russia. These figures show that in the middle of the seventies, the Jews constituted a little over 4 per cent, a figure corresponding to their percentage of population.[16] Another survey of political crimes published in the revolutionary organ *Literatura Partii "Narodnoi Voli"* (The Literature of the People's Will) corroborates these figures, giving the percentage of Jews participating up to the year 1878 as 4.4 and showing a slight decrease to 4.1 from that year to 1880.[17]

Jewish revolutionaries participated in every phase of revolutionary activity. In the early seventies, when the slogan of the revolution was "Go to the people," Jews also took part in this crusade to propagandize the peasantry. Among the sons and daughters of the Russian nobility and the intellectual aristocracy who abandoned homes and careers to live and work among the peasants were to be found Jewish young men and women who also left families, studies and professions to gain converts for the cause among Russia's tillers of the soil. To approach the Russian masses, these Jews had to overcome numerous barriers. In order to gain the confidence of the peasants and become a part of them, as the program of the

13. Quoted in *Hist. Schr.*, III, 136.
14. *Rol Evr. Rus. Rev. Dviz.*, pp. 32–33.
15. *Hist. Schr.*, III, 152–171.
16. *Katorga i Ssylka*, 1928, No. 38, pp. 29–56. Summary of figures on Jewish participation also on p. 47 in supplement.
17. *Literatura Partii "Narodnoi Voli,"* 1905, p. 356.

Narodniki demanded, it was necessary for these missionaries of the revolution to learn farming, master various handicrafts, study the peasants' folk-lore and manner of speech and even to dress as mujiks.

How difficult it was for Jews to disguise their Jewishness is related by Lev Deich, one of the most Russified of the Jewish revolutionaries. Dressed as a mujik, he had been working in a village preparing the ground for propaganda, when one day he was asked point-blank, "Are you not a *Zhid?*" (Jew). To this query Deich was obliged to remain silent.[18]

But there were those who prepared themselves even for such emergencies. To integrate themselves with the Russian masses, they resorted to conversion which, they believed, would establish a spiritual kinship between them and the peasants. An insight into the psychology of these zealots is given by one of the earliest *Narodniki,* O. Aptekman. "I am a Jew," he said to himself. "How will the Russian people receive me? Will they trust me?" After embracing the Greek-Orthodox faith, he went forth on his mission with greater confidence. "Now I am going to the Russian masses not as a Jew but as a Christian. I am at one with the people." [19] But neither Russification nor the affectation of peasant garb nor conversion was of much avail in bridging the gulf between the Jewish revolutionist and the Russian peasant.

Nor were the Jews particularly well suited for the terroristic activities upon which the *Narodniki* embarked in the late seventies after their efforts to stir up rebellion among the peasantry had failed. In this activity the number of Jews was small and those who participated showed a particular aversion for their task. Centuries of submissiveness to force, coupled with a religious training that bred an abhorrence of bloodshed, may be said to have been responsible for their reluctance to engage in violent action. As Deich puts it: "Neither by our nature nor by our training were we qualified to shed human blood." [20]

The first of the small number of early Jewish terrorists was Solomon Wittenberg, who organized a revolutionary circle in his native city. In a biographical sketch, a friend characterizes him as cultured, highly ethical, and of broad interests.[21] Wittenberg's fervent faith in the cause, as well as his deeply religious nature, are

18. *Za Polveka,* pp. 201–202.
19. O. Aptekman, "Moi Pervye Shagi na Puti Propagandy" (My First Steps as a Propagandist), *Popular Library of Magazine Kat. i Ssyl.,* Nos. 28–29, pp. 13 and 49.
20. *Zukunft,* 1916, p. 119.
21. A. Moreinis, *Kat. i Ssyl.,* 1929, No. 56, pp. 47–67.

evidenced in his farewell letter to his comrades before his execution. "Our blood will nourish the seed of socialism—of that I am certain," he writes. Quoting the words ascribed to Jesus, "Forgive them, for they know not what they do," he charged his closest friends not to seek revenge for his death.[22]

It is interesting to note that not only the early Christian *Narodniki* but the Jewish revolutionists as well were deeply imbued with the teachings of the New Testament and the spirit of Jesus. Aptekman relates in his memoirs that he often found the youth praying and weeping over the Gospels in preparation for their revolutionary mission. Considering the atheistic and nihilistic background of the movement, this deeply religious evangelism presents a curious paradox.[23]

While Wittenberg was the first Jewish terrorist, Aaron Gobet of Vilno was the first Russian Jew to pay the supreme penalty for such activity. In 1878, as a result of his efforts, the first strike organized by a revolutionary circle took place in a large textile factory in St. Petersburg. The famous George Plekhanov said of Gobet, who was an ordinary workingman, that he was worth as much as a revolutionary circle.[24] The Jewish terrorist was executed in 1879, when his plot to assassinate Alexander II was discovered.[25] Among the six terrorists sentenced to die for the assassination of Alexander II on March 1, 1881, was a Jewish woman, Hessie Helfman, whose sentence was commuted to hard labor. She died in the fortress of Petropavlovsk.

Of the few Jews who succumbed to police grilling and betrayed their comrades, Grigori Goldenberg (1855–1880) was the most notorious. He occupied an important position in the revolutionary movement, having served on the executive committee of *Narodnaia Volia*[26] which he helped organize. Goldenberg shot and killed Governor-General Kropotkin, of Kharkov, and participated in planned attacks on the life of the emperor. After five months of incarceration in the fortress of Petropavlovsk, he broke down and revealed the identity of his colleagues. From the confession which he wrote in prison, it appears that it was not fear and torment alone that led him to betray his comrades.[27] It seems that his sensitive, sick, and

22. Letter published in *Literatura Partii "Narodni Voli,"* 1905, pp. 11–12.
23. See, for example, Stepniak, *Underground Russia,* p. 23.
24. *Hist. Schr.,* III, 141.
25. *Ibid.,* III, 140–141.
26. *Narodnaia Volia* (The People's Will) is the name of the revolutionary party organized in 1879. It used terrorism as a political weapon, and, though small in number, managed to commit a number of political murders, including that of the tsar.
27. Confession published by R. Cantor in *Krasny Arkhiv,* 1928, XXX, 117–183.

tortured soul could not endure the suffering of those involved in the terroristic acts, particularly since he came to the conclusion that these acts were entirely futile. In his confession he justifies himself thus:

> The wailing of mothers and sisters of the political prisoners . . . the arrests, exiles and executions so shattered my spirit that I could see no way out. . . . I know that the disclosure of these secrets was terrible, but even more terrible, it appeared to me, was the existence of secrets which were the cause of so much misery and torture.[28]

It is believed that the sly promises made by the authorities about granting a liberal constitution to Russia and amnesty for all political prisoners as a reward for his information, contributed to his breakdown. The cheering words which Goldenberg spoke to a fellow prisoner about to be exiled indicate how much reliance he placed on the pledges made to him by the officials: "Do not despair, pretty soon you will all be freed. I am negotiating with the government about a constitution."[29]

Contemporaries as well as his latest biographer maintain that Goldenberg cannot be regarded simply as a traitor. According to the testimony of his comrades, he was not treacherous by nature. Not overwise or strongly principled, Goldenberg, though unduly self-confident, was essentially a sincere and honest person.[30] A modern writer suggests that the moral collapse which led to betrayal and then to suicide was due not alone to personal weakness of character, but also to the fact that methods of bloody terror were altogether too new to the Jewish revolutionary and still alien to his spirit.[31]

It was in the organizational phases of revolutionary activity, for which Jews were much more suited, that they were most successful. One of the outstanding organizers of the seventies was Mark Natanson, who in 1869 organized in the capital the first of the revolutionary-educational units commonly known as the Chaikovsky cells. Although it is generally assumed that the student Chaikovsky was the originator of these widespread socialist groups, it has been established that Natanson was really their founder.[32] In 1876, he amalgamated the various cells into a unified organization known as "The Northern-Revolutionary Narodny Group," from which later there emerged the revolutionary party *Zemlia i Volia*.

28. *Ibid.*, 160–161, 166.
29. A. Bialovesky, *Byloe,* 1906, August, p. 204.
30. *Ibid.*
31. *Hist. Schr.*, III, 148.
32. Deich, *Rol Evr.*, pp. 30–31, pp. 166–167.

In her memoirs, the famous Vera Figner speaks of Natanson as an "incomparable propagandist" and as a "wise and energetic leader" who headed *Zemlia i Volia*.[33] In a monograph on his life she asserts that no one else in his time could measure up to him in revolutionary achievement.[34]

The leader of the Moscow Chaikovsky cell, second in importance to that of St. Petersburg, was the Jewish student Simon Kliachko. This cell played an important rôle in the distribution of illegal literature among the revolutionary groups in Russia.[35] In the printing, distribution, and importation of illegal literature from abroad, Jewish revolutionists took a leading part. The center of their activity was Vilno, which in the seventies functioned as an important medium for the illegal political traffic between Russia and Western Europe.[36]

The cradle of Jewish socialist propaganda was the rabbinic seminary of Vilno, where such outstanding figures as Aaron Lieberman, Aaron Zundelevich, Vladimir Iokhelson,[37] and Arkadi Finkelstein were initiated into the movement. Finkelstein, who organized an illegal library at the seminary,[38] was expelled, as were the other revolutionary students when discovered by the school authorities. Zundelevich organized a Jewish revolutionary circle consisting mostly of expelled rabbinic students. Among its members was also Anna Epstein, referred to in revolutionary literature as "chief smuggler and nurse of the revolution." [39]

Energetic and efficient, Zundelevich pioneered in organizing illegal transportation on a large scale. This revolutionary smuggler, sometimes described as "The Minister of Foreign Affairs of the Revolution," was among the organizers of *Zemlia i Volia* and later became a member of the executive committee of *Narodnaia Volia*.

33. Vera Figner, *Polnoe Sob. Sochin.*, I, 113. Figner is referring to the revolutionary party *Zemlia i Volia,* which was organized in the later seventies and which engaged in revolutionary propaganda among the peasantry.

34. V. Figner, *Kat. i Ssyl.*, 1929, no. 56, pp. 141–150.

35. Aptekman, *Russkoe Proshloe,* 1923, Bk. II, 89–103. See also *Istoriko-Revoliutsionny Sbornik,* I, 38.

36. V. Iokhelson, *Byloe,* 1918, July, pp. 58–59.

37. Vladimir Iokhelson, who spent many years in Siberia for his revolutionary activities, developed there an interest in ethnology and anthropology. His studies of little known tribes residing in Siberia were published by the Imperial Russian Geographical Society and the Imperial Academy of Sciences. From 1912 to 1922 he was associate curator of the Museum of Anthropology and Ethnology at the Academy of Sciences in Russia. In 1922 he came to the United States, where he was associated with the Carnegie Institute until his death in 1937. See *New York Times,* Nov. 2, 1937, p. 28.

38. *Ist.-Rev. Sbor.*, I, 37.

39. She is also noted for having been the first Jewish woman in a Russian university. *Hist. Schr.*, I, 471.

It is noteworthy that even before the creation of this party, he had advocated the use of terror as a political weapon and had assisted in the perpetration of two terroristic acts. Zundelevich urged closer coöperation with the Social Democrats of Germany, who were exceedingly unpopular with the Russian socialists of the seventies.

A letter written by Alexander Mikhailov, leader of *Narodnaia Volia,* characterizes Zundelevich not only as practical and energetic but also as one who had the most ideal relationships with his comrades. "A more tender, a more humane man could not be found among us," he declares. The sentiments he inspired may be judged from the outcry with which Mikhailov's letter ends: "Our dear Moshe, where are you now? What has happened to you?"[40]

In his desire to establish closer connection with the Western European socialist movement, Zundelevich was supported by Paul Akselrod, a close friend and associate of Plekhanov with whom he established the first cell of the Russian Social Democratic party.[41] Akselrod and Zundelevich, recognizing the importance of the West European workers' movement, were the only two in the seventies who served as intermediaries between West European and Russian socialism. Thus it was, a modern historian observes, that Jews performed a special function in the history of Russian socialism.[42]

Jewish revolutionaries not only served as intermediaries between Russian and West European socialism, some of them were also responsible for the creation of such movements in European countries. Constantine Katz of Ekaterinoslav, who, under the assumed name of Gera Dobrodzanu, became famous as literary critic, publicist, and authority on Roumania's agrarian problem, is regarded as pioneer of the socialist movement in that country.

Another Russian-Jewish political emigré, Anna Rosenstein, under the adopted name of Kuleshov, together with her husband Turati, organized the Italian Socialist Party. She also founded and edited for thirty-five years the central organ of the party, *Kritica Sociale.* It is interesting to note that when this Jewish woman revolutionary, the first female student in the Polytechnique of Zurich, was exiled from France for anarchistic propaganda, the famous Russian writer, Ivan Turgenev, interceded in her behalf.[43]

Russian-Jewish revolutionaries were also instrumental in the

40. *Hist. Schr.,* III, 159–160.

41. Deich, *Rol Evr.,* p. 136.

42. *Hist. Schr.,* III, 163.

43. On Katz-Dobrodzanu see Dr. Joseph Kisman, *Hist. Schr.,* III, 447–484; also M. Rosenbaum, *Mi-Zikronotov shel Soziolist-Revoluzioner,* p. 222. On Anna Rosenstein see *Hist. Schr.,* III, 165, and sketch of her life in final chapter of Deich's *Rol Evr. Rus. Rev. Dviz.,*

creation of the first Jewish socialist organization in the world, The Hebrew Socialist Union, established in London in May, 1876. Among its founders was Aaron Lieberman (1845–1880), a former student of the rabbinic school in Vilno and a member of the first revolutionary circle of that city. Lieberman, a colorful, gifted, and dynamic personality, occupied a central and unique position among the Jewish socialists of the seventies. He was born in a small town in the province of Grodno and very early in life came under the influence of the *Haskalah* literature. When the revolutionary circle of Vilno was discovered by the police, he fled to Königsberg, where he lived for a time. Emigrating to London, he made the acquaintance of Peter Lavrov,[44] famous Russian socialist, and became one of his collaborators on the bi-weekly publication *Vpered* (Forward). Previously, Lieberman, who was given to dramatic gestures, sent Lavrov his hat as a token of admiration. "Since I cannot send you my head, I am sending you my hat," [45] an accompanying note stated.

The first to conceive the idea of a Jewish revolutionary party, Aaron Lieberman was a unique phenomenon in his time because of his strong Jewish sentiments. His comrade Zundelevich describes him as a "highly educated and original personality who combined progressive European ideas with national-Jewish sympathies." [46]

Evidence of Lieberman's Jewish attachments was his special fondness for the Hebrew language, which he mastered. When the question of the creation of a Jewish socialist literature arose in the Vilno revolutionary group, he insisted that the medium be Hebrew. The others opposed socialist work among Jews, but insisted that if such propaganda were undertaken, the language used should be Yiddish—the speech used by the masses. Lieberman urged the use of Hebrew because he considered it the best literary vehicle for the training of Jewish leadership among Talmudic students.[47]

Unlike his comrades, who disdained these students, Lieberman had a high opinion of their cultural status and idealistic potentialities. Contrasting them to the opportunistic assimilationists, he praised the *yeshibah* students as "the pillars upon which rests the honor of Israel." [48]

The first socialist proclamation written in Hebrew and addressing itself "to the intelligent Jewish youth" was issued by Lieberman

44. Peter Lavrov (1823–1900), theoretician of the *Narodniki* movement, was a political emigré in England.
45. Zinberg, *Perez.*, I, 236.
46. B. Frumkin, *Ev. Star.*, 1911, p. 235.
47. V. Yokhelson, *Byloe*, 1918, July, p. 57.
48. *Ha-Emet*, 1877, no. 2, p. 23.

in July, 1876, as a supplement to *Vpered*. This propaganda pamphlet found its way to the group he sought to reach, for a Jewish writer states that many of these manifestoes were surreptitiously concealed between the pages of the Talmud.[49]

While his use of Hebrew for propaganda may be explained on grounds of expediency, there is no doubt that sentimental reasons also moved him. This is especially borne out by the fact that he wrote the by-laws for the London Hebrew Socialist Union in Hebrew first, translating afterward for practical purposes into Yiddish.[50]

Lieberman's Jewish sentiments expressed themselves also in his regard for Judaic teachings. His attitude is revealed in the first correspondence he published in *Vpered*. The article which proclaims the equality of all nations and races and hails the Russian peasants as "our brothers," with whom as Russians, Jews share common interests and common customs, points with pride also to the fact that socialist ideals are inherent in Judaism and form an integral part of Jewish tradition. "The *Obshchina* [village commune] is our very existence, revolution is our tradition, the commune is the foundation of our legislation," he declares, elaborating upon these assertions by citing Biblical laws. He points to Marx and Lassalle and other socialist leaders as products of the Jewish spirit, and exhorts his fellow-Jews to follow their teachings with the same fearless defiance of persecution which their ancestors exhibited in the Middle Ages.[51]

To encourage and facilitate Jewish participation in the socialist movement, Lieberman advocated the formation of special Jewish sections. These groups were to be federated with the Russian Socialist party as well as with the socialist parties of Western Europe. He sent formulation of this plan, together with by-laws for the contemplated Jewish branches, from London to his comrades in Vilno. Because of the break-up of the revolutionary circle in that city, Lieberman's idea, the first of its kind to be suggested, did not materialize. It may rightly be regarded, however, as the forerunner of the Jewish socialist movement of a later date.[52]

The first socialist organ in Hebrew, *Ha-Emet* (The Truth), was also issued by Lieberman. This monthly, which he published in Vienna under the assumed name of Arthur Freeman, appeared in May, 1877. One of Lieberman's close collaborators on the periodical

49. L. Zitron, *Drei Liter. Dorot,* II, 18. A complete Yiddish translation of this proclamation is found in *ibid.*, pp. 15–18. Also in *Roter Pinkes,* 1924, II, 167.

50. A copy of the by-laws both in Hebrew and in Yiddish is found in *Hist. Schr.*, I, 541–544.

51. *Ev. Star.*, 1911, p. 237.

52. Plan and by-laws are published by N. Bukhbinder in *Istoriko-Revoliutsionny Sbornik,* I, 44–51.

was a well-known revolutionary and gifted Hebrew-Yiddish publicist, Leizer Zukerman.[53] *Ha-Emet* had a short-lived existence, which ended after the third number was confiscated and barred from admission to Russia.

Morris Winchevsky, who edited *Asefat Hakamim* (The Assembly of the Wise), the Hebrew socialist publication which appeared next, describes *Ha-Emet* as a "fine and honest literary undertaking." Since all articles were written anonymously, he observes, the idealistic standard of the magazine was unmarred by personal ambition.[54] Speaking of Lieberman's literary style, Winchevsky says, "From his writing one could see that in spite of his Western culture, he remained a learned, sharp-witted Talmudist who enjoyed making his readers wrinkle their foreheads trying to understand him." [55]

Despite these sentiments and traits, Lieberman was completely at variance with the ideology of both the religious and the national Jew, believing in the preservation neither of the Jew nor of Judaism. Against both viewpoints he protested strongly:

> At a time like this when the cry on every tongue is bread and work, when the problem of the knife and the fork is of greater importance than all other problems put together, at such a time our literature finds nothing more important to discuss than the question of religion and nationality and other such worthless things which every sensible person has ceased to be interested in.[56]

He urged the Jews to get closer to and to assimilate with the peoples in whose midst they resided. But unlike other assimilationists of his time, he did not believe that Russification and fusion with the peoples of the world would of itself solve the Jewish problem. The redemption of the Jews, like that of the rest of the world, depended on the solution of the economic problem. "It is because of this unsolved question," he asserted, "that Jewish blood has been shed in all lands of Europe." [57]

Like most revolutionaries, Lieberman led a stormy and turbulent life. A dramatic highlight in his career was his trial, together with a group of other socialists, in Berlin in 1879. Referred to as "The trial of the Russian Nihilists," the case attracted wide attention. Lieberman was sentenced to six months' imprisonment and deporta-

53. *Ev. Star.*, 1911, p. 530.
54. *Zukunft,* 1907, Feb., p. 46.
55. *Ibid.*, p. 48.
56. Introductory editorial to *Ha-Emet,* p. 2.
57. *Ibid.*, no. 3, p. 34.

tion from Prussia. In 1880, he committed suicide in New York for some unknown reason.[58]

Although Lieberman, as has been pointed out, was practically the only Jewish socialist retaining Jewish sentiments or interests—the others having completely dissociated themselves from Jewish life, some even to the extent of conversion[59]—the entire Jewish community was reviled both by the anti-Jewish press and by the government[60] for the activity of the revolutionists. ***Russky Evrei*** commented bitterly on the irony of the situation: "Jewry, scoffed at and rejected by its errant sons, is yet held accountable for these very renegades! This makes it imperative that we exert all our energies to combat these enemies of the general peace and welfare." [61] The memoirs of A. Lessin, poet, publicist, and for many years editor of the Yiddish monthly, *Zukunft*, reveal how widespread this resentment against the Jewish rebels was among the Jewish masses, and how genuine was their loyalty to the régime of Alexander II. Lessin maintains that he cannot recall a single "good word" ever spoken by a Jew about the socialists, who were never even spoken of as "socialists," but merely as "they." The sympathy of the people was decidedly on the side of the emperor and his government. Lessin recalls that his father used to speak of Loris-Melikov[62] as a man with a heart of gold praying "that the Lord grant both him and the tsar long life." [63]

The editor of *Zukunft* also recounts how sorrowfully news of the assassination of Alexander II was received by the Jews. His family was engaged in celebrating the Jewish festival of Purim when his father, ashen and trembling, announced the news. Genuine grief gripped the celebrants and the home turned into a house of mourning. How differently Jews had reacted to the death of Nicholas I was

58. On Lieberman, see Zinberg, *Perez.*, I, 233–263; B. Frumkin, *Ev. Star.*, 1911, pp. 234–248, pp. 513–533; Zitron, *Drei Liter. Dorot*, II, 3–50; Cherikover, *Hist. Schr.*, I, 469–532.

59. Among these converts women constituted the greatest number. Most women married out of their faith. See *Hist. Schr.*, III, 133–134.

60. According to the testimony of Deich, there was no discrimination made by the government in its treatment of Jewish political prisoners. "No matter how poor our Russian or how Jewish our appearance," he states, "we were never insulted as Jews." *Zukunft*, 1916, p. 158.

61. 1880, no. 9, editorial.

62. As head of a government committee to suppress the revolutionary movement, Loris-Milikov (1825–1888) sought to stamp out rebellion through liberal concessions to public opinion. He prepared a plan of a modified form of representative government, which was to be promulgated on March 1, 1881. Because Alexander II was assassinated on that day, the plan, which is known as Melikov's Constitution, was never put into effect.

63. *Hist. Schr.*, III, 177, 179.

recalled by one of his uncles: "Then, it was an occasion for joy; now it brings darkness and gloom." [64]

That the Jews as a whole were nevertheless held responsible for Jewish socialists is to be seen in the following incident related by the poet E. Zunser. In 1872, after the arrest in Vilno of a group of young Jews charged with nihilism, Governor-General Potapov summoned a number of Jewish representatives of that community. "In addition to all the other good qualities which you Jews possess, about the only thing you need is to become nihilists too," he complained. "We! Nihilists?" a member of the group asked. "Your children are, at any rate," Potapov replied. "They have become so through the bad education you are giving them." "Pardon me, General," Jacob Baritt answered, "this is not quite right! As long as we educated our children there were no nihilists among us. They became nihilists only when you took the education of our children into your hands." [65] According to Zunser, Baritt's reply was directly responsible for the shutting down of the rabbinic schools of Vilno and Zhitomir. The *ukaz* closing the two seminaries came shortly after the governor-general reported Baritt's statement to St. Petersburg.[66]

The increased activities of the revolutionaries in the later seventies intensified the hostility of the press and the government against the Jews. "Everyone knows," declared *Novoe Vremia*, "that these Jews, since time immemorial the representatives of the revolutionary spirit, now stand at the head of the nihilists." [67] Reflecting the attitude of the government was a report submitted by the governor of Minsk in 1878, which pointed to increased anti-government activity among Jewish youth and urged that educational opportunities for Jews be restricted.[68]

Thus did the Jewish revolutionists, whose ultimate aim, however indirectly, was the solution of the Jewish problem, complicate the Jewish situation and add another vexing problem to those already in existence.

64. *Ibid.*, III, 182–183.
65. *A Jewish Bard*, p. 32.
66. On closing of the seminaries see above page 95.
67. Quoted in Zinberg, *Ist. Ev. Pech.*, p. 248.
68. Gessen, *Ist. Ev. Nar. v Ros.*, II, 212.

XII

ECONOMIC POSITION OF THE JEWS IN THE REIGN OF ALEXANDER II

THE reign of Alexander II saw an improvement in the civic and cultural status of the Russian Jew, but neither government policies nor the various Jewish movements for emancipation brought any amelioration of their economic position. Their poverty was aggravated both by the industrialization of Russia, which began in the fifties of the nineteenth century, and by the new rural economy resulting from the liberation of the serfs.

Both Jewish and non-Jewish sources supply ample testimony to the unmitigated poverty of the Jews. Levanda gives us a glimpse into a typical Jewish household of the Northwest: "Three families crowded into a rickety hovel. . . . Half-naked, hungry children huddled on an unheated oven. . . . The riotous joy of children when the father comes home with a loaf of bread in his hands." [1]

A Russian scholar made a special study in the forties of the Jewish communities in the Pale and reported that only three out of a hundred Jews possessed capital of any consequence, while the rest led a half-starved, miserable existence.[2] A government committee appointed in the eighties to investigate the condition of the Jews reported that 90 per cent of them constituted "a proletariat living from hand to mouth, in poverty and under the most trying and unhygienic conditions." [3]

A Russian statistician's survey of the province of Grodno records that "the bulk of the Jews there are poor. . . . It is not uncommon for a three- or four-room dwelling to house as many as twelve families. . . . In most cases a pound of bread, a herring, and a few onions represent the daily fare of an entire family. . . . The average earning of a Jewish breadwinner amounts to fifteen kopeks a day." [4] Conditions were not better in other parts of the Northwest, D. Afanasiev's study of the province of Kovno revealed. He

1. *Razsvet,* 1860, no. 1, p. 8.
2. B. Miliutin, *Ustroistvo i Sostoianie Evr. Obshchestv v Ross.,* pp. 225–6; quoted in *Sbornik Mater. ob Econ. Paloz. Evr. v Ross.,* Preface, p. xxi.
3. Quoted by A. Subbotin, *Ev. Bib.,* X, 76–77.
4. P. Bobrovsky, *Grodnenskaia Guberniia,* I, 858–9.

too noted that the Jews lived in crowded quarters, and that it was not uncommon for several families to occupy one small room.[5]

In 1857, a survey by the Provincial Board of Finance of Minsk of the occupations of the Jewish population of that city established that out of every hundred Jews 2.3 per cent were merchants, 4.3 per cent engaged in agricultural pursuits, 22.8 per cent were artisans, 48.4 per cent were burghers with definite occupations, and 22.4 per cent had no occupation whatsoever. The Russian economist and statistician, Zelensky, commenting on these figures, maintained that a percentage of 22.4 for the unemployed was far from accurate. The figures, he pointed out, did not take into account the large number of idle Jews who, fearful of being drafted for military service because of their unemployment status, falsified their economic position. Zelensky contended that one half, if not three-quarters, of the Jewish population could be described as living a useless and parasitic life as brokers and hucksters. This situation he ascribed not to laziness or indisposition to work, but rather to the lack of means or opportunity of engaging in productive labor.[6]

Because of the smaller number of Jews in the Ukraine and more favorable natural conditions, the economic position of the Jews was always somewhat better in that region than in the northwestern provinces. But even in the Ukraine, poverty was the common lot. A Russian economist and statistician reports that in the province of Chernigov most of the Jews lived in poverty and squalor, their food consisting generally of bread and vegetables.[7] According to the testimony of a landowner in the province of Kiev, most of the Jews of that territory were poorer than the peasants, and their existence was a most precarious one.[8]

The low economic status of the Russian Jews is clearly evidenced by their disproportionately small representation in the commercial and industrial life of the country. According to official figures of the year 1864, the number of Jewish owners of factories and industrial establishments in western Russia was far below their proportion in the population. In the province of Vilno, Jews constituted eight-thirteenths of the urban populations but owned only one-fourth of the shops and industrial plants. In Mogilev, they comprised six-sevenths of the city population but owned only one-sixth of the industrial establishments; and in Vitebsk, where Jews com-

5. *Kovenskaia Gub.*, pp. 582–3.
6. I. Zelensky, *Minskaia Gub.*, I, 658–661.
7. Domontovich, *Chernigov. Gub.*, p. 541. Quoted in *The Jewish Question in Russia*, by Prince Demidoff San-Donato, tr. by J. Michell, p. 89.
8. *Vest* (The Message), 1869, no. 312, quoted in Orshansky, *Evrei v Rossii*, p. 141.

prised one-third of the city population, they owned one-fourth of such establishments.

Even in the Southwest, where their condition was somewhat more favorable, the percentage of Jewish industrialists was still proportionately smaller than the non-Jewish. In the province of Kiev, Podol, and Vohlyn, where the percentages of the Jewish city population were respectively four-fifths, two-thirds, and nineteen-twenty-seconds, the proportions of Jewish factories and manufacturing plants as compared with non-Jewish were respectively 1:6½, 1:2¼ and 1:2.[9] It should also be noted that a goodly number of these Jewish "factories" were petty artisan shops, which the Russian statistician Zelensky refused to classify under the term factory.[10]

Statistical studies, notes Orshansky, prove that with few exceptions Jews were represented only in those branches of industrial activity which required small capital, simple machinery, and few employees. These industrial establishments, he points out, were nothing more than artisan workshops.[11]

Significant also are the statistics regarding Jewish home ownership. In Brest-Litovsk, the 7,510 Jews out of the total population of 8,829 owned 887 of the 1,139 houses in the city. In Slonim, where Jews numbered 5,476 of a total of 6,407, they owned 509 of the 734 houses.[12] The government committee which studied Jewish conditions in the eighties reported that not only was the proportion of houses owned by Jews smaller than that of non-Jews, but the homes they inhabited were usually rated as "dangerous for occupation." [13]

The density of the Jewish population as compared to that of the non-Jewish in the same area is another index to their relatively greater poverty. During the forties, 100 houses in the province of Kiev were occupied by 410 to 510 Christian inhabitants, whereas the same number of dwellings housed 1,299 Jewish occupants. This made the living space of the Jews one-third that of their Christian neighbors.[14] The same situation obtained in Poland, where official testimony revealed that Jews lived in miserable congestion and squalor.[15]

These conditions were due to the fact that space was restricted

9. Stolpiansky, *Deviat Gub. Zapadno-Russ. Kraia, 1864 goda,* pp. 34, 52, 93, 117, 137, 160, 182. Quoted in *Evr. v Ros.,* pp. 17–18.

10. I. Zelensky, *Minskaia Gub.,* II, 242.

11. *Evr. v Ros.,* p. 20.

12. *Ibid.,* p. 147.

13. A. Subbotin, *Ev. Bib.,* X, 77.

14. I. Funduklei, *Statis. Opis. Kiev. Gub.,* I, 247–8.

15. *Evr. v Ros.,* p. 150.

and that restricted areas were in the most populated sections of the Russian Empire. In provinces where Jews were allowed to reside, an average of 1,584 persons inhabited each square mile, while in the regions barred to Jews, the number of people per square mile ranged from 1,154, the highest figure, to as low as 10.[16] The approximately one and a half million Jews residing in the seventeen provinces of European Russia, exclusive of the By-Vistula region, constituted 2.1 per cent of the total population of Russia, but were so unevenly distributed that they averaged 7.85 per cent of the populations of those areas where they had legal residence. In some provinces their proportion ran as high as 13 per cent.[17] In the By-Vistula region, where there were 612,098 Jews, they formed 12.5 per cent of the total population.[18]

Authoritative historians and statisticians maintain that these averages were really higher, since many births were not recorded because of laxity in birth registration among Jews during that period. Referring to the difficulty in getting accurate figures, a statistician who made a survey of the province of Vilno ironically remarks: "To make a survey of the number of Jews here is no easier a task than to determine the population of the days of King David. . . . The Jewish community is a veritable abyss, where people are simply swallowed up without leaving a trace." [19]

The statistician Zelensky, too, complained about the difficulty of arriving at correct statistics regarding Jews. In his opinion, at least one out of every three was not registered.[20] The Jewish economist Jacob Lestchinsky suggests that in order to avoid excessive and discriminatory taxes imposed upon them, as well as to escape dreaded military service during the Nicholas régime, many Jews deliberately failed to register.[21]

The concentration of Jews in the cities and towns of the Pale intensified the demoralizing competition and poverty there. The ratio of Jewish city dwellers to non-Jewish ranged as high as 94 per cent in the case of the province of Mogilev.[22] In sharp contrast was the low ratio of Jews to Gentiles among the village population of the Pale, exclusive of the By-Vistula region. In 1881, this percentage ranged as low as 1 per cent, the highest being 6.2 per cent.[23]

16. Prince Demidoff San-Donato, *The Jewish Question in Russia*, pp. 77–78. Quoted from the *Statistical Register of Ministry for the Interior.*

17. *V. P. S. Z.*, XL, no. 42,264.

18. *Schriften far Economic un Statistic*, I, 93.

19. A. Korev, *Vilensk. Gub.*, p. 306.

20. *Minsk. Gub.*, I, 651.

21. *Schriften far Econ. un Statistic*, I, 4–5.

22. Prince Demidoff San-Donato, *J. Question in Rus.*, pp. 78–79.

23. *Sbor. Mat. ob Ec. Pol. Ev. R.*, Preface, pp. xxxvii-xxxviii.

Illuminating as to the extent of Jewish poverty are statistics of tax delinquencies. In the years 1855–57, the government was obliged to cancel the taxes of the cities of the province of Grodno, where the population consisted mostly of Jews, because of the inability of those cities to make any payment.[24] In the province of Minsk, where registered Jews represented only one-twelfth of the total population, the proportion of their tax arrears in 1860 was one-quarter of the total sum. Because more than one-half of the Jewish inhabitants of the province, who were themselves charity cases, could not pay the special tax for government-supported philanthropic agencies, the Jewish communities were obliged to assume this responsibility.[25]

The inability of the Jews to meet their taxes was due not alone to their poverty but also to the discriminatory extra taxes that were imposed upon them. The government was aware of this situation, as was evident from a report of the Ministry of the Interior which ascribed Jewish delinquency in meeting their special candle tax to disproportionate taxation.[26]

Because of their extreme poverty, the health of the Jews was inferior to that of the Christian population. Describing the village of Kobyliu in the province of Vohlyn, the priest Morachevich said of the physical condition of the Jews: "Most of them are emaciated and pale. . . . Many of them are frail and unfit for physical labor." [27]

The Russian statistician, Bobrovsky, too, noted the inferior health conditions of the Jews. In the city of Slonim, he points out, 11 per cent of the total Jewish population resorted to medical aid, while only 4 per cent of its Christian residents applied for such help. Though this more widespread application for medical care, the writer observes, may be partially attributed to their superior enlightenment, it is nonetheless true that conditions caused by their extreme poverty exposed Jews to greater disease and mortality.[28]

A study made by the War Department in 1875 revealed that Jews had twice as many physically deficient individuals as non-Jews. Recruiting records of the same year showed that two and a half times as many Jews were physically unfit for military service as non-Jews.[29]

24. P. Bobrovsky, *Grodnen. Gub.*, II, 753.
25. I. Zelensky, *Minsk. Gub.*, I, 660–1.
26. *Z. M. V. D.*, July, 1867, quoted in *Minuvshee*, pp. 22–23.
27. *Etnog. Sbornik*, 1853, I, 296, quoted in *Ev. v Ros.*, p. 152.
28. *Grod. Gub.*, I, 858; II, 871–2.
29. Subbotin, *Ev. Bib.*, X, 76.

The rate of mortality, too, was relatively higher among the Jews. From 1844 to 1847, according to official figures, their death rate was twice as high as that of the Greek-Orthodox population residing in the Pale.[30] A statistical survey of the province of Grodno revealed that in its cities, largely populated by Jews, the mortality was eight times higher than in the country towns. "Death," says Bobrovsky, "was more successful in the crowded dirty hovels inhabited by Jews, who comprise one-eighth of the population of the state. Look into one of these hovels, which is about to collapse and bury as many as fifteen male and female souls, and you will be struck by the filth and stench. The swarm of half-naked children can hardly find room in this dark hut, three-quarters of which is taken up by the stove, bed and table. . . . Tuberculosis, asthma, nervous fever, nose bleed, and hemorrhoids find not a few victims among these Jews." [31]

As has been stated, the social and industrial reforms initiated in the sixties, far from improving the economic situation of the Jews, made it even worse. Hitherto large numbers of them had earned their livelihood as sales agents and managers for landowners whose profits from serf labor permitted them this luxury. The liberation of the serfs curtailed their income, and the landowners were obliged, as a measure of economy, to dispense with the services of these middlemen. With the financial assistance of rural credit institutions created in that period, the landowners began to manage their estates themselves.

The peasants no longer resorted to the Jews for disposal of their surplus produce. Having as a result of their emancipation become more enterprising and frugal, they undertook to perform those tasks themselves. The peasant also became a less frequent visitor at the Jewish inns which had depended on his patronage. Thus a considerable number of Jews who had hitherto eked out a living serving the landowners and the peasants were now left without means of subsistence.

The initial steps in the industrialization of the country also affected the economy of the Jews adversely. With the exception of a small number who acquired fortunes as railroad builders and financiers, the greater part of Jewry suffered from these changes. As a result of the expansion of rail and steam facilities for transportation, for example, numerous Jewish innkeepers and coachmen who had made a living from coach travelers lost their source of livelihood.

30. *Sbornik Stat. Sved. o Ros.*, 1865, Bk. I, quoted in *Ev. v Ros.*, p. 153.
31. *Statis. Opis. G. Grodno,* 1860, pp. 43, 57, quoted in *Ev. v. Ros.*, pp. 153–154.

It should be noted that though these social and industrial reforms had an unsettling effect upon the already rickety economic structure of Russian Jewry, the changes could have been beneficial had the Pale been removed and opportunity given to Jews to adapt themselves to the new conditions.

Statistics on the ratios of the Jewish to the non-Jewish population and on the economic opportunities open to the two groups indicate how much better was the lot of Jews outside of the Pale of Settlement than within it. In provinces where Jews had permanent legal residence, there was on the average one Jew to nine non-Jews, while in the other parts of Russia the ratio ranged from one to 326 to as low as one to 4,813.[32] Government officials who advocated the removal of the Pale for artisans pointed to the demoralizing competition to which Jews were subjected in restricted and congested areas. A contrast in opportunity is afforded by the following figures. In the provinces of Kursk and Iaroslav, which were barred to Jewish residence, for each one thousand inhabitants there was respectively 0.8 and 0.9 of an artisan, while in the province of Kiev, which, with the exception of the capital, was within the Pale, there were 2.6 artisans for the same number of inhabitants.[33]

Stressing the economic advantages of a more widely diffused Jewish population, Orshansky called attention to the fact that where Jews lived in relatively smaller numbers their income was higher.[34] In the western provinces where the ratio of the Jewish population to that of the non-Jewish was six times higher than in the South, the number of well-to-do Jews was three and one half times less. How the economic condition of Jewry operated in inverse proportion to its percentage of population is further illustrated by contributions to the special government taxes. While the average annual payment of an individual Jew from the western provinces to the tax imposed for specific Jewish charities was 1.96 kopeks, in the South it amounted to 16.85 kopeks.[35]

Aware of this situation, prominent government officials and Jewish leaders advocated the lifting of residence restrictions as an immediate measure for improving the economic position of the Jews. In 1861, Vasilchikov, governor-general of Kiev, under whose jurisdiction resided 600,000 Jews—almost half of the entire Jewish population of Russia—submitted a memorandum to the central government urging that the right of residence throughout Russia be

32. Demidoff San-Donato, *J. Ques. in Rus.*, pp. 77–78.
33. *V. P. S. Z.*, XL, no. 42,264.
34. *Ev. v Ros.*, p. 145.
35. *Ibid.*, pp. 144–145.

extended to all Jews with a secondary education. One of the reasons that prompted him to intervene on behalf of the Jews, he stated, was his desire to relieve congestion in the area he administered.[36]

That the Pale was a harmful factor in the cultural and material progress of the Jews was also the opinion of Postels, an official of the Ministry of Public Education. In a report he prepared for the ministry upon completing an inspection tour of the special Jewish schools, Postels stated that the limitation of residence privileges was responsible not only for the failure of the program of Russification which was the primary purpose of the Jewish government schools, but also for the depths of poverty into which the Jews were sinking ever deeper day by day.[37]

The progressive deterioration of the economic position of the Jews made their leaders more insistent in their demands for the removal of residence restrictions. The same group of wealthy Jews who in 1856 were satisfied with concessions for university graduates and first-guild merchants, reported to the government six years later that the privileges granted to small groups had made no tangible change in the position of the Jews. They pleaded that all Russia be opened at least to Jews acquiring a secondary education.[38] The Jews of the Northwest went even further in their demands; in 1866, Jewish representatives of Vilno notified the governor-general of the region that this petition did not express their views, for, they insisted, "it was necessary to allow all Jews to earn a livelihood throughout Russia." [39]

The government, however, as has been indicated in a previous chapter, clung to its original policy of granting minor legal privileges only to select groups of the Jewish population. During the reactionary period of Alexander's reign, the anti-Jewish press, too, vigorously opposed the extension of Jewish rights, supporting the government's determination to retain the Pale. The following observation made by *Syn Otechestva* (Son of the Fatherland) is typical of the arguments advanced by the opposition: "It is evident that if civic equality should be granted to that mass of usurers and hucksters of doubtful honesty, the Jewish tribe will burst en masse into the centers of Russian industry and into the untrammeled patriarchal regions, enriching themselves at the expense of the gullible Russians." [40]

36. Gessen, *Ist. Ev. Nar. Ros.*, II, 157–158.
37. *Otchot Postelsa po Obozreniiu Evreiskikh Uchilishch,* pp. 64–65.
38. Gessen, *Ist. Ev. Nar. Ros.*, II, 158.
39. *Ibid.*, II, 160.
40. Quoted in Orshansky, *Ev. v Ros.*, pp. 71–72.

There is, however, ample evidence that Russian merchants and peasants did not share this distrust of Jews or fear their competition. In November, 1866, Russian newspapers reported that a group of prominent Christian merchants of St. Petersburg had petitioned the government to make it easier for Jews to trade in the capital as well as in all other parts of Russia.[41] In a study of the fairs of the Ukraine, the Russian writer, I. Aksakov, states that Russian merchants were on the best of terms with their Jewish competitors, even helping them circumvent the law forbidding Jews to trade there.[42]

Surveys made by Russian economists and statisticians also serve to refute charges of anti-Jewish publicists as to the menace of greater Jewish opportunity. One of these scholars concludes that the small towns of New Russia and the Ukraine would have dwindled to villages had it not been for Jewish activities.[43] Another writer speaks of the Jews of Bessarabia as being indispensable to the functioning of all branches of industrial activity.[44] A government official who served in New Russia and collected information on Jewish activities there observes: "One can definitely say that in general the Jews in the region of New Russia, far from being a burden on the Christian population, are on the contrary rather useful." [45] S. Maksimov, a noted authority on Russian economy, thus comments on the Jews of Siberia: "The Jews are bringing a great deal of industrial life into Siberia. The Jew is both fit and useful for Siberia." [46]

A comparison between the standards of living of the Christian populations within and outside the Pale points to the conclusion that the non-Jewish population, too, would have benefited from the opening of the ghetto. This was made clear by the financier and writer, I. Blioch, in a five-volume study entitled *Sravnenie Materialnago i Nravstvennago Blagosostoianiia Guberni Zapadnykh, Veliko Rossiskikh i Privislianskikh* (A Comparative Study of the Material and Moral Status of the Western, Great Russian and By-Vistula Provinces). The data in this work were based on material gathered by a special government committee which studied Jewish conditions for five years. Appointed in 1883 by Tsar Alexander III, this body, headed by Count Palen, a former minister of justice, was known as the High Commission and is sometimes referred to as the Palen Commission. The material it assembled on the economic and legal

41. *Ibid.*, pp. 72–73.
42. I. Aksakov, *Izsledovanie o Torgovle na Ukrainskikh Iarmarkakh*, p. 36.
43. V. Pavlovich, *Ekaterinoslavskaia Gub.*, p. 263.
44. A. Zashchuk, *Bessarab. Oblast*, I, 173.
45. *Chteniia v Mosk. Obshch. Ist. i Drev.*, 1866, III, 234.
46. *Vestnik Evropy*, 1868, III, 134.

status of the Russian Jews covers a period of over a hundred years.

In the introduction to his digest of Blioch's voluminous work, the Russian economist A. Subbotin lauds the study as an enlightening contribution to a question which is shrouded in darkness.[47] Deploring the benighted conceptions held by most people concerning the Jews, he quotes the following observation of the Russian writer Shchedrin: "In the matter of the Jewish question, we still walk in the dark, not having any facts, but only tales which, though long meaningless, still function in their full vigor." Of the scientific value of Blioch's work Subbotin has this to say: "In his analysis of the Jewish question, Blioch pursued the strictly scientific method of induction. All his judgments were based on a scrupulous study of the subject—not on facts selected at random in support of an isolated case but on classified and connected facts. His conclusions were based on that classification of facts as arranged and verified by the High Commission." [48]

Among other things, Blioch's work reveals that the growth of the non-Jewish population as well as its material status was greater in the Pale than outside of it. In the years 1863–1883, the Christian city population in the Pale of Settlement grew almost twice as fast as in the adjacent areas, and the village population increased one-third more than that outside of the Pale. From 1856 until the middle of the eighties, the decrease in livestock in the provinces where Jews were allowed to live was four times less than in the provinces from which Jews were barred. In 1877, the reserve food supplies were two and a half times greater than in non-Jewish provinces and cash for such supplies was twice as much, while the debt for these purposes was 50 per cent less in the Jewish than in the non-Jewish provinces.[49]

Blioch also states that a survey of the economic status of the Russian peasantry revealed that one-tenth of the peasant families in the Pale were found in "excellent condition," while in the areas adjacent to the Pale no peasant family of such economic status was to be found. Of those described as "in very good condition," 23.9 per cent of peasant families were in the Jewish provinces as compared to 0.5 per cent in contiguous provinces. In "good status" there were in the Pale 48.1 per cent, whereas in the eleven neighboring provinces there were only 13.8 per cent of such peasant households. Of "aver-

47. *Ev. Bib.*, X, 63–124.

48. *Ibid.*, p. 66.

49. Since olden times it was required by law that each community in Russia set aside a reserve supply of food or cash for emergency use in time of famine. See article "Prodovolstvie Narodnoe" (Public Alimentation) in *Entsik. Slovar,* XXV, 354–361.

age status" families, the Jewish regions had 18.5 per cent, adjacent provinces 66.2. No peasants in the Jewish Pale of Settlement were rated as in "unsatisfactory condition." Outside of the Pale, however, 19.4 per cent were rated thus.[50]

One of the factors responsible for the better economic condition of the peasants living in Jewish neighborhoods was the large market for their surplus produce to be found there. In the eastern regions of Russia, observes Zelensky, where, because of the absence of Jews, the urban population consisted of only 6 per cent of the total, the price of bread was very low on account of the small demand. In the western provinces, on the other hand, where the city population comprised 20 per cent of the total, the peasant had the advantage of obtaining a higher price for his products because of the larger demand. Zelensky also notes that the farmer of the Northwest had an additional advantage, since the Jew in the capacity of middleman helped him dispose of his surplus products abroad or in the Vistula and Baltic regions.[51]

Another Russian writer testifies that the peasants of the western provinces conceded that without the Jews, they could neither dispose of their meager produce nor procure money to finance their husbandry. "To forbid the Jews to go from farm to farm, from fair to fair," he contended, "would immediately put an end to the trade of the entire region which only they maintain." [52]

As regards the charges of the anti-Jewish press which agitated against the removal of the Pale on the ground that Jews were responsible for drunkenness among the Russian masses, statistics and official data prove quite the contrary. The High Commission, which established that the general well-being of the non-Jewish population was better in the Pale than outside of it, also found that there was less drunkenness among the peasants in the Jewish areas.[53] Another government committee, appointed by Alexander II in 1870 to study rural economy, reported that complaints about drunkenness among the peasants came primarily from the Great Russian provinces, fewer from the Ukraine and New Russia, and almost none from the western and Baltic provinces.[54] Since the lowest degree of intoxication existed in Jewish areas and the highest in non-Jewish regions, it follows that it was not the Jew who was responsible for this evil.

This conclusion had already been established in the latter part of

50. Subbotin, *Ev. Bib.*, X, 71–75. See also I. Bikerman, *Materialy K Zakonoproectu ob Otmene Cherty Evreiskoi Osedlosti,* pp. 3–5.
51. *Minsk. Gub.*, II, 43, 379.
52. Babst, *Ot Moskvy do Leiptsiga,* p. 7, quoted in *Ev. v Ros.*, p. 41.
53. Subbotin, *Ev. Bib.*, X, 85.
54. *Ibid.*, p. 88.

the reign of Nicholas I. In 1844, the Jews were expelled from villages on the allegation that the peasants were being demoralized and exploited by Jewish tavern and innkeepers. A study of a representative rural community, however, made in the years following the expulsion by a Russian economist and statistician of the University of Kiev, disproved the validity of the charge. His survey revealed that the eviction of the Jews was succeeded by an increase in both the price and the consumption of liquor. Thus the liquor income of the landowners, who now managed this business themselves, doubled between the years 1840–1850.[55]

Not only do figures prove less drunkenness among the Russian masses living in the proximity of Jews, but they also indicate less crime as well. Blioch's studies of comparative crime within and without the Pale show that there were one and a half times more criminal cases in the non-Jewish areas; that the number of premeditated cases of murder was lower in the Pale than in regions adjacent to it and 6 per cent less than in all of Russia. Other crimes, such as looting, robbing, and extortion, were lowest per capita in provinces populated by Jews.[56] The noted Russian writer, Leskov, similarly refutes the charge that the Jews were in any way responsible for the drunkenness of the Russian masses. Pointing to the larger number of crimes due to intoxication in the non-Jewish areas, he asserts that excessive drinking was an evil which the church had unsuccessfully tried to cure in Russia long before Jews settled there in considerable numbers.[57]

The foregoing facts about the relation of the Jew to the morality and the economic well-being of his non-Jewish neighbors prove how baseless were the objections to the removal of the Pale on the ground that it would have a bad effect on the Russian masses. A comparative study of the potential opportunities for livelihood outside the Pale, in contrast to the intolerable competition within the ghetto, leads one to the inescapable conclusion that the lifting of all residence restrictions was the reform most imperatively and immediately needed for the improvement of the sorry economic state of Russian Jewry.

55. I. Funduklei, *Statis. Opis. Kiev. Gub.*, II, 194–199.
56. Subbotin, *Ev. Bib.*, X, 74.
57. N. Leskov, *Ev. v Ros.*, pp. 30–32.

XIII

CONTRIBUTION OF RUSSIAN JEWS TO RUSSIAN LIFE AND CULTURE IN THE REIGN OF ALEXANDER II

THE limited rights and opportunities offered by the régime of Alexander II did little to improve the economic lot of Russian Jews. However, the reforms were responsible for the appearance of outstanding Jewish personalities, who made valuable contributions in various fields of Russian life. It should be borne in mind, however, that while the more liberal régime of Alexander II made possible the emergence of these personalities, the *Haskalah* movement, which had begun in the preceding reign, started some of them in pursuit of their respective careers. The Jewish jurists, medical men, and journalists who made their mark in the period of the Great Reforms came from that small portion of Russian Jewry who, unlike the bulk of their brethren, had responded to the program of the *Haskalah* and had availed themselves of the educational opportunities offered by the Nicholas government.

It will be recalled that secular education was frowned upon by the religious leaders of the period because of the fear that the acquisition of such knowledge unaccompanied by civic rights would tempt Jews, ambitious for a career, to desert their faith. That these apprehensions were justified is substantiated by the large number of conversions which occurred in the fifties and the sixties. Among the Russian Jews many embraced Christianity as a means of achieving an academic career, otherwise closed to Jews even in the reign of Alexander II. Some resorted to apostasy in order to rise in government service, while others did so for the sake of acquiring legal status and social position. To this last-mentioned group belonged the converts who came from among the richer Jews.

This wealthy class, which constituted only a fraction of Russian Jewry, made its initial appearance in the reign of Nicholas I. Through liquor concessions which the government then farmed out to private individuals, a small number of Jews accumulated large fortunes. Others amassed wealth during the Crimean War. Most of the Jewish magnates grew rich in the era of railroad-building which offered new opportunities for men of initiative and enterprise.

Outstanding among these Jewish financiers was the Günzburg

family. Its wealth dated back to the days of Nicholas I. Evzel Günzburg (1812–1878), who received the title of baron from the Grand Duke of Hesse-Darmstadt, established the first private banking institution in Russia. The Günzburg firm, which assisted the government in financial operations abroad and was instrumental in arranging loans for the building of railroads, played an important part in the development of banking in Russia.[1]

Another leading financier was Abraham Zack (died 1893), head of a Petersburg commercial bank, which under his leadership became the most powerful financial institution in the capital. Zack was often consulted in finance and railroad matters by the State Council and other government committees. He was offered the post of assistant minister of finance with a promise of promotion if he would embrace Christianity, but he refused.[2]

Jews were among the pioneer railroad-builders in Russia. One of them, the banker Samuel Poliakov (1836–1888), referred to as the "Railroad King," built several railroad lines and founded the first railroad school in Russia. In recognition of his achievements he was raised to the nobility and given the title of Privy Councilor. The same title was also conferred upon his two brothers, Lazar and Jacob, who were engaged in the same activities. The three Poliakov brothers were the first Russian Jews to be made members of the nobility and given honorary titles.[3]

In connection with the wide philanthropies of Samuel Poliakov for non-Jewish causes, it is interesting to note that two of his benefactions helped establish institutions from which Jews were excluded. The Katkov Lyceum, where Jews were not admitted, was built in Moscow principally by funds contributed by Poliakov and other wealthy Jews. The Poliakov Dormitory of the St. Petersburg University, which was founded through his gift, specifically barred Jews in its by-laws.[4]

Notable among the railroad-builders was the economist and writer Ivan Blioch (1836–1901), one of whose works was discussed in the previous chapter. This outstanding financier and railroad contractor participated in the construction of railways of the Great

1. On the Günzburgs see G. B. Sliozberg, *Perez.*, II, 94–115; S. M. Ginsburg, *Hist. Werk*, II, 117–163.

2. *Ev. Entsik.*, VII, 619–660; Sliozberg, *Dela Minuvshikh Dnei*, I, 141–142; also A. Paperna, *Perez.*, III, 353–354.

3. *Hist. Schr.*, III, 109–110; *Ev. Entsik.*, XII, 734; *The Memoirs of Count Vitte*, p. 20; Sliozberg, *Del. Min. Dn.*, I, 142–144. See also *K. P. Pobedonostsev i Ego Korrespondenty*, I, 734–738.

4. *Hist. Schr.*, III, 116; Sliozberg, *Del. Min. Dn.*, I, 142. Count S. Vitte, *Vospominaniia*, I, 251. About his other philanthropies for non-Jewish causes see *K. P. Pobedonostsev i Ego Korres.*, I, 25–26.

Russia Company and served as president of several railroads. He was also noted for his writings on such varied subjects as railroad finance, social reforms, Jewish rights, and international peace. A work dealing with the effects of railroads upon the economic conditions of Russia won him the award of a gold medal by the Paris Exposition in 1878 and membership on the Scholarly Committee of the Ministry of Finance. His book on international peace, published in 1898, is believed to have inspired Tsar Nicholas II to issue the famous peace declaration responsible for the first Hague Conference in 1899.

Though this versatile and talented Jew became a convert to Christianity, he used his literary gifts to champion Jewish rights. The opening declaration of Blioch's last will and testament, "I was my whole life a Jew and die as a Jew," expresses a sentiment that was undoubtedly shared by many Jewish converts of the period. Many of them even after conversion maintained an active interest in Jewish affairs and in Jewish culture. The Hebrew-Yiddish writer A. B. Gottlober, who was supported by the wealthy baptized Jew, Abraham Horowitz, once ironically remarked: "Would that all Jews were converts!" [5]

In the free professions, too, a considerable number of Jews made their mark in the reign of Alexander II. In an article discussing the part Jews played in the administration of justice during the period of the Great Reforms, a noted Jewish jurist states that there were between twenty to thirty Jewish lawyers engaged in various capacities in the newly reorganized courts. Considering the fact that the number of Jewish students in all branches of higher learning in 1865 totaled but 129,[6] this proportion of Jewish jurists attaining positions of importance in government service is impressive. Jews served as prosecuting attorneys, judges, and chief secretaries in various departments of the highest judicial body of Russia, the Senate Courts.[7]

Jewish lawyers participated not only in the preparation of the judicial reform of 1864, but also in the administration of the new courts. According to an eminent jurist and Jewish leader, the history of Russian justice has failed to record the significant contributions of Jews to Russian law.[8] One of these Jews was the jurist and journalist Arnold Dumashevsky (1833–1881), who served in various capacities in the Ministry of Justice. Refusing to renounce his

5. *Ev. Star.*, 1914, p. 435. On Blioch see *Jew. Encyc.*, III, 250–252; Sliozberg, *Del. Min. Dn.*, II, 169–172; *Mem. of Count Vitte*, pp. 20–21.

6. Posner, *Evr. v Obsh. Shk.*, Supplements, p. 55.

7. A. Litowsky (J. Galpern), *Perez.*, III, 108–198.

8. Sliozberg, *Del. Min. Dn.*, I, 136.

faith, he forfeited the opportunity for an academic career in the University of Petersburg, of which he was a graduate, as well as the chance of rising to any position of importance in the Ministry of Justice.[9]

Another jurist participating in the judicial reforms of 1864 was Herman Trakhtenberg (1839–1895). He was the first Jew to occupy an important post in the Ministry of Justice, and was accorded several honors for meritorious work in government service. Among the honors he enjoyed was the unusual distinction of being elected honorary justice of the peace of the district of St. Petersburg. As chief secretary of the newly formed Appellate Criminal Department of the Senate, he became the "soul" of this institution, and was largely responsible for its smooth and satisfactory functioning during the first and most difficult period of its existence. According to the noted jurist and eminent Jewish leader, Sliozberg, Trakhtenberg composed and wrote thousands of opinions in his own handwriting. Sliozberg speaks of these decisions as a veritable monument to the memory of this jurist, albeit an anonymous one, since officially the chief secretary took no part in the handing down of decisions.[10]

Gregori Verblovsky (1837–1900), who served as one of the first secretaries of the District Court of St. Petersburg, also figures prominently as an early Jewish jurist. A justice of the District Court of Voronezh for twenty years, Verblovsky served as member of the Appellate Division of Moscow and wrote numerous books and articles in the field of law.[11]

Other Jews occupying positions of importance included Jacob Teitel; Jacob Galpern, at one time president of the Society for the Promotion of Culture among Jews; and the brothers Jacob and Boris Utin, who were baptized Jews. Boris was a member of the Appellate Division of St. Petersburg.[12] According to Teitel and Sliozberg, the two noted senators Fuchs and Koni were also converted Jews.[13] Most distinguished of Jewish jurists was Alexander Passover (1840–1910), whose fame extended beyond the borders of Russia. This learned attorney was consulted by many government dignitaries and agencies, participated in the founding of many legal periodicals, and made numerous valuable contributions to Russian legal literature.[14]

9. *Ev. Entsik.*, VII, 375–376.
10. Sliozberg, *Del. Min. Dn.*, I, 132–136; *Ev. Entsik.*, XV, 11.
11. *Ev. Entsik.*, V, 503–504.
12. *Hist. Schr.*, III, 112.
13. *Ibid.*, III, 114; Sliozberg, *Del. Min. Dn.*, I, 239–243.
14. *Ev. Entsik.*, XII, 314–316; *Del. Min. Dn.*, I, 207.

Almost all of the jurists, including many of those who were converted to Christianity, took an active part in Jewish affairs either as supporters of the Society for the Promotion of Culture among Jews or as defenders of Jewish rights. Chief among these champions of Jewish emancipation during the seventies was the brilliant legal theoretician I. Orshansky, to whose works numerous references are made in this book.

In the field of medicine, for which Jews showed a special preference,[15] they also made valuable contributions. The physiologist I. F. Tsion (died 1912), who before his conversion was a lecturer in the University of Petersburg,[16] received an award from the Academy of Sciences in Paris for a physiological treatise. Author of many other works on physiology and on pure medicine, Tsion became unpopular with the university students because of his reactionary views, and was forced to give up his post as professor of physiology in the Medico-Surgical Academy, where he had taught since his baptism. He entered the service of the Ministry of Finance and, in the capacity of Russia's agent in France, obtained the first loan for his government from that country. He was an active proponent of the Franco-Russian alliance concluded in 1895.[17]

In the course of Tsion's political activities, he engaged in a vituperative campaign against Sergius Vitte, the finance minister of Russia, who was regarded as a moderate liberal in his day. Tsion's fight against the minister brought him into disrepute with the progressive elements of his country and with the government, which, influenced by Vitte, forbade his return to Russia.

The general impression one receives of Tsion's personality is that of a highly gifted, ambitious person rendered unsympathetic by his pugnacity and reactionary superpatriotism. Judging him from a political viewpoint, Vitte interprets his antagonist thus: "The difference between a scoundrel of the left wing and that of the right is this—the first commits his misdeeds out of principle, whereas the latter is motivated by greed and personal ambition." [18] From a psychological point of view it would not be illogical to suggest that Tsion's anomalous position as a converted Jew had something to do with the development of his ignoble characteristics.[19]

15. Fifty-eight per cent of the Jewish university students in 1878 were registered in the departments of medicine. *Hist. Schr.*, III, 112.

16. Jews were accepted as lecturers (*Privatdozents*) but not as professors in Russian universities.

17. W. L. Langer, *The Franco-Russian Alliance*, 1890–1894, p. 425.

18. S. Vitte, *Vospominaniia*, I, 255.

19. On Tsion see *ibid.*, pp. 249–255; also *Memoirs* of same author, pp. 49–50; *Ev. Entsik.*, XV, 820–821; *Hist. Schr.*, III, 114–115.

A physiologist and public servant of a different order was Nicholas Bakst (1842–1904), whose life was devoted to the advancement of science and the service of his people. Bakst wrote important works on physiology and was a lecturer on the subject in the University of St. Petersburg and in the School of Medicine for Women. He was a member of the so-called Scholarly Committee of the Ministry of Education and a contributor to the newspapers *Moscovskiia Vedomosti* and *Golos*.

The influence of this scholar, who was a lifelong champion of complete Jewish emancipation, changed the unfriendly attitude of *Golos* to the Jews. Dr. Bakst published among other works a book entitled *Russkie Liudi o Evreiakh* (Opinions of Russians about Jews) in which famous Russians expressed their advocacy of Jewish rights. As an ardent advocate of Jewish equality, the physiologist was concerned not only with the political problems of the Jews but with their economic ills as well. For the correction of the occupational abnormalities from which his people suffered, he urged the promotion of craftsmanship and agriculture among them. It was due to his efforts that Samuel Poliakov, whose adviser he was on Jewish matters, established and subsidized the organization to encourage agriculture and artisanship among Jews which later became known as the *Ort*.[20] Bakst carried on the work of this society until his death.

Among the outstanding medical men who started their careers in the reign of Alexander II, the name of Joseph Bertenson (1833–1895) must be mentioned. This distinguished physician, a convert to Christianity, spent the greater part of his life in government service in the field of public health. He was director of a number of medical institutions he had helped to create. Among his literary efforts may be listed his editorship of a medical journal and several volumes on problems of public hygiene and sanitary reform which are considered of great practical significance. His accomplishments earned him the title of Privy Councilor and the distinction of serving as court physician.[21]

Another contributor to the field of public health and hygiene was Benjamin Portugalov (1835–1896). He served as city physician in the province of Perm, and as sanitary supervisor of mining districts in the Ural Mountains. Portugalov, who devoted a great deal of his time to philanthropic work, especially in combatting drunkenness, was among the first in Russia to advocate socialized medicine.[22]

20. *Ev. Entsik.,* III, 698–701; A. E. Kaufman; *Ev. Star.,* 1913, pp. 333–334; Sliozberg, *Del. Min. Dn.,* I, 267–8.
21. *Jew. Encyc.,* III, 106; *Ev. Entsik.,* IV, 330–331.
22. *Hist. Schr.,* III, 81; *Jew. Encyc.,* X, 141.

The significant number of Jewish names in the medical profession connected with army service is commented upon by the non-Jewish historian M. L. Usov. He observes that an abundance of Jewish names such as Grossman, Shapiro, and Rabinowich figured in the list of awards in the Russo-Turkish War of 1877–78. In 1880, many Jewish physicians received the citation of "Imperial Favor" for their achievement in checking the then raging typhoid epidemic.[23]

Jews also distinguished themselves as soldiers in active service. This fact is attested to by General Kuropatkin, who stated that "both Tartars and Jews have demonstrated that like other Russian soldiers they were able and will be able to fight and die heroically." [24] A monument erected in Moscow in honor of the fallen heroes in the storming and capture of Plevna, includes seven Jewish names. It was to this memorial that a Jewish deputy in the Russian Duma referred in an ironic comment. If these soldier heroes were resurrected, he observed, they would not have the right to live in the city which had done them honor.[25]

The patriotism of many Jews remained undiminished despite the antisemitism from which they suffered. An example of this undampened ardor is furnished by the large number of Jews who volunteered in the Russo-Turkish War on behalf of the ideal of Pan-Slavism. This movement created a strong nationalist feeling which resulted in the intensification of antisemitism in Russia, yet Jews continued ardently to espouse the cause of the Balkan Slavs with both pen and sword.[26]

That Jews aspiring to become a part of Russian culture and the Russian people possessed the adaptability for this process is indicated by the contributions they made to Russian scholarship and literature. The significance of these contributions is best understood when one remembers that up to the middle fifties of the nineteenth century, Russian scholarship and literature were practically a closed world to the Jews. One of these new literary achievements was a work on Russian folk-lore entitled *Russkiia Narodnyia Pesni i Bylini* (Russian Folk Songs and Legends). This seven-volume study of the spiritual life of the Russian peasants from cradle to the grave was written by the ethnologist and linguist, Paul Shein (1826–1900), who in his youth was converted to Christianity.[27]

Another converted Jew, the famous Semitic scholar and Orientalist, Daniel Khvolson (1819–1911), oft-mentioned in these pages,

23. M. L. Usov, *Ev. v Armii,* p. 60.
24. *Voenny Sbornik,* 1883, no. 7, quoted in *Ev. Entsik.,* III, 167.
25. Usov, *Ev. v Arm.,* p. 13.
26. A. E. Kaufman, *Ev. Star.,* 1913, pp. 210–211.
27. *Ev. Entsik.,* XV, 950.

made an epochal contribution to the religious literature of the Russian people. Appointed by the Holy Synod to serve as a member of a committee of experts whose task it was to make the first Russian translation of the Old Testament, this gifted scholar himself produced two-thirds of the work.

In the field of Semitics and Oriental studies, to which he made lasting contributions, Khvolson was practically a pioneer in Russia. Some of his scholarly works were undertaken for the express purpose of defending the Jewish people and the Talmud against libelous charges. In refutation of the ritual murder charge made against the Jews of Saratov in 1857, he wrote his treatise *O Nekotorykh Sredne-Vekovykh Obvineniiakh protiv Evreev* (Concerning Some Medieval Accusations against the Jews). Following a similar charge against the Jews of Cutais in 1877, this Semitic scholar issued a revised edition of this work.[28]

Khvolson was the first noted scholar in Russia to take up the cudgels on behalf of the Pharisees.[29] According to him, the Pharisees spoken of in the Gospels were not representative of the Pharisees as a class. Those said to have been condemned by Jesus were a particular group of insincere rabbis whom the Talmud too characterizes as hypocrites. In that book which in his own German translation is called *Das Letzte Passamahl Christi und der Tag Seines Todes*, Khvolson advanced historic proof of the innocence of the Pharisees in the crucifixion. In support of his contention, he cited Talmudic laws of the time, proving that both the trial and the sentence of Jesus, as described in the Gospels, were contrary to Pharisaic law. Since in those days the Sadducees held the balance of power, Khvolson insisted, the Pharisees could not have decided the fate of Jesus. As further proof that they were not enemies of Jesus or of his followers, Khvolson pointed out that the Pharisees warmly defended the Apostle Paul at his trial and helped other early Christians who were persecuted by the Sadducees.[30]

In regard to the misrepresentations of the Talmud on the part of Christian scholars, the Orientalist stated that these perversions were due largely to ignorance of the original Rabbinic sources. He ex-

28. In 1901 Khvolson published his German translation entitled *Die Blutanklage und Sonstige Mittelalterliche Beschuldigingen der Juden.*

29. On the Pharisees from the point of view of modern research see: R. Travers Herford, *The Truth about the Pharisees;* George F. Moore, *Judaism in the First Centuries of the Christian Era;* Louis Finkelstein, *The Pharisees,* particularly the Foreword. On the Crucifixion see: Conrad H. Moehlman, *The Christian-Jewish Tragedy,* particularly pp. 212–245. Also by the same author, *Protestantism's Challenge,* particularly pp. 189–220; Joseph Klausner, *Jesus of Nazareth,* pp. 339–356; Samuel Zeitlin, *Who Crucified Jesus?*

30. *Das Letzte Passamahl,* pp. 115–121, *Die Blutanklage,* pp. 22–34.

plained that not all of the statements in the Talmud can be cited as authoritative or representative, since that monumental work comprises a collection of discussions and opinions of varying degrees of importance. He also called attention to the usual disregard of time, place, and circumstances connected with Talmudic statements contained in a compilation which covers a period of centuries. In scoring the absurdity of indiscriminately attributing Talmudic sanction to every individual opinion expressed in a vast literature, Khvolson draws the following apt comparison: "The phrase 'the Talmud states' may very glibly be used by beer-hall orators, but not by scholars. When I read that phrase, I picture someone saying: 'The stenographic report of the German Reichstag states that no standing army is necessary.' The question then arises: where was it spoken—in Berlin or Frankfort? When—in 1848 or in 1870? Finally, who said it—the minister of war or Bebel? Similar questions must be asked in judging statements quoted from the Talmud." [31]

Among other works this prolific scholar produced were studies in archaeology and in the history of religion. Khvolson held three professorial posts simultaneously—one in Petersburg University, another in the Greek-Orthodox Theological Seminary, and a third in the Roman-Catholic Academy. He was elected to honorary membership in the Academy of Sciences of St. Petersburg in 1910. His successful academic career brings to mind an ironic witticism attributed to him. In response to a query as to whether he had renounced his faith out of conviction, Khvolson is said to have replied: "Yes, it was out of conviction. I was convinced that it was far better to be a Gentile professor than a Jewish *melamed*." [32] But in spite of his conversion, this gifted son of Israel considered himself a Jew to the day of his death. It was related in Vilno, the city of his birth, that his dying words were: "Take me to my Rabbi, Rabbi Israel of Zareche." [33]

Another illustrious name in the field of Semitic scholarship is Albert Harkavy (1835–1919). Unable to obtain a professorial appointment because of his Jewish faith, he served as librarian of the Oriental Department of the Imperial Library, a post he held the greater part of his life. Harkavy's scholarly achievements in the field of history and Oriental studies were recognized by the Russian government, which conferred upon him many honorary orders and accorded him the rank of Councilor of State.

Through his Oriental studies, he made notable contributions to

31. *Das Letzte Passamahl,* p. 71.
32. M. Lipson, *Die Velt Derzehlt,* I, 57.
33. *Ibid.,* I, 57.

early Russian history. His graduation thesis, entitled (in English translation) *Narratives of Mohammedan Writers about the Slavs and the Russians,* formed the first part of an important work published two years later. In this work he collected and interpreted narratives about the Slavic tribes and the Russian people as related by Mohammedan authors who lived before the tenth century. The book furnished valuable material for Oriental scholars and for the historians of Russia.

In 1875, Harkavy created a sensation in the world of Semitics when he exposed as forgeries some of the Biblical manuscripts the Biblical library had bought from the renowned Karaite Orientalist, Abraham Firkovich.

A pioneer in the field of early Russo-Jewish history, Harkavy made some original contributions to this subject. Among these was the theory regarding the origin of Jewish life in Russia mentioned in the first chapter of this book. While the writer Levinsohn was the first to suggest that Jewish settlers originally came not from Germany but from the Eastern countries, it was Harkavy's scientific research that substantiated this conjecture. Harkavy also maintained that up to the middle of the seventeenth century, Slavonic speech was the vernacular of Jews residing in Slavonic lands—not the German-Jewish dialect as was generally believed. The theory that Slavic was used was supported by Bershadsky, a Gentile historian of Lithuanian Jewry, but is contested by Dubnow. In the course of his refutation, Dubnow expresses the opinion that Harkavy's viewpoint on the subject was that of an apologist, born of eagerness to prove that Russians and Jews shared a common cultural heritage.[34] While this may have been a motivating factor, it should be observed, that unlike other *maskilim,* who sought to establish such theories in the hope of facilitating mergence of the Jew into the Russian people, Harkavy never evinced such a desire. Of his Jewish loyalties his biographer has this to say: "As a Jew Harkavy clung with all his heart to his people and to his faith. . . . No winds had the power to shake his faith; not even a chair in the St. Petersburg University could triumph over him."[35]

Jewish participation in Russian journalism has been dealt with in Chapter VIII, where the literary contributions and personalities of men like Rabinowich, Orshansky, Levanda, Kulisher, and others are discussed. These journalists contributed to both the Russian-Jewish and the Russian press. A number of Jewish publicists, how-

34. *Ev. Star.,* 1909, pp. 7–41.

35. Moses Reines, *Dor Va-Hakomov,* I, 82–83. On Harkavy see also I. Berlin, *Ev. Star.,* 1910, pp. 592–598.

ever, wrote for the Russian press exclusively. Prominent among these was the convert, Osip Notovich (1849–1914), at one time editor and publisher of *Novoe Vremia,* and founder of the influential political organ *Novosti* (The News). He wrote on a variety of subjects and also issued a popular version of Buckle's *History of Civilization.*[36]

In the field of *belle lettres* there was no Jewish figure of importance in the Alexandrian period, perhaps because fiction was not a popular medium of Jewish literary expression and the Jew was a novice in the art and spirit of the Russian language.

But it has recently come to light that the noted poet, A. F. Fet, reared as a Christian and regarded by his contemporaries as a Christian by birth, was in truth born of Jewish parentage. The strange circumstances which veiled his Jewish origin were as follows: A Russian officer by the name of Shenshin, homeward bound from the Napoleonic wars in 1819, passed through the city of Königsberg, where he fell in love with the beautiful wife of a Jewish innkeeper. He took away with him this woman who, as subsequent events disclosed, was already with child. Having married her, he brought her to his estate in the Orlov province. A few months after her arrival, she gave birth to a son, later known as the poet Fet—his mother's family name—which he retained as his pen name till his death. His use of the matronymic was due to legal complications which arose from the unusual circumstances of his mother's marriage. The Lutheran ritual which solemnized her union with Shenshin in Germany was not considered valid in Russia and the child was born before the marriage had been sanctified by the Greek-Orthodox church, so Fet was considered illegitimate and was denied the use of Shenshin's name and title of nobility. It was not until 1873, when Fet was already advanced in years, that his battle for legitimacy was won. His struggle for legal status and his lifelong concealment of the secret of his real paternity weighed heavily upon him and may have contributed to his cynicism and misanthropy. An envelope which, according to his instructions, was opened after his death, established what his intimates had long suspected, that he was not a Shenshin but the son of a Jewish couple.[37]

Fet's reputation as a poet and master of pure lyrics was established in 1842, when a collection of his verses appeared in Moscow. In the later fifties, his contributions grew, and he came to be regarded as one of the most prominent literary figures in Russia.

36. *Novy Entsik., Slovar,* XXVIII, 898–899; Sliozberg, *Del. Min. Dn.,* II, 221–222; see also V. Korolenko, *Istoria Moego Sovremennika,* II, 258–263.

37. Igor Grabar, *Moia Zhizn,* pp. 252–254.

Among his lifelong friends and admirers were two famous writers, Tolstoi and Turgenev. A volume of Fet's verses was issued by a committee headed by Turgenev, who once observed that the poet was greater than Heine. In the sixties, in consequence of severe attacks on Fet's poetry by the critics of the Pisarev school, who opposed art for art's sake and who berated the lyrist for his reactionary economic and political views, Fet disappeared from the literary field for twenty years. During his years of silence, however, he did not give up writing. On the contrary, during his apparent inactivity his talent flowered and ripened to full maturity. Beginning with 1883, Fet again resumed publication, issuing a series of small volumes of poetry called *Evening Lights*. The Russian critic N. N. Strakhov, who speaks of Fet as "greatest magician and incomparable poet," characterizes *Evening Lights* as pages of pure gold.[38] Prince Mirsky, a historian of Russian literature, describes these lyrics as "the most precious diamonds of our poetry."

Mirsky interprets Fet as a dual personality whose life presented a sharp contrast to the nature and style of his poetry.[39] As a man he was cynical, materialistic, practical, and coldly reserved. As a poet he was deeply passionate, imaginative, and romantic. One is inclined to wonder whether the strange circumstances of Fet's birth and the secret of his Jewish origin which he carried locked in his heart did not have some bearing on the paradoxical dualism in his nature.

In the realm of music, where Jewish names figure prominently, the brothers Anton and Nicholas Rubinstein stand out not only as great musicians and composers but also as the founders of the first conservatories of music in Russia. Before their time, the country possessed a few musical societies which led a "miserable existence," but there were no properly functioning institutions of music. Anton Rubinstein (1829–1894), baptized in infancy by his grandfather, organized the Russian Musical Society in Petersburg in 1859. Three years later, the society under his directorship became the first Russian conservatory of music. A tribute paid him by *Russkaia Starina* (Russian Antiquities) in 1889, when the jubilee of his first appearance as a concert pianist was celebrated, read as follows:

Founder of the first "Russian Musical Society"—today called The Imperial—founder and first director of the first Russian conservatory, Anton Rubinstein, rendered enormous services to his country. He called to life a group of new workers and musical artists who, until his time, had, so to speak, no right of citizenship in Russia. He was the first to

38. *Polnoe Sobranie Stikhotvoreni A. A. Feta,* I, 11–12.
39. Prince D. S. Mirsky, *A Hist. of Russ. Lit.,* pp. 289–293.

lay the foundation of a proper, earnest, musical education in Russia, an education which is so important for the development of a nation, especially its younger generation. . . . Yes, this Russian, a colossus because of his mighty gifts, his name as well as the fruits of his creation will pass on from century to century unto the far-off generations of humanity, as long as man finds gratification in the world of sound.[40]

Though admitted into the Greek-Orthodox faith when a mere infant, Rubinstein was painfully aware of his Jewish origin all his life. As a youth struggling for achievement and fame, he learned that twice as much was required of him as of a Christian. Throughout his life, abroad and in his own country, he was unpleasantly reminded of his ancestral faith. He smarted at these allusions, whether by opponents who maliciously hinted at his Jewishness or by admirers who patronizingly remarked "we don't like Jews, but that doesn't mean Anton Grigorovich [Rubinstein]." When Alexander III conferred upon him the honorary title of *Excellenz*, Anton said to his mother: "I have a presentiment that I shall need this *Excellenz* some day against the very powers that gave it to me. For all your baptism at Berdichev, we are Jews, you and I and sister Sophie."

From his oft-repeated reproaches to his mother concerning the apostasy of the family, it is obvious that the conversion weighed heavily upon him throughout his life. For while Rubinstein resented the world's unkind reminders, he was by no means ashamed of his Jewish birth, nor did he seek to conceal it. One of his friends relates that the musician possessed an ivory-handled paper knife upon which Rubinstein's name was inscribed in Hebrew letters. It is common knowledge that many of his operatic themes were inspired by the Old Testament. He personally ascribed his deep love for the Bible to its great literary and artistic merits and to its dramatic grandeur. But one of his collaborators, the dramatist and poet Solomon Herman von Mosenthal, interprets Rubinstein's choice of Old Testament material as an expression of his Jewish sentiments. He believes that it was Rubinstein's aversion for Wagner and particularly his resentment of the latter's antisemitic pamphlet, "Judaism in Music," that prompted the Russian composer to concentrate on Judaic subjects.[41]

His brother, Nicholas Rubinstein (1835–1881), considered the

40. 1889, LXIV, 515–516.

41. Catherine Bowen, *"Free Artist"; The Story of Anton and Nicholas Rubinstein,* pp. 73, 183, 308, 309, 151, 152. Anton Rubinstein's autobiography is published in *Russ. Star.*, 1889, LXIV.

soul of the musical life of Moscow, was instrumental in founding in 1860 a Moscow branch of the Musical Society of St. Petersburg. Nicholas became director and professor of the conservatory which developed therefrom.[42]

In the world of art, the figure of Mark Antokolsky (1842–1902) looms as the greatest sculptor not alone of Russia but of his age. This world-acclaimed genius, who was awarded the highest prize for sculpture by an international jury at the Paris Exposition of 1878, drew upon Russian, universal, and Jewish subjects for his artistic creations. Among his religious and classical works are such studies as "Death of Socrates," "Christ Bound before the People," and "Mephistopheles." Most famous of his Russian studies are statues of "Ivan the Terrible" and "Peter the Great." For his "Ivan" he was appointed Academician of Arts at the express command of Alexander II. Antokolsky had previously declined the title of Honorary Citizen offered him by the Academy, which had refused at that time to elect him to membership, although it had awarded him two silver medals for his works. The first creations which launched his career as a sculptor were drawn from Jewish life. Famous among these is "The Jewish Tailor," which earned him one of his silver medals.

This ghetto-bred youth, born in Vilno, achieved early fame in spite of the hardships of poverty and the handicap of his faith, which he not alone never renounced, but piously adhered to throughout his life. He was concerned deeply with the fate of his people, particularly with the problems of young Jewish artists, whom he assisted in every way.

The Russian art critic, Stasov, in discussing the unique genius and personality of this artist, extols his militant Jewish loyalties in these words: "So great was the fearlessness of Antokolsky that, instead of seeking to smother his Jewishness, he loudly proclaimed it. It was Jewish subjects and Jewish types that he presented before the Academy, the judges, and the Russian public when he made his first appearance before them." [43]

A genius like Antokolsky was able to achieve fame in spite of his refusal to renounce his faith. The great majority of gifted Jews, however, were able to attain recognition and position only through conversion. What this compromise with their consciences cost them in terms of spiritual suffering and inner conflict has been indicated in the sketchy account of the converted Jews described in these

42. On Nicholas Rubinstein see Catherine Bowen, *"Free Artist"*; also *Ev. Entsik.*, XIII, 710–711.

43. V. Stasov, *Vest. Evropy,* April, 1883, p. 692.

pages. As for the numerous gifted sons of Israel who were doomed to "waste their sweetness on the desert air" because they refused to abandon their faith for the sake of a career, one can well imagine what unhappiness unfulfilled ambition and stifled talent caused them. But their deprivation was Russia's loss also. When we consider the remarkable contributions made by Jews in so short a span of time despite the limited opportunities open to them, we may well surmise how much greater would have been Russia's gain from an emancipated Jewry.

XIV

CONCLUSION

WHY, in the final analysis, did Jewish emancipation fail to materialize, and where does the responsibility for this failure lie? In this struggle three main forces were involved: the government, the *maskilim*, and the orthodox masses with their leaders. What was the responsibility of each of these for the unsuccessful outcome of these attempts to secure civic rights?

As to the government, it is clear that no régime gave any genuine evidence of its intention to grant the Jews emancipation. Neither in the most reactionary nor in the most liberal periods had the Jews of Russia any chance of acquiring civic equality *as long as they remained Jews*. Educational measures undertaken by the government of Nicholas I, ostensibly for the purpose of preparing Jews for citizenship through "moral" improvement, were only ill-concealed attempts at conversion. Though the educational system of Alexander II was free from missionary tendencies, the fact remains that in his régime, too, barring a few minor exceptions, a Jew could attain equality only by means of baptism.

On the whole, notwithstanding the minor concessions granted during the reign of Alexander II, his attitude toward the Jews was not very different from that of his predecessors. Whatever general or Jewish rights were granted during his rule must be attributed not to his liberalism but to the progressive spirit of the times. It was as a concession to this spirit that Alexander II, who was really distrustful of progressive ideas and was as deeply prejudiced against the Jews as the other tsars, yielded to the liberal demands for reforms. Had it been in the power of these liberal forces to grant the Jew emancipation, it is not unlikely that Russian Jewry would have won its battle during that period. But the determined opposition of the monarch, who refused under any circumstances to consider the abolition of the Pale, was the chief deterrent to the achievement of this goal. It may be stated, then, without any reservation that at no time up to the death of Alexander II was the civic emancipation of the Jews an even remote possibility.

The error of the *maskilim* lay in their belief that Russification would earn for the Jew the coveted prize of equal rights. How futile it was for these champions of enlightenment to pin any such hopes on a tsarist monarchy, even at its best, became most disillusioningly apparent in the rule of Alexander II. One cannot altogether blame them for their naïve optimism as to the efficacy of the *Haskalah* program or for their delusions about the government's intention—their eagerness to hasten the progress of emancipation blinded them to a more realistic understanding of the problem. At the same time one cannot help feeling that there was an element of cravenness in the tacit admission of the *maskilim* that the Jew had to earn rights which the non-Jewish population enjoyed without any such qualifications. There was far more dignity and wisdom in the stand of those Jewish leaders who demanded that emancipation should precede enlightenment and who contended that once equality was granted, the widespread pursuit of education would follow as a natural consequence.

Among the positive achievements of *Haskalah* should be listed first and foremost the opening of the door of secular culture for the ghetto Jew. To the efforts of the *maskilim* should be credited the interest in agricultural pursuits which their propaganda helped to stimulate. They were also responsible for the renaissance of the Hebrew language and literature, for the awakening of Jewish nationalism, and for the birth of the Zionist movement, through which spiritual and political self-emancipation in the ancient homeland was sought. Even Jewish participation in the revolutionary movement may in a measure be attributed to the influence of *Haskalah*. It is true that the political aspirations of the *maskilim* were essentially predicated upon a benevolent monarchy and that they strongly opposed revolutionary means. Nevertheless, one may still regard Jewish intellectuals who turned to revolutionary activities as products of *Haskalah*, for it was by way of secular education that they came upon the path of revolution.

Concerning the third element involved in this conflict, orthodox Jewry, one may interpret its opposition to enlightenment as motivated by both unconscious and conscious reasons. The great mass of orthodox Jews repudiated everything *Haskalah* represented because of instinctive and unreasoning resistance to any innovation which would upset their accustomed pattern of life, or which challenged the validity of their accepted beliefs. But there were also conscious and valid reasons for the opposition. Orthodox leadership saw in the doctrines of *Haskalah* a threat to the preservation of Judaism and the Jew. That these fears and suspicions were partly justified we have seen demonstrated in the eventual weakening of Judaism and in the derelictions from the Jewish ranks which followed in the wake of *Haskalah*. It should be borne in mind that it was the orthodox way of life that had thus far proved the most effective means of safeguarding both Judaism and the integrity of the Jewish people in the Diaspora. Nay, more than that, as long as the Jew was compelled to live in ghettos, traditional Judaism offered a spiritual sustenance which compensated for the disabilities imposed upon him. Many of the religious leaders were also aware of the spiritual frustration that awaited educated youth who through secular education were being equipped for a world that would not accept them but were at the same time rendered unfit for life in the ghetto.

Regardless of the cost in suffering, no generation of youth could be expected to desist from the pursuit of enlightenment for the sake of inner peace. Nor could it rightfully be asked of a people nurtured in traditions of learning that they shut out the light of the world about them, even were such a course the only means of preserving their spiritual heritage. It was foolhardy even to attempt to do so, for one could no more hope to stem the onrushing tides of progress than Canute could hold back the waves of the sea.

But orthodoxy's unyielding resistance to *Haskalah* was in no wise responsible for the retardation of Jewish emancipation just as the efforts of the *maskilim* were of little avail in securing that prize. To none of the factions in Jewry can that failure be ascribed, for the achievement of that goal depended not upon the efforts of the Jews but upon the will of the government. Clearly, then, it was not by "remaking" the Jew, but by a change in the form of government that Jewish emancipation had any chance of realization.

BIBLIOGRAPHICAL NOTE

This bibliographical note presents a topical arrangement of materials used in the preparation of this book with the works classified according to the main subjects treated in this study. It includes brief descriptions and appraisals of the most important publications but omits mention of those footnote references which are incidental to the theme of this work. The classifications are as follows: 1. Bibliographical aids; 2. General Russian history; 3. General history of the Jews in Russia; 4. Ancient and medieval history; 5. The Period of Alexander II; 6. Legal status; 7. Secular education; 8. Agricultural experiments; 9. Economic status; 10. The *Haskalah* movement; 11. Cultural and moral status; 12. Revolutionary movement.

Bibliographical Aids

There are two bibliographical guides in Russian on the periods covered by this book. They are: V. I. Mezhov, "Bibliografia Evreiskago Voprosa v Rossii s 1855 po 1874 Goda" (A Bibliography on the Jewish Problem in Russia from 1855 to 1874) in *Evreiskaia Biblioteka*, V, 37–49; *Sistematichesky Ukazatel Literatury o Evreiakh na Russkom Iazyke, 1708–December 1889* (A Systematic Index to the Literature about the Jews in the Russian Language from 1708 to December 1889), St. Petersburg, 1893. The first part of this work is devoted to a bibliography on Russian-Jewish history while the second deals with world Jewry.

General Russian History

For the student there is an extensive literature on Russian history even in the English language. The general reader will find the works on Russian history referred to in this study extremely helpful for an understanding of both Russian history and of the position of the Jew in Russia. A factual and comprehensive account from the founding of the Russian State until 1928 is provided by George Vernadsky, *A History of Russia*, New Haven, 1929. A detailed history from Catherine II to Nicholas II was written by Alexander Kornilov, *Modern Russian History*, two volumes, New York, 1916, translated by Alexander S. Kaun. The translator wrote a concluding chapter dealing with the reign of Nicholas II covering the period 1894–1916. The period of Alexander II, with which this book is primarily concerned, is described in a popular work by Stephen Graham, *A Life of Alexander II, Tsar of Russia*, London, 1935. That period from the point of view of a revolutionist is portrayed in Peter Kropotkin, *Memoirs of a Revolutionist*, Boston and New York, 1930. A scholarly account of the social movements of the period is found in A. A. Kornilov, *Obshchestvennoe Dvizhenie pri Aleksandre II* (Social Movements in the Reign of Alexander II), Moscow, 1909. The cultural and spiritual life of the Russian people is treated in D. S. Mirsky, *A History of Russian Literature*, New York, 1927, and in Thomas G. Masaryk, *The Spirit of Russia,* two volumes, translated from the German original by E. and C. Paul, London and New York, 1929. The last-mentioned work is a profound analysis of the religious and philosophical currents in Russian history.

Reference Works on Russia

The following encyclopediae furnish further material on all phases of Russian life and history: *Entsiklopedichesky Slovar* (Encyclopaedic Dictionary), chief editor, I. E. Andreevsky, 41 volumes, St. Petersburg, 1890–1904. Two volumes were added in 1906. *Novy Entsiklopedichesky Slovar* (New Encyclopaedic Dictionary), 29 volumes published, work incomplete, St. Petersburg, 1912–1916. *Bolshaia Sovetskaia Entsiklopediia* (The Large Sovet Encyclopaedia), chief editor, O. I. Shmidt, work begun in Moscow 1926; 32 volumes of the planned 65 have been completed.

General History of the Jews in Russia

Source material on the general history of the Jews in Russia is to be found in *Polnoe Sobranie Zakonov Rossiskoi Imperii. Sobranie Pervoe* (A Complete Collection of the Laws of the Russian Empire. First Collection), containing 45 volumes and listing the laws from 1649–1825; *Polnoe Sobranie Zakonov Rossiskoi Imperii. Sobranie Vtoroe* (A Complete Collection of the Laws of the Russian Empire. Second Collection), covering in 55 volumes the laws between 1825–1881. These two collections are official publications and, in addition to the laws, furnish statistical data and official observations concerning the Jews. A helpful guide to these collections is P. Levanda, *Polny Khronologichesky Sbornik Zakonov i Polozheni, Kasaiushchikhsia Evreev* (A Complete Chronological Collection of the Laws and Statutes Concerning Jews), St. Petersburg, 1874. Abundant historical information including source material is to be found in the following Jewish periodicals and collective volumes: *Evreiskaia Biblioteka* (The Jewish Library), place, date of publication, and nature of this magazine are described in Chapter VIII of this book. *Perezhitoe* (Experiences), an annual published in St. Petersburg between 1908–1912. Edited by a group of scholars, this periodical deals mainly with the history of the Russian Jews, particularly of the nineteenth century. *Evreiskaia Starina* (Jewish Antiquities), a quarterly published in St. Petersburg, 1909–1930, by the Jewish Historical Ethnographic Society. Edited by the historian S. M. Dubnow, the magazine concentrated on publishing studies on the history and ethnography of Polish-Russian Jewry. *Voskhod* (Sunrise), a monthly edited by Adolph Landau and issued in St. Petersburg between the years 1881–1906. *Historische Schriften* (Historical Writings), three volumes, volume I, Warsaw, 1929; volume II, Vilno, 1937; volume III, Vilno-Paris, 1939. The last-mentioned three volumes are the products of the Yiddish Scientific Institute, formerly of Vilno, presently in New York City, and are in keeping with the high standards of this institution.

The following secondary works provide a comprehensive account of the history of the Jews in Russia: S. M. Dubnow, *History of the Jews in Russia and Poland,* translated from the Russian by I. Friedlaender, three volumes,

Philadelphia 1916, 1918, 1920. It covers periods from earliest times to 1914. J. Gessen, *Istoria Evreiskago Naroda v Rossii* (The History of the Jewish People in Russia), Leningrad, 1925, two volumes in one. It contains a full account of Jewish life in Russian territory from the Middle Ages till the middle eighties of the nineteenth century. J. Gessen, *Evrei v Rossii* (Jews in Russia), St. Petersburg, 1906, deals with the social, legal, and economic aspects of Russian Jewry, with the first part entirely devoted to a study of the statute of 1804. S. M. Ginsburg, *Historische Werk* (Historical Works) three volumes, New York, 1937, is a collection of articles on various aspects of Russian-Jewish history. This work is particularly valuable because the author, a recognized Russian-Jewish historian, spent thirteen years in the government archives studying original documents made available to scholars after the Revolution of 1917.

Ancient and Medieval

Source material on ancient and medieval history is found in: *Regesty i Nadpisi* (Documents and Inscriptions), volume I, St. Petersburg, 1896, published by The Society for the Promotion of Culture Among Jews in Russia. A. Firkovich, *Abne Zikkaron. Mazebot al Kibre Bne Yisrael Bi-Krim* (Monuments on the Graves of the Israelites in Crimea), Vilno, 1872. A detailed account of the various theories concerning the origin of Jewish settlement on Russian soil as well as a history of the Jews in medieval Russia is given in I. Berlin, *Istoricheskiia Sudby Evreiskago Naroda na Territorii Russkago Gosudarstva* (The Fate of the Jewish People in the Territory of the Russian State), Petrograd, 1919. It is especially valuable for the abundance of sources cited by the author. A. Harkavy's *Ha-Yehudim U-Sefat Ha-Slavim* (The Jews and the Language of the Slavs), Vilno, 1867, represents an important contribution and a pioneering effort in the field of early Russian-Jewish history.

The Period of Alexander II

The period of Alexander II, central theme of this book, is treated in the Complete Collection of Laws as well as in the periodicals and secondary works cited in the section on General History of the Jews in Russia. First-hand information and contemporary opinion on this period may be gleaned from the publications described in Chapter VIII of this book. The exalted mood of the period as reflected in the contemporary Russian and Jewish press is described by S. M. Ginsburg in an excellent series of articles: "Zabytaia Epokha" (A Forgotten Era) in *Voskhod*, 1896, and "Zabytaia Stranitsa" (A Forgotten Page) in *Minuvshee* (Bygone Days), Petrograd, 1923. An analysis of the social and intellectual currents in Jewish life based upon the Jewish press was made by I. Sosis in "Obshchestvennoe . . . Reform" (Social Currents in the Period of the Great Reforms), *Evr. Star.*, 1914, and by S. M. Dubnow in *Pisma o Starom i Novom Evreistve* (Letters on Old and New Judaism), pp. 205–227, St. Petersburg, 1907. The problems of the day and the spiritual currents of the times are subjects of works of the following contemporaries: I. Orshansky, *Evrei v Rossii* (Jews in Russia), St. Petersburg, 1877, which deals mostly with economic and political problems. Michael Morgulis, *Voprosy Evreiskoi Zhizni* (Problems of Jewish Life), St. Petersburg, 1889, a collection of essays devoted chiefly to problems of education and Russification from the point of view of an ardent Russificator. Ioakhim Tarnopol, *Opyt Sovremennoi i Osmotritelnoi Reformy v Oblasti Iudaisma v Rossii* (An Essay on the Contemporary Reform of Judaism), Odessa, 1868. Civic rights, Russification, and religious reform are the subjects of this work. Z. Minor, *Rechi* (Addresses), first edition, Moscow, 1875, a collection of sermons and addresses representative of the ideology of the government rabbis. Leon Rosenthal, *Toldot Hebrat Marbe Haskalah Be-Yisrael Be-Erez Russyah* (History of the Society for the Promotion of Culture among Jews in Russia), two volumes in one, St. Petersburg, 1885. Two outstanding publicists and champions of Jewish rights, Orshansky and Rabinovich, are described by J. Gessen in *Gallereia Evreiskikh Deiatelei* (A Gallery of Jewish Leaders), first edition, St. Petersburg, 1898. Valuable material on the period is contained in the following memoirs: Pauline Wengeroff, *Memoiren einer Grossmutter*, volume I, Berlin, 1908; volume II, Berlin, 1910; Eliakum Zunser, *A Jewish Bard.*, translated by Simon Hirsdansky, New York, 1905.

Reference Works on Russian-Jewish History

The following Jewish Encyclopediae were consulted in the preparation of this study: *The Jewish Encyclopedia*, 12 volumes, New York, 1901–1906. (Very helpful in the use of these volumes is the guide prepared by Joseph Jacobs, *The Jewish Encyclopedia*, New York, 1906.) *The Universal Jewish Encyclopedia*, 10 volumes, chief editor Rabbi Isaac Landman, New York, 1939–1943. *Evreiskaia Entsiklopediia* (The Jewish Encyclopedia), issued by the Society for Scientific Jewish Publications, 16 volumes, St. Petersburg, 1906–1913. The last volume contains an index.

Legal Status

The previously mentioned Complete Collection of Laws, and Levanda's Guide provide sources for the study of the legal position of the Jews. N. Varadinov, *Istoria Ministerstva Vnutrennikh Del* (History of the Ministry of the Interior), 8 volumes, St. Petersburg, 1853–1863, contains legal information about Jews culled from the Complete Collection of Law and from reports of ministers. In addition to the historical works and periodicals listed in the section on the General History of the Jews in Russia which provide material on the legal status of the Russian Jews, books dealing exclusively with this subject are: I. Orshansky, *Russkoe Zakonodatelstvo o Evreiakh* (Russian Legislation Concerning Jews), St. Petersburg, 1877, a brilliant analysis of the legal history of Russian Jews from the time of Catherine II to the seventies of the nineteenth century. N. Golitsyn, *Istoria Russkago Zakonodatelstva o Evreiakh* (The History of Russian Legislation Concerning Jews), St. Petersburg, 1886, covers laws from 1649 to 1825. In spite of the author's obvious bias, the book is valuable for the source material. N. D. Gradovsky, *Otnosheniia k Evreiam v Drevnei i Sovremennoi Rusi* (The Treatment of Jews in Ancient and Contemporary Russia), St. Petersburg, 1891. The author makes the thesis that the spirit of intolerance to Jews is foreign to the historic traditions of Russia. The apologetic tendency sometimes mars the scholarly character of the work. Prince Demidoff San-Donato, *The Jewish Question in Russia,* translated from the Russian by J. Michell, London, 1884, a compact account of Russian-Jewish legislation from the days of the Muscovy Tsardom to the eighties of the nineteenth century, and a lucid analysis of the effects of the Pale on the economic life of the Jew. I. P. Kelberin, *Cherta Osedlosti* (The Pale of Settlement), Petrograd, 1914, a brief history of the legislation regarding the Pale and a plea for its removal. I. Bikerman, *Materialy k Zakonproectu ob Otmene Cherty Evreiskoi Osedlosti* (Material on the Projected Abolition of the Pale), St. Petersburg, 1911.

Secular Education

The policy of the government concerning the education of Jews is revealed in the Complete Collection of Laws and in: *Sbornik Postanovleni po Ministerstvu Narodnago Prosveshcheniia* (Collection of Regulations of the Ministry of Public Education), 6 volumes, St. Petersburg, 1865–1878. *Dopolnenie k Sborniku Postanovleni po Ministerstvu Narodnago Prosveshcheniia* (Supplement to Collection of Regulations of Ministry of Public Education), 1803–1864, St. Petersburg, 1867. *Sbornik Rasporiazheni po Ministerstvu Narodnago Prosveshcheniia* (Collection of Executive Orders of the Ministry of Public Education), 3 volumes, St. Petersburg, 1866–1867. All the foregoing are official publications. Secret instructions not published in the Collection of Laws appear in the three above-mentioned publications, and are therefore indispensable for a study of the special Jewish schools. *Zhurnal Ministerstva Narodnago Prosveshcheniia* (The Journal of the Ministry of Public Education), the organ of the Ministry of Public Education, appeared irregularly and under various titles from 1803 to 1833. From 1834 it is called *Zhurnal Ministerstva Narodnago Prosveshcheniia.*

The following studies represent critical analyses of the government's educational policies: A. Beletsky, *Vopros ob Obrazovanii Russkikh Evreev v Tsarstvovanii Imperatora Nicolaia I.* (The Problem of Jewish Education in the Reign of Nicholas I), St. Petersburg, 1894. M. G. Morgulis, "K Istorii . . . Evreev" (The History of Secular Education of Russian Jews) in *Evreiskaia Bibliot.,* volumes I, II, III; S. M. Ginsburg, "Russkoe . . . Veka" (The Russian Government and the Problem of Jewish Education in the First Half of the Nineteenth Century) in *Minuvshee,* Petrograd, 1923. See also the introductory essay by the same author in *Kazennye Evreiskie Uchilishcha* (Jewish Government Schools), edited by S. Lozinsky, Petrograd, 1920. S. Posner, *Evrei v Obshchei Shkole* (Jews in the General Schools), St. Petersburg, 1914, chapters I, II. David Philipson, *Max Lilienthal,* New York, 1915; chapters "The Russian Career" and "My Travels in Russia" are based on Lilienthal's memoirs.

Special studies of the government schools are furnished by: S. Lozinsky's above-mentioned *Kazennye Evreiskie Uchilishcha,* based on source materials, but containing many errors and needing careful checking. P. Marek, *Ocherki po Istorii Prosveshcheniia Evreev v Rossii* (History of Jewish Education in Russia), Moscow, 1909, important because of source material consisting of school records. *Otchot Postelsa po Obozreniiu Evreiskikh Uchilishch* (Postel's Report on the Jewish Schools), St. Petersburg, 1865, an unbiased report on the condition of the government schools written by an important official of the Ministry of Public Education. *Sbornik v Polzu Nachalnykh Shkol* (Collection of Essays for the Benefit of the Elementary Schools), St. Petersburg, 1896. A. Gordon, "Evreiskiia Uchilishcha" (The Jewish Schools), in *Z. M. N. P.*, 1862, CXV, 9, Div. I, pp. 254–283. L. Binshtok, "Vopros ob Evreiskikh Uchilishchakh" (The Problem of the Jewish Schools) in *Russky Vestnik* (Russian Messenger), 1865, nos. 11, 12, pp. 203–234 and 574–591. The contemporary Russian-Jewish and Hebrew press contains ample material on the subject.

Agricultural Policies

The government's agricultural policies concerning the Jews in the days of Alexander I and Nicholas I are set forth in G. Derzhavin, "Mnenie" (Opinion) in *Sochineniia Derzhavina* (Works by Derzhavin) volume VII, published by the Imperial Academy of Sciences, St. Petersburg, 1872. It served as the basis for the statute of 1804. The laws and decrees as well as occasional accompanying comments are contained in the Complete Collection of Laws and Varadinov's above-mentioned work which expresses the official view. Critical studies of these agricultural experiments were made by: V. N. Nikitin, *Evrei Zemledeltsy* (Jewish Agriculturists), St. Petersburg, 1887, a reliable study based on government records. S. J. Borovoi, *Evreiskaia Zemledelcheskaia Colonizatsia v Staroi Rossii* (Jewish Agricultural Colonization in Old Russia), Moscow, 1928, an excellent history of Jewish colonization based on colonial records. M. Kulisher, "Kto Vinovat" (Who Is the Guilty One?) *Evreiskaia Biblioteka*, IV, 91–113, a factual saga concerning a Jewish colony which collapsed after ten years of futile struggle. *Sbornik Materialov ob Economicheskom Polozhenii Evreev v Rossi* (Material on Economic Status of Jews of Russia), two volumes in one, St. Petersburg, 1904, published by the Jewish Colonization Association and edited and prepared by a staff of experts. Volume I, 1–188 contains figures and statistics on the Jewish agricultural settlements in Russia.

Economic Status

The last mentioned *Sbornik Materialov* gives an all-embracing picture including statistics and figures on the economic, social, and cultural structure of Russian Jewry. Other source material is provided by *Materialy dlia Geografii i Statistiki Rossii Sobrannye Ofitserami Generalnago Shtaba* (Material on the Geography and Statistics of Russia Collected by Officers of the General Staff). This series of original studies and surveys of various provinces and regions contains important material on the economic condition of Russian Jewry. Of this series the following were used for this book: D. Afanasiev, *Kovenskaia Guberniia* (The Province of Kovno), St. Petersburg, 1861; P. Bobrovsky, *Grodnenskaia Guberniia* (The Province of Grodno), St. Petersburg, 1863; A. Korev, *Vilenskaia Guberniia* (The Province of Vilno), St. Petersburg, 1861; V. Pavlovich, *Ekaterinoslavskaia*

Gubernia (The Province of Ekaterinoslav), St. Petersburg, 1862; A. Zashchuk, *Bessarabskaia Oblast* (The Region of Bessarabia), St. Petersburg, 1862; A. Zelensky, *Minskaia Guberniia* (The Province of Minsk), two volumes, St. Petersburg, 1864. An independent original study in the same category is I. Funduklei's, *Statisticheskoe Opisanie Kievskoi Gubernii* (A Statistical Survey of the Province of Kiev), three volumes, St. Petersburg, 1852.

Special studies of the economic condition of the Russian Jews are the subjects of: I. Orshansky, *Evrei v Rossii*, an excellent study and a pioneering effort in this field. I. Blioch, *Sravnenie Materialnago i Nravstvennago Blagosostoianiia Guberni Zapadnykh, Veliko-Rossiskikh i Privislianskikh* (A Comparative Study of the Material and Moral Status of the Western, Great-Russian, and By-Vistula Provinces). The character of this work is described in Chapter XII. This subject also receives attention in: I. Bikerman, *Materialy* . . . ; Prince Demidoff San-Donato, *The Jewish Question in Russia*, (both mentioned in the legal section); J. Gessen, *Istoria Evreiskago Naroda v Rossii* (listed under General History); and *Schriften far Ekonomic un Statistic* (Writings on Economics and Statistics), published by the Yiddish Scientific Institute and edited by Jacob Lestchinsky, Berlin, 1929, I.

The Haskalah Movement

Source material on *Haskalah* in Prussia and Galicia are provided by: *Ha-Measef* (The Collector), a monthly, Königsberg, 1783–1784. The nature of the magazine is discussed in Chapter II. *Bikkure Ha-Itim* (First Fruits of the Times), an annual, Vienna, 1820–1831. Edited for the first three years by the poet and dramatist Shalom Ha-Cohen, it subsequently had various editors and served as the organ of the best contemporary writers and scholars. N. H. Wessley, *Dibre Shalom Ve-Emet* (Words of Peace and Truth), Vienna, 1827, described in Chapter II. Abraham Goldberg, *Masa Zafon* (A Prophecy from the North), Lemberg, 1848.

The following periodicals are useful for a study of *Haskalah* in Russia: *Pirhe Zafon* (Flowers of the North), I, 1841, II, 1844, both published in Vilno. They are typical of the literary immaturity of that period. *Ha-Boker Or* (Light of the Morning), a monthly founded and edited by the poet A. B. Gottlober, appeared irregularly first in Lemberg from 1876 to 1879, then in Warsaw, 1880–1881. It contains contributions of the best writers of the time and the editor's autobiography, "Zikronot Mi-Yeme Neurai" (Memoirs of My Youth), which reflect the cultural history of Russian Jewry. The Hebrew weeklies of the sixties and seventies described in Chapter VIII also served as vehicles for *Haskalah*. Contemporary works reflecting the *Haskalah* ideology and program are: *Kol Shavat Bat Yehudah* (The Lament of the Daughter of Judah), described in Chapter III. I. B. Levinsohn, *Bet Yehudah* (The House of Judah), edited by B. Nathanson, Warsaw, 1878, and *Teudah Be-Yisrael* (A Testimony in Israel), edited by B. Nathanson, Warsaw, 1878, are discussed in Chapter III. The novels of Abraham Mapu and Peter Smolenskin, and the poetry of A. Lebenson, Micah Lebenson, and Leon Gordon provide material for this subject. All these are discussed in Chapters IX and X. *Igrot Yehuda Leb Gordon* (The Letters of Judah Leb Gordon), edited by I. Weisberg, 2 volumes, Warsaw, 1894. A. I. Kovner, *Heker Dabar* (A Critique), Warsaw, 1865, and *Zeror Perahim* (A Bouquet of Flowers) are discussed in Chapter IX.

A critical analysis of the history and literature of Russian *Haskalah* is set forth in: S. L. (Israel) Zinberg, *Istoria Evreiskoi Pechati* (The History of the Jewish Press), Petrograd, 1915, an excellent study of the various currents of thought up to 1881. Israel Zinberg, *Die Geschichte fun der Literatur bei Yiden* (The History of Jewish Literature), VII, book 2, Vilno, 1937. The last mentioned book is part of an eight volume study which is both in style and in content the best history of Jewish literature from the Middle Ages through the first half of the nineteenth century. Other valuable works on *Haskalah* include: I. Cherikover (E. Tcherikover), *Istoria Obshchestva dlia Rasprostraneniia Prosveshcheniia mezhdu Evreiami v Rossii* (History of the Society for the Promotion of Culture among Jews of Russia), St. Petersburg, 1913. J. Klausner, *Historyah shel Ha-Safrut Ha-Ibrit Ha-Hadashah* (The History of Modern Hebrew Literature), III, Jerusalem, 1913, is particularly valuable for its voluminous bibliographical material. The same author has written *Yozrim U-Bonim* (Creators and Builders), I, Tel Aviv, 1925, which contains short biographies of the creators of modern Hebrew literature, and *History of Modern Hebrew Literature*, translated by Herbert Danby, London, 1932. Myer Waxman, *A History of Jewish Literature*, III, New York, 1936, an exhaustive and carefully documented work. Chapters IV to VIII of book 4 deal with the *Haskalah* in Russia. Jacob S. Raisin, *The Haskalah Movement in Russia*, Philadelphia, 1913. Shalom Spiegel, *Hebrew Reborn*, chapters VII, VIII, book I.

Cultural and Moral Status

The above-mentioned literature of and about *Haskalah* reflects the standards and aspirations of a small worldly portion of Russian Jewry. For an insight into the cultural and moral standards of the masses and of their religious representatives the following writings are helpful: Pauline Wengeroff, *Memoiren einer Grossmutter*, I, Berlin, 1908, II, Berlin, 1910, a firsthand portrayal of the religious and social life of Russian Jews in the nineteenth century. Israel Cohen, *Jewish Life in Modern Times*, New York, 1914. Books II, V, VI give a faithful account of the morals, manners, and cultural standards of Russian Jewry of pre-revolutionary days. L. Mandelstam, "Iz Zapisok . . . Rossii" (Memoirs of the First Jewish University Student in Russia) in *Perez.*, I, 1–50. Abraham Paperna, "Iz Nicolaevskoi Epokhi" (Memoirs of the Nicholas Epoch) in *Perez.*, II, 1–53, III, 264–364. Louis Ginzberg, *Students Scholars and Saints*, Philadelphia, 1928, chapters on "The Jewish Primary School," "The Gaon of Wilna," and "Rabbi Israel Salanter." Jacob Mark, *Gedolim fun Unser Zeit* (Great Personalities of Our Time), New York, 1927. Though not a documented or objective study, the last-named work is of value for the glimpses it offers into the lives of the characters whom the writer knew personally. *Sbornik Mater.*, mentioned in the section on Economic Status, contains official statistics on communal institutions which serve as an index to the social responsibilities of the Jewish community. S. J. Abramovich, *Shlome Reb Hayem's* (Solomon, the Son of Hayem), vol. XVIII in the Collected Works of Mendele Moker Sefarim (Mendele the Bookseller), Warsaw, 1928. Practically all the works of this author provide an excellent source for the study of the life of Russian Jewry.

The *Hassidic* movement which played an important part in the religious and social life of a great portion of Russian Jewry is described in: S. M. Dubnow, *Toldot Ha-Hassidut* (The History of *Hassidism*), three volumes in one, Tel Aviv, 1930, a critical and complete account of the origin, development, and decline of the movement. It also includes a comprehensive and critical bibliography on the subject. S. A. Horodetzky, *Sefer Shibhe Baal Shem Tob* (The Book of Praises of the Baal Shem Tob), Berlin, 1922, an annotated edition of a book by that name published in 1815 by a disciple of the founder of *Hassidism*. The *Shibhe Baal Shem Tob*, the original version, is a collection of stories and legends about the Besht and is a primary source on *Hassidism*. Jacob Minkin, *The Romance of Hassidism*, New York, 1935, a lively and scholarly account of the movement. Solomon Schechter, chapter "The Chassidim" in *Studies in Judaism*, New York, 1920, I, 1–45, an excellent exposition of the doctrines of *Hassidism* and of the history of the movement.

Jews in the Revolutionary Movement

Jewish participation in the early revolutionary movement is treated in: Lev Deich, *Rol Evreev v Russkom Revoliutsionnom Dvizhenii* (Role of the Jews in the Russian Revolutionary Movement), Moscow, Leningrad, 1926. B. Frumkin, "Iz Istorii . . . 1870-ykh Godakh" (The History of Jewish Participation in the Revolutionary Movement in the Seventies of the Nineteenth Century) in *Ev. Star.*, 1911. S. L. Zinberg, "Pervye . . . Literature" (The First Socialistic Organs in Jewish Literature) in *Perez.*, I, 233–263. I. Cherikover, "Der Unhoib . . . Bavegung" (The Beginnings of the Jewish Socialist Movement) in *Hist. Schr.*, I, 469–532; "Yiden . . . 60-er un 70-er" (Jewish Revolutionists in Russia in the 60's and 70's) in *Hist. Schr.*, III, 60–172. This article is particularly useful for its extensive bibliography on this subject. *Historische Schriften*, III, comprises a collection of studies on the Jewish socialist movement in various parts of the world until 1897 and contains a number of articles dealing with that activity in Russia. S. L. Zitron, *Drei Literarische Dorot* (Three Literary Generations), II, Vilno, 1921, contains biographies and characterizations of the leading early Jewish revolutionists.

Memoirs and articles by contemporary revolutionists are to be found in: Paul B. Akselrod, *Perezhitoe i Perredumannoe* (Experiences and Reflections), Berlin, 1923. Lev Deich, *Za Polveka* (Half a Century), Berlin, 1923. O. Aptekman, "Moi Pervye Shagi na Puti Propagandy" (My First Steps as a Propagandist) in *Popular Library of Katorga i Ssylka*, nos. 28–29. Vladimir Iokhelson, "Dalekoe Proshloe" (The Distant Past) in *Byloe* (The Past), 1918, July, pp. 53–75. Morris Winchevsky, "Zhurnalistische Erinnerungen" (Memoirs of a Journalist), in *Zukunft* (The Future), from October 1906 to December 1907; *Ha-Emet*, (The Truth), monthly, Vienna,

1877, edited by Arthur Freeman, (pen name for Aaron Lieberman). This was the first socialist magazine in Hebrew. It is described in Chapter XI.

While the foregoing material deals almost exclusively with Jewish participation in the revolutionary movement, a good deal of incidental information on this subject is scattered in publications dealing with the general Russian Revolution. For bibliographical aid on this subject consult A. A. Shilov, *Chto Chitat po Istorii Russkago Revoliutsionnago Dvizheniia* (What to Read on the History of the Russian Revolution), Petrograd, 1922. For specific references to Jewish participation see pages 160–162; further material may be found by combing the general sources mentioned in the references.

INDEX

VOLUME II

1881-1917

EDITED BY MARK WISCHNITZER

CONTENTS

PREFACE

THE first volume of this book appeared in 1944. It deals with the struggle of the Russian Jews for political emancipation till the end of the reign of Alexander II (1881). Louis Greenberg died suddenly in 1946. He left a manuscript for the second volume which carries the story of the Jews in Russia up to the Bolshevik revolution in 1917. He did not finish his seventh chapter.

At the request of the editor of the Yale Historical Series, I undertook to read the manuscript, which was in draft form, with a view to making it ready for publication, and to do the essential minimum of editing. I have made practically no changes in the presentation of facts and the evaluation of political, socio-economic, and cultural developments except to eliminate obvious errors.

I checked quotations from sources, which had evidently sometimes been made from memory. I supplemented authors' names, titles, dates, and places of publication where, as often happened, they were either lacking or suggested by no more than a word or casual abbreviation. Sometimes one had to guess from such phrases as "the famous humorist" or "a reputable attorney" or "a former journalist" the man alluded to. I have brought the references up to date as far as this was possible. The fundamental source materials used are listed in the bibliography of Volume I. My textual changes and additions are in square brackets. Such changes as were made by the Editor of the Yale Historical Series and the editorial department of the Yale University Press to put the manuscript in shape for publication are of course not indicated in the text.

Professor George Vernadsky, who sponsored and guided Louis Greenberg's work as a graduate student, was kind enough to read the manuscript and to offer many valuable suggestions. I wish to express to him my grateful appreciation. My sincere thanks are due to Mr. William Horowitz, who organized the subscription committee, and to Mrs. Batyah Greenberg for her valuable assistance in placing at my disposal the card files of her late husband.

In transliterating from the Russian, Hebrew, and Yiddish, the author followed with slight modifications the method employed by the Yale University Library.

All Russian dates in this volume are according to the Julian calendar.

MARK WISCHNITZER

Yeshiva University, New York

I

HISTORICAL BACKGROUND

1. The Reign of Alexander III

THE assassination of Alexander II on March 1, 1881, created one of the great "ifs" in Russian and indirectly in world history. On the very day the tsar was murdered by a bomb thrown by a revolutionary, he had signed the so-called Loris-Melikov constitution. Although this document was far from a constitutional charter, it did contain the seeds out of which a democratic regime might well have grown. That does not mean to say that Alexander was inherently less autocratic than his tyrannical predecessors, or that his views were essentially more enlightened than those of his despotic father Nicholas I. In signing this document as in granting the famous reforms of the first part of his reign, he was yielding to the pressure of enlightened public opinion. Upon this sensitiveness to the currents of the times historians base their premise that, given time, he might, after contact with the representatives of the people, have instituted a constitutional monarchy. His violent death and the character of the heir who succeeded him precluded any such possibility within the next reign.

Because of the death of his first-born, the tsar's second son Alexander III inherited the throne. Trained primarily for a military career and, as one of his close friends and admirers characterized him, "a man of limited education" and lacking "in mental keenness," [1] the new tsar came to the throne ill equipped even for the traditional role of ruler. He was, to be sure, firmly fortified with the traditional faith in absolutism and in his own imperial destiny. Like his predecessors he regarded autocracy as a divine institution and himself as God-anointed. Since he was by nature averse to democratic innovations, the fears, suspicions, and hatreds engendered by his father's assassination only strengthened his resistance to demands of the people for a share in government.

To a large extent Alexander's inherently autocratic views were molded and directed by K. P. Pobedonostsev, his mentor and spiritual adviser. In the capacity of procurator of the Holy Synod and in-

1. *The Memoirs of Count Witte,* tr. from the original Russian manuscript and ed. Abraham Yarmolinsky (New York, Doubleday, Page and Co., 1921), p. 38. Hereafter cited as Witte, *Memoirs.*

timate friend of the tsar, this Machiavellian character did more than any other man to shape the policies of Russia in the last quarter of the nineteenth century. A brilliant jurist possessing the mentality and temperament of a medieval inquisitor, he was an implacable foe of democracy, which he designated "the great falsehood of our time."

He argued that the doctrine of democracy, which presupposes the capacity of people to understand the subtleties of political science, could be grasped only by the elite, the aristocracy of the intellect. According to Pobedonostsev, the mass always and everywhere is vulgar and its conceptions crude. He ridiculed the idea that in a popular government the elected representatives were the servants or agents of the people. Both in an autocracy and in a popular form of government the people, he contended, are ruled in the interests of privileged persons. The difference is only this: while the former provides sovereigns prepared from birth and trained by education to rule, the latter represents the rule of a party which happens to have a majority because its leaders have become adept at playing on the instincts and passions of the masses. "Parliamentarianism is the triumph of egoism, its highest expression," was his verdict.[2]

Pobedonostsev was vehemently opposed to freedom of the press, since he regarded the newspaper as "one of the falsest institutions of our times" and found it hard to imagine "a despotism more irresponsible and violent than that of the printed word."[3] Because of his bitter hatred of journalists and his considerable influence the special feature, "Among the Journals and Newspapers," which for a time appeared in the *Government Messenger* was eliminated.[4] This archreactionary was also opposed to secular education which he regarded as useless and burdensome for the masses. Only people, he argued, who were to be trained for higher education should receive instruction at an early age; the masses who lived by manual labor should be given physical training instead. He warned the advocates of universal education "that by tearing the child from the domestic hearth . . . for such a lofty destiny, they deprive his parents of a productive force essential to the maintenance of the home, while by raising before his eyes the mirage of illusory learning, they cor-

2. K. P. Pobedonostsev, *Reflections of a Russian Statesman,* tr. Robert Crozier Long (London, Grant Richards, 1898), pp. 35–36.

3. *Ibid.,* p. 62. [For an analysis of Pobedonostsev's policies see particularly Salo W. Baron, *Modern Nationalism and Religion* (New York, Harper and Brothers, 1947), pp. 176–185. Ed.]

4. ["Pisma K. P. Pobedonostseva k Grafu N. P. Ignatievu," *Byloe* (1925), N. S., Nos. 27–28, p. 61. Ed.]

rupt his mind and subject it to the temptation of vanity and conceit." [5] A fanatical champion of autocracy and the status quo, he fiercely contested any change that threatened to disturb the established order. In the words of a Russian journalist, "Pobedonostsev is an arch-bureaucrat, that is—a kind of wooden ruling machine in human shape, to whom the living units of mankind are nothing, while the maintenance of the bureaucratic 'order' is everything." [6]

Throughout the reign of Alexander III Pobedonostsev wielded great power, advising the emperor on all matters of state policy, writing many of his manifestoes, and thus helping to shape the course of Russian history. An uncompromising opponent of any concession to public opinion, he despised Alexander II, whose policies he consistently criticized to his son, the heir apparent and future emperor. A letter of Pobedonostsev's written to C. F. Tiucheva, on February 25, 1880, reads in part: "My God, how is he [the heir] going to govern? He has not even seen how men of strength and wisdom govern. The reign of his father which he sees is devoid of wisdom, strength, and will." [7] Alexander II in turn regarded Pobedonostsev as a bigot and never entrusted him with any important task. Curiously enough, it was at the insistence of the head of the Cabinet, Loris-Melikov, against whom Pobedonostsev directed his most venomous intrigues, that he was appointed by Alexander to the post of procurator of the Holy Synod. During Alexander II's lifetime and later Loris-Melikov had ample cause to regret his recommendation. It was due chiefly to Pobedonostsev's influence that Loris-Melikov's plan was rejected by the new emperor at a meeting of the Cabinet on March 8, 1881, and the author of the plan together with the ministers who supported him was dismissed from the government.[8] Pobedonostsev triumphed; Russia returned to militant reaction, and he held sway as chief adviser to the ruler.

The spirit of extreme reaction affected every branch of Russian life. The government reintroduced the system of class education which had prevailed in the pre-reform days. School authorities were advised to discourage children of the lower classes from seeking a secondary education; and in a notorious circular referred to as "cooks' children" the Ministry of Education instructed the heads

5. Pobedonostsev, *Reflections*, p. 79.

6. [*Free Russia*, organ of the Society of the Friends of Russian Freedom (London, January, 1900), p. 4. Ed.]

7. ["Pobedonostsev and Alexander III," *Slavonic Review* (June, 1928), p. 53. Ed.]

8. [For a firsthand account of the meeting of March 8, 1881, see *Iz Dnevnika E. A. Peretza*, Krasny Arkhiv, I (1925), 133–150; also *Byloe* (January, 1906), pp. 189–194. Ed.]

of secondary schools to deny admission to the children of coachmen, valets, cooks, small storekeepers, washerwomen, and the like. In order further to discourage higher education among the poor, university fees were raised.[9]

The determination of the government to keep the peasantry and the lower classes in subjection was also reflected in drastic changes in the judicial system. The principle of keeping the judiciary independent of the executive branch of the government was upset in the lower courts by the institution in 1889 of *zemsky nachalniks* (rural chiefs), an office which combined both administrative and judicial authority. Through this functionary the nobility was practically made master over the peasantry, since the zemsky nachalnik appointed by the governor from among the local nobility was both judge and administrator of the rural community. This chief not only was the supervisor of every individual peasant but was also given authority over all the local peasant institutions and peasant courts. In addition control of the zemstvos, the local self-government institutions which had been an outstanding feature of the reforms of Alexander II, was given to the nobility by a law promulgated June 12, 1890.

The ax of reaction wielded mercilessly by the government also fell upon the press. So oppressive did the censorship become that in a very short time almost the entire liberal press ceased publication. With the exception of a few liberal organs which operated under severe handicaps throughout the eighties, the reactionary journalists had the field of public opinion to themselves. The leader of these literati was M. N. Katkov, editor of *Moskovskia Vedomosti* (Moscow News), an intimate friend of Pobedonostsev.

A liberal and champion of western ideas and institutions in his early career, Katkov turned rabidly reactionary after the Polish uprising of 1863. Intolerant by nature, after he had "seen the light" he castigated with fanatical fervor both the reforms he had once advocated and his professional colleagues who remained faithful to these ideas. In the late sixties and seventies he denounced the reforms of Alexander II and advocated a complete return to the absolutism of Nicholas I. Trial by jury, the zemstvo, even such limited freedom of the press as existed were the objects of attack in the pages of his publication, whereas the censorship laws strangling the free press were hailed with the jubilant cry, "Arise gentlemen, the government is coming! The government is returning!" During the discussions of the Loris-Melikov plan Katkov sought to discredit

9. S. V. Rozhdestvensky, *Istorichesky Obzor Deatelnosti Ministerstva Narodnago Prosveshchenia. 1802–1902* (St. Petersburg, 1902), p. 619.

it with the charge that rebellion was brewing within the very gates of the government.

Discussing the ideology and political program of Katkov, K. K. Arseniev, noted publicist, writes: ". . . he opposed equality before the law in all its aspects. He demanded that in dispensing justice the courts pay special deference to persons of 'decent society.' The Ministry of Finance was deprecated for the abolition of the poll tax, and for the taxes it levied on government securities. Government regulation of the economic life of the country was declared an evil when it redounded to the benefit of the masses but hailed as a blessing when it favored the privileged minority." [10]

Another publicist, K. Leontiev, a contributor to the influential magazine *Grazhdanin* (The Citizen), formulated the program of monarchical reaction as follows: "The Russian people should be limited, screwed down, restricted anew in its freedom . . . Russia grew and developed simultaneously and in close connection with the growth of inequality in Russian society, with the establishment of serfdom and with the development of a hereditary officialdom." A *Grazhdanin* correspondent envisaged an ideal Russia: "The peasant tills the soil, the merchant conducts the trade, the warrior defends the country, the clergy worship God and serve His church, and gentlemen of the nobility, you rule the country in government posts." [11]

Nor did the literary champions of political, social, and racial inequality shrink from perverting the Judeo-Christian doctrines about the equality of man. In their struggle for emancipation, complained one of these writers, the Jews were eagerly clutching at such catch phrases as dignity, equality of man, protection under law. Man, in order to establish his just claim to such rights, had first to prove his human qualities. For by the term man is not meant every two-legged creature but an ideal moral being endowed with spiritual attributes and characteristics. What tribunal was to judge the fitness of man the writer did not suggest, but it went without saying that this prerogative belonged to the highest category of human beings—the nobility.

The doctrines preached by the reactionary publicists fitted in with the program of the government concerning racial and religious minorities. The emperor who proclaimed that "Russia should belong to the Russian people" laid down the following principle as a guide for the treatment of all non-Russian groups. Russian statehood, nationalism, language, and reverence for the faith professed by the

10. K. K. Arseniev, *Za Chetvert Veka* (*1871–1894*) (Petrograd, 1915), p. 332.
11. *Ibid.*, p. 495.

Russian people and its sovereign should prevail in all the land.[12] In line with these views the government embarked upon a policy of religious intolerance and militant nationalism. All religious sects were ruthlessly persecuted. Among the dissident Christian groups there were some who were noted for their high moral principles and exemplary conduct. Nevertheless, because the emperor and the procurator of the Holy Synod regarded them as a menace to the dominant church, these sects were hounded indiscriminately. In some cases they were forbidden to hold divine service and their children were even taken away from them. The policy of aggressive nationalism expressed itself in severe restrictions imposed on all non-Russian groups residing on the borderlands of Russia; Poles and other so-called foreign groups were subjected to compulsory Russification and the right of the Poles to government service was limited in the Polish provinces.[13]

To complete the account of the reign of Alexander III reference must be made to the few positive achievements which somewhat relieve the darkness of the period. The campaign against illiteracy which may be said to have begun in the sixties, during the early reign of Alexander II, made considerable progress despite the reactionary policies of Alexander III, although it must be stated that the dissemination of elementary education was primarily the work of the zemstvos whose efforts were often impeded rather than aided by the government. Thus, for example, while the zemstvos spent 5,307,000 rubles in 1891 on elementary education, the total outlay of the state for this purpose was 1,480,397 rubles. The high percentage of literates by the end of the nineteenth century attests the successful efforts of the zemstvos. Whereas in 1880 the percentage of pupils to the total population was 1.16, in 1891 it was 2.22, in 1894 2.80, and in 1898, 3.26. According to the census of 1897, 27.8 per cent of the population above the age of ten were literate, marking quite an advance from the practically universal illiteracy which had existed in Russia a few decades previously.[14]

As a result of the growth of factories and of an industrial proletariat during the reign of Alexander III, the eighties saw the emergence of the first factory legislation in Russia. The initial law

12. *Istorichesky Vestnik* (July, 1912), p. 274.

13. A. Kornilov, *Kurs Istorii Rossii XIX Veka* (Moscow, 1914) III, 193 ff.

14. P. N. Ignatiev, D. M. Odinetz, and P. J. Novgorotsev, *Russian Schools and Universities in the World War* (New Haven, 1929), p. 4; V. I. Charnolusky, in the collective work, *Istoria Rossii v XIX Veke,* VII, 165–166; T. J. Polner, *Russian Local Government during the War and the Union of Zemstvos* (New Haven, 1930), pp. 27–28; N. S. Timasheff, "Overcoming Illiteracy. Public Education in Russia, 1880–1940," *Russian Review* (Autumn, 1942), pp. 81–82.

passed on June 1, 1882,[15] as well as the subsequent legislation, was designed primarily to offer some sort of protection to women and children employed in industry; the laws fixed a maximum working day and regulated and in some instances completely barred night work. Special factory inspectors charged with the task of enforcing the new labor legislation were appointed.

On the whole, however, except for the advances noted, the period was one of political and social reaction in which the nobility regained many of their old advantages and entrenched themselves anew as the lords and masters of Russia. Describing the situation of the common people, a contemporary refers to the period as one of "stillness," when the masses, exhausted spiritually and physically, were unable to offer any resistance to the reactionary policies of the government.

On March 1 the Russian people were startled to learn of an attempt on the life of Tsar Alexander made by a group of university students. (Five of the group including A. I. Ulianov, elder brother of V. I. Ulianov-Lenin, were hanged after trial on May 8.) The press referred to this outbreak of terror as reminiscent of the heroic days of the Narodniks of the late seventies and likened it to the faint echo of a storm which had spent its force. But the storm broke forth with even greater force in the reign of Nicholas, who succeeded his father in 1894.

2. The Reign of Nicholas II

There were several vital events which made this eruption inevitable in the reign of Nicholas II. The emperor himself having been a most important factor in precipitating this bloody struggle, it is necessary to dwell at least briefly on his character and political views. Count Witte who knew the tsar intimately stated that he had rarely met a better-mannered young man than Nicholas II, but that his good breeding merely concealed his shortcomings.[16] Notable among these was his weakness of character and vacillating nature, on which the British historian Sir Bernard Pares, who was in a position to observe him at close range, commented as follows: "Nicholas was singularly open to reasonable argument, much more so than his father. The trouble was that he was so much so, that each new impression might efface the last." [17] Hence no minister felt secure in

15. *Polnoe Sobranie Zakonov Rossiskoi Imperii. Sobranie Tret'e* (Complete Collection of the Laws of the Russian Empire. 3rd Series), Vol. II, No. 931. Hereafter cited as *T.P.S.Z.*

16. Witte, *Memoirs*, p. 189.

17. Sir Bernard Pares, *The Fall of the Russian Monarchy* (London, Jonathan Cape, 1939), pp. 56, 58–59.

his position or could ever be certain that he was not being undermined in his position by "backstairs influence." Nicholas chose his most important officials not for their ability or integrity but usually because they were recommended to him by a "boudoir council" which consisted of his wife, a number of grand dukes, or a favorite of the moment. To maintain their posts ministers had to cater to courtiers and favorites who dominated the emperor. In spite of a superficial kindliness which marked his intercourse with people, Nicholas was essentially a cruel man. Count Witte relates in his memoirs, that during his premiership he received a dispatch from Sologub, the governor general of the Baltic provinces, describing the measures taken to suppress the uprising in the Reval district. The governor general requested Witte to exert a moderating influence upon Captain Richter of the punitive expedition, who was executing people indiscriminately without the least semblance of legality. Witte submitted this dispatch to the tsar who returned it to him with the notation opposite the lines describing the captain's bloody deeds: "Fine! A capital fellow!" [18] Similarly, the tsar warmly commended General D. F. Trepov, head of the police, who in order to suppress the peasant riots issued the famous order "not to spare cartridges." [19] The Russian liberal, I. I. Petrunkevich, characterized Nicholas II and his period as follows: "Nothing this man touched succeeded. Everything he did bore the stamp of egotism, insincerity, falsehood, cruelty, and indifference to the fate of Russia. The history of his entire reign contains not a single noble page." [20]

Weak willed, vacillating, fitful, and "constant only in his inconstancy," Nicholas was consistent throughout his rule in his refusal to allow his people a share in government. In unmistakable terms he made this determination clear at the outset. On the occasion of his marriage in the first year of his reign, on January 17, 1895, when he received a delegation of all classes who came to offer their felicitations, he said: "In several zemstvo assemblies there have been heard lately voices of men carried away by preposterous delusions concerning the participation of the representatives of the zemstvos in the affairs of the inner administration. Let everybody know that I shall guard the principle of the autocracy as firmly and uncom-

18. Witte, *Memoirs*, p. 189.

19. [*The Secret Letters of the Last Tsar. Being the Confidential Correspondence between Tsar Nicholas II and His Mother, Dowager Empress Maria Feodorovna*, ed. Edward J. Bing (New York and Toronto, Longmans, Green and Co., 1938), p. 187. Ed.]

20. [I. I. Petrunkevich, *Iz Zapisok Obshchestvennago Deatelia. Vospominania*, Arkhiv Russkoi Revolutsii, XXI (Berlin, 1934), 290. Hereafter cited as Petrunkevich, *Iz Zapisok*. Ed.]

promisingly as it was guarded by my never-to-be-forgotten deceased parent." [21] This speech was written by Pobedonostsev, who sought to make it clear at the beginning of Nicholas' rule as he had at the inauguration of his father Alexander that all hopes for a liberal regime were vain.

But circumstances now were quite different. At the beginning of the eighties, with the revolutionary forces crushed, the will of the masses to resist was completely broken. Toward the end of Alexander's reign the vitality of the people stirred again, and the will to reconstruct Russian life on more democratic lines began to reassert itself. In 1894 a secret political organization, the party of the People's Rights, issued a proclamation declaring its purpose to be the achievement of political freedom through the union of all forces opposed to the government. The party aimed at the establishment of a representative government, universal franchise, freedom of speech, press, assembly, and conscience, and also at national self-determination. In their public pronouncements the leaders of the zemstvos did not go so far. All they asked for was that they be consulted in matters of administration and be given the opportunity to present their needs directly to the emperor. Such in substance was the content of a petition submitted to the new tsar by the liberal leaders of the zemstvo of the province of Tver. It may well be, as some historians maintain, that the modest demands of the zemstvo leaders did not express their political aspirations but were only trial balloons designed to explore the reaction of the government. But the government was in no mood to listen to any suggestion for sharing its power with the people.

The answer of the people came early in the reign of Nicholas. In the course of the first ten years there were peasant riots, student disorders and workers' strikes; three ministers and Grand Duke Sergei Alexandrovich were assassinated by the revolutionaries. To squelch the disorders in the universities the government decreed the recruiting into the army of those university students who participated in antigovernment activities. It was in retaliation for this order that Minister of Education N. P. Bogolepov was shot and fatally wounded by a terrorist.

Among the assassinated ministers was D. S. Sipiagin, the minister of the interior. He was replaced by Viacheslav Plehve, a self-seeking, unscrupulous bureaucrat who set about crushing the revolutionary spirit by harsh measures. To put an end to the peasant

21. [Simon Dubnow, *History of the Jews in Russia and Poland* (Philadelphia, Jewish Publication Society of America, 1920), III, 8, Hereafter cited as Dubnow, *History*. Ed.]

riots which culminated in the burning or seizure of nobles' estates, Plehve introduced the principle of group responsibility whereby whole villages were punished for the participation of individual peasants in agrarian riots. Special assessments were levied on entire peasant communities to compensate the landowners for losses thus incurred, and in addition they were saddled with the burden of supporting special rural police created to maintain order in the villages. In order to crush the spirit of rebelliousness which was beginning to manifest itself among the factory workers, Plehve utilized the factory inspectors whose original duty it was to protect the rights of the workers.

But the severe measures of the government failed to halt the mounting flames of revolution. These fires were fanned by two revolutionary parties—the Social Democrats and the Social Revolutionaries, who, though at variance regarding the ultimate objectives and means, were united in their revolutionary opposition to the existing regime. These organized groups found a ready response among the masses whose hatred of the government was intensified by the war then being fought against Japan.

Unfamiliar with the issues of the war and knowing only that their sons were being sent to die in far-off Manchuria, the people felt growing resentment against their government as Russian armies suffered disaster after disaster on land and sea. Had they a voice in the matter, they thought, the war could have been either averted or more efficiently conducted. Thus the war with Japan, whereby Plehve and the tsar's advisers sought to bolster the autocratic regime, served only to weaken further the tottering structure of tsarism by uniting the entire people against the monarch and his court.

The opposition to the government reached the boiling point after "Bloody Sunday," January 9, 1905. Following the example of some zemstvo representatives who, in the fall of 1904, submitted petitions to the tsar pleading for an end to absolutism in Russia, the workers of St. Petersburg, too, decided to address the monarch in this fashion. The zemstvo representatives as well as the workers were encouraged by the so-called "political spring"—the relaxation of police repression—inaugurated by the moderate Prince P. D. Sviatopolk-Mirsky who on August 26, 1904, succeeded Plehve in the Ministry of the Interior.[22] Carrying icons and chanting prayers, about 200,000 workers—men, women, and children—led by the priest George Gapon, marched on the cold and windy morning of Sunday, January 9, to the Winter Palace. But instead of being received by the tsar the unarmed demonstrators were intercepted by

22. [Plehve was assassinated July 15, 1904, by the terrorist Sazonov. Ed.]

troops who fired at the huge crowd, killing several hundred and wounding more than a thousand.

Great excitement and tremendous unrest swept the country after this incident. N. N. Popov designates January 9 as the beginning of the first Russian revolution; [23] and the president of the first Soviet of Workers' Deputies, G. S. Khrustalev-Nosar, refers to that date as the turning point in the history of the revolution. "Up to January 9th," he observes, "there were movements in the working class; from January 9th on there began the movement of the whole working class." [24]

The weeks following Bloody Sunday witnessed an unprecedented wave of strikes throughout the country. Abolition of the autocracy and the convocation of a constituent assembly for the purpose of founding a democratic republic were the constant demands put forth by the workers of those days. Simultaneously with the strike movement of the urban proletariat, agrarian riots swept the countryside. In some localities government officials were forcibly ousted and their positions taken by committees chosen from among the peasantry. While the slogan of the striking city worker was "Constituent Assembly," the rallying cry of the peasant was *Zemlia i Volia* (Land and Freedom).

In an attempt to stave off revolution the government resorted to both repression and conciliation. The moderate Sviatopolk-Mirsky was replaced by the reactionary Bulygin whom Nicholas, on February 23, 1905, appointed as chairman of a committee charged with preparing a plan for the establishment of a consultative body of representatives. At the same time various organizations and private persons were permitted to make representations to the committee about the organization of the new consultative body. The Bulygin constitution published in the form of an imperial order on August 6, 1905, provided for the establishment of an advisory body, called the duma, without any legislative powers.[25] To assure its conservative character the electoral law was so formulated that only the well-to-do classes could participate in the choice of deputies.

The projected Bulygin duma satisfied neither the liberals nor the socialists. But whereas the former were willing to accept it in the hope of using the new institution as an instrument in their further struggle for a genuine parliamentary government, the latter de-

23. N. N. Popov, *Ocherk Istorii Vsesoiuznoi Kommunisticheskoi Partii* (Moscow, 1928), p. 85.

24. G. S. Khrustalev-Nosar, *History of the Soviet of Workers' Deputies,* in Russian (1910), p. 47, quoted in James Mavor, *An Economic History of Russia* (2d ed., London, J. M. Dent and Sons, 1925), II, 478.

25. *T.P.S.Z.,* Vol. XXV, Pt. I, No. 26,661.

cided to boycott the elections. Nor did the proposed duma have any effect upon the ever spreading wave of strikes, peasant disorders, and the fermenting spirit of revolt which penetrated into the army and the navy. In his memoirs Count Witte gives a graphic description of the chaotic conditions of the summer and fall of 1905:

"Anarchistic attacks directed against the lives of government officials; riots in the institutions of higher learning and even in the secondary schools, which were accompanied by various excesses; trouble in the army; disturbances among the peasants and workmen, involving destruction of property, personal injury and loss of life; and finally strike—such were the main conditions with which the authorities had to cope. . . . The universal exclamation was: We can live like this no longer! The present insane regime must be done away with!" [26]

Realizing that neither the pressure of public opinion nor individual acts of terrorism would compel the authorities to yield to the will of the nation, the people decided to declare a general strike against the government. A strike of the engine drivers on one of Moscow's railroads in the first week of October, 1905, spread with such rapidity that by the 12th of the month all the railroads of Moscow and St. Petersburg ceased operating and by the 13th the strike became general. On that day there came into existence in St. Petersburg the first Soviet Rabochikh Deputatov (Soviet of Workers' Deputies), which took over the management and direction of the strike. Like a tidal wave the strike soon engulfed the whole country, so that by October 17 all industries and utilities in Russia came to a standstill and it seemed as though life itself was suddenly suspended.[27]

Frightened out of their complacency, Nicholas and his advisers, who had been meeting for several days, could not decide whether to yield to the general demand for a constitution or to drown the revolution in blood. Witte's opinion in favor of submission finally prevailed because the military leaders could not guarantee the reliability of the troops. On the evening of October 17 all Russia was electrified by the news that an imperial manifesto, issued that very day, granted Russia a constitutional government.[28] According to this historic document the newly created Duma was to be a legislative and not merely a consultative body as had been stipulated by

26. Witte, *Memoirs*, pp. 269–270.

27. See Mavor, *An Economic History of Russia*, II, 481–498; S. Sverchkov, *Na Zare Revolutsii* (Moscow, 1922), pp. 93–106.

28. [Pares, *The Fall of the Russian Monarchy*, pp. 85–86; full text of the manifesto in English translation, App., pp. 503–504. Ed.]

Bulygin's project. This October manifesto, which invested the Duma with all the powers common to a parliament in a democratic regime, had an immediate effect. The general strike ceased.

Distrustful of the government, the revolutionary leaders were anxious to continue the strike in the hope of dealing tsarism a decisive blow. The proletariat, as they put it, "did not want a *nagaika* [a lead-tipped lash] wrapped up in a constitution." [29] This time, however, their efforts were abortive. Two attempts to call a general strike in St. Petersburg and an armed uprising organized in Moscow in December, 1905, were crushed by the police. For the revolutionary tide, having reached its high water mark in October, had begun to recede. Exhausted from the long period of strikes and social unrest, the masses were eager for a resumption of normal activity. In the first test of strength with the revolution tsarism obtained a temporary victory.

3. Between Two Revolutions: 1905–17

Events following the October manifesto amply justified the suspicions of the revolutionary leaders: Nicholas II never intended to keep faith with his people. Like Pharaoh he yielded under duress only to retract at the first favorable opportunity. Having gained confidence in its ability to deal with the revolutionary forces, the government set out to destroy both the spirit and the letter of the constitution which had just been wrested from it by force. Not that the constitution had made, even for a moment, the slightest difference in the conduct of the government. As a noted contemporary remarked: "Everything remained the same, there was not the least sign attesting to the reorganization, at the people's demand, of the form of government from absolutism to a constitutional regime." [30]

A decree restoring to the tsar practically all the powers he surrendered on October 17 and making the Duma virtually powerless was promulgated on April 27, 1906—three days before the Duma's opening—in an amendment to the Fundamental Laws of the Empire.[31] The local authorities used all the means at their disposal to effect the election of docile deputies; nevertheless, the elections to the first two Dumas resulted in complete victories for the opposition parties. As a result, neither of the first two Dumas was permitted to complete the five-year term; both were dissolved by imperial decrees after three months of existence. Determined to create a sub-

29. Mavor, *An Economic History of Russia,* II, 497.
30. Petrunkevich, *Iz Zapisok,* p. 434.
31. *T.P.S.Z.,* Vol. XXVI, Pt. I, No. 27,805.

missive Duma, the government on June 3, 1907, so amended the electoral law that the lower classes and the racial minorities were severely limited in their franchise.[32] The amendment, in the opinion of even so conservative a historian as Sir Bernard Pares, constituted a coup d'etat.[33]

The man responsible for this change was P. A. Stolypin, prime minister of Russia from the summer of 1906 till his assassination in 1911. The wave of disorders that broke out in the summer of 1906 following the dissolution of the first Duma prompted the emperor and his counselors to look for a strong administrator. Stolypin's forceful administration of the province of Saratov in the turbulent year of 1905 recommended him to the court for this office. Although the revolution was definitely on the decline, the socialist parties utilized the general disappointment caused by the closing of the first Duma, July 9, 1906, to stage a few weakly organized uprisings in the navy and to foment some political strikes. In addition, the revolutionaries embarked upon a crusade of political assassinations and thus converted the life of every government official from the highest to the lowest into a nightmare. During that period 3,611 government functionaries fell victim to assassins' bullets or bombs.[34]

To stamp out rebellion Stolypin created field courts-martial for the trial of political offenders.[35] In little more than two months after these courts were instituted assassins took 13,381 lives.[36] The country was placed under "special protection," and all civil liberties were "temporarily" withheld; during the election campaign for the second Duma the liberal press was so gagged by administrative order that no free discussion of public issues was possible.

To appease public opinion and retain the confidence of the conservative elements, Stolypin upon taking the premiership issued a declaration of policy in which he promised a number of vital reforms affecting the peasantry, racial groups, religious nonconformists, and others. Some significant measures, including the abrogation of the zemsky nachalniks' right to sentence peasant offenders without trial, were enacted into law even before the opening of the second Duma.[37] In his declaration the premier sought to justify the

32. *T.P.S.Z.*, Vol. XXVII, No. 29,240; cf. Samuel N. Harper, *The New Electoral Law for the Russian Duma* (Chicago, 1908), p. 56.

33. Pares, *The Fall of the Russian Monarchy*, p. 103.

34. *Russky Kalendar*, ed. A. Suvorin (1907 and 1908); *Vestnik Evropy* (November, 1906), p. 466.

35. *T.P.S.Z.*, Vol. XXVI, Pt. I, No. 28,252.

36. *Russky Kalendar* (1907).

37. *T.P.S.Z.*, Vol. XXVI, Pt. I, No. 28,392.

institution of the field courts-martial which he stated were directed against the extreme revolutionists and were essential for the pacification of the country. The refusal of the conservatives to accept government posts offered them by Stolypin is indicative of the people's distrust of the premier, despite his attempts at conciliation.

There is a difference of opinion regarding the character and political aims of Stolypin. Sir Bernard Pares, who either condones or, at most, is mildly critical of the most reactionary leaders of tsarist days, speaks in almost affectionate terms of the creator of the field courts-martial. Witte, on the other hand, describes him as "the embodiment of political immorality." [38] While Witte's judgment may have been somewhat colored by his enmity for Stolypin, who replaced him in the premiership, there is no doubt that his appraisal of the man is closer to the truth. In support of this characterization the writer points to Stolypin's toleration of the extreme nationalistic Union of Russian People, otherwise known as the Black Hundred (*Chornaia Sotnja*). Like the Nazis in a later period, the Black Hundred perpetrated wholesale massacres of Jews but also engaged in the assassination of leaders of the opposition.[39] The leaders of the union were shady characters and the membership consisted of "plain thieves and hooligans." [40] And whatever the avowed political views of Stolypin may have been, the fact remains that he was responsible for those electoral laws which destroyed the spirit of the October manifesto. In depriving the masses of the right to vote he was responsible for the election of the third Duma whose views coincided with those of the government and did not reflect the will of the people. Had Stolypin really reflected the political aspirations of the people, he would not have lasted longer than the first or the second Duma. A. A. Mosolov, a member of the court camarilla which ruled Russia, relates an incident typical of the attitude of the Imperial Court toward the real representatives of the people. At the opening of the first Duma all the deputies were invited to the Winter Palace, where the tsar delivered his speech from the throne. On the way home Minister of the Imperial Court Count Freedericksz observed to Mosolov: "The deputies? They give one the impression of a gang of criminals waiting for the signal to throw

38. Pares, *The Fall of the Russian Monarchy,* pp. 111–113; Witte, *Memoirs,* p. 367.

39. [*Soiuz Russkago Naroda. Po Materialam Chrezvychainoi Sledstvennoi Kommissii Vremennago Pravitelstva 1917 Goda,* compiled by A. Chernovsky (Moscow and Leningrad, 1929), pp. 4–13, 54, 55, 98. Also *Tsarism v Borbe s Revoliutsei* (Moscow), p. 237. Ed.]

40. Witte, *Memoirs,* p. 367.

themselves upon the ministers and cut their throats. What wicked faces! I will never set foot again among those people." [41]

In November, 1905, a truly hideous character, the notorious peasant G. E. Rasputin, became the master of the Imperial Court, dominating Tsarina Alexandra and through her the tsar, whom she greatly influenced. A high-strung, hysterical, but strong-willed woman, the empress harbored a fanatical faith in the sanctity of autocracy, which she believed her husband was divinely ordained to preserve. Even in the face of revolutionary upheaval and amid the universal clamor for some governmental reform, Alexandra fiercely clung to the prerogatives of absolutism. It is not clearly established when Rasputin's real influence began, but it seems that he was already firmly established at the court in 1913,[42] and was the virtual ruler of Russia until his assassination in 1916. A native of Siberia, where he was notorious for his debauchery and dishonesty, he was forced to flee his home village to escape arrest when he and his father were accused of stealing horses. After wandering for some time over various parts of Russia, frequenting monasteries where he acquired a smattering of canon law, he emerged as a "holy man" reputed to possess miraculous healing powers. It was because of this power attributed to him that Rasputin was called to the court to heal the sickly only son of the emperor, the heir Alexis. A strong personality, possessing hypnotic powers, Rasputin seems to have exerted a calming effect upon the ailing child. According to the testimony of court intimates the mere presence of Rasputin had a beneficent effect upon the young Alexis. Just as he held the boy in his spell, so too did this ignorant peasant exercise a powerful influence over the tsar and the tsarina. "When in trouble or assailed with doubts," the tsar once observed to Rodzianko, president of the fourth Duma, "I like to have a talk with him, and invariably feel at peace with myself afterwards." [43] To the superstitious and hysterical empress Rasputin became a veritable Christ upon whom the life of her only son depended. Aware of the abnormal hold he had upon the imperial couple, the shrewd muzhik in time made them believe that not only the life of the tsarevich but the dynasty of the Romanovs and the welfare of all Russia depended upon his prayers. Mosolov says that the tsar had seemed to have a superstitious fear

41. [A. A. Mosolov, *At the Court of the Last Tsar,* ed. A. A. Pilenco, tr. E. W. Dickes (London, 1935), p. 139. The Russian original of the memoirs, *Pri Dvore Imperatora,* appeared in 1937 in Riga. Ed.]

42. Pares, *The Fall of the Russian Monarchy,* pp. 137 and 151.

43. [M. V. Rodzianko, *The Reign of Rasputin: An Empire's Collapse* (London, A. M. Philpot, 1927), p. 11. Ed.]

of what might happen to them in the event of the "holy man's" death.[44]

Rasputin soon became the most important adviser to the tsar and began to wield great influence in the affairs of state. He made and unmade ministers, and in time no Russian statesman, no matter how important, could retain his post if he incurred the displeasure of this dissolute muzhik. Counts, princes, and members of the highest aristocracy would come to Rasputin's home to beg for political preferment. According to Aaron Simanovich, his Jewish secretary, Rasputin took special delight in humiliating the high placed, whether men or women, addressing them in vulgar, disrespectful language and playing humiliating pranks upon them.[45] His scandalous amours involving women of the highest society were common knowledge, but the protection of the tsar kept him immune from prosecution and placed him above the law. His revolting exploits, which brought shame upon Russia and her rulers who condoned them, finally brought about Rasputin's downfall. On December 17, 1916, he was murdered by a group of high-placed conspirators.

It was undoubtedly because of the dependence of the ministers on the good graces of this ignorant charlatan that from the death of Stolypin till the fall of the tsardom in 1917 not a single personality of outstanding ability filled a ministerial post in Russia. In the years immediately preceding the first World War and during the crucial years of the war second- and third-rate bureaucrats directed Russia's ship of state. Describing the final stages of the Romanov dynasty, the erudite Russian historian George Vernadsky observes: "At the most tragic moment of Russian history, the government was composed largely of incapable men having neither the ability nor the will to rule." [46]

As in 1904–5 during the war against Japan, so in 1917 the incompetent conduct of the struggle against the Central Powers united all the opposition factions against the autocratic monarchy. Though advocating different political programs all were united by a common determination to overthrow the existing regime. It was, however, the propaganda of the socialist parties among the workers and in the army that caused the final uprising which dealt the death-

44. Mosolov, *Pri Dvore Imperatora,* p. 149.

45. A. Simanovich, *Rasputin i Evrei* (Riga, *s.a.*), pp. 25–26. [These memoirs of Rasputin's secretary appeared in two German translations: *Rasputin, der allmächtige Bauer* (Berlin, 1928); *Der Zar, der Zauberer und die Juden* (Berlin and Leipzig, 1943). Ed.]

46. George Vernadsky, *A History of Russia* (New Haven, Yale University Press, 1929), p. 227.

blow to the regime of the Romanovs. Street rioting in Petrograd excited by a serious food shortage set off the revolt, March 12–16, 1917. Called out to quell the disturbances, the troops of the capital instead joined the rioters, thus giving the first indication that the government had lost the military support upon which its authority rested.

The official governing body created by the Duma soon after the outbreak of the revolution was composed of liberals, moderate conservatives, and one socialist, Alexander Kerensky. It was this government, known as the Provisional government, which asked for and received the formal abdication of Nicholas II. But the real power during this period of anarchy was the Soviet of Workers' Deputies which had been organized in 1905, suppressed that year, and now again revived. This group refused to accept posts in the Provisional government and awaited a chance to take office as a bloc. On November 7, 1917, the soviet under the leadership of Vladimir Lenin and Leon Trotsky deposed Alexander Kerensky and dissolved the coalition government he headed. At the order of the Ekaterinburg soviet, Nicholas II and his family were executed in that city on July 16, 1918, thus ending the reign of the Romanovs.

The fate of the Jews under the last two Romanovs and their subsequent emancipation by the Provisional government will be the subject of the following chapters.

II

ANTI-SEMITISM, 1881–1905

FOR Russia, the accession of Alexander III ushered in a period of militant reaction; to the Jews it brought a reign of terror and added new disabilities. Prior to his rule there had been a few sporadic pogroms, all of which occurred in the city of Odessa at widely separated intervals, one in 1820, another in 1859, and the third in 1871. Beginning with the regime of Alexander III the pogrom became an established, frequently recurring feature until the fall of the tsardom in 1917. These attacks upon Jews, although not directly engineered by the central government, were at all times tolerated by it despite an occasional face-saving protestation to the contrary. Undoubtedly no serious excesses could have occurred without the active participation or tacit consent of the authorities, for experience has demonstrated that the least show of force on the part of the police was sufficient to check the violence of the mob or nip a potential pogrom in the bud. That these outbursts were not spontaneous but planned and organized by higher-ups is obvious from the common pattern they pursued. The procedure was as follows: often before a pogrom started a rumor would spread through the town about coming disorders scheduled for a particular date. Alarmed, the Jews would ask the authorities for protection. They would be told to go home and reassured about their safety, but no steps were taken to forestall the possible riots. Then on the appointed day there would appear at the railway station a band of out-of-town hooligans under the leadership of a literate ringleader who had a prepared list of Jewish homes and business establishments. Having fortified themselves with liquor, the howling ruffians would swoop down upon the Jewish quarter, and there would follow an orgy of pillage and looting. In the south of Russia where most of the pogroms occurred in the eighties, this rabble was referred to as "the barefoot brigade." Harold Frederic, who spent some time in Russia studying the pogrom epidemic, referred to "A band of young men from St. Petersburg—young students, clerks and ne'er-do-wells generally who traveled about the country and invariably appeared in a town a day or so before the outbreak of the riot." [1]

In the first period of the pogroms the local rabble did not par-

1. Harold Frederic, *The New Exodus: A Study of Israel in Russia* (London, 1892), p. 116.

ticipate in the pillaging, they merely looked on and wondered; but gradually they joined the barefoot brigade and soon learned the art themselves. To incite the peasants against the Jews, secret agitators would read them extracts from the anti-Semitic press which openly called for the murder of Jews. They assured the peasants that the government permitted the pillage and murder of Jews and that only officials bribed by Jewish money sought to prevent the execution of that order. In most instances the local authorities of south Russia gave no evidence of such "faithlessness." Not only did they fail to make the slightest attempt to stop the riots but they called out soldiers to protect the mobs against the Jewish self-defense. In a number of instances the provincial authorities themselves participated in the organization and execution of pogroms or made it known to the local authorities that their connivance was expected.

The memoirs of a non-Jewish social worker and author who lived in the south of Russia at the time give a revealing account of the pogrom technique as he saw it in action in Kirovo (formerly Elisavetgrad), the first city to initiate this savagery. The anonymous author relates that the local police commissioner, an honest and fair-dealing man, received a visit from a high-ranking official from St. Petersburg who to his dismay asked whether in the event of a pogrom he could guarantee the safety of the non-Jewish population. The emissary absolved the commissioner in advance of any blame for outrages perpetrated against Jews, declaring that such assaults were to be interpreted as "unexpected outbursts of the people's wrath." Yet he warned that if Russian or German merchants were to suffer from mob violence or looting, the police would be held responsible for negligence.[2]

According to the writer the pogrom was organized by a gang dispatched to Kirovo for that purpose. It began on April 15, 1881, the day following the Greek Orthodox Easter celebration, when a drunken Russian was ejected from an inn by its Jewish owner. The mob, waiting nearby for provocation, raised the hue and cry that Jews were beating Russians and began attacking Jewish pedestrians. At this signal for the attack Jewish stores in the market place were smashed and looted. Although the riots were checked that night by the police, they were resumed the next day with increased vigor and with the police assuming a neutral attitude.[3]

2. [See "Vospominania o Yuzhno-Russkikh Pogromakh" (Memoirs on the Pogroms in Southern Russia) by an anonymous Russian author (P. Sonin), *Evreiskaia Starina* (Jewish Antiquities), II (St. Petersburg, 1909), 209. Ed.]

3. *Ibid.,* p. 211.

The pogrom in Kirovo was the prelude for a series of excesses in numerous other localities in south Russia. The pogrom in Kiev on April 23, according to the testimony of General V. D. Novitsky, chief of the state gendarmerie, was aided and abetted by the governor general of the southwestern region, General Adjutant A. P. Drenteln, "who hated the Jews from the bottom of his heart, and gave complete freedom of action to a savage mob which in the presence of the general and his troops continued to loot and plunder Jewish warehouses, stores, and market places." [4] Indeed, so demoralized did the soldiers become by their commander's inaction and by the atrocities committed as they looked on that they themselves joined the hooligans.

Although by no means a friend of the Jews, General Novitsky was nonetheless eager to put an end to these disorders. When out of fear of antagonizing his superiors the governor general refused to let him appeal to the central government in St. Petersburg, Novitsky approached Loris-Melikov, the minister of the interior. The latter threw the issue back into the lap of the chief of police, washing his hands of it with the suggestion that Novitsky contact his superior officer to stop the disorders. The pogrom, which practically destroyed the suburb of Podol, was finally halted by a detachment of troops which on its own initiative opened fire on the plundering mob.[5]

The official reports of the Austro-Hungarian consul in Kiev confirm the foregoing testimony. "The entire behavior of the police leads one rightfully to the conclusion that the disturbances are abetted by the authorities," he wrote to the minister of foreign affairs in Vienna. His account of the pattern of the pogrom and its preparations is similar to that described above; and he too mentions the inactivity of the governor general and police chief of Kiev who witnessed the disturbances.[6]

The pogrom in the city of Balta, in the province of Podolia, which surpassed in savagery the riots of 1881, was conducted with the open protection and assistance of police authorities. On the day the excesses began, March 29, 1882, the Balta Jews who far outnumbered the non-Jewish population caused the hooligans to retreat and seek shelter in the fire house. But no sooner did the police and troops

4. General V. D. Novitsky, *Iz Zapisok Zhandarma* (Leningrad, 1929), pp. 179–187. Hereafter cited as Novitsky. Quoted by E. Cherikover, "New Materials on the Pogroms in Russia in the Early Eighties," *Historishe Shriften,* in Yiddish, Vol. II (Berlin, YIVO, 1937).

5. Novitsky, p. 181.

6. [N. M. Gelber, "The Russian Pogroms of the Eighties in the Light of Austrian Diplomatic Correspondence," *Historishe Shriften,* in Yiddish, II, 466–496. Cited hereafter as Gelber, "The Pogroms." Ed.]

arrive than the mobs poured into the streets again to continue their attacks, this time aided by the police who beat the Jews with their swords and rifle butts. Someone then sounded the alarm bell as a signal to the local populace, who came streaming into the market place, accompanied by the local military commander, the police commissioner, the mayor, and a detachment of the city battalion. Turning toward the Turkish section of the city where the Jewish population was sparser and resistance might be less, the mob plundered and looted until in the space of a few hours there was nothing left to loot. A cordon of soldiers stationed at all points leading into that section headed off any Jews who sought to come to the aid of their fellows, while freely allowing all non-Jews to enter. The following morning about five hundred peasants from neighboring villages, called out by the district police captain, arrived in the market square armed with clubs. The Jews, at first hopeful of assistance, were bitterly disillusioned when the newcomers soon joined the local rabble in a renewed attack. At first the mob was restrained by the officers of the local battalion and by Bishop Radzionovsky who remonstrated with them, but with the arrival of the police commissioner the military commander and the district police captain were ordered to give the mob a free hand. After breaking into a nearby liquor store which they looted, the intoxicated crowd of peasants, soldiers, and police fell to their task of destruction and plunder, murder, rape, and general violence.[7]

As for the Balta pogrom, there is corroborative testimony that it too was planned in advance and was well known to the authorities and prominent Christian families of the city. For example, the marshal of the nobility in Balta tauntingly apprised his Jewish tenant that he was looking forward with pleasure to that event. When his tenant on the eve of the pogrom appealed to him for protection, he replied: "Do you want me to tell you everything? Well, I want you to know that I am an official serving under oath and I carry out all instructions precisely as directed. If I were ordered to murder my brother-in-law, I would do so. I cannot do anything for you."[8]

In the city of Berdichev, where the Jews were permitted by the

7. [See Dubnow, "Anti-Evreiskoe Dvizhenie v Rossii v 1881 i 1882 g.," *Evreiskaia Starina,* I (1909), 88–110 and 265–276. This is one of the main sources for the history of the pogroms of 1881 and 1882 and the discriminatory policies of the tsarist bureaucracy pursued at the same time. Hereafter cited as "Anti-Evreiskoe Dvizhenie." Cf. also *Materialy dlia Istorii Anti-Evreiskikh Pogromov v Rossii,* ed. G. Krasny-Admony, Vol. II: *Vosmidesiatie Gody* (Leningrad and Moscow, 1923). Also Cherikover, "New Materials on the Pogroms in Russia in the Early Eighties"; Y. Hessen, *Istoria Evreiskago Naroda,* II (Leningrad, 1927), 215–234. Ed.]

8. "Anti-Evreiskoe Dvizhenie," p. 93.

police to defend themselves, they managed to drive off the out-of-town rabble, in May, 1881, and avoid a pogrom. There was not a single case of rioting against Jews in the northwest because the governor general of that region, Count E. I. Totleben, made it clear that he would not countenance such disorders.[9] The absence of anti-Jewish excesses in the northwest at a time when 215 localities in the ten provinces of the southwest experienced such disorders in the course of a few months must be attributed to different attitudes of the respective administrations.

Although some Jewish historians maintain that the pogroms were organized by the central government itself, other historians of the period consider this assertion entirely without foundation.[10] No such evidence to substantiate it has been uncovered in the archives of the Police Department opened after the revolution of 1917. Furthermore, the marginal notations made by Alexander III on reports submitted to him seem to indicate his displeasure and concern over these disturbances. On April 5, 1882, the tsar noted on a report on riots in Kherson Province, "I hope that the uproar will soon be stopped." When informed about an officer who incited the mob, he observed, "A fine officer! A shame!" And on the report of the governor general of Kiev, who ascribed the pogrom to the deep-seated hatred of the populace, Alexander noted, "It surprises me." In another instance the emperor expressed his deep satisfaction over the cessation of a pogrom. "It is impossible to believe," he once wrote, "that no one should have stirred up the people against the Jews. It is necessary to conduct an investigation in this matter." [11]

There is still another circumstance which tends to disprove the theory that the central government instigated the pogroms. The first riots occurred while Loris-Melikov was still minister of the interior. Though not the liberal the reactionary court clique insinuated he was, his political views and general policies make it impossible to conceive of him as an instigator of pogroms. In fact, as Novitsky stated, the minister wired him to do everything in his power to check the riots and restore order.[12]

But that some power emanating from St. Petersburg was guiding and planning the pogroms seems to be indisputable. "A sinister

9. Dubnow, *History,* II, 276.

10. V. J. Yakovlev-Bogucharsky, *Iz Istorii Politicheskoi Borby* (Moscow, 1912), p. 219; *Die Judenpogrome in Russland,* ed. Commission of Research into Pogroms appointed by the Zionist Relief Fund in London (Cologne and Leipzig, Jüdischer Verlag, 1910), I, 24.

11. R. Cantor, "Alexander III o Evreiskikh Pogromakh," *Evreiskaia Letopis,* I (Leningrad, 1923), 149–158.

12. Novitsky, p. 181.

agitation was rife among the lowest elements of the Russian population, while invisible hands from above seemed to push it on toward the commission of a gigantic crime. In the same month of March, mysterious emissaries from St. Petersburg made their appearance in the large cities of South Russia," says the Russian-Jewish historian Dubnow. Who might that power have been? It must have been a body close to the highest circles, for its emissaries were in contact with the top government officials, and it undoubtedly wielded much power since its orders were obeyed by those high in authority.

Both logic and a number of circumstances point to a secret group of high officials, formed in March, 1881, under the name of the Sacred League as the directive force in this program of violence. This organization was built on conspiratorial lines and consisted of arch-reactionaries and rabid anti-Semites. Believing as they did that the Jews were the source of all rebellion against the government and the established order, they sought through terror and violence to destroy the leaven of the revolution. As a man who made and unmade ministers, Pobedonostsev, the moving spirit of the league, was in a position to command the obedience of provincial administrators. Count Nicholas P. Ignatiev, who became minister of the interior in May, 1881, was an active member.[13] Funds to hire the riff-raff which comprised the barefoot brigade were no doubt furnished by the wealthy nobles and high officials associated with the league.

It must emphatically be stated, however, that while there is no evidence of the central government's official sanction of this program, and though the conspiracy must be ascribed directly to the league, the government cannot be absolved of responsibility or guilt. This government, which exhibited so much energy and resourcefulness in dealing with revolutionary activities could have put a quick stop to the pogroms had it seriously wished to do so. The provincial authorities would not have countenanced these excesses if they had sensed a determined opposition on the part of the central government or had the tsar taken a firm stand in the matter. Though the monarch may have been disturbed by the excesses, he nevertheless found it distasteful to do anything about them. "The sad part about these disturbances," he observed, "is the necessity of the government to defend the Jews." Apparently the tsar's deep-seated hatred of the Jews and the intense anti-Semitism which permeated his regime paralyzed the will to check the undercover anti-Jewish machinations of the Sacred League and thus encouraged the

13. [Dubnow, *History,* II, 248. The league existed till the fall of 1882. Ed.]

provincial authorities in their criminal neglect or connivance. This encouragement to violence and whitewashing of official guilt was most flagrantly manifested when Ignatiev became minister of the interior. In a memorandum of August 25, 1881, concerning the establishment of provincial committees to review the Jewish problem,[14] which will be discussed later on, Ignatiev placed the blame for the pogroms entirely upon the Jews. He accused them of seizing not only the trade and business of the country but also considerable portions of land, and justified the attacks upon them as the natural reaction of an aroused people who were being exploited by the Jews. The Jewish communal leaders who in February, 1883, submitted their grievances to the Pahlen commission [15] scored the memorandum as an indictment of the entire Jewish people and as a government document of "a unique character which has no parallel in the annals of Russian administration."

The prejudiced attitude of the central government was also reflected in the trials of those arrested during the pogroms for robbery and murder. The light punishments meted out by the courts for serious offenses were a clear indication how the upper government circles felt about these pogroms. In Kiev the public prosecutor Strelnikov declared in open court that the Jews were free to leave Russia and that they could look for little protection from the law.[16] Jewish leaders called the attention of the Pahlen commission to the fact that the central government failed to grant even a token of material assistance to the victims of the excesses. An offer of aid, no matter how small, would have served as a protest against the violence committed and helped to repudiate the rumors about the imperial orders for pogroms. Instead of extending aid, the government forbade soliciting funds for this purpose; the governor of Odessa even refused to accept such a donation offered him by a wealthy Jew.[17]

After the pogroms had been checked the anti-Jewish excesses took a different form; numerous fires broke out in the Pale of Settlement bringing ruin and destruction upon the Jewish inhabitants of many cities. These widespread fires, probably the work of the

14. For the memorandum see "Anti-Evreiskoe Dvizhenie, pp. 99–100. Also Dubnow, *History*, II, 273.

15. [The High Commission for the Revision of the Current Laws concerning the Jews. Ed.]

16. "Anti-Evreiskoe Dvizhenie," p. 97.

17. *Ibid.*, p. 98. [It seems that the government was impressed by the representations made by the Austro-Hungarian ambassador in St. Petersburg, who pointed to the large number of Jewish refugees swarming into the neighboring towns of Austrian territory. The disorders ceased during the summer of 1882. Gelber, "The Pogroms," pp. 491–493. Ed.]

same mysterious groups which directed the pogroms, were officially described as accidents, but when Count Dmitry Tolstoi replaced Ignatiev in the ministry on May 30, 1882, both the fire and the pogrom epidemics ceased. Tolstoi dissolved the Sacred League in the fall of 1882 and made it clear to the provincial authorities that he would tolerate no mob violence against the Jews. In the history of the reign of Alexander III the appointment of Tolstoi to the Ministry of the Interior marks the triumph of complete and absolute reaction; for the Jews, however, his ministry brought at least temporary relief from the fear of attacks by savage hordes. Though pogroms occurred in 1883 in Rostov and Ekaterinoslav, and in 1884 in Nizhni Novgorod they were sporadic outbursts which the police quelled properly.[18] By that time the government had decided to fight its Jewish population by means of more intense discriminatory legislation and economic restrictions.

The pogroms were used as a pretext to impose new disabilities on the Jews and further limit their civil status and economic opportunities. To make the new legislation appear as a demand from the people, the government organized provincial committees to review the Jewish problem. One needs but examine the method of selecting delegates and the procedure of these committee meetings to discover their real purpose. Ignatiev's memorandum of 1881 which ordered the governors to convoke such committees not only outlined in advance the specific problems they were to take up but also indicated the decisions they were to reach. The minister advised the committees to gather statistical data on the Jews and make the proper recommendations for the curtailment of their "pernicious" activities. They were given just two months to accomplish this ambitious task. In addition to the published instructions, the government also sent secret directives regarding the choice of the delegates. The size of the committees varied from ten in some areas to sixty in others. Although the minister permitted the participation of Jews, no committee except that of the province of Kovno had more than two Jewish delegates. Consequently the Jews' point of view as well as their influence was negligible. While the mayors of the chief cities of the provinces were invited to sit in on the committee meetings, the mayor of Zhitomir, capital of the province of Volhynia, was not included because his views on the Jewish question did not suit the authorities. For the same reason the mayor of Grodno refrained from expressing his opinion at these meetings; instead, at the advice of the chairman, he submitted his opinion in writing. The proceedings and, in some cases, even the dates of the meetings

18. Dubnow, *History,* II, 360–362.

were kept secret; only in 1884 were some of the committees' proceedings published. The Jewish delegates were denied the right to study the memoranda and notes, so that they came to the meetings ill prepared to cope with the situation. All these precautions were taken by the government personnel of the committees in order to forestall any attempt on the part of the Jews to influence the decisions of the committees. At the same time every step taken was planned to prejudice the mind and inflame the emotions. The opening session of each committee meeting, for example, was devoted to a reading of Ignatiev's denunciatory memorandum, a procedure hardly calculated to create a judicial and objective atmosphere. Following this reading in the Kherson committee the provincial governor declared that the exploitation of the Christian population by the Jews was an established and irrefutable fact and he would brook no discussion of this subject; all that the members of the committee were expected to do was to answer the questions asked in the memorandum. The effect upon the Jewish delegates was crushing: they saw themselves representing three million Jews who were being tried in a closed court by prejudiced judges appointed by anti-Jewish administrators without being given an opportunity to present their case properly; they were convicted before court opened.

A few examples will suffice to show how unreliable and colored was the statistical material collected by the committees. According to the report submitted to the committee of Bessarabia, the Jews of Kishinev numbered 46,249 souls. A thorough count by the Jewish committee members revealed only 27,702. As for the number of Jewish artisans, the police, who were interested in minimizing the figure, reported 1,927 as against 2,317 computed by the artisans' bureau of Kishinev. The actual figure as established by the Jewish representatives of the committee was 2,465. Similar discrepancies were shown in other cities.

More significant was the information concerning the number of saloons owned by Jews. (A common charge by the government was that Jews were the cause of widespread drunkenness among the peasants.) The office of excises of the province of Bessarabia reported that 224 permits for the operation of saloons were issued to Jews in 1881. A canvas by the Jewish members of the committee revealed the number to be only 128. In the dispute which arose between the Jewish delegates and the director of the excise office, who was a member of the provincial committee, it came out that the management had "forgotten" that the permits were renewable every six months and had counted 96 permits twice.

Jewish leaders commenting to the Pahlen commission on these findings as experts charged that the entire plan of the committees was "a cleverly conceived comedy, a parody on an earnest attempt to solve one of the domestic problems of Russia." [19]

And yet, despite all the prejudice and hostility which clouded the proceedings, the conclusions arrived at were not entirely unfavorable for the Jews. Of the sixteen provincial committees involved, the findings of twelve were made accessible to the Jewish experts of the Pahlen commission in the eighties. A majority of these twelve committees voted to limit the rights of the Jews in but one field: the sale of strong drinks in rural settlements. This vote was undoubtedly influenced by the exaggerated notions concerning the number of Jewish inns and taverns, and by the baneful propaganda about Jewish responsibility for promoting drunkenness. Only six of the twelve committees voted to limit the right of Jews to petty trade in the villages. On permitting Jews to reside within villages and hamlets, a matter that vitally concerned half a million souls, only five committees voted in the negative, while seven refrained from making any proposal. Likewise, five committees voted to forbid Jews to acquire land; seven arrived at no conclusion. Five favored excluding Jews from both wholesale and retail trade in strong drink, while seven ignored the matter. Thus, apart from the liquor question, the majority of the twelve committees studied did not favor new restrictions for Jews in the matters considered.

Of even greater significance was the attitude of the committees to the most vital problem of Russian Jewry: the Pale of Settlement which circumscribed the area of their residence. Five committees voted to abolish the Pale, six uttered no opinion, and only one, that of Vitebsk, favored preserving the prevailing limitations of Jewish residence. The Vitebsk provincial committee as a body, the minutes of the session reveal, was predominantly in favor of doing away with the Pale, but voted adversely under pressure of the governor, the committee chairman. Thus, even assuming that all four of the committees whose proceedings were not available for study favored the status quo of the Pale, it would still leave the majority of the total number either opposed to retaining it or neutral. However much the government conspired to "pack" the committees and influence their judgment, they did not pronounce sentence of guilt upon their Jewish neighbors or support the government's allegation that the native population hated or resented the Jew.[20]

19. "Anti-Evreiskoe Dvizhenie," p. 106.

20. *Ibid.*, pp. 106–108. [Cf. also article "Gubernskia Kommissii po Evreiskomy Voprosu," in *Evreiskaia Enciclopedia,* Vol. VI, cols. 823–824; Dubnow, *History, II,* 269–275. Ed.]

But though these proceedings failed to provide the needed pretext for promulgating new anti-Jewish legislation, the government saw to it that a Central Committee for Review of the Jewish Question, established on October 19, 1881, carried out its task "correctly." The central committee, attached to the Ministry of the Interior, consisted of several high officials with Assistant Minister D. V. Gotovtsev as chairman. It was charged with the preparation of legislative projects to be submitted for approval to the State Council, Russia's legislative body. The committee's attitude toward the Jews as recorded in its minutes of January and February, 1882, resembled that of a public prosecutor toward a criminal. Permeated with prejudice and filled with historical inaccuracies, the minutes reiterated the hackneyed charges of Jewish clannishness and aggressiveness. Despite repeated exposure of allegations about the immoral character of the Talmud the committee renewed this charge. And they blamed the Jews with so abusing the civil rights granted them in the reign of Alexander II [21] that the population had risen up against them.

In a refutation submitted by the group of Jewish leaders previously referred to it was pointed out that the assertions about the Talmud were made by people who had never read that work either in the original or in translation. Of all the religious and racial minorities in Russia the Jews were the only ones whose merger with the Russians was a prerequisite for civil equality. The accusation of refusal to merge the Jewish leaders challenged with a demand for a definition of the term "merge." If it meant renunciation of their faith as the price of civil equality, there was no use expecting it; if it referred to social and civil assimilation, then let the government remove discriminatory legislation and merger would be effected of itself.

The central committee report recommended the complete revision of legislation concerning Jews. In the meantime, in order to calm the allegedly aroused populace, temporary measures were recommended, among them the following: 1) prohibition of new Jewish settlement in the villages of the Pale; 2) prohibition of owning or managing real estate and land outside city limits; 3) prohibition of wholesale or retail trading in strong drinks in villages or hamlets.

These measures, the committee stated, were proposed to protect the peasants from exploitation by Jews as well as to safeguard the Jews against the wrath of the exploited. In proof of the contention that the Jews aroused the peasants' wrath, the report asserted that Jewish saloons were the first object of attack. But as the Jewish

21. See *The Jews in Russia,* Vol. I, chap. VI.

leaders commented, the pogroms with few exceptions took place in the cities, not in the villages; and it was not Jewish saloons but business establishments and private residences that were the chief targets of attack. When saloons were looted it was not because of any particular grudge but in order to put the hoodlums in the proper mood for the occasion.[22]

Ignatiev did not risk submitting the committee's proposals to the State Council even though it was not a democratically chosen body but consisted of the tsar's appointees. Instead, he decided to present the projected disabilities as an administrative measure so that he could submit them to the Cabinet, of which he felt more certain. But the majority of the ministers were opposed to the proposals as they stood and compromised on a somewhat modified form. Their decisions having received the sanction of the emperor, the following three measures were enacted on May 3, 1882, as Temporary Rules:[23] No new Jewish settlers were allowed in the villages and hamlets of the Pale; Jews could not own or manage real estate or farms outside the cities of the Pale; Jews were not allowed to do business on Sunday or other Christian holidays. These "temporary" measures remained in effect until the fall of the tsardom in 1917.

It is interesting to note that Ignatiev did not regard the Jew as a menace to his own estates. It is reliably reported that while the May Rules were being drafted but before the tsar's signature was affixed to them he had arranged through his mother to renew all the contracts with his Jewish managers in the province of Kiev for a period of twelve years. Only after he had been advised by his mother that the deal had been concluded did he submit the May Rules for imperial sanction.[24] There is also reason to believe that Ignatiev was prepared to change his attitude toward the projected discriminations. S. M. Ginsburg, a friend of Baron Horace de Günzburg, leader of Russian Jewry, recounts that Ignatiev once remarked to the Baron, "I have heard that the Jews have collected a million rubles for me and have deposited it in your bank." The Baron, who did not believe in buying Jewish rights, quickly replied, "I know nothing about it. You were misinformed."[25]

Ostensibly promulgated with a view to safeguarding the Russian masses from exploitation by the Jews, the disabilities were bound to be a boomerang for those who were presumably to be protected. Because of the elimination of Jewish competition the value of real

22. ["Anti-Evreiskoe Dvizhenie," p. 94; Dubnow, *History,* II, 362. Ed.]
23. *T.P.S.Z.,* Vol. II, No. 854.
24. Frederic, *The New Exodus,* p. 130.
25. S. M. Ginsburg, *Historishe Werk* (3 vols., New York, 1937), II, 144.

estate in the villages inevitably dropped. When the services of Jewish middlemen were no longer available in the villages, the peasants had to resort to non-Jewish middlemen who, being scarce, commanded a higher price. Those who could not obtain such services were compelled to lose valuable time on trips to the city to dispose of their produce.[26] Blinded by an irrational hatred for Jews, Ignatiev and the court clique which supported him failed to realize that in inflicting economic ruin on one portion of the population they were bound to affect adversely the fortunes of the entire community. Even the pogroms, though directed exclusively against the Jews, inflicted serious financial loss on the non-Jewish population. A St. Petersburg newspaper calculated that as a result of the anti-Jewish disturbances the value of government bonds alone depreciated 152 million rubles.[27]

The chief sufferers from the new restrictions were, of course, the Jews. Although the Cabinet rejected Ignatiev's proposal to empower village assemblies to banish undesirable Jews who had lived in rural areas prior to 1882, the imperial ukase of May 3 specifically stated that no *new* Jewish settlers would be permitted. At the instigation of Christian merchant competitors, peasant leaders in many communities were persuaded to adopt hostile resolutions banishing their Jewish neighbors from their established places of residence. As a result many rural communities, especially in the provinces of the southwestern region administered by anti-Semitic Governor General Drenteln, ejected their old Jewish residents.

The May Rules were so interpreted by the authorities that even without a resolution from the village assembly many Jews suddenly found themselves homeless. Often a Jewish villager returning from a trip would be declared a new settler and forever barred from his home. It was customary for rural residents to repair to nearby cities for divine worship in the synagogues during the High Holiday season. Often these visiting worshipers were compelled to prove their legal right of residence before they were permitted to return home. According to Drenteln's interpretation of the May Rules Jewish villagers under his jurisdiction were not permitted to move from one village to another, and even a change of domicile in the same village resulted in the loss of residence rights. This governor general authorized his police to banish Jews who lived in rented houses, on the grounds that a renewal of lease was forbidden to Jewish tenants. Because of this arbitrary interpretation of the rules ten thousand Jews were threatened with expulsion from their homes in the cold

26. On the role the Jews played in the economy of Russia in the 1850's to seventies see *The Jews in Russia,* Vol. I, chap. XII.
27. ["Anti-Evreiskoe Dvizhenie," p. 275. Ed.]

of winter. Only after the greater part of these people had been banished and economically ruined did the highest court of appeals, the Senate, order the expulsions stopped.[28]

The restriction of movement from one village to another, confirmed by an imperial order of December 29, 1887,[29] worked cruel hardships. If a village was burned down or a factory closed, the Jews affected had no right to seek shelter or employment in another rural community but must move to some city or town. Children were not allowed to maintain enfeebled parents or widowed mothers in their homes if they happened to have lived in another village. Nor might a son come and manage a business or industrial establishment left him by his father in another village; he could not even claim ownership of a home left him by his parents in a village outside his legal residence.[30]

The small group of privileged Jews who resided outside the Pale also felt the aggressive hostility of the government of Alexander III. In the reign of Alexander II first-guild Jewish merchants, graduates of universities, and artisans were given the privilege of residence outside the Pale.[31] These privileged Jews were permitted by law to import a specified number of coreligionists from the Pale for their employ as clerks or domestics. Some Jews took advantage of this concession and after registering as employees of a privileged Jew would pursue their own calling or engage in trade. There were also no doubt cases where Jews registering as artisans in order to obtain legal residence did not practice their craft. But even in the reactionary period of Alexander II the government overlooked such infractions of the law. In fact, in 1880 the minister of the interior instructed the governors of the provinces outside the Pale not to expel into the Pale Jews found residing illegally within their provinces. This policy was completely reversed in the period of Alexander III. Under both Ignatiev and Tolstoi the police of the cities outside the Pale conducted periodic searches for illegal Jewish residents. St. Petersburg and Kiev distinguished themselves in this respect (only one district of Kiev, Podol, was open to Jewish residents). At the order of Gresser, the cruel police chief of the capital, the police kept up an unremitting hunt for these victims. Those who could not prove their rights of residence were given twenty-four to forty-eight hours to liquidate their business and make the necessary preparation for the expulsion. Among the evicted were people who had lived in the capi-

28. [Dubnow, *History,* II, 341. Ed.]
29. *T.P.S.Z.,* Vol. VII, No. 4924.
30. [Dubnow, *History,* II, 342. Ed.]
31. *The Jews in Russia,* Vol. I, chap. VI.

tal for many years and consequently found it impossible to terminate their affairs in such short order. In desperation many of them embraced Christianity to legalize their stay.

The surrender of their faith was the highest price Jews paid for such privileges. But there were other humiliations to which they subjected themselves for this purpose. Jewish writers, for example, registered as valets to Jewish attorneys, their duties consisting of shining shoes and carrying the portfolios of their masters. It was through such official employment that the famous Russian-Jewish poet Simon Frug managed to reside in St. Petersburg. An ironic instance is that of a young Jewess who in order to attend an institution of higher learning in the capital registered as a prostitute. She was banished when it was discovered that she was using the privilege of the yellow ticket, which permitted prostitutes rights of residence outside the Pale, to engage in the pursuit of learning.

The periodic hunts for "illegal" Jews were a lucrative source of income for the police who were the only beneficiaries of Jewish rightlessness. For a bribe a Jew sometimes managed to postpone or cancel the date of expulsion or escape having his home raided at night. Through the "good will" of an influential official some Jews succeeded for a time in circumventing the law. In this connection it is pertinent to observe however that Sir Bernard Pares highly exaggerates the effect of bribes upon the position of Russian Jewry under tsarist rule. In a brief discussion of their legal status in his excellent work, *The Fall of the Russian Monarchy*, he states: "But these exemptions were a fruitful source of demoralization for the Russian police, for by systematic bribing the Jews were able to *evade all restrictions*" (italics mine).[32] This is a careless, inaccurate, and misleading statement. The fact is that bribes were effective only in avoiding an arbitrary interpretation of the law. In a police state like tsarist Russia the local administration exercised both judicial and executive powers over its citizens; the Jews particularly were a rightless minority at the mercy of a hostile official. There is the authoritative testimony of N. Kh. Bunge, minister of finance during the reigns of Alexander II and Alexander III, that the severe manner in which both the old and new laws were executed under Alexander III was most distressing to the Jews for in the preceding regime they had always been applied with greater consideration.[33]

When one considers that the bulk of Jews lived in the Pale, that they were kept out of villages even within the Pale, that the doors of educational institutions remained closed to the great majority of

32. Pares, p. 65.
33. [See *Evreiskaia Enciclopedia,* Vol. I (St. Petersburg, 1908), col. 836. Ed.]

Jewish young people, and that with a few rare exceptions no Jews were employed in any department of government service, it is obvious that the role of bribery was a very limited one and it did not, as Pares said, enable Jews to "evade all restrictions."

In its campaign to reduce to a minimum the number of Jews residing outside the Pale, Alexander's administration decided to cut down as much as possible the number of Jews in government service. That Jewish physicians enjoyed the status of officers in the army was particularly irksome to the authorities. Admitted to army service in the previous regime, these doctors had earned their promotions for distinguished service in the Russo-Turkish War.[34] On April 10, 1882, the minister of war issued an order limiting Jewish physicians in the army to 5 per cent of the total number, with the stipulation that none of these be appointed to the western provinces. To add insult to injury, the order gave as reason their failure to discharge their duties conscientiously and their adverse influence upon hygiene in the army.[35] As a result of this offensive order many Jewish physicians in the army resigned their posts. Dr. S. Yaroshevsky wrote in his letter of resignation: "As long as the government will not retract the gratuitous aspersion cast upon Jewish physicians, each extra minute spent by them in the service adds to their shame. Out of respect for their human dignity, Jewish physicians should not remain where they are spurned." [36] For this courageous stand Yaroshevsky was arraigned before a court of justice.

Pursuing its policy of revoking all concessions granted Jews in the previous reign, the government of Alexander III set about limiting their educational opportunities. By offering special privileges to professionally trained Jews the preceding regime had encouraged the pursuit of higher learning. Now in its anxiety to eliminate Jews from the free professions and at the same time to reduce the number entitled by profession to unrestricted residence, the government began to curtail their number in the schools producing the professional intelligentsia.

Originally the recommendation for a Jewish *numerus clausus* came from provincial authorities, with the complaint that Jews were responsible for the dissemination of revolutionary ideas in the schools. These suggestions found a ready response in the emperor, who ordered the Cabinet to consider the matter. At first the Cabinet held that this change should be made through legislative channels and referred the question to the Pahlen commission, then in session, with

34. *The Jews in Russia,* Vol. I, chap. VIII.
35. See *Evreiskaia Starina,* IX (1916), 21.
36. *Idem.*

instructions to give the charge immediate attention. But then without waiting for a report the Cabinet, prompted by the emperor, instructed the minister of education, I. D. Delianov, to begin limiting Jewish students in secondary schools and universities.[37] The authorization was superfluous, for the minister of the interior had anticipated this move by so advising the minister of education, who in turn so instructed his local administrators. Thus before the numerus clausus became official law it was put into effect by administrative order in a number of secondary schools (*gymnasia*) and universities in the years 1885 and 1886.[38] The official limitation of students in schools was inaugurated on July 1, 1887, and on July 10 it was extended to the universities.

In connection with this decision to bar the mass of Jewish youth from educational institutions it is important to point out that it did not reflect popular opinion. That fact is made clear when one examines the attitudes toward this question taken some six years earlier by the provincial committees created in 1881 for a discussion of the Jewish question. Although these groups consisted of "trustworthy" men hand picked by the governors of the respective provinces, a majority of them registered their disapproval of impeding the education of Jewish youth: six were opposed to any limitations, five recommended limitations of a more favorable nature, and only two favored a numerus clausus.

The opinions of some of the committees on the subject are worthy of note. In its resolution opposing any such projected discriminations the committee of Kherson commended the Jews for their educational aspirations, the majority agreeing that instead of discouraging these ambitions the government ought to encourage them. It was also suggested that more schools be opened to accommodate both Jews and non-Jews. In a similar vein the mayor of Kishinev in Bessarabia Province observed that it would be unfair to put any limitations on the number of Jews in the schools since they contribute their proportional share toward the maintenance of educational institutions. The committee of Chernigov objected to the proposed curtailments on the ground that the schools served as an effective medium for eliminating religious and racial traits which set the Jews apart from the rest of the population. By a majority of fourteen to one the committee of Kiev not only rejected the numerus clausus but suggested that parents of children attending

37. [See *Evreiskaia Enciclopedia,* Vol. I, col. 835. Also *The Legal Sufferings of the Jews in Russia,* ed. Lucien Wolf (London, 1912), pp. 15 ff. Ed.]

38. *Zhurnal Ministerstva Narodnago Prosveshchenia* (Journal of the Ministry of People's Education), *235* (1884), 77–78. Hereafter cited as *Z.M.N.P.*

schools located outside the Pale be granted the right of residence there. That this suggestion emanated from one of the provinces under Governor General Drenteln is of particular significance. The minority opinion among the committees which approved the numerus clausus voiced objections similar to those discussed above. In one of these committees it was argued that if the government barred the schools to so many Jews it was bound to permit Jews to open their own schools, and that since such a procedure was contrary to the best interests of the country the proposed restrictions should not be put into effect.

The Pahlen commission did not approve the numerus clausus. Appointed in 1883 by an imperial ukase, the commission was officially named the High Commission for the Revision of the Current Laws concerning the Jews. Count K. I. Pahlen presided over it during the greater part of its existence. The rest of the commission consisted of high-ranking government officials. In the five years of its existence, 1883–88, the commission assembled valuable material concerning the Jews of Russia, including information furnished by representative Jews. In essence the commission recommended continuation of the policies of Alexander II, which meant a gradual elimination of Jewish disabilities. Because the views of the majority of the commission were unacceptable to the emperor, it was dissolved in 1888 and all its material placed in the archives.[39]

A. I. Georgievsky, a high-ranking official of the Ministry of Education and a member of the Pahlen commission, reporting on the subject of educational limitations for Jews, repudiated the charges of atheism and lack of patriotism leveled against Jewish students. He suggested on behalf of the commission that instead of indiscriminately limiting the number of Jewish students in the secondary schools regardless of their economic status, only those of the lower classes be assigned quotas. There would be no necessity for limiting university students, since they would be affected in turn by reductions in the lower schools. These recommendations, be it observed, were inspired by neither religious nor racial prejudice but were an expression of a class philosophy which regarded those on a low economic level, whether Jew or Gentile, as unfit for higher education. But by the time these conclusions were submitted to the Cabinet the matter had already been disposed of in accordance with the wishes of the tsar and his anti-Semitic clique.[40]

The numerus clausus created a peculiarly vexing problem for the

39. [See *Evreiskaia Enciclopedia,* Vol. I, article on Alexander III, cols. 825–839, and Vol. V, article on the Pahlen commission, cols. 862–863. Ed.]

40. S. Pozner, *Evrei v Obshchei Shkole* (St. Petersburg, 1914), pp. 71–78.

Jews. Their admission to the schools was dependent upon the number of non-Jewish students, whether in areas preponderantly populated by Jews or otherwise. In the secondary schools their chances for admission were even slimmer than in the elementary schools, since a great proportion of the Christian population did not give their children a secondary education. There were cases where parents in their anxiety to raise the basis for the Jewish quota undertook to pay the tuition fee of a Christian student and to maintain him at their expense. In a monologue called "Gymnasie" the famous Yiddish humorist Sholem Alechem describes the frustrations brought about by this regulation and describes the ingenious plots and ludicrous situations created by an ambitious mother determined to get her son into the coveted institution. The following passage from that story, although written in humorous vein, suggests the heartaches suffered by Jewish parents and the tragedy of Jewish youth. The harassed father, driven by his determined wife, had tried every possible avenue toward the goal, but in vain. The story then runs:

And the Almighty had compassion, and sent me a Gymnasiye [*sic*] in Poland, a "commercial" one, where they took in one Jew to every Christian. It came to fifty per cent. But what then? Any Jew who wished his son to enter must bring his Christian with him, and if he passes, that is, the Christian, and one pays his entrance fee, then there is hope. Instead of one bundle, one has two on one's shoulders, you understand? Besides being worn with anxiety about my own, I had to tremble for the other, because if Esau, which Heaven forbid, fails to pass, it's all over with Jacob. But what I went through before I *got* that Christian, a shoemaker's son, Holiava his name was, is not to be described. And the best of all was this—would you believe that my shoemaker, planted in the earth firmly as Korah, insisted on Bible teaching? There was nothing for it but my son had to sit down beside his, and repeat the Old Testament. How came a son of mine to the Old Testament? [41] Ai, don't ask! He can do everything and understands everything. With God's help the happy day arrived and they both passed. Is my story finished? Not quite. When it came to their being entered in the books, to writing out a check, my Christian was not to be found! What has happened? He, the Gentile, doesn't care for his son to be among so many Jews—he won't hear of it. Why should he, seeing that all doors are open to him anyhow, and he can get in where he pleases? Tell him it isn't fair? Much good that would be! "Look here," says I, "how much do you want, Pani Holiava?" Says he,

41. [In Sholem Alechem's original the Russian term "Zakon Bozhy" for the school subject "religion" is used but not "Bible teaching" and "Old Testament" as employed by the translator. Ed.]

"Nothing." To cut the tale short—up and down, this way and that way, and friends and people interfering, we had him off to a refreshment place, and ordered a glass, and two, and three, before it all came right! Once he was really in, I cried my eyes out, and thanks be to Him whose Name is blessed, and who has delivered me out of all my troubles.[42]

Thwarted in their attempt to enter gymnasia, a large number of Jewish students covered the course of studies with the aid of private tutors and presented themselves for examination at a recognized school. Upon passing the examination they would receive a diploma qualifying them for admission to a university. In most cases the diploma proved unavailing, for the percentage of Jewish applicants admitted to universities was pathetically small. The more enterprising or well-to-do young people traveled abroad in quest of knowledge or a professional career. In the universities of France, Germany, and particularly Switzerland were to be found Russian-Jewish students, many of whom endured extreme poverty.

Without waiting for the school quota system to accomplish in time the purpose of reducing the number of Jews in the professions, the government set about eliminating those who had already acquired their professional qualifications. Obviously from dissatisfaction that so many Jewish jurists enjoyed an enviable reputation, an imperial order was issued on November 8, 1889, stating that in future the application of every non-Christian lawyer for permission to practice his profession must be confirmed by the minister of justice.[43] Although this order was not specifically directed at Jews, their applications were invariably denied while Mohammedans and Karaites met no obstacles.

During the first six years of this law's operation not one Jewish attorney was admitted to the bar.[44] Thus young men who had been permitted to spend years training for the legal profession in government schools were without warning deprived of the right to make use of their knowledge.[45]

The government of Alexander III waged a campaign against its three million Jewish inhabitants. In 1887 the cities of Rostov-on-Don and Taganrog, hitherto included in the Pale of Settlement, were

42. [Sholem Alechem's "Gymnasie" has been frequently printed. In the United States it was published in *Selected Works of Sholem Alechem* (New York, 1912), Vol. I, 243–258. An English translation in *Yiddish Tales,* by Helena Frank (Philadelphia, Jewish Publication Society, 1912), 162–179. Ed.]

43. *T.P.S.Z.,* Vol. IX, No. 6331.

44. M. I. Mysh, *Rukovodstvo po Russkim Zakonam o Evreakh* (St. Petersburg, 1904), pp. 410–412; *Evreiskaia Biblioteka,* IX, 469.

45. On Jewish contributions to the legal field in Russia see *The Jews in Russia,* Vol. I, chap. XIII.

barred to new Jewish residents.[46] Step by step the economic opportunities of the Jew were narrowed. Loyal discharge of the duties a full-fledged citizen owes his state were demanded of him, while the state placed him in the position of a second-class citizen and constantly cast aspersions upon his loyalty.

A common charge against the Russian Jew was that he sought to evade military service. Indeed, the government gave him good cause for aversion to such service. In the army he was placed in an inferior position, he could never attain the rank of a commissioned officer, and upon discharge he could not remain in the city where he served his term if it happened to be located outside the Pale. Nevertheless the charge of Jewish delinquency was not borne out by figures. While the male population of the Pale constituted 11 per cent of the total male population, Jews supplied 12 per cent of recruits.[47] This percentage would be even larger if the statistics took into account Jews who died before reaching military age or those who migrated because of persecutions. Many of these names were not removed from the records, so that the basis for the military quota was inaccurate. As a result of this fictitious discrepancy between the required number and those available the draft boards refused to grant exemptions to those who were entitled to them by law.

In order further to curb the alleged tendency to evade military service, the government issued a ukase in 1887 holding the entire family responsible for the failure of a recruit to report for duty.[48] If a Jewish boy of military age emigrated in quest of the opportunities and rights denied him in his native land, his relatives had to pay a fine of 300 rubles. If they were unable to meet this obligation the government auctioned the household goods to collect it. This fine which applied only to Jews worked havoc with a number of Jewish families to whom 300 rubles was a fabulous fortune.

The campaign to destroy the last remaining reforms of the preceding reign, conducted at an accelerated tempo in the last years of Alexander III, was aimed with special cruelty against the Jews. The tsar's miraculous escape when his train was derailed at Borky station on October 17, 1888, intensified his religious fanaticism and fostered a spirit of mysticism in the court. Pobedonostsev impressed upon the monarch that God had saved his life in order that he might keep Russia pure of any Western influence. Consequently when in 1890 a high dignitary submitted a memorandum pointing to the

46. [*Evreiskaia Enciclopedia,* Vol. VII, cols. 301–302; Dubnow, *History,* II, 346. Ed.]
47. [M. L. Usov (Trivus), *Evrei v Armii* (St. Petersburg, 1911), p. 35. Ed.]
48. [Dubnow, *History,* II, 356–357. Ed.]

miseries inflicted upon an innocent and unoffending people and calling attention to the bad impression this maltreatment of the Jews created abroad, the tsar noted upon the margin of the document: "We must never forget that it was Jews who crucified our Lord and spilt his precious blood." [49] The court clergy publicly preached that it was sinful for Christians to be on friendly terms with Jews and backed up their exhortations by quotations from the Gospels. The fate of the Jews was now in the hands of two rabid reactionaries, I. N. Durnovo, who became minister of the interior following the death of Tolstoi in 1889, and V. Plehve, who assumed the post of Durnovo's assistant. Familiar with all the intricate workings of the Police Department, of which both had been former chiefs, they set about utilizing the intense anti-Jewish sentiment in the court.

The provincial administrators were quick to take the cue and institute a veritable hunt against the Jewish population. Many small towns in the Pale were declared villages and thus barred to new Jewish residents. In the category of new residents were included all those who had settled in those areas following the Temporary Rules of May, 1882. There were cases where Jewish soldiers upon being discharged from the army were barred from their native villages on the ground that they were new settlers.

The life of those who lived outside the Pale was made unbearable. Particularly affected by this intensified police vigilance were the artisans and petty traders. On the least suspicion that they were deviating from the pursuits permitted them by law, they were summarily deported to the Pale. The presence of Jews in the two capitals, St. Petersburg and Moscow, was a special source of irritation to the reactionary government leaders. Unable to order a wholesale expulsion of those who had legal residence there, Gresser, the police chief of St. Petersburg, resorted to all sorts of ingenious devices to make life there unendurable. In 1890 he issued an order that signs on Jewish stores and workshops must carry the full Hebrew names of the owners and of their fathers. When the names appeared in small type police ordered them changed to bolder type. Then the authorities ordered that the names appear not in the dignified proper form but in the intimate diminutive. This ingenious device of humiliation was quickly copied by other administrators. Gresser, who openly declared that he was above the law,[50] issued a decree forbidding the Jews of St. Petersburg to teach their children a trade. This order was undoubtedly motivated by the intention to deport the

49. Frederic, *The New Exodus*, p. 173. [The name of the high dignitary is not given. Ed.]
50. *Ibid.*, p. 248.

children of artisans as soon as they reached maturity. In the meantime the policy of ridding St. Petersburg of as many Jews as possible was relentlessly pursued. From two independent sources Frederic estimated that between May and November, 1891, close to two thousand Jews were expelled from the city. Some of these deportees were sent out from the city in chains like criminals.[51]

The greatest blow, however, was reserved for the Jewish community of Moscow. Early in 1891 it became known that the Grand Duke Sergei, a brother of the tsar, had been appointed governor general of Moscow. A rumor was circulating that the tsar had decided to make Moscow the capital of Russia again and that he was sending his brother there to take the appropriate steps. Whether in preparation for removing the imperial seat to Moscow or in honor of the arrival of the new governor general, who in addition to having an unsavory reputation shared the anti-Jewish prejudices of the court, the administration decided to expel the Jews who had settled in Moscow in accordance with the law of 1865.

The edict of expulsion was published March 29, 1891, the first day of the Jewish Passover. Whether by design, to add a touch of refined cruelty, as some historians maintain, or because of bureaucratic inefficiency, the order of exile was issued in two parts on successive days, March 28 and 29. The first part stated that henceforth no Jewish artisan would be permitted to settle in Moscow. The Jews of Moscow, who learned the news at the Passover service in the synagogues, strange as it may seem sighed with relief. Agitated and fearful over dark rumors of an evil decree impending over the Jewish community, Moscow Jewry almost welcomed news that the new order did not affect the old residents. Even the part of the ukase published the next day sustained their hope. It stated that measures would be taken for the gradual removal of the "above-mentioned Jews" to the Pale. The phrase was naturally taken by the Jewish community to refer to the new arrivals, cited in the first part of the edict; there was still no hint of threat to the old residents of Moscow.

The ambiguous formulation of the ukase was not accidental; it was designed to hide the arbitrary and illegal character of the new enactment. The Jewish artisans resided in the old Russian capital by virtue of the law of 1865. Normally the new laws were promulgated or old ones revoked through the State Council. The decision to revoke the residence rights of Moscow Jews had not even been submitted to the Cabinet. This resolution to uproot the thirty thousand Jews of Moscow was adopted by the tsar at the suggestion of the minister of the interior. In unreasonable cruelty it even surpassed the May

51. *Ibid.*, p. 249.

Rules of 1882. The latter closed the rural area of the Pale only to new settlers; the edict of 1891 was made retroactive. The secret instructions accompanying the published ukase ordered the banishment of all Jews residing in Moscow.

The following procedure for the execution of the edict was laid down by the Moscow authorities. Illegal and semi-illegal residents were to be deported at once, while artisans with legal residence were served notice to leave the city within a period of between three months and one year. Included in the decree of exile were the so-called circular Jews, for example those who had lived in Moscow before 1880 and whose residence there was legalized by a special circular of the minister of the interior in 1880.

The fixing of a minimum and maximum period within which certain categories of artisans were to liquidate their affairs created a lucrative source of revenue for the police. The financial ability of the prospective deportee to bribe the proper authorities determined the time he was given to wind up his affairs.

The first to feel the sting of the new decree were the illegal Jews, most of whom lived in the Zaradie quarter, slum and home of the poorer Jewish population. In this section of the city also stayed out-of-town Jews who visited Moscow temporarily for business purposes. It is estimated that at least half the Jewish community of Moscow lived in the tenement houses of Zaradie.

At midnight following the promulgation of the decree of expulsion this entire section was surrounded by police, cossacks, and firemen led by Cossack General Yourkovsky. The object of the raid was to discover first the Jews who were subject to immediate deportation. Harold Frederic, at that time correspondent of the London *Times* in Moscow, gives the following description of the raid:

> Under Yourkoffsky's personal supervision, the whole quarter was ransacked, apartments forced open, doors smashed, every bedroom without exception searched, and every living soul, men, women, and children routed out for examination as to their passports. The indignities which the women, young and old alike, underwent at the hands of the Cossacks may not be described . . .
>
> As a result, over 700 men, women and children were dragged at dead of night through the streets to the *outchastoks* or police stations. They were not even given time to dress themselves, and they were kept in this noisome and overcrowded confinement for thirty-six hours, almost all without food, and some without water as well. Of these unhappy people, thus driven from their beds, and haled off to prison in the wintry darkness, some were afterward marched away by *étape*, that is, chained to-

gether with criminals and forced along the roads by Cossacks. A few were bribed out of confinement; the rest were summarily shipped to the Pale . . . They were chiefly artisans and petty traders. There was no charge of criminality or of leading an evil life against any of them. They were arrested and banished whether their passports were in order or not, and with them, alike to the *outchastoks* and into exile went their children and womenkind.[52]

Frederic adds that it was by good luck no larger number of Jews was arrested. At the risk of severe punishment, a police officer who was a Christian convert forewarned his former coreligionists of the coming raid. Many Jewish dwellers of Zaradie did not come home that night; some of them went to the cemeteries, others kept moving through the city, and many respected Jews sought refuge for their wives and children in houses of ill repute.[53]

In his memoirs I. I. Petrunkevich relates that upon publication of the ukase of expulsion from Moscow there began a terrible search for Jews. No Jew could feel secure. During the night the police would break into Jewish homes in search of new arrivals, ordering the sleepers to get up and present their passports for examination whether or not their owners had the proper residence qualifications. He tells how the wife of a university graduate who had legal residence in the city was not allowed to attend the funeral of her husband on the ground that upon the death of her husband she had lost the right to stay in Moscow.[54]

Many reputable Jews who because of failure to wind up their affairs were caught after the expiration of their period of grace were marched to the railway station in manacles and in the company of criminals. The *New York Times* of December 7, 1891, listed the names of eighty-eight Jews who were thus deported from Moscow. Even sickness did not procure postponement of the day of deportation; the patients were brought on stretchers to the railway station. No mercy was shown, no special merit on the part of a Jew could earn a cancellation of deportation or even postponement. A few weeks after the raid on Zaradie the tsar, while visiting Moscow with his wife and family, received a pathetic petition from a Jewish veteran. Israel Deyel, a corporal in the reserve, pleaded that Jewish soldiers who had served in the army should not be expelled from their native city.[55] It is reliably reported that Alexander III read the letter. As a result the veteran was imprisoned, and expulsion

52. *Ibid.*, p. 200.
53. *Ibid.*, p. 201; also Dubnow, *History*, II, 403–404.
54. Petrunkevich, *Iz Zapisok*, pp. 280–281.
55. For a copy of the petition see Frederic, *The New Exodus*, pp. 287–289.

proceeded with fiercer determination.[56] To encourage the vigilance of the police in tracking down "illegal" Jews, an announcement by the *Messenger of the Moscow Police* promised rewards for the arrest of rightless Jews. The reward for one such Jew was the same as for two criminals charged with looting.[57] Unable for lack of time to dispose of their property adequately, many Jews were virtually forced to give it away for a few rubles.

The expulsion of about twenty thousand Jews—two-thirds of the Jewish community—also had grave economic consequences for the general population. The Jews of the circular class alone employed about twenty-five thousand Russian workmen. Several industries experienced a severe crisis owing to the banishment of the Jews and the prohibition of their coming to Moscow even on business. The manufacture of silk all but ceased, the volume of business having been curtailed by 100,000,000 rubles. In 1893 representatives of large merchant and manufacturing groups pleaded in a special memorandum that Jews be permitted to come to Moscow for business purposes. Despite the shift of business from Moscow to Leipzig, the petition was refused by the police chief.[58]

Only about a third of Moscow's Jewry—people with a higher education, first-guild merchants born there, and children of soldiers who had served under Nicholas I—was allowed to remain. But even these lived under severe disabilities and in humiliating circumstances. The following incident illustrates the administration's attitude. Rabbi Solomon Minor, the spiritual leader of the Jewish community, was often called to account for registering Jewish children under Christian names. The authorities insisted that instead of using the Russian equivalent of biblical names, like Isaac, Moisei, as was his wont, he employ humiliating diminutives such as Itske, Moshka, etc. Because the rabbi "dared" to insist on his right to employ the standard Russian translation he came to be regarded as a political suspect and was subsequently dismissed from his post and deported to the Pale by personal order of the tsar.[59]

The fate of the remaining Jewish community in Moscow is reflected in the unhappy history of its synagogue, which merits a brief description since it epitomizes the status of the entire Russian-Jewish community under Alexander III.[60]

56. *Ibid.*, pp. 221–222.
57. *Byloe* (September, 1907), p. 157.
58. *Ibid.*, pp. 155–156.
59. [Dubnow, *History*, II, 424, gives another reason for the dismissal and deportation of Rabbi Minor: his wilful opening of the Moscow synagogue. The order of the tsar was dated September 23, 1892. Ed.]
60. See A. S. Katsnelson, "From the Martyrdom of the Moscow Community" (The Synagogue of Moscow in the years 1891 to 1906), *Evreiskaia Starina*, I, 175–188.

In 1891 the old Moscow synagogue, chartered in 1861, moved into its new building constructed with the permission of the authorities. The new structure was built in Byzantine style with a cupola bearing the traditional shield of David. The building finished, there immediately came an order from the administration to remove the cupola. This order, which might have been prompted by a desire to erase the possibility of mistaking the synagogue for a Greek Orthodox church with its traditional cupola, was executed within a few days. That was only the first episode. The anti-Jewish mood then prevailing in Moscow could not tolerate the existence of a decent-looking synagogue. On July 23, 1894, the synagogue administration was informed by the police that the institution was temporarily closed and forbidden to hold divine service or any other public functions until further notice. That notice came two months later in the form of a ukase which gave the Jewish community the choice of selling their synagogue or converting it into a philanthropic institution.

Unwilling to sell their house of worship, which was built with common funds, the synagogue leaders accepted the second alternative and decided to transfer the Jewish trade school to the newly constructed synagogue. For this the synagogue had to be remodeled. Although the plans were approved by the proper authorities, the building had to undergo several renovations. And then, while the synagogue was still in process of being made over, the police chief of Moscow, in 1895, issued an order closing the school.

To save the synagogue, it was decided to move into it the Talmud Torah maintained by the Moscow community. New plans for remodeling were drawn and approved by the government. By two years later, when the remodeling was completed, the director of the school had been deported to the Pale and the Talmud Torah was closed by order of the governor general. Again the synagogue officials were confronted by the government with the choice of selling or converting into a philanthropic institution or hospital. There began a tragi-comedy of rebuilding the synagogue to adapt it to all conceivable sorts of philanthropic institutions. It was constantly under reconstruction: each time it was remodeled to fit a specific charitable institution the institution turned out to be either nonexistent or superfluous, and when on the other hand an institution was pronounced useful by the government the synagogue building was declared unsuitable.

The continuous repairs of the synagogue impoverished the Jewish community of Moscow. Matters reached such a pass that the salaries of the religious functionaries could not be met on time. The building contractors had to sue for their claims. Communal interest and public activity among the Jews were paralyzed. The synagogue was saved from bankruptcy through the death of a wealthy Jew who left it a considerable bequest. In fact, the only field of public activity in which the Jews could show a "live" interest was the cemetery. The police did not impose their invariable limitations on this branch of Jewish life. They evidently recognized the Jewish cemetery as a useful institution.

During the years that the synagogue was closed, the ten thousand Jews of Moscow were allowed to maintain five chapels which accommodated 816 persons. Since the number of Jewish soldiers stationed in the Moscow garrison who were permitted to attend services on the High Holidays exceeded one thousand, the majority of Moscow Jews had no place of worship even during these festivals. The government not only did not allow an increase in the number of chapels, it even forbade a change of locale. Aware of this situation, the landlords in whose premises the chapels were located kept on raising the rent. In one case the Moscow administration had allowed a removal because the building was old and deteriorated, but upon discovery that the new room was somewhat larger than the old chapel permission was withdrawn.

Deprived of the opportunity of worshiping in the open, the Orthodox element of the city held secret religious services during Rosh Hashana and Yom Kippur. The Moscow police were not unaware of these illegal gatherings, but sometimes the benevolent attitude of the lower police officials was of no avail. Then a raid would be ordered and some of the worshipers would be fined, jailed, or even deported from the city. In police circles the High Holidays were known as days of "hunting the Jews."

A. Katsnelson, whose study of the Moscow synagogue serves as the basis for this account, records the following incident at a secret religious service. One Yom Kippur afternoon, when the worshipers were already weary from fasting and continuous prayers, the cry suddenly rose, "A raid!" The news passed through the room like an electric current. Candles were put out, prayer shawls removed, and the crowd pressed to the doors. They were stopped by a strong contingent of uniformed police and plain-clothes men. Women fainted; men milled around; some were panic-stricken. One convert was there who observed the Jewish faith secretly. In those days the discovery of a baptized Jew at a Jewish religious service could result in grave consequences both for himself and for the Jewish community. While the police were busy examining the passports of the congregants, an elderly worshiper pushed his own passport into the hands of this man. This unselfish gesture through which the elderly Jew subjected himself to a series of unpleasant experiences saved the baptized man and the community from more than mere embarrassment.

Other attempts were made by the Moscow Jewish community to have the synagogue reopened. In 1895, the coronation year of the new tsar, Nicholas II, they petitioned the governor general for permission to hold a public service in the synagogue in honor of the new emperor. The police chief regarded the request as an act of arrogance, summoned the Jewish representatives to his office, and severely rebuked them. The community was not even allowed to open the synagogue when an imperial ukase granted freedom of religious worship to all denominations. The misadventures of the Moscow synagogue ended in 1906, in the short period of the existence of the first Duma, when it was finally legalized. The chronicle of the synagogue concludes this recital by saying: "This house, called the Moscow synagogue, saw much sorrow and many, many tears." [61]

The history of the Moscow synagogue may indeed serve as a parable of the experiences of Russian Jewry during the reign of Alexander III. The one comforting thought which brightens this gloomy picture is the knowledge that the Russian people themselves were not responsible for the hardships and cruelties imposed upon the Jews. The guilt for these injustices must be ascribed to the emperor, Pobedonostsev, Ignatiev, and the small clique of court dignitaries who were in complete charge of Russian affairs.

It has been established beyond a shadow of doubt that the pogroms of the eighties were not organized by the local Christian population, certainly not by the peasants whom the government allegedly sought to protect from Jewish "exploitation." The May Rules of 1882 which further narrowed the Pale by one-tenth were a temporary measure decreed by imperial ukase although only a minority of the Cabinet favored it. Not even the bureaucratic State Council was asked to sanction the measure, nor was it consulted on the numerus clausus. There is good reason to believe that if it had been left to the provincial committees, although their members were selected by the government itself, or even to the bureaucrats of the Pahlen commission,[62] the Jews would not only have been spared the harsh disabilities but in time have attained civil equality.

Nicholas II

The Jews had little reason to mourn the passing of Alexander III on October 20, 1894: his reign had brought them pogroms, expul-

61. [*Ibid.*, I, 188. Ed.]
62. [See above, pp. 26–28. Ed.]

sions, and humiliations. But the rule of his son Nicholas II was no better for them. On the contrary, it intensified the campaign against the Jews. In the eighties the anti-Jewish outbreaks were mostly limited to plundering and beatings; comparatively few murders were committed during those excesses. But during the reign of the last Romanov the pogroms became wholesale massacres. As for expulsions and humiliations, there was no end to the cruel decrees and indignities that were heaped upon the hapless Jewish population.

The spiritual adviser of Nicholas II was the same Pobedonostsev who had inspired the anti-Jewish policies of his father. This administrative head of the Russian church is said once to have stated that he hoped to solve the Jewish problem as follows: one-third of Jews to be destroyed, one-third made to emigrate, and the rest to be swallowed up by the Russian people. Here too as with Alexander III Pobedonostsev's advice fell on receptive ears. So deep-seated was Nicholas' hatred for the Jews that even arguments setting forth the advantages for the Russian people in the abolition of Jewish disabilities had no effect upon him. Thus when Count Pahlen, governor of Vilna, proposed the abolition of the Pale in order to weaken the influence of the Jews who constituted a majority in the cities of the northwest, the emperor refused to listen to him. Also rejected was the advice of Count Witte that for the sake of expediting the assimilation of Jews certain educational restrictions be removed. The Cabinet favored this recommendation but not so the tsar. Even as strong a statesman as P. A. Stolypin did not influence the emperor in this direction. In October, 1906, when the Cabinet under his presidency decided that it was necessary to enter upon the road of a slow and gradual abolition of Jewish disabilities, Nicholas refused to approve the minutes.[63]

On the whole the tsar was rarely troubled by his ministers on behalf of the Jews. He generally surrounded himself with underlings who did his bidding and anticipated his slightest wish. Of this clique were Durnovo, Goremykin, Sipiagin, and Plehve, all of whom at one time or another held the important post of the minister of the interior and all of whom were infected with deep prejudices against Jews. Then again, the increased revolutionary activities in which Jewish students and workers played their part added fuel to the existing hatred and caused the government to intensify its war upon the entire Jewish population.

The war against Jews was waged on all fronts. Because of the May Rules which barred Jews from the area outside the city limits,

63. Witte, *Memoirs,* pp. 383–384.

practically all summer resorts were closed to them. No exceptions were made for the sick who were prescribed cures in the watering places outside the Pale. In 1896 a law was passed forbidding Jewish soldiers to spend their furloughs anywhere outside the Pale. According to this law, a soldier who was serving in a regiment situated outside the Pale could not remain during his leave in the city where he was performing his military duties.

At the same time the government increased its vigilance over the privileged Jews who lived outside the Pale. The city of Kiev was the object of the strictest police surveillance, since Jews were permitted to come there for short business visits. Every week late at night the police would stage raids on Jewish hotels in search of illegal Jews. To pay for the extra police force necessary for these periodic searches, the Jewish community of Kiev was taxed 15,000 rubles annually. This appropriation was made from the tax levied on kosher meat to maintain Jewish philanthropic and educational institutions. Even the anti-Semitic newspaper *Kievlianin* (July, 1901) decried this action of the government as "hardly conceivable." [64]

In the field of education the restrictive interpretations of the numerus clausus robbed Jewish youth of the limited opportunities provided for them by law. With all other professions closed to the Jews, the youth flocked to the departments of medicine and law in the higher schools. In order further to reduce the number of vacancies open to Jews under the quota system, the Ministry of Education resorted to this cunning device. It ordered that beginning with the academic year 1899–1900 the percentage of Jews eligible for admission should be calculated in relation not to the total student body but to that of each department.[65] This circular specifically stated that the new ruling was a result of the participation of "non-Russian" elements in disturbances within the university. In 1901 the ministry ordered the reduction of the general quota on the ground that the number of Jewish students exceeded the legal proportions.[66]

The never ending ministerial circulars limiting free movement and exercise of the most elementary human rights in practically every branch of activity had their inevitable effect upon the attitude of the Russian masses toward their Jewish neighbors. The Jew came more and more to be regarded as a citizen of a special class to whom the general law did not apply. This, coupled with the traditional intolerance of an illiterate or at best semiliterate Christian popula-

64. Dubnow, *History,* III, 20.
65. Pozner, *Evrei v Obshchei Shkole,* Supplement, No. 12, p. 5.
66. *Ibid.,* No. 13, p. 6.

tion, explains the ease with which ordinarily peaceful and decent folk could be aroused to plunder and murder Jews. As in the days of Alexander III, the mobs which destroyed Jewish lives and property were frequently under the impression that they were executing an order of the tsar. A Ukrainian peasant, arrested and brought before a court of justice for having taken part in anti-Jewish excesses, expressed his astonishment at his arrest as follows: "They told us we had permission to beat the Jews, and now it appears it is all a lie." [67]

The closing years of the nineteenth century witnessed a renewal of the pogroms in the familiar pattern. As in the eighties, the attacks on Jewish life and property met no disapproval from the local authorities. Their only action was directed toward preventing the Jews from defending themselves. Again the scene of these outrages was the Ukraine; the severest pogrom took place in the city of Nikolaev during the Easter Festival, April, 1899, and lasted for three days.

That a pogrom could be nipped in the bud if there was the will to do so was clearly demonstrated in the Polish city of Chenstokhov. At the instigation of an anti-Semitic priest a large mob of Polish pilgrims, gathered in the city for worship at one of the Catholic shrines, tried to stage a pogrom. The rioters were confident that the customary immunity accorded to Russian plunderers would be accorded them too. But the Poles miscalculated, for the Russian authorities welcomed this opportunity to inflict punishment upon a crowd who they knew harbored little love for the Russians. A detachment of soldiers was ordered to fire upon the mob, and one volley proved enough to disperse them. But such display of energy in suppressing anti-Jewish riots was a rare phenomenon during the reign of Nicholas II: the regime of the last Romanov employed the pogrom as a means of diverting the growing disaffection of the people and of checking the ever growing revolutionary activities. By placing the blame for the misery of the masses upon Jewish shoulders, the government hoped to cover up its corruption and inefficiency which was the real cause of that misery.

Kishinev, the capital of Bessarabia, was the first city after the turn of the century to experience a big pogrom; on April 6 to 8, 1903, fifty were killed and several hundred wounded. The local yellow sheet *Bessarabets* (The Bessarabian) prepared the ground for these massacres, for months hurling all sorts of vile accusations against the Jews. So pleased was Plehve with P. Krushevan, the editor of the paper, that he offered him a government subsidy for

67. Dubnow, *History,* III, 34.

the publication of a similar sheet named *Znamia* (The Banner), which he began publishing in St. Petersburg in 1902.

Krushevan's propaganda became particularly vicious in the early months of 1903 when the rumor spread that Jews had slain a peasant boy for ritual purposes in the town of Dubosary. Although judicial investigation established that the murdered boy was the victim of a greedy uncle, *Bessarabets* charged the Jews with the crime and called upon the Christian populace for vengeance. Soon the familiar rumors were circulating about an order from the tsar to murder Jews. The police did nothing to check it for they themselves were among the organizers of the pogrom which broke out on April 6, the first day of the Easter Festival. For two days the fifty thousand Jews of the city of Kishinev were at the mercy of hoodlums who committed every conceivable atrocity upon them. According to official figures, seven hundred Jewish homes and six hundred stores were wrecked, but there can be no estimate of the terror and savagery let loose upon a helpless people.[68]

The Kishinev massacre aroused a universal outcry in Russia as well as abroad. The liberal press and the most distinguished Russian writers expressed their horror at the outrages. Count Leo Tolstoi squarely placed the responsibility upon the government, the bigoted clergy, and corrupt officials for poisoning the minds and the sentiments of the Russian masses. As the details of the barbarities became known abroad, mass meetings of protest were held in England and the United States, and funds for the victims of the massacre were raised. The Russian government was charged with direct complicity in these riots, instigated and organized by Plehve. To appease public opinion the governor of Bessarabia, General von Raaben, was replaced by Prince Urussov.

There is no doubt whatsoever that Minister of the Interior Plehve was the instigator of the pogrom. Prince Urussov, a fair and conservative man who made a careful study of the causes of the Kishinev

68. V. Korolenko, *Dom No. 13* (*Epizod iz Kishineuskago Pogroma*), first printed illegally by the Bund in Russia, 1903, second edition published by the Bund in London; Nedelnaia Khronika Voskhoda (St. Petersburg, 1903), No. 16 and subsequent issues; *Memoirs of a Russian Governor. Prince Serge Dmitriyevich Urussov,* tr. and ed. Herman Rosenthal (New York, 1908), *passim,* hereafter cited as Urussov, *Memoirs;* Michael Davitt, *Within the Pale.* (*The True Story of Antisemitic Persecution in Russia,*) (Philadelphia, 1903), Pt. II, "The Kishineff Massacre"; *Russia at the Bar of the American People. A Memorial of Kishinef.* Records and documents collected and edited by Isidore Singer (New York, 1904).

[The main source for the history of Kishinev pogrom, published after the fall of the tsarist empire, is *Materialy dlia Istorii Anti-Evreiskikh Pogromov v Rossii,* Vol. I: *Dubossarskoe i Kishinevskoe dela 1903 Goda,* ed. G. Krasny-Admoni and Simon Dubnow (Petrograd, 1919), pp. 358. See also *Die Judenpogrome in Russland,* Vols. I–II. Ed.]

massacre, states that for a long time he doubted Plehve's direct complicity in these bloody excesses. Subsequent events dissipated his misgivings and confirmed his lingering suspicions.[69] Witte, who knew Plehve intimately, reports that the minister of the interior, a Jew hater during whose regime the tides of pogroms rose to an unprecedented height, justified these riots as counterrevolutionary outbreaks.[70]

During the trials of those arrested for rioting it was obvious where the sympathy of the court lay. Light sentences were meted out to those whose guilt was undeniable, and the court so hampered the attempts of the defense to get at the real organizers of the massacre that they were impelled to resign in protest. The court also rejected all civil claims against the government for damages. This verdict was upheld by the Senate where the defendant, Governor von Raaben, frankly stated that the granting of monetary compensation to pogrom victims would establish a dangerous precedent; it might mean an additional annual expense of several million rubles to the treasury.

The government had good reason for refusing to establish a precedent like this, for in spite of the outraged protests of the civilized world the ruling clique of Russia had no intention of relinquishing the pogrom as a weapon to fight the revolution. In the summer of 1903, a few months after the horrifying pogrom at Kishinev, a similar outrage took place in the city of Gomel in the province of Mogilev.

A new phenomenon in the history of these onslaughts was the self-defense of the Gomel Jews, which was organized to meet the emergency. Had not the troops obstructed the gallant attempt by shooting at the defenders and killing and wounding scores of them, the pogrom would have been checked at the outset. But with the protection given the rioters, it continued the whole day and left many wounded and dead in its trail as well as hundreds of wrecked homes and business establishments.[71]

Realizing that they could not rely upon the authorities for protection, Jews began after the Kishinev massacre to organize self-defense groups in every community. Had the police given these defenders a free hand instead of aiding the aggressors, Russian Jewry would have been spared many a tragedy in the first decade of this century. But again, had the police frowned upon pogroms there would have been no need for self-defense. Since the pogrom was an

69. Urussov, *Memoirs,* pp. 81–82.

70. Witte, *Memoirs,* pp. 380–381.

71. [Dubnow, *History,* III, 87–89. Also Cyrus Adler, *The Voice of America on Kishineff* (Philadelphia, 1904) and the sources cited above in n. 68. Ed.]

integral part of the anti-Jewish policies of Nicholas II, the courageous resistance proved for the most part futile. But it did help to maintain the morale and self-respect of a people whom the government sought in every way to degrade and crush.

The attacks on Jews were not interrupted even during the political spring when Prince Sviatopolk-Mirsky, Plehve's successor, sought to pacify public opinion through gestures at reform. Although Mirsky was undoubtedly opposed to anti-Jewish excesses, they had become such an institution that the minister found himself powerless to check the series of violent outbreaks in the fall of 1904. This time the excuse for the riots was the allegation of the anti-Semitic St. Petersburg daily, *Novoe Vremia* (New Times), and similar anti-Jewish publications that the Jews were conspiring with the enemy against the fatherland. Heedless of the disproportionately large number of Jews fighting and dying for the fatherland in greater Siberia, where they had no right to reside, the anti-Semitic press wrote inflammatory articles charging the Jews with evasion of military service.

These malicious falsehoods brought results. In many cities troops mobilized for war service staged violent attacks on Jews before departing for the front. Thus the homes of many reservists who were at the front fighting for their country were wrecked by their colleagues about to join them on the battlefield. This time the pogroms were not limited to the south; the mobilized troops staged riots also in White Russia. In some localities of the northwest rioting crossed religious lines, and soldiers who had begun with attacks upon Jews ended by attacking even the police. It may well be that the government was wary of resorting to stringent measures in the suppression of pogroms lest it antagonize troops whose hearts were not in the war and who resented being sent to die in a far-off land. While the departure of the troops for the front was marked thus by anti-Jewish excesses, the mobilization of Jewish reservists outside the Pale was an occasion for the expulsion of their families by the government. The minister of the interior ruled that the wives and children of physicians or artisans forfeited the right to remain in the territory forbidden to Jews as soon as their husbands or fathers had left their homes. The fact that these "privileged" Jews were called away to fight or perhaps to die for their country was not taken into account by the bureaucrats of Nicholas II. Owing to the pressure of public opinion this ruling was subsequently changed to permit the families of the reservists to remain in the privileged area for the duration of the war.

The disastrous defeat of the Russian forces by the Japanese

on land and on sea in 1904–5 was a further cause for bloody pogroms. In addition to the unbridled campaign against Jews by the anti-Semitic press, which invented all sorts of fantastic accusations, the Black Hundred declared as its program the extermination of the Jews. This organization, to be described in a subsequent chapter, was called into being by the government to save the tottering throne of Nicholas II. Owing to the combined efforts of the reactionary press and the Black Hundred, both of which had the support of the government, pogroms in which Cossacks and soldiers took part broke out in a number of cities in the spring of 1905. Particularly murderous was the pogrom in the city of Zhitomir in Volhynia, where for three days the hordes of the Black Hundred with the aid of the police and troops subjected the Jewish population to savage attacks. The heroic efforts of the Jews in self-defense proved of little avail in the face of the military protection afforded the hooligans. Thus a group of young men on their way from a nearby town to aid their brethren were intercepted by a mob that had been told Jewish murderers were on their way to slaughter Christians. A number of the young men were killed by the mob and the rest were viciously beaten.

The summer of 1905 again witnessed a series of pogroms in various parts of the Pale. These bloody incidents were but a faint prelude to the violence perpetrated by the Black Hundred which broke loose upon the Jewish populace the day after the publication of the October 17 manifesto. But before these outrages, which were unparalleled in the annals of tsarist persecution, are described, space must be given to the reaction of the Jews to the pogroms of the eighties, as well as to the history of Russia under the so-called constitutional regime.

III

THE EMIGRATION QUESTION, 1881–1905

A SQUALL passed through, thunder and lightning . . . and then a stillness followed as though everything in nature had died. Everything it seems is under the impact of one common feeling." Thus did the Russian-Jewish weekly *Razsvet* (Dawn) describe the mood of Russia following the assassination of Alexander II on March 1, 1881.

The pogroms that quickly followed in the wake of the assassination amply justified the gloomiest forebodings. Panic seized all the Jewish communities throughout the land—even those of the northwestern region, which were not smitten with the scourge of pogroms. A correspondent reporting from the city of Mariupol to *Razsvet* thus represents the mood of the Jews by paraphrasing passages of the Pentateuch: "In the morning the people were awaiting the coming of the evening, and in the evening they were anxious that the morning should come . . . The sound of a shaken leaf made them frightened and they lost all trust in life." [1]

To the fear of pogroms were added disquieting rumors about fresh discriminatory legislation contemplated by Minister of Interior Ignatiev. The convening of the provincial committees for a discussion of the Jewish problem seemed to substantiate the ominous reports circulating in the Pale.[2]

Unable to defend themselves otherwise, the Jews resorted to the aids traditional in days of stress and storm: prayer and fasting. Public fast days were declared in many communities and special services held at which penitential prayers from the High Holidays' liturgy and pertinent passages from the Bible were read. The press described a service in Odessa, a city whose Jews were not counted among the Orthodox: "When the cantor chanted the prayer, 'All the nations reside on their land but Israel wanders the earth like a shadow finding no rest, receiving no brotherly welcome,' the sobbing of the men and women in the synagogue was heart-rending." [3] A resident of St. Petersburg gave his impressions of the public service held in the synagogue attended by many Jewish intellectuals who

1. (St. Petersburg, 1881), No. 24.
2. [See above, Chapter II. Ed.]
3. *Nedelnaia Khronika Voskhoda,* (1882), No. 7, col. 158.

had long ago drifted away from Jewish observances. As the preacher in a broken voice spoke of the sad condition of Jewry, a protracted cry as if from one voice rose from the assemblage. All wept, young and old, the poor clad in their shabby gaberdines and those dressed in the height of fashion.[4]

The burial of scrolls desecrated during the anti-Jewish excesses was another occasion for expression of the grief which filled the heart of Russian Jewry. "The air was filled with heart-rending sobbing, tears were streaming from everyone's eyes when the gravediggers lowered our sacred scrolls into the grave," recounted an eyewitness.[5]

The excesses created a spiritual crisis in the lives of the Jewish intelligentsia. The pogroms shattered a dream cherished for more than a generation, that Russification would earn for the Jew civil and eventually social equality. Most deeply hurt were the extreme Russificators, one of whom expressed his disillusionment thus:

The "enlightened" Jews had repudiated their history, forgotten their traditions, and come to despise everything that made them conscious of belonging to an eternal race. Without an intelligent understanding of Jewish ideals and burdened by Judaism even as an escaped convict is hampered by heavy chains, what could compensate for their belonging to a tribe of "Christ killers" and "exploiters"? How pathetic is the position of those who advocated fusion with the Russian people through national self-abnegation. Life and the logic of events demand that the Jew define his position, for it has become impossible to occupy a seat between two chairs. Either one openly declares oneself a renegade or one decides to share the sufferings of his people.[5]

Another representative of the intelligentsia poured out his heart:

When I think of what was done to us, how we were taught to love Russia and the Russian word, how we were lured into introducing the Russian language and everything Russian into our homes; that our children know no other language but Russian, and how we are now rejected and hounded . . . my heart is filled with corroding despair from which there is no escape. This terrible insult flung at us is destroying me. It seems to me that even if I succeeded in settling in a country where all were equal and where no lootings, no Jewish committees existed, I would still remain spiritually crushed to the end of my days.[6]

4. *Razsvet* (1882), Nos. 3 and 4, quoted by Dubnow, "From the History of the Eighties," *Evreiskaia Starina,* IX (1916), 2.

5. Correspondence from the town of Berezovka, in the province of Kherson, in *Russky Evrei* (St. Petersburg, 1881), No. 41.

6. See *Razsvet* (1881), Nos. 31, 32, and 35. Also quoted partly by Dubnow, "From the History of the Eighties," pp. 24–25.

Another such penitent admitted that those who had joined the Haskalah were much happier today than those who had rejected that path. The former now pointed out to errant ones that they had no right to be angry or bitter; they had simply been mistaken, they should not be so deeply disappointed. We have no moral support, was his lament.[7]

The attitude of Russian public opinion served only to increase the spiritual torment of the Russificators. Jewish contemporaries speak of the indifference and hostility of even enlightened portions of Russian society toward their Jewish compatriots. In his memoirs the Russian-Jewish writer Ben Ami states that the worst aspect of the pogroms was that not only the general press but the best elements of the Russian public both indirectly and directly approved the anti-Jewish movement. At the height of the Odessa pogrom all his former high-school teachers, including the most liberal, regarded the excesses as justified revenge of the people against the Jews. The Ukrainian socialist writer M. Dragomanov pointed with a measure of pride to the fact that the pogroms took place only in the Ukraine. His anti-Semitism found fresh fuel in the resistance of the Ukrainian Jew to his advice that they intermarry with their non-Jewish neighbors.

Even more shocking was the stand taken by the revolutionary organization called the Narodnaia Volia (People's Will). In the barbarous attacks of the peasants upon the Jews, who were the poorest and most underprivileged element in the population, this group saw the realization of their most cherished dream: the rising of the Russian peasantry against their oppressors. To encourage the masses in what they termed a "revolt" the Narodnaia Volia issued a proclamation calling upon the tillers of the soil to destroy both the Jews and the landowners.

Commenting on the attitude of the liberal press toward these outrages, a prominent attorney and Jewish leader, Henry Sliozberg, recalls that not one of these publications put up a fight against the official anti-Semitism of the government. Nor did any of them refute the charge that the economic activities of the Jews were harmful to the country. Only occasionally was there a feeble comment from among them that the pogrom was not the proper means of solving the Jewish problem.[8] The one protest that was raised, submitted by the Moscow merchants to the minister of finance, pointed out the financial losses that resulted from the disorders.

7. *Nedelnaia Khronika Voskhoda* (1882), No. 1.

8. H. B. Sliozberg, *Dela Davno Minuvshikh Dnei. Zapiski Russkago Evreia* (Paris, 1933), I, 107.

"Where are the Russian writers and preachers of love and brotherhood whom our youth have idolized?" lamented a writer in *Razsvet*, voicing the bitterness and disillusionment of the Jewish intelligentsia. That Tolstoi and Turgenev, the two giants of Russian literature at that time, should fail to raise their voices on behalf of a martyred people was a crushing blow.[9] The one honorable exception was the famous writer M. E. Saltykov-Shchedrin, who in moving words expressed his horror at the bestialities committed against the Jews and his sympathy for the victims.

History has never recorded upon its pages a more difficult, a more inhuman, and a more painful problem than that of the Jew. The story of man is a record of never ending martyrology but at the same time it is also a chronicle of never ending enlightenment. While in the sphere of martyrdom the Jewish people occupy first place, as far as human enlightenment is concerned they are outside its reaches so that the rays of enlightenment do not touch them. There is nothing more heartbreaking in this tale of man's inhumanity to man.[10]

What was the underlying reason for this paradoxical behavior on the part of the liberal press and the Russian intelligentsia? *Russky Evrei* analyzed it as follows. Like the reactionary press, the progressive press were scantily informed on Jewish matters. The only difference in their presentation was that the latter measured their words with some care while the former did not hesitate to invent all sorts of lies about the hated objects of the calumnies. Again, the liberal press were occupied in waging battle against the reactionaries on purely Russian affairs, which absorbed their energies to the exclusion of other interests. And they did not wish to be branded pro-Jewish, as the opposing publications were quick to do whenever a generous word was recorded on behalf of the Jewish people. Lack of knowledge of the character of the Jewish people and of the conditions of their life, coupled with a deep-rooted prejudice which affected the thinking and emotions of even the most enlightened Christians, explained the anomaly of liberals and revolutionaries countenancing and encouraging violence against a people who were themselves the victims of injustice.

Faced with a hostile government which was determined to undermine even their partial rights, and surrounded by an inflamed population and a uniformly unfriendly press, the Jews found themselves

9. [Later, after the Kishinev pogrom of 1903, Tolstoi vigorously protested against the government. See above, p. 51. Ed.]

10. [Dubnow, "From the History of the Eighties," p. 24, quotes from Russian-Jewish papers of 1881 and 1882. Ed.]

in a hopeless and helpless position. They could not look even to their coreligionists abroad for aid: news of the pogroms was slow to reach the general public in the outside world. Strict censorship kept the full story even from the Russian public. E. Cherikover found in the archives of the censors' office in Kiev a number of secret circulars issued by the chief of the Press Bureau in St. Petersburg between May and September, 1881, ordering the suppression of articles dealing with the pogroms. The publication of information on the work of the provincial committees was also forbidden.[11]

It was through the Jewish refugees who fled from the scenes of carnage that the outside world learned of the happenings there. English Jewry was the first to receive a full account from the lips of a group of immigrants who on the way to the United States stopped off in Liverpool in October, 1881. About that time influential English Jews were beginning to receive confidential information forwarded secretly by a group of Orthodox leaders headed by Rabbi Isaac Elhanan Spector of Kovno. To bring the plight of their people to the attention of the civilized world these Jews in Russia formed a secret organization which not only gathered material on the pogroms but also compiled valuable data on the general situation of Russian Jewry. This information they sent secretly to the religious leaders of British, German, and French Jewry, implored them to lay the cause of Russian Jewry before the conscience of civilization.[12]

In response to this request Nathaniel Rothschild, noted Jewish financier, forwarded the material he received to the *Times* of London which utilized it for two articles, published on January 11 and 13, 1882, entitled "Persecution of the Jews in Russia." The *Times* story was taken up by the press in other countries, and expressions of condemnation of the Russian government and sympathy for the victims of the pogroms appeared in many newspapers. As a result of the *Times* articles an impressive mass meeting was held at the Mansion House in London on February 1; the lord mayor of London presided, and church and academic dignitaries participated in the denunciations and protests. This meeting raised over £100,000 for the victims of the pogroms. Similar meetings took place in a number of other large cities in England, and demands that the government intercede on behalf of Russian Jewry were made in both Houses of Parliament, where the Russian government was severely condemned for its barbarities.

In the United States, too, public opinion was aroused to a high

11. Cherikover, "New Materials on the Pogroms in Russia in the Early Eighties," *Historishe Shriften,* II, 458–459.
12. *Ibid.,* p. 460.

pitch of indignation which found expression at mass meetings, in the press, and in Congress. On the day the mass meeting was held in London a similar one took place in New York City, and there was one a month later in Philadelphia. In response to the many petitions that Congress intercede on behalf of Russian Jewry the following resolution submitted by James B. Belford of Central City, Colorado, was adopted on March 6, 1882:

Whereas the people of the United States have learned with sorrow and indignation of the miseries inflicted upon the Jews in Russia, especially in Elisabethgrad, Kieff, Odessa, Warsaw and at some three hundred other towns and villages in said Empire; and: whereas the people of the United States in the interest of civilization and humanity protest against the spirit of persecution thus revived in Russia against the Hebrews, who, as a race, have shown themselves loyal and faithful citizens and subjects wherever accorded equal rights of manhood and citizenship.

Therefore: Resolved by the Senate and House of Representatives of the United States of America in Congress assembled, that the President of the United States be requested to submit to his Imperial Majesty the Czar, the friendly assurances of the people of this nation and to request His Imperial Majesty to exercise his august power for the sake of humanity to protect the Jewish subjects from violence of their enemies and to extend to them his protection as the late lamented sovereign, his father did over the Christians of Bulgaria at a time when said Christians had been the victims of a like persecution.[13]

Acting upon this resolution, President Chester A. Arthur on April 15 instructed the chargé d'affaires, Mr. Wickham Hoffman, to bring to the attention of the Russian government in the most courteous manner the concern of the United States over the persecution of the Jews.

Embarrassed by this storm of protests, the Russian government tried to justify its conduct in the traditional anti-Semitic manner by putting the blame upon the Jews themselves. Hoffman reported to Washington that in a personal conversation Ignatiev informed him the provincial committees which had been called for a discussion of the Jewish problem unanimously recommended the expulsion of all Jews from Russia. Ignatiev further stated that the hostility of the population to the Jews made the position of the government extremely difficult. Since Hoffman had no access to the proceedings of the committees, which were kept under lock and key, he could not know that Ignatiev was lying to him about their conclusions. Igna-

13. [*Joint Resolution,* No. 151, 47th Congress, First Session. Also *Congressional Record,* Vol. 13, Pt. 2, p. 1647. Ed.]

tiev's duplicity was matched by Hoffman's naïveté when he wrote to Washington: "I am satisfied that the Russian government is truly anxious to put a stop to these riots." [14]

But public opinion in the United States was not as easily appeased as was the American representative in Russia. The press, church unions, and various other bodies continued to manifest their sympathetic interest in the Jews of Russia. Congressman Samuel S. Cox of New York delivered a lengthy address in the House on July 31, 1882, giving expression to American resentment of the maltreatment suffered by the Jews in Russia. Besides condemning anti-Jewish policies, the address contained much information on the pogroms as well as on the position of the Russian Jewry. Cox tried to prove that the government of the United States had a legal right to intercede with the Russian government on behalf of its Jewish subjects.[15]

None of these protests and resolutions would have been made in England or America without pressure, since, as is well known, governments are always reluctant to interfere with what they call the internal affairs of other countries. In spite of the fact that all foreign powers were apprized of the pogroms by their accredited representatives immediately after they occurred, none of them voluntarily interceded on behalf of the Jews. Even when urged by public opinion in England, Gladstone, the liberal premier of Great Britain, refused to make representations to the Russian government on behalf of the Jews nor would he present to Alexander III the petition of English Jewry on behalf of their Russian coreligionists. The American chargé d'affaires, Hoffman when ordered to bring the matter to the attention of the Russian government, was reminded: "This instruction devolves a delicate duty upon you, and a wide discretion is given you in its execution." [16]

14. [*Papers Relating to the Foreign Affairs of the United States.* Transmitted to Congress, with the Annual Message of the President, December 4, 1882 (Washington, Government Printing Office, 1883), p. 452. Ed.]

15. The Address was printed in the *Congressional Record, 13,* App., p. 651; also as a separate pamphlet. [According to E. Cherikover, *History of the Jewish Labor Movement in the United States,* in Yiddish, I (New York, 1943), 152, n. 27, Cox did not deliver the speech but transmitted it for publication in the *Congressional Record.* It may be pointed out that Congressman Cox had addressed Congress before that, on May 21, 1880, on the condition of Russian Jewry. Cf. Wischnitzer, *To Dwell in Safety: The Story of Jewish Migration since 1800* (Philadelphia, Jewish Publication Society, 1949), pp. 35–36. Ed.]

16. [*Papers Relating to the Foreign Affairs of the United States,* p. 451. On the intercession of the American government with the Russian government over the anti-Jewish excesses, see Cyrus Adler and Aaron M. Margalith, *With Firmness in the Right. American Diplomatic Action Affecting Jews, 1840–1945* (New York, American Jewish Committee, 1946), pp. 208 ff. Ed.]

The mass of Russian Jewry were unaware of the diplomatic intervention on their behalf and entertained no hope of foreign aid in improving their lot. Hopelessness turned to panic when in January, 1882, Count Ignatiev in an interview with Dr. Isaac Orshansky suggested that the only salvation for Russian Jewry lay in emigration. "The Western border is open to the Jews" was his sardonic invitation.[17]

Jewish leadership was sharply divided on the question whether officially to sponsor mass emigration. Although those favoring this course were strengthened by Ignatiev's statement, they were outvoted at a meeting in St. Petersburg in April, 1882. This gathering, called by Baron Horace de Günzburg with the permission of the minister of the interior, is sometimes referred to ironically as the Conference of Notables since it included a number of wealthy Jewish financiers.[18]

The Jewish upper bourgeoisie and their spokesmen were fearful that an attempt to organize, encourage, and regulate emigration from Russia might be regarded by the government as unpatriotic act. The majority of the delegates agreed that acceptance of emigration as a solution would undermine the struggle for emancipation. Some even expressed the fear that mass emigration would increase pogroms and encourage looting of the belongings and property of those planning to leave. One speaker held that all was not hopeless for Russian Jewry; the fate of three million people could not be decided by the whim of a Russian official. The Jew would never leave Russia voluntarily. Expressing the opinion of the minority which favored mass emigration, Dr. Max Mandelstam of Kiev bluntly asserted: "Either we get civil rights or we emigrate. Our human dignity is being trampled upon, our wives and daughters are being dishonored, we are looted and pillaged; either we get decent human rights or else let us go wherever our eyes may lead us."

The division of opinion was reflected in the press, where controversy raged for several years. Soon after the first wave of pogroms in 1881 *Russky Evrei*, a weekly paper, called upon Jews not to lose hope but to wait patiently for that better day "when our enemies are disgraced and all Russia realizes that we too are entitled to human rights. Pogroms are a result of rightlessness and when that has been obviated the attendant evils will vanish with it. By supporting mass emigration the Jews would be playing into the hands of their enemies, who hope that they will flee from the field of bat-

17. [Wischnitzer, *To Dwell in Safety*, p. 39. Ed.]
18. The minutes of the conference were published in *Nedelnaia Khronika Voskhoda* (1882), Nos. 32, 33, 34, and 36.

tle." [19] "Only anti-Semites," said another issue of the paper, "are blinded to the fact that our youth and even a considerable portion of our adults have become so completely Russianized that they are incapable of thinking of any other fatherland save Russia." [20] Even after Ignatiev's statement *Russky Evrei* did not change its stand but encouraged the Jews to wait patiently until their rights should be granted them. In answer to the warning of those who predicted that Jewry was faced with imminent destruction unless the people left the country, the paper predicted that the Jews of Russia would achieve the status of full-fledged citizens sooner than was thought and that in any case mass emigration could not be accomplished in a short time.[21] If Jewish emigration were to become a mass movement sanctioned by responsible leadership, it would be tantamount to admission that there was no hope of solving the problem of those remaining in the country; it would mean that "we renounce our claim to full citizenship in Russia, a right we have acquired by virtue of our sojourn here for many centuries and because of our proportionate contribution to the growth and development of the Russian state." [22]

Voskhod was also opposed to mass emigration. Prior to Ignatiev's statement the paper had advocated the establishment of special committees to regulate the chaotic flight of refugees; but now, a year later, when wholesale emigration was proposed, *Voskhod* changed its attitude. Emigration would injure the cause of emancipation and would furnish the anti-Semites with a means to discredit the loyalty of the Jews. The charge would be raised "that at the first reverses the Jews take flight and their best leaders through all possible means encourage emigration." [23]

Even in the most critical pogrom periods *Voskhod* did not relax its forthright efforts on behalf of Jewish equality. It conducted the fight with dignity and courage, and scored the self-abasing manner in which the Conference of Notables implored the government for "an authoritative word" to check the aroused animal instincts of the mob. Only a demoralized and spiritually degraded leadership, it declared, would, instead of sharply protesting the pogroms and horrible discriminations, be satisfied with soliciting, imploring, and suggesting to the government.[24]

Razsvet was the only journal which preached mass emigration as

19. *Russky Evrei* (1881), No. 31, editorial.
20. *Ibid.,* No. 24.
21. *Ibid.,* No. 25, editorial.
22. *Ibid.* (1882), No. 21, p. 786.
23. *Nedelnaia Khronika Voskhoda* (1882), No. 9, editorial.
24. *Ibid.* (1882), No. 39, editorial.

a policy. After the first pogroms in 1881, it too had for a while objected to large-scale exodus. Discussing the proposal, it made an eloquent if rhetorical plea:

Shall we flee because of the savage shouts "Beat the Jew!" Shall we move out en masse? Shall we desert the skies which witnessed our birth and the earth under which are buried our fathers who suffered not less than we did? . . . Shall we forsake the spaces which our forefathers cultivated when the *Ermaks* were still hunting wild animals? Who has a right to suggest such a thing to the Jew? The Jew will remain in Russia . . . because Russia is his fatherland, the soil of Russia his soil, the sky of Russia his sky. The Jewish problem is a Russian problem.[25]

But toward the end of 1881 *Razsvet* began to change its attitude and became the champion of organized emigration. The journal served as the medium of expression for all the broken and disillusioned in the Pale who saw in emigration their only hope for survival and rehabilitation. Without direction from any central organization, circles favoring spontaneous emigration sprang up in all parts of the Pale immediately after the pogroms. Fearful for their lives, thousands of Jews fled over the borders of Russia. Because of insufficient funds many of the would-be emigrants to the United States were stranded in European ports. Correspondents of *Razsvet* urged the establishment of central committees to direct and facilitate the movement of emigrés. Such voices became more vociferous and admonishing when the Conference of Notables decided against mass emigration. A group of Odessa university students wrote a collective letter to *Razsvet* declaring emigration the only way out. Everywhere the people were organizing and with their poor pennies maintaining emigration centers. All they were asking from the intelligentsia was information on conditions in the United States, Palestine, and other possible centers of immigration.[26] A letter with forty signatures from Nikolaev defiantly declared that the best elements in Jewry turned with repugnance from those who hampered the cause of the resurrection of the Jewish people (meaning emigration). A letter signed by the leaders of the synagogue and Talmud Torah of a town in the province of Kherson spoke of emigration as the only solution and challenged the leaders in St. Petersburg with the Talmudic query, "If not now, when?" [27] Similar letters from numerous other cities were received and published by

25. *Razsvet* (1881), No. 19. [The Cossack Ermak was a successful conqueror in Siberia in 1581. Ed.]
26. *Ibid.* (1882), No. 40.
27. *Ibid.*, No. 11.

Razsvet. A letter describing the sad condition of the Jewish villagers in the southern agricultural settlements is worthy of note. Owing to the hostile attitude of the Christian peasantry the Jewish husbandmen were fleeing to the cities or emigrating to the United States or Palestine. The letter pleaded for direction and information to guide these emigrants. "The Jewish peasant is ready and willing to work," the correspondent wrote; "he is not the spoiled and enfeebled resident of the city. He is the son of the fields, the dweller of the village, the plough and the harrow are familiar instruments to him. He needs no cities, he is in need of village life." [28]

The bitterness of the "country" against the capital grew as the Jewish leaders in St. Petersburg refused to reverse their stand on emigration. The Hebrew author Mordecai Kagan charged that the wealthy Jews refused to sponsor and direct emigration not from principle but for selfish reasons. They were unwilling, he asserted, to assume the financial burdens of such an undertaking. While it is possible that this motive may have existed, it cannot be gainsaid that the chief concern was fear of weakening the Jewish position in Russia. This certainly was the motive that prompted the selfless and devoted servant of his people, Rabbi Isaac Elhanan Spector, to vote against emigration at the Conference of Notables.

The attitude of Jewish leadership on this issue had no effect upon the masses. Driven by fear of pogroms, confined to an ever narrowing ghetto and hampered by growing economic restrictions, they yearned for a chance to build a new life for themselves in friendlier climes. The two countries which figured prominently as centers of refuge were the United States and Palestine, the first for the economic opportunities offered by its vast underpopulated areas and the second because of its sentimental historical appeal. The problem of emigration, which at first was considered from the economic and political angles, soon began to be considered also from national and cultural points of view. The question was raised whether America or any other country offering hospitality to Jewish refugees would serve as a permanent or fully satisfying solution to the problem of Jewish insecurity, both physical and spiritual. Could it guarantee the perpetuation and development of the religious and cultural values of the Jewish heritage? Did Judaism and the Jewish way of life have any chance for survival outside the Pale and in any land other than that associated with historic memories and national aspirations? These were the questions posed by the Jewish nationalists who advocated the rebuilding of Palestine as a national home as the only solution to both the economic and spiritual problems of the

28. *Ibid.,* No. 10.

Jew. Thus it came about that in the early eighties political and cultural Zionism was formulated and the Zionist movement launched in Russia.

The change of policy inaugurated with the accession of Alexander III, and the insecurity and hopelessness of the Jewish position in Russia, led the intellectuals to take stock of the condition of Jewry throughout the world. Their status even in those countries where complete or partial civil rights had been achieved caused grave concern to discerning observers. In Germany, where the Jews were emancipated in 1869, a strong and well organized anti-Semitic movement was launched in the seventies. Its aim was not only to deprive the Jews of their hard-won civil rights but in addition to impose new disabilities upon them and alienate them from the political and cultural life of the German people. It was in these years that the so-called theory of racism later adopted by the Nazis was formulated by Wilhelm Marr, Eugen Dühring, and other anti-Semitic theorists. This was the time when anti-Semitism was launched as an international movement. In 1882 an international anti-Semitic Congress was held in Dresden, with representatives from Germany, Hungary, and other countries. In central and eastern Europe anti-Semitism became a political movement threatening to undermine the position of the Jew in all European countries.

The mood of some of the Jewish intellectuals of the period is reflected in a letter of the Hebrew writer A. Friedberg, in the summer of 1881. Describing the plight of Russian Jewry who found no defenders even among the higher classes of Russian society, he observed: "Our status is shaky not only here in the land of utter darkness but also in Germany, the land of science and reason, as well as in Hungary and Galicia." The Jews of France and Great Britain enjoyed comparative security only because their number was small. The two potent factors militating against the Jewish minority in every country were economic competition and religious intolerance, which Friedberg believed would never cease. It was high time therefore for the Jew to cease being a tolerated guest in strange lands, serving as scapegoat for the sins of others. "It is high time," he exclaimed, "for Israel to obtain a place of security in the land of his ancient inheritance where the dove will find a resting place for her feet." [29]

Prominent among those who embraced Zionism and helped to formulate its philosophy was Moses Leb Lilienblum, who in his earlier years was a follower of the Haskalah, a battler for religious

29. A. Druianov, *Ketabim Letoledot Hibat Zion Veyishew Ezetz Israel,* I (Odessa, 1919), cols. 2–3.

reforms, and a disciple of the famous radical Russian thinkers G. G. Chernyshevsky and D. I. Pisarev. In a series of articles in *Razsvet* advocating the reacquisition of Palestine as a Jewish homeland, Lilienblum advanced arguments which became classic in Zionist ideology. The fundamental cause for Jewish persecution, he maintained, was the fact that in all lands the Jew was regarded as a stranger. Irrespective of the antiquity of a Jewish community, and even when the settlement of Jews antedated that of the so-called native population, the Jew was nonetheless regarded as a foreigner by the dominant nationality. In the Middle Ages he was considered a stranger in Christian Europe because of his faith; in the nineteenth century he is regarded as a stranger because of the intense nationalism of the modern state. A nation, Lilienblum maintained, is like a large family which tolerates a stranger in its midst only so long as he does not inconvenience the members of the family. As soon as he becomes burdensome he is in one manner or another asked to leave. Because of his second-class citizenship the Jew was barred from occupations engaged in by the native population. At the time when trade was considered beneath the dignity of the upper classes, the Jews were permitted to be the traders or moneylenders. But as soon as the "strangers" managed to save up some money and the native population began to engage in trade, there rose the murmur, "Had it not been for the Jew, all the wealth and trade would be ours." That banishment or massacre of the Jews brought no material gain to the country but on the contrary, as in the case of Spain, economic decline made no impression upon the Christian countries. As the anti-Semitic wave which originated in Germany swept over Europe, culminating in the pogroms in Russia, terror-stricken Jews asked: "Are the Middle Ages returning?" "I believe so," stated Lilienblum: "The cries of 'Down with the foreigner' and 'Hep Hep, *Juden heraus*' (out with the Jew) now resounding in Germany, Hungary, Russia, and Romania will continue for a long time. When the national bigotry which followed the religious intolerance of medieval times shall have exhausted itself, who knows what form the new group fanaticism will take? Naturally the Jews who have lived in Russia for centuries, whose ancestors were born and buried there, and whose sons have shed their blood for that country do not consider themselves strangers, but that does not affect the attitude of the dominant ethnic group toward them. The only solution is for the Jews to cease being strangers and acquire a homeland for themselves." In their anxiety to rid Europe of Jews the European powers would help them regain their ancient homeland, Lilienblum believed; but should they refuse to do so the Jew ought not to be deterred from colonizing Palestine, so that within a century all the Jews would be able to remove from unfriendly Europe to the land of their forefathers. All emigration efforts should be directed toward Palestine, to which Jews have a historic claim, and not toward the United States where they may again be regarded as strangers. "We need a corner of our own, we need Palestine, we need a real centre there . . . we need energy and activity. We are qualified for such an undertaking. To work!" [30]

Another convert to the cause of Zionism was the gifted novelist and publicist Lev Levanda, an ardent champion of Russification throughout the reign of Alexander II. The first wave of pogroms in 1881 shattered his dream of Russification and assimilation. In an article which appeared in 1882 in *Russky Evrei* he took to task those who were still preaching the gospel of assimilation. For the last thirty years, he reminded his readers, "our ablest men have lectured us on the benefits of assimilation in which they saw a panacea for all our ills. . . . But what shall we do if those with whom we seek to merge repulse us hand and foot, with hands armed with brass knuckles and feet shod with iron heels?" Levanda took to task the critics of the Zionist movement which was then beginning to gain its first adherents. Although he himself regarded Zionism as a fantastic dream and did not yet see it as an answer to the Jewish problem, he wanted the assimilationists to understand that desperation was impelling Jews to seek a homeland. At that time he saw only the negative motivation of the Zionist idea and thought of it solely as a counsel of despair and bewilderment on the part of a panic-stricken people. "Panic," he cautioned, "instead of extricating one from a dangerous situation only complicates matters and makes things worse." [31]

The savage pogrom in Balta in the last days of March, 1882, destroyed Levanda's final hope for a solution of the Jewish problem in Russia and caused a complete change in his attitude to Zionism. Describing the pogroms as a black cat that had crossed the path between the Jews and the Russians, he declared that it did not matter to him who had let the black cat out; what mattered was that it would be decades before the physical and moral havoc of the pogroms would be repaired. He now embraced the Zionist ideal and became its ardent exponent and consecrated servant.

In a series of feuilletons variously entitled "Flying Thoughts of

30. *Razsvet* (1881), Nos. 41–42. This article and others which Lilienblum wrote for *Razsvet* appeared in a volume, *O Vozrozhdenii Evreiskago Naroda na Sviatoi Zemle ego Drevnikh Otsov* (2d ed., Moscow, 1886).

31. *Russky Evrei* (1882), No. 1.

One Perplexed," "Dream of the Perplexed" and "Flying Comments" (signed with the initial "W"), he delivered himself of his new convictions. Instead of crawling like a worm in the dark and cringing before every passer-by pleading for pity and tolerance, the Jew must undertake to help himself; he must learn to stand on his own feet as others do. If he is to struggle and suffer, let it be for a lofty ideal and not for a miserable piece of bread. What Levanda meant by lofty idealism and self-help he made more specific in a description of a dream.[32]

In that dream he saw himself as the embodiment of the Jewish people standing as a defendant before Clio, the muse of history. She sternly warned him that some day the nations would put this question bluntly to him:

> What are you and who are you? If you consider yourself a part of us, then dissolve within us completely without any reservations or rationalizations. If on the other hand you do not wish to do so, then be yourself completely, assume the definite status of a people, and we shall gladly accept you on terms of equality as an independent link in the chain of the nations. We will not tolerate your stumbling about among these links, clutching now at one, now at another, declaring "*Ubi bene, ibi Patria* (where I thrive, there is my fatherland). If things go ill with me in Hungary, I shall go to America; if I fare badly there I shall go to Africa or Australia." In thus doing you accomplish nothing but serve as an impediment to the complete soldering of all the links in the family of nations. We should like to have you as a neighbor, a colleague, a collaborator but not as a gypsy.

Clio thereupon reminded him that he was not born a gypsy but was reduced to that state and remained thus due to the insecurity of his position everywhere and because he was lacking in vision. "You need but wish to change your status," she assured him, "and you will not find it impossible to do so." [33]

The same year that Levanda issued a call to his people to seek self-fulfillment in a national center of their own, another Russian Jew, Leo Pinsker, issued a brochure which is regarded as the canon of the Zionist movement. Published in Berlin in 1882, under the title *Auto-emanzipation, ein Mahnruf an seine Stammesgenossen* (Auto-emancipation, an Appeal to His People) and signed "by a Russian Jew," the booklet not only formulated the program of Zionism but presented a keen analysis of the Jewish position.

Pinsker, a distinguished physician and contributor to Russian-

32. *Razsvet* (1882), No. 27.
33. *Ibid.*, No. 31.

Jewish publications, had previously been an advocate of Russification. The new policies of the government and the anti-Jewish outbreaks caused a complete change in his views.

The crux of the Jewish problem, according to Pinsker, lay in the distinctive character of the Jews, who live among people with whom they are unable to merge. Normalization in their position in the family of nations was the solution, for the abnormal position of the Jews, a people without a territorial center, was the cause of their misfortune; the lack of a Jewish homeland was responsible for the ubiquitous hatred of the Jews. With the loss of their national independence the Jews had lost the status of a living nation. Ordinarily loss of the state results in the disappearance of the nation identified with it. The Jews, contrary to that rule, continued to live on spiritually as a nation even after the destruction of their physical state. The nations of the world were thus confronted with the anomalous spectacle of what they regarded as a dead nation walking in their midst. This ghostlike existence of the Jewish people strangely affected the imagination of the world; it created fear of the Jew, a fear that has passed down through the centuries and culminated in widespread Judaeophobia.

Pinsker described anti-Semitism as a variety of demonopathy and a psychic aberration which is hereditary and incurable. This abnormal attitude toward the Jews explains the variety of fantastic charges that have been made against them throughout the ages. The fact that most of the accusations were proved to be groundless did not stop the anti-Semite from inventing new and more fantastic charges. These were necessary to quiet the evil conscience of the Jew baiters, "to justify the condemnation of an entire nation, to prove the necessity of burning the Jew, or rather the Jewish ghost, at the stake."

From his analysis of Judaeophobia as a hereditary form of demonopathy, Pinsker drew the significant conclusion that combating anti-Semitism by means of polemics was useless, a waste of time and energy, "for against superstition even the gods fight in vain." Prejudice or instinctive ill will, he maintained, is not moved by rational argument, however forceful and clear.

In addition to the psychological factor, Pinsker listed two other causes breeding ill will toward the Jew. Having no country of his own, the Jew is subject to all the handicaps experienced by the foreigner in addition to those impediments resulting from his national status. While no people is fond of foreigners living in its midst, as an act of reciprocity and out of sheer self-interest each nation feels duty bound to accord hospitality to the nationals of other countries.

But the Jew, because of his national homelessness, is not subject to this general rule. There is no country where he can offer hospitality to non-Jewish nationals; he is in the position of a beggar who is not expected to repay the favors he receives. In the land of his birth the Jew is regarded neither as a native nor as a foreigner; he is, as Pinsker puts it, "in very truth, the stranger *par excellence.* He is regarded as neither friend nor foe, but as a stranger of whom the only thing known is that he has no home."

This insecurity makes him particularly vulnerable in economic competition. Since the native is usually given preference over the foreigner, the Jew who is on a lower plane than the ordinary alien has the least opportunity to earn a livelihood. Pinsker thus describes the unenviable position of the Jew in the economic struggle for existence: "With what irritation the beggar must be regarded who dares to cast longing glances upon a land, the home of others, as upon a beloved woman guarded by distrustful relatives. And if he nevertheless prospers, and succeeds in plucking a flower here and there from its soil, woe to the ill-fated man! Let him not complain if he experiences what the Jews in Spain and Russia have experienced."

In summarizing the sad state of his people, the author of *Autoemancipation* states: "For the living, the Jew is a dead man, for the natives an alien and a vagrant, for property-holders a beggar, for the poor an exploiter and a millionaire, for the patriot a man without a country, for all classes a hated rival."

Pinsker did not believe that the legal emancipation of the Jews would radically alter the situation: he pointed out that emancipation was never granted to the Jew either as a matter of course or as the spontaneous expression of human compassion. Rather it was offered as a munificent gift flung to a poor, humble, and wandering beggar. The only effective and permanent escape from the indignity of Jewish life he saw in self-emancipation; in the determination of the Jew to build a territorial center for himself and cease playing the "hopeless role of the Wandering Jew." The Jewish people "are everywhere in evidence and nowhere at home."

To achieve this purpose Pinsker urged the Jewish leaders to seek to awaken the atrophied national consciousness among the Jews and to stimulate the desire for national rejuvenation in their own land. He realized that this first step in the emancipation of Jewry would be a difficult one. Because of the traditional belief in the coming of the Messiah who would bring about their national resurrection on the soil of their ancient homeland, no attempt had been made to encourage national self-liberation. Then again, centuries of homelessness and bitter struggle for existence had caused "the people without a *fatherland* to forget their *fatherland*." Pinsker believed, however, that it was possible to arouse their dormant national consciousness and that the example of other subject and oppressed nationalities which were able to regain their independence would serve as an inspiration to the Jews and stimulate the will for national restoration.

It should be noted that the author of *Auto-emancipation* did not suggest Palestine as the territorial center of the Jews. The goal of our present endeavors must be not the Holy Land but "a land of our own." It may be in any part of the world large enough to accommodate "the Jews of all lands who must leave their homes."

To implement these ideas Pinsker suggested that a national congress or directorate be formed. This organization consisting of the leaders of Jewry should be entrusted with the selection and direction of immigration into the new Jewish homeland as well as with the general management of the affairs of world Jewry.[34]

Thus, fifteen years before the program of political Zionism was laid down by its founder, Theodor Herzl, at the first Zionist Congress in Basle, Pinsker had formulated the essential ideals and aims of Zionism in a book which for its lofty style and depth of thought has been unequaled by any subsequent work on the subject. It is in the words of Ahad Haam "the fons et origo" of all Zionist ideas and policies.

The writings of the early exponents of Zionism found a warm response in the hearts of Russian Jews. In many cities Zionist circles were formed whose program included, in addition to fund raising and propaganda, preparing *chalutzim* (pioneers) for settlement in Palestine. These clubs were soon united in a national organization, Hobebe Zion (Lovers of Zion).

Because of the difficulties the Turkish government raised against Jewish immigration as well as the slight absorptive capacity of the country at that time, the number of Jewish emigrants to Palestine in the eighties was negligible. The main stream of emigration flowed to the United States. To Russian Jews seeking a refuge from massacre and persecution America was the promised land, the land of opportunity and freedom.[35] The contemporary press gives a lively description of the emigration fever that seized the Jewish popula-

34. [An English translation, *Auto-emancipation—an Admonition to His Brethren by a Russian Jew,* D. S. Blondheim, Jr., appeared in New York, in 1896 and 1906. All quotations from this translation. A new translation was published by Masada, New York, 1939. The pamphlet is also included in *Writings and Addresses of Leo Pinsker* (New York, Scopus Publishing House, 1944). Ed.]

35. [Simon Dubnow was a champion of the mass movement to America. See Wischnitzer, *To Dwell in Safety,* p. 52. Ed.]

tion throughout Russia. In their eagerness to leave the country Jews disposed of their belongings for practically nothing. Particularly smitten with this fever were the petty traders and those with no special occupation. Enthusiastic letters received from those who had reached the shores of America accelerated the movement for emigration.[36] A correspondent from Kovno stated that almost the entire Jewish youth of that city, including high-school students, were preparing to emigrate. "Yesterday two hundred families passed Kovno en route to the United States," he wrote, "and tomorrow thirty families are leaving from our own city." [37]

Abraham Cahan, an emigrant of that period, recounted that even Jews of good financial status joined the emigrants. He described the enthusiasm of the emigrants as "religious," since to most of them it was not merely a quest for personal salvation; they were concerned with establishing a new home for the entire Jewish people.[38]

The stream of emigration from Russia to America proceeded uninterruptedly throughout the eighties. The number of Jewish immigrants to the United States from Russia in the years 1881–90 totaled 135,003 souls.[39]

In 1891 the movement from Russia assumed even greater proportions as a result of the rumors circulating in the spring of 1890 about impending Jewish disabilities. The expulsion from Moscow and the economic crisis in Russia intensified Jewish anxiety to seek a new haven. The economic depression was particularly disastrous for the population of the Pale, where as a result of the influx of Jews driven from Moscow and other parts of the interior, competition was bitter and unemployment widespread.

On March 3, 1891, Charles Foster, secretary of the United States Treasury, appointed two commissioners, John B. Weber and Dr. Walter Kempster, to investigate the causes leading to emigration to the United States from Europe. They spent several months in Russia touring the most important cities in and outside the Pale. The report they submitted to the secretary [40] included a brief survey of the history of the Jews in Russia. After a careful study of the Jewish community of Moscow following the expulsion of the major-

36. *Hameliz* (St. Petersburg), October 6 and 27, 1881.

37. *Ibid.*, April 27, 1882.

38. A. Cahan, *Bleter fun mein Leben* (New York, 1926), II, 18.

39. Samuel Joseph, *Jewish Immigration to the United States from 1881–1910* (New York, Columbia University, 1914), p. 93.

40. [Cf. *Letter from the Secretary of the Treasury, transmitting A Report of the Commissioners of Immigration upon the Causes Which Incite Immigration to the United States*. Vol. I, Reports of Commissioners (Washington, Government Printing Office, 1892), in *The Executive Document 235 of the House of Representatives 1891–92*, 52d Congress, First Session, Pt. 1. The report was the work of commissioners J. B. Weber and Dr. Walter Kempster who visited Russia in 1891 for that purpose. Hereafter cited as Weber and Kempster, *Report*. Ed.]

ity of its members,[41] the commissioners found that the overpowering desire of those left was to emigrate.

Nearly all of them are artisans or have been business men of some kind, and in general their appearance indicates industry and character. All told the same story: the tailor, whose customers have left; the butcher, whose business has been ruined because of the exodus; old men, women and children importuning the committee [Moscow Jewish Relief Committee] to give heed to their cries and help them get away from their surroundings, any place being better than here where they are living in constant terror of persecution. Homes are destroyed, business ruined, families separated, all claiming that they are not criminals except that they are charged with being Jews; all expressing a willingness and an anxiety to work, begging for the opportunity to begin life somewhere, where they do not know nor do they care. The overpowering desire on the part of all of them is to get away from here, whether it is to America, Brazil, Africa or the Argentine Republic.[42]

The same pressure for emigration the commissioners found everywhere in the Pale. In Minsk they were told that the overcrowded labor market, due to the influx from the interior, was compelling numbers already there to leave for Africa, Australia, Palestine, the Argentine, and America.[43]

The place America held in the imagination of Russian Jewry is described in the following passage: "Aside from a small proportion of Jews who look longingly and hopefully toward Palestine, next to their religion and their persistent eagerness for education, America is the present hope and goal of their ambition, toward which their gaze is directed as earnestly as that of their ancestors toward the promised land."[44] To the tormented and persecuted Jews of tsarist Russia America was not only a land of greater economic opportunity but held out the hope of religious and political equality. A Jewish contractor in fairly good circumstances stated to the American officials that soon after the promulgation of the May Rules he began to study English to "learn the language of a nation where men are regarded as human beings."[45]

The accelerated flow of emigration in the nineties was in no small measure due to the readiness of relatives who had settled in America in the previous decades to aid emigrants in their passage. "We found," the commissioners said, "that America was by no means an

41. *Ibid., passim.*
42. *Ibid.*, p. 58.
43. *Ibid.*, p. 67.
44. *Ibid.*, p. 71.
45. *Ibid.*, p. 73.

unknown country to them, and that many of the families have relatives and friends in the United States."[46]

In 1891 Baron Maurice de Hirsch attempted to divert Jewish emigration to other countries suitable for receiving new settlers. One of the wealthiest men of his time, the baron devoted the greater part of his life to philanthropy.[47] A German Jew by birth, he was interested in the plight of his fellow Jews throughout the world, particularly those suffering from persecution. Believing that Jews could rebuild their lives through agriculture and as artisans, he offered to establish a fund of 50,000,000 francs in Russia for the organization of farm and trade schools. When the Russian government insisted on administering the fund, Hirsch withdrew his offer and decided to encourage the emigration of Russian Jews to underpopulated lands suitable for colonization. In 1891 the baron founded the Jewish Colonization Association in London, with a capital of £10,000,000, for the purpose of assisting the emigration of Jews from countries of persecution to any other part of the world, particularly to countries in South and North America where they could establish colonies of new settlers. For this purpose he commissioned a group of experts to explore the absorptive capacity of various South American countries. The Argentine Republic was selected as the most suitable place for the project. The population was sparse, there was an abundance of good land, and the government was willing to receive new immigrants. By relieving the pressure of immigration to the United States through diverting at least part of it to the Argentine, the philanthropist hoped to avoid the racial friction which a heavy influx of aliens might create in America.

The Argentine experiment proved abortive. In spite of the careful selection of emigrants by Hirsch's agents in Russia, the new settlers could not cope with either the climate or their new environment. Unlike Palestine, which though barren and neglected for centuries held its settlers by virtue of historic memories and the will to rebuild themselves as a nation, and unlike the United States which held forth the hope of a life of freedom and equality, the Argentine had nothing spiritual to offer the first Jewish pioneers. Thus only a trickle of emigration was diverted there, while the main stream continued to flow to the United States. This stream was not checked when Russia, through the October manifesto of 1905, became a so-called constitutional monarchy. On the contrary, it continued to swell as Russia plunged deeper into reaction.[48]

46. *Ibid.*, p. 71.
47. See his article "My Views on Philanthropy," *North American Review* (July, 1891), No. 416, pp. 1–4.
48. [See Wischnitzer, *To Dwell in Safety*, pp. 81–82, 105–107. Ed.]

IV

THE FIRST REVOLUTION AND THE PERIOD OF REACTION, 1905–17

NICHOLAS II never intended to keep the pledge he made to his people in the manifesto of October 17. He had been forced to make a conciliatory gesture because of the general strike which paralyzed every activity in the country. But the emperor and his camarilla had decided to crush the revolutionary spirit by diverting it toward bloody attacks upon the Jews. The day after the issuance of the manifesto a wave of pogroms broke out in more than three hundred cities with casualties running up to the tens of thousands.

Organized by the monarchist Union of Russian People actively assisted by the local authorities, the pogroms in each city started with a prearranged signal. Someone, supposedly of course a Jew, would fire upon a patriotic procession carrying a portrait of the tsar, and the mob infuriated would fall upon the Jewish population. The pogrom usually lasted three or four days, while the police professed their helplessness to check the fury of the crowd. But on the fourth or fifth day, when the police finally intervened, the mob was dispersed and order restored in many areas without a shot being fired.[1]

Addresses delivered from the rostrum of the first and second Dumas, which sent their own commissions to study the causes of pogroms in several Russian cities, made the guilt of the police authorities apparent. Criminal connivance and negligence were also substantiated by a number of official communications which came to light during the era of the pogroms. The revelations made by the special investigating committee formed by the Provisional government immediately after the collapse of the Romanov regime in March, 1917, only confirmed what was common knowledge during the existence of the tsardom: the government of Nicholas II itself engineered and perpetrated periodic massacres upon its Jewish citizens.

The conduct of the authorities of Odessa during the pogrom that lasted there from October 18 to 22 is typical. An account submitted to Nicholas II by Senator Kuzminsky, who was commissioned to investigate the excesses there, serves as an indictment of the city

1. See Dubnow, *History,* III, 124 ff.

government despite the senator's efforts to cast the blame upon the Jewish inhabitants who, he alleged, provoked the onslaught by offending the patriotic sensibilities of the Russian people. In his eagerness to absolve the local authorities, the senator involved himself in glaring contradictions. At one point he stated that he could find no proof of the charge made by the local populace that the patriotic demonstration which set off the pogrom was sanctioned by General D. B. Neidhart, the police chief of the city. At another point he mentioned the testimony of the district attorney of Odessa that Neidhart had confessed to him how on the morning of October 18 he had issued a permit for the demonstration.

The procession, according to Kuzminsky's report, stopped at the residences of the commander of the military forces, General A. V. Kaulbars, and of the police chief, and was greeted by both in a friendly manner. Then followed the usual procedure. Someone fired at the procession and killed the boy who carried the ikon. The mob immediately responded with cries of "Beat the Jews!" "Death to the Jews!" Rioters proceeded to loot business places and break into Jewish homes where they perpetrated brutal crimes. Prominent gentile citizens of Odessa, eyewitnesses to these atrocities, testified. One Russian physician said that he witnessed the murder of a young Jewish girl, that the rioters hurled children from second and third stories into the street, and that one of them, seizing a child by its feet, smashed its head against a wall.

What was the attitude of the police and the military during the pogrom? To punish the population for attacks upon policemen by revolutionaries Neidhart ordered all police taken off the streets, so that during the four days of rioting there were none on duty. And whenever the police did appear on the scene, instead of curbing the mob they directed the pillaging and murdering, in many instances supplying weapons. One army officer reported that when a detachment of soldiers under his command sought to drive off a band of pillagers a policeman tried to dissuade him from interfering with the mob. An army captain stated that in answer to his question why the pogroms were not stopped a policeman replied that the authorities had permitted the beating of Jews for three days. Another policeman informed the same officer that when he telephoned to his precinct about the outbreak of the disorders he was told it was "not his business" and was ordered not to interfere. There were also instances where policemen fired into the air or at the ground and then, charging that the shots had come from Jewish residences, ordered troops to fire into homes and dispose of the inhabitants.

The head of a naval school at Odessa testified to Senator Kuzminsky that he and a relative saw police not only participating in pogroms but actually engineering them. On October 20 several "patriotic" processions carrying the tsar's portrait and ikons emerged from a police station and in the presence of the policemen accompanying them fell to looting Jewish stores. The military detachment that patrolled the neighborhood made no attempt to interfere.[2]

The criminal activity of the troops during the pogrom was a direct consequence of the attitude of the police. Noting the benevolent manner of the police toward the hoodlums, the soldiers drew the logical conclusion that the crowd had the sanction of the authorities. Consequently, instead of dispersing the mob, they fired at the Jewish defenders. A gentile physician reported that an army officer, who looked on indifferently while a band of ruffians were torturing a group of Jews to death, observed with satisfaction, "Well, you wanted no government, so you have none." It was also established by eyewitness accounts that soldiers themselves participated in looting and murdering Jews.[3]

According to official figures, more than 500 people were killed during the Odessa pogrom, of whom around 400 were Jews, and of the 289 wounded 237 were Jews. The senator's report states, however, that since it was difficult to ascertain the exact number of all the pogrom victims it might safely be assumed the actual number exceeded the official figures.[4]

The behavior of the Odessa authorities was typical of that of the police throughout the country during those fateful days of October 18–22. Official documents which later came to light show that the local authorities did not act on their own responsibility. A report from the chief of the Central Police Department, A. A. Makarov, to P. N. Durnovo, minister of the interior, dated February 15, 1906, is revealing. It states that with the knowledge and approval of the Central Police Department Budogovsky, assistant to the chief of the gendarmerie of Ekaterinoslav Province was preparing a pogrom in one of the cities of that province. To arouse the masses he distributed leaflets in which the "genuine Russian People" were called upon to destroy the Jews and the revolutionaries, "monstrous creatures" who, with the Social Democrats, had so distressed the "little father," the tsar, that he had become prematurely grey.

2. See *Materialy k Istorii Russkoi Kontr-Revolutsii* (St. Petersburg, 1908), I, 137. Henceforth cited as *Materialy*.

3. *Ibid.*, I, cxlviii–clvi. Also J. Lawrinowitsch, *Kto Ustroil Pogromy v Rossii?* (Wer ist der Urheber der Pogrome?) (Berlin, 1908), pp. 95–100.

4. *Materialy*, I, clxvi.

"Wake up, arise great Russian people, organize fighting brigades, arm yourselves . . . and go forth in defense of your tsar, your fatherland, and the Greek Orthodox faith." [5] For his patriotic services, Budogovsky was recommended for reward by his superiors in St. Petersburg.

A few weeks after the opening of the first Duma on April 27, 1906, a bloody pogrom broke out in the city of Bialystok, which lasted from June 1 to 3. On June 2 an interpellation was addressed in the Duma to Stolypin, minister of the interior, regarding the disorders in Bialystok and the steps the government had taken to check them. A number of deputies used that occasion for a general discussion of the government's policies respecting pogroms. V. D. Nabokov, a member of the liberal Cadet party, charged that the central authorities were often the instigators of mob violence against the Jews.[6] Leaders of other parliamentary factions openly accused the government of engineering the pogroms as a counterrevolutionary measure and absolved the Russian people of any responsibility for the outrages committed upon Jewish citizens.[7]

Dr. Shmarya Levin, a deputy, pointed out that the Jews were singled out for attack by the government because they were the weakest element in the body politic and were identified with the classes of Russian society struggling for freedom.[8]

The Duma decided to appoint a commission from its own membership to investigate the origin and causes of the pogrom in Bialystok. But before the committee had returned with its report the question of complicity of the government was again raised in the Duma in connection with the accusation that the St. Petersburg police were printing and distributing inflammatory literature among the peasantry and the army. A number of prominent deputies, among them Prince S. D. Urussov, former assistant minister of the interior and governor of Bessarabia, bluntly pinned the blame for the pogroms on the government. So convincing was Urussov's address that at its conclusion many deputies shouted "pogrom makers" at the ministers. A formal vote by the Duma denounced the government as responsible for the pogrom.[9]

The report of the commission on the Bialystok affair served as another occasion for the first Duma to discuss the pogroms. Accord-

5. See *ibid.*, I, lxxxvii–xcii, for the full text of the report.
6. *Gosudarstvennaia Duma. Sessia Pervaia. Stenograficheskye Otchoty* (Stenographic Reports) (St. Petersburg, 1906), II, 952–953.
7. *Ibid.*, II, 957.
8. *Ibid.*, II, 953–954.
9. *Ibid.*, II, 1129–1132.

ing to the findings of the committee, the pogrom in Bialystok was the work of the Black Hundred actively assisted by the police and military authorities. In his address the chairman of the committee, deputy Arakantsev, rejected the charge of the Bialystok authorities that the riots were caused by the people's resentment of Jewish activity in the revolutionary movement. He emphatically denied the existence of any enmity between Jews and Christians in Bialystok. The pogrom in which soldiers and police joined the mob was planned and executed, he asserted, by the state and municipal authorities.[10] The debate on the Bialystok affair lasted for several days and terminated with the adoption of a resolution which put the entire responsibility for the pogrom upon both the local and the central authorities and demanded the resignation of the Cabinet.[11]

In a truly parliamentary regime such an expression of censure and lack of confidence in the ministry would have brought about the fall of the government; in tsarist Russia it was not the ministry but the Duma that was dismissed. Two days after the passage of this resolution an imperial placard posted on the doors of the Duma announced its dissolution because the deputies meddled in affairs out of their jurisdiction and presumed to investigate the conduct of authorities responsible only to the tsar.

The disbanding of the Duma called forth a fresh outbreak of revolutionary terror which Stolypin sought to crush in turn by terror—the field courts-martial. To combat the revolutionary spirit among Jewish youths the government continued to rely on its old and tested method, the pogrom. In August troops massacred Jews in the city of Sedlets. The casualties came close to two hundred. An official report submitted by an army officer to the governor general of Warsaw in September, 1906, which described the barbarities committed, specifically named a Colonel Tikhanovsky as responsible for the planning and execution of the massacre. Instead of punishing the criminal officer, however, General Scalon, the governor general of Warsaw and chief of the armed forces of the Warsaw region, commended his activity and expressed genuine gratitude.[12]

"After the hideous crimes of Bialystok and Sedlets," wrote J. Lawrinowitsch, "the pogroms which occurred in 1906 in Gomel, Vologda, Tsaritsin [now Stalingrad], Simbirsk [Ulianovsk], and Murom, and the innumerable smaller pogroms engineered by the Black Hundred in Odessa, will appear as child's play. But these

10. *Ibid.*, II, 1583–1603.

11. *Ibid.*, II, 2087–2088. For the English translation of the commission's report and the resolution adopted by the Duma, see *American Jewish Year Book, 5667 (1906/07)* (Philadelphia, Jewish Publication Society of America), pp. 70–89.

12. *Materialy*, I, 405–414.

'games' cost tens of human lives, the destruction of entire districts in many a city, and millons in material damages." [13]

The moral deterioration of the tsarist regime went on apace. In 1905 the attacks on the Jews were conducted by the Union of Russian People under the protection of the police and soldiers; in 1906 they were directly organized and conducted by the army. From benevolent neutrality toward the Black Hundred in their war on the Jews in 1905, the government turned the following year to open belligerence.

The manner in which the government conducted the trials of the pogrom makers is additional proof of its direct responsibility for the Jewish massacres. Generally only professional thieves or ignorant peasants apprehended on the last day of the pogrom received any sort of punishment. Induced or actually ordered in the tsar's name by the local police to pillage and murder Jews these victims of ignorance and bigotry were made the scapegoats of tsarist "justice." At the same time the real engineers of the massacres were rewarded for their "services" to the country, most of them receiving promotions or special bonuses. The cases of D. B. Neidhart, police chief of Odessa, P. G. Kurlov, the governor of Minsk, and Komissarov, of the Central Police Department, are typical. Komissarov had been responsible for installing in the Police Department the press for printing the inflammatory literature already referred to. Exonerated by the courts, Neidhart and Kurlov were promoted to higher posts; and Komissarov, whose subversive activity was the subject of an acrimonious discussion in the first Duma, received a gift of 10,000 rubles from a special secret fund.[14]

The shamelessness of the government was particularly glaring in its treatment of those Jews who had been arrested while defending themselves during the pogroms. These gallant young men who had risked their lives to save brothers and sisters from murder and rape were given harsh sentences. Under the influence of I. G. Shcheglovitov, minister of justice, who interceded on behalf of all those accused of participating in the pogroms, the courts meted out severe punishment to Jews guilty of resisting. In Odessa a military court which sentenced a group of such youths to a long term of penal servitude justified its action on the ground that the defendants were members of the Jewish proletariat which sought to overthrow the government by armed attacks upon the army and police. A higher military court upheld this specious verdict, and similar ones were issued by the courts in every city where Jews were tried for resisting. In

13. *Kto Ustroil Pogromy v Rossii?*, p. 40.
14. *Ibid.*, pp. 196–197.

a literal sense the court was quite right in asserting that these Jews were engaged in antigovernment activity, for by resisting the pogromists who were abetted by the police and the troops they were also resisting the government at whose instigation and instructions these armed mobs operated.

Along with the physical attacks in the streets came legal assault on the Jews, with such endlessly adverse interpretations of laws affecting them that life in the period following the revolution of 1905 became a nightmare for them. It is significant that Stolypin himself favored a milder treatment. In the capacity of minister of the interior he had in 1907 instructed the governors of the interior provinces by circular to stop the expulsion of Jews who had settled there before August 1, 1906. When he assumed the premiership after the dissolution of the first Duma, the Cabinet under his presidency adopted a resolution in favor of the gradual abolition of all Jewish disabilities. But upon the emperor's rejecting this,[15] Stolypin quickly changed his attitude and embarked upon a course of militant anti-Semitism.

The third or Black Duma, convoked on November 1, 1907, did nothing to alleviate the brutal arbitrariness of the police toward the Jewish populace. Whereas the first two Dumas heard noble addresses in defense of the Jews, reactionary deputies in the third Duma echoed the vicious and scurrilous charges made in the yellow sheets of the Black Hundred. From the rostrum of that Duma such notorious anti-Semites as V. M. Purishkevich, N. E. Markov, and others preached their gospel of hatred and bigotry to millions of Russians.

Typical of these attacks was an interpellation about the Stolypin circular of 1907. A group of deputies entered on November 26, 1908, an urgent interpellation charging that the government was showing favoritism toward the Jews because it had been bribed by them. During the ensuing debate Markov spewed his usual venom at the Jewish people. A deputy from the left correctly observed that it was a cruel joke to accuse of friendship for the Jews a government that subjected them to pogroms, robbed them of the most elementary human rights, and made them pariahs. One who is shameless enough to make such statements, he said, passes the bounds of minimum decency and he loses his claim to be called human.[16]

It was in the third Duma that the suggestion was made to eliminate Jews from the army, which would invalidate their claim to citizen-

15. Witte, *Memoirs*, p. 384.

16. *Gosudarstvennaia Duma. Stenograficheskye Otchoty Tretei Dumy, Vtoraia Sessia, Chast I* (Third Duma, Second Session, Pt. I) (St. Petersburg, 1908), pp. 1850–1857.

ship. This recommendation provided an occasion for the hackneyed charges of disloyalty, cowardice, evasion of military service, and corruption of the morale of the armed forces. The brilliant defense by liberal and socialist deputies, who sought to prove statistically that the Jews contributed more than their share of recruits and that Jewish soldiers fought bravely and earned rewards for distinguished service, failed to impress Judaeophobes bent on heaping calumnies upon their hated victims.[17]

Jew-baiting from the platform of the Duma strengthened the prevailing impression that the victim was a defenseless creature to be mistreated with impunity, and tsarist officials lost no time in exploiting Jewish helplessness. A case in point is the arbitrariness with which many governors interpreted Stolypin's circular. One clause permitted local officials to judge the fitness of Jews to remain in their provinces, provided they held innocuous political views, were acceptable to their gentile neighbors, and had established settlement before August 1, 1906. Accordingly, anti-Semitic governors so twisted the interpretations of this law as to expel Jews with permanent rights of residence. There were even instances where people who had never been previously arrested for political offenses were exiled. The ludicrousness of some of these charges was highlighted when an investigation revealed that two sons of one family accused of political propaganda were minors, aged fifteen and eight.[18] Others in the community who had every right to live there were subjected to extortion by the so-called "good officials" to obtain a clean bill of political health.

There were other opportunities for officials, particularly those in charge of areas outside the Pale, to terrorize Jewish inhabitants. Since the residence of most Jews there was contingent upon their practicing a particular profession or craft, their lives were subject to constant scrutiny and uncertainty. One governor, for example, ordered the expulsion of a group of midwives because of too few births to warrant their presence. "The Jewish question," writes L. Kliachko, "occupied the administration both day and night. During the daytime they checked whether Jews engaged in occupations which entitled them to rights of residence and at night they staged raids for those Jews who either had no rights or had lost them owing to change of status." [19]

In some instances, as the following episode illustrates, governors

17. [Cf. "Duma Gosudarstvennaia," *Evreiskaia Enciclopedia,* Vol. VII, cols. 374–375; also Dubnow, *History,* III, 155–156. Ed.]
18. Cf. L. Kliachko, "Za Chertoi," *Evreiskaia Letopis,* III, 156–158.
19. *Ibid.,* p. 159.

would expel Jews for personal reasons. A. Khvostov, governor of Nizhni Novgorod and later minister of the interior, once summoned the rabbi of Novgorod and threatened to banish a Jewish family from his province each time *Rech* (Speech), the organ of the Cadet party, attacked the government and his administration.[20]

The sharp surveillance of the "sacred" area outside the Pale was not left entirely to the discretion of the local administration. Watchful eyes in the Ministry of the Interior were always on the alert for the slightest infraction of residence privilege. In a report to the Senate Stolypin in 1909 called attention to the fact that Jewish merchants who enjoyed the privilege of temporary visits to the capital for business purposes often bought merchandise in which they did not deal within the Pale. He asked the Senate about the legality of a tobacco merchant's purchasing a shipment of fish in St. Petersburg.[21] The next year Stolypin raised the question whether Jews were entitled to live in summer resorts outside of city limits, localities ordinarily barred to Jews even within the Pale. The Senate replied that the law was clear on the subject and left the matter to the discretion of local authorities who no doubt interpreted it to suit themselves.[22]

The brazen manner in which corrupt officials exploited the lack of Jewish rights furnishes many tragi-comic instances. There were a few apartment houses in St. Petersburg where, by bribing the police, Jews could spend a few days and sometimes prolong the privilege for months or even years. The police captain or his assistant would receive his "salary" on a weekly or monthly basis. One man who had been paying a monthly tribute for such protection decided to secure legal rights of residence through baptism, and confronted the police sergeant with a baptismal certificate when he next came to collect his bribe.

For a substantial remuneration some government officials would go so far as to hide Jews in their own homes. It was common knowledge among Jews that a certain police captain in St. Petersburg ran his ten-room house as a hotel for "illegal" Jews, charging them 10 rubles a day. This debauchee and drunkard boasted of his tolerance and affection for Jews and encouraged his guests to observe their religion in his home. So Jews with prayer shawls and phylacteries were to be found chanting the ancient Hebrew prayers in the home of the district captain not far from the police station.[23]

20. J. V. Gessen, *V Dvukh Vekakh. Zhiznenny Otchot,* in Arkhiv Russkoi Revolutsii, XXII (Berlin, 1937), 297.
21. *Evreiskaia Letopis,* II, 117.
22. *Evreiskaia Enciclopedia,* Vol. X, cols. 420–421.
23. *Evreiskaia Letopis,* II, 120–122.

The Jews not only were a source of enrichment for the greedy servants of the tsar but also served as a means to political advancement. No wonder the notorious Plehve stated that expulsion of all Jews would be vigorously opposed by both government officials and the Black Hundred.[24] That Plehve himself used anti-Semitism to achieve promotion is attested by Witte from his intimate knowledge of him. "Personally he had nothing against the Jews," wrote Witte. "This I know from my numerous talks with him on the Jewish question. He possessed enough intelligence to understand that he was following an essentially wrong policy. But it pleased Grand Duke Sergei Alexandrovich and apparently His Majesty. Consequently, he exerted himself to the utmost." Thus the man who according to Witte was the leading spirit in the anti-Jewish policy and author of all the anti-Jewish laws and administrative measures under both Ignatiev and Durnovo pursued this course against his own convictions in order to curry favor with the tsar and his court advisers.[25] As we have seen, Stolypin, too, although privately favoring the gradual removal of Jewish disabilities, reversed his policy the moment it met with Nicholas II's disapproval. Accordingly, the expulsions of Jews from areas outside the Pale and from villages inside the Pale assumed a mass character. In the spring of 1910 twelve hundred Jewish families were exiled from Kiev in the most brutal manner with neither the aged nor infants spared.

The numerus clausus, introduced for Russian schools for the first time in 1887 as an administrative measure,[26] was never rigidly observed until after the revolution of 1905. Even the minister of education, Delianov, who inaugurated the restrictions and instructed the administrators to enforce them strictly, made many exceptions. Of the 82 Jewish students who were admitted in 1897 to the University of Odessa, 71 were registered above the quota at the personal instructions of Delianov. To be sure, many deserving Jewish students were barred from institutions of higher learning by the quota system, since not all of them could obtain the personal interviews with Delianov which usually resulted in admission. Thus only 45 out of 80 applicants were admitted to the University of Kiev in 1897.[27] The ministers who succeeded Delianov were not as amenable to personal appeals, and his immediate successor further limited the number of Jewish students by applying the quota system to individual departments. The political spring, however, brought con-

24. *Ibid.*, III, 156.
25. Witte, *Memoirs*, p. 380.
26. See pp. 34–35.
27. S. Pozner, *Evrei v Obshchei Shkole*, p. 89.

siderable relief to Jewish students. As a result of the general relaxation of police repression, both central and local educational authorities adopted a more liberal attitude. And when the institutions of higher learning were granted autonomy in 1905, their administrations began to disregard the numerus clausus altogether. The leading Russian academicians, it should be noted, frowned upon educational restrictions for Jews. They made their attitude clear at the convention of representatives of Russian universities in 1906. Assembled to prepare new statutes for the institutions of higher learning, the elected representatives unanimously adopted a resolution that their doors be open to all eligible candidates without regard to sex, faith, or national origin.[28]

But the reactionary policy inaugurated by Stolypin was soon reflected in the treatment of Jewish students. In the fall of 1907 the minister of education instructed the authorities of Odessa University to abide by the 10 per cent quota. On September 16, 1908, an imperial decree confirmed the numerus clausus as law. Stolypin did not submit the measure to the third Duma, which was then in session; as in preconstitution days it was passed by a decision of the Cabinet and approved by the emperor. On August 22, 1909, it was also fixed in the secondary schools. Instead of the former 3 per cent, 5 per cent of Jewish students were to be admitted into the secondary schools of Moscow and St. Petersburg; in the schools within the Pale the percentage was raised from 10 to 15, while the 10 per cent quota in schools outside the Pale was left undisturbed. The mild concessions made by the new statute were vitiated by extension of the numerus clausus to private schools enjoying the status of government schools. On March 11, 1911, the percentage norm was extended to the "externs." It is to be kept in mind that large numbers of Jewish youths who were denied entrance into secondary schools had previously been able to take final examinations at such schools after covering the prescribed curriculum under private tutors. Diplomas awarded to those externs who had successfully passed the examinations would qualify them for admission to a university either in Russia or abroad. But as the number of Christian externs was practically nil, the ukase of March 11 barred the last avenue by which Jewish students might escape their educational disabilities.[29]

These restrictions were in line with the intensified anti-Jewish campaign which followed the suppression of the revolution of 1905. The periodic pogroms which kept the Jews in a state of terror, the expulsion from areas outside the Pale, the never ending ministerial

28. *Ibid.*, p. 94.
29. [Dubnow, *History*, III, 158–159. Ed.]

circulars and senatorial interpretations piling disability upon disability, and the narrowing opportunities for education marked the Stolypin period as the worst in the history of Russian Jewry. In this counterrevolutionary era the Jews suffered more than any other element in the population. Deputy N. M. Friedman recalled in the Duma in February, 1910, that even in the harsh days of Plehve Jews were not subjected to such cruel treatment.[30]

Evidently to justify its extreme anti-Jewish policy and to discourage attempts made by liberal and socialist groups in the third Duma to raise the question of Jewish equality, the government conceived a monstrous plan to deal the Jews a mortal blow. On February 9, 1911, liberals and socialists opened discussion on a bill proposing to abolish the Pale. It met with violent opposition from the rightist groups. During the ensuing debate Markov, one of the leading spirits in the Union of Russian People, branded the Jews a criminal race and enemies of mankind: only the government was powerful enough to keep them in check and protect the defenseless Russian people against their machinations. He delivered a similar diatribe before the Congress of the United Nobility then convening in St. Petersburg, of which he was also a member. The political platform of this organization, which represented the most reactionary elements of the wealthy landowners, resembled that of the Union of Russian People. The program formulated in 1911 not only demanded the retention of all existing restrictions but advocated the systematic and complete elimination of Jews from the country. The congress reinforced its demand with the charge of ritual murder. No civilized and cultured society, it stated, could tolerate so barbaric a people. "All the Jews must be driven within the Pale, this is the first act. The second act is to drive them out of Russia entirely." [31]

The rightist press gave wide and sympathetic publicity to the proceedings of the congress, and of its own accord made even more drastic demands: "The government must recognize that the Jews are dangerous to the life of mankind in the same measure as wolves, scorpions, reptiles, poisonous spiders, and similar creatures which are destroyed because they are deadly for human beings; such destruction is even favored by law. The Jews must be placed under such conditions that they will gradually die out. This is the present task of the government and of the best men in the country." [32]

The demands of the monarchist organizations and their press

30. [*Ibid.*, p. 157. Ed.]

31. Alexander B. Tager, *The Decay of Tsarism. The Beiliss Trial* (Philadelphia, Jewish Publication Society of America, 1935), pp. 19–20.

32. *Ibid.*, p. 21. [The debasing name "Zhids" was used for the Jews. Ed.]

were the signal for the new and barbarous attacks the government was preparing against the Jews. Testimony gathered by the special investigating committee formed by the Provisional government in 1917 after the collapse of the tsarist regime confirmed what had been known at the time: that the Union of Russian People and similar "patriotic" organizations were subsidized by the government. Markov admitted to the committee that he himself had received a monthly subsidy of 12,000 rubles to publish *Zemshchina*, the organ of the United Nobility, and that this allowance came from the government's special secret fund of 10,000,000 rubles.[33]

Hired patriots prepared public opinion for the new blow the government was to deal Russian Jewry. As a spearhead for the assault they planned to use the medieval ritual murder charge raised in the Congress of the United Nobility and in the rightist press. In place of the accusation of revolutionary participation, which was growing stale, it was necessary to conduct a campaign along new lines in order to divert the people's rising dissatisfaction with the government; for toward the end of his career Stolypin's reactionary policies united virtually all classes and parties in Russia against the government. Owing to the scandalous exploits of Rasputin, who had such control of the emperor and his wife that he enjoyed unbridled power,[34] even the conservative Octobrists became dissatisfied with the government. The great majority of them favored the anti-Semitic policies of the government, and they had, in 1909, proposed that Jewish jurists be ineligible for the post of justice of the peace on the ground that Russia was a Christian state. But they opposed the zemstvo measure submitted to the Duma by Stolypin in 1911, which provided for the introduction of rural self-government in some western provinces, excluded Jews from participation in the zemstvo elections, and disqualified them from being chosen zemstvo deputies. In protest the Octobrist leader, A. I. Guchkov, resigned as president of the fourth Duma.[35]

Since, therefore, the government had lost the support of the entire Duma, with the exception of the monarchists whose "patriotism" was handsomely rewarded from secret funds, it had to justify its policies afresh and rally popular support. For this purpose a humble and obscure Jew by the name of Mendel Beilis was chosen as a scapegoat. In his person the government of Nicholas II attempted to implicate the entire Jewish people in the charge of ritual murder.

The conspiracy against Beilis began with the murder of a Chris-

33. *Ibid.*, p. 20. Also *Soiuz Russkago Naroda,* pp. 136–140.
34. [See above, pp. 16–17. Ed.]
35. [Cf. Tager, *The Decay,* p. 23. Ed.]

tian lad, Andrei Yushchinsky, by a band of criminals on March 12, 1911. The boy, whose corpse was thrown into the river Dnieper, had possessed incriminating information about the doings of the gang, which was headed by a notorious thief and fence, Vera Cheberiak. On March 20, when the body was discovered, and even before an investigation was conducted, the monarchist press in Kiev and St. Petersburg charged that the boy was the victim of a Jewish ritual murder. Soon the reactionary press throughout the country began publishing inflammatory articles accusing the Jews of killing a number of Christian children annually for purposes of ritual and warning against granting Jews civil equality.

The following examples are typical of the propaganda the press kept feeding the Russian public. "May Russia be saved from Jewish equality even more than from fire, sword, and open invasion of enemies. The slobbering liberals seem not to understand what kind of species the Jews they are dealing with are." The newspapers quoted falsified extracts from Jewish religious books, charging that in them was to be found "a horrible commandment converting the Jewish people as an entity and every single Jew as an individual into murderers." But it was not only Judaism, "externally hostile to Christianity," which corrupted the morality of the Jew. His anthropological and sociological traits conditioned him to live a parasitic and criminal life. Calling upon the Christian world to awaken to the danger of harboring such a people, the anti-Semitic press kept driving home the argument that they had "the right to accuse the whole of Jewry as accomplices of ritual torturers and consumers of Christian blood."

The conclusions to be drawn were obvious: "It is evident that there will hardly be found even in our Imperial Duma volunteers who will agree to be equalized in their rights with the murderers after the tortures of the martyred Yushchinsky." The press demanded that Jews be deprived of whatever privileges they possessed, forbidden "to be artisans, dentists, assistant surgeons, and technicians in other fields," and barred "from any possibility of receiving instructions." [36]

Alexander B. Tager, who spent many years studying the Beilis case in the tsarist archives made accessible by the Soviet government, states that the police quickly established the identity of the murderers of the Yushchinsky boy. The authorities refrained from apprehending the criminals because of the conspiracy to pin the guilt upon a Jew. Among the leading conspirators were Minister of Justice Shcheglovitov and the procurator of the Supreme Appellate

36. *Ibid.*, pp. 29–30.

Court of Kiev, Chaplinsky. Determined to frame a Jew for the murder, the authorities intimidated any police official who sought to solve the case honestly. One of these, the attorney of the Kiev Superior Court, Brandorf, was dismissed by Shcheglovitov because he opposed the version of ritual murder. Moreover, when the journalist S. I. Brazul-Brushkovsky with the aid of experienced detectives tracked down the real murderers in a private investigation, Chaplinsky refused to make any arrest. In fact, after Brazul-Brushkovsky had published his revelations which were received as convincing both in Russia and abroad, Chaplinsky made contact with Cheberiak and her band for the purpose of shielding the murderers. Tager comments on this strange alliance: "No 'queen of thieves' ever had a knight more devoted to her than had Cheberiak in the person of Chaplinsky." [37]

Instead of arresting the criminals, the police on the night of July 21–22, one month after the Brazul-Brushkovsky story appeared in the press, arrested Mendel Beilis, charging him with murder for ritual purposes. It should be noted that the investigating magistrate, Fenenko, and attorney Brandorf of the Kiev Superior Court, both of whom became thoroughly familiar with the Yushchinsky case, waged a long and bitter struggle against the arrest of Beilis. Of the nine judges of the Supreme Appellate Court who voted on the indictment two, who actually studied the case, wrote a dissenting opinion in which they pointed out the baselessness of the charge; the other seven, who did not study the case, deferred to the wishes of the higher authorities and voted accordingly.

The innocent Beilis remained in prison for more than two years while the tsarist machinery worked frantically to build up a case against him. After the arrest and indictment the government could no longer release him and give up the entire affair without losing face. And it still hoped to retrieve its political fortunes by a "successful conclusion of the ritual murder trial." Indeed those fortunes were deteriorating at an alarming pace. Not only within the country but internationally too the prestige of the Russian government was declining. Thus in 1911 on account of the Jewish policies America broke her commercial treaty with Russia.

The diplomatic conflict arose as a result of a Russian law forbidding the residence of foreign Jews in Russia. In December, 1911, the United States House of Representatives by a vote of 300 to 1 passed a resolution urging the president to break off the commercial treaty with Russia because of discrimination against American citizens of Jewish faith. The Senate unanimously approved the action

37. *Ibid.*, pp. 68, 70, 96, 119, 125, 142.

of President Taft, who notified the Russian ambassador of his intention to abrogate the treaty.[38]

The Beilis case, too, created ill feeling for Russia throughout western Europe and in the United States. In France, Germany, England, and the United States public protests signed by eminent leaders in all branches of thought denounced the Russian government for its attempt to revive a medieval fiction about the Jew. The protest issued by a group of Czech scholars headed by Thomas G. Masaryk declared that never before in history had a government sanctioned and supported a prejudice believed in only by ignorant masses.[39] It is worthy of note that S. D. Sazonov, minister of foreign affairs, to whom world opinion was reported by the Russian ambassadors abroad, made no attempt to interfere with the development of the Beilis case.

In Russia itself, moreover, the trial of Beilis aroused general indignation. With the exception of the rightist parties, all factions from conservative Octobrists to radical Bolsheviks were lined up against the government. *Russkoe Bogatstvo* (Russian Wealth), edited by the famous writer V. G. Korolenko, stated that "the present Russian nationalism will not cleanse itself of the shame with which it has covered itself, even when this nationalism is dead," and that "the very pit which it has dug for the Jews will be the one into which it will fall." The Bolshevist *Za Pravdu* (For the Truth) asserted that the trial had caused a universal revulsion because a simple, average worker had been branded by the government as a cannibal and a vampire engaged in drinking children's blood in accordance with a supposed injunction of his religion. "The proletariat of Russia," the paper stated, "has been in the front ranks of those who raised their voices in defense of the trampled honor of the Russian people." [40]

The underground press of the revolutionaries attacked the government in even more vehement language. "The Beilis trial," one leaflet asserted, "must justify all the inhuman persecution which the Russian government has applied and intends to continue to apply to the Jewish people. Again all democratic Russia protests and accepts this bloody challenge, this bloody weapon, one end of which

38. For a full account of this diplomatic episode see *American Jewish Year Book, (5672) 1911/12,* pp. 19–128, and *(5673), 1912/13,* pp. 92–210. [Also *With Firmness in the Right,* Adler and Margalith, pp. 255 ff. Also Nathan Schachner, *The Price of Liberty. A History of the American Jewish Committee* (New York, 1948), pp. 43 ff. Ed.]

39. *American Jewish Year Book, 5675 (1914/15)*, pp. 65–82, contains complete texts of the protests.

40. Tager, *The Decay,* pp. 150–151.

is pointed against the Jewish people, while the other is turned *against the whole of struggling Russia.* The very object of creating this terrible affair was to shatter the Russian democracy." [41] As the time of the trial approached, the illegal revolutionary groups organized mass protests through strikes in factories and in universities.

The universal excitement made no impression on the government; Beilis was finally brought before the court on September 25, 1913.[42] As the archives disclosed, Judge F. A. Boldyrev, a man of extremely rightist tendencies chosen to preside over the trial, was promised an important promotion by the minister of justice should Beilis be convicted. The noted Russian-Jewish lawyer, Oscar O. Gruzenberg, counsel for the defense in the Beilis case, describes this judge as a man known for his willingness to please the authorities. As chief prosecutor, a judicial official of German extraction, O. J. Vipper, was appointed. Gruzenberg's description of him suggests the Hitlerian types who later gained the upper hand in Germany.[43] The lists of the jurymen were sifted with a view to eliminating candidates not regarded as completely "reliable." The government's mistrust of members of the intelligentsia is evident in the report submitted to the Central Police Department in the capital by its Kiev representative: "Procurator Vipper is evidently an experienced man for he succeeded [by means of challenges] in eliminating the entire intelligensia from the personnel of the jury." [44]

As an expert on the Jewish religion, the prosecution secured a Polish priest, Father Justin Pranaitis, author of a pamphlet charging Jews with ritual murder.[45] At the time his pamphlet appeared, in 1893, critics had pointed out that Pranaitis was a totally ignorant man and that his Hebrew quotations contained in abundance the crudest mistakes and falsifications. This ecclesiastical "expert" also had a record as an extortioner. The government resorted to his services because, as the archives show, no important Russian priest could be found to support its case.[46] Prosecutor Vipper unwittingly paid the Russian clergy a high compliment when at the trial he declared that the choice of a Polish priest as a government expert was due to the fact that "no one so learned, courageous, and steadfast was to be found among the Greek-Orthodox clergy." [47] The

41. *Ibid.*, p. 154.
42. [The trial lasted until October 23. Ed.]
43. Oscar O. Gruzenberg, *Vchera* (Paris, 1938), p. 119.
44. Tager, *The Decay*, p. 177.
45. [*The Christian in the Jewish Talmud; or the Teachings of the Rabbis about Christians* (in Latin), Ed.]
46. Tager, *The Decay,* p. 203; Gruzenberg, *Vchera,* p. 127.
47. Tager, *The Decay,* p. 208.

defense headed by Gruzenberg included the best legal minds of the bar associations of St. Petersburg and Moscow. Outstanding representatives of Russian science and scholarship volunteered their services as experts, refusing any remuneration and traveling at their own expense.

Judge Boldyrev tried in every way to prejudice the jury against the defendant, hampered the work of the defense, and even came to the assistance of the witnesses for the prosecution. His summation to the jurors resembled the address of a prosecutor rather than that of an objective jurist. Everyone feared the effects of the court's charge upon the simple-minded jurors. But the twelve peasants were not swayed by the judge's insinuations; their verdict was not guilty. Thus the conspiracy prepared by the government over two years was defeated by twelve ordinary citizens. As Gruzenberg remarked: "The plain peasants proved to be higher in their moral sensitiveness than many representatives of the contemporary judiciary." [48]

The government regarded the acquittal as a shattering blow to its prestige. "The trial of Beilis was the Tsushima of the administration which will never be pardoned," was the confidential opinion of the Police Department.[49] To "rehabilitate" its honor the ministers of the interior and of justice entered into a new conspiracy to create another ritual case which, they hoped, would ultimately prove the government's charge. Out of its secret funds the Ministry of the Interior with the approval of the tsar paid the notorious anti-Semite G. G. Zamyslovsky, one of the lawyers of the prosecution and deputy of the Duma, 75,000 rubles for the publication of his book, *The Murder of Andrei Yushchinsky.* This volume, which sought to prove the guilt of Beilis and to justify the stand of the government, appeared in 1917 on the eve of the revolution.[50]

The huge grant to Zamyslovsky served another purpose: it was a reward for his services in the Beilis case (in spite of its failure the government handsomely rewarded all who loyally assisted in the case). Arnold D. Margolin, a Kiev attorney who was intimately connected with the case even long after it had ended, relates that promotions and rewards were showered as if from a horn of plenty on all who had in one way or another managed to please Shcheglovitov, "beginning with Chaplinsky, who was appointed a senator, and ending with the common messenger of the jury room, who was

48. *Ibid.,* p. 216.

49. *Ibid.,* p. 219. Near the island of Tsushima the Russian fleet suffered a disastrous defeat during the Russo-Japanese War in 1905.

50. *Ibid.,* p. 224.

promoted to the post of sheriff."[51] Boldyrev, the judge, not only received the promised promotion but was also given a watch by the emperor as a "special gift."[52]

The generous rewards for "faithful services" made by the central government encouraged other officials to similar endeavors. When less than a month after the conclusion of the Beilis trial the corpse of a boy was found in a village not far from Kiev, the acting chief procurator of the Kiev district proceeded to engineer a new ritual trial with a zeal that exceeded that of Chaplinsky, his predecessor in office. The case, however, collapsed after an honest investigator discovered that the murdered boy was the son of a Jewish tailor. The murderer, a notorious criminal hired to commit the crime, had mistaken the identity of his young victim; instead of killing a Christian child he blundered and killed a Jew.

Doubtless the government would finally have succeeded in staging another ritual trial had not World War I broken out some nine months after the termination of the Beilis case and diverted its attention to more urgent matters. The outbreak of war against Germany on July 19, 1914 (Julian calendar) united the Russian people behind the government and all political differences were temporarily put aside. Not only the liberals but even the socialist parties (excepting the Bolsheviks) pledged their support in the prosecution of the war. Forgetting all their grievances against the tsarist regime, the Jews too rallied with genuine patriotism to the call of their fatherland. *Novy Voskhod* (New Sunrise) stated their position on July 24, 1914:

> We were born and grew up in Russia, here rest the remains of our fathers . . . The bearers of the ideals of our fathers, the nucleus of world Jewry —the Russian Jews—*are at the same time inseparably allied with our mother country where we have been living for centuries and from which there is no power that can separate us—neither persecution nor oppression.* In this historical moment, when our fatherland is threatened by foreign invasion, when brute force has armed itself against the great ideals of humanity, the Russian Jews will manfully step forward to the battlefield and do their sacred duty.

From the rostrum of the Duma the Jewish deputy N. M. Friedman declared on July 26: ". . . in the great enthusiasm which has seized upon the nation and peoples of Russia, the Jews are marching to the battlefield shoulder to shoulder with all the peoples of

51. A. D. Margolin, *The Jews of Eastern Europe* (New York, 1926), p. 231.
52. Tager, *The Decay,* pp. 173, 222.

Russia; there are no forces that can tear the Jews away from their fatherland to which they are bound by ties centuries old."

The sincerity of these pronouncements appeared in the fact that during mobilization the Jewish population delivered its full quota of reservists, and large numbers of Jews volunteered. Many Jewish youths studying abroad on account of the numerus clausus in Russian schools returned to their native country to join the colors, while others enlisted in the armies of the Allies. This response to the call to arms was quite understandable. In spite of their disabilities the Jews of Russia were attached to the land of their birth. The mistreatment they had suffered at the hands of the government had not prejudiced them against the Russian people. The tsarist regime and the Russian people were at no time one and the same thing to the Jews. They knew that the pogroms, the limitations on their rights, and the endless legal persecutions were not the work of the people. Naturally they entertained a hope that their patriotic services might help to mitigate their bitter lot; the very fact that Russia was arrayed on the side of the democracies strengthened that hope. *Novy Voskhod* gave guarded expression to this simple faith: ". . . the Jews trust that with the vanishing of the mailed fist the German spirit of militarism, which swallows up the prime of the nation, will also be destroyed and that humanity will come nearer to the ideals of the ancient prophets." [53]

But almost immediately the government showed that it contemplated no change in Jewish policies. The reactionary press, uncertain about what course to pursue toward the Jews, at first spoke of the necessity of forgetting past grievances and the desirability of a united front among all the elements of the Russian population; but at a hint from the government it quickly changed its tune. Instead of receiving gratitude for their patriotic services, the Jews were charged with "trading" their patriotism for civil equality. Jewish soldiers wounded on the battlefield were sent to the Pale; the families of Jewish privates stationed outside the Pale were refused the privilege of visiting their wounded relatives at their place of service.[54]

53. *Novy Voskhod,* August 1, 1914, quoted in *Evreiskaia Starina* X (1918), pp. 200–201.

54. [Cf. *The War and the Jews in Russia* (New York, National Workmen's Committee on Jewish Rights, 1916), pp. 42–118. The documents and press reports quoted are literal translations from the Russian original on the oppression of Russian Jewry during World War I. For more detailed documentary evidence see especially pp. 63, 65, 75, 76, 77, 81, 83, 84, 94, 95, 96; also "Iz Chornoi Knigi Rossiiskago Evreistva. Materialy dlia Istorii Voiny 1914–1915 g," *Evreiskaia Starina,* X (1918), 194–296. Ed.]

Not content with these humiliating restrictions, the authorities hurled charges of espionage against the Jews, with the result that they were expelled wholesale from their places of residence. In a report to the central committee of the Cadet party the noted attorney and Jewish leader Maxim M. Vinaver pointed out the dangers of such accusations. Since cases of espionage in wartime were tried in secret and no record of the proceedings kept, accusations might have dire consequences. They were particularly ominous, Vinaver asserted, when directed at a group against which there existed ancient prejudice.

Most charges against the Jews of treason originated in the staff of the Russian armies in the north, Vinaver said. Attached to that army was a Colonel Miasoedov, who had supplied the Germans with information which contributed to the defeat of the Russian armies by Hindenburg. To avert suspicion from him, Miasoedov's agent had deliberately circulated slanderous rumors against the Jews. The colonel was subsequently convicted of treason and hanged.

The belief that charges of disloyalty also originated with those members of the general staff who were of Polish and German extraction was expressed by the chief rabbi of Vilno, Isaac Rubinstein, who had many occasions during the war to appear before the general staff either on behalf of Jewish communities threatened with expulsion or in order to plead for the return of exiles to their former homes. He held that from the beginning of the war these generals foresaw the dismemberment of the Russian Empire and sought through expulsion to rid the future Polish or Baltic states of their Jewish citizens.

Other occasions for charges of espionage were provided in tsarist Poland, where for a number of years before the outbreak of the war a hostile relationship existed between Poles and Jews. The boycott of Jewish goods advocated by Polish agitators fanned this hostility to hatred. In the war the Poles found an opportunity to wreak vengeance upon their Jewish neighbors and rid themselves of hateful competitors. There were special factors which made the Polish Jews easy objects of suspicion. Their Yiddish speech, which resembled German, and their peculiar attire, so unlike that of the general population, excited the suspicions of the Russian armies. Hostile Poles hastened to exploit these circumstances to the utmost and poisoned the minds of the Russian soldiers with fanciful rumors of Jewish espionage. Stories were spread, for example, of gold being sent in coffins to Germans; of a Jew making signals while riding on a white horse in front of Russian troops; of windmills giving mysterious signals; of secret telephone lines laid for tens of miles by means of thick wires and cords.

As a result Russian officers, without bothering to check the accuracy of these malicious charges, ordered wholesale expulsions of Jews from the war zones. Thus, ten days after war was declared two thousand individuals, representing the entire Jewish population of the town of Myshinets, in the province of Lomzha, were banished. The military commandant refused to reconsider his decision even after the governor of Lomzha let the Jews return to their homes. Banishments continued to increase with no exceptions made for the families of reservists. In Grodzisk, province of Warsaw, the four thousand Jewish inhabitants were ordered at 11 A.M. to evacuate the city before night. Among them were three hundred families of reservists. In one town where both the Jewish and Polish populations were expelled the Polish inhabitants were allowed to return after two days but the Jews were ordered to stay out. These evacuations not only proved disastrous to the masses of Jewry but resulted in serious dislocation of the economic life of the affected regions, thus seriously injuring the war effort.

Soon after the outbreak of war the military commanders began to make hostages of leaders among the Jewish population and held them responsible for the loyal conduct of their coreligionists. Among these hostages were some who had distinguished themselves for meritorious service, such as a Mr. Gokhbez who had been cited from the rostrum of the Duma by Cadet deputy N. V. Nekrasov for splendid assistance to the Union of Zemstvos.

The system of hostages, immoral in itself, led to all sorts of abuses. In some instances hostages were executed without knowing the cause; in other cases the rich were put up for ransom and others taken in their place. Vinaver describes this trafficking in human lives as follows: "At first the richest people were taken; these were then discharged for a certain ransom and in their place a second group was designated; this in turn was released for another payment and a third group arrested."

Military orders regarding the seizure of Jewish hostages reveal the confusion which characterized the High Command's thinking. In January, 1915, a proclamation appeared in the streets of the city of Lvov (Lemberg), which had been captured from the Austrians, stating that "the progress of the war has disclosed an open hostility on the part of the Jewish population of Poland, Galicia, and Bukovina." This indiscriminate lumping together of the Jews of Poland, subjects of the Russian Empire, with those of temporarily occupied enemy territory showed the prejudiced and irrational attitude of the accusers. The source of the information regarding Jewish treachery, moreover, suggested either gullibility or ill will. An order of the High Command called attention to articles appearing in German newspapers that stated the German army to have found faithful allies among Russian Jews. In Russia those seeking pretexts to justify their anti-Semitic policies seized eagerly upon this obvious attempt to undermine the confidence of the government in a group of its citizens.

Numerous official orders of the day testify to the hostile campaign of the High Command against the Jewish population—who at that time were supplying 400,000 soldiers to the Russian army and seeking loyally to fulfill their duties in the war. One order placed Jewish physicians under special surveillance because, allegedly, they had been corrupting the troops with revolutionary propaganda. Still another order, issued by a general of infantry, imposed more severe penalities for frauds committed by Jews than by offenders of other nationalities.

On the other hand, acts of heroism or sacrifice on the part of Jews were played down or censored in the press. In the editorial offices of the liberal press long columns of such news were canceled by the censors. An item in the progressive daily ***Rech***, citing a Jewish noncommissioned officer for an exploit, had the word Jewish deleted by the censors, and in another newspaper photographs of Jewish soldiers who earned the Cross of St. George were suppressed.

Particularly severe was the treatment accorded the Jewish weekly *Novy Voskhod* for its attempt to publicize acts of valor by Jewish soldiers. The censors either suppressed the lists of such soldiers or after considerable bargaining permitted only partial publication. In some cases only initials were permitted. When *Novy Voskhod* announced its intention to print a special volume, *The War and Jews*, recording the full story of Jewish contributions to the war effort, it was shut down.

It is obvious that this bias against publicity about Jewish heroism and the wide publicity given wholesale accusations of Jewish treason were intended as a prelude to the expulsion of Jews from the war zones. Since the Pale of Settlement was situated chiefly in the border areas constituting the zones of military operation, the greater part of Russian Jewry was affected by the orders of expulsion.

One particular edict which carried an indictment of the entire Jewish people, issued toward the end of March, 1915, forbade the settlement of Jews on the shore of the Gulf of Finland. The

Jewish communities addressed a memorandum to the tsar pointing out the grave implications of this prohibition, asserting that the Jews themselves would eject from their midst those guilty of treasonable activity, and recalling that never in all history had a wholesale charge of treason been leveled against an entire Jewish population. "At a time when our children are fighting in the ranks of the gallant Russian army for the honor and glory of Russia, we, their parents, are subjected to a common responsibility on the level of outlaws, and are subjected to penalities for abominable deeds which are aimed at the betrayal of our children." The memorandum concluded: "We dare address your Imperial Highness in the hope that our humiliations will not be enforced any longer; that we may be relieved from the stigma of outcasts, and be allowed the right as loyal sons of the fatherland to exert all our efforts to combat our common enemy."

The address remained unanswered. Russian public opinion and the Duma, however, did not remain indifferent to the expulsions and general mistreatment of the Jews during the war. Of particular note is the investigation of the Kushi affair conducted by two deputies of the Duma. The story of the Kushi incident is as follows. On May 18, 1915, a report in the official army organ *Nash Vestnik* (Our Messenger) stated that during an attack made by the Germans on the night of April 29 at Kushi, province of Kurland, there was discovered "shocking treachery against our forces by a certain part of the local population, particularly the Jews." According to the report, the Jews of Kushi had concealed German soldiers in their cellars; at the approach of the Russian detachments, the Germans emerged at a given signal from their hiding places and set Kushi on fire from all sides. "This regrettable incident once more confirms the fundamental requirement of field service . . . that is, the necessity that the utmost attention be given to guard duty, especially at those important points that were formerly held by the enemy and are inhabited mostly by Jews."

By military order the Kushi incident was brought to the attention of the entire army. The story was posted on placards in many cities and reprinted in the entire press. Editors who refused to publish it were compelled to do so under threat of administrative punishment.

The investigation undertaken by Alexander Kerensky and N. M. Friedman proved this story to be pure fabrication. Only three of the forty homes of Kushi belonged to Jews; and when the Germans were attacking Kushi there were no Jews in the town. *Every Jewish house had been destroyed by fire.* Kerensky reported in the Duma:

"After a year's war we see before us the Jews crucified through hatred and slander. I proclaim from this tribune that I personally went to investigate the accusations alleged against the Jews of Kushi, that they had committed treason against the Russian army. I must reiterate that it is a mean slander and that such a thing could not, because of local conditions, have happened there!"

At the same session Paul Miliukov, leader of the Constitutional Democratic party, denounced the government's treatment of the Jews. He charged that the usual policy of discrimination practiced by the tsarist government against all minority groups had assumed unheard of dimensions during the war under the guise of military necessity. When compared with the atrocities perpetrated against the Jews, all other government misdeeds paled into insignificance. A people who had been animated by patriotic enthusiasm at the beginning of the war had become the objects of mockery. The wholesale charges of treason and the taking of innocent people as hostages were reminiscent of the Dark Ages. The leader of the Social Democrats, N. S. Chkheidze, also expressed his horror: "Was there ever a government so cynical as to take hostages from its own subjects? I declare this act has no precedent in history." As for finding traitors, he advised the government to look within its own ranks.

A bitter indictment of the government came from deputy Friedman. He told of a Jewish soldier who had returned from the United States to join the Russian army. Upon his getting home after losing an arm in battle his mother and relatives were ordered to leave town. "Tell the gentlemen of the right that I do not mourn my lost hand, but that I mourn deeply the lost human dignity that was not denied to me in alien lands," Friedman read from the man's letter. The deputy cited instances where Jewish soldiers wounded in the war were deported from cities to which they had gone for cures, because these cities were outside the Pale. He described the cruel treatment of Jewish refugees and asserted that the persecution of Jews in Russia surpassed that of the Spanish Inquisition. The source of Jewish suffering was not the Russian people, Friedman declared, but the Russian government. "Before the face of the entire country, before the civilized world, I declare that the calumnies against the Jews are the most repulsive lies and chimeras of persons who will have to be responsible for their crimes." [55]

There followed a formal interpellation on the treatment of Jews, submitted by the Constitutional Democrats, the Peasant Labor group, and the Social Democrats. The government was asked to ac-

55. [*The War and the Jews in Russia,* pp. 81, 84. Ed.]

count for the expulsions, the Kushi affair, and the taking of hostages. During the debate it was charged from the tribune of the Duma that in order to protect traitors within their own ranks the military authorities sought to create fictitious traitors among the Jews. "A screen is thereby put up for the Miasoedovs and other of our traitors behind which they may take shelter."

Chkheidze declared that the Russian people and the world knew who was responsible for the tragic position in which the country found itself both at the front and behind the battle lines. They knew it was not the Jews, "but those who fatten on government contracts in connection with the supply of the army."

What justice is this that requires that a Jewish volunteer, who has been several times in battle, and is now crippled and mutilated should be sent out within twenty-four hours from places in Russia where he is looking for employment? What humanity is this which forbids the offering of food to hungry Jewish fugitives kept in sealed wagons at the stations, as our authorities have done? What freedom is this to have the whole Jewish press suppressed and destroyed by a single stroke of the pen? What brotherhood is this when a part of the army is set against the Jewish soldiers who are risking their lives in the same trenches with the others? What ethical or aesthetic principle underlies the outraging of a Jewish woman within the precincts of the synagogue, whither she flew in the hope of escaping her terrible fate? (Shouts from the Right: "What? Shame!") Shame indeed, but this is a fact! [55]

The interpellation on expulsion, slander, and taking of hostages was referred to a committee whose findings declared all three practices illegal.

But the committee's findings had no effect on the government. The regime still needed a scapegoat upon whom to fasten the responsibility for its own incompetence and corruption. And such was the belief of members of the opposition in the Duma as well as other agencies of Russian public opinion. The Military Industrial Committee of Trade and Professional Organizations, formed in May, 1915, to integrate the nation's economic resources for a more successful prosecution of the war, openly condemned the incompetence of the government. At a meeting held on August 25 the president of that organization charged that the conduct of the war had from the very beginning been in incompetent hands. Asserting that the army was suffering heroically, he expressed his fear that "the time may come when our courage will fail." [56]

The outbreak of war had intensified the widespread demand for

56. *Rech,* July 28, 1915, quoted in *The War and the Jews in Russia,* p. 93.

Jewish emancipation. Some 225 leading Russian men of letters and journalists issued a manifesto demanding complete civil equality for Russian Jewry. Declaring that the Jews had not only always shared the trials and tribulations of Russians but given ample evidence of their sincere love for Russia and their eagerness to render service to the common cause notwithstanding grievous injuries done them by prejudice, the writers stated that the emancipation of the Jews "shall form one of the conditions of a truly constructive regime."

Numerous municipalities both outside and within the Pale, zemstvo assemblies, university officials, merchants, trade and professional organizations petitioned the government and the Duma to remove all Jewish disabilities.[57] "The sons of the Jewish nation are now fighting side by side with the Russians for their country," a speaker declared at a meeting of the Military Industrial Committee. "Unfortunately, this country has until now been only a stepmother to them." The speaker offered a resolution to abolish all restrictive laws against the Jews. It was received with prolonged applause and adopted.[58]

The Free Economic Society, the principal economic organization of Russia, joined the chorus demanding Jewish emancipation. A resolution adopted unanimously at a meeting in 1915 stated in part that "if in time of peace these restrictions, which are harmful economically and offensive morally, are recognized as a relic of barbarism that must be abolished, it is all the more difficult to reconcile ourselves with them at the present time, when hundreds and thousands of Jews serve under the Russian banners on the battlefield." The meeting decided that the Council of the Society ask the government to abolish all Jewish disabilities "immediately and permanently by legislative enactment."[59]

Many other commercial and technical organizations urged the government to remove the Jewish disabilities, which they regarded as the cause of the economic backwardness of Russia. All the replies to an inquiry on this subject addressed by the Merchants Association to its county members advocated abolition of the Pale of Settlement.[60] Almost every national convention of various industries urged the government to emancipate the Jews.[61]

57. *Novy Voskhod,* September 4, 1914, April 24 and May 24, 1915, quoted in *The War and the Jews in Russia.*

58. *Rech,* July 28, 1915.

59. *Razsvet,* January 25, 1915, quoted in *The War and the Jews in Russia,* p. 94.

60. *Evreiskaia Nedelia* (1915) No. 5, quoted in *The War and the Jews in Russia,* p. 95.

61. *The War and the Jews in Russia,* pp. 94–95.

But the government gave no indication of intention to change in any way its Jewish policies. In fact, when the journal *Evrei i Rossia* (The Jews and Russia) canvassed the opinions of the ministers, representative deputies of the Duma, and prominent Russian leaders regarding prospects for the Jews after the war, the replies of the members of the Cabinet were evasive. The statement of the Octobrist leader and president of the Duma, M. Rodzianko, was not more reassuring. Judging by the prevailing state of affairs in the government, he saw no ground for hope of a change for the better. Neither the fourth Duma nor the bureaucracy, he held, gave any such indication. A number of other progressive leaders questioned by the journal shared Rodzianko's view.[62]

Indeed, no change in the status of Jews was likely under Nicholas II, who blocked and discouraged every attempt to ameliorate the condition of his Jewish subjects. He made his unalterable decision in respect to this issue emphatically clear. His guilt in the countless pogroms, persecutions, and oppressions endured by Jewry during his regime is manifest beyond shadow of a doubt. Ample proof of his responsibility may be adduced from the many imperial pardons he granted to *pogromshchiks* (the perpetrators of the riots) and the promotions and gifts he bestowed upon police officials responsible for the organization of pogroms. Even in prerevolutionary days his open fraternizing with the notorious leaders of the Black Hundred, engineers of Jewish massacres, showed where his sympathy lay. His guilt was clearly established by the evidence found in the archives, after the revolution of 1917, and by the memoirs of tsarist dignitaries. So deep rooted was his anti-Semitism and that of Nicholas Nicholaevich, his second cousin and commander in chief of all the Russian armies, that no sacrifice of the interests of the Russian people was too great provided it worked to the injury and detriment of Jewish subjects.

General A. N. Kuropatkin, former minister of war, states in his diary that after the Kishinev pogrom of 1903 both Plehve and the emperor told him the Jews deserved this lesson on account of their revolutionary activities.[63] Count Witte relates that after the pogrom in Gomel the Cabinet under his presidency decided to initiate judical proceedings against a police officer whom investigation had disclosed as organizer of the pogrom. But the tsar noted marginally on the minutes of the decision submitted to him: "How does this business concern me?"

A. Lopukhin, former head of the Police Department, supplied in-

62. *Evrei i Rossia,* (1915), Nos. 1 and 3.
63. [See *Dnevnik A. N. Kuropatkina,* Krasny Arkhiv, II (1922), 43. Ed.]

formation which incriminated the tsar himself as the inspirer of pogroms. He reported a conversation between the emperor and General Drachevsky who had been appointed police chief of Rostov-on-Don. "You have a lot of Jews there in Rostov and in Nakhichevan," the tsar observed. The general remarked that many of them had died during the revolutionary disturbances and pogroms. "No, not enough," Nicholas II retorted. "I expected that more would die." [64] Lopukhin added correctly that here was a hint to the new boss of Rostov to contrive further pogroms in the city under his jurisdiction.

The tsar disclosed his attitude to pogroms by open patronage of the Union of Russian People, which instigated such outrages. He was an honorary member of the society, wore the party emblem, and at every opportunity gave it public support.[65] Grigoriev, the police chief of Odessa who was dismissed because he refused to cater to the Black Hundred, was stunned when the tsar, who received him in audience, appeared wearing the insignia of the union. He took this act as a silent rebuke for his refusal to cooperate with the organization of pogromists.

In his enmity toward the Jews the tsar was strongly influenced by his wife. The empress too was a notorious anti-Semite. It was "disgusting," she remarked, that a "genuine" Jew, G. E. Weinstein, should have been appointed to the State Council. So deep seated was the imperial couple's hatred for the Jews that even Rasputin with his extraordinary sway over them could effect no change in their attitude. If one is to believe his Jewish secretary, Simanovich, Rasputin sought on many occasions to intercede on behalf of the Jewish people but was discouraged by the emperor from doing so. The tsar would often complain to Rasputin about Jews on whom his ministers rendered adverse reports. Simanovich states that he had to exert much tact to keep Rasputin from falling under the anti-Semitic influence of the royal pair. He knew that Rasputin's enmity could prove fatal to Jewry.

Simanovich declares that he had the confidence of Jewish leaders and that he arranged two meetings between them and Rasputin to discuss the Jewish problem. Rasputin advised them to seek to acquire civil equality by bribing the government. He was visibly affected by the stories of expulsions and atrocities committed by the army against Jews, and it was due to his influence, Simanovich as-

64. A. Lopukhin, *Otryvki iz Vospominanii. Po Povodu Vospominanii Witte* (Moscow, 1923), p. 86.
65. Witte, *Memoirs*, p. 192.

serts, that Nicholas Nicholaevich was removed from the command of the army.[66]

Both Simanovich and Rasputin exacted a promise from A. D. Protopopov that if he was appointed minister of the interior he would improve the condition of Jewry; as a result of this promise he got his appointment.[67] Not only does Simanovich confirm the well-known fact that for several years Rasputin had the power of appointment of the highest officials of the state but he supplies some amusing incidents which throw an interesting light on the last years of Romanov rule.

Finding the task of supplying ministers to the tsar a difficult one, Rasputin asked his secretary to keep his eyes open for suitable candidates. The monarch would often demand of his favorite an immediate recommendation, whereupon Rasputin would gather a conference in which a motley assortment of people participated, sometimes his nieces or others far removed from government circles. In one instance a certain Volkonsky was made assistant minister of the interior because his name was mentioned by Simanovich's son who happened to be at Rasputin's home.[68]

It may well be that Simanovich exerted a good influence over Rasputin in respect to his feeling for Jews; and also no doubt Rasputin's own strong and independent nature kept him from being infected with the anti-Semitic virus which permeated the court circles. In this matter Rasputin showed more courage than the leading ministers who served under Nicholas II. To please their master and strengthen their position almost all these ministers either tolerated or pursued anti-Jewish policies. It may be stated without reservation that with the exception of Sviatopolk-Mirsky there was no leading minister who possessed independence of spirit or moral courage at least concerning Jews.

Witte did not show much moral courage in his treatment of the Jewish problem nor was he entirely free of anti-Jewish bias, as can be gathered from a communication addressed to Minister of the Interior A. A. Makarov in 1912.[69] As a practical statesman Witte did not permit his personal feelings to interfere with his public policies. It was his opinion that many of the anti-Jewish laws "did much harm to Russia and the Russians." In dealing with Jewish legislation, he asserts, he never considered the advantages the Jews

66. Simanovich, *Rasputin i Evrei,* pp. 52–57, 73–81.

67. *Ibid.*, p. 131.

68. *Ibid.*, pp. 114–115.

69. See L. M. Aisenberg, "Na Slovakh i na Dele. Po Povodu Memuarov Witte i Lopukhina," *Evreiskaia Letopis,* III (1924), 24–43.

would derive from a particular measure but rather the effect of this or that measure upon Russia as a whole.

On one occasion when Tsar Alexander III asked him, "Is it true that you are in sympathy with the Jews?" Witte answered, "The only way I can answer this question is by asking Your Majesty whether you think it possible to drown all the Russian Jews in the Black Sea. To do so would, of course, be a radical solution to the problem. But if Your Majesty will recognize the right of the Jews to live, then conditions must be created which will enable them to carry on a humane existence. In that case, gradual abolition of their disabilities is the only adequate solution of the Jewish problem." [70] Nevertheless, a brief examination of his record reveals that Witte never had the courage to defend his policies and that he suffered from the same lack of statesmanlike firmness he saw in his opponents.

While Witte was minister of finance, it was suggested that Jews be barred from membership in the merchant's guild of Moscow. Witte at first agreed with the special committee of the ministry which rejected this. Following a conference with Grand Duke Sergei Alexandrovich he changed his mind and with "a lackey's desire to please" arranged for the measure to pass.[71]

It is common knowledge that Witte was the author of the declaration of December 12, 1904, which promised mild reforms to the Russian people. When a delegation of representative Jews complained of his failure to make any specific reference to Russian Jewry, he put the blame on his colleagues of the State Council who, he said, failed to realize that an improvement of the Jewish position would prove beneficial to the whole country. Because of their utter lack of confidence in Witte, the leaders of Russian Jewry decided that it was useless to see him again following the issuance of the October manifesto, which also failed to hold out any specific promise to the Jews.[72]

Witte's fear of antagonizing the tsar and the court clique was especially evident during the October pogroms of 1905 which broke out during his premiership. Visibly embarrassed, he said to a committee of the League for the Attainment of Complete Equality for Russian Jewry, "Tell me what measures to undertake, I am ready to do anything." "Let the central government immediately publish in *Pravitelstvenny Vestnik* [Government Messenger] a warning that it will hold every administrator personally responsible for

70. Witte, *Memoirs,* pp. 376–377.
71. Aisenberg, "Na Slovakh i na Dele," p. 26.
72. *Ibid.,* p. 34.

a pogrom in the area of his jurisdiction, and the pogroms will cease immediately," was the reply. Witte agreed and suggested that the committee draft a statement for publication. The statement when it appeared a few days later had been changed beyond recognition. When the Jewish delegation again called on him in hope of getting some action in response to the cries for help that came from all over the Pale, he impressed them as being a confused and helpless man who was powerless to check the pogroms.[73]

Not only did Witte lack the courage to take energetic measures in his capacity of prime minister to put an end to the bloody massacres of October, but when an opportunity presented itself to assert his authority he used it rather to ingratiate himself with his master. When Lopukhin informed Witte in January, 1906, that proclamations inciting to riots against Jews were being printed and disseminated by Komissarov in the Police Department it had a crushing effect upon the premier, who felt hurt and humiliated that such activities took place behind his back. Intimates of Witte's told Lopukhin that he had suffered a shock as a result of the revelation.[74] Yet not only did he lack the courage to punish the guilty official but, noting, as he put it, "that His Majesty was silent and appeared to be familiar with all the details of the matter," Witte, undoubtedly anticipating his majesty's wishes, pleaded for clemency. The tsar graciously accepted the plea of his prime minister and pardoned the man.[75]

Ethically, Lopukhin states, the tsar and Witte were not far apart; and that their difference lay in their temperament. Witte's moral laxity and weakness of character stemmed, he believed, from his love of power, for which he depended on the good graces of the tsar. A warm reception from the tsar would leave him in an exalted and happy mood for a week, whereas a cool reception would plunge him into gloom.

Witte's anxiety to please the emperor created much distrust on the part not only of socialists but even of honest conservatives like D. Shipov, who refused to accept a post in Witte's Cabinet.[76]

Stolypin, who stood at the helm of the government during the five most crucial years of Russian history, 1906–11, showed no greater sturdiness of heart respecting the Jewish question. His chief

73. *Ibid.,* pp. 35–36.
74. Lopukhin, *Otryvki iz Vospominanii,* p. 89.
75. Witte, *Memoirs,* pp. 332–333.
76. D. Shipov, *Vospominania i Dumy o Perezhitom* (Moscow, 1918), pp. 461–480; I. T. Polner, *Zhizneni Put Kniazia G. E. Lvova* (Paris, 1932), pp. 123–124; V. I. Gurko, *Features and Figures of the Past* (Stanford University Press, 1939), pp. 491–493, App. 4, pp. 717–721.

desire, despite his opinions, seems to have been to keep the favor of the tsar. Professing to be a moderate conservative, he protested but tardily the tsar's open fraternization with the monarchist Black Hundred. He never took energetic measures against the lawlessness and violence of this notorious organization. In spite of the information furnished him by Grigoriev, the honest chief of police of Odessa, concerning the terrorist activities of the Odessa branch of the Union of Russian People, which consisted of criminals and pimps, Stolypin made no effort to suppress the organization.

On the contrary, as late as 1909, when the revolution was already crushed, he reminded Grigoriev's successor in an official communication that the Union of Russian People had played a great, "one may say a historic role," in the troubled years 1905–6. He did not believe, he said, that the time had yet come when the organization could be regarded as superfluous.[77] At a special investigation undertaken by the Provisional government in 1917 it was established that Stolypin had himself approved government subventions to the Black Hundred for its activities.[78]

Stolypin's policies betray his lack of sincerity and his anxiety to keep in the good graces of the emperor at whatever cost to conscience or conviction. Mention has been made of the decision of the Cabinet during Stolypin's premiership to remove some Jewish disabilities. In his memoirs, the then finance minister, V. N. Kokovtsov, supplies interesting details about that episode.

To the meetings of the Cabinet held in October, 1906, Stolypin gave a number of valid reasons why some restrictive measures should be abolished. The suggestion met with the approval of all the ministers, each of whom undertook to compile a list of those disabilities which came in his jurisdiction. But the tsar, as has been indicated, disapproved of the step and explained his unfavorable decision in a letter to Stolypin:

> Despite most convincing arguments in favor of adopting a positive decision in this matter, an inner voice keeps on insisting more and more that I do not accept responsibility for it. So far my conscience has not deceived me. Therefore, I intend in this case also to follow its dictates. I know that you too believe that "A tsar's heart is in God's hand." Let it be so. For all laws established by me, I bear a great responsibility before God, and I am ready to answer for this decision at any time.[79]

77. *Soiuz Russkago Naroda,* pp. 226–229, 241–242.
78. *Ibid.,* p. 277.
79. *Out of My Past. The Memoirs of Count Kokovtsov,* ed. H. H. Fischer (Stanford University Press, 1935), pp. 166–167.

Although Stolypin believed, as Kokovtsov stated, that restrictions against Jews were of no real service to the Russian population, he lacked the necessary courage even to attempt to change the emperor's opinion. Moreover, to show his concern for the good name of the tsar, he informed Nicholas that he had altered the minutes of the session to read that the ministers, not the tsar, had decided against making any change in the status of Russian Jewry.

If Witte and Stolypin, the two strongest personalities in the reign of Nicholas II, bowed to their master in the matter of treatment of the Jews, it is small wonder that the petty bureaucrats who followed Stolypin in the last years of the tsarist regime made no attempt to change this traditional course. The position of the Jews deteriorated especially during the war, when in addition to expulsions, defamations, and atrocities committed by the army their destiny was guided by changing ministers who were minions of Rasputin.

Because of the expulsions and evacuations brought about by military exigencies, large masses of Jews accumulated in the interior provinces outside the Pale. To legalize their presence in forbidden territory, the Cabinet at its session on August 4, 1915, temporarily abolished the Pale except in the capitals and other specified areas. It stipulated, however, that the removal of residence restrictions was a temporary war measure which in no way changed the legal status of the Jews. And to impress this fact upon them other restrictions, such as that on admission to the bar, were applied with greater severity outside the Pale than within.[80]

Some local administrators altogether ignored the decision of the government and refused to admit Jews into their territory,[81] well knowing that they would not be tried for insubordination. A district chief of police in St. Petersburg aptly expressed the tsarist official's sense of mastery over the Jews. Asked why he stamped the passport of every new arrival with red ink, a designation for banishment, he replied, "I know you have residence rights, but I also know I will not be held accountable for Jews." [82]

The anti-Semitic administrators never doubted that the end of the war would restore the Pale; but this time they miscalculated. Abolished as a temporary war measure by the tsarist government, the Pale was not restored. After the collapse of the tsarist regime in the February revolution of 1917, the Provisional government on

80. *Pravo,* November 1, 1915, p. 2819, quoted in *The War and the Jews in Russia,* p. 109.
81. *Pravo,* October 19, 1915, p. 2671; November 1, 1915, p. 2822.
82. Cf. L. Kliachko, in *Evreiskaia Letopis,* II, 116.

March 22 conferred complete civil equality upon the Russian Jews, abolishing all restrictions against them and placing them on an equal footing with the rest of the population.[83]

The abolition of all Jewish disabilities was hailed by the entire Russian press as an act of long-delayed justice. The attitude of *Novoe Vremia* reflected the spirit of the times and the change brought about by the revolution. This semi-official organ of the tsarist government had always been in the forefront of the anti-Semitic publications which poisoned public opinion against the Jews. Now, to ingratiate itself with the new government, it executed an about-face and hypocritically acclaimed the decree of Jewish equality:

> The new regime could not tolerate even for a day the artificially erected barriers between the various nationalities inhabiting Russia . . . nothing evoked more hatred against the former government on the part of Russian society than the persecution of minority groups and religions. Who can say how much Russia suffered in her cultural and economic development as a result of her racial policies which were not only meaningless but also foolish! . . . The old regime menaced Russia with internal disunity; the new freedom will unite all her forces and make her ten times stronger.[84]

The decree of Jewish emancipation, promulgated three days before the Jewish Passover which commemorates the deliverance from Egyptian bondage, was received with jubilation by Russian Jewry. In some Jewish homes on the Seder nights of that year the emancipation proclamation was read instead of the traditional Haggada.

The reaction of the Jewish press was one of restraint and dignity. A detailed analysis of it appears in the next chapter which deals with the struggle for Jewish emancipation in the years 1905–17.

83. [*Vestnik Vremennago Pravitelstva* (Official Gazette of the Provisional Government), No. 15 (61), Petrograd, March 22 (April 4), 1917. There is an English translation of the document in Raphael Mahler, *Jewish Emancipation. A Selection of Documents* (New York, American Jewish Committee, 1941), pp. 63–65. Ed.]

84. Quoted in S. M. Ginsburg, *Amolike Peterburg* (New York, 1944), pp. 251–252.

V

THE DUMAS AND THE STRUGGLE FOR EMANCIPATION, 1906–17

THE Jewish struggle for emancipation in Russia had a long and checkered history. In some ways it resembles the battle of western European Jewry for political equality, but it differs in technique and program. In the early stages of this campaign for civil rights—in the 1840's and fifties—the leaders placed special emphasis on the acquisition of secular education. It was the belief of these *maskilim* (followers of Haskalah or Enlightenment) that once their brethren had gained a knowledge of secular culture and modernized their religious observances and system of education, the Russian government would willingly bestow full citizenship upon them. During these early years no attempt was made to appeal to Russian public opinion. Jewish intellectuals in the days of Nicholas I did not yet possess an adequate knowledge of the Russian language. Besides, it is doubtful whether there would have been much chance of reaching the ears of a suppressed people.

In the reign of Alexander II the champions of Jewish rights introduced the appeal to Russian sympathy as a new weapon in their struggle. By this time there had grown up a generation of Jews educated in modern rabbinical seminaries or Russian universities. They were acquainted with the Russian language and, moreover, regarded themselves as full-fledged members of the Russian nation. The first Russo-Jewish publication, *Razsvet,* that was established for the above-mentioned purpose appeared in 1860 in the city of Odessa. Its chief function, like that of subsequent, similar organs of public opinion, was to familiarize the Russian world with the plight and problems of the Jew and to enlist gentile support for Jewish equality. At the same time these periodicals served as a forum of defense for the maligned Jews, refuting libelous charges and seeking to explain and interpret the Jew to the gentile world. The Jewish writers as well as the gentile ones who came to espouse their cause pleaded for the removal of all Jewish disabilities not only on the ground of justice and humanity but also in the enlightened self-interest of the Russian masses.

When the government of Alexander III reverted to a policy of militant anti-Semitism, the Russo-Jewish press stood as the only means of defense available to the Jews. It was here that Jews expressed their sorrow and resentment over the pogroms of the eighties. In it appeared scathing refutations of government charges that these excesses were the natural result of Jewish "exploitation." The May Rules of 1882, which further narrowed the Pale of Settlement and imposed new disabilities upon the Jewish population, were also subjected to blistering criticism by all these publications.

As Chapter III has shown, after the outbreak of the first wave of pogroms there began a movement to solve the problem of Russian Jewry through emigration. While none of the Russo-Jewish organs opposed emigration as a solution for individual Jews, all insisted that Russian Jewry continue the battle for equality in Russia, their native land. Only those blinded by hatred, *Russky Evrei* declared,[1] can fail to comprehend the attachment which binds the heart and soul of the educated Jew to Russia, the land of his birth, from whose midst he has no desire to depart in search of another homeland. Even after Ignatiev's brutally frank suggestion to a Jewish leader that the Jews leave the country since they had nothing to look forward to in Russia, *Russky Evrei* asked for patience.[2] "Emigration as a national policy," it maintained, "would be tantamount to giving up the claim to equality acquired as a result of our residence here for many centuries and our contributions together with her other citizens to the growth and development of Russia." [3]

With noteworthy courage the press continued the struggle for Jewish rights in the face of pogroms and growing disabilities. *Voskhod*, as has been indicated, rebuked the Conference of Notables in St. Petersburg for its groveling plea that the government help quiet the passions of the raging mobs.[4]

To circumvent censorship, which often made direct criticism of government policies impossible, the Russo-Jewish press resorted to circuitous methods. Thus *Voskhod* was for fifteen years the only Russo-Jewish organ to conduct a weekly "Review of the Russian Press" in order indirectly to criticize tsarist policies. S. M. Ginsburg, who for a number of years was closely associated with *Voskhod*, called attention to the misunderstanding which existed in the minds of many Jewish critics concerning this indirect criticism. Some Jewish writers ridiculed the polemical battles with the anti-Semitic press, asserting that there was no use in arguing with malicious detractors.

1. (1881), No. 24, p. 933.
2. *Ibid.* (1882), No. 5, pp. 162–164.
3. *Ibid.*, No. 21, p. 786.
4. *Nedelnaia Khronika Voskhoda* (1882), No. 39; see above, p. 63.

These critics, however, quite missed the point, for the polemics were aimed not so much at the anti-Semitic journalists as at the anti-Semitic government. There had to be some means of expressing resentment of libelous charges and refuting them. The writer of the "Review of the Russian Press" never engaged in apologetics but rather attacked and indicted traducers and maligners of Jewry; the Russian press often quoted him.[5]

But *Voskhod* did not always confine itself to the indirect approach. It often threw discretion to the winds and protested Jewish mistreatment in no ambiguous terms. In an editorial summarizing the year's events of 1883, a writer complained that he could not find

> one green oasis in the dry and arid desert of the past twelve months. The policies of the last two years developed and produced the fruits of the present year: the same pogroms with their concomitant wanton destruction, the same cruel expulsions and the same arbitrariness of the administration. Moreover, these cruel persecutions no longer have the "charm of novelty." In the beginning the world was aroused and protested, now the world stands by and is silent. The critical illness which physicians sought to heal in its early manifestations has now become chronic.

Nevertheless he urged the reader to begin the new year with faith in progress and in the inevitable triumph of truth and light over bigotry and darkness.[6]

During the entire reign of Alexander III and in the preconstitutional period of Nicholas II the struggle for civil equality consisted in appealing to the conscience of the Russian people and in arousing foreign public opinion. The Bureau of Defense, a committee organized in the early years of the twentieth century by a group of leaders in St. Petersburg, had as its purpose not only self-defense but also the dissemination of accurate information concerning Russian Jews. Through foreign as well as Russian organs of public opinion the bureau worked to counteract anti-Semitic propaganda and prodded the conscience of Europe to bestir itself on behalf of Russian Jewry. Because of its need for frequent loans from abroad tsarist Russia was highly sensitive to foreign public opinion.

A drastic change in the character of this campaign for emancipation took place in the political spring of 1904 when the Russian people made a bid for their own political freedom. Following the appointment of Sviatopolk-Mirsky as minister of the interior on August 26, 1904, numerous political meetings were held throughout

5. S. M. Ginsburg, *Amolike Peterburg,* pp. 179–180.
6. *Nedelnaia Khronika Voskhoda* (1883), Nos. 51–52, pp. 1441–1444.

the country. These demanded the abolition of autocracy and the introduction of a constitutional regime. The Jews too now voiced their demands in stronger and bolder terms.

A "Declaration of Jewish Citizens" sponsored by six thousand Jews stated in part:

We expect to receive civil equality, and we expect it not on the ground that it would make the Jews more useful citizens nor because it would benefit others. Neither do we expect equality as a reward for the blood our brethren are shedding on the fields of Manchuria even as their brothers shed theirs in former wars; we do not even demand civil equality on the basis of our centuries-old residence in territories which are today a part of the Russian Empire. We demand civil equality and equal obedience to the general laws as men who in spite of everything are aware of their human dignity and are conscientious citizens of a modern state. We do not expect that right to be bestowed upon us as an act of grace or magnanimity or as a matter of political expediency, but as a matter of honor and justice.[7]

A memorandum that thirty-two communities sent to Witte, president of the Cabinet, spoke of "the offended human dignity which will not be appeased by half measures." And an even sharper declaration by twenty-six other communities stressed the futility of seeking to appease the Jewish population with partial reforms. In March, 1905, a national conference of Russian Jewry was held in Vilno for the purpose of formulating a program of demands to be presented to the government. Except for the Jewish socialists, who were represented in the Bund, all elements of the Jewish community sent representatives to the conference. At that meeting there was formed the League for the Attainment of Complete Equality for Russian Jewry. The society proceeded to demand political and national rights.[8]

By the term "national rights" was meant communal autonomy and official recognition of both the Jews' national language and national schools. Although the last of European Jewries to receive civil and political equality, the Russian Jews, it should be noted, were the first to demand national rights.

There were a number of reasons for this courageous stand on the part of Russian Jewry. The French Jews' surrender—for the sake of obtaining civil equality—of all claims to nationhood, at the famous gathering called by Napoleon in Paris in 1807, was often severely criticized by Jewish writers. Furthermore, the rapid assimi-

7. *Pravo* (1905), No. 9.
8. Simon Dubnow, *Kniga Zhizni* (2 vols., Riga, 1934 and 1935), II, 21–26.

lation of west European Jews, who in their struggle for civil freedom in the nineteenth century renounced their national identity, served as a warning to their brethren in the east. Ahad Haam, a leading Russian-Jewish thinker, described the abasing form that assimilation took among some elements of emancipated western Jews as "slavery in freedom."

There was too, of course, the impact of the general struggle for national self-determination of various minority groups, whose intensified efforts in that direction in the latter part of the nineteenth century greatly encouraged Jewish emulation. Another helpful factor was the modification of the conception of nationhood which had previously implied territorial possession. In the beginning of the twentieth century there was a tendency to define it also in spiritual and cultural terms, as a group bound by common historic experiences and a common language or culture.

In Russia Simon Dubnow published in the nineties a series of articles in which he developed his conception of a Jewish people as a spiritual community held together by historical, cultural, and religious ties. Although they had lost their political independence, the Jews did not cease to exist as a national group because of the common spiritual interest uniting the various portions of Israel scattered throughout the world. Further to preserve the identity of the Jewish nationality Dubnow urged that the Jews be given the opportunity in each country to foster their religious and cultural institutions. As against the Zionists, who advocated the establishment of a Jewish national center in Palestine where the perpetuation of both Judaism and Jewry would be assured, Dubnow advanced his ideas of autonomy, according to which the Jewish people could preserve their national existence in the lands of the Diaspora.[9]

The manifesto of October 17, 1905, offered Russian Jewry the first opportunity to wage an organized political battle for civil equality. While the Bund, together with the parties of the left, decided to boycott the elections to the first Duma, by means of which, they contended, tsarism was seeking to save its tottering structure from the growing might of the revolution, the League for the Attainment of Complete Equality resolved to participate. An energetic campaign conducted throughout the country under its leadership resulted in the election of twelve Jewish deputies. Nine of these were Cadets (Constitutional Democrats) and three joined the Trudoviki (Labor group), a newly formed faction supported chiefly by peas-

9. [Koppel S. Pinson, "The National Theories of Simon Dubnow," *Jewish Social Studies* (October, 1948), pp. 335–358. Ed.]

ants, with a program somewhat resembling that of the Social Revolutionaries.

The leader of the parliamentary Jewish group was M. M. Vinaver, chairman of the league and one of the leaders of the Cadet party. Another outstanding member was Shmarya Levin, who later attained fame as a leader in the Zionist movement. The Jewish deputies did not form a bloc in the first Duma, but they worked as a unit on matters of Jewish interest, consulting the central bureau of the league on Jewish measures to be submitted to the Duma.

The opening of the first Duma in St. Petersburg on April 27, 1906, was an event of great historical significance for Russia. For the first time the Jews had a public platform where they could present their case to the representatives of the Russian people as well as to the entire country. Eager to utilize this opportunity for which they had waited so many years, some Jewish deputies and leaders outside the Duma pressed for immediate action. The Jewish press urged the deputies to make clear that Jews would not be satisfied with less than complete equality. Shmarya Levin urged that the Jewish question should take precedence over that of the peasantry.[10]

The method of procedure was also a matter of serious disagreement. Some deputies and Jewish leaders maintained that since the Jews were the most rightless of minority groups their case merited special and separate treatment, while others held that the removal of Jewish disabilities should be effected through a general law abolishing all religious and national discrimination in Russia. Trudovik deputy Leonty M. Bramson relates that the majority of the deputies, Cadets by party affiliation, were opposed to a separate declaration on behalf of the Jews because they feared lest some anti-Semitic deputy utilize the occasion to make an anti-Jewish speech.[11]

While the cause of the Jews in its entirety was not presented to the Duma, the question of Jewish rightlessness was brought to the attention of that body on several occasions. A number of deputies criticized the government because in his declaration of policy I. L. Goremykin, president of the Cabinet, failed to make any reference to the government's intentions regarding the Jewish problem. Vinaver, speaking for the Jewish deputies, expressed amazement that the government could completely avoid allusion to Jewish inequality. "We Jews, representatives of one of the most tormented nationalities in the land, have never uttered a word about ourselves, because we did not consider it fitting to speak in this place about civil inequality," he declared. The Jews had hoped that the government

10. Shmarya Levin, *The Arena,* tr. Maurice Samuel (New York, 1932), p. 287.
11. Memoirs, in *Novy Put* (1916), No. 15.

would not forget them, but from its attitude to the Jewish question it was obvious that the administration intended to cling to its old habits.[12] Heated pleas for Jewish emancipation were made in the Duma during the debate on the appointment of a committee to prepare a bill on civil equality. Contrary to the leaders of the conservative Octobrists, who urged caution in dealing with the Jewish problem, the Cadet party advocated immediate removal of all Jewish disabilities.[13] Another occasion for protests against mistreatment of Jews was afforded by the pogroms in Bialystok and Sedlets.[14]

In an article on the first Duma Vinaver relates how it afforded some Russian deputies their first lesson in Jewish history. When the Jewish question came up for discussion in the committee on civil equality two bulky volumes were brought in, one a source book on Russian-Jewish history *Regesty i Nadpisi* (Digests and Inscriptions) and the other a collection of discriminatory laws against the Jews in Russia. One deputy measured the book of statutes with his eyes as if to say: "Did we really create all these restrictions?" Several times he attempted to read it but each time put it back. When Vinaver opened the first page of *Regesty i Nadpisi*, pointing to the statement that Jews had lived in Russia since the earliest known times, two Octobrists near him rose from their seats to look at the page as though they could not believe their eyes. As the report on the Jewish status was concluded, a liberal deputy, speaking in the hush that had fallen upon the listeners, said, "When will the time finally come when we Russians will not have to blush before you Jews?"[15]

Deputy Bramson testifies to the eagerness of the Trudovik peasant deputies to confer civil rights upon their Jewish neighbors. It seems that a few days before the opening of the first Duma a deputy from Grodno had provided living quarters for a group of peasant deputies whom he sought to influence against the Jews and in favor of the government policies. The peasant deputies moved out in protest as soon as the Trudoviki quarters opened. Bramson also recounts how in a party caucus the statement of a peasant deputy that Jews could not be made the equals of the Russian peasants was met with jeers by the majority. When the two Jewish deputies present asked for the floor, Christian deputies pleaded for the privilege of answering first. The speakers asserted that they came to the Duma determined to fight

12. *Gosudarstvennaia Duma. Sessia Pervaia. Stenograficheskye Otchoty* (1906), I, 338–339.

13. *Ibid.*, II, 1050–1052, 1006–1010.

14. See above, Chapter III.

15. "Tenth Jubilee Number of *Rech*," quoted in *Novy Put* (1916), No. 16, pp. 11–12.

any attempt to punish a people for their faith or nationality or to continue the tradition of pinning all guilt upon the Jews. When the question of granting the Jews complete equality was brought to a vote, 3 voted in the negative, 10 abstained, and over 100—the majority of whom were peasants—voted in the affirmative.[16]

Had a vote been taken on the floor of the Duma on this question it would have passed by a majority, since the Duma was composed chiefly of liberals. Of a total of 486 deputies, the Cadets controlled about 200, the Trudoviki 94, other leftist groups some twenty-odd deputies, the Octobrists 38, and the extreme rightists had but a handful. Very likely the bill would have been vetoed by the State Council and certainly blocked by the tsar, but the vote of the Duma would have been a moral victory for both the Jews and the Russian people. It was due to the timidity of the majority of the Jewish deputies and to the hesitancy of the Cadet party in bringing the matter to a vote that the representatives of the Russian people assembled in the first Duma did not formally repudiate the anti-Jewish policies of the tsarist government.

The precedent established by the first Duma was followed by the second, which convened on February 20, 1907. In this Duma there were only four Jewish deputies. One had been elected on a non-Jewish party ticket, the other three by Jewish constituencies; all were comparatively unknown to the Jewish world. (The prominent Jewish leaders who served in the first Duma were disqualified for election to the second because all of them had signed the Vyborg manifesto.) [17] The question of Jewish equality was presented to the second Duma only once: in considering a bill submitted by the government proposing to abolish all religious discrimination except that against Jews, the Committee on Freedom of Conscience amended it to include the Jews. Because of the short life of the second Duma this bill, like that in the first Duma, failed to come before the plenary session for a final vote. Thus the first two Dumas, which would have voted civil equality for Russian Jewry, never had an opportunity to register the will of the Russian people. As for the third and fourth Dumas, which on account of the election law of June 3, 1907, did not represent the masses of the Russian people, there was neither the intention nor the possibility of securing justice for the Jews through these.

In previous chapters mention has been made of how the extreme

16. Bramson, memoirs in *Novy Put* (1916), No. 15.

17. [The Vyborg manifesto of July, 1906, signed by the parliamentary opposition in protest against the dissolution of the first Duma, called upon the Russian people to stop paying taxes. Ed.]

rightists utilized the rostrum of the third and fourth Dumas to heap abuse upon the Russian Jews and to disseminate vicious propaganda against them. It will be recalled that the third Duma raised the question of eliminating Jews from military service because of their allegedly harmful influence upon the morale of the soldiers. The Jews could not even find support among the conservative Octobrists who formed the party of the center and in the last two Dumas exercised a dominating influence. Their attitude to the Jews is apparent in their objection to the appointment of Jewish jurists as justices of the peace on the ground that it would be incompatible with a Christian state.[18]

The Jews, moreover, were inadequately represented in the third and fourth Dumas. Because of the pressure exerted upon the electorate by local administrations, and the terroristic methods of the Black Hundred, only two Jewish deputies were elected to the third and three to the fourth Duma. The chief task of these deputies, who were not particularly note-worthy individuals, was to defend the Jews against the attacks of the extreme right. In the third Duma the Jewish deputies did manage to collect 166 signatures for a bill to abolish the Pale of Settlement; it was submitted to the Duma which after some debate sent it to committee where it was buried.

The fourth Duma never even considered abolishing Jewish disabilities. One of the factors that militated against friendly endeavor on behalf of the Jews was the Beilis trial which inflamed anti-Semitism; another was the outbreak of the war which suspended all factional strife and opposition to the government.

But when as the war progressed Russia suffered alarming defeats, a critical attitude toward the government began to manifest itself. As a result, the so-called Progressive bloc was created in August, 1915. It consisted of Octobrists, right Nationalists, and the Cadets —who formed the radical element. Its purpose was to create a Cabinet that would lean more on the support of the people. On the Jewish question the Cadets, whose program called for the immediate removal of all religious or national restrictions, agreed for the sake of political expediency to the formula of "slow embarkation on the road to Jewish equality." For a time they thus gave up the battle for Jewish rights altogether. Subsequent events caused not only the Jews but all progressive circles in the country to lose faith in the Progressive bloc.

In their anxiety to preserve the bloc the Cadets, who as a party were never militant about Jewish emancipation, became even more amenable to compromise. They had voted, as we have seen, against

18. [Dubnow, *History,* III, 153–156. Ed.]

an interpellation regarding an anti-Semitic circular sent by the minister of the interior to all local administrations. To secure the passage of reforms they favored they agreed to retain temporarily the existing limitations against the Jews. They were criticized for this betrayal by a liberal Russian organ which charged the party with adopting the methods of the Octobrists of the third Duma in matters of Jewish policy.[19] The Social Democratic deputy Chkhenkeli sarcastically suggested that the Cadets declare themselves openly as either anti-Semites or political charlatans.[20] So too did the Jewish Cadet deputy Friedman upbraid his party for faithlessness to its program and, appealing to progressive Russia, implied that there could be no room for Jewish deputies in the Progressive bloc. The Jewish press in condemning the Cadets for their "retreat" observed that only the parties of the left were ready to solve the Jewish problem and that they alone were the real friends of the Jews.[21]

Jewish resentment at the attitude of the bloc was strongly voiced in the spring of 1916, when the Duma rejected the interpellation regarding the anti-Semitic circular. In an open letter to their deputies a group of Jewish leaders protested the action of their coreligionists who had voted against the interpellation. "People tortured by persecution expect from you not only defense from violence but a courageous battle."

It should be noted that some prominent members of the Cadet party dissented from the policy of yielding to the majority of the Progressive bloc on the Jewish question. During the debate on the bill for rural self-government F. I. Rodichev, a leading Cadet and veteran champion of Jewish rights, protested against the Jewish restrictions: "Each inequality breeds hooliganism;" in depriving the Jews of their human rights, the Russians cannot truthfully assert to their enemies that they are battling for the freedom of small peoples.[22]

Reference has been made a number of times to the support Jewry found among the Russian people in their battle for emancipation. There was the petition to the government for Jewish equality submitted by the Military Industrial Committee representing most industries, trades, and professions. There was an appeal signed by one hundred writers in support of Jewish freedom. A volume of

19. Quoted in *Novy Put* (1916), No. 19, p. 112.

20. *Stenograficheskye Otchoty Gosudarstvennoi Dumy. Chetvorty Sozyv* (Fourth Duma), July, 1916.

21. *Novy Put* (1916), No. 20.

22. *Stenograficheskye Otchoty Gosudarstvennoi Dumy. Chetvorty Sozyv* (Fourth Duma), December 8, 1916.

essays published in 1916 by the Russian Society for the Study of Jewish Life merits special attention. Entitled *Shchit* (The Shield) and edited by such men of letters as Maxim Gorky, Leonid Andreev, and Feodor Sologub, the book contains expressions of opinion, sketches, and studies of Jewish life by Russia's foremost writers, economists, and philosophers.[23] It is a valuable study of anti-Semitism, its causes and cures.

In an article on "Russia and the Jews" Gorky, who approached the subject from a humanitarian point of view, castigated his compatriots for their indifference to the fate of their Jewish neighbors. "The situation," he wrote, "of the Jews in Russia, which is a disgrace to Russian culture, is one of the results of our carelessness, of our indifference to the straight and just decrees of life. In the interests of reason, justice, civilization, we must not tolerate that people without rights should live among us; we would never have tolerated it if we had a strong sense of self-respect." Paying tribute to the Jewish people for "its manly idealisms, its unconquerable faith in the victory of good over evil," he said: "The Jews—mankind's old, strong leaven—have always exalted its spirit, bringing into the world restless, noble ideals, goading men to embark on a search for fine values."

In a deeply moving essay entitled "The First Step" Andreev depicted the spiritual torments which he, as a Russian intellectual and "a happy representative of the sovereign race," suffered as a result of Jewish persecution. Although he was not directly responsible, shame and sin oppressed him. All his fervent pleas, "the sincerest tears of compassion and outcries of indignation unfailingly broke against a dull, unresponsive wall." He could not rid himself of a sense of guilt: "all powerlessness, if it is unable to prevent a crime—becomes complicity; and this was the result: personally guiltless of any offence against my brother, I have become in the eyes of all those unconcerned and those of my brother himself, a Cain." While to the Jews the Pale and other disabilities were a fatal and impregnable fact which deformed their entire life, they were for Andreev, the Russian, like a hump on the back, which disfigured him both physically and spiritually. He was forever conscious of its presence. It robbed him of peace of mind both day and night. And he described his feeling of relief and exaltation when he read about the possibility of the imminent removal of a number of Jewish disabilities.

Both the religious philosopher Dmitry Merezhkovsky and the

23. Tr. A. Yarmolinsky (New York, Alfred A. Knopf, 1917). [All quotations are from the English translation, pp. 5–6, 8, 24, 57–58, 68, 70–71, 86, 90–91. Ed.]

novelist Feodor Sologub asserted the moral responsibility of all Russians for the mistreatment of the Jews and stressed Russia's concern in the solution of the Jewish problem.

While these writers and thinkers approached the problem primarily from a humanitarian and ethical point of view, Paul Miliukov made a historical and political analysis of anti-Semitism. He called attention to the fact that with the exception of Romania and Russia all modern countries had granted the Jews civil rights. Religious and racial differences no longer created disabilities in civilized countries, and wherever anti-Semitism still existed in western countries its aims were political. "The problem of Jewish equal rights in Russia is the problem of the equal rights of all our citizens in general . . . That is why the anti-Semitical [sic] parties in Russia have a larger political significance and importance than the anti-Semitical parties of the West. In our country they almost coincide with anti-constitutional parties in general, and anti-Semitism is the banner of the old régime, of which we still struggle in vain to rid ourselves. That is why the Jewish problem has come to occupy the center of our political stage."

Following a survey of Jewish fortunes in Russia, Miliukov correctly observes that however ancient the instincts upon which the anti-Semite sought to play, anti-Semitism as a motto and a political weapon was a comparatively new phenomenon in Russia. It arose with the struggle of the Russian people for political freedom; it was the product of the constitutional epoch. When the people asserted their will to participate in national affairs, the government appealed to hatred of the Jews to divert their attention. "Antisemitism," Miliukov wrote, "says to the ignorant masses: 'There is your enemy, fight the Jews and you will improve your life conditions.' "

In Russia, as he pointed out, anti-Semitism was also used by the demagogue as a means of frightening the authorities. With this in view the "legend of the Jew as the creator of the Russian revolution" was formed. As a proud Russian Miliukov indignantly rejected this charge which carried the obvious implication that without the Jew the Russian nation would not have sought its own political liberation: "No, however great my respect for the exceptional gifts of the Jewish people may be, I will not refuse the Russian nation the ability of taking the initiative in the cause of its own freedom."

M. V. Bernatsky, a professor and writer on economic topics, urged full equality for the Jews in a scholarly essay on "The Jews and Russian Economic Life." Describing the harmful effect of the anti-Semitic policies upon both the victims and the general economy of the country, he wrote: "Antisemitism from the economic standpoint is nothing but a tremendous waste of the country's productive powers." Because Jews formed an integral part of Russia's economic organism, the blows directed at them affected in an equal if not greater degree the mass of the Russian people. Emigration of all the Jews would hurt Russia's economic development. He concluded with an appeal on behalf of Jewish freedom:

Whoever has our economic welfare at heart, whoever dreams about the mighty development of our country and of its real emancipation from foreign influence,—inasmuch as this is generally possible,—must understand that anti Semitism is the worst foe of our economic prosperity, that, in short, the Jewish question is a Russian question. Full rights for the Jews, equal with those that the rest of the population of the Empire enjoy, are an indispensable condition for our peaceful cultural development. Only on that basis can we achieve the broad ideals which have come into prominence in this tragic struggle with German imperialism.

The diagnosis of the Jewish status in Russia as a problem of the Russian people coincided with the approach to the question of Jewish emancipation on the part of the enlightened elements of Russian Jewry and their leaders. For in contrast with those champions of equality in Haskalah days who pinned all their hopes on the government, Jewish leaders of the later period appealed to the Russian people, of whom Russian Jewry formed an integral part. A brief sketch of the two Jewish political leaders who for almost two decades led the struggle for emancipation will reveal the methods employed to champion Jewish rights in that era.

Among the so-called bourgeois Jewish leaders [24] Maxim M. Vinaver (1862–1926) was the most eminent. Born and trained in Warsaw, he settled in St. Petersburg soon after his graduation as a lawyer from the university of his native city. His legal practice and scholarly contributions to reputable journals soon made him an eminent figure in the world of jurists. He was a contributor to the Studies of the Juridical Society of the University of St. Petersburg and editor of *Vestnik Prava* (Legal Messenger), journal of the civil department of that society.

Vinaver's entrance into politics began in the political spring of 1904, when he took an active part in the various conferences then being held. He presided at the constitutional convention at which the Cadet party was formed, and was a member of the central committee until the dissolution of the party. Chosen deputy from St.

24. The leadership of the Bund and other socialist groups will be discussed in the following chapter.

Petersburg in the first Duma on the Cadet ticket, Vinaver was one of the leaders of that faction in the chamber. He was the author of the Duma's reply to the emperor's address delivered from the throne.

After the closing of the Duma Vinaver signed the Viborg manifesto, for which offense he was sentenced together with the other signers to serve a three-month prison term and lose his elective rights. Disqualified to stand for election, he nonetheless continued to influence the Cadet party through his position in the central committee and active participation in the annual party conferences.

Vinaver was also a guiding spirit of the party after the February revolution of 1917 and during the existence of the short-lived Provisional government. He was appointed senator by that government and served in the presidium of the committee charged with framing the bylaws for the Constituent Assembly to which he was elected as a Cadet representative.

After the October revolution of 1917 Vinaver, a militant liberal, fled to the Crimea where he accepted the post of minister for foreign affairs in the Crimean regional government, which was organized for the purpose of fighting the Bolshevik government with the help of the Allied armies. Upon the defeat of the White armies and their expulsion from the south of Russia by the Red forces, Vinaver fled to Paris where he died in 1926.[25]

Simultaneously with his activity in Russian politics Vinaver distinguished himself in Jewish public affairs. Soon after he settled in the capital he began to show a keen interest in the plight of his people. In the early nineties when the harsh regime of Alexander III permitted no political activity, the young lawyer began to serve his people in the spiritual and cultural field.

At the suggestion of Simon Dubnow, then residing in Odessa, Vinaver with a group of others started to collect material on the history of Russian Jewry. These young intellectuals also organized a historical-ethnographic committee which held periodic meetings at which papers were read on various aspects of Jewish history. These meetings served not only as a spiritual focus for the Jewish intelligentsia of the capital but also as a training ground for Jewish leaders. At Vinaver's suggestion the Historical-Ethnographic Society was founded in 1908; he was its president until 1917. The society published the quarterly *Evreiskaia Starina* which grouped around itself the most competent students of Russian-Jewish history.[26] In 1902

25. *M. M. Vinaver i Russkaia Obshchestvennost Nachala XX Veka* (Paris, 1937); a volume of essays on the life and work of Vinaver, including a biographical sketch.

26. [Vinaver, "Kak My Zanimalis Istoriei," *Evreiskaia Starina,* Vol. I (1909); Wischnitzer, "Pamiati S. M. Dubnowa," *Evreisky Mir* (Union of Russian Jews, New York, 1944), pp. 55–68. Ed.]

Vinaver also undertook the publication of *Voskhod*, which throughout the tsarist regime conducted a gallant fight for Jewish equality.

Vinaver attracted national attention and gained wide popularity among Russian Jewry at the trial that followed the pogrom in Gomel. Because of the open bias of the court the counsel for the defense, who included some of the best representatives of the legal profession in Russia, decided to withdraw from the trial in protest. Charged with the task of stating the case for the attorneys, Vinaver gave such a brilliant presentation that his address to the court made a profound impression on the entire country.

The conference of Jewish representatives held in Vilno in March, 1905, called at Vinaver's initiative and conducted under his chairmanship, further increased his popularity among the masses of Russian Jewry. Dubnow, who met Vinaver for the first time at this conference, relates that this brilliant jurist impressed him as a born political leader. "His political wisdom and tact made themselves evident in the conduct of the conference," Dubnow writes, and he tells how in spite of the varying opinions and temperaments of the sixty-seven representatives Vinaver managed to hold them together, to calm heated passions, and create a common ground for collective action. "His speeches were enchanting, not by virtue of superficial brilliance but because of their lucidity and captivating logic; he coined phrases that were unique and memorable." [27]

Vinaver always looked upon the struggle for Jewish freedom as an integral part of the general Russian struggle for political emancipation. This view was expressed in a resolution which he sponsored and the Vilno conference adopted: that the complete realization of the program undertaken would be made possible only with the introduction of civil liberties and the establishment of a truly parliamentary regime. Through his own struggle for equality, Vinaver stated, the Jew at the same time contributed to the success of the general cause of Russia's freedom.

In his memoirs Witte relates that when he assumed the presidency of the Cabinet a Jewish deputation called upon him regarding the matter of Jewish equality. In the course of the interview Witte informed his visitors that he himself favored gradual equalization of the Jews with the rest of the Russian population, but that to enable him to present their case for consideration the Jews should refrain from participating in the revolutionary movement. He told the delegation: "Of late years the Jews have come to the fore as leaders of various political parties and advocates of the most extreme political ideas. Now, it is not your business to teach us. Leave

27. Dubnow, *Kniga Zhizni,* II, 22.

that to Russians by birth and civil status and mind your own affairs." [28]

According to Witte Baron Günzburg, the head of the delegation, and a few others agreed with him. Vinaver on the other hand dissented. He declared that the time had come when the Russian people were going to obtain full rights for all citizens irrespective of race or faith, and that it was the duty of the Jews to offer every possible support to those Russians who were fighting for the political emancipation of the country.

Vinaver urged this same argument upon his fellow Jews. "Let us not succumb to the prevailing panic," he wrote in 1906, "our efforts and our faith will render a great service not only to the Jewish people but also to the general struggle for freedom in Russia." [29] And in his reply to the address from the throne he chided the government for omitting all reference to the Jewish problem, asserting that this silence indicated the government's intention to continue its old policies in the general affairs of the country: "By your failure to take notice of the cry of despair coming from the souls of six million people, you have declared your intention to tread the old path. Let it be known that we Jews are joining the chorus of those voices which say unto you: 'Go away.' We shall follow only that government which will reflect the will of the people."

Like all other Jewish intellectuals who were products of the Russian school system and had the opportunity to come into close contact with their Russian neighbors, Vinaver had a profound love for the Russian people and a deep faith in their sense of justice. In his attacks on the government for its anti-Jewish policies he always differentiated between the administrative authorities and the Russian people. During the debate on the Bialystok pogrom he declared, "We profoundly believe that the Russian people bear no enmity toward us; our enemy is only the ruling clique, which for its own pernicious purposes seeks to incite the people against us. These criminally blinded people fail to realize that by their actions they undermine not only our position but also the sound body of the great mass of the Russian population as well as the entire state organism." He concluded the address with the declaration: "We Jews are a small people but we have one powerful weapon—the weapon of despair, and we have one great ally—the genuinely humane Russian people."

Disqualified, as we have seen, for election to any Dumas after the first, Vinaver took a leading part in the election campaigns and in

28. Witte, *Memoirs,* pp. 381–382.
29. *Voskhod* (1906), No. 7, p. 29.

the formulation of Jewish policies. As a result of the decision adopted by the Zionists at their conference in Helsingfors in 1906 to intensify their political activity on behalf of Jewish emancipation in the Diaspora under the banner of their own organization, Vinaver with a group of non-Zionists formed the Jewish People's group. The organizational conference of that group, held in St. Petersburg in February, 1907, adopted a program similar to that of the dissolved League for the Attainment of Complete Equality. In addition to political emancipation the People's group announced as its aim the development of the spiritual powers of the Jewish people and demanded the right to use their national language and to have autonomy in the field of education.

Although no Zionist, Vinaver viewed the Jewish people as a national group united by common historic experiences and a common culture. Attached to his people by historical, religious, and cultural ties, Vinaver at the same time regarded himself as a member of the Russian people with whom he shared a common political destiny. Dubnow aptly characterized him as one in whom the Jewish and Russian elements were inseparable and, as he put it, "the hand of Jacob took hold on Esau's heel." [30]

Of a similar conviction was Leonty M. Bramson (1869–1941), deputy of the first Duma. Born in Kovno where he received his elementary and secondary education, he studied law in the University of Moscow. Upon graduating in 1890 he settled in St. Petersburg, where in addition to his private practice he engaged in Russian and Jewish public service. In his student years Bramson already showed a keen interest in the plight of his people. At the same time he was strongly influenced by Russian culture, particularly by those currents which gave rise to the movements for freedom and equality. These twin influences of Jewish and Russian culture left their mark on the activities of the future Russian-Jewish leader.

Soon after his arrival in the capital Bramson became an active member of the Free Economic Society and of the Society for the Promotion of Culture among Jews. In the later nineties he took an active interest in the Russian branch of the Jewish Colonization Association, which had its headquarters in Petersburg,[31] and for a number of years he managed the practical work of the association. As a lawyer Bramson joined the Bureau of Defense which sought to render legal aid to Jews against illegal and arbitrary acts on the part of tsarist officialdom.

30. *Kniga Zhizni,* I, 393.

31. J. Brutskus, "Bramson—Organizator Russkago Evreistva," *Evreisky Mir* publication of the Union of Russian Jews, II (New York, 1944), pp. 21–22.

The revolutionary year 1905 opened a new field of activity for Bramson. His love of Russia drove him into joining the movement for political freedom through participation in various political organizations. He took a leading part in the League for the Attainment of Complete Equality and later in the People's group, organizations which sought both to achieve full equality for the Jews and to make Jewish public life more democratic.

Elected to the first Duma as a candidate from his native province of Kovno, Bramson joined the Trudoviki and thereby virtually became one of the leaders of the Russian peasantry. Deprived like Vinaver of the opportunity to serve in the following three Dumas because he had signed the Viborg manifesto, he continued to influence the Trudoviki, with whom he kept in close contact. According to F. Brutskus, he was "soul and organizer" of the group.[32] At the same time he served as a permanent member of a committee of leaders who advised the Jewish deputies on purely Jewish policies.

During World War I Bramson was an active leader of Ekopo, a relief organization which rendered aid to refugees driven from their native towns.[33] He became particularly active in Ort, the organization which aimed at the rehabilitation of Jews through training them as artisans and agriculturists.[34] Bramson's work in Ort, to which he attracted large groups of the Jewish intelligentsia and representatives of the working class, gained him wide popularity among the younger generation of Jews. When he left Russia after the October revolution because of his opposition to the new government, Bramson devoted his entire activity to Ort. Under his energetic leadership this developed into a large organization with branches in all European and American countries. He held its presidency from 1923 until 1941, the year of his death in France.

Bramson never showed any interest in the Zionist movement. Brutskus asserts that a family incident was responsible for his prejudice against the Palestinian experiment. Bramson's father, a pioneer Zionist of Kovno, had made an unsuccessful attempt to organize a cooperative colony in a wild region of northern Galilee. The failure, which had unpleasant consequences for its organizers, gave the son a distaste for Palestine which lasted until 1935 when he paid a personal visit to the Holy Land.[35]

32. *Ibid.*, p. 23.

33. [Ekopo is the abbreviation of Evreiski Komitet Pomoshchi (Central Committee for the Relief of Jewish War Sufferers). Established in 1916, Ekopo developed a vast program of relief and rehabilitation. Ed.]

34. [Founded in 1880 in St. Petersburg, this organization was reorganized in 1921 as World Ort Union. Ed.]

35. *Evreisky Mir,* p. 15.

With this single exception, Bramson was active in every phase of Jewish life. In a sketch of his life and work Brutskus pays him this tribute: "For more than a half century Bramson gave himself unstintingly to his people. On all the hills and valleys of that long and hard road there are to be found the traces of Bramson. He was everywhere the organizer, originator, and unflagging worker." [36]

Vinaver and Bramson were the pre-eminent representatives of the so-called democratic and political leadership of Russian Jewry. Both men were chosen by their respective communities as delegates to the conference at Vilna, where the League for the Attainment of Complete Equality was formed in 1905. The program adopted at that conference and urged by these leaders upon the Russian government and public opinion represented in great measure the expression of the organized will of Russian Jewry.

But there were other Jewish representatives, who, although not officially delegated by the community, often spoke and acted on behalf of their Jewish compatriots. These self-appointed leaders, known as *shtadlanim* (intermediaries) and in modern days contemptuously referred to as backstairs diplomats, were products of the political conditions of their time. For a people constantly harassed by hostile governments and unfriendly local administrations, and until the spring of 1905 lacking democratically organized political leadership to intercede on their behalf, individual Jews, prominent chiefly on account of their wealth, would assume the function of shtadlanim. Beginning with the year 1857 there are to be found in the archives of the various Russian ministries constant references to petitions of individual Jews pleading for concessions and favors for their people. The petitioners had no authorization from those on whose behalf they pleaded.[37] In many instances some of these self-appointed leaders came to be recognized by the authorities as spokesmen of the Jewish community, and they rendered a much needed service.

One shtadlan who was known throughout the Pale and recognized for many years by the tsarist government as a spokesman was the banker Baron Horace de Günzburg (1833–1903).[38] He was initiated into the role by his father Evzel, who was for many years a self-appointed but recognized spokesman for Russian Jewry. In the first volume of this study reference was made to the memoranda Evzel de Günzburg submitted to the government about extending

36. *Ibid.,* p. 24.

37. [H. B. Sliozberg, "Baron G. O. Günzburg i Pravovoe Polozhenie Evreev," *Perezhitoe,* II (St. Petersburg, 1910), 97. Ed.]

38. [On the hundredth anniversary of the birth of Günzburg there appeared in Paris *Baron Gorazi O. Günzburg. Ego Zhisn i Deatelnost* (1933), 165 pp. Ed.]

special rights to select groups of Jewry. According to Sliozberg, his petition of 1862 initiated the inquiry about the Jewish problem sent out by the central government to the local administrations which subsequently led to the law of 1865 opening the interior provinces of Russia to artisans.[39] Both Evzel and his son Horace rendered a great service to Russian Jewry during the projected military reform passed in 1874. It was due solely to their intercession that the contemplated discriminations against the Jews were eliminated from that reform.[40]

Horace de Günzburg was particularly active on behalf of his people in the dark days of Alexander III and Nicholas II. After his father's death he took over the mantle of leadership. Having been invited to head a small group of select Jewish deputies to appear before the Pahlen commission, Günzburg supplied the commission with factual data on various phases of Jewish life, gathered by competent scholars. This material, supplemented by Günzburg's statements, played an important role in the findings of the Pahlen commission. It should be remembered that the commission was preceded by Ignatiev's provincial committees before which, at the inspiration of the government, charges were made not only that the economic activity of the Jews harmed the "native" population but that loyalty to Judaism could not go hand in hand with loyalty to the state. It was only because fair-minded Senator Pahlen, chairman of the commission, gave the Jews an opportunity to present their side of the case that the work of the commission took the turn it did. The commission's decision in favor of gradual abolition of all Jewish disabilities—which caused it to be dissolved—was greatly influenced by Günzburg and his associates.

The dissolving of the Pahlen commission was followed by the creation of a new committee, headed by Plehve, charged with preparing legislation to make permanent the Temporary Rules of May 3, 1882. Eager to please both the anti-Semitic emperor and Pobedonostsev, Plehve submitted a series of fresh restrictions designed to make the existence of Russian Jews even more unbearable. It was again due to Horace de Günzburg, who managed to secure the cooperation of Minister of Finance A. I. Vishnegradsky, that Plehve's projected anti-Jewish measures were rejected.[41]

Describing Günzburg's incessant efforts on behalf of Russian Jewry in the early nineties during the expulsions from Moscow and

39. Sliozberg, "Baron G. O. Günzburg," pp. 98, 99.

40. *Ibid.*, pp. 99–100; also Sliozberg, *Dela Davno Minuvshikh Dnei,* I, 93–94; S. M. Ginsburg, *Historishe Werk,* Vol. II.

41. Sliozberg, "Baron G. O. Günzburg," pp. 107–108; Ginsburg, *Historishe Werk,* II, 147–148.

the areas outside the Pale, Sliozberg writes: "One may think of these days as of an epidemic which kills right and left, and among the fallen and the wounded one sees the mighty figure of Baron Horace de Günzburg rushing aid wherever it was needed, seeking to alleviate pain and wipe away a tear." [42]

Both the authors from whose monographs this information about the baron is drawn were his close friends and admirers. Although they were conscientious and reliable historians, the portrayal of their friend was no doubt colored by their affection for him; in fact the portrait more often resembles a eulogy than an objective account. While these writers were in a position to report on the numerous representations made to the government regarding Jewish matters, they lacked the means of ascertaining the effectiveness of these intercessions. It may nevertheless be accepted with a fair degree of certainty that Günzburg's contacts with high government authorities must have been productive of some good results.

In addition to his political activity the baron made concrete and constructive contributions to his people's welfare in other fields. Upon the death of his father he became president of the Society for the Promotion of Culture among Jews. He financed the publication of a number of valuable works on Judaism and supported needy students and writers. The organizations that sought to train Jews for agricultural pursuits and as artisans received his moral and financial support. Sliozberg summarizes the role of the baron in Russian-Jewish life thus: "In the person of Horace Günzburg there departed from us a part of Jewish history in Russia. For almost half a century that history was bound up closely with the name of Baron Günzburg." [43]

A shtadlan of a different character was H. B. Sliozberg (1863–1937). After graduating from the law school of St. Petersburg University he spent several years in Germany doing postgraduate work. A scholar by inclination, he would have preferred an academic career but that was barred to him in his native land on account of his faith. In consequence he practiced law. He was an active member of the Juridical Society, contributed to scientific journals, and for a number of years edited the most prominent legal organ, *Vestnik Prava*. For more than ten years he was compelled to practice his profession as assistant to an attorney, because after 1889 no Jewish lawyer could be admitted to full professional status without special authorization from the minister of justice.

Early in his career Sliozberg met Baron Horace de Günzburg,

42. Sliozberg, "Baron G. O. Günzburg," p. 108.
43. *Ibid.*, p. 94.

whose adviser he became on matters concerning Russian Jewry. At Günzburg's suggestion he edited and published a study of the Jewish colonies in Kherson and Ekaterinoslav provinces. The purpose of this study was to refute the hostile charges made in anti-Semitic government circles against the Jewish farmers.

The official visit to Russia of the two American commissioners of immigration, John B. Weber and Dr. Walter Kempster,[44] afforded Sliozberg his first opportunity to become intimately familiar with the everyday life of the Jews in the Pale. Upon their arrival in St. Petersburg the commissioners sought out Baron Horace de Günzburg, who suggested that Sliozberg advise them during their stay in Russia. In his memoirs Sliozberg relates how hard it was to explain to the Americans the laws governing Jewish residence in Russia. Citizens of a free country, they could not conceive how whole families could be banished from their place of residence because of legal technicalities or adherence to a certain faith. Even a verbatim translation of statutes left them incredulous. It was only after their arrival in Moscow where they witnessed the mass eviction of Jewish artisans that they were finally convinced such cruelties were possible in a modern state.[45]

As has been told in Chapter III, after the stay in Moscow the American commissioners toured the Pale and visited a number of Jewish centers, where they made a thorough study of the economic and legal conditions of the Jewish population.[46] Sliozberg, who accompanied them, was deeply impressed by these direct contacts with his people. Reminiscing about this experience, he observed that a firsthand acquaintance with the life of the Jewish masses should be a prerequisite for Jewish leadership. "I felt myself attached heart and soul not only to the spirit which kept that people alive for thousands of years but also to the human mass which lived by that spirit." "Throughout my life," Sliozberg continued, "there would appear before my eyes images of the various types I met on that tour. I would see Jews rolling logs over the Nieman up to their waists in water; the Jewish lads, pale faced, emaciated, with wise and luminous eyes, turning the linotype machines in the printing houses in Vilno —and the expelled Jews on the Brest railway station in Moscow." After this he vowed to himself to do everything possible to alleviate the material and spiritual suffering of his brethren. His now intimate knowledge of human misery also strengthened within him the

44. See above, p. 73.

45. Sliozberg, *Dela Davno Minuvshikh Dnei,* II, 47.

46. [Weber and Kempster, *Report, passim;* also Sliozberg, *Dela Davno Minuvshikh Dnei,* II, 54 ff. Ed.]

desire not only to give collective aid but to serve the individual. Subsequently he had many occasions to render this kind of service, a service which some contemptuously dismissed as mere philanthropy.

The two American commissioners must have been strongly impressed with Sliozberg's high qualities, for at the termination of their mission in Russia they urged him to emigrate to the United States. Knowing that he was thwarted in his career by being a Jew, they assured him that in America a man of his talent could render useful service to his coreligionists and at the same time be free of all the disabilities of tsarist Russia. In later years Sliozberg confessed that in moments of depression, when the struggle for Jewish rights seemed hopeless, this tempting suggestion came to his mind. But always the love of Russia would prevail. "Had I left Russia," he confessed, "I would always have felt like one who deserted his suffering brethren." [47]

The "attorney for Jews," as he was dubbed, did not desert them but stayed to continue the struggle for freedom and to stand guard over the meager rights which the tsarist regime afforded the Jews. His battleground was primarily the first department of the Senate. To that department he would take his appeals against illegal expulsions and all sorts of discriminatory actions or arbitrary interpretations of the statutes governing the Jews. Armed with an expert knowledge of the law, he waged incessant legal battle against the lawlessness and corruption of tsarist officialdom.

Sliozberg relates that in the early years of his career, a time when the Appeal Department of the Senate was in the charge of fair and unbiased men, his work was quite fruitful and morally gratifying. But as the regime gradually deteriorated and grew desperate, even the highest court was handed over to venal bureaucrats as corrupt as the administration itself. In these circumstances Sliozberg's work was practically futile. Still, he would not yield and continued the struggle to the end of tsarism.

Besides the numerous appeals which he brought to the Senate on behalf of communities and single individuals, Sliozberg, as a member of the Bureau of Defense, also participated in all the pogrom trials. It was primarily owing to his efforts that non-Jewish expert testimony was introduced in the Beilis case.

In addition to the legal and literary service he rendered to the Jews, Sliozberg engaged in purely philanthropic work. Following the October pogroms in 1905, together with Horace de Günzburg he organized a relief committee which distributed close to 6,000,000 rubles among the victims. During World War I he was among the

47. Sliozberg, *Dela Davno Minuvshikh Dnei,* II 65–67.

organizers of Ekopo,[48] which spent about 50,000,000 rubles for relief of refugees.

In 1920 Sliozberg, who was by political conviction a rightist Cadet, settled in Paris. There he continued his philanthropic work, this time for needy Russian-Jewish intellectuals. The organization which he founded for this purpose was called Ohel Yakob (Tent of Jacob). During his visits to the United States he lectured in a number of Jewish communities on the plight of European Jewry. Shortly before his death he contemplated a manuscript on the ethical ideals of Judaism. In his last letter to S. M. Ginsburg he wrote, "Let our youth know what Judaism has contributed to humanity."

Just as with Vinaver and Bramson, so too with Sliozberg love of his people went hand in hand with love of Russia. A non-Zionist throughout his life, he was a Diaspora nationalist with a deep attachment for Judaism and its religious and cultural values. The leader of the Zionist Revisionists, Vladimir Jabotinsky, asserts that to Sliozberg the concept of the Jew merging with the Russian people was not inconceivable. He considered Russia not only the creation of the Russian people but the common state of all the nationalities inhabiting its territory, a sort of commonwealth of nations of which Russian Jewry formed an integral part. Sliozberg believed anti-Semitism to be foreign to the nature of the Russian people and its history. In his opinion the government found the initiative for its anti-Semitic policies among the Poles and the Germans of the Baltic provinces.[49] In Sliozberg's presence, Jabotinsky declared, no one could speak ill of Russia; that land formed the basis of all his thoughts and dreams.

This love of Russia and her culture coupled with a devotion to the Jewish faith and people also characterized another Jewish benefactor of that day, the distinguished lawyer Oscar O. Gruzenberg (1866–1940). In his early youth he came in contact with the disabilities which plagued Russian Jews, and being a fighter by nature he conceived a mortal hatred for tsarist arbitrariness and vowed resistance.

During his student years in the University of Kiev the police raided his home in the dead of a winter night. Searching for illegal Jews, they discovered that his mother lacked right of residence. Young Gruzenberg defended her presence in his house by insisting that children having right of residence had a moral obligation to care for an aged mother. The officials ordered him to mind his own business and arrested his mother. For several days she was kept

48. [*Ibid.*, Vol. III, chap. 14. Ed.]
49. *Ibid.*, I, 261.

in jail in the company of prostitutes and criminals. "After this painful incident," Gruzenberg wrote, "everyone who rose against this arbitrary absolutism with all its cruelties was my brother and ally, to whose aid I was duly bound to hasten in times of suffering." [50]

Gruzenberg remained loyal to his sense of duty throughout the existence of the tsarist regime. Upon achieving fame as one of Russia's foremost lawyers he appeared on behalf of some of the most noted political leaders, liberals as well as revolutionaries. He defended some of the famous literary figures, V. G. Korolenko and Paul Miliukov among them, who as editors of opposition organs had incurred the wrath of the government and were in consequence brought to trial. His unusual talent as counsel for the defense wrested many a political criminal from tsarist dungeons or execution chambers. In his memoirs Gruzenberg describes the awful responsibility he felt toward those he undertook to defend. "Only those who trod the painful path of the everyday struggle for justice, who battled for the cause of individuals in the courts in the ministerial chancelleries, and against all the mighty of this world, know what it means to give away one's heart piece by piece." [51]

And a very great heart Gruzenberg gave to the defense of his people. Early in his career he came face to face with their want and defenselessness. A short stay in a small town inhabited by Jews gave him yet another opportunity to witness the arbitrary treatment of his people by tsarist officials. He then came to the conclusion that a people charged with the crucifixion of Christ and ill will toward non-Jewish neighbors had few friends in the world. At the risk of being branded a nationalist Gruzenberg decided to heed the admonition of the rabbinic sage: "If I am not for myself, who will be?" [52]

He took a leading part in the ritual and pogrom trials. Indeed he participated in practically all the trials of Zionist leaders charged with antigovernment activity, following one of Plehve's circulars of 1903, when Zionist activity was banned and declared subversive.

In the trial of Beilis Gruzenberg was the leading attorney. His defense brought him international fame. He spent two years investigating the details of the case, for which service he received no renumeration, even as he refused compensation for defending the literary figures of Russia charged with political crimes.

50. Gruzenberg, *Vchera,* pp. 20, 21.

51. Gruzenberg, *Ocherki i Rechi,* ed. Alexis Goldenweiser, with introductory articles by E. M. Kulischer, I. A. Naidich, A. Y. Stolkind, and I. L. Citron (New York, 1944), p. 48.

52. *Vchera,* pp. 23–24.

The stirring and masterful six-hour address which Gruzenberg delivered at the Beilis trial contained some unique passages. Referring to the attempt of the prosecution to defame the Jewish faith, he said, "In the courtroom an attempt has been made to turn the God of Israel into a Kiev Jew upon whom a raid was staged. But the Jewish religion is an old anvil upon which many heavy enemy hammers have been broken." And to the defendant he addressed himself thus: "Hardly two centuries have passed since the time when on such charges our ancestors would perish at the stake. Fearlessly, with a prayer on their lips, they would go to their undeserved death. Why then are you, Beilis, better than they? You too should walk to your end as they did. Repeat the words of the final prayer: 'Hear, O Israel, the Lord our God, the Lord is one.' "

"Gruzenberg's defense," wrote I. A. Naidich, "was heard throughout the world. Proudly every Jew felt in that oration the significance of the term 'Eternal Israel.' The entire Jewish people saw in Gruzenberg the defender of their dignity and honor." [53] In recognition of the great services rendered to the Jewish people, Tel Aviv, the first all-Jewish city of Israel, named one of its streets after Gruzenberg. Naidich recalls that on a visit to Tel Aviv in 1924 he stopped a youthful Jew on Gruzenberg Street and asked him if he had heard of the famous man after whom the street was named. Unhesitatingly the youth replied, "He was a great defender of Jewry." [54]

Gruzenberg had a profound love for Russia in spite of the fact that he was barred from a professional appointment and like Sliozberg had to practice as assistant to an attorney. He was born in the period of Alexander II, when Haskalah had already succeeded in making inroads in the Pale and many Jewish homes became culturally Russified. The first words spoken to him were Russian; the first children's songs, nurses, playmates, all were Russian. Beginning with the fourth grade in secondary school, he devoted himself with love and perseverance to the study of Russian literature. Aware of the discriminations against Jews in the academic field, his teacher of Russian literature shamefacedly asked him whether he would pursue his literary studies. The young student would have loved to give himself to the study of the Russian language and literature, but the humiliating thought troubled him: "Where are you trying to push yourself? Who wants your love? Your persistence will only make you ridiculous and pathetic." The mere thought of buying his way to a teaching career through the only means open—the desertion

53. *Ocherki i Rechi,* p. 39.
54. *Ibid.,* p. 44.

of his faith—filled him with shame, "as though one were bodily struck with a whip." [55]

This disappointment and the rebuff he received when, graduating with distinction from the University of Kiev in 1884, he was denied a professorial chair by reason of his faith, neither embittered him nor prejudiced his judgment of the Russian people. Describing the anti-Jewish attitude of one teacher, Gruzenberg states, "He was an anti-Semite but like the majority of the Russian anti-Semites never harmed a single Jew." [56] Not even his battles in the Russian courts of law (which beginning with 1906 became obedient instruments of the government) could undermine his respect for the Russian legal profession. "One does not have to blush for the Petersburg, Moscow, and the general Russian bar." [57]

Like most of the Jewish intelligentsia who were products of Russian culture and knew the Russian people well, Gruzenberg distinguished the people from their rulers. "What connection was there between the creative Russian spirit and its tsars and their governments!" he exclaimed in a description of the Russian legal profession. Gruzenberg also paid particular tribute to the intelligentsia and workers of St. Petersburg as the two forces which, fearing no one but their own conscience, were instrumental in the creation of a better world. Through repressive measures these forces could be temporarily bent but not broken; it was impossible, he reflected, to cause those who had grown to full stature to crawl on all fours.[58]

Although Bramson belonged to the more radical Trudoviki, Gruzenberg, Vinaver, and Sliozberg sided, either by active affiliation or in their political views, with the Constitutional Democratic party. They were all liberals who struggled for the cause of freedom, both for Russia and for the Jews. But there were considerable numbers of Jews who took an active part in the general revolutionary movement. There was also an important socialist Jewish organization, which although a part of the Social Democratic party, conducted its revolutionary activity primarily among the Jewish workers. The following chapter will be devoted to a study of the part Jews played in the revolutionary movement in Russia.

55. *Vchera,* p. 6.
56. *Ibid.,* p. 5.
57. *Ibid.,* p. 44.
58. *Ibid.,* p. 40.

VI

THE ROLE OF THE JEWS IN THE REVOLUTIONARY MOVEMENT, 1881–1917

THE role of the Jews in the revolutionary movement of the sixties and seventies was described in Volume I of this study. This chapter will sketch the activities of the Jewish revolutionaries from the eighties till the February revolution of 1917. In this period Jews not only participated in the general socialist movements but also formed special organizations which conducted revolutionary activity primarily among the Jewish masses and played a significant role in the overthrow of the tsarist regime.

Following the crushing of the Narodnaia Volia (People's Will) in the early eighties, revolutionary émigrés in Geneva in 1883 formed a new socialist organization, Grupa Osvobozhdeniia Truda (Group for the Emancipation of Labor). Headed by George Plekhanov, it included the Jewish socialists Paul B. Akselrod and Lev Deich. The first revolutionary circle to adopt a Marxian program, the Emancipation of Labor laid the foundation for the birth and development of the Social Democratic Workers' party, which played a dominant role in the collapse of the tsarist regime.

The emergence of the Emancipation of Labor marked a break with the revolutionary tradition which prevailed in Russia in the sixties and seventies, and in its place introduced socialism along Marxian lines. According to the old tradition, as expressed through the Narodniki, Russia, unlike the countries of western Europe, was to effect the transformation from a semifeudal agricultural economy to a socialist society without passing through the intermediate stage of industrial capitalism. Because of her unique historical traditions and institutions, especially because in the *obshchina* (the village commune) the Russian peasant shared his land with the other members of the community and was therefore trained for a collective economy, Russia was historically prepared for a socialist society, the Narodniki argued. In contrast to Marxism, which looked to the industrial proletariat as the class destined to lead the revolutionary struggle against exploitation and usher in the socialist society, the Narodniki placed their faith in the redemptive mission of the Russian peasant, the traditional rebel and collectivist. "Let us bless the Lord that our fate was not like that of Europe. We do not want her kind of proletariat or nobility or forms of government. We want to preserve the collective form of ownership of the obshchina," stated the proclamation issued by the leaders of the Narodniki in 1861.

The Narodnik philosophy was strongly colored by Slavophilism which held that, "uncontaminated" by the decadent capitalist West, Russia was destined by history to follow her own unique course and thus serve as an example to the world. The reactionary Pan-Slavs regarded the tsar, the people, and the Greek Orthodox Church as bound to one another by historical and mystic ties and as the instruments of that divine mission. The spiritual fathers and leaders of the Narodniki likewise believed in the unique mission of Russia, but in their utopian philosophy it was the peasant who was the carrier of the mission.

The founders of the Emancipation of Labor disavowed both the program and the methods of the Narodniki. Former Narodniki themselves, they now subjected that revolutionary philosophy to a critical analysis and found it completely out of date not only with scientific socialism but also with the industrial and economic development of Russia. In his pamphlet on *Socialism and the Political Struggle*, published in 1883 and regarded as the manifesto of the Emancipation of Labor, Plekhanov sarcastically compared the Narodnik belief that Russia would skip the capitalist stage to the biblical story of the sun standing still at Joshua's command. Pointing to the fact that, in spite of the utopian theories of the Narodniki, Russia had already entered the capitalist phase of its economic development, Plekhanov advised all those wishing to become real revolutionaries to revolutionize their own minds first. For this purpose, he asserted, it was necessary to understand and anticipate the natural course of historic events instead of pleading with lady history to stand in one place and wait until the would-be leaders should have prepared for her new, more direct, and beaten paths.[1]

Plekhanov also outlined the successive forms which the revolutionary struggle in Russia would take and the part the working class would play. Upon the establishment of a constitutional regime the proletariat must seize control of the government in order to lead the struggle for complete and ultimate emancipation. The role of the revolutionary intelligentsia was to be the teachers and leaders of the working class, which in turn must be trained to act as an independent party immediately after political freedom had been achieved.[2] The indispensability of the working class in the politi-

1. *Socialism and the Political Struggle,* pp. 7 and 15.
2. *Ibid.,* p. 72.

cal struggle in Russia was again stressed by Plekhanov at the International Socialist Congress held in Paris in 1889: "The revolutionary movement in Russia will triumph only as a movement of the working class. There is no other, nor can there be any other way." [3]

In similar vein P. B. Akselrod defined the mission of the working class and the role of the Social Democratic intelligentsia. He regarded the Social Democrats as the pioneers and central force in the revolutionary struggle of the working class, who should always keep before the workers the final aim: capture of political power for the introduction of socialism. In order that the proletariat might fulfill its historic mission there must exist within it a working-class party capable by virtue of numerical strength, intelligence, and popularity among the masses of seizing power at the opportune moment. To achieve this objective Akselrod urged the training of leaders from among the ranks of the more intelligent of the proletariat.[4]

The publications of the Emancipation of Labor and the official program they published in 1885 reached but few of the revolutionary circles in Russia. Living abroad, the leaders of this group were in no position to make easy contact with the masses of their native land. The possibility of communication with socialist circles in Russia lessened with the arrest in 1884 of Lev Deich, the most experienced organizer of the group. Nevertheless the organization did manage to establish some contact with sympathizers in a number of Russian cities whom it supplied with socialist literature.

Almost simultaneously but independently of the Emancipation of Labor, another small Social Democratic circle was organized in St. Petersburg, headed by a Bulgarian revolutionary, Blagoev. Lacking the intellectual leadership of men like Plekhanov or Akselrod, the group was unable to formulate a clear and precise program. Its salient feature was the emphasis it placed on the importance of the working class conducting its revolutionary struggle as an independent party. In contrast to the Emancipation of Labor, which could reach only Russian university students studying abroad and

3. M. N. Liadov, *Kak Nachala Skladyvatsia Kommunisticheskaia Rossiskaia Partia* (Moscow, 1924), p. 43.

4. Letter of Akselrod to the Social Democratic circle in Odessa in 1887, in *Materialy dlia Istorii Revolutsionnago Dvizhenia,* Vol. II *Iz Arkhiva P. B. Akselroda,* eds. V. S. Voitinsky, B. I. Nikolaevsky, and L. O. Zederbaum-Dan (Berlin, 1924), 231–235. A detailed and comprehensive study of this circle and its connection with Marxist circles in Russia in the seventies is given by N. A. Buchbinder in *Istoriko-Revolutsionny Sbornik,* ed. V. Newski, I (Moscow, 1923), 37–67.

a few socialist circles in Russia, the Blagoev group succeeded in reaching small groups of workers in Russia.

The effect of the Emancipation of Labor on the course of socialist work in Russia in the eighties as well as the extent of the inroads Marxian thought had made in that decade in Russia is still a subject of speculation. The memoirs of contemporary revolutionists and the archives of the Police Department have now definitely established that in spite of the severe regime of Alexander III there existed small Social Democratic circles in a number of Russian cities, chiefly in industrial centers. The aim of these groups, led by revolutionary intellectuals, was to prepare intelligent leadership for the coming political struggle. They studied popular socialist pamphlets in addition to general subjects such as history, geography, mathematics, and the natural sciences.

The eighties also saw the first stirrings of revolutionary activity among the workers. Far from skipping the stage of capitalism, Russia had already reached a high degree of industrial and capitalist development. The country offered an attractive field for capitalism because of a number of conditions: the protectionist policies of the government, abundance of raw materials, the ban on unions, and a large supply of cheap labor made possible by the impoverishment of the peasantry during the agrarian crisis of the eighties. The growth of heavy industries in this period and the corresponding increase of the industrial proletariat have already been described. The rise of a factory proletariat was accompanied by the first large-scale strikes. Particularly noteworthy was the stoppage of the big Morozov textile factory in Moscow in 1888. These industrial conflicts offered favorable opportunities for the early Social Democratic agitators.

In the Pale, too, the eighties saw the beginning of what later became a well organized and influential Social Democratic movement. It started with small circles of intellectuals and small groups of intelligent workers, and its development followed the lines of the general revolutionary movement. The eighties also saw the sharpening of class differentiation in the ghettos. Before the rise of the big cities and the growth of factories the Jewish proletariat consisted of unskilled workers or artisans. The relationship between the master artisan and his few employees was patriarchal and more or less friendly. Because the artisan employee regarded his position as merely temporary and looked forward to the time when he would open a workshop of his own and be his own master, no class solidarity or class consciousness developed among the employees in these workshops. But the industrialization of the country, the growth of railways and factories, quickly changed the economic life of the Pale. There too the sixties, seventies, and eighties witnessed the growth of large cities and factories and the emergence of the factory worker.

The new capitalistic economy also revolutionized the small artisan workshop and changed the traditional relationship between employer and employee. Instead of working directly for the consumer, the master artisan now began to work for the store that supplied the owner of the workshop not only with raw materials but often with the machinery of production. The store sought to sell its products not only in the local market but in other towns now accessible by railway. The prospect of passing from worker artisan to master craftsman became ever slimmer and in some trades almost impossible. The bulk of the Jewish craftsmen, employees as well as small employers, were reduced to the status of permanent proletarians.

Industrialization caused growing unemployment and depressed wages. The effects of the economic change were especially disastrous in the Pale during the reign of Alexander III. Owing to the May Rules of 1882 and the rigid enforcement of anti-Jewish legislation, Jewish workers were bound to the ever narrowing space of the Pale. As a result of the oversupply of labor and the keen competition for jobs, exploitation reached inordinate proportions. According to a report submitted to the International Socialist Congress in London in 1896 by the Bund, the average working day of a Jewish worker was between fourteen and sixteen, and sometimes even eighteen hours, while the pay was as low as 2 to 3 rubles a week.[5]

The Jewish proletariat, among whom the pioneers of the socialist movement sought to spread their revolutionary doctrines, consisted of the industrialized artisans, workers in textile factories in such large cities as Bialystok and Lodz, and employees in the tobacco industry and other branches of manufacture. But the occasional strikes of Jewish workers in the seventies or eighties, it should be noted, were in no way due to the small and conspiratorial revolutionary groups.

In the eighties there existed a number of socialist circles scattered throughout the Pale. Almost every big Jewish community had one. In these secret circles, which were really study groups, the workers were taught reading, writing, arithmetic, the natural sciences, and the elementary principles of socialism. Where the groups were large, there were also advanced courses for the more educated workers. The language of propaganda was Russian.

5. M. Rafes, *Ocherki po Istorii Bunda* (Moscow, 1923), p. 4.

In the content of propaganda there was nothing that distinguished Jewish from non-Jewish revolutionary circles. Jewish problems received no special attention in the early groups. The leaders of these cells usually consisted of intellectuals exiled by administrative decree to cities of the Pale, where they were to be under police supervision. These men, who frequently came from assimilated families and had begun their careers as agitators in the general revolutionary movement, sought through these cells to spread the doctrines of socialism. They had no intention of training workers for special activity among Jews.

The significance attached to the circles by the workers is evident from the following statement made by a worker in an address delivered in Vilno on May 1, 1892:

> We dare not sit with folded hands and wait for assistance from above. We shall be saved and emancipated only through our own efforts. As far as possible each should seek to educate himself and others and thus contribute toward the formation of at least small socialist groups, for the time being. Through these circles we shall be able to become members of the great universal struggling workers' party which acting in unison will achieve its human rights. Then shall be inaugurated genuine freedom, fraternity, and equality for all mankind, Jews not excluded.[6]

In spite of the fact that the early revolutionary cells primarily stressed the economic aspects of socialism, the membership quickly realized the importance of the struggle for political freedom. Another worker at the same May Day celebration said:

> And so to work! The entire enlightened world marches forward and is approaching the new order of the future. Only our beloved Russia is still far from the goal . . . so it is up to us to pave the way with our young forces. We must first explain to our sisters and brothers that the emancipation of each individual worker will be achieved only upon the emancipation of the entire working class. But in our country we are greatly handicapped by lack of freedom of the press, assembly, and organization. Our first step, therefore, has to be the achievement of a constitution.[7]

Following the economic depression of the eighties and the severe famine of 1891, there began in 1893 a strong economic upswing which accelerated the development of industrial capitalism on an

6. *Pervoe Maia 1892 Goda* (Geneva, 1893), quoted by N. A. Buchbinder, *Istoria Evreiskago Rabochago Dvizhenia v Rossii* (Leningrad, 1925), p. 63. Hereafter cited as Buchbinder, *Istoria.*

7. *Ibid.* [Also the Yiddish translation of four speeches made in Vilno on May 1, 1892, in "Memoirs of Grigory Gurevich," *Historishe Shriften,* in Yiddish, III (Vilno, YIVO, 1939), 610–625. Ed.]

unprecedented scale. In the last decade of the century the number of industrial workers more than doubled, rising from 720,000 to 1,600,000. In 1900 the production of cast iron, steel, coal, and oil trebled, and the rail system increased from 28,000 to 49,500 versts. The general industrial prosperity was reflected in the Pale, where the Jewish proletariat almost doubled and the stream of emigration began to recede.

The economic improvement was accompanied by a series of industrial conflicts that in most cases ended to the satisfaction of the workers. In the first few years of the strike movement the government remained neutral. Its indifference may have been partly due to the fact that the chief issue involved was the establishment of the twelve-hour work day invoked from an old statute of 1779. But soon, as the strike fever gripped ever wider masses of workers and assumed alarming proportions, the authorities began to resort to repressive measures. Strike leaders were arrested, arraigned in court, and many exiled to Siberia by administrative decree. The forcible interference of the administration failed to halt the strike wave but it succeeded in bringing home to the workers the interdependence of freedom and the economic struggle.

Important aid in these strikes was offered by the chest funds of what were originally fraternal and benevolent societies composed of both employers and employees. In time, these societies changed to purely workingmen's associations, at first for mutual aid and then for maintaining strikers' chest funds. The revolutionary leaders sought later to gain access to these popular workers' organizations in order to influence and direct the strikes.

The outbreak of the strike movement caught the revolutionary leaders unprepared; it raised the issue of propaganda among the masses as against small select circles. The leaders quickly sensed the opportunity offered by the mass struggle of the workers and decided to change the personnel as well as the content of studies of the secret circles so as to adapt them to the new situation.

L. or Y. Martov (the pseudonym of Y. O. Zederbaum), who remained active in the secret circles of Vilno during the nineties despite police supervision, describes in his memoirs the opposition to the new trend. "The thought," he wrote, "that the circle would now consist primarily of agitators and that the subject matter taken up by their circles would be calculated to prepare the students for activity among the masses was entirely unacceptable to the greater part of the working youth." [8]

The opposition was based partly on ideological and partly on

8. *Zapiski Sotsial-Democrata,* I (Berlin, 1922), 227; appeared also in 1924 in Moscow.

personal grounds. The admission of the rank and file into the cells, the opposition argued, would defeat their main purpose, which was to prepare select and qualified revolutionary leaders. Others who found here a congenial atmosphere for the pursuit of studies among intellectually compatible companions objected to widening the circles for fear of lowering their cultural level.

To counteract this opposition and point out the value of utilizing the economic conflicts for the dissemination of socialist propaganda on a mass scale, Arkady Kremer, the leading socialist of Vilno, wrote a brochure, *Ob Agitatsii* (About Mass Propaganda). This pamphlet, so often quoted in socialist literature of the period, served as a guide among both Jewish and Russian socialists of the nineties.[9]

The chief task of the proletariat was to capture political power. Kremer pointed out that the daily economic struggle taught them the importance of possessing that power, for in the struggle to improve his economic position the worker realized more and more clearly how an unfriendly political administration could block his path. It was unreasonable to expect the Russian workers to be convinced of the necessity of the political struggle from a merely theoretical exposition. "The masses of the people are drawn into battle not by theoretic arguments but by the concrete logic of things, by the natural course of events which forces them into the struggle."

On May 1, 1895, in Vilno Martov delivered an address in which he supported Kremer's ideas. An important document in Russian-Jewish socialist literature, it was later published by the Bund in a brochure variously entitled *A Turning Point in the Jewish Labor Movement* or *A New Epoch in the Jewish Labor Movement*. Martov asserted that the successes socialism was able to record were due to the introduction of democratic and economic elements into the movement. Discussing the economic phase of the workingman's struggle, he pointed out that the socialist leaders did not expect their cause to triumph because of the all-powerful might of its ideal and theory; the hope of socialism was based rather on the solution it provides for the needs of the masses. And the economic struggle of the workingman must naturally lead him to battle eventually for political freedom.

Martov's speech is also noteworthy because for the first time it urged the organization of a special Jewish workingmen's party. Its organization followed from the democratic principle upon which the movement was built: in order to reach the Jewish masses the

9. Extract published in Rafes, *Ocherki po Istorii Bunda,* pp. 31–32.

spoken and written propaganda must be changed from Russian to Yiddish, the only language understood by the Jewish worker. The Jewish proletariat should not depend upon the Russian or Polish working class for its liberation, but in compliance with the democratic slogan "through the efforts of the people themselves" work for their redemption as Jews. In Martov's opinion the indifference of the Jewish masses to the fate of their nation was a handicap to the development of their class consciousness: if a people was not willing to battle for its proper status as a nation neither would it attempt to rise from its inferior class status. National consciousness must go hand in hand with the awakening of class consciousness.

But Martov was careful to qualify his Jewish nationalism. While he scored the Jewish bourgeois intellectuals for their apathy toward nationhood and contemptuous attitude to their people, he rejected nationalism as a "bourgeois gift." "We can boldly stress the specific Jewish character of our movement," he declared, "without running the risk of turning aside from the universal workers' movement in general and the Russian in particular."

Yiddish, or *jargon* as it was then called, now became the medium of oral and written propaganda, and proclamations issued to the workers were written in that tongue. But as the number of intelligent workers grew a demand arose for more advanced works on economic and social subjects. To fill this need a "jargon committee" was created in Vilno in 1895 to promote a Yiddish literature. It also had the task of organizing libraries to spread these works in the cities of the Pale.

In 1896 the first illegal Yiddish newspaper appeared in Russia: *Di Arbeiter Stime*, which later became the official organ of the Bund. Strangely enough, this novel illegal publication which the socialist-minded workers received with joy owed its appearance to the ingenuity and enterprise of a Jewish locksmith, Israel Michael Kaplinsky, a man who subsequently became an agent of the Okhrana (secret police) and for his treasonable activity was shot in 1918, when the Soviet government came to power.

The growing number of socialist cells in the various cities of the Pale in the northwest and the Polish provinces created the need for a central organization to direct and unify their activities. Both the strikes and May Day, which beginning with the nineties grew in popularity and became an established holiday, required preparation and direction. Inaugurated as a workingman's holiday at the International Socialist Congress held at Stuttgart in 1889, May 1 was celebrated for the first time in Russia by the Jewish workers of Vilno. A few years later the observance spread to other cities of the

Pale. The same year, 1895, that Martov delivered his memorable May Day address in Vilno, there was held there a secret conference of socialist leaders who decided to proceed with the formation of a Jewish Social Democratic party. Its chief aims were to develop the political and socialist consciousness of the Jewish masses and to stress civil equality for the Jews.

Two years later, at a conference held in Vilno, there was founded the General Jewish Workingmen's Party of Russia, Poland, and Lithuania, popularly known as the Bund. A number of cities sent accredited delegates to that conference, but the leading group, which had called the meeting, came from Vilno. By this time Vilno was the center of the Jewish workingmen's movement and the distributing center which supplied communities in the provinces with illegal literature.

Arkady Kremer, a founder of the Bund and one of the three original members of the central committee, has furnished interesting information on the importance of Vilno as a center for both the Jewish and the Russian revolutionary movement. He asserts that although the Bund officially came into existence in 1897, it had actually existed since 1895: from that time or earlier the Jewish socialist circles of the northwest had acted as a group with Vilno as their center. The conference of 1897 simply ratified an existing situation. "It should be remembered," Kremer wrote, "that Vilno was then the center not only of the Jewish but of the entire Social Democratic movement in Russia. The Vilno method of mass propaganda formulated in my brochure *About Mass Propaganda* was then also adopted in St. Petersburg, Moscow, and Kiev." [10]

Although specifically a Jewish organization, the Bund always regarded itself as an integral part of the Russian Social Democratic party. Some prominent and active Bundists took a leading role in the formation of the party itself. In fact the leaders of the Bund were among the organizers of the meeting held in Minsk in 1898 at which the Russian Social Democratic Workers' party was founded; and of the three delegates selected to serve on its central committee two were Jews, one of them being Kremer.

Among those present at the Minsk meeting was an agent of the Okhrana; and soon afterward the leaders of the new party and those of the Bund were arrested. The spying was directed by S. Zubatov, then the chief of the Okhrana in Moscow. When he was convinced that the complete list of socialist leaders had been submitted to him, he ordered simultaneous arrests throughout the Pale.

10. *Bund Almanach* (Warsaw, 1922), quoted in Rafes, *Ocherki po Istorii Bunda,* pp. 41–42.

Some seventy of the most important members of the Bund were rounded up in 1898. In spite of this unexpected blow the movement did not collapse. Both numerically and spiritually the workers' movement had reached that stage of development where the arrest of even the principal leaders could not destroy it. "The losses sustained by the Jewish proletariat," writes Buchbinder, "only hardened its will and soon caused the emergence of new battlers for the social revolution." [11]

Only a few weeks after the wholesale arrests the second conference of the Bund was held. The delegates reported that in spite of the blows dealt the movement the work had not ceased; on the contrary, the number of workers joining was continually growing, the demand for illegal literature had doubled or even trebled within the year, and strike activities were being conducted as successfully as before the arrests.

In addition to the attacks from without, the Bund had also to wage a long and bitter fight against those within its ranks who threatened to emasculate its revolutionary character. This struggle reflected the bitter controversy raging from the mid-nineties to the first years of the new century between the so-called Economists, or Revisionists, and the orthodox Marxists. Because of the considerable economic gains won by the workers as a result of the strike wave in the prosperous period of the late nineties, there came to the fore within the party a school of thought insisting that the struggle of the working class should be confined to economic ends. Citing the concessions obtained from employers by means of the strike, the advocates of economism asserted that it was not necessary for the workers to conduct a political struggle against the government in order to improve their economic condition; the purpose could be achieved through banding together in labor unions. This theory gained particular force after the political arrests and after the law of June 2, 1897, fixed the working day for adults at eleven and a half hours.

Arguing for a united front in achieving labor advances, a writer in *Rabochaia Mysl* pointed out the advantage of mass strikes as compared to isolated ones. "The government and the industrialists," he said, "have formed a union for the purpose of fighting the employees; with the combined forces of the police, the military, and the priesthood they hoped to resist the demand of the workers. Consequently in order to resist the united enemy we too have to unite the workers . . . Then instead of the managers, the minister

11. Buchbinder, *Istoria*, p. 82.

himself guarded by police and troops will open negotiations with the strikers." [12]

Envisaging the potential power of the proletariat, the advocates of economism believed that the chances of improving their lot would increase if they refrained from antagonizing the government by fighting autocracy. An exponent of this theory summed up what in his opinion should be the position of the proletariat toward the problem of socialism: "You workers concern yourself with your immediate needs and let your grandchildren take care of themselves." [13]

There were also among the Economists those who for tactical reasons stressed the phase of the proletarian struggle for economic betterment. These socialist thinkers maintained that the battle for economic improvement of the masses would inevitably bring them into collision with the tsarist regime, the defender of the capitalist class. Then, thwarted by the government in their efforts to better their economic position, the proletariat would recognize the significance of the political struggle as a prerequisite or companion to the economic struggle.

In a pamphlet entitled *Credo*, issued around 1899, the advocates of economism sought a revision of the Marxist program of the Social Democratic party which stressed the political struggle of the proletariat as alone leading to the overthrow of tsarism and to the social revolution. *Credo* declared:

> We hope that intolerant, negating, and primitive Marxism which unduly stresses and exaggerates the class character of society will become more democratic in its conception and will radically revise its attitude toward society within which it functions and assume a more positive attitude to society as a whole. . . . The Social Democratic party should emerge from its narrow sectarian interests and dedicate itself to reforming contemporary society along democratic lines and to the defense of all working classes.[14]

The writer suggested that the Social Democratic party be dissolved.

Credo provoked a vigorous denunciation from a group of Social Democratic leaders who saw in economism an attempt to dilute the Marxian program and to entice the working class from its revolutionary path. Their reply, known as the *Protest of the Seventeen*, is said to have been the work of Lenin, then in exile in Siberia. "We

12. *Rabochaia Mysl* (July, 1898), No. 3, quoted in Liadov, *Kak Nachala,* pp. 254–255.

13. *Ibid.*, p. 258.

14. See V. I. Lenin, *Sochinenia* (2d ed., Leningrad, 1926), II, 472 ff.

do not know," it declared, "how widely the views [expressed by *Credo*] are shared by Russian Social Democrats," but fearing they might gain adherents the writers felt compelled to protest. They warned their comrades that such views constituted a perversion of Russian Social Democracy as well as a threat to its appointed course, namely, the organization of an independent political workers' party whose program of class struggle was inseparable from the battle for political freedom. True to the fundamental tenet of Marxism which conceived of the economic and political struggle of the working class as forming one integral unit, *Protest* declared: "The proletariat must strive to form independent political workers' parties for the chief purpose of capturing power and organizing the socialist society." The authors of *Protest* also rejected the charge of *Credo* that Social Democracy refused to cooperate with the nonproletarian classes of Russian society in the struggle against absolutism. On the contrary, Marxist socialists always sought to participate in all phases of social life and to encourage every revolutionary movement against the autocratic government. The call of *Credo* to the working class to re-examine its attitude toward other classes was really, *Protest* charged, an attempt to weaken the class consciousness of the workers.[15]

The charge that *Credo* attempted to divert the proletariat from the class struggle and to effect a reconciliation between the workers and the capitalist class was not without foundation. The liberal middle class and intelligentsia who sought to democratize the state so that it might represent all classes of Russian society were eager to enlist the support of the working class for the attainment of political liberty. But they feared that the rising power of the workers might subsequently be turned against them to establish a dictatorship of the proletariat.

A spokesman for this liberal school was P. B. Struve. An adherent of Marxism in early life, he later abandoned the ranks of the Social Democrats to become one of its leading opponents. In contrast to the Marxists who invested the working class with the Messianic mission of the ultimate redemption of humanity, Struve stressed the dignity and the natural rights of the human being, irrespective of class.[16]

Struve also rejected another fundamental tenet of Russian Social Democracy, that the destruction of tsarism and the establishment of a democratic regime was "chiefly or even primarily" the task

15. Both *Credo* and the *Protest* were published in *Istoriko-Revolutsionnaia Khrestomatia* (Moscow, 1923), I, 327–339.

16. P. B. Struve, *Na Raznia Temy* (*1893–1901*) (St. Petersburg, 1902), p. 524.

of the proletariat. He insisted that the reorganization of Russian life took precedence over class interests and therefore demanded the wholehearted cooperation of all creative elements of Russian society. To the intelligentsia he assigned a particularly important role in the remaking of Russia.[17]

The anti-Marxian currents in the Russian labor and socialist movements found their adherents in the ranks of the Jewish proletariat. Here, too, there were labor leaders arguing that for the sake of economic advantages the Jewish worker should abandon all political activity against the government. The opponents of Marxism pointed to the disadvantage of antagonizing their powerful enemy, the government, which might otherwise be neutral or even take a benevolent attitude toward the economic struggle.

This view was shrewdly fostered among Jewish socialist leaders by the chief of the Moscow Okhrana, Zubatov. Following the arrest of the Bund leaders in 1898, Zubatov urged them to dissociate antigovernment activity from the struggle for economic improvement. He assured them that if they would abandon their battle against the government the authorities would assist the Jewish workers in their struggle for better working conditions. This propaganda was effective, and a number of the arrested socialists promised when freed to spread his ideas among the Jewish workers.

It should be observed, however, that this change of heart was not due solely to Zubatov. A contributing factor was no doubt economism. It must also be borne in mind that the revolutionary philosophy of Marxism and particularly the close connection between the political and economic struggle of the working class were still new concepts to the majority of Jewish socialist leaders. Whatever the reasons, a group of the imprisoned revolutionaries not only betrayed their comrades and pledged their loyalty to Zubatov but also undertook to form nonpolitical organizations in their respective communities. The leading figure among these was Mania Vilbushevich, a high-strung, sickly Jewish girl who was an excellent organizer and gifted speaker. Following her arrest in Minsk in 1900 she soon became one of Zubatov's favorites as a result of the valuable information she gave the Okhrana. She was the moving spirit of the Jewish Independent Workingmen's Party, a nonpolitical workers' union formed in 1901 along the lines of economism.

In the preamble to the constitution of the new organization the founders asserted that no theory justifies gaining adherents who do not understand its aims. It was criminal to jeopardize the material interests of the masses for the sake of political goals at present com-

17. *Ibid.*, p. 314.

pletely foreign to them. For this reason the founders of the new party had left the Bund which according to them utilized the economic struggle chiefly to incite the workers to revolution. The new party, on the other hand, disavowed political goals, its primary interest being in raising the economic and cultural standards of the Jewish masses.

The Bund, because it was an illegal and conspiratorial party, could not choose its leadership through democratic methods; the identity of the members of its central or local committees was for obvious reasons never known to the rank and file. But the Independent party was organized along democratic lines; it did not fear the police, and, as the police archives opened after the revolution of 1917 revealed, kept the Okhrana informed of its activities.

The Jewish Independents were successful for a time in Minsk, where they organized a number of legal professional organizations and conducted a series of successful strikes. In spite of the bitter fight waged against them by the Bund they succeeded in attracting large numbers of workers, who welcomed the opportunity to obtain better working conditions through a strike sanctioned by the police. In fact, so successful was the party in Minsk that Vilbushevich was called to St. Petersburg in May, 1902, and instructed by Plehve himself to found a branch in Vilno, the citadel of the Bund. But the Independents could gain no foothold there because of the high intellectual caliber of the workers and the strong revolutionary tradition that prevailed; after several unsuccessful efforts the attempt was abandoned.

Simultaneously an attempt was also made to organize a branch of the Independents in Odessa. With the approval of the police they organized a number of strikes there but soon lost control over them. Under the influence of the local Social Democrats the strikes, which had begun as economic measures, soon assumed a political character and developed into practically a city-wide stoppage of industry. Alarmed at this unexpected development, the authorities decided to suppress the Independents and arrest its leaders, thus bringing police socialism among the Jewish workers to an inglorious end.[18]

Having successfully overcome the menace of the Independents, the Bund ran into more serious internal difficulty at the second congress of the Russian Social Democratic party in London in 1903.

18. On the history of the Jewish Independent Workingmen's party see Buchbinder, *Istoria,* pp. 179–252; Rafes, *Ocherki po Istorii Bunda,* pp. 73–80; B. Frumkin, "Zubatovshchina i Evreiskoe Rabochoe Dvizhenie," *Perezhitoe,* III, 199–230; D. Zaslavsky "Zubatov i Mania Vilbushevich," *Byloe* (1918), No. 9, pp. 99–129.

At that congress, which saw the split of Russian Social Democracy into Menshevik and Bolshevik factions, the Bund decided to pursue its revolutionary activity independently among the Jewish workers. The withdrawal of the Bund from the party which it had helped to found was the climax of a clash that had begun in 1900. At its fourth conference, held in Bialystok, the Bund had asked for cultural autonomy for the Jews of Russia and demanded that the Social Democratic party recognize the Bund as the sole representative of the Jewish proletariat. It had suggested that the Social Democratic party be organized along national lines and the Jews be accorded the status of a nationality. A country like Russia, one of the resolutions stated, made up of a multiplicity of nationalities, should be reorganized into a federation of national groups, each enjoying complete autonomy. The program of Social Democracy implies opposition not only to the suppression of one class by another and to the government's tyrannizing over the citizenry but also to the domination of one nationality or language over another.

This resolution brought down upon the Bund the wrath of *Iskra* (The Spark), a magazine founded in 1900 in Geneva by the theorists of the Social Democratic party. It scored the stand of the Bund as reactionary, chauvinistic, and an impediment in the path of assimilation, which it regarded as the solution of the Jewish problem. Lenin, who was the moving spirit of *Iskra* until the autumn of 1903 when the editorial board passed over to the Mensheviks, took the Bund leaders to task for what he regarded as their separatist tendencies. According to him the cultural and spiritual isolation of the Jewish proletariat was the result of the discriminatory policies of the tsarist government. "That accursed autocratic government," he wrote, "passed on to us as an inheritance the estrangement of the proletariats of the various nationalities which it mistreated and suppressed." This divisiveness of the working classes Lenin regarded as the greatest hindrance in the struggle against the government. Only in a united assault upon autocracy could he see any hope of victory. Lenin therefore vehemently opposed the desire of the Bund to divide the Social Democratic party into national groups.

Lenin also refused to acknowledge the idea of Jewish nationhood. He maintained that the conception of the Jews as a nation was both politically reactionary and scientifically untenable. Jewish assimilation had set in in other lands since the emancipation; he could see no reason why Russia, where emancipation would be even more complete because of the heroic awakening of the Jewish proletariat, should be an exception in the respect. It was no accident, he asserted, that in both Russia and western Europe the most reactionary elements of society were mobilizing their forces to prevent the assimilation of the Jews.[19]

At the 1903 congress of the Social Democratic party in London the Bundists offered a resolution which would have given their party the status of an independent Social Democratic organization and made it the sole representative of the Jewish working class. When this was defeated by an overwhelming majority the delegates of the Bund decided to leave the congress and withdraw from the party. It is interesting to note that the chairman of the committee which prepared the negative report on the resolution was the same Martov whose May Day address in 1895 had contributed to the formation of the Bund.[20]

Upon the secession of the Bund the Social Democratic party attempted to organize general Social Democratic committees in the regions of the Pale in order to gain converts among the Jewish workers and thus weaken the influence of the Bund. These committees failed to make much headway, and the Bund continued to play the leading role among the Jewish proletariat. Its tremendous revolutionary influence on the Jewish masses was particularly evident in the months following the Bloody Sunday of 1905 in St. Petersburg. At the call of the Bund a wave of political strikes and street demonstrations was organized throughout the Pale. Some demonstrations led to clashes between workers and police. Because in the Pale the police acted with particular ferocity and savagery in suppressing political demonstrations, the Bund organized armed detachments of workers to resist the police and troops and defend the demonstrating workers. In a number of cities these workers fought with great gallantry against soldiers and Cossacks. According to Buchbinder, "the Jewish workers manifested great revolutionary heroism, fearlessness, and readiness to die in the struggle against absolutism." The widespread revolutionary activity of the Jewish workers served to popularize the Social Democratic ideas among the general population and won many new adherents to the ranks of the revolutionaries.[21]

It was again primarily under the leadership of the Bund that political stoppages were organized in October, 1905. The Jewish population readily responded to the strike call and, as everywhere

19. For a fuller exposition of Lenin's views on Jewish nationalism see *Iskra* (July 15, 1903), No. 44; (Oct. 22, 1903), No. 51.

20. Rafes, *Ocherki po Istorii Bunda,* p. 108; see also p. 38.

21. Buchbinder, *Istoria,* pp. 294–295.

else in Russia, industrial and commercial activity in the Pale ceased too. Throughout that area bloody encounters with the police occurred; the fallen workers were buried in mass funerals at which revolutionary addresses were delivered. The revolutionary ardor of the Jewish masses was dampened soon after the promulgation of the October manifesto when at a given signal a wave of pogroms broke out throughout the Pale. Here again the Bund in conjunction with other Jewish socialist parties organized self-defense groups which bravely fought both the pogromists and their protectors, the police and the military.

The common struggle against the regime raised the issue of a closer union between the socialist groups of the various nationalities inhabiting Russia and of the readmission of the Bund into the Social Democratic party. Both sides having shown a willingness to compromise, the Bund was readmitted in 1906 as a Jewish Social Democratic organization unlimited in its activities by territorial boundaries. In 1912 the party recognized the plank of the Bund program regarding national cultural autonomy for the Jewish people.

In the period of the Stolypin reaction which followed the crushing of the revolution of 1905 the Bund too was forced to suspend its antigovernment activities. The struggle in the Social Democratic party between those who insisted on preserving the underground revolutionary cells and those who advocated disbanding them in order to concentrate all forces on the economic struggle of the workers was reflected in the Bund. Here, too, there appeared the so-called "liquidators" who urged converting the remaining conspiratorial committees into legally functioning groups. In spite of strong efforts the influence of the Bund as a revolutionary organization virtually ceased. During World War I, as a result of the expulsions and the decimation of the Jewish communities, the Bund deteriorated still further. Reports of the provincial gendarmerie during those years generally contained the stereotyped phrase, "no activity on the part of the Bund organizations was noted."

Of particular significance among the Bund's achievements is its role in bringing the Jews out of their spiritual isolation. Through the spirit of revolt against class and national oppression the downtrodden masses achieved a new dignity. In the struggle against exploitation and tsarist autocracy the workers of the ghetto found themselves united not only with non-Jewish comrades in Russia but with a worldwide movement. The fact that Jews who had always quaked at the appearance of the police or the Cossacks now dared openly to defy the authorities and to offer armed resistance to these dreaded forces is ample testimony to the Bund's effectiveness.[22]

The story of Hirsh Leckert illustrates the spiritual change that came over the Jewish workers with the appearance of the Bund. Leckert, a humble, unlettered cobbler and active member of the Bund, fired two shots at von Wahl, governor of Vilno, because he had ordered the flogging of a group of Jewish workers arrested for participating in a demonstration on May 1, 1902. Condemned to die by the hand of the hangman, Leckert met his death with heroism.

The glory of this transformation has been set down in poetic prose by David Einhorn:

First there was the word, the word stirred the consciousness, consciousness called to action, and action came like lightning. In Vilno there lived a shoemaker whose name was Leckert and he had a wife and child. By day he worked with his last and awl, and at night he would go to secret meetings to listen to the message concerning his fellow toilers. And one day when the cup of suffering was filled to the brim his comrades went forth into the street in a demonstration to proclaim the coming of a better day for the workingman—a day which would see neither rich nor poor but equality for all.

And those in power who feared these messengers of the oppressed sent out their lackeys who arrested, imprisoned, and tortured these men and women. So there awoke within this humble cobbler a holy wrath; quietly he procured weapons and unknown to anyone and without a word of farewell to wife or child went to the theater where the tyrant was enjoying himself. As this tyrant emerged from the theater this cobbler shot him, seeking to wash out with his blood the shameful indignity perpetrated against his humiliated sisters and brothers.

In the middle of the night they hanged Leckert in the field called Voennoe Pole. No one knows where his grave is, for he did not die. There in the field of execution he came to life again to proclaim to the world the honor and the dignity of the Jewish workingman.

From that day forth every blow upon the body of the Jewish worker became transformed into a mark of honor, and the yellow badge shone with the radiance of the sun. And in that radiance there gleamed four letters: Bund. And wherever these letters appeared they testified to the birth of a new Messiah—the Jewish workingman.[23]

The period of heroic revolutionary activity of the Bund was rather short-lived, lasting from about the mid-nineties to 1905, when

22. *Ibid.,* p. 375.

23. [H. Leivick wrote a play in Yiddish *Hirsh Leckert* (Vilno, 1931). See also Jacob Pat, *Hirsh Leckert,* in Yiddish, (Warsaw, 1927). Ed.]

it reached a peak. After Stolypin's defeat of the revolutionary forces the Bund never recovered the influence it had exercised in its heyday.

It produced a number of zealous and able leaders who made their mark in the history of the Russian revolution. Prominent among these was Arkady Kremer (1865–1935), generally regarded as the founder of the Bund. Kremer was endowed with a good deal of practical wisdom and energy which he gave unstintingly to the cause of the revolution and which gained him his reputation among leaders and rank and file—for he possessed no oratorical or literary gifts; a shy person by nature, he shunned the platform.[24]

A more colorful figure was Vladimir Medem (1879–1923), gifted orator and publicist. The son of a baptized military physician who reared him in the Greek Orthodox faith, Medem returned to his people to lead the Jewish workers. Unable to speak or understand Yiddish until he reached maturity, he came to be one of the fervent champions of Jewish cultural autonomy and of the Yiddish language.

Medem's revolutionary career began when he was expelled from the University of Kiev for antigovernment activity. In Minsk, where he was sent to live under police supervision, he joined the Bund and quickly rose to a position of leadership. He represented the Bund at a number of Social Democratic congresses and was a frequent contributor to the party publications. Most of his writings dealt with the problem of Jewish nationalism.[25]

Besides the Bund, there were also a number of minor socialist parties which placed emphasis on the national aspect of the Jewish problem. The Poale Zion (Workers of Zion), first organized in Ekaterinoslav in 1900, saw the solution for the Jewish worker in the establishment of a Jewish homeland in Palestine built on cooperative lines. Within a few years this party managed to establish branches all over the Pale. Out of these scattered branches which failed to develop a clear-cut and unified program there emerged in 1904 a

24. See *Arkady: A Collection of Essays in Memory of the Founder of the "Bund," Arkady Kremer (1865–1935)*, in Yiddish (New York, 1942), p. 415. [Koppel S. Pinson, "Arkady Kremer, Vladimir Medem, and the Ideology of the Jewish Bund," *Jewish Social Studies* (July, 1945), pp. 233–264. Ed.]

25. See *Vladimir Medem on the Twentieth Anniversary of His Death*, a collection of articles in Yiddish (New York, 1943). [Mention is to be made of the following recent contributions to the history of the Bund: Koppel S. Pinson, "Arkady Kremer, Vladimir Medem"; A. L. Patkin, *The Origins of the Russian Jewish Labor Movement* (Melbourne and London, 1947); Abraham Menes, "The Jewish Socialist Movement in Russia and Poland" (from the 1870's to 1897), in *The Jewish People. Past and Present*, II (New York, 1948), 355–368; and Raphael R. Abramovitch, "The Jewish Socialist Movement in Russia and Poland (1897–1919)," *ibid.*, II, 369–398. Ed.]

new organization called Socialist Zionists. Pointing to the fact that in all capitalist countries the Jewish worker is denied employment in the basic industries and hence reduced to pauperism, the Socialist Zionists advocated the acquisition for the Jewish people of a territorial center where under normal economic conditions the masses could live their own political and national life. They differed from the Poale Zion in not insisting that the territory be ancient Palestine. Both parties agreed that the problem of the Jewish worker would remain unsolved even after political liberty had been achieved and the condition of non-Jewish workers improved.

Both the Socialist Zionists and the Poale Zionists took part in the revolutionary activities of 1905 and exercised considerable influence on the workers' unions. They also enrolled in the self-defense groups which fought the pogromists.

The relations between Socialist Zionists and the Bund were extremely hostile. The Bund denounced Zionism as a reactionary and petit bourgeois movement. It was particularly intolerant of organizations which in its opinion were misleading Jewish workers by diverting them from the struggle against tyrants and capitalists. The enmity between the rival groups often led to physical clashes. There were occasions when Bund members tore up the Socialist Zionists' May 1 proclamations or fired at their gatherings; on one occasion a member of the Socialist Zionists was murdered by a Bundist.[26]

Opposed to Jewish nationalism in any form, many Jewish revolutionaries who saw the solution of the Jewish problem in the political emancipation of Russia did not join any of the Jewish socialist organizations. They were to be found in either the Social Democratic or the Social Revolutionary party. The most prominent Jewish Social Democrats were Paul Akselrod, L. Martov, and Leon Trotsky. The first two were among the founders and active collaborators on *Iskra*, which combated the nationalistic and, as they termed it, separatist tendencies of the Bund. Trotsky never showed any interest in the plight of his people. When in the course of a debate Medem asked him whether he regarded himself as a Jew or a Russian, Trotsky replied: "Neither! I am a Social Democrat, and that is all!" [27]

In the Social Revolutionary party, too, there were a number of Jews who never identified themselves with any Jewish cause. Two such, Gregory Gershuni and Michael Gots, helped to found the party in 1901. In contrast to the Marxian socialists who saw in the proletariat the class destined to overthrow tsarism and ultimately effect

26. Buchbinder, *Istoria*, p. 346.
27. See *Vladimir Medem on the Twentieth Anniversary of His Death*, pp. 10–11.

the social revolution, the Social Revolutionaries believed that the liberation of Russia was the common task of all laboring groups and the revolutionary intelligentsia. As the spiritual successors of the Narodniki, they also adopted terror as a means of overthrowing the regime.[28] *Iskra* fought the party bitterly for its rejection of the dictatorship of the proletariat and its use of terror.[29]

Comparatively few Jews were members of the fighting brigade which was organized to execute the sentences of government officials condemned to death by the party. Among these few were Evno Azev, subsequently exposed as a notorious agent provocateur, and Gregory Gershuni (1890–1908), bacteriologist and social worker.[30] There were also few Jews among the theorists and contributors to the publications of this party.

In conclusion it may be said that while the Jewish masses, as the greatest sufferers of the tsarist regime, readily joined the ranks of the revolution and made significant contributions to its cause, the chief thinkers and leaders of the revolution were non-Jews. The spiritual leader of the Social Revolutionaries was the writer and critic, N. K. Mikhailovsky. The two greatest writers and political leaders of the Social Democratic party were Plekhanov and Lenin.

28. For the program of the Social Revolutionaries see V. Ivanovich, *Rossiskia Partii, Soiuzy i Ligi* (St. Petersburg, 1906), pp. 8–13.

29. See Lenin's essay, "Why the Social Democrats Must Declare Determined and Relentless War on the Social Revolutionaries," in *The Struggle for the Bolshevik Party* (*1900–4*) Selected Works, (New York, International Publishers), II, 193–196.

30. Gershuni's memoirs, *Iz Nedavnago Proshlago* (Paris, 1908; Moscow, 1928).

VII

THE ORIGINS OF ZIONISM IN RUSSIA

THE earliest nationalistic stirrings among Russian Jews appeared in 1881, after the first series of pogroms had swept over the Ukraine. The first to declare war on the assimilationists and to call on Jewish youth to return to their people was the Hebrew novelist and publicist, Perez Smolenskin (1842–85). In Volume I of this work it was pointed out that, as a result of disappointment at the government's failure to grant the Jews civil equality, Smolenskin's nationalistic doctrine found a ready response among some of the Jewish youth. Nationalistic sentiments were also fed by the intensified anti-Semitism which followed the close of the Russo-Turkish War.[1]

Since Smolenskin's influence was limited to that small segment of the Jewish intelligentsia who could read Hebrew, the ideological trend toward nationalism was not very widespread. There was, however, an unformulated awakening of national consciousness among some elements of the Russified Jewish intelligentsia. The feeling expressed itself in a concern for the economic welfare of their brethren and a desire to ameliorate the wretched poverty among the Jewish masses. Many young Jews who had hitherto been completely indifferent to the fate and fortunes of their people now, spurred by indignation at the pogroms, began to take an interest in the program of vocational and agricultural training for the masses.

In his reminiscences about the first pogrom in Odessa in 1881, Ben Ami described the change that came over the Jewish students after the first anti-Jewish outbreaks. When in 1880 he had approached his fellow students for contributions toward the establishment of a Jewish trade school he found no sympathetic response. Some refused to contribute on principle, asserting they would give nothing to specifically Jewish causes, and those who did give gave reluctantly. However when the pogrom occurred the students were the first to organize a self-defense group, and the number of those interested in the plight of their people steadily grew. "These were the first meetings," Ben Ami wrote, "at which the Jewish youth gave thought to their own unfortunate brethren." [2]

1. See *The Jews in Russia,* I, 139–143.
2. *Evreisky Mir* (St. Petersburg, May, 1911), p. 26.

Similar sentiments were shown by students throughout the country. A letter written by a Jewish student in Kiev to a friend abroad states that the students of St. Petersburg University were the first to respond to the public fast day proclaimed by the Jewish community of St. Petersburg and that large numbers of them attended the service of intercession held in the synagogue that day and delivered addresses in Yiddish and Russian in which they promised to give their all for the cause of their people. The appearance of the young men in their university uniforms and their sincere and impassioned orations made a tremendous impression on the throng that filled the synagogue.[3]

In his memoirs Abraham Cahan furnishes some interesting details about a service in Kiev. He reported that a Jewish student by the name of Aleinikov addressed the congregation in Russian as follows: "We are your brethren, we are Jews just as you are. We repent of the fact that we regarded ourselves as Russians and not as Jews. The events of the last years have shown us that we were sadly mistaken. Yes, we are Jews." [4]

Another contemporary, J. H. Lipshitz, a leader of the orthodox wing, was struck by the spirit of piety that gripped the Jewish student youth in those days. "Many of the youth who had turned their backs on Judaism and had put their faith in Haskalah began to realize that they were relying on a broken reed and returned to the God of their fathers." [5]

It may be safely assumed that the return to Judaism on the part of the intelligentsia—how widespread this movement was is difficult to establish—was prompted by national rather than by religious sentiment. Through participation in prayers Jewish youth sought to identify themselves with their people. This disillusionment of the maskilim protagonists of Haskalah and the assimilationists after the pogroms has been described in Chapter III of this volume. The bitter mood of those who had hoped that secular education and Russification would open the doors to civil and social equality for the Jews was expressed by the poet J. L. Gordon, himself a staunch advocate of Russification. In a short poem entitled "Mahalat Hazikkaron" (The Malady of Memory) he cried, "I believed that Haskalah would surely save us, but that blessing was turned into a curse, and the golden cup of which we drank was flung into our faces."

In an article directed particularly to Jewish socialist youth,

3. *Iz Arkhiva P. B. Akselroda,* p. 228.
4. *Bleter fun mein Leben,* I, 500.
5. J. Lipshitz, *Zichron Jacob,* III (Frankfort on Main, 1931), 76.

M. L. Lilienblum exclaimed, "Of what concern is socialism to us? We are regarded as strangers in a capitalist society and we shall be treated as strangers in a proletarian regime. Granted that capitalistic society is responsible for Henry the drunkard and Arthur the non-drunkard, but what matters it to us? Each of them will loot our home, destroy our furniture, tear our pillows, and chase us with cries of hep! hep!" [6]

Lilienblum's diatribe against the socialists was undoubtedly the result of the attitude of the Narodniki to the pogroms. Mention was made in Chapter III of the proclamation issued by the central committee of the Narodnaia Volia calling upon the Ukrainian people to rise against the Jews who allegedly robbed and exploited the peasants. It has been established that the author of the proclamation was the journalist Romanenko, subsequently a notorious anti-Semite and on the editorial staff of the yellow sheet *Bessarabets* which was largely responsible for the pogrom in Kishinev in 1903. The same Romanenko was also the author of a number of anti-Jewish pieces which appeared in the organ of the Narodnaia Volia.

It may be noted that the affairs of the Narodnaia Volia at the time of the appearance of the pogrom proclamation were no longer in the hands of the responsible leaders of the party, who either were languishing in the prisons of Russia or had been executed. The movement was led now by a small group of newcomers whose revolutionary loyalty and moral integrity had not been established as yet. In addition, some of the few older members of the party had turned traitor and joined the ranks of the monarchists, as Romanenko eventually did.[7]

That the anti-Semitic articles in the *Narodnaia Volia* may be traced to an anti-Semitic coeditor who abused his authority in no wise detracts from the fact that Russian socialist youth was infected with anti-Jewish prejudice and either openly sympathized with or remained completely indifferent to the plight of the Jews. M. B. Ratner, a noted leader of the Social Revolutionaries and a close student of the Russian revolution, states that there was evidently a definite anti-Semitic current in the ranks of the early Russian socialists, including the Narodniki. This prejudice of the pioneer revolutionaries he ascribes not so much to anti-Semitic feeling per se as to lack of understanding of the Jewish position and to immature economic and political views. It stemmed from inability to distinguish between the real oppressors and exploiters of the peasantry—the nobility and the

6. *Hameliz* (1883), No. 60.
7. D. Shub, "Evrei v Russkoi Revolutsii," *Evreisky Mir,* pp. 129. ff.

government—and their imagined foes, the Jews who were themselves the wretched victims of a common oppressor. No doubt the Jewish Narodniki were also in a measure responsible for this attitude. Estranged from their people and unfamiliar with the historical background of Jewish economic life, the assimilated radical youth looked with contempt upon the petty Jewish traders whom they regarded as swindlers and exploiters. Immature politically, a good many of these Jewish Narodniki saw in the pogrom the rising of the people against their oppressors. Beginning with attacks upon the Jews, they believed, the revolt would spread to an attack upon the non-Jewish bourgeoisie and the government.

Ratner cites the instance of a Jewish Narodnik who, wearing a red blouse to hide his Jewish identity, paraded among the pogromists in Kiev. But when he saw that the mob, having attacked and ruined the poorest quarters of the Jewish population, showed no like hostility for either the wealthier classes of Russian society or the government, this misguided revolutionary suffered a nervous breakdown. Ratner also points to another extenuating factor in the anti-Semitism of the Narodniki. They did not yet know that the government was using the pogrom as a smoke screen, as a diversionary and counterrevolutionary measure. Despite these explanations, however, the Narodniki cannot be excused for their indifference to the glaring misery of the Jews and the rivers of Jewish blood shed on Russian soil.[8]

While Ratner's analysis is in general acceptable, the most influential factor shaping the attitude of the Narodniki toward the pogroms was the outright traditional anti-Semitism which pervaded all classes of Russian society. As was pointed out in Volume I, with very few exceptions the famous Russian authors suffered from an anti-Jewish bias. Since the Narodniki had made no special effort in their literature to break down either racial or religious prejudice among their followers (as was done later by the Social Democrats), radical Russian youth had not been trained to comprehend the Jewish problem.

Most of the Jewish Narodniki were stunned by the open anti-Semitism revealed in the ranks of their Russian comrades, a sentiment directed even against the Jewish socialists. Because of this hostility Jewish revolutionaries left the ranks of the Narodniki, some even joining the newly formed Zionist groups.

A brochure written by Paul Akselrod in 1882 revealed the spiritual

8. M. B. Ratner, "Evolutsia Natsionalno-politicheskoi Mysli v Russkom Evreistve," in *Sbornik* (*Almanach*) *SERP* (abbreviation of Sotsialisticheskaia Evreiskaia Rabochaia Partia) (St. Petersburg, 1908), II, 24–26.

crisis experienced by the radical Jewish youth. He asserted that the pogroms and especially the reaction of Russian intellectuals shocked the Jewish socialist intelligentsia into a new conception of themselves and their people. For a long time they had believed that the Jews were not a nation but constituted an organic part of the Russian people. Now they suddenly realized that the majority of Russian society regarded them as a separate nation. Moreover in the opinion of these Russians all Jews, whether orthodox or assimilationist, petty bourgeois or proletarians, or socialists ready to risk their lives or freedom for the deliverance of Russia, all were "Zhids" constituting an element harmful to the country. The undisguised approval of the pogroms shown by the radical Russian intelligentsia suddenly brought home to the Jewish cosmopolites and assimilationists how mistaken was their idea of the status of their people. They now also realized that the bulk of the non-Jewish masses had not yet reached that stage of class consciousness where they could understand the identity of interests among all the lower classes of the various nationalities of Russia. Although an assimilationist by conviction, Akselrod failed to see any immediate benefits in assimilation for the Jews of Russia. Only by assimilation with a culturally superior society as in western Europe or the United States did the Jew stand to gain anything. In Russia, where the Christian population stood on a lower cultural plane than the Jews, there was no reason for the latter to assimilate with the former. Their merger must await social and political reforms that would raise the cultural status of the Russian masses.[9]

Akselrod's sentiment regarding his people and the change in his attitude after the pogroms become particularly apparent when compared with his views at the beginning of his revolutionary career in the seventies. Discussing his reasons for devoting himself to the Russian revolutionary movement in preference to the struggle for Jewish emancipation, he stated then that for him the Jewish problem shrank into insignificance before the era of equality and fraternity which the coming enthronement of the poorest and most downtrodden promised to inaugurate.[10] His conclusion after the pogroms, that the Jews constituted a distinct and separate national group whose problem could not be solved by assimilation but required special treatment and attention from the Jewish revolutionaries, was a repudiation of his former belief and his Russian colleagues in the revolutionary movement. Because Peter Lavrov, the spiritual leader of the Narodniki, and other leading members of the party feared that Akselrod's state-

9. *Iz Arkhiva P. B. Akselroda,* pp. 220, 221–226.
10. P. B. Akselrod, *Perezhitoe i Peredumannoe* (Memoirs), I (Berlin, 1923), 75.

ment might hurt the cause of the revolution, his brochure was not published until 1924, more than forty years after it was written.[11]

The noted Russian Narodnik Stepniak, whose pen name was Sergei Kravchinsky, described the mood of the Jewish revolutionaries in the period of the pogroms in his novel, *The Career of a Nihilist.* In a conversation with a Russian colleague the hero of the novel, who is modeled after the revolutionary Aaron Zundelevich, openly admits that he feels no attachment to the Russian people:

> We Jews, we love our race, which is all we have on earth. I love it deeply and warmly. Why should I love your peasants, who hate and ill-treat my people with blind barbarity? Who tomorrow will perhaps loot the house of my father, an honorable working man, and brutally assault him, as they have done to thousands of other poor hard-working Jews? . . . As to so-called society, the upper classes, why! what but contempt can one feel for such wholesale cowards? No, there is nothing in your Russia worth caring for. But I knew the Nihilists, and I loved them even more than my own race. I joined and fraternized with them, and that is the only tie which binds me to your country.[12]

The national awakening of a subjugated people in its own territory, such as the Italians, Czechs, Poles, or Balkan nationalities, expressed itself in an attempt to achieve independence and throw off the foreign yoke. Among the Jews of Russia national consciousness took other forms. Some of the Jewish Narodniki expressed their solidarity with their people by abandoning the ranks of the party in protest against their colleagues' indifference to Jewish suffering. Others who saw the only hope of the Jews in the cause of the revolution set out to organize their own socialist groups to work among the Jewish masses. It is noteworthy that in spite of the general desertions in the early eighties the numbers of Jewish revolutionaries actually increased considerably. While in 1873–77 Jews constituted only 6 per cent of all political prisoners, the percentage jumped to 14 in 1884–90, 579 out of the total number of 4,307.[13]

Others, having lost all hope of improving conditions in Russia, decided that the solution for Russian Jewry lay in emigration to the United States, where Jewish life might be rebuilt on new economic and social foundations. To execute this program of emigration a

11. "O Zadachakh Evreiskoi-Sotsialisticheskoi Intelligentsii," *Iz Arkhiva P. B. Akselroda,* p. 219. Reprinted in Yiddish in *Zukunft* (New York, September, 1924), under the title "Pogromen un di Revolutsionere Bavegung mit 43 Yor Zurick."

12. *The Career of a Nihilist* (New York, Harper and Brothers, 1889), p. 47.

13. Cherikover, ed., *History of the Jewish Labor Movement in the United States,* II (1945), 195.

movement known as Am Olam (Eternal People) was started in 1881. The founders were at first undecided whether Palestine or the United States should be the new objective, but they soon settled on the latter.[14] The name of the movement and its emblem of a plow and the Ten Commandments are indicative of its nationalistic character and purpose. The plow symbolized the agricultural pursuits through which the founders hoped to build Jewish economy on a sound and stable basis. The attempt to raise the economic status of Russian Jewry through training its youth in agriculture and crafts was a cardinal plank in the program of the Haskalah and was adopted by the Jewish intellectuals of the seventies and eighties. Through such economic readjustment the leaders also hoped to disprove the common charge of the anti-Semites that the Jew engaged in "unproductive occupations" such as trade and brokerage. Dubnow, who in his youth was a symapthizer of Am Olam, thus described the idealistic character of its founders: "They were indeed heroes and not ordinary fortune seekers . . . Scholars, students, teachers, they exchanged their free professions in the land of tyranny for field labor in the land of freedom in order to serve as an example for the masses of the emigrants who would follow them." [15]

The diary of one of their members gives us a glimpse into the psychology of those people: "Our motto is labor in the fields, and our goal is the physical and spiritual rejuvenation of our people. In free America, where people of various nationalities live in amity, we Jews too shall find a corner in which to rest our heads. We shall prove to the world that we are qualified for physical labor." [16]

The enthusiam with which the nationalistic-minded Ben Ami, under the pseudonym Resh Galuta, reported the founding of the organization reveals the high hopes which it inspired in some elements of Jewish youth. Describing its emblem of a plow and the Decalogue surrounded by the words Am Olam, he interpreted it to signify a call to the Jewish people: "Eternal People, arise from the dust! Shake off the contempt of the nations, for the time has come!" [17]

The contemporary Jewish press abounds in reports of Am Olam groups that were formed in numerous cities of the Pale. The Berdichev group "consisted exclusively of intelligent young people who aimed to labor in the field." [18]

14. A. Druianov, ed., *Ketabim Letoledot Hibat Zion Veyishuv Eretz Israel,* I (Odessa, 1919), 19–21.

15. Dubnow, *Dibre Yeme Israel Bedorot Haachronim* (History of the Jews in the Last Generation), III (Tel Aviv, 1924), 194.

16. *Nedelnaia Khronika Voskhoda* (1885), Nos. 45–46.

17. *Ibid.* (1882), No. 6.

18. *Razsvet* (1882), No. 17.

Some leaders of Am Olam, particularly those who came from the revolutionary ranks, not only stressed agricultural work; they also insisted that the colonies in the United States be established on communistic principles, modeled on the Russian mir or obshchina rather than on the system of private property which in their opinion was the greatest evil of the prevailing economic order. Of the two motives which animated the founding of the movement, the national and the socialist, the latter was predominant. While prompted by a fervent desire to redeem their people from political oppression and economic misery, the founders never showed concern for the perpetuation of the Jews as a nation or for the continued growth and enrichment of Jewish culture. Cherikover correctly observes that the intelligentsia of the movement were closer to Russian radicalism and Russian culture than to the life of the Jews.[19]

This affinity with Russian culture and its spiritual representatives was made evident by a group of Am Olam from Odessa who, while stopping in the Austrian frontier station of Brody on their way to the United States, deliberated how to force the release of G. G. Chernyshevsky, the famous Russian philosopher of the Narodniki, from his imprisonment in Siberia.[20] Even the idealization of the United States by the leaders of Am Olam was undoubtedly influenced by the Russian Narodnik intellectuals, many of whom believed that democratic America would be fertile soil for the establishment of collective agricultural communes fashioned on the obshchina.[21] In his memoirs Grigory Gurevich, a Jewish revolutionary, refers to the high regard which the radical Russian intelligentsia of the seventies had for the United States and its democratic institutions.[22] Some of the Narodniki emigrated to the United States and there established a few colonies on communistic principles. But neither the Narodnik communes founded in Kansas nor those of Am Olam founded in Louisiana, South Dakota, and Oregon proved successful. Both lacked the material means and practical experience for such pioneering ventures. Abraham Cahan, who devotes a chapter to the most successful of the Am Olam colonies, New Odessa, Oregon, asserts that the settlers were neither physically nor spiritually suited for pioneer life in an agrarian commune. The failure of that colony in 1887 virtually marked the end of Am Olam as an organized group.[23]

19. *History of the Jewish Labor Movement in the United States,* II, 183.
20. H. Burgin, *Geshikhte fun der idisher Arbeterbawegung* (New York, 1915), p. 73.
21. V. L. Debagory-Mokrievich, *Vospominania* (Paris, 1894) pp. 9–10.
22. "Memoirs of Grigory Gurevich," *Historishe Shriften,* III, 226.
23. A. Cahan, *Bleter fun mein Leben,* II, 297–303; Abraham Menes, "Di Am Olam Bavegung" in *History of the Jewish Labor Movement in the United States,* II, 203–238. [Also Wischnitzer, *To Dwell in Safety,* pp. 60–64. Ed.]

Another association that arose in Russia in the early eighties as a direct result of the pogroms was the Hibat Zion (Love of Zion) movement which subsequently became world-wide and led to the establishment of Palestine as an important Jewish center. In contrast to Am Olam which never formulated a national program, the founders of Hibat Zion were primarily Jewish nationalists interested in solving not only the problem of the Jew but also that of Judaism. The Hebrew linguist Ben Yehuda, who advocated the building of the Jewish homeland in Palestine even before the pogroms,[24] declared in 1881: "Three things are engraved in letters of fire on the flag of nationalism: country, national language, national culture; he who rejects any of these betrays the very existence of the nation." And stressing the importance of Hebrew as the national language of the Jewish people, Ben Yehuda asserted: "Hebrew is our national language. For each of its words, letters, and vowels the blood of our fathers was shed like water and the chosen of their children were led to slaughter. The Hebrew language is the most precious treasure that was left to us from all ancient glory. Shall we abandon it?"[25]

Perez Smolenskin, editor of the Hebrew *Hashahar* (The Dawn) who soon after the pogroms embraced the cause of Zionism, now stressed the importance of Palestine not only as a refuge for the persecuted Jews of Russia but also as a territorial and spiritual center of the Jewish people. Comparing the relative values of Palestine and the United States as centers of emigration, Smolenskin asserted that Palestine was the symbol of the existence and unity of the Jewish people and, when inhabited by a sizable Jewish population, would also become their spiritual center. Urging all those who were sincerely interested in the rehabilitation of the Jew to decide upon Palestine as the center of emigration, Smolenskin declared: "Even if that land were inferior to all other countries, even if much work and effort be required to build its waste lands, we still should choose Palestine for that land is the symbol of our nationhood."[26]

Ben Yehuda, Smolenskin, Lilienblum, Pinsker, and Levanda were the principal literary advocates of Zionism in the early eighties. As indicated in Chapter III, Lilienblum embraced the ideal of Zionism immediately after the first pogroms, while Pinsker and Levanda first suggested the acquisition of any territorial center and only later joined the Hibat Zion movement. The call of these writers and of lesser literary figures who supported them found a ready response.

24. See *The Jews in Russia,* I, 144–145.
25. *Hamaggid* (1881), Nos. 35–37. Cf. *Sefer Hazionut,* Vol. II, *Tekufat Hibat Zion* (Tel Aviv, 1942), Pt. I, p. 84.
26. *Hashahar* (Vienna, 1882), No. 7, p. 354.

Under different names there sprang up in various cities groups or clubs with Zionist programs. Among the student youth, too, groups were founded whose purpose was to foster the Zionist ideal. Jewish students formed the first group of Zionist pioneeers known as Bilu, for the Hebrew words *Beth Yakob le-khu be-nelkha,* "Oh House of Israel, come ye, and let us go." (Isaiah 2:5.)

A declaration sent by forty students to Chief Rabbi Nathan M. Adler of London and to the Alliance Israélite Universelle in Paris reflects the mood and the spirit of consecration to the cause on the part of the nationalistic-minded youth. Asserting that their most fervent aim was to dedicate their physical and spiritual powers to the land of their fathers, to rebuild her ruins and restore her to her ancient glory, they pleaded for support and guidance from the leaders of Israel. Convinced that they were expressing the desire of thousands and tens of thousands of Jewish youth throughout the country, the signers of the address concluded with the fervent appeal: "People of Israel, lift up your eyes and see your loving children, who united stand ready to serve you and restore you from captivity into a life of happiness in your own country. Awake and permit these sentiments of your children to be translated into reality." [27]

The first Bilu group was founded in Kharkov in January, 1882, most of the members consisting of university students. Twenty of its members were charged with recruiting new adherents to the cause. Following a tour which took the missionaries of Bilu to various cities of the Pale, a number of societies were formed with a total membership of over five hundred. According to M. M. Ussishkin a branch was organized in the spring of 1882 in Moscow with twenty-five student members. In contrast to the other Hibat Zion groups whose purpose was popularization of the ideal of Zionism among the masses of Jewry that would lead to the ultimate establishment of Palestine as a Jewish homeland, the program of Bilu stipulated that its members themselves immediately emigrate to the Holy Land. Like Am Olam, Bilu aimed at establishing cooperative colonies that would serve as models in social living for future settlers. A circular of the Kiev group presents the socialistic aspect of the movement. Describing the land ownership problem as the greatest evil of the old civilization, it warned against building the new colonies on the "rotten foundation" of the old world. "Do not forget that the renaissance must be not only along national but also along economic lines." [28]

Through their central office, which was transferred from Kharkov to Odessa with a branch in Constantinople, the Bilu groups negoti-

27. *Hameliz* (April 16, 1882), No. 17, cols. 331–334.
28. S. L. Zitron, *Toledot Hibat Zion* (Odessa, 1915), I, 129.

ated with influential Jewish leaders abroad and with the British writer, politician, and traveler, Lawrence Oliphant, regarding their settlement in Palestine. While touring the Holy Land in 1879 Oliphant had conceived the idea of establishing an autonomous Jewish province under the suzerainty of Turkey, then the mistress of Palestine. In Constantinople he had conversations with high officials regarding his plan and he was received by the Sultan, whose assent he sought. After a year of fruitless negotiation he returned to England where he completed the book *Land of Gilead,* in which he pleaded for the realization of his plan.

Oliphant's active and even more intense interest in Zionism was resumed in 1882 with the establishment in London of the Mansion House Fund to provide relief for the refugees from Russia and facilitate their emigration. Appointed to the executive committee of the fund, he was selected as a special emissary to eastern Europe to direct the emigration of a large group of Jews to the United States. In a letter to the London *Times* Oliphant expressed the belief that only by putting an end to Jewish homelessness would the Jewish problem be solved.[29] He also wrote to the editor of the Hebrew *Hamaggid,* David Gordon, a staunch and consistent champion of Zionism, assuring him of his support to the cause. Evidently familiar with the psychology of wealthy Jews, who, as will be seen later, opposed the re-establishment of Palestine as a Jewish center, Oliphant cautioned against placing any faith in the rich Jews of England. If the Jews will only manifest a real desire to return to the land of their fathers, Christians in England are ready to spend many hundred of thousands of pounds sterling to assist them in the consummation of this "great and worthy cause," Oliphant declared.[30] He was reported to be intending to open an office in Constantinople to facilitate Jewish emigration to Palestine.[31]

Oliphant's public promise of large-scale financial aid from Christians for Jewish colonization in Palestine caused a furor and evoked eager hope among the masses of Russian Jewry. Rumors spread that Oliphant himself, said to be a man of tremendous wealth, was ready to contribute fantastic sums of his own to the cause of Zionism. Not only did the masses of the Pale, hungry for any crumb of hope, snatch eagerly at the rumor but even sober publicists and social leaders gave it credence. Rabbi Samuel Mohilever, a pioneer Russian Zionist,

29. S. Dinaburg, *Sefer Hazionut,* p. 47. The letter to the *Times* is referred to in *Hazefirah* (Warsaw), March 7, 1882.
30. Dinaburg, *op. cit.,* p. 47.
31. *Ibid.,* pp. 47–48; *Hamaggid* (1882), No. 16.

came away from an interview with Oliphant impressed with his sincerity. Upon his return home the rabbi published a letter in which he sought to correct the current impression that Oliphant was ready to spend 500,000,000 rubles to gain the consent of the Sultan for Zionist plans. But the rabbi reported his faith in Oliphant's promise that as soon as the wealthy Jews of Russia and Poland embarked on a program of large-scale purchases of land in Palestine, his Christian friends would make £50,000,000 available for the purpose.[32] Thus did a responsible and respected rabbi and Zionist leader confirm the legend of the Oliphant miracle.

Great was the hope which the masses of Jewry placed in the "saintly gentile," and keen disappointment followed when Oliphant's promises turned out to be fable. The first to experience that disappointment were the members of Bilu, whose central office in Constantinople submitted a memorandum requesting material and moral assistance for the colonies they sought to establish. It turned out that Oliphant could do nothing for these pioneers, since, as he declared, any help from an Englishman at that time when relations between England and Turkey had become strained would only prove a boomerang to Bilu.[33] Though disheartened by the unexpected blow, these Jewish zealots decided not to give up their idealistic venture. The Constantinople office, after apprising the followers in Russia that no land was prepared for them in Palestine, warned: "The weak and soft-hearted who are not sure of themselves should stay home. We are now in need only of those who are ready to sacrifice themselves for their people." Those who felt strong enough to face these conditions were invited to Odessa to receive instructions for their journey to the Holy Land.[34]

After numerous fruitless appeals for financial assistance for settling Bilu volunteers in Palestine, the organization adopted a new set of bylaws which completely changed its character. Instead of being limited to young idealists who were ready to become pioneers in cooperative colonies in Palestine, membership was now open to sympathizers willing to contribute to Bilu as well as to middle-class Jews who would settle in the Holy Land on their own private farms. But still the organization failed to attract adherents and it quickly deteriorated.

32. Dinaburg, *Sefer Hazionut,* p. 50.

33. [In another statement, made on April 21, 1882, Oliphant referred to the replacement of Lord Beaconsfield in 1880, by Gladstone, who was not friendly toward Turkey, as the reason "the matter was dropped." See Wischnitzer, *To Dwell in Safety,* p. 58. Ed.]

34. Druianov, *Ketabim,* I, 40–42.

The less than two dozen Bilu members who managed to get to Palestine lived a hard pioneering life which overtaxed their physical endurance without giving them any spiritual satisfaction. Instead of working in a cooperative colony of their own which was to serve as a model and an inspiration to Jewish youth throughout the world, they eked out a miserable existence as hired farm laborers in a colony established by the Alliance Israélite Universelle.[35] Disappointed and broken in spirit, a number of the group returned to Russia, while others severed their connection with the organization.

The Bilu experiment in Palestine proved as abortive as the Am Olam in the United States. Neither has left its imprint on the turbulent period of the past fifty years of Jewish history.[36]

Of more enduring value for the Zionist movement and the subsequent rebuilding of Palestine were the Hibat Zion clubs which under various names sprang up in a number of cities in the early eighties. The membership of these groups generally consisted of middle-class Jews with some Hebrew background. Some of these early Zionist clubs also managed to attract the more nationalistic elements of the academic youth.

The program of these Zionist groups consisted of propaganda among the masses and collecting funds for the support of the few Jewish colonies then existing in Palestine. These clubs arranged courses for adults in the Hebrew language, Jewish history, and the Bible. Jewish festivals were made occasions for Zionist celebrations and singing Palestinian songs. In some communities where the Hobebe Zion (Lovers of Zion) had many members they would organize synagogues of their own. In this connection it is of interest to note that Lilienblum was opposed to the establishment of Zionist synagogues on the ground that coveting honors and offices might weaken the movement.

These special synagogues were not the only ones to play a part in the Zionist movement. Ever since the birth of Zionism the synagogue as such has had an important role in fostering the movement; being virtually the only public place where the people could congregate, it offered the most convenient forum for spreading Zionist

35. H. Khessin, "The Diary of an Emigrant to Palestine," *Voskhod* (1889), No. 1; later it was published in a separate volume, in Hebrew, under the title *Miyoman Ahad Habiluim* (Tel Aviv, 1925).

36. [This judgment of Bilu is too harsh. The colony of Gederah, founded by Bilu people in 1884, exists till our days. Ed.]

On Bilu see Dinaburg, *Sefer Hazionut,* pp. 34–35, 55, 217–219, 229–235; Zitron, *Toledot Hibat Zion,* I, pp. 127–132, 205–208; Druianov, *Ketabim, passim;* Israel Belkind, *Di Ershte Shrit fun Yishub Eretz Israel* (2 vols., New York, 1917). [Vol. I contains valuable source material. Also Samuel Kurland, *Biluim. Pioneers of Zionist Colonization* (New York, 1943). Ed.]

propaganda. It was also a fruitful field for gaining adherents to the movement, since the bulk of the Jews in the eighties attended synagogue. In some synagogues the custom was introduced of having special collection plates on the eve of Atonement for the benefit of the colonies in Palestine. Because in those days the rabbis exercised considerable influence on the masses, the Zionist leaders sought to obtain their good will and participation.

Hibat Zion also received moral support from a great part of the Hebrew press. The nationalistic *Hashahar* soon after the pogroms began to advocate the resettlement of Palestine by Jews. The weekly *Hamaggid* was a consistent supporter of the Zionist ideal. The influential *Hameliz*, which at first hesitated to take a stand on the issue because of the opposition to the movement on the part of the wealthy Jews, sensed the warmth of interest of the masses and soon joined the upholders of the cause. Of the Russian periodicals, *Razsvet* was the ardent champion of Zionism, while *Voskhod* represented those elements of the Jewish intellectuals and the upper bourgeoisie who were either lukewarm or opposed to re-establishing the Jews on their ancestral soil.[37]

From the very beginning Zionism met strong opposition within Jewry, some of it for ideological reasons and a part of it motivated by fear. The Bundists fought Zionism because they regarded it as an attempt to divert the interest of the masses from the class struggle which in their opinion was the most important means to the ultimate redemption of the Jewish proletariat. The assimilationists frowned upon Zionism because it retarded the process in which they saw the key to the solution of the Jewish problem. Wealthy Jews regarded the movement with disfavor primarily out of fear lest it impugn their patriotism and make their status of citizens in their respective countries less secure. With few exceptions the upper classes in every country were either indifferent or hostile.

The following episode reflects the hostility felt by at least some of the wealthy Russian Jews. In 1885 the Hobebe Zion of St. Petersburg, who were primarily university students and other intelligentsia, decided to arrange a literary-musical evening, the proceeds to be used for the support of the struggling colonies in the Holy Land. Groups of enthusiastic students volunteered to visit the homes of wealthy Jews in the capital selling tickets. When a delegation called on the Jewish financier A. I. Zack, he ordered them out of the house. The next morning the leader of the delegation met the financier at the entrance to his bank and demanded an apology. Zack refused, and the student struck him. As a result of the public dis-

37. See above, Chapter III.

turbance that ensued the impetuous young Zionist was expelled from the university and banished from the capital.[38]

In the eighties the wealthy Jews of Russia had an additional reason for shunning the Hibat Zion movement: the refusal of the government to legalize it. For this reason the Russian Hibat Zion was founded at a convention in the city of Kattowitz (Katowice) in Upper Silesia. Dr. Leo Pinsker, author of *Auto-emancipation*, was elected the first president. The organization was partially legalized in February, 1890, as a philanthropic society, Committee for the Support of Jewish Tillers of the Soil and Artisans in Syria and Palestine, and was permitted to open an office in Odessa; hence the popular name "the Odessa Committee."

The truly practical achievements of the Hibat Zion of Russia in the fifteen to sixteen years of its existence preceding the launching of political Zionism in 1897 by Dr. Theodor Herzl were rather meager. The following figures of total contributions made by them toward the work in Palestine are indicative: in 1880, 45,799 rubles; in 1891, 36,279; in 1892, 26,445; in 1893, 40,280; in 1894, 42,873; and in 1895, 50,000.[39] A number of factors hampered the development of the young movement. Not only did the government's refusal to legalize the organization retard its growth, since the groups could not conduct propaganda campaigns for their cause; but the hostile attitude of Turkey, which on several occasions barred the Holy Land to Jewish immigration, undermined the faith of the Jewish masses in the feasibility of resettlement.

But despite the small practical accomplishments of Hibat Zion, its spiritual contributions were highly significant. To the hounded and persecuted Jews of Russia, particularly to the disillusioned intellectuals, it offered a program which held out the hope of ultimate redemption from degradation and humiliation. It prepared the ground for the subsequent emergence of political Zionism with Theodor Herzl, by not only popularizing the idea among the masses of Jewry but by formulating the ideology of Zionism and producing a number of thinkers and leaders who later guided and directed the movement. In addition to Pinsker, Smolenskin, and Lilienblum, Hibat Zion produced Ben Yehuda, who made his permanent mark in the cultural renaissance of modern Palestine; Ussishkin, a leader in the Zionist movement; and Asher Ginzberg, known by his pen name of Ahad Haam (One of the People).

Born in Budapest and with a degree in law from the University of Vienna, Theodor Herzl (1860–1904) was a playwright and

38. Zitron, *Toledot Hibat Zion,* I, 289–290.
39. Izhak Broides, *Vilno Hazionit ve-Askenohu* (Tel Aviv, 1939), p. 45.

journalist. In his early years he became interested in the Jewish problem as a result of the strong current of anti-Semitism then prevalent in western Europe. At one time he even advocated the wholesale baptism of the Jews of Austria. According to this fantastic plan all the Jews of Austria were to submit their children to baptism into the Catholic faith in a mass ceremony. In order to remove the stigma of opportunism or betrayal and to invest this act with a selfless altruism aimed at solving the Jewish problem for future generations rather than for themselves, Herzl suggested that the adult generation remain within the Jewish fold but submit their children for conversion before the act could bear the character of "cowardice or interested scheming." [40]

The Dreyfus affair had a shattering effect upon the sensitive Herzl. As the Paris correspondent of the *Neue freie Presse* of Vienna, he attended the ceremony at which the Jewish captain convicted of treason was publicly disgraced prior to his exile to Devil's Island. Herzl, who at that time believed Dreyfus to be guilty and was not yet aware that he was the victim of an anti-Semitic plot, was grievously shocked at the gleeful and malicious pleasure exhibited by the public at Dreyfus' degradation. He was convinced that this exhibition resulted solely from one fact: the deposed officer was a Jew. It was then that Herzl conceived of political Zionism as the only solution to the homelessness of the Jews. He soon set to writing his *Judenstaat*, which was published in 1896.

Herzl described anti-Semitism as a deep-rooted and ubiquitous prejudice ineradicable through assimilation, emigration, or any other means. Whether the Jews like it or not, they are and will always remain a distinct people, "a historic group with unmistakable characteristics common to us all." Even if the Jews wanted to dissolve in the surrounding nations, the world would not permit them to do so. Accustomed to consider the Jews as the most contemptible among the poverty-stricken, the world is provoked when it sees some Jews prosperous, and fails to realize that security and material well-being lead to the weakening and disintegration of Judaism. "It is only pressure," Herzl declared, "that forces us back to the parent stem; it is only hatred encompassing us that makes us strangers once more." [41]

Having come to the conclusion that the Jews will never be allowed to live in peace and security among the nations, Herzl suggested that they be given a territory large enough to satisfy their national need.

40. Alex Bein, *Theodore Herzl* (Philadelphia, 1940), pp. 94–95.
41. *The Jewish State: An Attempt at a Modern Solution of the Jewish Question*, tr. Sylvie d'Avigdor (1896), p. 24.

He did not specify Palestine. "We shall take what is given us, and what is selected by Jewish public opinion." But from his comparison of the Argentine and Palestine it is evident that for historic and sentimental reasons he favored the latter. "Palestine," he observed, "is our ever-memorable historic home. The very name of Palestine would attract our people with a force of marvelous potency." [42]

As the first step in the realization of his plan, Herzl stressed the necessity of obtaining the consent of the great powers to Jewish sovereignty over a neutral piece of land; then Jews would open negotiations for purchase. The attempts at colonization being made in the Argentine and Palestine, he asserted, were being conducted on "the mistaken principle of a gradual infiltration of Jews" which was bound to end in disaster. "It continues," he declared, "until the inevitable moment when the native population feels itself threatened, and forces the government to stop a further influx of Jews. Immigration is consequently futile unless based on an assured supremacy." [43]

Herzl believed that his plan would prove a boon to the world by relieving the nations of the scourge of anti-Semitism, and would at the same time be helpful to those Jews seeking assimilation, who "would be rid of the disquieting, incalculable and unavoidable rivalry of a Jewish proletariat driven by poverty and political pressure from place to place, from land to land." The nations would put greater faith in the loyalty of those Jews who had chosen to remain in their land of adoption and would regard them as "assimilated to the very depths of their souls." [44]

Although both his analysis of the Jewish question and his solution resembled Pinsker's, Herzl at the time of writing the *Judenstaat* was unaware of the existence of the *Auto-emancipation*. He read the brochure for the first time in February, 1896, after the appearance of the *Judenstaat*, and noted in his diary: "Remarkable agreement on the critical side, great similarity on the constructive." In fact, he later observed that had he known of Pinsker's pamphlet he might not have written his own.

The appearance of the *Judenstaat* made a tremendous impression on world Jewry and caused a stir among the Hobebe Zion in Russia. The fact that an assimilated Jew from the West, a noted publicist who had made his mark in the gentile world, had returned to his people to champion its cause and work for its national redemption filled *Hameliz* with renewed confidence in the eternalness of Israel. But

42. *Ibid.,* pp. 28–29.
43. *Ibid.,* pp. 27–28.
44. *Ibid.,* pp. 25, 10.

having paid tribute to Herzl's idealism, the Hebrew weekly cautioned against excessive optimism. A novice in Zionist work, a man unfamiliar with the temperament and ways of his people to whom he had so recently found his way, Herzl would soon realize that a nation cannot be rebuilt in a day.[45]

Nahum Sokolow, whose opinions carried weight in the Jewish world, was also skeptical of Herzl's plan. He warned against the possible dangers in Herzl's ideas just as he had cautioned against overconfidence in the Hibat Zion movement in the eighties. Herzl's publicized plans, he contended, would provide the anti-Zionist Turkish government with a pretext to repress the colonies in Palestine. Sokolow declared that it was his duty publicly to brand the author of the *Judenstaat* as a visionary and his project as a fanciful dream.[46]

The political implications of Herzl's bold and unprecedented plan filled the Russian Hobebe Zion with trepidation. Fearful lest the anti-Semitic press seize upon the appearance of the *Judenstaat* as an excuse to oppose granting civil equality to Jews, *Hameliz* emphasized that even if a Jewish state should be established the bulk of Jewry would still remain in other lands, and consequently a solution to their problem would have to be found for them in the Diaspora. Pointing to the fact that after the return from Babylon only an insignificant minority went up to Palestine, *Hameliz* dismissed Herzl's plans as a chimera offering no solution of the Jewish problem.[47] In the same spirit of concern for civil rights in Russia, Sokolow declared that the Jews of Russia would have nothing to do with Herzl's scheme until the government should have had a chance to study and express an opinion regarding it.[48]

Herzl's call for a Jewish world congress at first met with a cool reception among the Hobebe Zion of Russia. He was especially disappointed that the most influential Jewish philanthropists such as the Rothschilds, Baron de Hirsh, and others upon whom he had counted should have adopted a negative attitude toward his plan. He therefore decided to enlist the organized support of world Jewry for the establishment of a Jewish state. But his call for the convening of a Jewish assembly met with strong opposition not only from antinationalist Jews but also from devoted adherents of Hibat Zion. Some of the latter who hoped to reclaim Palestine as a Jewish homeland by a slow process of Jewish colonization feared that Herzl's

45. *Hameliz* (1896), No. 49.
46. *Hazefirah* (1896), No. 218.
47. *Hameliz,* (1896), No. 152.
48. *Hazefirah* (1896), No. 142.

method would result in the complete closing of the Holy Land to Jewish immigration by the Turkish government. Disquieting affirmation of such a possibility was furnished by a report in *Hazefirah* that the Pope had asked Constantinople to bar the influx of Jews into Palestine since Zionism went counter to the teachings of the ancient prophets who declared that Israel was destined to be an eternal wanderer. In Russia the anti-Semitic press used the appearance of the *Judenstaat* and its author's call for a Jewish world congress as an occasion for slandering the Jews. An article in the anti-Jewish *Novoe Vremia* which "traced" the descent of the English people from the ten lost tribes of Israel and designated the British kings scions of the House of David charged the Zionists and the English with forming a conspiracy against Russia.[49]

Yet in spite of their hesitations and vacillations the Russian Hobebe Zion decided to participate in the congress and sent ninety delegates.[50] Originally scheduled to convene in Munich, the first Zionist Congress assembled in Basle, Switzerland, owing to the public protests of the Munich Jewish community against holding it in their city.

The congress formulated the Zionist program as seeking for the Jewish people a national home secured by public law. It looked to achieve this end through promoting the colonization of Palestine by Jewish agricultural and industrial workers. It also stressed the importance of strengthening the Jewish national consciousness.

The Basle congress inaugurated political Zionism and marked a break with the policies of Hibat Zion. Whereas the latter sought to rebuild Palestine gradually as a Jewish homeland through assisting old and creating new Jewish settlements in the Holy Land, political Zionism laid emphasis on procuring a charter from the Turkish government for the immediate opening of Palestine to large-scale immigration. The program adopted at Basle followed Herzl's plan as outlined in his *Judenstaat*, save for the reservation that Palestine alone should be the future Jewish state.

This Zionist Congress impressed the Jewish world. Because it was the first assembly of world Jewry since the destruction of the second Temple, many Jews regarded the congress as the revival of the ancient Jewish Sanhedrin (Supreme Court of Law). The impressive personality of its president, whose handsome figure and personal magnetism captivated the delegates, contributed greatly to the effect of the congress. Even a sober and practical man like Sokolow was so taken with the charm of Herzl's personality that

49. Quoted in Broides, *Vilno,* p. 58.
50. *Ibid.,* p. 58.

he abandoned some of his former skepticism respecting the author of the *Judenstaat* and allowed himself to be converted into an ardent follower of political Zionism. His first account from Basle in *Hazefirah* revealed his change of heart. Reminding his readers of his critical attitude to the program of the *Judenstaat*, which he asserted he had not entirely changed, he proceeded to pay tribute to Herzl as a man and leader. He described him as a person of charm and great culture, whose tall and handsome figure, deep black eyes, and manner of speech "express grace and humility, aristocracy of spirit and highmindedness"; not only a dreamer but a practical statesman as well.[51]

The effect on the Jewish masses was even greater. They made Herzl a legendary figure, particularly after the diplomatic missions he undertook on behalf of the cause. His audiences with the Sultan of Turkey, Emperor William II of Germany, and high government dignitaries of other countries invested his personality with an aura, and they held him in awe. The love and admiration of the Russian-Jewish masses were demonstrated during Herzl's brief visit to Vilno after he had met Minister Plehve in St. Petersburg. Although the visit was not publicized the rumor of his coming brought thousands of Jews to the streets. An official report to the governor of Vilno stated that the few days Herzl spent in the city were a holiday for the hundred thousand Jews of the community. After a reception given him by the Jewish lay and religious leaders, who also presented him with a scroll of the Torah, the police captain who was present to see that no antigovernment speeches were made observed to his Jewish acquaintances: "Messrs. Zionists! What do you want? Palestine has not yet been given to you, but a king you already have. Truly, he is a king! His tall figure and appearance, his eyes and beard declare that he is a ruler of men, irrespective of what nation they be." [52]

After the Basle congress Zionist activity was greatly stimulated in the Pale. New clubs and groups under various nationalistic names sprang into existence, while those already in existence intensified their activity.

In addition to propaganda and education, the clubs and societies now engaged in the sale of shares of the Jewish Colonial Trust established by the World Zionist Congress to further new colonization in Palestine. At the first meeting in Vilno that was called to arrange for the distribution of these shares, there were some who

51. *Hazefirah* (1897), No. 191.
52. Broides, *Vilno,* p. 164.

were ready in their enthusiasm to invest their entire capital in the enterprise.[53]

The growth of the Zionist movement was revealed at the convention of Russian Zionists in Minsk in 1902, which was attended by over seven hundred delegates from all parts of Russia and Palestine. According to one delegate the representatives were full of enthusiasm and for seven days discussed various projects connected with rebuilding Palestine.[54]

Soon after the convention the Russian government outlawed the Zionist organization and forbade any activity on behalf of Palestine. In a confidential circular to the governors Plehve charged that the Zionists, instead of expediting the emigration of Russian Jews, were engaged in fostering national sentiment, thus weakening the patriotism of Russia's subjects. It was in the hope of getting the restrictions on Zionist work removed that Herzl undertook the trip to St. Petersburg. His visit to Plehve caused much resentment in radical Jewish circles. In their opinion he humiliated the Jews in the eyes of the world by conducting negotiations with Plehve shortly after the Kishinev massacre for which he was generally held responsible. Moreover, so rumor said, Herzl had promised Plehve that Russian Jews would abstain from all participation in the revolutionary movement if the government would revoke the restrictions on Zionist activity in Russia.

Unfortunately the archives of the Russian Ministry of Interior are silent respecting the substance of the Plehve-Herzl conversations. From the address Herzl delivered to the St. Petersburg Zionists who arranged a reception for him it is evident that he urged Russian Jewry, instead of dividing its energies, to concentrate all efforts on realizing the Basle program.[55]

The restrictions were not removed. But Zionist activity did not cease in Russia, nor did Zionist influence diminish in the Jewish communities where since the Basle congress the Zionists had become an important element in social, religious, and educational life. During the political spring the Zionists aligned themselves with the liberal factions of Russian Jewry in their struggle for equality. They conducted the election campaign to the first two Dumas as a united block. They played a significant part in the League for the

53. *Ibid.*, p. 71.

54. Israel Katzovich, *Sechzik Yor Leben Erinerungen* (New York, 1919), pp. 306–309.

55. Ginsburg, *Historishe Werk,* II, 220–232. [Also the same author's article "Poezdka Teodora Gerzlia v Peterburg," *Evreisky Mir,* pp. 197–209. Ed.] "Documents from the Archives of the Vilno Police on Herzl's Passage There," in *Miyamim Rishonim,* ed. A. Druianov, I (August, 1934), 63–72.

Attainment of Complete Equality; and their influence was revealed in 1906 when they caused the dissolution of the league as a result of a decision to conduct political work adopted at a conference held in Helsingfors.

In the years of the Stolypin reaction the government intensified its repressive actions against the Zionists. A decision of the Senate in 1907 officially outlawed all Zionist groups; as a result a number of leading Zionist leaders were prosecuted. The deterioration of the tsarist regime in the years before World War I was marked by severe persecution of the Zionists.

The political prospects of the Zionists outside Russia were not bright in that period. Having lost all hope of obtaining a charter for Palestine from the Sultan, they were encouraged by the Turkish revolution of 1908 when the Young Turks came to power. But the new rulers proved just as averse to Jewish national aspirations in the Holy Land as their autocratic predecessor.

The World War only aggravated the political situation of the Russian Zionists. As a province of Turkey, a country aligned with the Central Powers, Palestine was now enemy territory with whose subjects Russian Jews could have no communication. But during the war a couple of Russian Jews were responsible for two events which opened a new chapter in the history of Zionism. One was the organization of the Jewish Legion by Vladimir Jabotinsky, later founder of the militant Zionist faction known as the Revisionists. Fighting side by side with the British armies for the conquest of Palestine from the Turks, this Jewish military unit consisting exclusively of volunteers strengthened the claim of the Jewish people to the Holy Land. Another Russian Jew, Chaim Weizmann, who made a valuable contribution to the cause of the Allies was in great measure responsible for the issuance of the Balfour Declaration on November 2, 1917. Besides Weizmann and Jabotinsky, a number of other Russian Jews were among the leaders of the World Zionist movement, and have helped shape and guide the destinies of world Jewry in the last two generations. The following pages will be devoted to a brief sketch of these personalities and their achievements.

The pre-eminent thinker of the Zionist movement, at once its most incisive critic and a great teacher of national revival, was Asher Ginzberg (1856–1927). The son of a Hassidic family, Ginzberg in his youth received the traditional Jewish education. He also became interested in medieval Jewish philosophy and the Haskalah literature which he chanced to find. For a number of years he attended, as a free auditor, courses in history and philosophy in several universities abroad.

An article called "Lo Ze Haderek" (The Wrong Way), published over Ginzberg's pen name, Ahad Haam, in *Hameliz* in 1889, attracted wide attention and immediately gained him the reputation of a keen thinker. Subjecting Hibat Zion to a severe and searching analysis, he asserted that the basic approach of the movement was fallacious and it was therefore bound to end in disappointment and disillusion. In his opinion it was wrong for the leaders to seek converts to their cause by appealing to the economic interests of the Jews; owing to conditions in Palestine, that could lead only to frustration. The first and primary goal of the Hobebe Zion should be to awaken the national consciousness of the Jews and so inspire them with new and fresh enthusiasm for the general well-being of their people that they would not be discouraged by obstacles and setbacks.

Following a historical analysis of the national sentiment which, he maintained, had prompted the ancient Jews to argue that Moses never appealed to the self-interest of the individual but rather to the general welfare of the community, Ahad Haam deplored the decline of that national emotion after the destruction of the Temple. Whereas all the blessings and curses in the Law of Moses have but one unvarying promise—the happiness of the community of which each individual felt himself to be an integral part—the religious ordinances of post-Exilic days attempted to appeal to the self-interest of the individual. Subsequent oppressions and migrations had intensified the anxiety of the Jew for his safety and tended further to enfeeble his national loyalty. Even Jews who were occasionally moved to work for their people could not completely subordinate their own interests to those of the nation. "The demon of egoism," Ahad Haam declared, "—individual or congregational —haunts us in all that we do for our people, and suppresses the rare manifestations of national feeling, being the stronger of the two." [56]

In these circumstances, Ahad Haam argued, the first step of the Hobebe Zion should have been an attempt to bring about a revival of the national sentiment, "to inspire men with a deeper attachment to the national life, and a more ardent desire for the national well-being." Such would have been the sound, the right way for Hibat Zion to extend "the empire of its ideal in Jewry" and train "genuine, whole-hearted devotees," qualified to work for the practical realization of a great but difficult national task. Describing the weakening of the movement as a result of the first failures in Pales-

56. Ahad Haam, *Ten Essays on Zionism and Judaism,* tr. from Hebrew by Leon Simon (London, 1922), pp. 11–12.

tine, Ahad Haam said: "What wonder, then, that so great an ideal, presented in so unworthy a form, can no longer gain adherents; that a national building founded on the expectation of profit and self-interest falls to ruins when it becomes generally known that the expectation has not been realized, and self-interest bids men keep away?"[57]

Emphasizing his central point that "the heart of the people is the foundation on which the land will be regenerated," Ahad Haam appealed: "Instead of adding yet more ruins, let us endeavor to give the idea itself strong roots and strengthen and deepen its hold on the Jewish people, not by force, but by the spirit. Then we shall in time have the possibility of doing actual work."

Revival of the national sentiment of the Jewish people as a prerequisite for practical Zionist work and the emphasis on the cultural rather than on the political aspects of Zionism, the two ideas which formed the thesis of the first of Ahad Haam's published articles, became the burden of all his writings. In fact he looked to Zionism for solution not only of the problem of the Jew but also of that of Judaism. Observing the progressive deterioration of Jewish culture and the Jewish way of life in western Europe and the gradual weakening of the loyalty to Jewish values among Russian Jews, Ahad Haam sought to create in Palestine a refuge for the Jewish spirit where, unhindered and unhampered by foreign influence, it might develop and thrive on its historic and native soil. Such a center would bring into one place Jews of the most diversified talent and genius and thus raise Jewish culture to greater heights; it would moreover infuse fresh vitality into all portions of Jewry and result in a reawakening of Jewish sentiment.

But Ahad Haam, it must be said, did not advocate the renunciation of political Zionism which aims to establish a Jewish state in Palestine. The difference between him and Herzl lay primarily in method and approach. Believing that Palestine offered no solution to the problem of the Jews, the bulk of whom would continue to live in the Diaspora for many generations to come, Ahad Haam urged that the Zionists concentrate their energies on raising in Israel's historic land a Jewish community which would be a "true miniature of the Jewish people," where there shall appear once more the genuine type of Jew, whether he be a rabbi, scholar, writer, farmer, artisan, or merchant.[58]

In a special article entitled "A Spiritual Center," published in 1907, Ahad Haam sought to clarify his views and to refute the

57. *Ibid.*, p. 14.
58. Ahad Haam, *Al Parashat Derakhim* (Berlin, 1921), I, 73–74.

erroneous interpretations given his idea of a spiritual center as excluding all other general activities characteristic of a normally functioning state. While the relation of the center of Palestine to the circumference—the Jewish communities throughout the world—would be of a spiritual character, it should be self-evident, he declared, that the center itself "would be a place like other places, where men were compounded of body and soul, and needed food and clothing, and that for this reason the center would have to concern itself with material questions and to work out an economic system suited to its requirements, and could not exist without farmers, laborers, craftsmen, and merchants."[59]

Briefly stated, Ahad Haam's theory looked to Zionism for a solution first of the problem of Judaism and then of the problem of the Jew. As a first step in Zionist work he advocated the reawakening of national sentiment which would prompt Jews to settle in Palestine, where, in spite of obstacles and political conditions, they would build up a sizable Jewish community. In time that community, where the genuine Jewish spirit must again flourish, would serve as the national center radiating fresh enthusiasm for Judaism and Jewish values to all parts of Jewry.

Even this sketchy outline of Ahad Haam's conception of Zionism shows why he was a consistent opponent of Herzl. His impressions of the first Zionist Congress, published in *Hashiloah* in 1897, were written in such a critical vein that they aroused a storm of indignation in the Zionist world. According to Ahad Haam, the greatest achievement of the congress was its spiritual significance. The ringing call of that assembly to establish a national home in their ancestral land, he asserted, was of great moral value both to the Jews and to mankind. Jewish representatives from all parts of the world had met in the first assembly of its kind since Israel was driven forth; they had now publicly declared their intention to build a secure home for their people in the land of their ancestors and thus solve the problem of the Jews. The declaration was bound to serve as the initial step toward "emancipation of ourselves from the inner slavery and spiritual degradation which assimilation has produced in us, and the strengthening of our national unity by joint action in every sphere of our national life, until we become capable and worthy of a life of dignity and freedom *at some time in the future*."[60] But the "exaggerated, unrealistic hope of imminent redemption" aroused by Zionist leaders, the kindling "of the false fire of a feverish enthusiasm," robbed that historic conclave "of its bloom

59. *Ten Essays*, p. 125.
60. *Ibid.*, pp. 25–31.

and made it a mockery." Moreover the national sentiment of the Jews, so Ahad Haam thought, was atrophied to such an extent that they would not be ready to receive the gift of a Jewish state even if it were offered to them. The purpose of the congress, as he saw it, was to proclaim the desire of the Jewish people to live so that not only would the world heed but that "we ourselves may hear the echo of our cry in our inmost hearts, and perhaps be roused thereby from our degradation." But because those directing the congress were men skilled in the art of diplomacy, he sarcastically observed, they created the impression that the Messiah was about to appear. As for himself, he sat at the congress "like a mourner at a wedding feast." "The salvation of Israel will be achieved by *prophets* not by *diplomats.*"

In order to train qualified leaders for the dissemination of Zionist ideology among the masses, Ahad Haam in 1889 organized a society called Bnei Moshe (Sons of Moses). In consonance with the teachings of its founder this society aimed at quality rather than quantity. The qualifications for admittance were rigid: each member was expected to exemplify in himself the highest ideals of Judaism. The Bnei Moshe must be distinguished by the love of truth, justice, generosity, love of peace, and humility. Each applicant was carefully investigated as to his family background, source of livelihood, and Jewish attitudes, and at initiation he was required to swear to comply with the bylaws of the organization and not disclose the identity of its members.

The long-range program of Bnei Moshe called for the revival of the Jewish people in the land of Israel through the reawakening of national sentiment and an increased devotion to Jewish cultural values and institutions. The members of the group were required to work for the improvement of the Jewish settlements in Palestine and at least once in their lifetime to visit the Holy Land. Seeking to produce a group of spiritual aristocrats, they counted among their members some of the most distinguished Zionists of Russia.[61]

The relationship between Ahad Haam and the members of Bnei Moshe was that of master and disciples. They consulted him on all sorts of personal and family matters and were expected to hide nothing from their leader. The following episode related by one of Ahad Haam's intimate friends, the noted Talmudist Chaim Tchernowitz, known as Rav Tzair, is typical of the personal interest the head of Bnei Moshe took in his followers. The wife of a member complained that her husband was spending his nights in his club at the chess table. In order to help him break the habit, Ahad Haam went

61. Zitron, *Toledot Hibat Zion,* I, 358–364.

to the home of his disciple late in the evening and stayed through the night waiting for the prodigal husband. At dawn when the man arrived he was stunned to find his spiritual mentor who, casting a rebuking glance at the offender, silently departed. The man soon mended his ways.[62]

The active literary career of Ahad Haam lasted for about fifteen years. During that period he was at one time head of the editorial board of the Hebrew publishing house Ahiasaf, and in 1897 he founded and edited the Hebrew monthly *Hashiloah.* The name of the magazine was significantly derived from a river in Palestine mentioned by the prophet Isaiah (8:6) as one whose "waters flow softly." The journal maintained high literary standards and was open to all branches of Jewish thought.

Ahad Haam was not a prolific writer; his entire literary output, aside from his correspondence, consisted of four modest volumes entitled *Al Parashat Derakhim* (At the Crossroads). But his unique and masterful Hebrew style of classical simplicity, his originality of thought, and keen, analytical mind made Ahad Haam not only the spiritual leader of the Zionist movement but also one of the truly great writers of modern Hebrew literature. In Palestine, where he had settled in 1922, he was revered by all factions of the Jewish community. His death in 1927 was mourned by Jews the world over.

Another Zionist leader, in many ways the direct antithesis of Ahad Haam, was the journalist and essayist Nahum Sokolow (1860–1936). Regarded as the creator of modern Hebrew journalism, Sokolow was a prolific writer and linguist who employed almost every form of literary expression. Born in the province of Plock, in Russian Poland, young Sokolow received training which his parents hoped would qualify him for the rabbinate. In spite of unusual erudition in rabbinics he chose journalism, however, went to Warsaw where he joined the staff of the Hebrew weekly *Hazefirah,* and later became its owner and editor. In the eighties the periodical under his management became a daily and for a number of years enjoyed great popularity among the Hebrew-reading public.

In pre-Herzlian days *Hazefirah* was skeptical of the Hibat Zion movement. After the congress at Basle, as has been said, Sokolow had a change of heart and eagerly used his paper to promote the cause of Zionism. Sokolow himself became a leading figure at Zionist congresses and occupied important posts, including that of secretary general, in the World Zionist Organization. At his suggestion the organization undertook to publish the Hebrew weekly *Haolam*

62. Rav Tzair, *Masekhet Zikhronot* (Book of Memoirs) (New York, 1945), p. 74. Hereafter cited as Rav Tzair.

(The World), which he edited for the first two years of its existence (1907–8).

During the first World War Sokolow rendered a great service to the cause of Zionism. Conversant with the ways of diplomacy and by temperament and inclination a skilled statesman, he cooperated with Weizmann in the negotiations which led to the issuance of the Balfour Declaration. In 1917 he was granted an interview with Pope Benedict XV who subsequently issued a declaration favorable to the Zionist cause.[63] From 1931 to 1935 Sokolow served as the president of the Jewish Agency of Palestine.

Sokolow's literary achievements, political activities, and wide range of intellectual attainments have astounded all his critics. His writings included Hebrew textbooks on geography and the English language, a history of anti-Semitism, a scholarly work on Baruch Spinoza, an essay on mass psychology (a subject comparatively new in Hebrew literature), a three-volume study of scholars and distinguished personalities both Jewish and non-Jewish, and a two-volume history of Zionism in English. From time to time there would also emerge from his pen a short story or novel. Sokolow's productivity is even more remarkable in view of his having written some of his most important works while traveling by plane or steamer. His Zionist activities took him to many parts of the world, where he would appear at public mass meetings on behalf of various Zionist funds.

Sokolow was greatly esteemed by his contemporaries. Shmarya Levin relates that in the literary circles of Warsaw in the early nineties it was a common saying that Sokolow had memorized all knowledge. Referring to Sokolow's reputation as a leading authority on world politics, Levin observes that if the Jews had a state of their own "Sokolow would have been its most distinguished diplomat." [64] In an essay on Sokolow entitled "As Colorful as the Rainbow" Menahem Ribalow, editor of the Hebrew weekly *Hadoar* (The Post), called him a many-faceted intellect whose wide field of interests stretched into infinite space with perfect harmony." [65]

Whether from the point of view of the advancement of human thought and culture specialization is to be preferred to versatility is a subject for speculation. It is possible that had Sokolow devoted himself to one particular branch of Jewish literature or scholarship he might have made a more enduring contribution to that particular field. But Sokolow himself did not believe this. In a critical appraisal

63. [Florian Sokolow, "Nahum Sokolow and Pope Benedict XV" *Zion* (Jerusalem, Jan.–Feb., 1950), Vol. I, Nos. 5–6. Ed.]
64. Levin, *The Arena,* p. 93.
65. *New Palestine* (New York), May 22, 1936.

of the writer David Frishman he averred that the creativeness of those endowed with versatility would be impeded by imposing limitations.[66] By not limiting himself to a specialized field Sokolow made his mark in many fields and became one of the foremost personalities of two generations.

Summarizing his reminiscences about Sokolow, Chaim Tchernowitz compares him to some of the great personalities in Jewish history, to Isaac Abravanel, Menasseh Ben Israel, and others who were both the spiritual guides and political leaders of their generation. This type of leader, in whom Jewish erudition blended so harmoniously with general culture and who was at ease in the company of all sorts of diplomats, is gone forever from the Jewish world Tchernowitz declares. "Such a personality was a miracle in our period . . . and with his death there came an end to a great and shining era." [67]

A leader of an altogether different mold was Menahem M. Ussishkin (1863–1941), generally known as the "iron man" of the Zionist movement. Born in Dubrovna, a town in the province of Mogilev in White Russia, Ussishkin was raised and educated in Moscow where his father, a wealthy merchant, had moved in 1871. Young Ussishkin was drawn into the Zionist movement while still a student at secondary school, during the controversy then raging in the Jewish press regarding America versus Palestine as a center of Jewish emigration. Already a strong devotee of Zionism, Ussishkin and his friend Y. Chlenov, who later became a leader of the Zionist movement, formed the Society of Immigrants to the Land of Israel. This group soon merged with Bilu and elected five pioneers for Palestine. During his student years at the Technical High School of Moscow Ussishkin was an active member of Bnei Zion, a group formed for the purpose of spreading Zionist propaganda among the academic youth.

Ussishkin took an active part in the early conferences of the Hobebe Zion among whom he soon became a leading figure. Following his marriage in 1891, two years after his graduation as an engineer, a trip to Palestine further strengthened his attachment to the land. Describing his visit to the Wailing Wall before leaving the country, he wrote: "It seems to me that anybody who has stood beside the Wall and has seen it once in his life will know no rest in his soul until he returns here again." [68]

66. *Hatekufah* (1923), Vol. 16.
67. Rav Tzair, p. 216.
68. Joseph Klausner, *Menahem Ussishkin, His Life and Work* (New York, Scopus Publishing Co., 1942), p. 39.

Although a member of Bnei Moshe and a strong adherent of cultural Zionism, Ussishkin also stressed the importance of political work. He was among those who urged that Russian Zionists heed Herzl's call and send delegates to Basle. But at the first meeting he clashed with the leader on the formulation of the Zionist program. Fearing that a clear and unequivocal statement of the ultimate Zionist aim in the spirit of Herzl would jeopardize the status of the existing settlements in Palestine and hamper their gradual growth, Ussishkin urged caution in the formulation of the Zionist program. The program adopted was in the nature of a compromise between the two opposing views, although with the emphasis on political Zionism. Ussishkin, who counted himself among the spiritual Zionists publicly demonstrated his displeasure with it. As Hebrew secretary of the congress, sitting on the platform, he conspicuously failed to join in the enthusiastic ovation given Herzl by the entire assembly at the conclusion of the session.

Ussishkin revealed his fighting qualities, strength of character, and unswerving loyalty to principle during the famous Uganda controversy which threatened to split the Zionist organization. The question at issue was whether the Zionists should accept an offer made by the British government to allow Jews to colonize Uganda in East Africa and guaranteeing them a certain measure of autonomy in their internal affairs. The Russian Zionists, who were inclined to distrust Herzl on account of his west European assimilationist background, suspected that he was now willing permanently to give up Palestine in favor of Uganda. Herzl's solemn assurance that he was interested in Uganda only as a temporary refuge failed to calm his opponents. The decision of the sixth Zionist Congress (1903) to appoint a commission to explore the possibilities of the East African territory was regarded by the adherents of Palestine as a betrayal of the Zionist cause.

It is interesting to note that the bulk of the Russian Zionists, whose kinsmen were then more in need of a haven of refuge than any other portion of Israel, were lined up with the opposition. Ussishkin himself had been in Palestine during the session of the sixth congress; upon his return to Russia he called a special conference of the anti-Ugandists and formed a group known as the Zionei Zion (Zion Zionists). In spite of the vigorous campaign conducted against him by some outstanding Zionists, supporters of Herzl, Ussishkin persevered in his battle against any plan that might prevent Palestine, the historic center of Judaism and the symbol of the Jewish spiritual renaissance, from becoming the future national homeland of the Jews.

A dramatic clash between the two principal opponents occurred in Vienna, where they met for the last time in April, 1904, at a meeting of the Greater Actions Committee.

"Do you suppose that we shall get Palestine?" Herzl asked. Ussishkin answered with conviction. "Yes. And if you don't believe it, there is no place for you at the head of the Zionist movement." When Herzl said to Ussishkin, "You are strong, but I am even stronger," the latter responded, "The idea is stronger still!" [69]

Ussishkin's bitter struggle was crowned with success at the seventh congress, held at Basle in the summer of 1905, a year after Herzl's death. At that assembly the Uganda project was officially rejected with due acknowledgment to the British government. A general principle was also adopted that Zionists as Zionists might not engage in any settlement activity whatever outside Palestine.

A highlight in Ussishkin's career was his appearance before the Versailles Peace Conference in 1919, as a member of a delegation of five which included Weizmann and Sokolow, to state the Jewish claim on their ancestral home. The moral effect of this address was tremendous, since it was the first appearance before the nations of the world of a Jewish representative demanding in the classical Hebrew language the restoration of the ancient Jewish homeland to its people.

In 1919 Ussishkin went to Palestine as the head of a delegation chosen by the Zionist organization and approved by the British government to supervise the affairs of the Jewish community there. A man of strong and forthright character, he soon came into conflict with the British administration which, he charged, was pursuing a policy hostile to the letter and spirit of the Balfour Declaration. To strengthen the Jewish position in the country he urged that Zionist endeavors be directed mainly toward purchasing land and increasing immigration. Conservative in his political and economic views, he nevertheless facilitated the establishment of cooperative settlements, a form of colonization he believed most suitable for a barren and neglected land.

The most lasting contribution Ussishkin made to the reclamation of Palestine for his people was as chairman of the board of the Jewish National Fund, a post he held from 1924 until his death in 1941. Established by the fifth Zionist Congress in 1901, this fund, called in Hebrew Keren Kayemeth Leyisrael, was intended for the acquisition through purchase of the soil of Palestine as the national and inalienable property of the Jewish people. National Fund land may never be sold to individual owners; it can only be leased

69. *Ibid.*, p. 70.

to individual or collective settlers on condition that they make their homes on the land and cultivate it. The dynamic head of this fund did not limit his activities to the work of managing only, he also undertook extended tours of the far-flung Jewish communities of the Diaspora to collect funds for his land purchasing agency.

The following figures reveal the growth of the popularity of the National Fund among the masses of Jewry, an achievement in no small measure due to Ussishkin's leadership. In 1921 when he was elected a director of the fund it owned 22,000 dunams of land (a dunam is about one-fourth of an acre) while upon his death in 1941 it possessed 561,000 dunams. The fund provided land for about 60 per cent of all the agricultural settlements in Palestine. These colonies are either communal or collective villages, or small holders' settlements.

Uncompromising to the point of intolerance, a relentless fighter for the ideas he championed, Ussishkin had many enemies in and outside the ranks of the Zionists. During the heated controversy that raged in the first decade of this century among east European Jews over the national supremacy of the Hebrew or the Yiddish language Ussishkin waged a bitter battle against the advocates of Yiddish. A zealous champion of Hebrew culture and the Hebrew language which he regarded as the only national language of the Jewish people, he had the temerity to oppose the election of the famous Hebrew-Yiddish novelist, Mendele Mocher Sefarim (Mendele the Bookseller), to honorary membership in the Society of Lovers of the Hebrew Language in Odessa, because Mendele had not opposed Yiddish.[70] Differences of opinion notwithstanding, friend and foe alike acknowledged the moral sturdiness of this "man of iron" and admired his boundless devotion to the ideas that animated his activities.

Ussishkin, like Sokolow and others of his kind, belonged to a type of Russian-Jewish leadership that is not likely to be duplicated elsewhere or at another time. Summarizing Ussishkin's life and achievements Joseph Klausner writes: "His Hebrew and general education amid a Jewry of millions, his deep roots in the soil of tradition, his boundless love for historical Judaism, his fervent Messianic vision—all these fitted him to be one of the leading fighters for the idea of redemption, the redemption of the land and the redemption of the people; and one of those most devoted to the national faith, language and literature of Israel in the Diaspora as in Palestine." [71]

70. *Ibid.*, p. 92.
71. *Ibid.*, p. 152.

A Russian Jew who gained world-wide fame both as a scientist and as the leader of the Zionist movement after World War I is Chaim Weizmann. Born in 1874 in Motol, a small town near Pinsk, he received his early training in the secondary school of that city where he developed an interest in the sciences. Upon graduation at eighteen, he studied in universities abroad and specialized in chemistry. He received the degree of doctor of science at the University of Freiburg, Switzerland, in 1900 and did research work at the University of Geneva, where he also lectured until 1904. After his marriage in that year he settled in Manchester, England, having been appointed lecturer and reader in biological chemistry at Victoria University. In 1916 he made his home in London and entered the service of the British Admiralty as director of the Admiralty Chemical Laboratories.

His first Zionist inspiration Weizmann received from his father, an adherent of Hibat Zion, and from his Hebrew teachers from whom he learned Talmudic and Hebrew literature in his secondary school days. He embraced the Zionist ideology and was among those who urged that the Russian Zionists participate in the congress at Basle. He himself attended a Zionist congress for the first time in 1898. Weizmann was the founder of the Democratic Fraction, a group which demanded more democratic procedure in the organization and advocated cultural activity, practical work in Palestine, and political propaganda. Like Ussishkin, Weizmann opposed Herzl's policy of stressing diplomatic work to the neglect of "small" work in Palestine. To him the practical work was a means to further the political objective. Weizmann was also among those who opposed the Uganda project.

From the death of Herzl to the first World War Weizmann took no leading part in Zionist work. His Zionist activities were mainly of a cultural character. During World War I political circumstances moved him into the central position of Zionist leadership. Because the Zionist leaders in Berlin, the center of the movement until the war, could not communicate with the branches in the lands of the Allied Powers, Weizmann became the head of a political committee in London which emerged as the headquarters of Zionism.

His personal acquaintance with prominent British statesmen, among them Arthur Balfour and David Lloyd George, as well as the scientific services he rendered the English government during the war made Weizmann the logical representative to negotiate for a British commitment regarding Jewish aspirations in Palestine. Weizmann believed that a pledge on the part of Britain to advance the cause of Zionism in the event of an Allied victory would secure the good will of world Jewry for the Allied cause. Lloyd George and a number of other high-ranking English statesmen who as late as 1917 were not at all sure as to the outcome of the war and believed that the support of the Jewish people, particularly in Russia and the United States, would be of considerable help to the Allies, were won over to Weizmann's views. Referring to that period in his war ministry, the former Prime Minister of Britain writes: "The fact that Britain at last opened her eyes to the opportunity afforded to the Allies to rally this powerful people to their side was attributable to the initiative, the assiduity and the fervour of one of the greatest Hebrews of all time: Dr. Chaim Weizmann. . . . Dr. Weizmann enlisted my adhesion to his ideals at a time when, at my request, he was successfully applying his scientific skill and imagination to save Britain from a real disaster over the failure of wood alcohol for the manufacture of cordite." [72]

During the summer of 1917 Arthur James Balfour, then foreign secretary of Great Britain, with the enthusiastic assent of the prime minister began to conduct negotiations with the second Lord Rothschild, president of the British Zionist Federation, regarding Zionist aims in Palestine. On behalf of the American Zionists, Supreme Court Justice Louis D. Brandeis took an active part in these conversations. Both sides having finally agreed on a formula, the Balfour Declaration was issued on November 2, 1917, in the form of a letter addressed by Balfour as foreign secretary to Lord Rothschild as head of the British Zionists. In this brief and historic document the British government pledged itself to facilitate the establishment of a Jewish national home in Palestine, "it being clearly understood that nothing shall be done which may prejudice civil and religious rights of existing non-Jewish communities in Palestine, or the rights and political status enjoyed by Jews in any other country." The latter stipulation was inserted to appease the wealthy Jews who, fearful that the creation of a Jewish commonwealth in Palestine would increase anti-Semitism and endanger their sheltered position, had waged a bitter fight against Zionism. In England Edwin Montagu, secretary of state for India, was among the chief opponents in the cabinet of a favorable commitment on the subject of Zionism.[73]

Following the issuance of the Balfour Declaration Weizmann became the head of the Jewish "state," its ambassador and tax collector. Tremendous funds were needed to begin immigration to Pales-

72. David Lloyd George, *Memoirs of the Peace Conference* (New Haven, Yale University Press, 1939), II, 722.

73. *Ibid.*, II, 726, 732–733; Blanche E. C. Dugdale, *Arthur James Balfour* (New York, G. P. Putnam's Sons, 1937), I, 156–157, 170; [Chaim Weizmann, *Trial and Error* (Philadelphia, Jewish Publication Society, 1949), I, pp. 202, 204, 206. Ed.]

tine on a large scale, between 70,000 and 80,000 people annually as he envisioned it. For this purpose a special agency, Keren Hayesod (Palestine Foundation Fund), was formed at the Zionist conference in London in 1920. To obtain the necessary funds for this organization Weizmann came to the United States in 1921, where he was given a royal welcome by the masses of American Jews. To these shores where since World War I there exists the most influential and prosperous Jewish population in the world, Weizmann continued to make frequent visits, appearing in almost every Jewish community to plead for the cause.

Weizmann was Palestine's most effective ambassador not only to Jews but also to the gentiles. On his visits to the United States he managed to enlist the active support of distinguished non-Jews on behalf of the Zionist ideal. His deep conviction of the justice of the cause and his persuasiveness helped him to win over many influential and wealthy Jews in this country. The cooperation of the non-Zionist elements in Jewry in the building of the Jewish homeland was necessary not only as a means of procuring greater financial resources but also to satisfy a proviso of the Palestine Mandate which stipulated that the Zionist organization "secure the cooperation of all Jews who are willing to assist in the establishment of the Jewish national home."

In Louis Marshall (1856–1929), American-Jewish leader for more than a generation, Weizmann found a sympathetic and invaluable friend for his cause. A representative of Reform Jewry, Marshall nonetheless had a warm appreciation of traditional Judaism and was keenly concerned with the fate of his people. He was a cofounder of the American Jewish Committee whose program was the defense of Jewish rights. As head of the United States Jewish delegation to the Peace Conference at Versailles, Marshall played a leading part in securing minority rights for the Jews of east European countries. Although a non-Zionist, he became interested in Jewish developments in Palestine after the Balfour Declaration.

It was at Marshall's suggestion that Weizmann initiated negotiations with influential non-Zionist Jews in the United States as well as in other countries that led to the formation of the extended Jewish Agency for Palestine, with equal representation for Zionists and non-Zionists. The official organization of the agency took place in Zurich in the summer of 1929 and was marked by extraordinary enthusiasm on the part of all assembled. It was a great occasion in Jewish history for it marked the first time since the Dispersion that all factions of Jewry had united for the rebuilding of their historic homeland.

The establishment of the extended Jewish Agency was a personal triumph for Weizmann. It was his diplomatic skill and perseverance that managed to bring together two opposing factions, one nationalistic in outlook and temperament, the other antinationalistic by sentiment and ideology. To accomplish this difficult task he had to overcome the stubborn resistance of leading Zionists who opposed the inclusion of non-Zionists in the agency.

Having finally succeeded in realizing one of his cherished ambitions, Weizmann soon experienced a series of heartbreaking disappointments. The sudden death of Louis Marshall in Zurich shortly after the founding of the Jewish Agency was a severe blow to the Zionist cause. In Palestine the political situation took an alarming turn. As a result of bloody riots staged by Arabs following the events at Zurich, the British government initiated a series of investigations which finally led to the repudiation of the promise made to the Jews in the Balfour Declaration. Since the British administration had from the very beginning shown marked hostility to the growth of Jewish influence in the Holy Land, the charge was made in responsible Zionist quarters that the British authorities countenanced the disorders, perhaps even engineered them, in order to be provided with an excuse for stopping Jewish immigration into Palestine. Weizmann had often been criticized for acquiescing in British interpretations of the Mandate; he now, in October, 1930, resigned from the agency in protest against the Passfield White Paper which declared that since the absorptive capacity of Palestine had reached the saturation point the purchase of land by Jews and their immigration into the country would be terminated. To appease the world-wide protests raised against this ruling Prime Minister Ramsay MacDonald sent Weizmann a letter on January 31, 1931, in which he somewhat modified the restrictions of Passfield's statement.

Still, the Jewish position in Palestine continued to decline during the thirties. Britain in line with the appeasement policy she adopted in that decade continued to favor the Arab chieftains at the expense of Jewish interests. The anti-Jewish policies culminated in April, 1939, in another White Paper issued by Colonial Secretary Malcolm MacDonald. This stipulated the complete stoppage of Jewish immigration at the end of April, 1944, permanently freezing the ratio of Jewish population to the Arab at one to two. Asserting that His Majesty's Government "now declare unequivocably that it is not part of their policy that Palestine should become a Jewish state," the White Paper repudiated the pledge made in the Balfour Declaration.

As a result of the restrictive immigration policy enunciated in the White Paper, Jews in the Hitler-dominated countries during World War II were denied a haven of refuge in Palestine where they could have saved themselves from the Nazi extermination centers. [In February, 1942, the small, unseaworthy *S.S. Struma*, packed with 769 refugees who were refused entrance to Palestine, blew up after leaving the harbor of Istanbul and all passengers except one woman perished in the open sea. Ed.] Many hundreds of homeless Jews who sailed on the *Struma* and other boats found a watery grave near the land which, according to the Balfour Declaration, was to become their national home again.[74]

Even the invaluable aid the Jewish community in Palestine rendered the cause of the Allies during the war [75] failed to effect any modification of Britain's Palestine policy. In the postwar period, the British Labor party, which on many occasions had denounced the White Paper as a shameful repudiation of a solemn promise and had pledged itself to rescind it, came to power and reversed its own stand. It continued to keep the doors of Palestine closed to the more than a million Jews left alive after the Hitler terror.

It has been mentioned that Weizmann had been accused of being too conciliatory toward the British government. His critics averred that his failure to take a stronger stand on occasions when the Jewish position was threatened encouraged the mandatory power continually to infringe upon Jewish rights. Yet it is difficult to conceive how a statesman whose only weapons were faith in the justice of his cause and public opinion could have made a show of "strength" against an empire engaged in power politics and the advancement of what it regarded as its best interests.

Whether Weizmann's leadership could have been more effective is a question the future historian may be able to answer. Yet despite all the criticism leveled against him Weizmann stands out as an impressive personality and as the foremost builder of Zion. Although far from being an orator, he probably gained more adherents to the cause of Zionism than any Zionist orator. Weizmann captivated his listeners by the charm of his personality, by his wit, clarity, and persuasiveness. By a historic coincidence the same British statesman who affixed his signature to the Balfour Declaration had during his premiership offered Uganda to the Zionist organization. Unable to understand why his offer had been refused, Arthur Balfour during a visit to Manchester in 1905 invited the young lecturer in chemis-

74. [Wischnitzer, *To Dwell in Safety*, pp. 242–243. Ed.]
75. Pierre van Paassen, *The Forgotten Ally* (New York, Dial Press, 1943), chap. 4.

try at Victoria University to call on him. Weizmann according to his own account found explanation rather difficult since he had not yet mastered the English language. But finally an idea came to him and he said, "Mr. Balfour, if you were offered Paris instead of London, would you take? Would you take Paris instead of London?" Balfour looked surprised and said, "But London is our own!" Weizmann countered, "Jerusalem was our own when London was a marsh." Balfour agreed.[76]

It was also undoubtedly due to Weizmann's influence that Balfour formed a genuine attachment for Zionism. At the end of his life he said to his niece "that on the whole he felt that what he had been able to do for the Jews had been the thing he looked back upon as the most worth his doing." [77]

The large audience that Weizmann attracted flocked to hear him not only because of his fame and the high position he held in the Zionist movement but also because of the originality of his addresses, which were embroidered with pertinent homilies and illuminating observations. Urging upon his listeners the necessity of a homeland, he recalled that the Jew is sometimes called the salt of the earth. Salt, he observed, is good when used in small quantities, while an excess spoils the food so that "you throw out the food and the salt with it." Likewise, certain countries find that they can digest only a certain number of Jews; having reached that point they ask the Jews to leave. The Jews are also sometimes called the leaven or ferment responsible for some extraordinary ideas or for initiative and energy. But here again he reminded his audience of the "very fine difference between a ferment and a parasite. If the ferment is increased by ever so little beyond a certain point, it becomes a parasite. So those who wish to be polite call us 'ferments,' others, who are not so scientific, prefer to call us 'parasites.' " [78]

Describing Weizmann, the propagandist Louis Lipsky wrote: "He drew his thoughts out of the depths of his soul, conscious of his historic responsibility. There was a stateliness in his speech which was unique. He spoke, *ex cathedra*, for the silent Jewish people. He was their interpreter. It was not a man speaking, but a cause that had found expression." [79]

[In 1937 Weizmann settled in Rechovoth, Palestine, as head of the Sieff Institute. On May 15, 1948, he was elected president of the Pro-

76. Dugdale, *Balfour,* I, 324–325; [Weizmann, *Trial and Error,* pp. 109–110. Ed.]
77. Dugdale, *Balfour,* II, 171.
78. *American Addresses of Dr. Chaim Weizmann* (New York, Palestine Foundation Fund, 1923), p. 28.
79. *Chaim Weizmann,* ed. Meyer W. Weisgal (New York, Dial Press, 1944), p. 177.

visional Council of the State of Israel; and Israel's first Constituent Assembly, the Knesset, elected him president of the state on February 14, 1949. Ed.]

The chief opponent of Weizmann was Vladimir Jabotinsky (1880–1940). The former was judicious by temperament, restrained in speech, moderate and patient, while his opponent was dynamic, given to extravagant language, and an extremist averse to compromise. Jabotinsky was born in Odessa to a semi-assimilated family which gave him a secular education. In his early youth he manifested literary ability, and while still in secondary school he contributed to the *Odesskia Novosti* (Odessa News). He studied law in Bern, Switzerland, and in Rome, while serving as foreign correspondent in those cities for Russian newspapers.

Attracted to Zionism in his early years, he did not take an active part in the movement until the pogrom in Kishinev in 1903. In the years following that pogrom he became the most popular figure among the nationalistically minded Russian-Jewish youth. A gifted orator, poet, playwright, and contributor to important Russian newspapers, Jabotinsky occupied a prominent position among Russian-Jewish leaders. At the Zionist conference in Helsingfors in 1906 he was among those who urged the Zionists to adopt a program of minority rights. He was among the leading champions of a maximum Jewish education for Jewish children, demanding that two-fifths of the curriculum in Jewish day schools be given to Jewish subjects and that the language of instruction be Hebrew.

At the outbreak of World War I he was sent abroad as foreign correspondent by the Moscow newspaper *Russkia Vedomosti* (Russian News). Believing that as a result of her alignment with the Central Powers Turkey would be deprived of Palestine, Jabotinsky conceived the idea of forming a Jewish military unit that would participate in the war against Turkey and share in the liberation of the Holy Land. After long deliberation the British government finally consented to the organization in 1917 of the first Judean regiment which under the command of Colonel Patterson saw active combat in the conquest of Palestine.

Soon after the conclusion of the war strained relations developed between the originator of the Jewish Legion and the military government in Palestine. Suspecting that Sir Louis Bols, head of the administration, was encouraging Arab opposition to Zionist aspirations and inciting pogroms against the Jews, Jabotinsky organized the Haganah, a Jewish self-defense unit. For leading this group in the riots of 1920 he was sentenced to fifteen years at hard labor. This harsh and unjust sentence was subsequently commuted as a result of the storm of indignation raised in England and throughout the Jewish world.

At the very outset of the building of the national home in Palestine sharp differences of opinion arose between Weizmann and Jabotinsky. The latter demanded an immediate program of large-scale Jewish immigration, the maintenance of a Jewish military unit to afford security to the Jewish settlers, and a more militant attitude on the part of the Zionist leadership in their negotiations with the British government. He rejected the official Zionist policy which concentrated on practical work in Palestine and preferred to seek through gradual infiltration and the strengthening of the economic position ultimately to build up the Jewish commonwealth. Supported by a group of prominent Zionists, Jabotinsky advocated a revision of the Zionist program and a return to the ideas of Herzl. The founder of political Zionism, it will be recalled, sought to create political conditions that would make possible a mass transference of Jews to Palestine and the speedy creation of a Jewish state there.

At a convention of Zionists sympathetic to Jabotinsky's views held in Paris in 1925 the World Union of Zionist Revisionists was formed. The WUZR also created a special branch for young people, called Betar after the Palestinian city which figured prominently as a fortress in the Bar Kokhba rebellion in 132–5 A.D. Jabotinsky as president of the Revisionists toured the Jewish communities throughout the world, lecturing and writing in Zionist and non-Zionist newspapers and periodicals on behalf of his program. Revisionism made a particular appeal to the Jewish youth of eastern Europe because of the wretched economic and political conditions prevailing in those countries in the period between the two wars.

Jabotinsky's program alienated the labor elements which played an important role both in the Zionist organization and in the building of modern Palestine. Revisionism advocated that until the Jews should have reached a majority in Palestine compulsory arbitration ought to be adopted as a means of settling class strife. Charging discrimination against their followers in the distribution of employment, Revisionist workers seceded from the influential Palestine Jewish Labor Federation (Histadruth) and formed their own National Labor Federation. The creation of the rival labor organization led to occasional physical clashes between the opposing camps and made the Revisionists unpopular in the Jewish homeland.

In the meantime, having become ever more critical of the official Zionist leadership which he charged with betrayal of Zionist ideals, Jabotinsky decided to sever his connections with the organization and to form a new one on more militant lines. At his call a convention of delegates purporting to represent over 700,000 Zionists founded the New Zionist Organization in Vienna in the summer of 1935. Jabotinsky settled in London where as the head of the new organization he sought to enlist the support of interested governments for an ambitious plan of solving the Jewish problem. According to this scheme all Jews desirous of settling in Palestine were to be evacuated from the countries of their residence and assisted in emigrating to the Jewish homeland. This program contemplated that within a period of ten years a million and a half Jews would be settled in Palestine. Having thus achieved a majority there the Jewish state, Jabotinsky believed, would be finally established.

Jabotinsky was a tragic personality, a combination of realist and dreamer. As a realist with the courage to face the truth it was clear to him that Britain's policies, accepted by the Zionist leadership, could not lead to the realization of the Zionist program in the forseeable future. But as a dreamer who lived in a world of illusions he refused to accept as fact the obvious truth that the Zionist leaders were not the masters of the situation. It was because of his seeming lack of perception for realities that Jabotinsky, in spite of all his unusual gifts, was always the leader of a small minority. Able to make people listen to him, he was unable to make them follow him. Paraphrasing the answer the Israelites gave to Moses at Sinai, "We shall do and we shall listen," Menahem Ribalow describes the attitude of the Zionists to Jabotinsky: "We shall not do but we shall listen." Zionists flocked to hear him because he gave expression to their resentment and accumulated wrath against the injustices of the mandatory power. But they failed to follow him, because Jews realized that the ultimate destiny of Palestine did not depend on them alone.[80]

In spite of his apparent failure Jabotinsky's achievements are significant. In his younger days he was one of the most effective champions of the national revival. His masterly translation of Bialik's poetry into Russian aroused a wide interest in the Hebrew language among the academic youth. The Jewish legion conceived by him, as well as his constant demands that the British government live up to its word, undoubtedly encouraged and stiffened the Zionist leaders in their dealings with that government. Even in a period that was rich in striking personalities Jabotinsky stands out as a unique and colorful figure.

The Zionist movement and its principal Russian-Jewish representatives thus far described were mostly of the middle class and

80. Menahem Ribalow, *Ketabim u-Megillot* (New York, Ogen Histadrut, 1942), p. 307. [Also Shalom Schwartz, *Jabotinsky, Lohem ha Umah* (Jabotinsky, the People's Warrior) (Jerusalem, 1943). Ed.]

liberal in political ideology. In fact, the leading Russian Zionists were affiliated with the Cadet party. But Jewish nationalism, as has appeared, made inroads also into the proletarian and socialist elements of Russian Jewry. The Poale Zion and the Socialist Zionists, the two socialist branches of the Zionist movement, were briefly described in the previous chapter. A sketch of Nachman Syrkin and Ber Borochov, whose careers reflect the history and development of the radical wing of the Zionist movement, will further clarify the ideology of Socialist Zionism.

Nachman Syrkin (1868–1924) was the first Russian-Jewish socialist who sought the solution of the Jewish problem in a synthesis of socialism and Zionism. As a mere youth he came under the influence of Hibat Zion. In his secondary school years in Minsk, where his parents moved from Mogilev, his birthplace, he took an active interest in the movement. Upon his graduation from school he went abroad to pursue his education. He studied at the university in Berlin, soon becoming a familiar figure in the Russian-Jewish student circles. In the heated and interminable debates that were raging in the eighties and nineties among the Jewish students abroad on the questions of Zionism and nationalism versus cosmopolitan or international socialism, Syrkin was a fervent upholder of the Socialist Zionist point of view. He attended the first Zionist Congress at Basle where he declared that if the projected Jewish state was to succeed it would have to be built along socialist lines.

Syrkin developed his philosophy of Socialist Zionism in *Die Judenfrage und der sozialistische Judenstaat* (1898). In a critical survey of modern history he lashed out at the upper and middle classes of Jewish society which in the hope of gaining civil equality betrayed their Jewish loyalties and bartered away their historic heritage. In an attempt to appease the growing anti-Semitism the Jewish assimilationists waved the flag of patriotism and loyalty to their respective countries. Superpatriotism, however, Syrkin declared could not save the Jew from the hatred of a society where the exploitation of the weak is the accepted rule. "As long as society rests on the might of the strong, and as long as the Jews are among the weak, want and misery will be the inevitable Jewish fate." [81]

[The manuscript left by Dr. Greenberg stops at this point. The reader will find further information about Syrkin's philosophy of Socialist Zionism in the Hebrew edition of his writings.[82]

81. Nachman Syrkin, *Geklibene Tzionistish-sotzialistishe Shriften* (New York, Central Committee Poale Zion, 1926), II, 144.

82. [*Kitvei Nachman Syrkin. Luktu Wesydru Bidei B. Kazenelson we-Jehuda Kaufman* (Tel Aviv, 1939). Ed.]

As to Ber Borochov (1881–1917), the leader of the Poale Zion movement, it may be noted that he carried great weight among his followers. He clearly foresaw that Palestine, and no other territory, "will become the land of concentrated Jewish immigration." [83] Borochov lived to see the Balfour Declaration proclaimed—and died in December, 1917.

Both Syrkin and Borochov promoted the labor movement in Palestine which was a driving force toward the establishment of the state of Israel. Both ranked among the foremost champions of Zionism in the former Russian Empire. Ed.]

83. [See *Nationalism and the Class Struggle: A Marxian Approach to the Jewish Problem.* Selected Writings by Ber Borochow, Introduction by A. G. Duker (New York, 1937). Ed.]

INDEX